INTRODUCTION

This book is intended to be used with good highway maps, and it's a good idea to get more than one map. State tourist authorities supply free official state highway maps—handy for small towns, secondary roads, pioneer trails, or points of interest.

Hours listed here are as accurate as possible, but are listed for general guidance only and should be rechecked locally; weather, local events, and other circumstances may change them. Although large institutions maintain strict hours, small local museums will often open on demand if you write or ask the local tourist authority.

As prices are subject to frequent change, exact amounts have been avoided; instead, admission is indicated as: a) free; b) sm adm (a small admission charge, or where moderate admission for a car includes all occupants); or c) adm (moderate to expensive entry fees). GEP means entry is free with a Golden Eagle Passport (issued at Federal recreation areas).

For additional information, write: **Alabama** Bureau of Publicity & Information, State Capitol, Montgomery 36104. **Alaska** Division of Tourism, Pouch E, Juneau 99801. **Arizona** Office of Economic Planning & Development, 1645 W Jefferson, Room 428, Phoenix 85007. **Arkansas** Department of Parks & Tourism, 149 State Capitol, Little Rock 72201. **California:** Southern California Visitors Council, 705 W 7th St., Los Angeles 90017. San Francisco Convention & Visitors Bureau, 1390 Market St., San Francisco 94102. San Diego Convention & Visitors Bureau, 1200 3rd Ave., Suite 824, San Diego 92101. Redwood Empire Association, 476 Post St., San Francisco 94102. **Colorado** Visitors Bureau, 225 W Colfax Ave., Denver 80202. **Connecticut** Department of Commerce, 210 Washington St., Hartford 06106. **District of Columbia** Area Visitors Bureau, 1129 20th St. NW, Suite 200, zip 20036. **Delaware** State Division of Economic Development, 45 The Green, Dover 19901. **Florida** Department of Commerce, Direct Mail Room 402, 107 W Gaines St., Tallahassee 32304. **Georgia** Tourist Division, P.O. Box 38097, Atlanta 30334. **Hawaii** Visitors Bureau, 2285 Kalakaua Ave., Honolulu 96815. **Idaho** Department of Commerce & Development, Capitol Bldg., Boise 83707. **Illinois** Division of Tourism, 222 S College St., Springfield 62706. **Indiana** Tourist Division, 336 State House, Indianapolis 46204. **Iowa** Tourism Division, 250 Jewett Bldg., Des Moines 50309. **Kansas** Travel Division, State Office Bldg., Topeka 66612. **Kentucky** Department of Public Information, Capitol

Annex, Frankfort 40601. **Louisiana** Tourist Development Commission, Box 44291, Baton Rouge 70804. **Maine** Department of Commerce & Industry, State Capitol, Augusta 04330. **Maryland** Tourist Division, 2525 Riva Rd., Annapolis 21401. **Massachusetts** Division of Tourism, Leverett Saltonstall Bldg., 100 Cambridge St., Boston 02202; provides minimal information; write instead to regional offices: Cape Cod Chamber of Commerce, Hyannis 02601. Berkshire Hills Conference, 100 North St., Pittsfield 01201. Pioneer Valley Association, 38 Gothic St., Northhampton 01060. Mohawk Trail Association, Charlemont 01339. Nantucket Chamber of Commerce, Nantucket 02554. Martha's Vineyard Chamber of Commerce, Martha's Vineyard. **Michigan** Tourist Council, Lansing 48926. **Minnesota** Tourist Information Center, 480 Cedar St., St. Paul 55101. **Mississippi** Travel & Tourism Department, P.O. Box 849, Jackson 39205. **Missouri** Tourism Commission, Box 1055, Jefferson City 65101. **Montana** Department of Highways, Dept. OW-45, 1315 8th Ave., Helena 59601. **Nebraska** Department of Economic Development, Box 94666, Lincoln 68509. **Nevada** Department of Economic Development, Carson City 89701. **New Hampshire** State Division of Economic Development, State House Annex, Box 856, Concord 03301. **New Jersey** Promotion Office, Box 400, Trenton 08625. **New Mexico** Department of Development, 113 Washington Ave., Santa Fe 87501. **New York** State Travel Bureau, Suite 1005, 99 Washington Ave., Albany 12210. **North Carolina** Travel & Promotion Division, Raleigh 27611. **North Dakota** Travel Department, Capitol Grounds, Bismarck 58501. **Ohio** Department of Economic & Community Development, Box 1001, Columbus 43216. **Oklahoma** Publicity & Information Division, 504 Will Rogers Memorial Bldg., Oklahoma City 73105. **Oregon** Travel Information Section, 102 State Highway Bldg., Salem 97310. **Pennsylvania** Travel Development Bureau, 432 S Office Bldg., Harrisburg 17120. **Rhode Island** Tourist Promotion Division, Roger Williams Bldg., Hayes St., Providence 02908. **South Carolina** Department of Parks, Recreation, & Tourism, Box 133, Edgar A. Brown Bldg., Columbia 29201. **South Dakota** Travel Director, Tourism Development, Pierre 57501. **Tennessee** Division of Tourism, Room 1028, Andrew Jackson Bldg., Nashville 37219. **Texas** Travel & Information Division, Box 5064, Austin 78763. **Utah** Travel Council, Council Hall, Capitol Hill, Salt Lake City 84114. **Vermont** Development Agency, Montpelier 05602. **Virginia** State Travel Service, 6 N 6th St., Richmond 23219. **Washington** Travel Development Division, General Administration Bldg., Olympia 98504. **West Virginia** Travel Development Division, State Capitol, Charleston 25305. **Wisconsin** Travel Division, Box 450, Madison 53701. **Wyoming** Travel Commission, 2320 Capitol Ave., Cheyenne 82002.

Although information listed here was as accurate as possible at press time, some errors must have crept in and some changes will have occurred since publication; for these, the author apologizes.

Americans·Discover·America Series

American Travelers' Treasury

Treasury

A Guide to the Nation's Heirlooms

BY SUZANNE LORD

William Morrow & Company, Inc. New York, 1977

To JCF, for his more than unobtrusive support
and tramontane perspective.

Library of Congress Catalog Card Number 77-292

ISBN 0-688-03130-7

CONTENTS

INTRODUCTION 5
ALABAMA 7
ALASKA 13
ARIZONA 17
ARKANSAS 25
CALIFORNIA 32
COLORADO 62
CONNECTICUT 72
DELAWARE 85
DISTRICT OF COLUMBIA 89
FLORIDA 97
GEORGIA 114
HAWAII 127
IDAHO 132
ILLINOIS 136
INDIANA 153
IOWA 165
KANSAS 171
KENTUCKY 178
LOUISIANA 186
MAINE 195
MARYLAND 201
MASSACHUSETTS 209
MICHIGAN 234
MINNESOTA 245
MISSISSIPPI 253
MISSOURI 259
MONTANA 270
NEBRASKA 277
NEVADA 282
NEW HAMPSHIRE 289
NEW JERSEY 294
NEW MEXICO 302

NEW YORK	313
NORTH CAROLINA	348
NORTH DAKOTA	360
OHIO	365
OKLAHOMA	385
OREGON	395
PENNSYLVANIA	405
RHODE ISLAND	432
SOUTH CAROLINA	441
SOUTH DAKOTA	451
TENNESSEE	460
TEXAS	473
UTAH	505
VERMONT	514
VIRGINIA	520
WASHINGTON	547
WEST VIRGINIA	562
WISCONSIN	567
WYOMING	580

ALABAMA

ANNISTON: Church of St. Michael & All Angels (18th St. & Cobb Ave.), a Gothic Episcopal church with cloisters; lovely Carrara marble altar with alabaster reredos surmounted by 7 angels; striking hand-carved ceiling; open daily 8:30-5; free.

ATHENS: Houston Memorial Library (Market & Houston Sts.), former home of Alabama Governor George S. Houston, is being preserved by the county government with the family furnishings intact; open Tues.-Fri. 10-noon, 2-5, Sat. 9-noon; closed hols; free. On the campus of Athens College, **Founders Hall Chapel** contains wood carvings of major religious figures by a native Alabamian; open daily 6 am-10 pm; free.

BIRMINGHAM: Arlington Antebellum Home & Gardens (331 Cotton Ave. SW), built by slaves of handmade brick, was a 4-room home enlarged to 8 rooms in 1842; period furnishings; the colorful history includes a female spy who hid in the attic; open Tues.-Sat. 9-5, Sun. 1-6; closed Jan. 1, Dec. 25; adm.

    Birmingham Museum of Art (2000 8th Ave. N at 20th St.) houses a vast and varied collection ranging from Egyptian and Indian artifacts to modern painting. Italian Renaissance paintings, Rives Collection of Palestine art, primitive art, Remington bronzes, porcelain, silver, iron-work, prints, and changing exhibits are highlights. Open Mon.-Sat. 10-5, Sun. 1-6; closed Jan. 1, Dec. 25; free.

CAMDEN: White Columns, an antebellum mansion with period furnishings, is open spring and summer 1-6; closed hols; adm.

CULLMAN: On campus of St. Bernard College (1 m E, off US 278) is the **Ave Maria Grotto,** over 150 miniature religious buildings on a terraced hillside. Open daily 7-sunset; adm.

DAUPHIN ISLAND: (30 m S of Mobile via bridge and causeway) is rich in stories of pirates and lost treasure. **Fort Gaines,** a 5-sided fort built 1821-50, was a strategic point during the Civil War; the Battle of Mobile Bay began here on Aug. 5, 1864, when Adm. David G. Farragut's Union warships entered the bay. Confederates failed to stop the Federal fleet with their torpedos. Confederate Museum (open daily 9-5, with longer hrs in summer; closed Dec. 25); adm.

DECATUR: Mooresville (6 m E on SR 20): many 19th-C buildings preserved; walking tour available at the Post Office (open daily 6-10, 4-5; closed hols). Free.

DEMOPOLIS: Gaineswood (805 S Cedar St.), a stately stone mansion built between 1842-60, open by appointment only. **Bluff Hall** (Commissioner St.) is a restored Greek Revival mansion built by slaves in 1832; open Sun. 2-5; adm.

EUFAULA: Shorter Mansion (340 N Eufaula Ave.) is a fine 1906 Greek Revival building furnished with 18th-19th-C antiques. Open Mon.-Sat. 10-noon, 1-4, Sun. 1-4; closed hols; adm. Many lovely old antebellum homes may be seen during Pilgrimage Week in Apr., and at other times by contacting the Chamber of Commerce.

FLORENCE: Indian Mound and Museum (S Court St.): The mound is one of the largest in the Tennessee Valley; the museum of artifacts is open Tues.-Sat. 9-12; 1-4; closed hols; sm adm. **W. C. Handy Home & Museum** (620 W College St.) is the composer's restored birthplace. The piano on which the "father of the blues" composed *St. Louis Blues,* and other mementos, are on display; open Tues.-Sat. 9-12, 1-4; closed hols; sm adm. **Pope's Tavern** (Seminary St. & Hermitage Dr.), built in the early 1800's as a stage stop, later served as a hospital; open Tues.-Sat. 9-12, 1-4; closed hols; sm adm. **Karsner-Kennedy House** (303 N Pine St.), a restored 1828 town house, is open Mon.-Fri.; adm. **Rosenbaum Residence** (117 Riverview Drive) was designed by Frank Lloyd Wright; not open to public.

FORT MORGAN STATE PARK: (21 m W of Gulf Shores via SR 180) preserves the star-shape fort designed by one of Napoleon's officers and constructed of slave-made bricks 1819-34. In Aug. 1864 it was captured by the Union in the Battle of Mobile Bay, and was used by the military as late as WW II. A museum houses guns, maps, uniforms, and military items. Open daily 8-5 (8-6 in summer); closed Dec. 25; picnic area; fee for park includes museum and fort.

GREENSBORO: Magnolia Grove (1 Main St.), an 1838 mansion built of bricks made on the estate, was the birthplace of Admiral Richard P. Hobson, a hero of the Spanish-American War. Features include cast-iron Corinthian columns, an unsupported winding staircase, family furnishings, and mementos from abroad. Open Tues.-Sat. 9-12, 2-4, Sun. 2-4; donations.

HORSESHOE BEND NATIONAL MILITARY PARK: (12 m N of Dadeville on SR 49) commemorates Andrew Jackson's defeat of the Creek Nation on March 27, 1814, ending the Creek Indian War. The **Visitor Center** displays Indian relics and guns; a 3-m interpretive road runs through the battlefield; open daily exc. Dec. 25 from 8-4:30 (later in summer); park road open until dusk. Free.

HUNTSVILLE: Alabama Space & Rocket Center (W on SR 20) highlights simulated travel to the moon and has indoor and outdoor exhibits. Many displays can be activated. NASA tours of **Marshall Space Flight Center** are available on a combination ticket. Open daily exc. Dec. 25 from 9-5 (to 6 in July-Aug.). Adm.

Burritt Museum (3131 Burritt Dr.) is an unusual 11-room house built in the shape of a Maltese cross; displayed are Indian artifacts, many items of local historic interest. Grounds contain gardens and a pioneer homestead. Open Mar.-Nov., Tues.-Sun. 1-5; donation.

JACKSONVILLE: Francis-Doctor's Office & Apothecary is a tiny museum of antebellum medical and pharmaceutical items; open Tues.-Fri. 2-5, Sat. 9-5; adm.

MALBIS: Malbis Memorial Church (S off US 90 on County road 27), modeled after a Byzantine church in Athens; impressive interior. Open 9-12, 2-5 daily; tours available; free.

MOBILE: Bienville Square, most colorful at Mardi Gras, is a little park from which radiate many fine old homes with iron balconies. **Church Street East Historic District** is a more modest residential area of 19th-C buildings which were falling into decay and have recently been renovated; a few buildings can be entered, but many are private residences; the Church Street Graveyard, with some headstones in French and Spanish, is especially interesting. The city is best seen during the **Azalea Trail Festival** (mid-Feb.-Mar.), when many events are scheduled; the trail is a 35-m marked route through city streets where azaleas are especially profuse; a self-guiding map of historic sites is available from the Jaycee Tourist Information Center (751 Government St.), open 8:30-5 weekdays plus weekends during the festival; guides also available.

Carlen House (54 Willcox St.) is an 1842 Creole cottage authentically furnished; open Tues.-Sat. 10-5, Sun. 1-5; closed hols; free. **City Hall** (111 S Royal St.), a Greek Revival-style brick building constructed in 1858 as a marketplace, is open, free, during business hours.

Oakleigh (350 Oakleigh Pl., follow signs from Government St.), an antebellum mansion surrounded by oaks, was built by slaves of handhewn lumber and handmade bricks between 1833-38; unusual outside cantilevered staircase, antique silver made in Mobile, 19th-C jewelry, and period furnishings. Open daily 10-4, Sun. 2-4; closed hols, Christmas week, Mardi Gras; adm.

Richards-Dar House (256 N Joachim St.), a town house in Italianate style, is best known for the iron lace decorating the facade; interior features include chandeliers, glass, and marble mantels. Open Tues.-Sat. 10-4, Sun. 1-4; adm.

Mobile Art Gallery (in Langan Park) has good collections of 19th-20th-C American and European paintings, prints, and changing exhibits. Open Mon.-Sat. 10-5, Sun. noon-5; closed hols; free.

Phoenix Fire Museum (203 S Claiborne St.), once the home station house for the Phoenix Steam Fire Co. No. 6, is now a museum of fire-fighting equipment with memorabilia of the volunteer companies of Mobile. Open Tues.-Sat. 10-5, Sun. 1-5; closed hols. Free.

Battleship Alabama Memorial Park (E on US 90) is a memorial to the state's veterans. Berthed here is the USS *Alabama,* which you can tour from bridge to engine room, as well as the submarine USS *Drum.* Open daily 8-sunset; adm.

MONTGOMERY: Alabama State Capitol (Bainbridge Ave. between Washington & Monroe Ave.), built in 1851, is where the Ordinance of Secession was passed in 1861 and where Jefferson Davis was inaugurated President of the Confederacy. Inside, 2 cantilevered spiral staircases flank the Rotunda, and 13-ft-high murals depict state history. On grounds are trees replanted from Civil War battlefields, statue of Davis, Confederate Monument; open daily exc hols 8-5; free. **Alabama State Archives** (624 Washington Ave.) has pioneer, Civil War, and other historic relics; open Mon.-Fri. 8-4:30, Sat. & Sun. 9-11:30, 12:30-4:30; closed hols; free.

First White House of the Confederacy (opposite the Capitol) is the 2-story, white, clapboard home used by Jefferson Davis and his family for only 3 months (until the Confederacy's capital was moved to Richmond, Va.); period furnishings and many personal belongings. Open Mon.-Fri. 9-4:30, Sat. & Sun. 9-11:30, 12:30-4:30; closed hols; free.

Ordeman-Shaw Complex (304 N Hull St.): several pre-Civil War houses restored and furnished with period antiques. **Ordeman-Shaw House** was built between 1848-53 by Charles Ordeman, a German architect taken with Italian styling. The Gothic-style **DeWolf-Cooper Cottage** is the information center for the Montgomery Chamber of Commerce; film and information on the city's history. Open Tues.-Sat. 9:30-4, Sun. 1:30-4; closed hols; adm.

Teague House (468 S Perry St.) is an 1848 Greek Revival mansion with 6 Ionic columns; period pieces. It served as headquarters for Wilson's Raiders in 1865. Open Mon.-Fri. 10-3; closed hols; free. **Murphy House**

(22 Bibb St.) is an 1851 Greek Revival home built by a cotton merchant now used for government offices; open office hours Mon.-Fri.; closed hols; free. **Lomax House** (235 S Court St.) an 1848 Greek Revival building now housing offices, is open Mon.-Fri. exc hols during business hours; free. Other antebellum homes that are privately owned but can be viewed from the outside are: **Taylor-Ponder-Bibb Home** (511 S McDonough St.), **Tyson House** (333 Mildred St.), and **Winter-Thorington House** (52 Goldthwaite St.).

Montgomery Museum of Fine Arts (440 S McDonough St.) houses Indian arts, early American portraits, period rooms, firearms, silver, and contemporary works; open Tues.-Sat. 10-5, Sun. 2-5; closed hols and 2 weeks in Aug.; free.

W. A. Gayle Planetarium (1010 Forest Ave.) features programs simulating space travel. Open Tues.-Fri. 8-5, Sat. & Sun. 1-4; free. Shows every afternoon June-Aug., and weekend afternoons Sept.-May. Adm.

MOULTON: Pioneer House Museum, with local historical displays, is open Tues.-Sun. 9:30-5; closed hols; adm.

MOUNDVILLE: Mound State Monument and Museum is an attractive site on the Black Warrior River. Some 40 mounds were built as bases for temples and other important structures 1200-1400 AD. A reconstructed temple; several typical huts. The Archaeological Museum was constructed over two burial sites. Open daily 9-5; closed Dec. 25; sm adm.

OZARK: Army Aviation Museum (SW via SR 249 at Ft. Rucker) has a large collection. Open Mon.-Fri. 9-4; Sat., Sun., & hols 1-5; closed Dec. 25; free.

RUSSELL CAVE NATIONAL MONUMENT (8 m NW of Bridgeport off US 72 via marked local roads 91, 75) is a large cave first occupied by nomadic hunters 6550-6145 BC. Visitor Center rangers demonstrate ancient skills, and let you try your hand at them. Open daily 8-5, an hr longer in summer; closed Dec. 25; free.

SELMA: Cahaba (9 m SW on SR 22, then 4 m S on unimproved road), now a ghost town, was chosen as the state capital in 1819, but disastrous floods caused the capital to be changed to Tuscaloosa in 1826; brick walls and chimneys remain, plans to restore the site. Open daily sunrise-sunset; free.

Sturdivant Hall (713 Mabry St.) is a restored neoclassic brick home built in 1853. Inside are fine Chippendale, Sheraton, and other antiques.

Slave quarters, wine cellar, smokehouse, carriage house, and garden. Open Mon.-Sat. 9-4, Sun. 2-4; closed Jan. 1, Dec. 25; adm.

THEODORE: Bellingrath Gardens & Home (off US 90, 20 m S of Mobile) is one of America's greatest gardens, 65 acres planted to be colorful year round, with ponds, special gardens, bird watching, river and bayou; self-guiding map at the entrance. Large collection of Boehm porcelain sculpture. The handsome, exquisitely furnished home can be seen by guided tour for an extra charge. Open daily 7-dusk; adm.

TUSCALOOSA: University of Alabama (on US 11), founded in 1831, was burned by Union troops in 1865. Only 3 antebellum buildings survived the fire: **George Home,** an 1829 brick house with 2 curved iron stairways named for Confederate Gen. Josiah Gorgas, who was president of the university, and his son Dr. William C. Gorgas, who helped conquer yellow fever; Spanish Colonial silver and historic exhibits; open during academic year, Mon.-Sat. 10-noon, 2-5, Sun. 3-5; free. The **President's Mansion,** built about 1840 in Greek Revival style, and the nearby **Denny Chimes Tower** with a 305-bell carillon. The **Little Round House,** a sentry box, was erected in 1860. **Museum of Natural History** (in Smith Hall) exhibits South Pacific and Central and South American cultures, fossils, minerals, and geological periods depicted in dioramas; open Mon.-Sat. 8-4:45, Sun. 1-4:30; closed hols; free.

   Old Tavern (University Blvd.), built in 1827, is open Tues.-Sun. 2-5; sm adm. **Friedman Library** (1305 24th Ave.) was originally a home, built about 1862 in Italian style; open daily exc. hols; free. Other handsome antebellum buildings are reminders of the days when Tuscaloosa (from Choctaw, meaning Black Warrior) was the state capital (1826-46) and prosperous cotton center. Some can be seen during Tuscaloosa Heritage Week (Apr.); write the **Tuscaloosa County Preservation Society,** Box 1665.

TUSCUMBIA: Ivy Green (300 W N Common) is where Helen Keller was born in 1880; personal possessions are displayed. Open Mon.-Sat. 8:30-4:30, Sun. 1-4:30; closed hols; adm. In July and Aug. the William Gibson play *The Miracle Worker* is performed Fri. nights.

TUSKEGEE: Tuskegee Institute, founded by Booker T. Washington, the former slave who became an educator and reformer. **The Oaks,** built in 1899 of handmade bricks, now houses university offices, but his study is still intact; open Sun. 1:30-4; sm adm. *The Chapel,* designed in 1969 by Paul Rudolph, has an interesting ceiling and lighting which changes throughout the day; open daily 10:30-noon, 1:30-3; free. **George Washington Carver Museum** contains exhibits of the agricultural research Dr. Carver conducted and his collection of native birds and flora; also dioramas on the contributions by blacks to Western culture, exhibits of African art, and changing collections. Open Mon.-Sat. 10-4, Sun. 1-4; closed major hols; free.

WETUMPKA: Jasmine Hill Gardens (5 m SE off US 231), with cherry trees and reflecting pools, is designed to show off copies of ancient Greek and Roman statues, including a copy of the Temple of Hera in Olympia; open daily in daylight; free.

ALASKA

ANCHORAGE: Anchorage Historical & Fine Arts Museum (121 W 7th Ave.) offers excellent displays on prehistory, exploration, and contemporary arts and crafts. Open in summer, Mon.-Sat. 9 am-8 pm, Sun. 1-5; in winter, Tues.-Sat. 9-5, Sun. 1-5; closed hols; free.

Heritage Library (National Bank of Alaska Bldg., 5th St. & E St.) has a superb collection of documents on Alaska's history; also Sydney Laurence paintings; open Mon.-Fri. 1-4; closed hols; free. **Z. J. Loussac Public Library** (427 F St.) also has fine material on Alaska.

Alaska Transportation Museum (3833 Airport Rd.) has kayaks, planes flown by bush pilots, and other unusual items; open daily; closed Thnks, Dec. 25.

EAGLE: The Eagle Historical Society maintains **Roald Amundsen's Cabin,** where the Norwegian explorer stayed after his ship *Gjoa* was iced in 1905 and from where he cabled news of his successful navigation of the Northwest Passage. Tours are given daily, June-Labor Day.

FAIRBANKS: Alaskaland (between Airport Way and the Chena River): 40-acre park re-creates a gold rush town, a mining town, and other examples of Alaskan life and architecture; historical museum; craft demonstrations. Open Memorial Day-Labor Day, noon-8; rest of year 10-5.

University of Alaska (at College, ½ m S on Anchorage-Fairbanks Hwy.): **Museum** displays include ethnology and archaeology of the Eskimo, natural history, minerals, fossils, ivory carvings, Russian and gold rush history, native wildlife. Open in Summer 9-5, in winter 1-5;

closed hols; free. **Library-Fine Arts Complex** houses outstanding books and other materials on the state. At **Brooks Memorial Mine Bldg.** you can examine and buy maps and geologic reports. Inquire at the Museum for campus tours and hours for the Arctic Research Center, Experimental Farm, and other departments.

HAINES: Sheldon's Museum contains pioneer and Eskimo artifacts; open daily in summer 1-4; sm adm. **Fort William H. Seward,** the first permanent U.S. Army post in Alaska, is open daily; free. **Totem Village** (Port Chilkoot) features a replica of a tribal ceremonial house, totem poles, exhibits of pelt drying, and tours of artisan workrooms; open weekdays; closed hols; adm.

JUNEAU: Nestled against the mountains and overlooked by the Alaska-Juneau gold mine, this town of narrow winding streets boomed after the Joe Juneau-Dick Harris gold strike of 1880. **Chamber of Commerce** (200 N Franklin at 2nd St.) has maps for self-guiding tours. The **Alaska State Historical Museum** (Whittier St., at the harbor) has splendid collections of Eskimo and other native ethnology, geology, natural history, and history; art gallery. Open Mon.-Fri. 8-4:30, Sat. & Sun. 12-4:30; in summer also 7-10 pm; closed Jan. 1, Easter, Dec. 25; free. **Alaska-Historical Library,** one of the best in the state, includes the Wickersham Collection of many rare volumes.

Interesting buildings include the unpretentious frame **Governor's mansion** with a Tlingit totem pole beside it and the 1894 onion-domed **Russian Orthodox Church** (326 5th St.) with ancient icons, vestments, documents (open June-Sept. and when cruise ships are in port; adm.). The privately owned **House of Wickersham** (213 7th St.) gives daily tours of its historical collection (spoons, ivory, gold, documents); reservations necessary; usually open May-Sept.; adm. **Federal Building** houses arts and crafts (3rd floor; open business hours; free).

KENAI: This town grew from a 1791 fortified Russian post, and in 1869 the U.S. built Fort Kenai, now a community center housing the **Kenai Historical Society Museum. Russian Orthodox Church** (Mission St.), built in 1896; 3 onion-shape domes; icons, wedding crowns, other relics.

KETCHIKAN: This fishing center is built on such a narrow strip of land between mountain and water that many buildings are on pilings. This area is noted for its many colorful totem poles. Examples include the Chief Johnson Pole (corner Mission & Stedman Sts.), erected during a 1901 potlatch; Chief Skowl pole (W end of the Front St. tunnel), moved here from old Kasaan; and Chief Kyan pole (head of Main St.) a reproduction.

Ketchikan Historical Museum (Centennial Bldg.) displays more than 1000 items related to Indian life, mining days, and local history; arts and crafts. The fine city library is also in this building. Open summers Mon.-Fri. 11-5, Sat. & Sun. 1-4; winters, Tues.-Fri. 1-5, Sat. & Sun. 1-4; also when cruise ships are in port; free. Behind the building is a memorial to Fort Tongass. **Totem Cultural Center** has totem poles, artisans demonstrating skills, other attractions.

Totem Bight State Historic Site (10½ m N off Tongass Hwy.) has a cluster of totem poles depicting Tlingit legends and a brightly painted, intricately carved community house; open daily.

Saxman Indian Village (2½ m S on the S Tongass Hwy) has several handsome totem poles. The Cape Fox Dancers perform Tlingit dances during cruise ship season.

KODIAK: Russian explorers discovered this island in 1673 and Alexander Baranof established a settlement in 1792; many residents are descendants of these Russian settlers. Kodiak served as Alaska's capital 1792-1804. **Baranof House Museum,** built about 1793 to store sea otter pelts and later used as a dwelling, is the oldest Russian structure in Alaska; Russian displays and Aleut artifacts. Open in summer Mon.-Fri. 11-3, Sat. & Sun. 1-4, with extra hours when ferries dock; in winter, Wed., Fri., Sat., Sun. 1-3; closed Jan. 1, Dec. 25; free.

SEWARD: The State & City Office Building (5th Ave. & Adams St.) displays photographs of the devastating 1964 earthquake. Resurrection Bay Historical Society Museum (in the basement) houses pioneer and Indian artifacts, and mining exhibits. Open summers, Mon.-Sat.; free. **Seward Community Library** (diagonally across the street) has some nice Russian icons and paintings by Alaskan artists Sydney Laurence and Eustace Ziegler. **St. Peter's Episcopal Church** (2nd Ave. & Adams St.) has a 1925 painting of the Resurrection using Resurrection Bay as a background and local people as models.

SITKA: One of Alaska's most beautiful and interesting cities, this was an important Russian settlement and served as Alaska's government center until Juneau was chosen capital in 1900. The **Centennial Building** (at the harbor) has a model of the town as it appeared in 1867, exhibits on the city's history. Visitor information available here from the Chamber of Commerce (open daily in summer 9-9, in winter 9-5); Russian folk dances performed in summer.

Sheldon Jackson Museum (at the harbor): Artifacts dating back to Russian times and an extraordinary collection of Eskimo, Aleut, Tlingit,

Haida, and Athabascan material; fine research library; open in summer
Mon.-Sat. 10-12, 1-5, Sun. 1-5; open in winter Mon.-Fri. 1-4; sm adm.

St. Michael's Cathedral (Lincoln St.), an 1848 Russian Orthodox
Church that burned in 1966, has been reconstructed and houses icons,
chalices, vestments, wedding crowns, and other treasures; open daily
June-Aug.

Pioneers' Home (at the harbor), with pioneer relics and surrounded by
a garden of native plants, is on the site of the old Russian parade grounds.
Behind it is the old Russian cemetery with some headstones dating back to
the early 1800's. Here a Russian blockhouse has been reconstructed. The
nearby Russian mission was built in 1842.

SITKA NATIONAL HISTORICAL PARK (6 m N of Sitka) preserves
and interprets the history of Russia's North American venture and serves
as a memorial to the Tlingit. Visitor Center (Metlakahtla & Lincoln Sts.)
exhibits depict Tlingit history and culture, and life during Russian days;
native craftsmen at work; audiovisual and other programs; open daily
8-5; closed Jan. 1, Thnks, Dec. 25. At the Visitor Center, and along a
self-guiding trail into the forest behind it, are totem poles from Haida,
Tsimshian, and Tlingit villages, and other exhibits.

SKAGWAY: An International Klondike Gold Rush Park—to include
Skagway, the nearby ghost town of Dyea, the Chilkoot Trail, and historic
sites from Whitehorse to Dawson—is a cooperative effort by the U.S. and
Canadian governments.

Trail of '98 Museum (a block E of Broadway on Spring St.) is housed
in a rather grand building with Gothic windows; outstanding displays of
pioneer life and history of the city and gold rush; open summers 9-6 daily,
in winter by appointment only; sm adm. Soapy Smith's Parlor & Museum
(2nd Ave. off Broadway) also houses historic relics; Soapy Smith, the
town's best-known outlaw, died in a shootout on the Skagway waterfront;
open daily in summer; adm. Gold Rush Graveyard (Skagway-Carcross
Rd., just N of the town center) contains the graves of Soapy Smith and
other pioneers.

Dyea (Skagway-Carcross Rd. to Milepost 2.6, then 7½ m on Dyea Rd.)
is now a ghost town, but from 1896 until the White Pass & Yukon Railroad
was built in 1902 it was the town from which backpacking prospectors left
to climb the Chilkoot Trail on foot over 3739-ft Chilkoot Pass. Once over
the pass, miners could raft or boat along the Yukon River to the gold fields
at Dawson. In 1898, an avalanche killed more than 60 gold seekers; they
are buried in Slide Cemetery at Dyea. The state has restored and marked
Chilkoot Trail from the Taiya River to the summit.

The **White Pass & Yukon Railroad,** Alaska's first railway, offers a thrilling ride (summer only) over the historic Trail of '98 from Skagway to Whitehorse (or reverse), with lunch at Lake Bennett ghost town.

WRANGELL: Shakes Island (reached by footbridge) has a number of restored totem poles, including 4 of the state's oldest, surrounding Chief Shakes' Community House; also Tlingit tools and other artifacts. Open in summer; by appointment in winter. **Wrangell Museum** (2nd St.) has early historical displays, exhibits on Indian life and crafts. Open Mon., Wed., Fri. 7-9; Tues., Thurs., Sat. 2-4; also when tour ships are in port.

ARIZONA

CANYON DE CHELLY NATIONAL MONUMENT (at Chinle, off SR 63): This spectacular red sandstone canyon, still used by Navajo as farm and grazing land, contains ruins of prehistoric villages, most built AD 350-1300, of Basketmaker culture; White House (1 m to a house built into a canyon crevice) and other trails; 15-m canyon rim drive. Visitor Center has archaeological displays; open daily 8-5; closed Jan. 1, Dec. 25; free.

CASA GRANDE RUINS NATIONAL MONUMENT (off SR 87, 1 m N of Coolidge, midway between Phoenix and Tucson) contains Casa Grande, a unique 4-story building probably used as a ceremonial center, built c. 1350 by Hohokam farmers, as well as remains from many ruined villages. The Visitor Center, with interpretive displays, provides conducted tours and a self-guided trail leaflet; open daily 7-6; sm adm or GEP.

CORONADO NATIONAL MEMORIAL (at the Mexican border, off SR 92, 25 m W of Bisbee) commemorates the expedition led by Francisco Vasquez de Coronado in 1540 in a vain search for the Golden Cities of Cibola. Interpretive displays in headquarters and on trails; living history programs and other events; rangers on duty 8-5 daily.

DRAGOON: The Amerind Foundation, Inc., dedicated to archaeological research, houses a superb collection of material from southern Arizona and Sonora, Mexico. Open Sat. & Sun. by appointment only (write to the foundation, Dragoon, Az 85609). Free.

FLAGSTAFF: Museum of Northern Arizona (3 m NW on US 180) has excellent material on prehistoric and contemporary Indians; fossil and geologic displays; Indian arts and crafts displayed and sold. Open Mar.-mid-Dec., Mon.-Sat. 9-5, Sun. 1:30-5; free. **Northern Arizona Pioneers' Historical Museum** (2m NW on US 180) depicts local history; open mid-Apr.-mid-Oct., Mon.-Sat. 9-5, Sun. 1:30-5; free. **Lowell Observatory** (W to end of Santa Fe Ave., then N to top of hill), where noted astronomical achievements included discovering Pluto in 1930, gives guided tours Mon.-Fri. 1:30-2:30; closed weekends and hols; free.

FLORENCE: Pinal County Historical Society Museum (2201 Main St.) is open Wed.-Sun. 1-5; closed Aug., hols; free.

FORT BOWIE NATIONAL HISTORIC SITE (22 m S of Willcox on SR 186, then on graded road leading E into Apache Pass; then 1½-m trail to ruins) was focal point of military operations against the Chiricahua Apaches led by Cochise and Geronimo; laundry, bakery, barracks, and other buildings; self-guiding booklet; open all yr; free.

FORT HUACHUCA (obtain visitor pass at main gate, just W of Sierra Vista, or at N gate in Huachuca City), established in 1877 by the U.S. Cavalry to combat Indians and outlaws, is now headquarters of the U.S. Army Communications Command. A museum (Bldg. 41401, at Boyd & Grierson Aves.) recounts its history; open Mon.-Fri. 9-4, Sun. 1-4, closed hols. Free.

FORT VERDE STATE HISTORIC PARK (off I-17 in Camp Verde): original buildings of the military post which served as a base for cavalry patrols and Indian scouts in the 1870's campaigns against the Apache. Open daily exc. Dec. 25, 8-5:30; sm adm.

GLEN CANYON NATIONAL RECREATION AREA: Lee's Ferry (off US 89-A, N of Marble Canyon) was established in 1873 to facilitate Mormon emigration westward and played a significant role in wagon-train movements and in the Glen Canyon gold rush of 1883-1914. Roadside exhibits interpret the history.

GRAND CANYON NATIONAL PARK: The **Visitor Center** (off US 180), with interpretive displays, is open daily 8-5. **Yavapai Museum** (1 m E), with geologic displays, is open daily 11-5. **Tusayan Museum,** with exhibits on the canyon's early human history, is open summer only, 8-5; nearby are the ruins of a pueblo built about 1185. All free.

HOPI INDIAN RESERVATION (on SR 264) is a rough square surrounded by the Navajo reservation about 75 m NE of Flagstaff. Most of the old towns are on 3 mesas: On the first mesa (reached via twisting road from Polacca) is the most beautiful town, **Walpi;** terraced pueblo begun about 1680, seems hardly changed since its founding. On the second mesa are **Shongopovi, Shipaulovi,** and **Mishongnovi.** On the third mesa is **Oraibi,** the oldest continuously inhabited community in the U.S., dating from 1100; old kivas and other ruins. Other pueblos here are **Hotevilla** and **Bacobi.** Farther west is **Moenkopi,** where residents can direct you to dinosaur footprints. Information on festivals and other attractions is available at **Hopi Indian Agency** at Keams Canyon (eastern end of SR 264) or **Hopi Cultural Center** (on SR 264 near Oraibi). At the latter, the meticulously crafted silverwork and colorful kachina dolls are for sale at Hopi Silvercraft & Arts & Crafts Cooperative Guild.

HUBBELL TRADING POST NATIONAL HISTORIC SITE (1 m W of Ganado, near jct SR 264, 63), on the Navajo Reservation, consists of 11 buildings on about 150 acres homesteaded by John Lorenzo Hubbell in 1878. For many Navajo, this trading post was their only link to the white world. In the trader's office and rug room, crafts are still for sale; tours are given of the home, which overflows with rare collections of Americana. Open all yr exc. Jan. 1, Thnks, Dec. 25, from 8-5; open later in summer. Free.

JEROME (on US 89A SW of Flagstaff) became a ghost town when the copper mines closed in the 1950's. Cracked and tilted buildings perch precariously on the mountainside. In **Jerome State Historic Park** the Douglas Memorial Mining Museum depicts life in the boom days. Open daily exc. Dec. 25, 8-5; sm adm.

KINGMAN: Mohave Museum of History & Art (400 W Beale Plaza). Items of local history; open Mon.-Fri. 10-noon and 1-5; Sat., Sun. 1-5; donation.

KITT PEAK NATIONAL OBSERVATORY (53 m SW of Tucson via SR 86, then SR 386): on the Papago Indian Reservation; 158-in. stellar telescope, 63-in. solar telescope; museum; open daily exc. Dec. 25, 10-4. Free.

MONTEZUMA CASTLE NATIONAL MONUMENT (48 m S of Flagstaff, off I-17): One of the best preserved prehistoric Indian pueblos, it consists of 5-story apartment dwellings—Montezuma Castle with 20 rooms, and Castle A with some 45 rooms—built by dryfarming Sinagua people and occupied c. 125-1450. Montezuma Well (7 m NE) is a sink tapped for irrigation. Open daily 8-5; free.

MONUMENT VALLEY NAVAJO TRIBAL PARK (N of Kayenta off US 163): spectacular formations rising from the desert and many prehistoric ruins. The Visitor Center (4 m E of US 163) provides information on self-guiding or guided tours; exhibits; crafts for sale; open all year 8-6; sm adm.

NAVAJO NATIONAL MONUMENT (22 m SW of Kayenta via US 160, then 9 m on SR 564) has a visitor center describing the Anasazi people who built and abandoned 3 cliff dwellings here 1250-1300. **Betatakin Cliff Dwelling** can be seen from an overlook; a close-up requires a 3-hr, ranger-led, strenuous hike (available Apr.-Oct). **Keet Seel Cliff Dwelling** is open May-Sept.; 8-m trail on foot or horseback; advance reservations required.

NOGALES: Pete Kitchen Museum (5 m N on US 89) houses relics of pioneers, Indians, Spanish mission period (including a memorial to Father Kino); open daily exc Mon. 10-5; closed Dec. 25; sm adm.

PHOENIX: Arizona State Capitol (17th Ave. & W Washington): in a beautifully landscaped park, with a statue of Winged Victory topping its classic copper dome. Murals in the Library and Archives depict Arizona's early days; historical and geological exhibits. Open Mon.-Fri. exc. hols, 8-5; free.

   Heard Museum of Anthropology and Primitive Arts (22 E Monte Vista Rd.), in Spanish colonial buildings, has fine ancient and contemporary arts and crafts of Southwestern tribes; Sen. Barry Goldwater's collection of over 400 Kachinas; mural reproduced from a Hopi kiva; some displays from Plains Indians, Mexican and South American cultures; Spanish colonial displays; open Mon.-Sat. 10-5, Sun. 1-5; closed Aug., hols; sm adm.

   Phoenix Art Museum (1625 N. Central Ave.) has a good collection of Oriental art (including Chinese ivories and tomb figures), medieval, Renaissance, French Baroque, modern works; also costumes, decorative arts, unique series of miniature rooms. Open Tues.-Sat. 10-5, Sun. 1-5; closed hols. Free.

   Phoenix Museum of History (1242 N Central Ave.) displays items related to early history of the city and state. Open Tues.-Sat. 9-5; free. **Arizona Museum** (1002 W Van Buren): Relics of Arizona pioneer days, Indian arts, historic maps. Open Nov. 1-June 1, Wed.-Sun., 2-5; donation. **Arizona History Room** (First National Bank Bldg., 1st Ave. &

Washington St.): changing exhibits of early Arizona life. Open Mon.-Fri. exc hols, 10-3; free. **Arizona Mineral Museum** (1826 W McDowell Rd. at Fairgrounds) is open Mon.-Fri. 9:30-5, Sat. & Sun. 12:30-4:30. Free.

Mystery Castle (foot of South Mountain, at end of S 7th St.) was built by a Seattle businessman. Open Tues.-Sun. 10:30-5; adm.

Duppa-Montgomery Homestead (116 W Sherman) is a brush-roofed adobe residence believed to have been built about 1867. **Bayless Cracker Barrel Store Museum** (118 W Indian School Rd.) is a well-stocked country store of the 1890's. Open Tues.-Sat. 10-6, Sun. noon-5. Free.

Pueblo Grande Municipal Monument (4619 E Washington St., 6 m, off US 60): Ruins of the Hohokam, who built a large network of irrigation canals to farm this area. Museum, mound, ball court. Open Mon.-Fri. 9-5, Sun. 1-5; closed hols; free.

Taliesin West (E on Camelback Rd to Scottsdale Rd., then N 5½ m to Shea Blvd., then E 5½ m to 108th St., then N to school), western architectural school and winter home of Frank Lloyd Wright, has guided tours in winter for those interested in architecture; phone 948-6670 for information.

Paolo Soleri Cosanti Foundation (6433 Doubletree Rd.), studios and craft workshops of architect Paolo Soleri, exhibits model and photographs of town of Arcosanti; ceramic and bronze windbells are cast during week. Open 9-5; tours by appointment.

Mission San Xavier del Bac (9 m S on Papago Indian Reservation), called the "White Dove of the Desert," was one of 29 established by Father Kino. Two dazzling white towers flank a richly decorated facade; unique blend of Byzantine, Moorish, and Spanish Renaissance; fine craftsmanship inside; murals; elaborate altar; still in use. Franciscans conduct tours every ½-hr, 9:30-4:30. A road E of the church leads to a replica of the shrine at Lourdes.

PIPE SPRING NATIONAL MONUMENT (on SR 389, 14 m SW of Fredonia on the Paiute's Kaibab Indian Reservation): Mormon missionaries to the Indians had originally camped here because of the spring, and in 1871 built Winsor Castle around the spring as a protection against Indians. Later it was used as a cattle ranch and travelers' rest; today ranching skills are demonstrated. Open daily 8-5; sm adm.

PRESCOTT: Old Governor's Mansion and **Sharlot Hall Museum** (400 W Gurley St.), home of Arizona's first territorial governor and state capital until 1867, is a museum with pioneer, Indian, and mineral displays. Open Tues.-Sat. 9-noon and 1-5, Sun. 1-5; closed hols; donation. **Smoki Museum** (Arizona Ave.), built to resemble a pueblo, contains an extraordinary collection of artifacts from Tuzigoot and other local ruins. Open June-Aug., Mon.-Sat. 10-4, Sun. 1-5, closed hols. Free.

QUARTZSITE: Hi Jolly Monument (in the cemetery on US 60 E of town) honors the Arab camel driver Hadji Ali (nicknamed Hi Jolly) who took part in an unsuccessful 1850's U.S. War Dept. attempt to use camels in the Arizona desert.

TEMPE: Arizona State University: Matthews Center Galleries, with outstanding American art (Andrew Wyeth, Bellows, Remington, Audubon, Innes, Homer, Stuart), including ceramics, sculpture, and prints. Open Mon.-Fri. 7 am-11 pm, Sun. 10 am-11 pm. **Grady Gammage Memorial Auditorium,** designed by Frank Lloyd Wright, has tours 1:30-3:30 when concerts or other events are not scheduled; apply at office. Free.

TOMBSTONE NATIONAL HISTORIC SITE: In 1877, prospector Ed Schieffelin, who had been warned that all he would find in this hostile Apache territory was his tombstone, named his first claim Tombstone— and the name stuck to the wild town that grew to over 10,000 population as other prospectors rushed in. Although mining lasted less than a decade, its bawdy houses and saloons attracted nationwide attention, and its lawlessness brought a threat of martial law from the President of the U.S. It drew a dazzling array of the famous and infamous, from Bat Masterson and the Earps to Diamond Annie and Big Nose Kate.

   Tombstone *Epitaph* (5th St.), founded in 1880 and Arizona's oldest continuously published newspaper, opens its offices daily to visitors; free.

   Tombstone Courthouse State Historic Monument and Museum (Toughnut & 3rd Sts.) preserves relics and documents. The 2nd-floor courtroom, used in many Western films, was the scene of many famous trials. Reconstructed gallows in rear. Open daily 9-5; sm adm.

   Schieffelin Hall (4th & Fremont Sts.), once the scene of the better dramas and concerts, contains the Tombstone Historama—an animated diorama with film—which tells the town's history. Open daily with frequent shows; adm. **Crystal Palace** (Allen & 5th Sts.), the most famous of more than 60 saloons, has been authentically restored. Open Mon.-Sat. 10-1 am, Sun. noon-eve. **Bird Cage Theatre** (6th & Allen Sts.), a lusty cabaret with private box seats suspended from the ceiling, has been preserved; original furnishings; open daily 9-5; sm adm. **O.K. Corral** (Allen St. at 4th St.), restored stagecoach office where the Earp-Clanton shootout took place, has lifesize figures of the gunmen. Inside are a blacksmith shop and other artifacts. Open daily 9-5; sm adm. **Wells Fargo Museum** (511 Allen St.) contains lifesize wax figures of some of Tombstone's famous characters, plus items of local history; sm adm. **Rose Tree**

Inn Museum (Toughnut and 4th Sts.), named for the white rose tree, planted about 1885, that blooms in Apr., displays original furnishings. Open daily 9-5; sm adm. **Wyatt Earp Museum** (Toughnut & 5th Sts.) contains Earp memorabilia. Open daily 8:30-6; sm adm. **Underground Mine Tours** (Toughnut & 5th Sts.) of a silver mine are conducted daily at 2; adm. **Boothill Graveyard** (N on US 80) contains the graves of many outlaws; many epitaphs are interesting. Open daily in daylight; donation.

A nearby ghost town is **Charleston** (9 m SW; park at the San Pedro River Bridge and walk about ½ m), with ruins of its silver mill and adobe buildings still standing.

TONTO NATIONAL MONUMENT (on SR 88, the Apache Trail, 28 m from Globe or 48 m from Apache Junction of which 25 m are unpaved): The Salado, a Pueblo people, entered this area about AD 900; 3 villages built in caves are preserved, and a self-guiding trail leads to the 20-room Lower Ruin and 12-room Lower Ruin Annex. Visiting the 40-room Upper Ruin requires a rough 3-m, 3-hr round trip hike for which reservations must be made 5 days in advance. The Visitor Center displays items made and used by the Salado. Open daily 8-5.

TUBAC PRESIDIO STATE HISTORIC PARK (on US 89, 45 m S of Tucson): Tubac, first European settlement in Arizona, was a mission ranch in the 1730's, a garrisoned presidio under the Spanish 1752-77, and mining headquarters in the 1850's; museum traces its colorful history. Open daily exc. Dec. 25, 8-5:30. Sm adm.

TUCSON: Arizona Historical Society (949 E 2nd St.) houses a museum of colorful exhibits of pioneer days, period rooms including a gambling casino and hotel lobby, and a research library. Open Mon.-Fri. 8-5, Sat. 8-1, Sun. 2-5; closed hols. Free.

Arizona State Museum (just inside University Blvd. entrance to Univ. of Arizona): one of the world's finest collections of archaeological and ethnological material on the Southwest. Open Mon.-Sat. 10-5, Sun. 2-5; closed hols; free.

Old Tucson (12 m W on Tucson Mt. Pk. Rd.), erected in 1939 by Columbia Pictures for the film *Arizona* and since used for many films, contains over 100 adobe and frame buildings; open 9-sundown; adm.

Fort Lowell Museum (E Ft. Lowell & Craycroft Rds.) in Fort Lowell Park, has fort ruins, reconstruction of the commanding officer's quarters; exhibits of uniforms and period furnishings; open Tues.-Sat. 10-4, Sun. 2-4; free.

Mission in the Sun (6300 N Swan Rd.), built in honor of Our Lady of Guadaloupe, patron of the Yaqui Indians, by noted local artist Ted De

Grazia, has painted interior walls. Open daily, free. Other work by De Grazia is shown in the adjacent Gallery in the Sun.

Old Adobe (40 W Broadway), built as a residence in 1868, is one of the few buildings remaining from Territorial days; it now houses restaurants and shops. Old buildings you can see from the outside are **Stevens Home** (155 N Main Ave.), an early Territorial example, **Otero Home** (219 S Main Ave.), an adobe house from 1859, and **Fish Home** (119 N Main Ave.), with adobe walls 3-ft thick.

University of Arizona (University Blvd. & Park Ave.): **Museum of Art** includes the Kress Collection of Renaissance art; a fine 19th-20th-C American collection; and many French painters (Matisse, Dubuffet, Leger); open Mon.-Sat. 10-5, Sun. 2-5. The university collection of **Arizona History** (including the range-cattle industry) is in the Main Library (3rd floor, room 320); open Mon.-Fri. 8:30-4:30, Sat. 8:30-noon. **Mineral Museum** (Geology Bldg.) has same hours as library. History of Arizona **Pharmacy Museum** (Pharmacy-Microbiology Bldg.) is open Mon.-Fri. 10-4.

TUMACACORI NATIONAL MONUMENT (48 m S of Tucson on US 89): This typical frontier mission church, constructed by Spanish Franciscans in the late 1700's near the little Pima village of Tumacacori, was used until the 1840's. A museum depicts early Indian and Spanish history; living history demonstrations. Open daily 9-5. Sm adm or GEP.

TUZIGOOT NATIONAL MONUMENT (about 2 m E of Clarksdale): A trail from the Visitor Center—whose museum houses grave offerings, including rare turquoise mosaics, and other objects—leads to the rambling 92-room hilltop Tuzigoot ruins. Open 8-5, longer in summer. Sm. adm. or GEP.

WALNUT CANYON NATIONAL MONUMENT (off I-40 7½ m E of Flagstaff, then 3-m park rd): The Sinagua cliff dwellings here can be seen from a canyon rim trail. A self-guiding, paved trail—¾-m round trip, requiring a 185-foot climb—leads to 25 of the rooms. Open daily 8-5 (8-7 in summer); snow can temporarily close the roads in winter. Sm adm or GEP.

WICKENBURG: Desert Caballeros Western Museum (20 Frontier St.) reconstructs, with a typical saloon, assayer's office, and other buildings, that rush that began in 1863 after discovery of the Vulture Gold Mine southeast of the city. Open Mon.-Fri. 9-4:30, Sat. 10-4, Sun. 1-4; donation. **The Jail Tree** (Center & Tegner Sts.) is an old mesquite to which prisoners were chained before a jail was constructed.

WINDOW ROCK: Navajo Tribal Museum describes natural history and prehistoric peoples, but emphasis is on Navajo history and way of life;

research library; photo collection; educational programs; zoo; open daily 8-5; closed Jan. 1, Easter, Thnks, Dec. 25; free. **Navajo Arts & Crafts Guild** (on SR 264, S of Hdqurs) is a showcase of high quality Navajo rugs, silverware, and other arts and crafts; even if you don't intend to buy, it's worth looking at; mail-order brochure available. Open daily 8-5 (longer hrs in summer); closed some hols; free. Smaller branches are in Betatakin, Cameron, Chinle, Kayenta, Monument Valley Tribal Park, and Teec Nos Pos, all on the reservation.

WUPATKI NATIONAL MONUMENT (30 m N of Flagstaff off US 89, or via Sunset Crater): Of some 800 ruins here, the most impressive is Wupatki (Hopi for Tall House); in the 1100's it contained over 100 rooms and was 3 stories high; nearby amphitheater and ball court. Trails lead to Wukoki, Nalakihu, Citadel, other ruins. Visitor Center open daily 8-5 (8-6 in summer); free.

YUMA TERRITORIAL PRISON STATE HISTORIC PARK (off US 80, E of Main St.), built in 1875, was known as the "Hell Hole of Arizona" during the 34 years that some of the West's most famous badmen were jailed here. Museum; you can tour cell blocks and dungeons. Open daily exc Dec. 25, 8-5:50; sm adm.

ARKANSAS

ALTUS: Swiss and German immigrants planted vineyards here in the late 1880's and built wineries and homes in Swiss-German style. Atop St. Mary's Mountain are **St. Mary's Church**, noted for ornate gold-leaf decoration and paintings, and **Wiederkehr Wine Cellars, Inc.**, with guided tours daily exc Sun. 9-4:30; closed hols; free.

ARKANSAS POST NATIONAL MEMORIAL (on SR 169, off SR 1, midway between De Witt & Dumas) is a wildlife sanctuary. Here Henri de Tonti, an Italian who accompanied LaSalle, established a trading post that became the first white settlement in the lower Mississippi Valley. In 1719-20 it was the site of John Law's Mississippi Bubble, an attempt to establish a duchy. The settlement thrived and in 1819 became capital of the Arkansas Territory; but the coming of railroads and the diversion of the river doomed the town. A Visitor Center tells the story with exhibits and audiovisual program; self-guiding auto trail; ½-m Historic Walking Trail; open daily 8-5; closed Dec. 25; free.

BERRYVILLE: Saunders Museum (314 E Madison): large and unusual collection of Colt and other guns; guns of Pancho Villa, Annie Oakley, and others; silver; lace; a tent woven by a harem for an Arabian sheik; open mid-Mar.-Oct. 9-5; adm.

BUTTERFIELD OVERLAND MAIL ROUTE, in its day the longest stagecoach line in the world—2651 m from St. Louis to San Francisco— ran N-S in Arkansas, where its traces can still be seen, from Elkhorn Tavern at Pea Ridge National Military Park to Fort Smith. Historic markers along the route; a few old buildings still remain.

CAMDEN: Now an industrial city, this town has many antebellum homes; Ouachita County Historical Assn. sponsors tours in May and Oct. Open all year is **Chidester House** (926 Washington St.), built as a stage stop in 1847; Civil War period furnishings; open Mon.-Fri. 9-5; closed hols; adm.

CONWAY: Greathouse Home (Faulkner St.) is a restored 1830 farmhouse that became an inn on the Butterfield Overland Mail Route; period furnishings. Open Apr.-Oct., Sat. & Sun. 3-5; free.

EUREKA SPRINGS: Called the "Little Switzerland of America," this is a lovely town with streets that twist and wind up and down hillsides, many never intersecting. Many buildings have multilevel entrances, such as St. Elizabeth Church, which can be entered through the bell tower. Many old buildings boast Victorian gingerbread; these are being restored by the artists and antique dealers who make this town their home. The 63 springs are free. **Eureka Springs Historical Museum** (95 S Main St.) is in an 1889 structure that started the town fad for Victorian architecture; artifacts of everyday life before the turn of the century. Open May-Oct. daily 10-5; adm.
    Hatchet Hall (35 Steel St.) was the last home (1908-11) of temperance leader Carry Nation; she made her last speech here and had intended to start a school for prohibitionists here. Now an art gallery; open Mar.- Nov., daily exc Sun. 9-5; sm adm. **The Rosalie** (282 Spring St.) was built about 1880 of handmade bricks; period furnishings; open mid-Mar.-mid- Nov., daily 9-6; adm. **Miles Mountain Musical Museum** (1½ m NW on US 62): music boxes, early phonographs, nickelodeons, player pianos from the 1800s; handmade dolls; Indian artifacts; tours May-Oct. daily 9-5; adm. **Bible Museum** (3 m E on US 62) has more than 10,000 volumes, including words on papyrus and clay dating back to 2000 BC; open Easter-Oct. daily 9-5; adm.

FAYETTEVILLE: University of Arkansas: University Hall or "Old Main," whose 150-ft mansard towers can be seen for miles; the top floor houses exhibits of Arkansas archaeology, geology, and natural history; outstanding early American glass collection; open Mon.-Fri. 8-5, Sat. 8-noon; closed hols; free. **Fine Arts Gallery** (Garland Ave.) designed by Edward Durell Stone, houses traveling shows; open Mon.-Sat. 8 am-10 pm, Sun. 2-5, closed hols; free.

Headquarters House (118 W Dickson St.): Greek Revival home built in 1853; used by both Union and Confederate forces during the Civil War; period furnishings; open June-Oct., Tues.-Sun. 2-4; sm adm.

FORT SMITH: Chamber of Commerce (613 Garrison Ave.) offers a booklet describing walking tours of the old sections, where residences built in the late 1800's have been restored; some may be visited. Several of these are on Free Ferry Road. **Fort Smith Art Center** (423 N 6th St.), built as a home in 1855 and now housing changing exhibits, is open Tues.-Sat. 10-4, Sun. 2-4; closed hols; free.

FORT SMITH NATIONAL HISTORIC SITE (Rodgers Ave. & 2nd St.): Belle Point was site of the first fort, built in 1817 overlooking the Arkansas River, not only to protect traders and settlers but also to separate the Osage to the N from the Cherokee to the S. A second fort was begun in 1838, and now only the stone commissary remains; it houses Indian and pioneer artifacts. Fort Smith became a major gateway to the West, especially after the California gold rush started; along with miners came assorted outlaws, and Fort Smith became the only outpost of law and order for the entire Indian Territory. Judge Isaac C. Parker was sent to restore order, and he presided here from 1875-1896. He delegated over 150 deputy marshals, sentenced 160 men to death and hanged about 79 of them, and during the first 14 years he presided there was no appeal from his decisions—all of which earned him the label, "the hanging judge." His courtroom and gallows have been restored (open daily 8:30-5, longer hrs in summer, closed Dec. 25; free), and he himself is buried in the National Cemetery (open daily 8-5; free).

HARRISON: Rally Hill Museum & Heritage Center (8 m SE via US 65 to Valley Springs, then 3 m E) depicts frontier life in furnished cabins; open May-Nov., Mon.-Sat. 9-4, Sun. 1-4; adm. **Bryant Art Center Galleries** (6 m S on SR 7), with works by American and European artists from the 17th C to the present, is open mid-Apr.-mid-Nov., Mon.-Sat. 9-5, Sun. 1-5; adm.

HELENA: This riverport on the Mississippi, the state's only outlet to the sea, has many antebellum homes—such as Hornor House with Civil War bullets embedded in its walls—along Great River Road; these are sometimes open for tours. **Phillips County Museum** (623 Pecan St. adj to public library) contains Mound Builder artifacts, Revolutionary era glass, silver, china, paintings, and costumes, an Edison exhibit, and relics from the time Helena was a key to Union control of the river during the Civil War; open Mon.-Sat. 9-5; closed hols; free.

HOT SPRINGS: Wildwood (808 Park Ave.) is a restored 1884 Victorian mansion featuring hand-carved woodwork; period furnishings; open Mar.-Nov., Mon.-Sat. 10-4, Sun. 1-5; adm.

HOT SPRINGS NATIONAL PARK: Indians, who called this the Valley of Vapors, considered this sacred ground where many tribes could bathe in peace. DeSoto visited here in 1541; later it was claimed by both France and Spain; a spa developed after the Louisiana Purchase of 1803. Today, 45 of the 47 springs are sealed off so that water can be piped to bathhouses and therapy rooms. Two springs, called the Display Springs, have been kept open on the Promenade. You can also get hot spring water from fountains along Reserve Ave. or Bathhouse Row. The **Visitor Center** (Reserve & Central Ave.) depicts the history of the park with exhibits and slide programs; also evening programs and nature walks. The self-guiding Promenade trail starts here; it leads along the Promenade and Bathhouse Row (where you can get a tour of a bathhouse).

JACKSONPORT STATE PARK (3 m NW of Newport on SR 69) is located at a big bend in the White River that had long been a crossing on an Indian trail and in 1822 became the site of an Indian trading post. The city was established in 1833 and became a thriving river port, but when the residents refused the railroad right of way in the 1870's, it turned into a ghost town. Today only the red-brick, 1869 **Jacksonport Courthouse Museum** remains; the courtroom trappings were often pushed aside for gala parties; doors and windows are memorials to Jackson Co. pioneers; period rooms illustrate local history from Indian days; carriage house. On the courthouse square is a brick outhouse, once lined with black walnut paneling and considered the most elegant privy in Arkansas. At the landing, the old White River steamboat *Mary Woods No. 2* is moored. Open Tues.-Sun. 2-6; closed Jan. 1, Dec. 25; sm adm.

JONESBORO: Arkansas State University Museum has natural history displays, including mounted waterfowl that use the Mississippi Flyway; good exhibit on the prehistoric people of Arkansas with a cutaway of a temple mound from the Ballard Site dating from 700-800 AD. Open Mon.-Fri. 9-5, Sun. 1-5; closed hols; free.

LITTLE ROCK: The historic area, bounded by the Arkansas River on the N, Fourche Creek on the S, the airport on the E, and the present State Capitol building on the W, is called the Quapaw Quarter (named for the native Indians who had a village here). Within this 3-sq-m area are: **First State Capitol** (300 W Markham St.), a Greek Revival building completed in 1836 and designed by Gideon Shryock. Except while Little Rock was occupied by Union forces during the Civil War, it served as the capitol from 1836-1911. Open Mon.-Fri. 8-4:30, Sat. & Sun. 1-5; closed Dec. 25; guided tours available; free. **Arkansas State Capitol** (W Capitol and Woodlane) is open Mon.-Fri. 8-4:30, Sat. & Sun. 1-5; closed hols; free.

Arkansas Territorial Restoration (E 3rd at Scott) is one of the nation's best restorations; 13 buildings, with carriage houses and other outbuildings, dating from the 1820's and 1830's, capture the lifestyle of frontier Arkansas. Among the buildings is the 2-story Jesse Henderliter House, originally built of logs and later covered with clapboard, and the home and printing office of the founder of the *Arkansas Gazette,* the oldest surviving newspaper W of the Mississippi. Open Mon.-Sat. 9:30-4:30, Sun. 1:30-4:30; closed hols; adm.

Albert Pike House (E 7th at Rock) is a beautiful antebellum home built in 1840, later used as a school, and furnished with Victorian, Art Nouveau, and other styles; open Tues., Thurs. 2-5; closed hols; tours by residents; free. **Angelo Marre House** (Scott at 14th) is a marvelously elaborate Victorian home with Italian influences built in 1881 by saloon-keeper Angelo Marre; frescoed ceilings have been restored; crystal chandeliers, ornate brasswork, period furnishings, paintings by local artists, a Battenburg lace bedspread, and old tapestries. Open Sun. 2-5; Tues., Thurs., Sat. 1-4:30; closed hols; adm. **Mount Holly Cemetery** (S Broadway at 12th) contains the graves of many noted Arkansans; map of the grounds available at the Victorian bell house; open daily sunrise to sunset; free.

Arkansas Arts Center (MacArthur Park) houses many American works and some European paintings; library; open Mon.-Sat. 10-5, Sun. 1-5; closed Dec. 25; free.

Museum of Science and Natural History (E. 9th in MacArthur Park), housed in an old U.S. arsenal where Gen. Douglas MacArthur was born in 1880, has particularly good exhibits on the history of glass and collections of pressed glass; early textiles; guns; birds; Indian artifacts; small planetarium; open Tues.-Sat., 10-5, Sun. 2-5; closed hols; free. **River Museum** (111 E 3rd) commemorates Little Rock's days as a steamboat stop; scale model paddlewheeler; modern Arkansas River projects; open Mon.-Fri. 9-5; closed hols; adm.

MORRILTON: Museum of Automobiles (on Petit Jean Mountain) contains the fine Winthrop Rockefeller collection of antique cars dating from 1899; more than 40 cars, including a 1907 Rolls-Royce and a 1914 Stanley Steamer, are attractively housed. Open daily 10-5; closed Jan. 1, Dec. 25; adm. **Winrock Farms,** established by Winthrop Rockefeller to breed Santa Gertrudis cattle, is also on the mountain; reception room, show barn, corrals, and stables are open daily, all year, sunrise-sunset; free. Auctions are held in May.

MOUNTAIN VIEW: Ozark Folk Center (2 m N, near jct SR 66, 9, 14), operated by the Arkansas Dept. of Parks & Tourism, is an 80-acre living museum of the arts, crafts, music, and lore of the area. Here 59 buildings of cedar and native stone house a Visitor Center for information, an auditorium, seminar rooms, and workshops, plus demonstrations of crafts such as shuckery, rail splitting, doll making, quilting, and blacksmithing, and craft sales. Festivals and other programs are given frequently. Open daily May-Oct. 10-6, with some weekend activities in winter, but hrs may be changed, depending on demand.

NORFORK: Wolf House, built about 1809 with Indian labor, is a 2-story log house that served as the first courthouse in Arkansas and also as an inn; pioneer household items and tools on display; open mid-May-mid-Oct., Mon.-Sat. 10-4, Sun. 2-5; adm.

OLD WASHINGTON STATE HISTORICAL PARK (9 m NW of Hope on SR 4): Washington, strategically located on the Old Southwest Trail, was a rest stop for many Texas-bound settlers in the early 1800's, and its cemetery contains many pioneer graves. Among the buildings are: **Confederate State Capitol,** built in 1841, where the Confederate Legislature met from 1863-5 while Little Rock was occupied by Federal forces; uniforms and memorabilia of the Civil War. The reconstructed 1824 **Old Tavern,** where Sam Houston plotted the drive to make Texas independent. The reconstructed 1831 **Blacksmith Shop,** where Col. Jim Bowie had the cutler fashion the first Bowie knife. The **Gun Museum,** with a good collection of antique weapons; many Bowie knives too. The **Schoolhouse,** housing the Pioneer Washington Restoration Foundation, which maintains this site, displays fabric and clothing from pioneer days to the Civil War.

Several homes with fine period furnishings have also been restored: **Block-Catts House,** handmade by slaves in 1828-32 of bricks produced here, has much of the original woodwork intact. **Garland House,** an 1836 Greek Revival home, belonged to a former state governor. **Royston House,** built in 1845, includes many Chinese pieces among its furnishings.

All buildings are open Mon.-Sat. 9-4, Sun. 1-5; closed Easter, Thnks, over Christmas; adm.

PEA RIDGE NATIONAL MILITARY PARK (10 m NE of Rogers via US 62): During the Civil War, Missouri was crucial to both sides. Brig. Gen. Samuel R. Curtis started a push to send pro-Confederate forces over the border and the battle ended here at Elkhorn Tavern on March 7-8, 1862, after 3 Confederate generals fell. The Visitor Center (open daily 8-dark; closed Jan. 1, Dec. 25) can give you information on the 7-m self-guiding auto tour of battlefield features and the restored Elkhorn Tavern.

PINE BLUFF: Founded in 1819 as a trading post by Joseph Bonne, this town claims that the first shot of the Civil War was fired here, shortly before Ft. Sumter. The **Civic Center,** with art galleries, library, and municipal offices, was designed by Edward Durell Stone. **Southeastern Arkansas Arts & Science Center** (200 E 8th St.) has art galleries with changing exhibits; open Mon.-Sat. 10-5, closed hols; free. **Du Bocage** (4th Ave. & Linden St.) is a restored Greek Revival mansion built in 1866, with period furnishings; open weekends 1-5; adm.

PRAIRIE GROVE BATTLEFIELD STATE PARK (8 m SW of Fayette-ville on US 62) commemorates the battle, that ended inconclusively, with many dead and injured, between Union and Confederate forces on Dec. 7, 1862. Hindman Hall Museum is devoted to the battle. Nearby is a re-created Ozark Mountain village.

ROGERS: Daisy International Air-Gun Museum (Victor Comptometer Corp., 1 m S on US 71): more than 2000 items, airguns from Napoleonic times to the present; open Mon.-Fri. 9-5; closed hols; free; plant tour free.

SPRINGDALE: Shiloh Museum (118 W Johnson Ave.) has local artifacts and Indian material; library; open Tues.-Sat. 10-5; closed hols; free.

TEXARKANA: Texarkana Historical Museum (219 State Line Ave.) is open Mon.-Fri. 10-4, Sat. 10-2, Sun. noon-3; closed hols; free.

WILSON: This is a company-owned town, built in English Tudor style, completely surrounded by the huge R.E.I. Wilson Plantation. The **Henry Clay Hampson II Museum of Archaeology** here houses Indian material from the Nodena Mound site and nearby areas in the Mississippi Valley. Open Tues.-Sat. 10-noon, 1-5, Sun. 1-5; free.

CALIFORNIA

ALTURAS: Modoc County Historical Museum (508 S Main St.) has a huge collection of Indian arrowheads, antique guns, and items related to local history. Open May-Oct. daily 9-5; Nov.-Apr., Mon.-Fri. 9-5; closed hols; free.

ANGELS CAMP: Angels Camp Museum (SR 49, 2 blocks N of Angels Creek): equipment from gold rush days; logging equipment, old vehicles; open June-Sept., Tues.-Sun. 10-6; rest of yr, weekends only; sm adm.

Mark Twain stayed here while gathering information for his "Celebrated Jumping Frog of Calaveras County," and a statue of him is in the town park. In May there is an annual jumping frog contest.

ANZA-BORREGO DESERT STATE PARK (on US 78, E of San Diego) contains a historic marker on the trail of Juan Bautista de Anza, who wanted to make Coyote Canyon an inland passage from Mexico north in 1774; Yaqui Well area of lost mine legends; Box Canyon Historical Area.

ARCADIA: Los Angeles State & County Arboretum (301 N Baldwin Ave.) offers the 1839 Hugo Reid Adobe Home, and 1879 coach house, and an 1881 Queen Anne Cottage; open daily 8-5; closed Dec. 25; free.

ARCATA: Chamber of Commerce (City Hall, 7th & F Sts.) has a booklet describing self-guiding auto tour past Victorian houses (Bret Harte stayed in one).

AUBURN: Placer County Historical Museum (Fairgrounds off High St.) houses gold-rush era displays; open June-Labor Day, Tues.-Sun. 10-4; rest of yr, Sat. & Sun. 10-5; closed hols; free. **Chamber of Commerce** offers a booklet for self-guiding tours of Old Town.

BAKERSFIELD: Kern County Museum & Pioneer Village (3801 Chester Ave.) offers a 12-acre restored village complete with jail, saloon, hotel, other buildings, and vehicles; open Mon.-Fri. 8-3:30; Sat., Sun., hols, May-late Oct. noon-5:30, late Oct.-Apr. noon-3:30; sm adm. The museum has archaeological finds, local plants and animals; open Mon.-Fri. 8-5; Sat., Sun., hols, May-Sept. noon-7, Oct.-Apr. noon-5; free. Both closed Jan. 1, Thnks, Dec. 25.

BARSTOW: Calico Ghost Town Regional Park (7 m E on I-15, then 3 m N on Ghost Town Rd.) preserves the school, saloon, assay shop, and other buildings of a town that boomed for about 5 years after silver was discovered in 1881; open daily 9-6, longer in summer; closed Dec. 25; parking fee plus charges for rides.

BENICIA CAPITOL STATE HISTORIC PARK (1st St. at G St., Benicia): Rather grand 1853 Greek Revival statehouse (1853-4); open daily 10-5; closed Jan. 1, Thnks, Dec. 25; sm adm.

BERKELEY: University of California campus covers more than 1000 acres E of San Francisco Bay. The **Campanile** (Sather Tower) is open daily 10-5; closed hols; sm adm. **Robert H. Lowie Museum of Anthropology** has a vast collection of anthropological material, changing exhibits; open Mon.-Fri. 10-4; Sat., Sun. noon-4; closed hols; sm adm. **Art Museum:** Hans Hoffmann paintings, Oriental art objects, and many European and American works; open Wed.-Sun. 11-6; closed major hols; free. **Earth Sciences Bldg.** has mineral and paleontological collections; open Mon.-Fri. 8-5; also weekend afternoons during academic year; closed hols; free.
   Palestine Institute Museum (Pacific School of Religion, 1798 Senic Ave.) has collections from the Holy Land dating from over 3000 BC; John Howell Bible Collection. Open Mon.-Fri. 8:30-5; free. **Judah L. Magnes Memorial Museum** (2911 Russell St.) collects materials related to Jewish life and culture with special emphasis on the American West. Open Sun.-Fri. 10-4; closed Jewish and legal hols; free.

BIDWELL MANSION STATE HISTORIC PARK (525 Esplanade, Chico), the ornate, 26-room home of John Bidwell, founder of Chico, was completed in 1868; fine period furnishings. Open daily 10-5; closed major hols; sm adm.

BISHOP: Laws Railroad Museum & Historical Site (5 m NE via US 6, then ½ m E on Silver Canyon Rd.) has indoor and outdoor exhibits from the days when Laws was a terminal of the Southern Pacific Railroad; open daily 10-4; closed major hols; donation.

BLOOMINGTON: San Bernardino County Museum (18860 Orange Ave.): Prehistoric and historic Indian displays, hall of mammals, birds' eggs; open daily 1-5; closed some hols; free.

BODIE STATE HISTORIC PARK (7 m S of Bridgeport on SR 395, then 13 m on unpaved Bodie Rd.): Authentic remains of gold town that boomed in 1859 and gained a reputation for wickedness; from the town jail and Chinatown to the morgue and segregated cemeteries; open all year, weather permitting.

CABRILLO NATIONAL MONUMENT (Point Loma, San Diego) commemorates the Portuguese explorer, first European to explore the W Coast (1542). Visitor Center displays on Cabrillo and whales (which migrate here Dec.-Feb.); open daily 9-5:15; free.

CALABASAS: Leonis Adobe (23537 Calabasas Rd.) was the home of the "King of Calabasas," a Basque sheep rancher; open Wed., Sat., Sun. 1-4:45; closed hols and mid-Aug.-mid-Sept.; free.

CALISTOGA: Napa County Historical Society Museum (1435 Oak St., fairgrounds) exhibits local memorabilia, Indian artifacts, collection of bells; open Sat., Sun. 12-4; free.

CARLSBAD: Alt Karlsbad Hanse House (2802 Carlsbad Blvd.) features the tunnel housing the mineral well, sunk in 1882, that made this a spa similar to its Czechoslovakian namesake; paintings and a replica of Bohemian King Karl IV's crown. Open Tues.-Sat. 10-5, Sun. 1-4:30; adm.

CARMEL: Mission San Carlos Borromeo del Rio Carmelo (3080 Rio Rd.), founded by Fray Junipero Serra in 1770, was built by Indian converts, who also decorated the interior; open Mon.-Sat. 9:30-5, Sun. & hols 10:30-5; closed thnks, Dec. 25; donation.

CHERRY VALLEY: Edward Dean Museum of Decorative Arts (9401 Oak Glen Rd., 4 m N of town) has a fabulous collection of 17th- and 18th-C European and Oriental decorative arts displayed to give the impression of a home rather than a museum. Open Tues.-Sat. 1-5; closed Mon., hols, 2 wks after Labor Day; free.

COALINGA: R. C. Baker Memorial Museum (297 W Elm St.): Indian and pioneer, oil, and mineral displays; open Mon.-Fri. 9-5, Sat. 11-5, Sun. & hols 1-5; closed hols; free.

COLONEL ALLENSWORTH STATE HISTORIC PARK (on SR 43, between Wasco and Corcoran) preserves California's only town founded, financed, and governed by blacks. It was founded by Col. Allensworth in 1908, but was abandoned after he died in an accident in 1914. The town is being restored with school, Allensworth's home, shops, and other buildings, and will be a research center on black history, with library and museum. Open daily 10-5; closed Jan. 1, Thnks, Dec. 25; free.

COLUMBIA STATE HISTORIC PARK (4 m N of Sonora on SR 49): This gold town boomed in 1850, with a typical combination of one church and 30 saloons. The preserved buildings, many with recreated interiors, were built with fire-resistant doors and shutters after a disastrous 1854 fire—Fallon Theater, Eagle Cottage boardinghouse, Wells Fargo office. Most buildings open daily 8-5, longer in summer; closed Thnks, Dec. 25; some shops closed weekdays.

COSTA MESA: Briggs Cunningham Automotive Museum (250 E Baker St.) exhibits a select collection of some 100 cars dating from 1898 to the present; open Wed.-Sun. 9-5; closed hols; adm.

CRESCENT CITY: Crescent City Lighthouse (Battery Point), one of the oldest on the Pacific Coast, was erected in 1856; museum; open Mar.-Nov., daily exc Fri. and hols, during daylight hours *at low tide;* free. **Del Norte County Historical Museum** (577 H St.), in the county jail, houses Indian exhibits; open summers Mon.-Sat. 1-4, spring & fall Wed.-Sat. 1-4, closed hols & Dec.-Feb.; free. **McNulty Pioneer Memorial Home** (710 H St.), built in 1897, has period furnishings; open Mar.-Nov., Wed.-Sat. 10-noon; closed hols & Dec.-Feb.; free. All maintained by Del Norte County Historical Society.

D. L. BLISS-EMERALD BAY STATE PARKS (SW end of Lake Tahoe): The remarkable, 38-room **Vikingsholm** is an authentic copy of a Norse fortress of about 800 AD; detailed replicas of Scandinavian furnishings; open July 1-Labor Day, 10-4:30; sm adm.

DONNER MEMORIAL STATE PARK (E edge of Donner Lake, 2 m W of Truckee): **Emigrant Trail Museum** recounts the conquest of the Sierra Nevada by whites and the trials of the Donner Party. In 1846 this 20-wagon party tried to take a mountain shortcut to California but were trapped by snow; 42 died in crude shelters or attempting to escape before rescuers reached them in 1847; open daily 10-4; sm adm.

ESCONDIDO: Palomar Observatory (35 m NE) has a museum and visitor gallery; open daily 9-5; closed Dec. 25; free.

EUREKA: Chamber of Commerce (2112 Broadway) booklets describe auto tour of gaudy Victorian homes. Carson Mansion (143 M St.), ornate, native-wood home built in 1855, is worth seeing from the outside; not open to public.

FORT HUMBOLDT STATE HISTORIC PARK (off US 101 at Eureka): Fort, constructed in 1853 to protect settlements that served as coastal supply bases for gold diggings on the Trinity River, was abandoned in 1870. Ulysses S. Grant was stationed here but was forced to resign after 5 months because of his drinking. The reconstructed buildings house historic and archaeological displays; also a logging camp display; open daily 8-5; closed Thnks, Dec. 25; free.

FORT ROSS STATE HISTORIC PARK (on US 1, 11 m N of Jenner): Established by the Russian-American Co. in 1812, the fort was later sold to John A. Sutter and became a ranch. The Manager's House, a museum, still retains elements of the original Russian construction and some of the original lavish furnishings; also Russian chapel, other buildings; open daily 9-5; closed Jan. 1, Thnks, Dec. 25; sm adm.

FORT TEJON STATE HISTORIC PARK (on SR 99, 36 m S of Bakersfield): Established by the US Army in 1854 to intercept cattle rustlers and bandits and to protect miners, this fort became a social and political center and a stop on the Butterfield Overland Mail; it stabled camels for the Camel Corps experiment. Barracks and officers' quarters are preserved; open daily 9-5; closed Jan 1, Thnks, Dec. 25; sm adm.

FREMONT: Mission San Jose de Guadalupe (43300 Mission Blvd.), established in 1797, now consists only of the padre's living quarters, converted into a museum; open daily 10-5; closed Dec. 25; sm adm.

FRESNO: Kearney Mansion (7160 W Kearney Blvd.) houses the County Historical Society in an 1890's home with blacksmith shop and other period exhibits; open Mar.-Dec., Wed.-Sun. 2-4; adm. **Fresno Arts Center** (3033 E Yale Ave.) features contemporary American works; also some Oriental, Mexican, and African material, and an 18th-C Swedish folk painting. Open Tues.-Sun. noon-4; closed hols & Aug.; free. **Fresno Museum of Natural History** (1944 N Winery Ave.) features birds and animals (some live) in natural settings, and Yokut Indian displays; open Tues.-Sat. 9-5, Sun. noon-5; closed major hols; sm adm.

GLENDALE: Forest Lawn Memorial Park (1712 S Glendale Ave.) is open 8:30-5:30; free; proper dress required. Among the attractions are the **Hall of the Crucifixion-Resurrection,** with 2 of the world's largest oil paintings (open daily 10-5; doors locked during showings; donation); **Forest Lawn Museum** (with gems, every coin mentioned in the Bible, and a reproduction of Ghiberti's Paradise Doors); **Memorial Court of Honor** (stained-glass copy of Leonardo da Vinci's *The Last Supper* with hourly lectures, 9-4); **Church of the Recessional,** copied from the one in England where Rudyard Kipling worshiped and containing a collection of manuscripts and mementos belonging to Kipling); other churches, stained-glass windows, and Carrara marble statuary.

GOLDEN GATE NATIONAL RECREATION AREA (Fort Mason, San Francisco): **Promenade** runs from the Golden Gate Bridge to Aquatic Park. Museum in **Fort Point** (within the Presidio via Lincoln Blvd.), erected to guard the Gate in 1853-61; open daily 10-5; free. **Alcatraz** (ferry from Fisherman's Wharf), built as a fortification and military prison, gained fame as a federal penitentiary (1934-63); tours include cells, mess hall, library, solitary, yard, guard towers. Ferries run daily 9-3 (longer hrs in summer) exc Jan. 1, Thnks, Dec. 25; reserve in advance (phone 398-1141).

GRASS VALLEY: **Rough & Ready** (4 m W on SR 20) was a gold strike named for Old Rough and Ready (Gen. Zachary Taylor); this area once tried to secede from the Union to form an independent republic. **Pelton Wheel Mining Exhibit** (114 Mill St.) houses mining displays; open mid-May-mid-Oct. daily 11-5; sm adm.

HEARST-SAN SIMEON STATE HISTORICAL MONUMENT (30 m N of Morro Bay on SR 1, 1 m E of village of San Simeon) was such a passionate hobby with William Randolph Hearst that though he lived here for 29 years after it was begun in 1919 he never considered it finished. This 100-room Hispano-Moresque mansion, La Casa Grande, was designed as a shell around entire rooms Hearst acquired from European castles. The Gothic Suite, his personal living and working quarters, takes up a relatively small part of the house; the 86-ft-long Assembly Room, 5200-volume Main Library, Doge's Suite, and North Wing were for the use of guests, as were 3 Mediterranean Renaissance style guesthouses. The house overflows with priceless tapestries, furnishings, and decorative arts, and is rather overpoweringly ornate. On the grounds are 2 swimming pools, marble statuary, elaborate staircases and terraces, sarcophagi, and fountains in the beautifully landscaped gardens. Open daily 8-3:30 by conducted tour only; you have a choice of 2-hr tours. Reservations are advised on weekends, holidays, and in summer from Ticketron or the Reservations Office, State Dept. of Parks and Recreation, 1416 9th St., Sacramento; price varies according to tour. Closed Jan. 1, Thnks, Dec. 25.

HENRY W. COE STATE PARK (from Morgan Hill on US 101, 14 m E via Dunne Ave.), a ranch homesteaded in 1883, contains the remains of Madrone Soda Springs spa and a museum on ranching; park open daily, museum on weekends 1-4.

INDEPENDENCE: Eastern Sierra Museum has Indian, local historical, and natural history displays; open daily 10-5, longer in summer; closed hols; free.

JACK LONDON STATE HISTORIC SITE (off SR 12, midway between Sonoma & Santa Rosa): House of Happy Walls, a memorial to her husband built by Charmain London in 1919, contains his personal effects and South Sea collection; furnishings were intended for Wolf House, the 26-room, volcanic rock mansion that burned before he could move in; London's grave is marked by a lava boulder; open daily 10-5; closed Jan. 1, Thnks, Dec. 25; sm adm.

JACKSON: Amador County Museum (225 Church St.) has exhibits on the history of this gold rush area where many camp ruins remain. The **Emigrant Trail,** blazed by Kit Carson, has been marked off the highway above Red Lake. Just N is Sutter Creek, where the Lincoln Mine produced the fortune that enabled Leland Stanford to finance the Central Pacific Railroad and Stanford University, and where Hetty Green made a fortune. **Amador City,** site of the fabled Keystone Mine, has many restored gold rush buildings. Nearby **Volcano** is another picturesque mining town.

JOHN MUIR NATIONAL HISTORIC SITE (jct SR 4, Alhambra Ave., S of Martinez): Home of the great naturalist, who was born in Scotland in 1838, from 1890 until his death in 1914; tours of his house and other structures (including the 1849 Martinez Adobe), audiovisual program on his life and work. Open daily 9-4:30; closed Jan. 1, Thnks, Dec. 25; sm adm.

KING CITY: Mission San Antonio de Padua (20 m SW in Jolon), founded in 1773, is a large adobe compound with restored gristmill, workshops, and wine press, and an 1813 chapel; a museum houses vestments, mission artifacts, Indian crafts. Open Mon.-Sat. 9-4:30; Sun. 11-5; donation; fiesta held in June.

LA JOLLA: T. Wayland Vaughan Aquarium-Museum (at Scripps Inst. of Oceanography, 8602 La Jolla Shores Dr.) features tanks of local fish and invertebrates plus splendid exhibits devoted to oceanographic research; open daily 9-5; free.

    La Jolla Museum of Contemporary Art (700 Prospect St.) highlights modern American and European art in a collection of more than 3000 works; open Tues.-Fri. 11-5, plus eve on Sat. & Sun; closed major hols; free.

LAKEPORT: Lake County Museum (175 3rd St.) has local Indian artifacts; open Mon.-Sat. 1-4; closed hols; sm adm.

LA PURISIMA MISSION STATE HISTORIC PARK (on Lompoc-Casmalia Rd., 3 m E of SR 1 in Lompoc): Well-restored church, shops, dwellings of this large 1812 mission; museum of Indian relics; 1821 cemetery; open daily 8-5; closed Jan. 1, Thnks, Dec. 25; sm adm.

LAVA BEDS NATIONAL MONUMENT (30 m SW of Tulelake off SR 139): Here Captain Jack's 70 fighting Modoc Indians and their families held off some 400 Federal and volunteer troops for nearly 6 months in 1872-3. Museum explains the Modoc War, only Indian war fought in California, and signs mark battlefield sites.

LOMITA: Lomita Railroad Museum (Woodward Ave. & 250th St.): 1902 steam locomotive, scale models, and other railroad items in a Victorian depot; open Wed.-Sun. 10-5; closed Dec. 25; sm adm.

LONG BEACH: Municipal Auditorium (300 Ocean Blvd.), built to resemble the Roman Coliseum, has a promenade on the 3rd floor with good views of the harbor. **Long Beach Museum of Art** (2300 E Ocean Blvd.) has a good collection of modern painting and sculpture; open Wed.-Sun. noon-5; closed major hols; free.

Queen Mary (Pier J) has self-guiding tours of bridge, engine rooms, typical staterooms, a marine museum, and the Queen Mary museum; open daily 10-3:30; adm.

La Casa del Rancho los Cerritos (4600 Virginia Rd.), a furnished 1844 adobe home, and **Rancho Los Alamitos** (6400 Bixby Hill Rd.), a furnished 1806 adobe home with large pressed glass collection, blacksmith shop, and barns, are open Wed.-Sun. 1-5; closed hols; free.

LOS ANGELES: El Pueblo de los Angeles State Historic Park marks the site where the city was founded in 1781 by settlers from Mexico. Restored buildings surround the Old Plaza (Sunset Blvd. & Los Angeles St.); this is the best place to start; conducted tours Tues.-Sat.; area open all year; free. Many special events take place here throughout the year; among the most colorful are the Blessing of the Animals on the Sat. before Easter, when children bring their pets to the Old Plaza Church to be blessed, and Las Psadas, a 9-day festival in December, when the drama of Mary and Joseph is reenacted. The center of this historic district is Olvera St., where stalls and shops re-create the atmosphere of a Mexican street market. Among the many buildings are: **Avila Adobe**, built in 1818 and the oldest dwelling in Los Angeles, was used by Gen. Fremont as the first seat of U.S. government in the late 1840's. **Nuestra Senora La Reina de los Angeles,** built about 1822 over an older structure, is the oldest church in the city and still active. **Pico House,** built in 1870, was the city's first hotel. The 1884 **Firehouse** houses old fire-fighting equipment.

Casa de Adobe (4605 N Figueroa St.) is a replica of a Spanish colonial ranch house of 1800, with period furnishings and historical items; open Wed., Sat., Sun. 1-4:45; closed major hols and mid-Aug.-mid-Sept.; free.

Lummis Home State Historical Monument (200 E Ave. 43, 5 m N off SR 11), home of historian and archaeologist Charles F. Lummis, contains some of his Indian artifacts; open Sun.-Fri. 1-4; closed hols; free.

Los Angeles County Museum of Art (5905 Wilshire Blvd.) consists of 3 modern galleries set in a landscaped garden with fountains and a sculpture garden. The outstanding collections include ancient Egyptian, Indian, and Oriental ceramics, paintings, and sculpture; American paintings dating from the 18th C to the present; Matisse bronzes, Rembrandt, and other European works; medieval, Renaissance, and Baroque paintings, tapestries, glass, and sculpture. The Frances and Armand Hammer Wing has permanent and changing exhibits of contemporary art. The Leo S. Bing Center features a theater, music, films, and a cafe. Open Tues.-Sun. 10-5; closed Jan. 1, Thnks, Dec. 25; free exc for special shows; free guided tours. Information on city buildings of architectural interest and occasional tours to these.

University of California at Los Angeles **Art Galleries** (405 Hilgard Ave.) has English and European painting plus a landscaped sculpture park with 20th-C masterpieces by Calder, Arp, Lipchitz, Rodin, and David Smith, among others; open Tues.-Sun.

University of Southern California (University Park) has art galleries with a good collection of 17th-C Italian, Dutch, and Flemish works, 18th-C British paintings, 19th-C French paintings, and a 19th-C American collection highlighted by the Hudson River school; open during academic yr, Mon.-Fri. Free.

Los Angeles Municipal Art Gallery (4804 Hollywood Blvd. in Barnsdall Park) has contemporary works; open Tues.-Sun. 12-5; adm charged for special showings.

Music Center (1st St. & Grand Ave.), with facilities for concerts and plays, has a pool reflecting the Lipchitz bronze *Peace on Earth.*

Bradbury Building (3rd & Broadway), commissioned in 1892, is a showpiece of glazed brick walls, tile floor, and fine wood paneling; the interior court is especially interesting, with wrought-iron grillwork balconies, cage elevators, and staircases; open Mon.-Fri. 9-5; closed hols; free.

Watts Towers (1765 E 107th St.): built over 33 years by Simon Rodia, an Italian immigrant; 8 spires of reinforced steel covered with cement, encrusted with bits of bottles, seashells, tiles, and other junk to create a structure praised as folk art; open daily 10-5; sm adm.

Southwest Museum (234 Museum Dr. in Highland Park): archaeology and ethnology of North and South American Indians; especially good material on the SW; open Tues.-Sun. 1-4:45; closed hols & mid-Aug.-mid-Sept.; free.

Los Angeles County Museum of Natural History (900 Exposition Blvd.) features fine exhibits on California's archaeology, history, natural history, fossils; armor; open Tues.-Sun. 10-5; closed Thnks, Dec. 25; free.

California Museum of Science & Industry (700 State Dr.) has energy, space agriculture, health, and other exhibits you can operate; open daily 10-5; closed Thnks, Dec. 25; free.

Griffith Observatory & Planetarium (Griffith Park) has planetarium shows daily (adm), telescopes you can use after dark to 10 (free), and a Hall of Science (Mon.-Fri. 2-10, Sat. 10-10, Sun. 1-10; free). The complex is closed Dec. 24, 25, Mon. from mid-Sept.-late June.

Rancho La Brea Tar Pits (Wilshire Blvd. & Curson Ave.), a rich source of Pleistocene fossils, has an observation pit open Tues.-Sun. 10-5; free. Statues of animals found here are scattered in surrounding Hancock Park.

Chinatown (N Broadway near College St.) has Chinese shops and restaurants lining the Gin Ling Way. **Little Tokyo** (between 1st & 3rd Sts., and San Pedro & Central) has Japanese restaurants, shushi bars, and Buddhist temples; Nisei Week is celebrated in August.

Hollywood Visitor Information (Hollywood & Vine) has information on tours of stars' homes, tickets to tv shows, and information on guided tours of **CBS Television City** (7800 Beverly Blvd. at Fairfax Ave.) and **NBC Studios** (3000 W Alameda Ave., Burbank). **Universal Studios** (Lankershim Blvd. off Hollywood Fwy.) has 2-hr tram ride past movie and tv sets; shows and special effects demonstrated after tour; daily 9-5 in summer, 10-3:30 in winter; closed thnks, Dec. 25; adm. **Walk of Fame** covers several streets, with the names of stars on bronze insets. **Mann's Chinese Theater** (6925 Hollywood Blvd.) has footprints and handprints of stars, beginning with Norma Talmadge in 1927. **Hollywood Cemetery** (Santa Monica Blvd. & Gower St.) is where Rudolph Valentino, Douglas Fairbanks, Sr., and others are buried.

First Baptist Church (Westmoreland Ave. at Leeward St.) has rose windows copied from those at the cathedral at Chartres, and a ceiling copied from a palace in Mantova, Italy. **Los Angeles Mormon Temple** (10777 Santa Monica Blvd.) is a huge structure surmounted by a 15-ft, gold-leaf statue of Angel Moroni; visitor center open daily 9-9; closed Jan. 1, Dec. 25; tours available; free. **St. John's Church** (514 W Adams Blvd.) is a copy of an 11th-C church in Toscanella, Italy, with a ceiling copied from the Church of San Miniato in Florence, an elaborate marble and mosaic altar, and an oak triptych. **St. Sophia Cathedral** (1324 S Normandie Ave.), believed by many to be the most beautiful Greek Orthodox church in the US, was built in 1952 in Byzantine style with a lavishly decorated, brilliant interior; open daily 9-4:30. **St. Vincent's Church** (Adams Blvd. & Figueroa St.) is in Spanish colonial style with Mexican tiling; open daily 6-6. **Wayfarers' Chapel** (5755 Palos Verdes Dr. S, on Palos Verdes Peninsula about 2 m E of Marineland), known as the "Glass Church," was designed by Frank Lloyd Wright as a memorial to the 18th-C Swedish mystic Emanuel Swedenborg, who had a vision of a sanctuary made of living trees; Wright designed the church to be mostly glass, so that trees and seascape seem to be part of the building; the 50-ft campanile is visible for miles at sea; open daily 11-4. **Wilshire Boulevard Temple** (3663 Wilshire Blvd.), a huge building with a massive dome inlaid with mosaics, contains art treasures from European synagogues; the interior has Byzantine columns of black Belgian marble, bronze chandeliers, stained-glass windows, and murals depicting the story of the Jewish people.

LOS ENCINOS STATE HISTORIC PARK (16756 Moorpark St., nr Balboa Blvd., Encino): This rest stop for a Spanish 1769 expedition became the rancho of Francisco Reyes some 25 yrs later; his stone hut is preserved along with the 9-room adobe home and 2-story French-style home (with a lake shaped like a guitar) of subsequent owners. Open Wed.-Sat. 1-4, Sun. 1-5; sm adm.

MALAKOFF DIGGINS STATE HISTORIC PARK (NW of Nevada City) began its history in a Nevada City saloon, where a prospector paid for his drinks with gold nuggets; miners followed him to establish shanties and tents on his panning stream. When nothing much was found, they called their camp Humbug; when a strike was made nearby, the name was changed to Malakoff (origin unknown). Although the 2600-acre park preserves some of the buildings of this boom town—including the St. Columncille (believed to be the patron of bartenders) Catholic Church—emphasis is on preserving the history of mining techniques, especially hydraulicking. A museum is open summers Tues.-Sun. 10-5, weekends in spring and fall 10-5; closed in winter.

MALIBU: J. Paul Getty Museum (17985 Pacific Coast Hwy) is a reproduction of Villa dei Papyri on the Bay of Naples, which was buried by Vesuvius. Getty had marble cut from quarries that had been closed for centuries and set by master craftsmen. All hardware, from massive bronze doors to lamps to door handles, was cast from Roman originals; copies of the villa's statuary were made; the trompe l'oeil portico walls are in a style popular with Romans; and many of the rooms are patterned after Roman originals and feature Greek and Roman antiquities. Other rooms feature 15th-18th-C European painting and French decorative arts. Also art lectures, facilities for scholars. Open Mon.-Fri. 10-5, but closes when parking space is filled (on Sat. or in summer this can be early in the day), so call ahead to reserve a parking space (phone 454-6541). Free.

MARSHALL GOLD DISCOVERY STATE HISTORIC SITE (at Coloma, NE of Sacramento on SR 49) is where THE gold rush started. Here in Jan. 1848, James Marshall found gold while working at Sutter's Mill on the American River.

Some 70% of the town of Coloma (pop: 200) is included in the historic site. A self-guiding trail includes the reconstructed Sutter's Mill; a museum tells the story of Sutter and Marshall and the gold rush, and houses Indian and pioneer relics; films are shown weekends. The Wah Hop store explains the Chinese contribution. Many of the trees in town were planted by former miners to commemorate the sites of their former dwellings. Buildings are open daily 10-5; closed Jan. 1, Thnks, Dec 25; sm adm.

MARYSVILLE: Bok Kai Temple (D St. at 1st St.) is a hundred-yr-old temple honoring the river god Bok Kai; the Marysville Chinese Community can arrange tours; donation; a Chinese festival takes place here in early spring. **Mary Aaron Museum** (D St. at 7th St.) is an 1854 home with relics of gold rush days, when this was one of the most important cities in the state; open Tues.-Sat. 1:30-4:30; closed hols; free. The **Chamber of Commerce** (429 10th St.) can supply additional information on historic sites here.

MODESTO: McHenry Museum (1402 I St.) has period rooms and historical exhibits; open Tues.-Sun. noon-4; closed hols; free. **Miller's Horse & Buggy Ranch** (10 m E on SR 132) has horse-drawn vehicles, old cars, general store, other buildings; open Mon.-Sat. in daylight, Sun. from noon; closed hols; sm adm.

MONTEREY: This beautiful town was named in 1602 by explorer Sebastian Vizcaino for the viceroy of Mexico. The Spanish king intended it to be capital of California, but in 1822 it became part of Mexico and in 1846 the U.S. flag was raised. It became a whaling and fishing center, inspiring John Steinbeck's *Cannery Row* (now lined with restaurants and shops rather than canneries); today the harbor is still colorful with fishing boats. A map of a 3-m walking tour (**"Path of History"**) past more than 40 historic sites (some open to the public) is available from the Chamber of Commerce (Monterey Fairgrounds Travelodge, 2030 Fremont Ave.). Two properties under the aegis of the National Trust for Historic Preservation are the 1834 adobe-and-redwood log house **Casa Amesti** (516 Polk St.) and the adjacent **Cooper-Molera Adobe**, which served as a store and saloon as well as a dwelling.

Royal Presidio Chapel of San Carlos Cathedral (Church at Figueroa St.), with a highly ornate facade, is the only presidio chapel left in California and has been in continuous use since 1795; open daily 8 am- 7 pm; free.

Monterey Presidio (Pacific St.), founded in 1770 by Capt. Gaspar de Portola, is now a military language school. It contains the U.S. Army Museum of local and presidio history, Army exhibits. Open Wed.-Sun. 10-5; closed Jan. 1, Thnks, Dec. 25; free.

Allen Knight Maritime Museum (550 Calle Principal) depicts the history of Monterey's whaling days with a fine collection of boat models, paintings, maritime artifacts; also research library. Open Tues.-Fri. 1-4 (also 10-noon in summer), Sat. & Sun. 2-4; closed hols; free.

Monterey Peninsula Museum of Art (559 Pacific St.) has collections of folk art; open Tues.-Fri. 10-4, Sat. & Sun. 1-4; closed hols; free.

MONTEREY STATE HISTORIC PARK (on the bay, with parking beside Municipal Wharf and Fisherman's Wharf) preserves many Spanish Colonial-style buildings, some modified by influences brought by New England seamen. A self-guiding booklet is available at the Customs house; most buildings are open daily 9-5; closed Jan. 1, Thnks, Dec. 25; sm adm covers all houses (Customs House is free). **Customs House** (Custom House Plaza) is a beautiful building erected in 1827 and enlarged in the mid-1800's; now a museum. **Pacific House** (Custom House Plaza) was built in 1847 as a home but later housed a variety of businesses. Now a museum devoted to California history and Indian artifacts. **Casa del Oro** (Scott & Olivier Sts.), so named because it was once rumored to be a gold depository, was a general store; restored and furnished. **California's First Theater** (Scott & Pacific Sts.), built as a roominghouse with a bar in 1846-7, became a smash hit as a theater when bored soldiers began to put on plays; plays are still given here. **Larkin House** (Jefferson & Calle Principal) is a handsome 2-story adobe home of the 1830's that became the model for Monterey architecture; many original furnishings; shown by guided tour only, daily exc Tues. **Stevenson House** (530 Houston St.), begun as a private home in the 1830's, is named because Robert Louis Stevenson stayed here in 1879 after it had become a roominghouse. Several rooms are devoted to Stevensoniana. Shown by guided tour daily. **Casa Gutierrez** (Calle Principal near Madison), an 1841 adobe home, is now a restaurant. Several other houses are not yet open to the public (but the charming Casa Soberanes at 336 Pacific is worth seeing from the outside).

NEVADA CITY: Settled by goldminers in 1849, this town didn't close its gold mines until 1942; it is a picturesque city, with many old buildings. The **Chamber of Commerce** (132 Main St.) can give you a self-guiding tour booklet. **National Hotel** (211 Broad St.), with balconies over the sidewalks, reportedly sold $1000 worth of booze a day during the gold rush; it still functions as a hotel. **Nevada County Historical Society Museum** (214 Main St.), in an old fire house, has exhibits on local history, including a temple altar belonging to the Chinese community; open all year, weekday afternoons, weekends 11-5; sm adm. See also Malakoff Diggins State Historic Park.

OAKLAND: Oakland Museum (10th & Oak Sts. on Lake Merritt) is a modern museum featuring the history, arts, and culture of California; open Tues.-Sun. 10-5, closed Jan. 1, Thnks, Dec. 25; free.

Jack London Square (at the harbor at the foot of Broadway), the colorful waterfront around which the city grew, has undergone considerable renovation and landscaping since Jack London hung out here; but still standing is Heinold's First and Last Chance, a bunkhouse for oystermen built from materials salvaged from a wrecked English whaler and later a saloon in which London drank and wrote.

Dunsmuir House & Gardens (2960 Peralta Oaks Ct.): 1899 mansion; period furnishings; open Apr.-Oct., Sun. 1-4 plus early Dec. daily; closed hols; adm. Separate adm for gardens.

OCEANSIDE: Mission San Luis Rey de Francia (4 m E on SR 76) is one of the largest and most beautiful missions. Built in 1798 and still in use, it is noted for the interior decoration done by the mission Indians; early vestments and other historical items on display; gardens, Indian cemetery; picnic sites. Open Mon.-Sat. 9-4, Sun. 11:30-4; closed Thnks, Dec. 25; sm adm. Festivals in summer.

OJAI: Ojai Valley Historical Society & Museum (338 E Ojai Ave.) has displays of local history and Chumash Indian material; open Wed.-Mon. 1-5; closed Jan. 1, Dec. 25; free.

OROVILLE: Chamber of Commerce (1789 Montgomery St.) has information on historic sites. **Chinese Temple** (Broderick St. at Elma St.), built in 1863 when Oroville had a Chinese population of 10,000; contains treasures donated by the Emperor of China; pagoda; rare tapestries and rugs; jewelry; costumes. **Judge C. F. Lott Memorial Home & Sank Park** (1067 Montgomery St.), a Victorian frame house built in 1856, is furnished with family antiques. Both open Fri.-Tues. 10-noon, 1-4, Wed. & Thurs. 1-4; closed Dec.-mid-Jan.; sm adm includes both bldgs.

Butte County Pioneer Memorial Museum (Relic Bldg., Montgomery & Oliver Sts.) is devoted to the history and folklore of the gold rush era; open Sun. 1:30-4; sm adm.

Oregon City (N on Cherokee Rd.) is a ghost town with abandoned mines and an old graveyard. **Cherokee** (jct SR 70 & Cherokee Rd.), a town that has mined diamonds as well as gold, has a small museum and old cemetery.

PACIFIC GROVE: Chamber of Commerce (Forest & Cathedral Aves.) sponsors tours of historic homes in Mar. **Pacific Grove Museum of Natural History** (Forest & Central Aves.) has outstanding exhibits of birds, sea life; Indian relics; open Tues.-Sun. 10-5; closed hols; free.

PALA INDIAN RESERVATION: Mission San Antonio de Pala (on SR 76, 7 m E off I-15) an asistencia of Mission San Luis Rey de Francia (see Oceanside), was abandoned and reestablished several times, and today is the only mission still serving Indians. Bell tower duplicating one in Juarez, Mexico; museum with mineral display. Open daily 10-5; closed hols; donation for museum, grounds free.

PALM SPRINGS: Palm Springs Desert Museum (135 E Tahquitz-McCallum Way) displays desert natural history, Cahuilla Indian artifacts, primitive and folk art; open late Sept.-May, Tues.-Sat. 10-5, Sun. 2-5; sm adm.

PALO ALTO: Stanford University has attractive buildings in Spanish mission style; the Medical Center was designed by Edward Durell Stone. A booklet for self-guiding tour, and guided tour services (2 pm daily exc hols), are available at the Information Center (Quadrangle, main entrance). On campus are:

Museum of Art: Ikedia collection of oriental art, pre-Columbian American art, Egyptian antiquities, primitive art, European works, and Stanford family mementos such as the Golden Spike driven to connect the first transcontinental railroad in 1869; open Tues.-Fri. 10-5, Sat. & Sun. 1-5; closed hols; free. The **Thomas Welton Stanford Art Gallery** houses American and European works; open Tues.-Sat. 10-5, Sun. 1-5; closed hols and part of the summer; free.

Stanford Memorial Church: Venetian mosaics, made in Italy and set here by Italian workmen; stained-glass windows; open daily 8-5; free.

Hoover Institution on War, Revolution & Peace: Pres. Hoover began this collection of documents on world conflicts; Hoover memorabilia; 285-ft observation tower; open Mon.-Sat. 8-5, Sun. noon-5; elevator closed lunchtime & hols; sm adm.

PASADENA: Pasadena Historical Museum (470 W Walnut St.) contains historical artifacts; a replica of a 200-yr-old Finnish farmhouse contains Finnish folk art; open Tues., Thurs., some Sun. 1-4; closed hols; adm.

Pasadena Museum of Modern Art (Orange Grove & Colorado Blvd.) has one of the finest collections of German Expressionist painting (Klee, Kandinsky, Jawlensky, Feininger); other fine 20th-C works; open Tues.-Sat. 10-5, Sun. noon-5; closed major hols; adm.

California Institute of Technology (1201 E California Blvd.) has guided tours from the Public Relations Office during the academic year; Mon., Thurs., Fri. at 3, Tues. & Wed. at 11; free.

Mt. Wilson Observatory (25 m NE via SR 2 in Angeles Ntl. Forest) has a visitors' gallery and museum open daily 10-5; closed Dec. 25; free but parking fee.

PETALUMA ADOBE STATE HISTORIC PARK (W of Sonoma on San Pablo Bay): Chief residence for Rancho Petaluma, the 100-sq-m empire that helped make Gen. Mariano Guadalupe Vallejo one of the richest, most powerful men in the Mexican Province of California. His adobe home, begun in 1836, was unfinished in 1846 when he was jailed and stripped of his property during the Bear Flag Revolt. House construction and furnishings show the transition from hand-made to industrial era materials; open daily 10-5; closed Jan. 1, Thnks, Dec. 25; sm adm.

PIO PICO STATE HISTORIC PARK (6003 Pioneer Blvd., Whittier) was home of California's last Mexican governor. Open Wed.-Sun. 10-5; closed Jan. 1, Thnks, Dec. 25; sm adm.

PLACERVILLE: The Chamber of Commerce (542 Main St.) can give you a tour guide to this old mining area, whose history also includes associations with railroad baron Mark Hopkins, meat-packer Philip D. Armour, and auto magnate John Studebaker. **Gold Bug Mine** (Bedford Park) is a municipally owned demonstration gold mine, with vein and stamp mill, that has been restored; picnic area; open daily 10-7, with tours Wed.-Sun. and gold panning demonstrations many afternoons; free.

PLUMAS-EUREKA STATE PARK (7 m W of Blairsden, off SR 89): Jamison City, a wild and wicked gold-mining town, continued to prosper after placer mining gave way to hard-rock mining; a bunkhouse serves as a museum of its mining history. The Plumas-Eureka Mill, said to have processed $8 million in gold, has been partially restored; the tramway built to carry ore to the main mill at Johnsville is believed to have served as the world's first ski lift. Museum open, weather permitting, daily all year 10-5; closed Jan. 1, Thnks, Dec. 25.

POINT REYES NATIONAL SEASHORE (on SR 1, at Point Reyes Station, Olema): In 1579, Sir Francis Drake is believed to have sailed his damaged *Golden Hind* into Drakes Bay for repairs. The name Punta de los Reyes was given by explorer Don Sebastian Vizcaino in 1603. **Headquarters** (Bear Valley Rd.) has displays on the San Andreas Fault, a seismograph, and Earthquake Trail along the fault; open daily 8-4:30, longer in summer.

POMONA: Adobe de Palomares (2 m NE at 491 E Arrow Hwy.) is a 13-room ranch house, typical of the 1850's and authentically furnished, with blacksmith shop, Indian artifacts, and ranch equipment; open Tues.-Sun. 2-5; closed hols; free.

RED BLUFF: Kelly-Griggs House Museum (311 Washington St.) is a renovated Victorian home with period furnishings; Pendleton Art Gallery; historical, Indian, and Chinese exhibits. Open Thurs.-Sun. 2-4, longer hrs in summer; closed hols; sm adm. Either here or at the **Chamber of Commerce** (100 Main St.) you can get a tour map of other Victorian buildings.

REDDING: Redding Museum & Art Center (810 Rio Dr. in Lake Redding-Caldwell Park) has prehistoric and recent Indian artifacts, historic and Columbia River stone sculpture displays; open Tues.-Sun., June-Aug. 10-5, Sept.-May noon-5; closed hols; free.

REDLANDS: Asistension Mission (26930 Barton Rd.) was begun as a mission in 1830 but abandoned 4 years later; it was used as a residence and then sold to Mormons. The 14 rooms include a wedding chapel, and house pioneer, Indian, and other historical exhibits, natural history displays; open Tues.-Sat. 10-5, Sun. 1-5; closed Thnks, Dec. 25; donation. Cactus and succulent garden; popular for weddings.

    Lincoln Memorial Shrine (Smiley Park, 4th & Eureka Sts.) contains manuscripts, books, artifacts on Lincoln and the Civil War; Tues.-Sat. 1-5; closed hols exc Lincoln's Birthday; free.

    San Bernardino County Museum (2024 Orange Tree Lane) has a huge collection of bird eggs, an exhibit on the endangered condor, historical murals, prehistoric Indian displays; cactus gardens; open Mon.-Sat. 9-5, Sun. 1-5; free.

RIVERSIDE: Mission Inn (3649 7th St), a mission-style hotel with patios, gardens, terraces, towers, Spanish cloisters, and a 200-yr-old altar in the chapel. Inside are Spanish antiques, paintings, dolls, hundreds of bells, crosses; tours daily 11:30, 2:30; adm.

Riverside Municipal Museum (3720 Orange St.): local archaeological, natural history, and history displays; open Tues.-Sat. 9-5, Sun. 1-5; closed hols; free.

ROSAMOND: Burton's Tropico Gold Mine & Mill offers restored buildings and museum of Tropico's gold rush era plus amusements. Some attractions open only Oct.-May, weekends and hols 9:30-4; others open all yr, Thurs.-Mon. 9:30-4; closed Thnks, Dec. 25; adm.

SACRAMENTO: California State Capitol (10th St. between L & N Sts.), beautifully landscaped, completed in 1874, has historical materials; open daily 7 am-9 pm; free. Governor's Mansion (16th & H Sts.), an ornate Victorian home built 1877-78, served as governor's mansion 1903-68; open daily 10-5; closed hols; adm. Sacramento City & County Museum (1009 7th St.) houses displays of local history in Pioneer Hall, an 1868 Greek Revival building; open daily 10-4; closed hols; free.

E. B. Crocker Art Gallery (216 O St.) exhibits European and American painting, graphic arts, sculpture, American decorative arts, and Oriental art objects in an imposing Italian Baroque-style building; open Wed.-Sun. 10-5, Tues. 2-10; closed hols; free.

ST. HELENA: Silverado Museum (1347 Railroad Ave.) contains Robert Louis Stevenson memorabilia; open Tues.-Sun., noon-4, closed hols; free.

SAN ANDREAS: Calaveras County Historical Museum (Main St.) is in a former courthouse; Indian, mining, and pioneer relics; open daily 9:30-5:30; free.

SAN DIEGO: Convention & Visitors Bureau (1200 3rd Ave.) provides a map of a 52-m scenic drive marked by blue seagulls that passes most attractions. Old Town, site of San Diego's original settlement in 1769, is centered around Old Town Plaza (San Diego Ave. & Mason St.); green markers on the streets lead you to the historic sites scattered among the many shops and newer buildings. Casa de Estudillo (SE of plaza), a 1-story adobe home (1820), has Mexican period furnishings. On the same block are Casa de Pedrorena (1864) and Casa de Altamirano (1868), first home of the San Diego *Union,* with old newspaper displays, trays of type, and the old press. Nearby are the 1865 Mason Street School, San Diego's first public school, the 1835 Stewart House, a restored adobe home, and the 1832 Casa de Machado. Presidio Park (N on Mason St. to Presidio Dr.) has mound marking the original Presidio and fort, the first construction in the city. Nearby is the Junipero Serra Museum, in a mission-style building, with splendid collections tracing the history of the city and missions;

library documents dating back to 1542; tower affords a vista of the city. **Whaley House** (2482 San Diego Ave. at Harney St.), a brick Greek Revival home completed in 1857, served also as a theater and courthouse; furnished with period pieces; on the grounds is a restored drugstore. Nearby are the **Derby-Pendleton House** (4017 Harney St.), a New England Greek Revival home shipped around the Horn in 1851, and 1850 **Little Adobe Chapel** (Conde & Congress Sts.), and **El Campo Santo** (San Diego Ave. near Arista St.), the old Spanish cemetery. **Seeley Stable & Roscoe E. Hazard Museum** is a reconstruction of an 1869 stable erected by A. L. Seeley, who operated a stage coach line between San Diego and Los Angeles; Old West memorabilia and horse-drawn vehicles. The plaza and surrounding blocks are a state park, and the **Visitor Center** (2660 Calhoun St.) can provide maps and information; walking tours are also available here. The Visitor Center and houses under state park jurisdiction are open daily May-Sept. 10-6, Oct.-Apr. 10-5; closed Jan. 1, Thnks, Dec. 25; free. Buildings not under state park jurisdiction may be closed Mon. and/or Tues. and charge sm adm.

    Mission San Diego de Alcala (10818 San Diego Mission Rd.) was California's first mission, founded in Old Town by Fray Junipero Serra in 1769 and later moved here for a better water supply, and is still in use. The museum has liturgical robes, records by Serra, and other relics. Open daily 9-5; closed Dec. 25; sm adm.

    Villa Montezuma (1925 K St.) is an 1887 Victorian mansion with stained-glass windows and unique interior decorating schemes, built by author Jesse Shepard; open Tues.-Fri., Sun. 1-4:30; closed hols; free.

    Balboa Park offers **Old Globe Theatre**, an authentic reproduction. **Reuben H. Fleet Space Theater & Science Center,** where multimedia productions simulate space flight, shooting rapids, and other experiences; action-oriented exhibits; open Mon.-Sat. 10-5, 7-9:30, Sun. 11:30-9:30; adm. **Natural History Museum,** with state exhibits; open daily 10-4:30; closed Jan. 1, Dec. 25; sm adm. **Museum of Man,** with ethnology of American Indians, physiology; open daily 10-4:45; closed Jan. 1, Thnks, Dec. 25; sm adm. **Aero-Space Museum,** with a reproduction of Lindbergh's *Spirit of St. Louis* and spacecraft; open daily 10-4:30; closed Jan. 1, Thnks, Dec. 25; free. **San Diego Art Institute Gallery,** with work by local artists, open Tues.-Sat. 10-5, Sun. 12:30-5; closed hols; free. **Spanish Village Art Center,** with artisans at work; open daily noon-4:30; closed some hols; free. **House of Pacific Relations,** with cultural exhibits from 20 nations; open Sun. 2-5; free. **Fine Arts Gallery** has an outstanding collection, including works by Rembrandt, Titian, and other masters through to modern artists such as Georgia O'Keeffe and Henry Moore, plus Oriental collection; open Tues.-Sat. 10-5, Sun. 12:30-5; closed Jan. 1, July 4, Thnks, Dec. 25; free. **Timken Art Gallery** specializes in Spanish

Baroque paintings and early Russian icons; open Tues.-Sat. 10-4:30, Sun. 1:30-4:30; closed Sept., hols; free.

Embarcadero & San Diego Bay, port for commercial and Navy craft, offers 3 ships of the Maritime Museum Association—1863 square-rigger *Star of India,* ferryboat *Berkeley,* and luxury yacht *Medea;* open daily 9-8; adm. Naval Training Center's maritime museum is open Mon.-Fri. 8-4:30, weekends & hols 1-4; free.

SAN FERNANDO: Mission San Fernando Rey de Espana (15151 Mission Blvd.) has been restored with church, workshops, living quarters, and monastery; Indian artifacts, ecclesiastical objects, and other historic material; open daily 9-5; closed Dec. 25; adm.

SAN FRANCISCO: Convention & Visitors Bureau (1390 Market St. nr Larkin) has booklets for 49-m scenic drive (marked with blue, white, and orange seagulls. Cable cars start at Powell & Market Sts. and at California & Market Sts. **Cable Car Barn** (1201 Mason St.), built about 1887 to house cable cars and the powerhouse, has been converted into a museum; historical displays; model cable cars. Open daily 10-6; closed Jan. 1, Thnks, Dec. 25; free.

Mission Dolores (16th & Dolores Sts.), founded in 1776 as Mission San Francisco de Asis, the 6th in the chain of Franciscan missions, is believed to be the oldest structure in the city and was the settlement from which the city sprang. The building combines Moorish, mission, and Corinthian elements; decorations and altar from Spain and Mexico. Alongside is a cemetery in which many prominent pioneers are buried. Open daily, May-Oct. 9-5, Nov.-Apr. 10-4; closed Thnks, Dec. 25; sm adm.

Civic Center (Van Ness Ave., Hyde, McAllister & Grove Sts.) includes: **City Hall** (1915), a grand French Renaissance-style building crowned with a copper dome. **Civic Auditorium,** connected to underground exhibit space in Brooks Hall. **War Memorial Opera House,** where the UN Charter was signed in 1945. **Public Library,** with outstanding collections, including fine material on the history of the city and state. **San Francisco Museum of Art,** specializing in contemporary works; open Tues.-Fri. 10-10, Sat. & Sun. 10-5, closed hols; free exc special exhibits. **Society of California Pioneers,** a library-museum devoted to the history of the state; open Mon.-Fri. 10-4, closed hols & Aug.; free. **Health Center** for the Chinese community has a sculptured Chinese dragon decorating the outside.

California Palace of the Legion of Honor (Lincoln Park), a replica of its Paris namesake, houses paintings from the 16th-20 C (with emphasis on French 18th-19th C), more than 40 sculptures by Rodin, decorative arts, and the huge print and drawing collections of the Achenbach Foundation for Graphic Arts. Open daily 10-5; free.

Palace of Fine Arts (Marina Blvd. & Naker St.), in a swan-filled lagoon, is a restored Greco-Romanesque rotunda built in 1915 for the Panama-Pacific International Exposition. It houses the Exploratorium of science, technology, and human perception. Open Wed.-Sun. 1-5, plus Wed. 7-9:30 pm; free.

Chinatown (bounded by Broadway, Bush, Stockton & Kearny) shelters the largest Chinese community outside of Asia. **Chinese Historical Society of America Museum** (17 Adler Pl. off 1140 Grant Ave.) is devoted to the history of the Chinese in America from pioneer days; open Tues.-Sun. 1-5; closed Jan. 1, Dec. 25; free. **Chinese Cemetery,** more than 100 yrs old, is across the bridge, bounded by the cities of S. San Francisco, Colma, and Pacifica.

Japan Center (bounded by Geary, Fillmore, Post, & Laguna Sts.) is a 5-acre complex of shops, cafes, and other buildings of the Japanese community; landscaped Peace Plaza with pagoda; open daily 10-6; closed Jan. 1, Dec. 25.

Pacific Coast Stock Exchange (301 Pine St. at Sansome St.) has a visitor gallery open Mon.-Fri. 9-2:30; closed hols; free.

Embarcadero Center (between Wall St. & the Ferry Bldg.) is an urban redevelopment complex replacing the old waterfront district with a new financial center; it is a multilevel pedestrian mall with plazas, promenades, shops, restaurants, galleries, a huge fountain, sculpture, and greenery.

Ferry Building (foot of Market St.) houses California Division of Mines & Geology Mineral Exhibit (open Mon.-Fri. 8-5; closed hols; free) and murals and products in the World Trade Center (Mon.-Fri. 9-3; closed hols; free).

California Historical Society (2090 Jackson St.), in an 1896 mansion that is an excellent example of the opulent homes of the Victorian era, houses period furnishings; an outstanding collection of paintings, prints, and photographs of California and the West; an excellent library with huge genealogical files. Open Tues.-Sat. 10-4; closed hols; free.

Octagon House (2645 Gough St. at Union St.), built in 1861, has been restored and authentically furnished by the National Society of Colonial Dames; open 1st Sun. each month, 2nd & 4th Thurs, 1-4; donation.

Haas-Lilienthal House (2007 Franklin St.), a stately Victorian mansion built in 1886, has period furnishings and changing exhibits; guided tours Wed. 1-3:30, Sat. & Sun. 12:30-4:30; adm. San Francisco's Architectural Heritage, which maintains this building, offers walking tours of the city's architectural landmarks.

Old Mint (5th & Mission Sts.), built in 1874, is now a museum restored with many original furnishings; exhibits trace the development of American money; numismatic items for sale; open Tues.-Sun. 10-4, closed hols; free.

Old St. Mary's Church (Grant & California Sts.), a handsome Gothic-style building erected in 1854 of New England brick, survived earthquake and fire; an inscription above the clock dial reads "Son Observe the Time and Fly from Evil."

Buddha's Universal Church (720 Washington St.), built by volunteers of the Pristine Orthodox Dharma, has an altar in the shape of a ship (symbol of truth), a 6-ft-high mosaic of the Buddha, and a bodhi tree grown from a slip of the one under which the Buddha is said to have found enlightenment; inquire for tour hours.

African American Historical Society (680 McAllister St.) houses permanent exhibits on African and Afro-American history as well as changing exhibits; research library; open Mon.-Fri. 9-5, Sat. noon-4; free.

Bank of California Collection of Money of the American West (lower level, 400 California St.) features pioneer ingots, coins, and currency; open Mon.-Fri. 10-3; closed hols; free.

Wine Museum (633 Beach St.) contains the Christian Bros. collection of drinking vessels from Roman times to the present, representations of Bacchus, drawings, sculpture, rare books, wine presses, and other displays related to the history of wine; open Tues.-Sat. 11-5, Sun. noon-5; closed hols; adm.

San Francisco Fire Department Pioneer Memorial Museum (Presidio Ave. at Bush) features antiquated firefighting equipment and illustrations of major holocausts; open daily 1-5; closed hols; free.

Wells Fargo Bank History Room (420 Montgomery St.) displays photographs and mementos from gold rush days; 1850 stagecoach; open Mon.-Fri. 10-3; closed hols; free.

A World of Oil (Standard Oil Co., 555 Market St.) presents the history of the oil industry through working models and dioramas; open Mon.-Fri. 10-4, closed hols; free.

Fisherman's Wharf (foot of Taylor St.): Docked at Pier 43 is the 1886 sailing ship **Balclutha,** a museum with maritime displays, and paddlewheel tug **Eppleton Hall,** maintained by San Francisco Maritime Museum; open daily 9:30 am-10 pm; adm.

San Francisco Maritime Museum (foot of Polk St. at Aquatic Park), in a building resembling a ship, houses fine ship models, figureheads, scrimshaw, and other maritime exhibits; research library; open daily 10-5; free. **San Francisco Maritime State Historic Park** (foot of Hyde St.) is a floating museum consisting of historic ships: *Eureka,* a side-wheel ferry built in 1890 and in use until 1957; the 1891 flat-bottomed scow schooner *Alma;* the 1895 *C. A. Thayer,* built to carry lumber from the Pacific Northwest; and the 1915 *Wapama,* a steam schooner that carried lumber and passengers along the West Coast. Open daily 10-6, with evening hours in summer; closed Dec. 25; sm adm.

Presidio (NW end of city near Golden Gate Bridge) has stood guard over San Francisco Bay since the Spanish established it in 1776; the adobe Officer's Club dates from that time. Historic markers; a museum contains uniforms and military artifacts; research library. Open Tues.-Sun. 10-5; free.

Ghirardelli Square (Beach & Larkin Sts., W of Fisherman's Wharf) is a multilevel complex of shops, restaurants, galleries, and theaters housed in refurbished brick buildings; it once was Domingo Ghirardelli's chocolate factory.

Golden Gate Park (between Lincoln Way & Fulton St., Stanyan St. & Great Hwy.) contains: M. H. de Young Memorial Museum (10th Ave. entrance) has a large collection of European and American art (incl Goya, Cellini, Tiepolo, Rubens, Watteau, El Greco); galleries housing artifacts from Africa, Oceania, and the Americas; and a wing devoted to temporary exhibits. A highlight is the exceptionally fine collection of Oriental works in the Asian Art Museum. Open daily 10-5; free. The California Academy of Sciences complex (across the Music Concourse from the de Young Museum) contains: Steinhart Aquarium, with one of the nation's finest collections of fishes and aquatic vertbrates, incl dolphins, Morrison Planetarium with daily shows; and several Halls of Science with botanic, mineral, dinosaur, and other specialties. The complex is open daily 10-5, with longer hrs in summer; sm adm; additional charge for planetarium shows.

SAN GABRIEL: Mission San Gabriel Arcangel (Mission Dr. & Junipero Serra Dr.), founded in 1771, was partially destroyed by an earthquake in 1812, and restored in 1815. This is a handsome mission with many original paintings, wooden statues, books, ecclesiastical objects, Indian artifacts, and other treasures. Open Tues.-Sun. 9:30-4, closed hols; sm adm.

SAN JOSE: Winchester Mystery House (525 S Winchester Blvd.) is a Victorian monstrosity built by Sarah L. Winchester, heiress to the Winchester Arms fortune, who had been told by a medium that she would never die as long as construction continued on the house. The house had 9 rooms when she bought it, but after 38 years during which carpenters worked round the clock, it had grown to more than 160 rooms, with 2000 doors, a secret passage, 50 staircases, and over 10,000 windows at the time of her death in 1922. Open daily Apr.-Oct. 9-5, Nov.-Mar. 9-4:30; closed Dec. 25; adm.

Rosicrucian Park (Naglee & Park Aves.) is headquarters of the Rosicrucian Order. The Egyptian Temple Museum, in a reproduction of an Egyptian temple, houses a copy of a 12th-dynasty tomb, mummies, art objects from Cairo and Luxor temples, and other Egyptian, Assyrian, and Babylonian antiquities. Open Tues.-Fri. 9-5, Sat.-Mon. noon-5; closed major hols; free. **Science Museum**, with physical science exhibits, has planetarium shows June-Sept., Wed.-Sun. 1-5; rest of yr, weekends only; adm.

Lick Observatory (on Mt. Hamilton, 25 m SE) has astronomical exhibits and a visitor gallery; phone 274-5061 for reservation. **San Jose Historical Museum** (Senter Rd. & Phelan Ave.): exhibits on Santa Clara Valley history; open Mon.-Fri. 10-4:30, Sat. & Sun. noon-4:30; closed hols; sm adm. **State House Museum** (Fairgrounds, 3 m S): displays of pioneer history; open Mon.-Fri. 1-5; closed hols; free. **New Almaden Museum** (21570 Almaden Rd. 12 m S in New Almaden): in an 1854 adobe; tours explaining quicksilver mining; minerals, Costanoan Indian artifacts. Open mid-Feb.-late Nov., Mon. & Wed.-Fri. 1-5, Sat. & Sun. 10-5; closed Easter vacation, Thnks; adm.

SAN JUAN BAUTISTA STATE HISTORIC PARK (in San Juan Bautista) records a long segment of the state's history. The earliest building was the 1797 **Mission San Juan Bautista** (2nd & Mariposa Sts.); the church, largest of its kind, is still in use today and contains many original relics; adj cemetery contains more than 4000 Indian graves. Open daily Mar.-Nov. 9:30-5:30, Dec.-Feb. 9:30-4:30; closed Jan. 1, Thnks, Dec. 25; donation.

Castro House (1840-1), originally home of a Spanish family, is furnished in the 1870's style of later occupants Patrick and Margaret Breen; the Breens, part of the ill-fated Donner Party, arrived here penniless, but a son's luck in the gold fields enabled them to buy this home. **Plaza Hotel,** built in 1858 by Angelo Zanetta within the adobe walls of an earlier structure, was an important stage stop until the railroad bypassed San Juan in 1876. **Zanetta House,** constructed in 1868 of adobe bricks from an earlier building, was a residence and dance hall. The park provides information on the history of San Juan; open daily 8-6 during DST and 8-5 at other times; closed Jan. 1, Thnks, Dec. 25; free. Sm adm to buildings.

SAN JUAN CAPISTRANO: Mission San Juan Capistrano, founded by Fray Serra in 1776, had two churches; the adobe Padre Serra's Church, built in 1778, is still in use; a larger cruciform church, said to have been the most beautiful of the mission churches, collapsed during the 1812 earthquake, killing 29 people. Tours of the church, ruins, Indian cemetery, and out buildings are given daily. This mission is celebrated for its swallows, which leave on or about Oct. 23 and return on or about Mar. 19; they are greeted with parades and other festivities.

The **Chamber of Commerce** (31793 Camino Capistrano, Franciscan Plaza) has maps for self-guiding tours of other historic sights.

SAN LUIS OBISPO: Mission San Luis Obispo de Tolosa (Monterey St. at Chorro) was founded 1772 by Fray Junipero Serra; he named it for nearby volcanic peaks that he thought resembled a bishop's mitre. The mission church, which is still active, contains some fine old statues and paintings. The museum contains Chumash Indian artifacts and early ecclesiastical items. Open daily, June.-Sept. 9-5, Oct.-May 9-4, closed Jan. 1, Dec. 25; donation.

San Luis Obispo County Historical Museum (696 Monterey St.) houses Indian artifacts, glass, material related to local history; open Tues.-Sun. 10-noon, 1-4; closed hols; free. Here you can obtain a self-guiding booklet for a **Path of History** that includes a 1897 cigar factory now a restaurant, the 1853 **Dallidet Adobe** built by a French vinter (open summer only, Sun. 1-4:30), the **Kundert Medical Building** designed by Frank Lloyd Wright in 1956, an 1889 **Southern Pacific Railroad depot,** and the **Ah Louis Store** (800 Palm St.). This last was built of hand-made bricks in 1874 by Ah Louis, a leader of the Chinese community; now a state historical landmark, it is still run by his family; open Mon.-Sat. 1-6; closed hols. **Sinsheimer Bros. Store** (849 Monterey St.) is one of the few cast-iron-front buildings in the area; fully restored to its 1874 appearance; open Mon.-Sat. 10-5:30; closed hols.

California Polytechnic State University at the N edge of town has a **Shakespeare Press Museum** (open Mon.-Fri. 10-2 during academic year) with antique printing equipment; free, but check at the Administration Bldg. for hours and tours.

SAN MARINO: Huntington Library, Art Gallery, and Botanical Gardens (1151 Oxford Rd.) houses the collections of railroad executive Henry Edwards Huntington. His mansion houses 18th-19th C British painting, French and English furnishings and decorative arts. The extraordinary library contains the Gutenberg Bible, rare printed books, manuscripts and hand-written letters by famous people. Open Tues.-Sun. 1-4:30; closed hols, Oct.; free.

El Molino Viejo (1120 Old Mill Rd.), housing the California Historical Society, was one of the state's first water-operated gristmills; exhibits paintings and graphic arts; open Tues.-Sun. 1-4; closed hols; free.

SAN MATEO: San Mateo County Historical Museum (1700 W Hilldale Blvd., College of San Mateo) has local historical exhibits; open Mon.-Sat. 9:30-4:30; closed hols; free.

SAN MIGUEL: Mission San Miguel Arcangel is of special interest for its well-preserved interior decoration which includes frescoes by Esteban Munras and Indian assistants, and the vaulted corridor; paintings, Indian and ecclesiastical artifacts; picnic area; open Mon.-Sat. 10-5, Sun. 11-5; closed Dec. 25; donation.

SAN RAFAEL: Marin County Civic Center (2 m N) is an especially handsome design by Frank Lloyd Wright; the Administration Bldg. has a garden in the skylight-covered central mall; a striking feature is the use of circular shapes indoors and out (such as the round courtrooms with curved tables); open Mon.-Fri. 9-5; closed hols; free.

Mission San Rafael Arcangel (1104 5th Ave. at Court St.) is a reconstruction of the original 1817 mission that ministered to sick Indian converts; open daily 11-4; closed Jan. 1, Easter, Dec. 25; free.

SANTA BARBARA: Mission Santa Barbara (upper end of Laguna St. at Los Olivos St.), founded in 1786, has been called "Queen of the Missions" because of its beauty and prosperity. Chumash Indians made the altar; many crafts they made here are also on display; fine examples of early Mexican art; beautiful Moorish fountain built in 1808; cemetery in which more than 4000 Chumash are buried. Open Mon.-Fri. 9-5, Sun. 1-5; closed Jan. 1, Easter, Thnks, Dec. 25; sm adm.

Historical Society Museum (136 E De la Guerra St.) offers lovingly displayed treasures from the city's history; open Tues.-Fri. noon-5; Sat. & Sun. 1-5; closed hols; free. The Society maintains 2 historic houses at 412-414 W Montecito St.: **Fernald House,** a 14-room Victorian mansion, has carved decorations and period furnishings. **Trussell-Winchester Adobe** was built in 1854 with adobe bricks and timber from the wrecked ship *Winfield Scott.* Both open Sun. 2-4; sm adm.

El Paseo (De la Guerra St. between State & Anacapa Sts.) is a shopping arcade in Spanish style built in and around the 1827 adobe **De la Guerra home** (described by Richard Henry Dana in *Two Years Before the Mast).* Across the street is *Plaza de la Guerra,* where the first City Council met in 1850. **Santa Barbara County Courthouse** (1120 Anacapa St.), one of the handsomest buildings in the West, is Spanish-Moorish style, with hand-painted ceilings, wrought iron chandeliers, murals, carved doors, imported tiles; set in garden. Open Mon.-Fri. 8-5; Sat., Sun., hols 9-5; free.

El Presidio de Santa Barbara State Historic Park (122 E Canon Perdido St.): foundations and scale model of the Presidio Real (royal fortress) and historic exhibits; El Cuartel, barracks once part of a row beside the fortress; open Mon.-Fri. 9-noon, 1-5; free.

Santa Barbara Museum of Natural History (2559 Puesta del Sol Rd., 2 blocks N of mission) has dioramas of prehistoric Indian life; geology, flora, fauna; planetarium. Open Mon.-Sat. 9-5, Sun. 1-5; closed Thnks, Dec. 25; free.

University of California at Santa Barbara (12 m N off US 101, near Goleta) has an **Art Gallery** (Arts Bldg.) with Renaissance and Baroque paintings, pre-Columbian artifacts, Islamic arts; open Tues.-Sat. 10-4, Sun. & hols 1-5; closed Jan. 1, Thnks, Dec. 25; free.

Santa Barbara Museum of Art (1130 State St.) has fine ancient sculpture, Oriental art, American painting and sculpture; open Tues.-Sat. 11-5, Sun. noon-5; closed hols; free.

Chamber of Commerce (1301 Santa Barbara St.) provides a map for a 12-block Red Tile Tour, a list of historic buildings, and information on Brooks Institute, Music Academy of the West, and other cultural institutions.

SANTA CATALINA ISLAND: Catalina Museum (in the casino in Avalon) has displays on the island's history; open mid-June-Nov., daily 1-4, 8-10; Dec.-mid-June, weekends only; free.

SANTA CLARA: Mission Santa Clara de Asis (on the Alameda, Univ. of Santa Clara), founded in 1777, is a replica with original roof tiles and statues; open daily, daylight hours; free. **de Saisset Art Gallery & Museum** (also on campus) houses rare artifacts and art works from the California mission period as well as paintings, sculpture, graphics, decorative arts, and furnishings; changing exhibits; open Tues.-Fri. 10-5, Sat. & Sun. 1-5; closed hols & Aug.: free.

Triton Museum of Art (1505 Warburton Ave.), set in a sculpture garden, has 19th-C English and American sculpture and paintings; local scenes by Theodore Wores; open Tues.-Sun. 2-4:30; free.

SANTA CRUZ: Mission Santa Cruz (126 High St.) is a reproduction of part of the original (destroyed by earthquake and fire); open daily 9-5; donation. **Santa Cruz Museum** (1305 E Cliff Dr.): seashells, Indian relics, costumes; open Tues.-Sat. 9-5; closed Jan. 1, Thnks, Dec. 25; free.

SANTA ROSA: Buddhist Temple (off SR 12, 5 m W in Sebastopol) was brought from the Orient in 1893 for the Chicago Exposition and later moved here. **Sonoma County Historical Museum & Codding Natural History Museum** (557 Summerfield Rd.) is open Tues.-Thurs., Sat., Sun. 1-5; free.

SHASTA STATE HISTORIC PARK (on SR 299, 6 m W of Redding) is what is left of the lusty "Queen City of the North" during the gold rush. The site was discovered by Pierson B. Reading, but armed prospectors from Oregon forced him off his claim after only about 6 weeks. By 1849, some 600 people were living in tents and shacks. The boom started because all roads from the south terminated here, but in 1857 a wagon road was pushed beyond Shasta, and people began to abandon the city during the next decade. The Courthouse, restored to its 1861 appearance, houses a historical museum; other buildings being restored; cemeteries have some interesting headstones. Open daily 10-5; closed Jan. 1, Thnks, Dec. 25; sm adm.

SOLVANG: Founded in 1911 by Danish educators from the Midwest, this town has many Danish-style buildings, shops featuring Danish specialties, windmills, a chiming windharp, an 1820 grist mill, artificial storks on rooftops, and a Danish festival in Sept. **Old Mission Santa Ines** (1760 Mission Dr.), founded in 1804, was heavily damaged by the 1812 earthquake and then set afire in 1824 by rebelling Indians but has been restored; many old wood carvings and paintings; a museum houses mission relics. Open Mon.-Sat. 9:30-4:30, Sun. noon-5; closed Jan. 1, Dec. 25; sm adm.

SONOMA STATE HISTORIC PARK is grouped mostly about Sonoma's handsome central plaza (between Spain St. & Napa St., 1st W and 1st E) where adobe buildings were constructed during the 1830-50's. Of the 1823 **Mission San Francisco Solano,** the chapel (built 1840-1 by Gen. Vallejo) and residence building remain. **Blue Wing Inn** (across the street) was a gambling room and saloon in gold rush days and today houses giftshops. **La Casa Grande** was Vallejo's first home, built 1836-40, where 11 of his children were born. The authentically furnished **Toscano Hotel** houses park headquarters and interpretive exhibits. The old Mexican army barracks and privately owned buildings also line the square.

 Lachryma Montis (½ m W) was Vallejo's main home, built 1851-2 beside a spring the Indians had called "crying mountain" and which Vallejo translated into Latin; a faddish frame Victorian house. Vallejo and his wife lived here for more than 35 years, in increasingly restricted economic circumstances, and here he wrote his 5-volume history of California. today the house serves as a museum and interpretive center.

 The buildings are open daily 10-5; closed Jan. 1, Thnks, Dec. 25; sm adm. Vallejo is buried in the little cemetery on the hill above Sonoma.

SONORA: Named by Mexican miners, this town was the gateway to the Mother Lode, and right in town (on what is now N Washington St.) was the largest pocket mine of all, Big Bonanza. Mark Twain and Bret Harte wrote stories set here and in the surrounding area. Although much of the town was destroyed by fire in 1852, many buildings erected soon after remain. The **Tuolumne County Chamber of Commerce** (158 W Bradford St.), in the old jail, has a museum of local history and can supply information on historic houses and cemeteries in town as well as on tours of the surrounding area. In almost any direction, there are many old mining camps: Just W is Shaw's Flat, an 1850's gold camp, where the 1850 Mississippi House contains the original bar and post office. W on SR 49 is Tuttletown, an early stage stop; on Jackass Hill is a replica of the cabin in which Mark Twain lived 1864-5 while gathering material for *Roughing It* and "Jumping Frog of Calaveras County." S on SR 108 is Jamestown, founded in 1848; just S of here, and E of SR 108 are the sites of Quartz Mountain and Stent camps, where miners found quartz more profitable than placer mines had been. Just beyond Yosemite Junction, SR 120 S goes to Chinese Camp, an 1850's center for stage lines and Chinese mining communities; to Groveland, originally called First Garrote for a horse thief hanged here, which still has adobe buildings dating from the gold rush; to Second Garrote, settled in 1848, with the Hangman's Tree where at least 12 men were hanged in boom days; and to others.

STOCKTON: Pioneer Museum & Haggin Galleries (1201 N Pershing Ave. in Victory Park) houses local historical displays and period rooms. Art gallery has 19th-C American and British paintings and graphics, Victorian and Oriental decorative arts. Open Tues.-Sun. 1:30-5; closed hols; free.

SUSANVILLE: Roop Fort & William Pratt Memorial Museum (75 N Weatherlow St.) was the fort built in 1854 by the first settler, Isaac Roop, who named the town in honor of his daughter; the town was capital of the Republic of Nataqua. The museum houses Indian artifacts. Open mid-May-Sept. daily 10-6; free.

SUTTER'S FORT STATE HISTORIC PARK (in Sacramento, on L St. between 27th & 28th Sts.): John A. Sutter, born in 1803 in Germany, left his wife and 4 children in 1834 to seek his fortune in America. The fort and community he established here became a stopover on the route between the Spanish colonies and the Sierras; in the mid-1840's, John C. Fremont and Kit Carson stopped here, and the survivors of the Donner Party were brought here to recuperate. Sutter contracted James W. Marshall to build a sawmill in 1847, and it was here that Marshall found the gold that started the gold rush (see Marshall Gold Discovery State Historic Park). Ironically, Sutter never profited; he was swindled and went into debt, and eventually retired to Lititz, Pennsylvania, where he died in 1880, disillusioned that he had failed to establish his dream community.

The reconstruction of **Sutter's Fort** here is based on a detailed plan published in Darmstadt, Germany, in 1848, in an effort to encourage German immigration to California; it contains exhibits of Sutter's life and daily pioneer existence, and a diorama of Fremont's 1844 arrival. Open daily 10-5; closed Jan. 1, Thnks, Dec. 25; sm adm.

On the grounds is the **State Indian Museum,** dedicated to California's 104 tribes; open same hrs as fort; sm adm.

VENTURA: Mission San Buenaventura (211 E Main St.): 9th and last mission founded by Fray Junipero Serra. At the baptistry entrance are Indian paintings, and over the altar is a statue of the patron saint; the crucifix is Spanish and believed to be 400 years old. The museum exhibits the wooden bells used in the missions, documents by Fray Serra, Indian-made artifacts. Open Mon.-Sat. 9-5; the church, still in use, is closed Sun., but the Museum is open; closed Dec. 25; donation.

Olivas Adobe (4200 Olivas Park Dr.): farm building from 1837 with chapel, gardens, period furnishings; visitor center. Open daily 10-4; closed major hols; free.

Ventura County Pioneer Museum (77 N California St.): local historical material, Indian artifacts, ship models, guns; open Mon.-Fri. 9-4:30, Sat. noon-4; closed hols; free.

VISALIA: Tulare County Museum (in Mooney Grove Park, S of town) houses historical exhibits, toys, Indian artifacts; open Apr.-Sept. daily 9-5; closed weekends & hols in winter; sm adm.

WEAVERVILLE: Weaverville Joss House State Historic Park (on SR 299) preserves the oldest authentic Chinese temple in the state. Begun in 1852, when there were at least 2500 Chinese in the area, it burned in 1873, was rebuilt 1874-5, and has been in continuous use ever since. Inside are many Chinese art objects; also rooms used for court and for temple attendants; tours given daily 10-4; closed Jan. 1, Thnks, Dec. 25; sm adm.

J. J. Jackson Memorial Museum (on SR 299) houses local historical materials; open May-Nov. daily 10-5; free.

WILLIAM B. IDE ADOBE STATE HISTORIC PARK (2 m NE of Red Bluff on Adobe Rd.): home of pioneer; exhibits of pioneer life; Indian and Chinese relics collected on the Lassen Trail; picnic site; open daily 8-5; closed Thnks, Dec. 25; free.

WILLITS: Mendocino County Museum (400 E Commercial St.): period rooms, Indian artifacts, exhibits on local history; open daily 10-5; closed hols; sm adm.

WILL ROGERS STATE HISTORIC PARK (15 m W of the Los Angeles Civic Center, just off Sunset Blvd. in Pacific Palisades): Ranch home of the Oklahoma-born crackerbarrel philosopher, maintained as it was when he lived here with his wife and 3 children; Western and Indian art, cowboy mementos; statue of Soapsuds, his favorite pony. Open daily 10-5; closed Jan. 1, Thnks, Dec. 25; free.

WILMINGTON: Banning Park (401 E M St.): 1864 home designed by Gen. Phineas Banning, who founded Wilmington, and built by clipper-ship carpenters; period furnishings; stables and coach house; open Apr.-Oct., Sun. 1-4:15 for conducted tours; sm adm.

WINERY TOURS: Wine Institute (717 Market St., San Francisco 94103) issues a free booklet describing the California wine regions and listing wineries open to the public, hours, picnic facilities, and whether the winery has tours or only winetasting and retail sales.

YOSEMITE NATIONAL PARK: Pioneer Yosemite History Center (Wawona) has historic buildings, living history demonstrations, horse-drawn vehicles. **Yosemite Travel Museum** (El Portal) has displays on early transportation in the area. Open daily; closed Dec. 25.

YREKA: Siskiyou County Museum (910 S Main St.) houses Indian and pioneer artifacts, reconstructed shops; open Tues.-Sat. 9-5, Sun. 1-5; closed hols; free. **Siskiyou County Gold & Gem Display** (4th & Lane Sts. in County Courthouse) of ores mined in the district is open Mon.-Fri. 8-5; closed hols; free.

YUCAIPA: Sepulveda Adobe (32183 Kentucky St.), an 1840 residence; period furniture; memorabilia; open Tues.-Sun. 1-5; closed Thnks, Dec. 25; donation.

COLORADO

ALAMOSA: Pike's Stockade (12 m S off US 285), a replica of the 1807 log stockade built by Capt. Zebulon Pike, is maintained by the State Historical Society. Open mid-May-mid-Oct. daily 9-4:30; free.

ASPEN: Aspen Historical Society Museum (620 W Bleeker St.) houses displays from the days when silver mines made this a boom town in the late 1880's to its collapse to a virtual ghost town after the Silver Panic of 1893 (even an 1840-lb silver nugget, largest in the world, didn't make the newspapers when it was found in 1894); open Tues.-Sun. 1-4; closed hols, 6 wks in spring & fall; adm. Nearby ghost towns include **Ashcroft** (12 m S on Castle Creek Rd.), once Aspen's rival but now just a dozen weatherbeaten buildings preserved by the Aspen Historical Society. **Marble** (30 m S of Carbondale on SR 133), a gold and silver camp in the 1880's, achieved greater fame after the marble quarries were opened in 1890; marble from here was used for the Lincoln Memorial and the Tomb of the Unkown Soldier.

BENT'S OLD FORT NATIONAL HISTORIC SITE (on SR 194, 8 m E of La Junta): Built in 1833 on the Santa Fe Trail as a fur-trading post, the fort became a rendezvous for Plains Indians and a military post for the conquest of what is now New Mexico; only remains of the walls still stand (restoration is planned); open daily; free.

BOULDER: University of Colorado Museum (Henderson Bldg.) has excellent material on prehistoric life, especially from the Plains and Southwest; geological exhibits; art gallery, botanical and zoological displays; open Mon.-Fri. 9-5; closed hols; free.

Pioneer Museum (1655 Broadway) is open daily in summer 2-5 and weekends rest of yr; closed hols; sm adm.

National Center for Atmospheric Research (1850 Table Mesa Dr.) has a slide show and exhibits on astronomy; open Mon.-Fri. 8-5; closed hols; free. **National Bureau of Standards & National Oceanic & Atmospheric Administration** (325 Broadway) allows self-guided tours of its laboratories; Mon.-Fri. 8-5; closed hols; free.

CANON CITY: Canon City Municipal Museum (612 River St., in the Municipal Bldg.) has exhibits on the history of the area from the time it was a favorite Ute camping ground, through gold mining days, to the collapse of the abortive film industry after a star drowned in the Arkansas River; open Mon.-Sat. 9-5, Sun. 1-5; closed hols; free. **Rudd Cabin** (behind Municipal Bldg.), birthplace of the first white child in the area; 1-room cabin built in 1860; many original furnishings; open same hrs as museum; free.

Robinson Mansion (12 Riverside Dr.) is a restored 1884 home with period furnishings; open mid-Apr.-mid-Nov., Tues.-Sun. 9-6; mid-Nov.-mid-Apr., weekends only, 1-5; adm.

CENTRAL CITY: This town, built on steep Gregory Gulch, site of Colorado's first important gold discovery in 1859, has drawn tourists as eminent as Pres. Grant, Walt Whitman, Oscar Wilde, and the Baron de Rothschild; tourists today help it retain the lively, gaudy

air it had when it labeled itself "the richest square mile on earth."
You can pan for gold, visit old mines, or visit buildings erected by
those who struck it rich and promptly imported architects and elegant
furnishings to the wilderness. The "Glory Hole" was blasted out by
dynamite to some 600-700 feet and is full of entrances to tunnels and
shafts; it is still being mined. **Central Gold Mine & Museum** (126
Spring St.) is open daily May-Sept. 9-5; mine tour given; adm.

Central City Opera House (Eureka St.) was built in 1878 by
mining families determined to have culture (Sarah Bernhardt and Edwin
Booth were among the notables they lured). Adjacent **Teller House,** once
an inn, still retains its lavish furnishings, but the famous "face on the bar-
room floor" was not painted until 1936. Tours of each are given daily
10-5; adm.

A monument, marking the site where John H. Gregory first found
gold, is on the boundary with **Black Hawk.** The old brewery on Eureka
Street, built in the early 1880's had a popular beer garden. Lace House,
built in the 1860's is replete with gingerbread trimming. Bobtail Tunnel can
be toured in summer on a burro-pulled train; adm. Gold Dust Village,
just below, was where the Chinese workers were segregated.

Nevadaville (2 m W) was laid out shortly after Gregory's gold find,
and its population once exceeded Denver's; today it is a ghost town
with the city hall, fire station, Masonic lodge, and other buildings
still standing.

COLORADO SPRINGS: The many mineral springs at the foot of
Pike's Peak, in what is now the Colorado Springs-Manitou ("Great
Spirit") Springs area, were long considered sacred by Indians, and
early settlers often found beadwork offerings in the streams here.
Later, white explorers and Pike's-Peak-or-Bust gold seekers found the
springs a convenient campsite before ascending the mountains to the
west. **Pioneers' Museum** (25 W Kiowa St.) features artifacts from Pikes
Peak area exploration; Indian displays; reconstructed rooms from the
1874 home of Helen Hunt Jackson. Open Tues.-Sat. 10-5, Sun. 2-5;
closed hols; free. **McAllister House** (423 N Cascade Ave.): 6-room
dwelling built in 1875 of bricks imported from Philadelphia; Victorian
antiques; open early June-early Sept., Tues.-Sat. 10-5, Sun. 2-5; sm
adm. **El Pomar Carriage House Museum** (Lake Ave., opposite Broad-
moor Hotel): vehicles, saddles, and riding accessories of the 1890's
West; open Tues.-Sun. 10-5; closed hols; free.

Colorado Springs Fine Arts Center (30 W Dale St.): prehistoric
art of the Southwest, smaller collections from around the world; open
Tues.-Sat. 9-5, Sun. 1:30-5; free. **Manitou Cliff Dwellings Museum**
(US 24 Bypass), cliff dwellings and artifacts dating from about 1100-
1300; summer, daily exc. Fri., 9-5; closed Oct.-mid-May; sm adm.

National Carvers Museum (14960 Woodcarver Rd., 10 m N on I-25): wood-carving demonstrations; exhibits; open Mon.-Sat. 9-5, Sun. 10:30-5; closed hols; adm.

American Numismatic Association (818 N Cascade Ave.) displays coins, tokens, medals, and paper money; open Mon.-Fri. 8-5; closed hols; free. **Clock Museum** (21st St. at Bott Ave.), with over 100 clocks, is open summers 9-sunset; inquire locally for winter hrs; adm. **Colorado Car Museum** (137 Manitou Ave.) features cars from 1900 plus custom-built models belonging to celebrities; open May-Sept., Mon.-Sat. 9-5 with longer hrs June-Aug., Sun. 10:30-5; Oct.-Apr., Sat. & Sun. 1-5; adm.

May Natural History Museum of the Tropics (8 m SW on SR 115): tropical invertebrates from all over the world. Open May-Sept. 8 am-9 pm; adm.

U.S. Air Force Academy (10 m N on I-25): **Visitor Center** (S entrance) has films, displays, schedule of events, and brochures for the self-guiding auto tour, "Follow the Falcon"; open daily 8-5; free.

CORTEZ: Four Corners Museum (City Library) displays fossils and Indian artifacts; open daily 8-6; free.

CRAIG: Chamber of Commerce (at entrance to City Park) is in the private railroad car once owned by railroad czar David H. Moffat; open business hours; free. **Moffat County Museum** (in courthouse) contains historical items; open Mon.-Fri. 9-5; free.

CRIPPLE CREEK: Cripple Creek Museum (on SR 67) houses relics from this gold town, where ore was discovered in 1890; by 1900 the town had 25,000 residents, and in 1901 $25 in gold was produced; open Memorial Day-early Oct., daily 10-5:30, weekends only in winter; sm adm. **Mollie Kathleen Gold Mine** (1 m N on SR 67) gives guided tours mid-May-Oct., daily 9-6; adm. **El Paso Gold Mine** (3 m SE on SR 67) gives tours in summer 10-6; adm. **Old Homestead** (353 E Myers Ave), a brothel during the 1890's, contains original furnishings; open Memorial Day-Oct., daily 10-5:30; adm. The **Imperial Hotel,** built in 1896 and still retaining some of its opulent furnishings, presents period melodrama from mid-June-mid Sept., Tues.-Sun.

DENVER: State Capitol (E. Colfax Ave. & Sherman St.) has a panoramic view from the dome, gold-leafed as a memorial to the early mining industry; inside are stained-glass portraits of Kit Carson, Ute Chief Ouray, other notables; rose-onyx wainscoting, rare marbles, brasses. Open all yr exc hols, free; guided tours in summer, weekdays 9-3:30, weekends 9:30-3:30, and less frequently rest of yr.

Colorado State Museum (E 14th Ave. & Sherman St.): collections arranged to depict the state's history; library. Open Mon.-Fri. 9-5, weekends and hols 10-5. Free.

Civic Center (W of Capitol Complex) includes the **Denver Public Library** (1357 Broadway) with outstanding materials on Western history and paintings; open Mon.-Thurs. 10-9, Fri.-Sat. 10-5:30, Sun. (Sept.-May) 1:30-5:30; closed hols; free. **Denver Art Museum** (100 W 14th Ave.), in an interesting modern building, has a vast and varied collection; Renaissance painting and sculpture; East Indian art objects; medieval sculpture; native Indian arts; decorative arts; Southwestern santeros; 17th-C Spanish Baroque material. Open Tues.-Sat. 9-5, Sun. 1-5; closed hols; free. Also in the Civic Center are the **Greek Theater** (an outdoor amphitheater in classic style used for square dancing and other events), the **City & County Building** (a massive structure in modified Roman style), the **Pioneer Monument** (the equestrian figure of Kit Carson surmounting figures of the Hunter, the Prospector, and the Pioneer Mother and Child) by Frederick MacMonnies, and the **Bronco Buster** by Alexander P. Proctor.

Larimer Square (Larimer St., between 14th & 16th Sts.), where Denver's founder William Larimer built his cabin, is a block of attractively restored buildings dating from the 1860's-1890's; they now house shops, art galleries, cafes.

U.S. Mint (W Colfax Ave. at Cherokee St.) gives ½-hr tours Mon.-Fri. exc hols, June-Aug. 8-11 & 12:30-3, Sept.-May 9-11 & 1-2:30; closed for inventory 2 wks before July 4th during which time only gold display on mezzanine can be seen. Free.

Forney Transportation Museum (1416 Platte St.) has over 250 cars and carriages dating from 1750; steam engines; rail coaches; cycles; airplanes; period costumes. Open daily exc Dec. 25, 9-6; adm. **Rippey's Veteran Car Museum** (2030 S Cherokee St.) has antique and classic cars dating from 1903; open Mon.-Fri. 9-5, Sat. 9:30-12:30; closed hols; free.

Molly Brown House (1340 Pennsylvania St.) is the ornate Victorian home of the socialite who survived the *Titanic* disaster and called herself "Unsinkable." Tours Tues.-Sat. 10-4, Sun. 12-4; closed hols; adm.

Denver Museum of Natural History (City Park & E 23rd Ave.): displays on prehistoric peoples; prehistoric animals; minerals; mounted mammal and bird collection; open Mon.-Sat. 9-4:30, Sun. noon-5; closed major hols; free. **Gates Planetarium** (City Park & E 23rd Ave.) has daily shows; advance reservations advised; adm.

EUREKA: Clarke Memorial Museum (240 E St.) offers an ornithological collection, fossils and minerals, Indian artifacts, local historical materials; open Tues.-Sat. 10-4; closed hols; free.

EVERGREEN: Bells of Granite Glen Museum (Upper Bear Creek Rd.) houses some 3000 bells dating from 1000 BC; open May-Sept., Tues.-Sun. 10-5; adm.

FAIRPLAY: South Park City (official name of Fairplay 1869-74), with some 30 authentically furnished buildings, is a fine reconstruction of a late 19th-C Colorado mining town; some buildings are on their original sites, others were moved from nearby ghost towns. Features include mining exhibits, complete railroad station, 1870's brewery serving as museum, and Chinese tong house. Open mid-May-mid-Oct. 9-5, longer hrs in summer; adm.

    Sheldon Jackson Memorial Chapel (6th & Hathaway Sts.), built in 1874 by missionary Sheldon Jackson, is an attractive Gothic-style chapel; open daily exc when services are being conducted.

FLORISSANT FOSSIL BEDS NATIONAL MONUMENT (35 m W of Colorado Springs via SR 24): Museum and information center (2.5 m S of Florrisant); nature trail. Preserved here is a rich fossil area with impressions of dragon flies, ants, butterflies, plant leaves, fish, birds and small mammals of the Oligocene. Open daily, June-Aug. 8-7, Apr.-May & Sept.-Oct. 8-4:30; open Mon.-Fri. 8:30-5, Nov.-Mar.; closed Jan. 1, Thnks, Dec. 25; free.

FORT COLLINS: Pioneer Museum (219 Peterson St.): prehistoric and contemporary Indian displays; local historical items; open Tues.-Sat. 1-5; closed hols; free.

FORT GARLAND: Fort Garland Museum (S of town off US 160): restored adobe fort built to protect settlers against Indian raids; later used to keep Confederates from Colorado's gold mines during the Civil War; was Col. Kit Carson's last command in 1866-67; a state museum, it features life-size mannequins in uniform. Open mid-Apr.-mid-Oct. daily 9-4:30; free.

GEORGETOWN: The only major mining town never destroyed by fire, Georgetown is unique in preserving an unusual number of period buildings. **Hotel de Paris,** whose French owner Louis Dupuy served gourmet meals in an elaborate setting of courtyards, diamond dust mirrors, imported china, and other luxuries; maintained with original furnishings as a museum. Open June 15-Sept. 15, 9-5:30; adm.

    Hammill House, one of the most luxurious homes in the Colorado Territory, was built over 13 yrs; many original furnishings; gold-plated door knobs; an onyx fireplace. Open May-Sept. daily 9:30-6; rest of year closed Mon.; adm.

Maxwell House (an 1880's Victorian home painted cream with pink and brown trim), Alpine House #2 Fire House (1874, with bell tower added 1880), several churches, and the old jailhouse are among other buildings still standing. The State Historical Society is developing an interpretive mining complex between Georgetown and Silver Plume (SW on I-70), called the Georgetown Loop Historic Mining Area.

GOLDEN: Colorado School of Mines (Illinois Ave. & 15th St.): Geologic Museum open Mon.-Fri. 8-5, Sat. & Sun. 1:30-4:30; closed hols; free.

Golden Pioneer Museum (911 10th St.) contains memorabilia of the city's history from the discovery of gold in 1859 through the time (1862-67) it was capital of the Colorado Territory; open Mon.-Fri. exc hols, 1-5; free.

Colorado Railroad Museum (17155 W 44th Ave.) covers 12 acres with steam locomotives and cars dating from the late 1800's; a replica of an early railroad station houses photographs and documents. Open daily 9-5, with longer hrs in summer; adm.

Man & His World—American Indian Museum (705½ Joyce St.) has collections of prehistoric to recent Indian artifacts; open daily 10-5; donation.

House of Carvings Museum (Lookout Mntn & US 40): wood carvings, miniatures to life-size; open May-Oct. 9-5; donations.

Lariat Trail is a scenic route leading to Denver Mountain Parks. Nearest of the parks is Lookout Mountain (5 m W); the road winds to the summit where William Cody (Buffalo Bill) asked to be buried; here there is his grave plus the Buffalo Bill Memorial Museum; open daily exc. Dec. 25, Oct. 1-Apr. 30, 10-5; May 1-Sept. 30, 9-7; free. The road continues past the Denver game preserve (deer, elk, buffalo) to the 8270-ft summit of Genesee Peak, Filius and Bergen parks, Evergreen, Bear Creek Canyon, Red Rocks Park, and to Denver.

GRAND JUNCTION: Historical Museum & Institute of Western Colorado (4th & Ute Sts.) has geological, anthropological, and historical displays; open June-Nov., Tues.-Sat. 10-5, Sun. 2-5; closed hols; free.

GREELEY: This town was named for Horace Greeley, who was so impressed with the area on a trip here in 1859 that he wanted to found a cooperative agricultural community; Nathan Meeker, agricultural editor of Horace Greeley's New York Tribune, founded the town. Meeker Memorial Museum (1324 9th Ave.), Meeker's home, contains many of his personal belongings and historical documents; open Mon.-Fri. 9-noon and 1-5; closed hols; free. Municipal Museum (in new city complex) has exhibits on local history; same hrs as above; free. (See also Meeker.)

HOVENWEEP NATIONAL MONUMENT (entry from Colorado side is off US 666 just S of Pleasant View, then 9 m on gravel road; Utah entry is via dirt road) contains pueblo ruins noted for their masonry towers; information available from the ranger at **Square Tower Ruin.** **Lowry Indian Ruins** (9 m W of Pleasant View via county road) are of an Anasazi village dating from about 1075; the Great Kiva is one of the largest ever found. Both open all year, weather permitting; free.

IDAHO SPRINGS: Named for Chief Idaho, who brought wounded or ill warriors here to bathe, this town is still popular for its radium baths. **Edgar Mine** (1 m W on US 40) is an experimental mine operated by the Colorado School of Mines; 45-min guided tours are given hourly, June-early Sept., daily 8:30-3:30; in winter you can make arrangements for tours with the Colorado School of Mines; free.

LA JUNTA: Koshare Kiva (18th & Santa Fe Ave.), a museum with Indian arts and crafts, is built in the form of a Pueblo kiva and maintained by an unusual troop of Boy Scouts who call themselves Koshares (Pueblo for fun makers). The Koshares, nationally known for their performances of authentic Indian dances, usually perform here Sat. evenings during July-Aug.; adm. The museum is open daily in summer 9-5, and in winter 11-5; free.

LEADVILLE: One of the most colorful towns in U.S. history, Leadville started as a gold camp when ore was discovered at California Gulch in 1860, but it reached its zenith after the later discovery of vast silver mines. By 1879 it had a population of 30,000, with 120 saloons, 19 beer halls, and 118 gambling houses—only 4 churches—and a reputation for sin and wickedness rivaled only by Dodge City and Abilene. The 9-m **Silver Kings Highway** circles the old mines; today the most famous is the molybdenum mine of the Climax Molybdenum Co. Horace Tabor, who started with a $17 grubstake and was soon accused of owning the whole town, lived here with his first wife Augusta and his second, tragic wife Baby Doe (whose story forms the basis of the opera *The Ballad of Baby Doe*). **Tabor Home** (116 E 5th St.) is the restored home of Tabor and Augusta, where they once entertained Pres. U. S. Grant. Open Memorial Day-Labor Day, daily 8:30 am-8 pm, rest of yr 9:30-5:30; closed hols; sm adm.
  Tabor Opera House (308 Harrison Ave.), built by Tabor in 1879, was said to be the most elegant in the West and hosted the N.Y.

Metropolitan Opera Co., Houdini, and many famous actors of the day. The Tabor box, the dressing rooms, the set stage, hand-painted scenery, and other authentic furnishings can be seen on a guided tour Memorial Day-Oct. Sun.-Fri. 9-5:50; adm.

The **Matchless Mine** (E of town on E 7th St.) at one time produced as much as $100,000 a month for Horace Tabor. Tabor lost his fortune in the panic of 1893 and died penniless 6 years later, but never gave up hope that the Matchless would again produce a fortune. His last words to Baby Doe were, "Hold on to the Matchless." For 36 years she struggled to keep the mine, living in a crude cabin beside it, where she was found frozen to death in 1935. Open Memorial Day-Labor Day, daily 9 am-7 pm; sm adm.

Healy House-Dexter Cabin (912 Harrison Ave.) are maintained by the State Historical Society. Healy House, built in 1878, displays red velvet upholstery, hand-carved furniture, diamond dust mirrors, and other symbols of Victorian opulence. The 2-room cabin, built in 1879 by mining millionaire James V. Dexter as a retreat, has a rough-hewn exterior, but contains a crystal chandelier, a Persian rug, and other lavish furnishings. Open June-mid-Oct., daily 9-4:40; free.

House With The Eye (127 W 4th St.) is named for the stained-glass window shaped like an eye in the roof; period furnishings; relics of mining days; a carriage house has a hearse and Baby Doe's buggy. Guided tours Memorial Day-Labor Day, daily 10-6; sm adm.

Heritage Museum & Gallery (9th & Harrison) features Leadville's history in dioramas, period costumes, mining memorabilia, geological displays, and changing exhibits of contemporary works by Western artists; open Memorial Day-early Sept., daily 10 am-9 pm; adm.

LITTLETON: Littleton Area Historical Museum (6028 S Gallup St.) open Mon.-Fri. 8-5, Sun. 1-5; free.

LONGMONT: Pioneer Museum (302 Kimbark) open Mon.-Sat. 9-5, Sun. 1-5; free.

MEEKER: Meeker Monument and **County Historical Society Museum** mark the site of the Meeker Massacre of 1879. Nathan Meeker, ex-agricultural editor of the *New York Tribune* (see Greeley), became an Indian agent here but was never popular with the Indians; finally, in 1879, he so enraged the Ute that they killed him and 19 settlers here. The massacre is reenacted every July 4 at the Range Call Celebration.

MESA VERDE NATIONAL PARK (10 m E of Cortez on US 160, then S on park road): here you have a unique opportunity to follow the story of centuries of prehistoric residence. At least 1300 yrs ago,

Basketmakers farmed this area. By the 8th C, their Pueblo descendents were building homes above ground. But abruptly something (possibly attacking foreign tribes) made these people leave their comfortable homes for defensible caves in the cliffs; these required incredible climbs up and down the cliff faces. Either the **Far View Visitor Center** (summer only; daily 8-5) or the **Chapin Mesa Visitor Center** (open all yr 8-5, longer in summer), with dioramas and artifacts, offers booklest for self-guiding trails and ranger-led trips to Cliff Palace (200 rooms, 23 kivas), Spruce Tree House (114 rooms, 8 kivas), and other ruins.

MONTROSE: Ute Indian Museum (2 m S on US 550), maintained by the State Historical Society, has fine collections. History of the Ute is told through dioramas, photographs, and artifacts; some prehistoric material. Also a memorial to the great peacemaking Ute chief, Ouray, and his wife Chipeta. Open May-mid-Oct., daily 9-5, with longer hrs in summer; free.

PLATTEVILLE: Fort Vasquez (1 m S on US 85), a fur trading post built in 1837, has been restored by the State Historical Society; a Visitor Center displays items related to the fur trade; open Apr.-Oct. 9-5; free.

PUEBLO: El Pueblo State Historical Museum (905 S Prairie Ave.): exhibits devoted to local history; section on iron and steel industry; life-size reconstruction of Fort Pueblo, where the Ute "Christmas Massacre" of 1854 took place, leading people to avoid the area for years, claiming it was haunted. Open Tues.-Fri. 9-5, Sun. & some hols 10-5; free.

Pueblo Metropolitan Museum (419 W 14th St.) is a 37-room brick mansion constructed in 1891; replete with Victorianisms such as gilded fireplaces and ornate chandeliers; open June 1-Sept. 1, Tues.-Sat. 9-5, Sun. & hols 2-5; Sept. 1-June 1, Tues.-Sun. 1-4; adm.

Southern Colorado State College Geological Museum (Chemistry-Geology Bldg.) is open during academic yr, Mon.-Fri. 9-5; closed hols; free.

SILVERTON: Many Westerns have been filmed on Blair St., with its hitching posts and false-front buildings. Among many reminders of mining days are the Grand Imperial Hotel, an 1880's showplace, and the gold-domed courthouse. The **San Juan County Historical Society Museum** (in the old jail on N Greene St.) is open Memorial Day-early Oct. 9-5; sm adm. Among the local ghost towns are **Eureka** and **Animas Forks,** both off SR 110.

72 CONNECTICUT

STERLING: Overland Trail Museum (1½ m E on US 6): large collection of branding irons; local pioneer exhibits; archaeological and palaeontological displays. Open late Apr.-late Sept., Mon.-Sat. 9:30-5, Sun. 10:30-5; free.

TELLURIDE: Known as the "City of Gold," this town is named for the local ore, tellurium, and is still a mining center. The 1891 **Sheridan Opera House,** which boasted stars such as Sarah Bernhardt, still stands. Nearby mining towns are **Ophir** (8 m S via SR 145) and **Camp Bird** (4 m E via SR 145).

TRINIDAD: **Baca House and Pioneer Museum** (opp Post Office on Main St.) are maintained by the State Historical Society. Baca House is a 2-story adobe residence built by rancher Felipe Baca in 1869; the museum contains exhibits relating to ranching; adjoining is **Bloom House,** .the restored Victorian home of a cattle baron of the 1880's. All are open mid-May-mid-Oct., daily 9-4:30; free.

Trinidad State Junior College Museum (on campus in Library Bldg) has prehistoric and recent Indian exhibits from the Trinidad area; open Mon.-Sat. 8-5 during academic year; free.

WALSENBURG: **Francisco Fort Museum** (in La Veta, 11 m W on US 160, then 5 m S on SR 12), in an 1862 fortified home, depicts pioneer life in the Colorado Territory. Open late May-mid Sept., daily 9-5; free.

CONNECTICUT

AVON: **Avon Congregational Church** (6 W Main St.), designed by Hoadley in 1818, is open Sun.-Fri. in daylight; closed in winter; free. (Other Hoadley churches are the 1809 **Christ Episcopal,** Amity Rd., Bethany; **First Congregational,** Church Dr., Cheshire; see New Haven.)

BRIDGEPORT: **P. T. Barnum Museum** (804 Main St.): personal effects of Barnum and Tom Thumb; carved Swiss village with moving parts; circus memorabilia; open Tues.-Sat. 12-5, Sun. 2-5; free. **Museum of Art, Science & Industry** (4450 Park Ave.): Indian artifacts, helicopter cabin, colonial interior, 1856 fire engine, planetarium, art gallery; open Tues.-Sun. 2-5; free.

BRISTOL: American Watch & Clock Museum (100 Maple St.): more than 600 timepieces, many locally made; the city's horologic tradition began in 1790 when Gideon Roberts crafted clocks and sold them on horseback; open Apr.-Oct., Tues.-Sun. 1-5; adm.

CANTERBURY: Prudence Crandall House (jct. Sr 14A & 169) was the state's first all-black school, established by a Quaker in 1833 with the aid of William Lloyd Garrison; inquire locally for hrs.

CANTON: Canton Historical Society (11 Front St., Collinsville) has period rooms and shops; other historical displays; open Wed.-Fri. 12-4, Sun. 2-5; adm.

CLINTON: Adam Stanton House (63 E Main St.), built about 1790, was part home and part general store operated until 1864; most furnishings are original; open May-June, Sept.-Nov. 2-5, July & Aug. 11-5; free.

COLEBROOK: Colebrook Historical Society (Town Hall) open daily 2-4; free.

COVENTRY: Nathan Hale Homestead (South St., off SR 31) is the 1776 home in which the patriot's father, a justice of the peace, held court; furnished with family heirlooms; open May 15-Oct. 15, daily 1-5; adm.

DANBURY: Danbury Scott-Fanton Museum and Historical Society (43 Main St.) is a museum of early American crafts and furnishings; adjoining 1770 Dodd House has displays of the beaver hat industry that began in this city in 1780; 1750 David Taylor House contains costumes, uniforms, clothing; Huntington Hall has changing exhibits; open Wed.-Sun. 2-5; closed hols; donation.

DARIEN: Bates-Schofield Homestead (Old King's Hwy. N) a classic saltbox (c. 1730), headquarters of the Darien Historical Society; period furnishings; fine library; open Wed., Thurs. 2-4, Sun. 2:30-4:30; donation.

DEEP RIVER: Stone House (S. Main St.): displays of local history; locally produced cut glass; open Tues., Thurs. 2-4 in summer; donation.

DINOSAUR STATE PARK (on West St. in Rocky Hill, ¾-m E of Exit 23 off I-91) preserves footprints of 2 smallish Triassic dinosaurs; one walked semierect and both were probably carnivorous; museum with models, other exhibits; self-guiding trail; open Apr.-Nov. daily 9-4 (limited exhibits rest of yr); free.

EAST GRANBY: Old New-Gate Prison and Copper Mine (Newgate Rd., off SR 20) opened in 1707 as America's first chartered copper mine. Requisitioned by Gen. Washington during the Revolution to house prisoners of war, it served as the first state prison 1776-1827. Tours of the restored mine and dungeons. The gatehouse is a museum of early American penology. Open Memorial Day-Oct. 31, Tues.-Sun.- 10-4:30; sm adm.

EAST HADDAM: Goodspeed Opera House (on SR 82 near E Haddam Bridge): built in 1876; lavishly decorated in the Victorian style of river steamboats; operates as a summer theater.

EAST LYME: The 1660 **Thomas Lee House** (SR 156) and **Little Boston School,** with period furnishings; open Memorial Day-Columbus Day, Wed.-Sun. 10-5; sm adm.

ESSEX: Pratt House (20 West Ave.): early 1700's, Griswold collection of handcrafted early American pieces; displays of local history; open June-Oct., Tues., Thurs., Sat. 1-5; closed hols; sm adm.

FAIRFIELD: Fairfield Historical Society (636 Old Post Rd., opposite Town Hall) open Wed. 9:30-4:30; free.

FARMINGTON: This elegant town, a colonial center for silversmiths, clockmakers, and other craftsmen, has been beautifully preserved. **Farmington Museum** (37 High St.) is in the 1660 Stanley-Whitman House, one of the finest houses of this period in the nation; painstakingly restored; exceptionally fine handcrafted furniture and household items; open Apr.-Nov., Tues.-Sat. 10-noon, 2-5; Dec.-Mar., Fri.-Sun. 2-5; closed hols; adm.

   Hill-Stead Museum (Mountain Rd.), an elegant mansion designed about 1900 by Stanford White for industrialist Alfred Pope, has outstanding Impressionist paintings; Ming Dynasty Porcelains; fine bronzes; other art objects; library. Open Wed., Thurs., Sat., Sun. 2-5; closed Thnks, Dec. 25; adm.

   First Church of Christ, Congregational (75 Main St.) is a fine 1771 meeting house; open Mon.-Fri. 9-4; closed hols; free.

FORT GRISWOLD STATE PARK (Monument & Park Aves., Groton): earthern remains of 1778 fort; on Sept. 6, 1781, Benedict Arnold led

British forces here to burn the fort and massacre the inhabitants; open daily 8-sunset; free. On grounds are **Groton Monument** (125-ft observation tower) and **Monument House** (reconstructed fort with displays of the Revolution and War of 1812); open mid-June-late-Sept., Mon.-Fri. 8:30-11:30, 1-4:15, Sun. 1-5; free.

GAY CITY STATE PARK (on SR 85 on the Hebron-Bolton town line): crumbling foundations and cemetery of the old mill town, Gay City, settled in 1796 by a religious sect led by Elijah Andrus. Sm adm weekends and hols.

GILLETTE CASTLE STATE PARK (off SR 148, W of Hadlyme): 24-room castle designed by actor William Gillette (famous for stage portrayals of Sherlock Holmes) took 20 men 5 yrs to build (1914-19); among the curiosities are many representations of cats (he owned at least 15 live ones) and a 3-m hobby railroad; open Memorial Day-late Oct., daily 11-5; sm adm.

GREENWICH: Bush-Holley House (39 Strickland Rd. off US 1 in Cos Cob): saltbox built before 1700 where Willa Cather and other artists and writers stayed; a hidden staircase; rare early American furniture. On grounds are a museum of John Rogers sculpture, barn with antique tools, artist workshop, and children's museum. Open Tues.-Sat. 10-noon, 2-5, Sun. 2-4; sm adm.
  Bruce Museum (Bruce Park off Steamboat Rd.): dioramas of prehistoric and recent wildlife, space exhibits, Indian artifacts, dinosaur tracks, among more than 20,000 exhibits; African, Etruscan, and Chinese art, European and American painting; changing exhibits. Open Mon.-Fri. 10-5, Sun. 2-5; closed hols; free.
  Putnam Cottage (243 E Putnam Ave.) was built about 1690; from here Gen. Israel Putnam escaped from the Redcoats in 1779; open Tues.-Sat. 10-noon, 2-5, Sun. 2-4; sm adm.
  Museum of Cartoon Art (384 Field Point Rd.): history of cartoons from 1899 to the present; open Tues.-Fri. 10-4, Sun. 1-5; closed hols; donation.

GROTON: U.S. Submarine Base (2 m N on SR 12): for 2-hr weekend bus tour of subs, museum, library, write in advance to Public Relations Office (Box 44, Groton 06340); commercial tours by boat past the installation are available spring-fall at docks under I-95 bridge.

GUILFORD: Henry Whitfield Museum (S off I-95 past Guilford Green on Whitfield St.), built in 1639, served as a parsonage, fort, and meeting hall for Puritans led by the Rev. Henry Whitfield, who founded the town; 17th-C furnishings; first tower clock in the colonies (made 1726); open Apr.-Nov., Wed.-Sun. 11-5; open Sat. & Sun. 11-4 rest of yr, but closed hols, Dec. 15-Jan. 15; sm adm. The 1735 **Thomas Griswold House Museum** (171 Boston St.), with historic displays and antiques, is open mid-June-Labor Day, Wed.-Sun. 11-4; sm adm. **Hyland House** (84 Boston St.), 1660 home with period furnishings, is open late June-early Sept., Tues.-Sun. 10:30-4:30; sm adm.

HARKNESS MEMORIAL STATE PARK (Waterford): 235-acre luxurious estate of Standard Oil heir Edward Harkness consisted of 27 buildings, including 30 servants' rooms, a game club, a garage housing a limousine turntable, and the 42-room mansion; half the estate is set aside as recreational land for the handicapped. The mansion, which displays changing exhibits of 874 watercolors of 1040 North American birds by Rex Brasher, is open Memorial Day-mid-Oct., weekdays 10-5, weekends & hols 10-6; sm adm.

HARTFORD: State Capitol (Capitol Ave.), designed in 1878 by Richard Upjohn, is open Mon.-Fri.; closed hols; tours available in spring and fall; free. **State Library** (opposite Capitol), Italian Renaissance-style, houses the Colt Collection of Firearms, Newcomb Clock Collection, Mitchelson Coin Collection, Gilbert Stuart portrait of George Washington, Indian artifacts, the original Royal Charter; state archives. Open Mon.-Fri. 9-5, Sat. 9-1; closed hols; free.

    Connecticut Historical Society (1 Elizabeth St.): outstanding 17th-18th-C Connecticut-made furniture, portraits (including Trumbull and Morse), lithograph prints (including the Kellog Bros.), tall clocks, 19th-C costumes, and silver. The library has more than a million documents related to state history; genealogical section. Museum open Mon.-Sat. 1-5, closed hols & Sat. aft. in summer. Library open Mon.-Sat. 9:30-5:30; closed hols & Sat. aft. in summer. Free.

    Wadsworth Atheneum (600 Main St.) is one of the nation's finest art museums. John Trumbull, Copley, Hopper, Shahn, Calder, Rauschenberg, and others; Wallace Nutting Collection of Furniture of the Pilgrim Century (1620-1720); J. P. Morgan's Greek and Roman bronzes and 18th-C porcelains; Lifar collection of Diaghilev Ballet costume and stage designs; European drawings, 17th-C Baroque painting, 19th-C French painting, and Italian Renaissance works. Also arms, armor, tapestries, decorative arts, special exhibitions. Open Sept.-July, Tues.-Sat. 11-4, Sun. 1-5; closed Jan. 1, July 4, Thnks, Dec. 25. Free.

    Nook Farm (351 Farmington Ave.) has a Visitor Center with changing exhibits. **Mark Twain House,** an 1874 Victorian fantasy reflecting the personality and grand lifestyle of the author, contains many Clemens family furnishings. Samuel Clemens lived here 1874-91 and wrote here 7 major works, including *Tom Sawyer* and *Huckleberry Finn.* The porch resembles the deck of a Mississippi steamboat. **Harriet Beecher Stowe House,** built in 1871, is more restrained; Mrs. Stowe lived here from 1873 until her death in 1896; family memorabilia. Stowe-Day Foundation research library is open to scholars. Open mid-June-Aug. daily 10-5; Mar.-mid-June & Sept.-Dec., Tues.-Sat. 10-5, Sun. 2-5; Jan.-Feb., Wed.-Sat. 10-5, Sun. 2-5; adm.

Old State House (800 Main St.), a classic Charles Bulfinch design, served as the state capitol 1796-1878 and as City Hall until 1915; restored offices and historical exhibits. Open Tues.-Sat. 12-4; closed hols; sm adm.

Butler-McCook Homestead (396 Main St.), built in 1782, reflects the evolution of taste in 4 generations of the same family; open May 15-Oct. 15, daily 1-5; adm.

Noah Webster House (227 S Main St. in W Hartford) is a simple frame dwelling built early 1700's; memorabilia of the author of the American Dictionary; open Thurs. 10-4; sm adm.

KENT: Sloane-Stanley Museum (1 m N on US 7): craft and domestic tools dating from the 17th C; open Memorial Day-Oct., Wed.-Sun. 10-4:30; sm adm.

LEBANON: On the unspoiled green is **Jonathan Trumbull House,** built in 1735, with period furnishings; behind it is **Wadsworth Stable,** moved from Hartford. The nearby **Revolutionary War Office** was used by Trumbull to direct the supply effort during the war; open May-Nov., Tues.-Sat. 1-6; adm.

LITCHFIELD: Founded in 1719, this town is noted for its many fine colonial houses. Most are privately owned, but can be seen on an annual tour (usually in July). **Litchfield Historical Society Museum** (on the Green) contains 18th-C paintings, a restored colonial kitchen, American fine and decorative arts, and Indian artifacts; open May 15-Oct. 15, Tues.-Sat. 11-5. Sun. 2-5; rest of yr, Tues.-Sat. 2-4; closed hols; free.

Tapping Reeve House & Law School (South St.): restored house, erected in 1773, with period furnishings; America's first law school in a little white cottage (graduates included Aaron Burr, 2 U.S. vice presidents, and 130 members of Congress); open May 15-Oct. 15, Tues.-Sat. 11-5, Sun. 2-5; closed hols; adm.

MADISON: Nathaniel Allis House (853 Boston Post Rd.): built about 1770; period furnishings, costumes, toys, ship models, library; open mid-June-mid-Sept., Tues.-Sat. 10-5; closed July 4; sm adm.

MANCHESTER: Cheney Homestead (106 Hartford Rd.): built about 1780 by a clockmaker and farmer; 18th-19th-C furnishings; open Thurs., Sun. 1-5; closed hols; sm adm. **Antique Auto Museum** (Slater St.) has 26 antique autos in operating condition; open daily 11-5 in summer, weekends rest of yr; adm.

MERIDEN: Andrews Homestead (424 W Main St.): saltbox dating from about 1760; antique furnishings, many made in Meriden; open Wed., Sun. 2-5; closed hols; adm.

MIDDLETOWN: Wesleyan University Davison Art Center (High St.): prints and printmaking from the early 15th C; contemporary works, some housed in the 1838-40 Greek Revival Alsop House with exterior trompe l'oeil figures and interior oil-on-plaster wall paintings that are unique in the U.S. Open when college is in session, weekdays 10-4, Sat. 9-12, 1-4, Sun. 2-5; free. **Olin Library** (Church St.): manuscripts and papers of Einstein, Yeats, Pound, Charles Wesley, and others; open daily; closed hols; free. **Russell House** (High St.), 1828 Greek Revival home built for a China trader; houses faculty offices; open during academic year, Mon.-Fri.

Submarine Library & Museum (440 Washington St.): memorabilia of submarine service, models, oceanography display; library; open Mon.-Fri. 10-1, weekends 10-5; free.

MOODUS: Amasa Day House (Moodus Green), 1816 house with period furnishings, open May 15-Oct. 15, daily 1-5; sm adm.

MYSTIC: One of the oldest shipbuilding and whaling ports in the country, Mystic has supplied some of America's fastest clipper ships and the first regular ironclad vessel, the *Galena*. Many handsome old houses built by prosperous captains and merchants still stand. **Denison Homestead** (Pequotsepos Ave.) contains 5 rooms reflecting the tastes of 11 generations of the Denison family, 1717-1941; furnishings are original; tours mid-May-mid-Oct., Tues.-Sun. 1-5; adm. **Whitehall Mansion** (SR 27, just N off I-95), 1771 country home, open Mon.-Fri. 2-4; adm.

Mystic Seaport (Greenmanville Ave, 1 m S off I-95) is a living museum with authentic homes, shops, and ships commemorating a maritime New England village of the mid-19th C. Seaport Street is lined with shops where old skills are demonstrated; maritime displays. Moored here are the *Charles W. Morgan,* a 19th-C wooden whaler, the square-rigged *Joseph Conrad,* and other ships. Summer riverboat cruises and a planetarium of celestial navigation are an extra charge. Open daily in summer 9-5; in winter 9-4; closed Jan. 1, Dec. 25. Adm includes most attractions.

NEW BRITAIN: New Britain Museum of American Art (56 Lexington St.): outstanding works from the Revolution to the present century; Thomas Hart Benton's *Arts of Life in America* murals, Wyeth family, Stuart, Copley, Eakins, Sloan, Whistler, Sargent; Sanford Low collection of illustrations. Open Tues.-Sun. 1-5; closed hols; free.

NEW CANAAN: New Canaan Historical Society (13 Oenoke Ridge) has restored a number of buildings, most open Tues.-Fri., Sun. 2-4; closed hols; adm: **Hanford-Silliman House,** begun in 1762 by a weaver and tavern keeper; rare old pewter; period furnishings. **John Rogers Studio Museum,** where the sculptor worked 1878-1904; works and personal belongings. **Antique Tool Museum and Old Printing Office** contains early craft utensils; printshop with a handpress.

    Silvermine Guild of Artists (1037 Silvermine Rd.): art galleries and craftsmen; New England Exhibition; chamber music concerts; open daily 12:30-5; closed Jan. 1, Thnks, Dec. 25; free.

NEW HAVEN: Yale University, founded in 1701, bounds the historic Green on the west. **Visitor Center** (Phelps Gateway, College St.) can arrange free tours; most buildings are open daily all yr. **Connecticut Hall** (Old Campus), built 1752 in Georgian style, is the only surviving pre-Revolutionary building. **Harkness Memorial Tower** (High St.), a Gothic-style carillon, contains a Memorial Room with the college history depicted in woodcarvings. **Marsh Hall** (360 Prospect St.), originally home of paleontologist Othniel C. Marsh, is an unusual combination of Gothic and Victorian. **Art & Architecture Building** (Chapel & York Sts.) is a rough concrete design by Paul Rudolph; inquire here for schedule of architecture tours. **David S. Ingalls Skating Rink** (Sachem & Prospect Sts.) is by Eero Saarinen.

    Yale University Art Gallery (1111 Chapel St.) is outstanding; Olsen Collection of Pre-Columbian art, African sculpture; Moore Collection of Near and Far Eastern Art; Jarves, Griggs, and Rabinowitz collections of Italian and Northern European painting; 20th-C painting and sculpture; also strong on American works—Revolutionary paintings, miniatures by Trumbull, Garvan collection. Open Tues.-Sat. 10-5, Sun. 2-5; also open Thurs. 6-9 pm in winter; closed Jan. 1, July 4, Dec. 25; free.

Peabody Museum (170 Whitney Ave.) is one of the world's greatest natural history museums; fossil vertebrates, bird hall, pre-Columbian hall are outstanding; excellent displays of the anthropology and natural history of New England. Open Mon.-Sat. 9-5, Sun. & hols 1-5; closed Jan. 1, July 4, Thnks, Dec. 25; sm adm charged some days.

Sterling Memorial Library and **Beinecke Rare Book & Manuscript Library** (Wall & High Sts.) have more than 4 million volumes; superlative collections of Americana, English and European literature, medieval manuscripts, and early books and newspapers. On display are illuminated manuscripts, a Gutenberg Bible, Audubon birds, changing exhibits. Open during academic year from 8:30 to 5 or later; shorter hours in summer; free.

Yale Collection of Musical Instruments (15 Hillhouse Ave.), one of the best in the nation, has many fine antiques; concerts are performed on old instruments during the academic year. Open mid-Sept.-mid-May, Tues.-Thurs., 2-4, Sun. 2-5; closed during college vacation; free.

On **The Green** are **Center Church on the Green** (with the colony's founding illustrated in a Tiffany window, 17th-C graves in crypt) and **Trinity Church** (vaulted ceiling and Tiffany windows), both designed by Ithiel Town. David Hoadley's 1815 **United Church** is considered his masterpiece; in 1855 Henry Ward Beecher's congregation supplied abolitionists going to join John Brown in Kansas with Bibles and "Beecher Bibles" (guns).

Grove Street Cemetery (between Prospect & Ashmun Sts.) contains graves of Eli Whitney, Noah Webster, Lyman Beecher, other prominent residents.

New Haven Colony Historical Society (114 Whitney Ave. at Temple St.) houses re-created colonial rooms, local historical exhibits; fine library; open Tues.-Fri. 10-5, Sat. & Sun. 2-5; closed Jan. 1, Easter, Dec. 25; free.

Morris House (325 Lighthouse Rd., 4 m SE) was built 1685 and rebuilt 1780 after the British burned most of it; period furnishings; open May-Oct., Mon.-Fri. 10-5, Sun. 2-5; closed hols; donation.

Branford Trolley Museum (3 m E on US 1 at 17 River St. in East Haven) displays more than 80 trolleys dating from 1878-1936; museum houses associated exhibits; open Apr.-Nov., Sat. & Sun. 11-6, hols noon-5; also open Mon.-Fri. 10-5 from late June-Labor Day; adm.

NEW LONDON: Founded in 1646 by Puritans, this became a privateer center; in 1781 Tories burned the wharves and waterfront. Benedict Arnold watched the burning from **Ye Ancientest Burial Grounds** (Huntington St.), which dates from 1653 and has colorful epitaphs. The

1678 **Hempsted House** (11 Hempstead St.) survived the burning; restoration is based on a detailed diary kept by the son of the builder; diary on display; open May 15-Oct. 15, daily 1-5; sm adm.

Old Town Mill and **Nathan Hale Schoolhouse** (Main & Mill Sts.): The school is where Hale taught before his service with the army and execution as a spy. The mill, dating from 1650, is the oldest industrial power plant in the nation; contains a museum of early industry. Open June-mid-Sept., Tues.-Sun. 1-4; free. **Shaw Mansion** (11 Blinman St.) served as the state's naval headquarters during the Revolution; history includes visits by Washington and Lafayette; library; open Tues.-Sat. 1-4; closed hols; sm adm.

Lyman Allyn Museum (100 Mohegan Ave, opp Coast Guard Academy): superb dollhouse and toy collection; early New England decorative arts; Egyptian, Greek, and Roman antiquities; Oriental collection; eclectic collection of paintings that includes Degas, Andrew Wyeth, Gris, Matisse, Braque, and Utrillo. Also research library on art history; tours, other activities. Open Tues.-Sat. 1-5, Sun. 2-5; closed hols; free.

U.S. Coast Guard Academy (on SR 32, 1 m N) gives guided tours by appointment, but the Visitor Center is open 8-5 daily; you can visit the training bark *Eagle* when it is in port; free.

NEW MILFORD: New Milford Historical Society (4 Aspetuck Ave. on the green): portraits and miniatures; fully furnished Victorian home; open Wed., Sat. 2-5; free.

NORFOLK: Norfolk Historical Society (on the green) open late June-mid-Sept., Sat. 10-12, 2-5, Sun. 2-5; donation.

NORWALK: Lockwood-Mathews Mansion (295 West Ave.): lavish 1864 blend of French chateau and Scottish manor house; octagonal rotunda beneath a 40-ft-high skylight; 63 rooms, a showcase of Victorian decorative arts. Open Sun. 1-4; sm adm.

NORWICH: Leffingwell Inn (348 Washington St.) was built in 1675 as a home and turned into a public house 25 years later; it became a meeting place for patriots during the Revolution; restoration is exquisite, with locally made period pieces. Open in summer Tues.-Sat. 10-noon, Tues.-Sun. 2-4; in winter Sat., Sun. 2-4; adm. **Norwichtown Historic District** (E Town St., Elm Ave., Washington St.) has more than 50 pre-1800 private dwellings on or near The Green.

Slater Memorial Museum and Converse Art Gallery (108 Crescent St., Norwich Free Academy) houses Greek, Roman, and Renaissance casts, 17th-20th-C American art and furniture, Indian artifacts, Oriental and African art, Egyptian textiles and art objects, and a gun collection. Open Sept.-May, Mon.-Fri. 9-4, Sat. & Sun. 2-5; June-Aug., Tues.-Sun. 1-4; closed hols; free.

OLD LYME: Florence Griswold House (Lyme St.), headquarters of Lyme Historical Society; 1817 Federal home, a gathering place for Barbizon Impressionists in the early 1900's (Old Lyme is still home to many artists); paintings by Hassam, Wiggins, Metcalf, and others; china; toy museum. Open mid-June-Labor Day, Tues.-Sun. 10-5; sm adm. Next door is the Lyme Art Association gallery. **First Congregational Church of Old Lyme** (Lyme St.) is a picture-postcard church, a copy of one built in 1816 that burned in 1907; believed based on a London church designed by Wren. Open daily; free.

PUTNAM MEMORIAL STATE PARK (jct SR 58, 107, SE of Danbury) was the winter camp site of Gen. Israel Putnam's Continental Army 1778-9. A **Revolutionary War Museum** contains historical displays, reconstructed log buildings; open daily 8-sunset; free.

RIDGEFIELD: Aldrich Museum of Contemporary Art (258 Main St.) open mid-Apr.-mid-Dec., Sat. & Sun. 2-5; adm. Sculpture garden open daily, free.

    Keeler Tavern (132 Main St.), also known as Cannonball House because a British cannon ball is imbedded in a corner post, was an inn from 1772-1907. During the 1777 Battle of Ridgefield, Benedict Arnold (not yet a traitor) set up barricades here. Pavilion and walled garden were added later by architect Cass Gilbert. Open Wed., Sat., Sun. 2-5; closed hols & Dec. 25-Jan. 1; adm.

RIVERTON: Hitchcock Museum (SR 20), in an 1829 church, houses antique painted furniture made by Lambert Hitchcock and other 18th-19th-C craftsmen. Hitchcock opened his factory here in 1826 to produce stenciled chairs at a reasonable price; whole families did the work, children rubbing the chairs with red priming to emulate rosewood; reproductions are still made in the old factory a short walk away. Open May-Nov., Tues.-Sat. 10-5; Dec.-Apr., Sat. only, 10-5; closed hols; free.

ROWAYTON: United Church of Rowayton (210 Rowayton Ave.), completed in 1962; redwood communion table is supported by a rock found on the site; colored glass panels in roof; open daily.

SHARON: Gay-Hoyt House (Main St.), a 1775 brick home; exhibits on county history; open June-Oct., Tues., Sat. 2-5; adm.

SIMSBURY: Massacoh Plantation, Simsbury Historic Center (800 Hopmeadow St.) is a complex of historic buildings depicting 3 centuries of Connecticut life; open May-Oct. daily 1-4; closed hols; adm.

STAMFORD: Hoyt Farmhouse (713 Bedford St.), built about 1690, contains period costumes, tools, dolls, other exhibits; library. Open Wed., Sun. 1-4; closed hols; sm adm. **First Presbyterian Church** (1101 Bedford St.), symbolically shaped like a fish; 1958 design by Wallace K. Harrison; beautiful stained glass; open daily 9-5; closed hols.

STONINGTON: Charming coastal village, a base for privateers and whalers; sea captain's homes still line the streets. Militiamen defended it against British bombardment in 1775 by manning guns in Cannon Square and it was attacked again during the War of 1812. **Old Stonington Lighthouse** has regional and seafaring memorabilia; open summers, Tues.-Sun, 11-4:30; sm adm.

STORRS: University of Connecticut William Benton Museum of Art: good collection; American and European painting; Kathe Kollwitz prints; open Mon.-Sat. 11-4, Sun. 1-5; closed hols; free.

STRATFORD: Capt. David Judson House (967 Academy Hill): 1723 home; period furnishings; slave quarters; genealogical library; open Apr.-Oct., Wed., Sat., Sun. 11-5; closed July 4, Labor Day; adm. Nearby is the **American Shakespeare Theater,** designed to resemble the Globe; drama presented in summer; library. **Boothe Memorial Park** (N Main St.) has a collection of unusual buildings from the state, including museum and blacksmith shop; free.

SUFFIELD: Hatheway House (Main St.): built in 1760, with additions in 1795; elegantly furnished to represent 3 periods of 18th-C decor; 1795 wing contains French handblocked wallpapers, Adamesque plasterwork; open May 15-Oct. 15, daily 1-5; closed hols; adm.

TERRYVILLE: Lock Museum of America, Inc. (114 Main St.): 5000 locks and keys dating from the early 19th C; open May-Oct., Tues.-Sun. 1:30-4:30; free.

WALLINGFORD: Samuel Parsons House (180 S Main St.), a 1759 gambrel-roofed house, once served as a stagecoach tavern; 18th-19th-C furniture; open Sun. 2-5; free.

WATERBURY: Mattatuck Historical Society Museum (119 W Main St.) has re-created 4 colonial and one Victorian rooms; paintings by

Connecticut artists; junior museum of Indian and colonial history; open Tues.-Sat. noon-5, Sun. 2-5; closed hols & Sun. in July & Aug.; free. **Clock Tower** (Meadow St.) is modeled after Mangia Tower in Italy.

WATERFORD: Eugene O'Neill Memorial Theater Center (SR 213) is a complex including the National Theatre of the Deaf, several other theaters, schools, workshops, and conference facilities; also O'Neill memorabilia and theatrical exhibits; performances in summer.

WETHERSFIELD: Old Academy Museum (150 Main St.), headquarters of the Wethersfield Historical Society, is open May 15-Oct. 15, Tues., Thurs., Sat. 1-4:30; closed hols; sm adm. A 1692 wooden warehouse, built for West Indies trade, is being developed as a maritime museum by the Society.

Joseph Webb House (211 Main St.), built 1752 and restored with fine furnishings; here George Washington and Count de Rochambeau in 1781 planned the Yorktown campaign that would end the Revolution. **Silas Deane House** (209 Main St.), home of our first Commissioner to France, who procured arms for the Continental Army; elegant 1776 building; period furnishings. **Isaac Stevens House** (213 Main St.), built 1788-89; fine wrought hardware; family furnishings; toys, bonnets. All open Tues.-Sat. 10-4; also, from mid-May-mid-Oct, open Sun. 1-4; adm.

Buttolph-Williams House (Broad & Marsh Sts.) is a wonderful garrison-design home built in 1692 and meticulously restored with period furnishings; open May 15-Oct. 15, daily 1-5; closed hols; adm.

First Church of Christ (Main & Marsh Sts.), built 1761-4, has been restored; free.

WILTON: Wilton Heritage Museum (249 Danbury Rd.) is a 1757 home open Sat. & Sun. 2-5; adm. It is owned by the Wilton Historical Society, whose library is in **Lambert House** (150 Danbury Rd.), a Tory-owned tavern that later served as a station on the underground railway; open Tues.-Fri. 10-5; closed hols, Aug.; adm.

WINDSOR: Oliver Ellsworth Homestead (778 Palisado Ave.) was visited by Washington, Adams and others; many original pieces; wine press cupboard; Gobelin tapestry presented to Ellsworth by Napoleon; open May-Oct., Tues.-Sat. 1-6; sm adm. **Flyer House and Wilson Museum** (96 Palisado Ave.): house, built about 1640 authentically refurbished; museum houses items of local historical significance, library; open Apr.-late Nov., Tues.-Sat. 10-noon, 1-4; closed hols; sm adm. **United**

Church of Christ (75 Palisado Ave.): 1794 classic Georgian; open daily in winter 9-3, in summer 9-noon.

WINDSOR LOCKS: Bradley Air Museum (3 m W at airport): fighters, bombers, helicopters, unmanned aircraft, other craft dating from WW II to the present; open Memorial Day-Oct. or Nov., weather permitting, daily noon-6; rest of yr, weekends and hols, noon-6; adm.

Trolley Museum (on SR 140, across the river from Windsor Locks, 1¼ m E of Warehouse Point) is an outdoor display of streetcars dating from 1892-1947; locomotives, railroad equipment. Open, subject to change and weather permitting, Sun. & hols all year (exc. Dec. 25) 1-5 (longer in summer); Sat., Mar-Nov. 1-5; usually also open July-Labor Day, Tues.-Fri. 11-4; free.

WOODBURY: Glebe House (Hollow Rd.), built c.1690 and enlarged 1740, has period furnishings and a museum of the Episcopal Church in America; open Wed.-Sat. 11-4, Sun. 1-5; closed Thnks, Dec. 25; free.

WOODSTOCK: Henry C. Bowen House, **Roseland** (SR 169): Gothic Revival, built 1845, colored pink; many original furnishings; open June-Oct., Tues., Thurs., Sat. 1-5; adm.

DELAWARE

DOVER: Laid out by William Penn, this has been the state capital since 1777. **Bureau of Travel Development** (45 The Green) has a map for the "Heritage Trail"; surrounding The Green are lovely 18th-19th-C homes (interiors of many can be seen during Old Dover Days in May). **Old State House** (The Green), built in 1722, was rebuilt 1787-92 with material from the original structure. **Hall of Records** (Legislative Ave.), with city and state documents, is open regular business hours.

Governor's House (Kings Hwy.), fine middle Georgian, built c.1790; stop on the Underground Railroad; period antiques; tours Tues. aft.

The Delaware State Museum (316 S Governors Ave.): 4 buildings include Swedish-style log cabin and phonograph museum; exhibits on state history, period costumes and furnishings, archaeology, industry. Open Tues.-Sat., 10-5, Sun. 1-5; closed Mon., hols. Free.

John Dickinson Mansion (6 m SE on US 113, ½ m E on Kitts Hummock Rd.): fine 18th-C plantation home of the "Penman of the Revolution"; period furnishings; open Tues.-Sat. 10-5, Sun. 1-5; closed hols; free.

Octagonal School House (on SR 9, 1½ m N of Little Creek) is a restored one-room schoolhouse built in 1836. Open Sat., Sun. 1-4. Free.

FORT DELAWARE STATE PARK (on Pea Patch Island): This large fort, built in 1859, is being restored; small museum of Civil War relics; film of its history. Open Apr. 30-Sept. 30, Sat., Sun., hols; boats leave noon-6 from Delaware City; boat fare modest.

LEWES: Settled by the Dutch in 1631, this has long been the home of Delaware River pilots and tales of shipwrecks and pirate treasure. **Zwaanendael Museum** (Kings Highway & Savannah Rd.), a replica of the Town Hall in Hoorn, Holland, was erected to commemorate the 300th anniversary of Dutch settlement; exhibits of Indian, Colonial, Dutch, maritime, and military history. Open Tues.-Sat. 10-5, Sun. 1-5; closed Mon. hols. Free. **Lewes Historical Society Restorations** include the Burton-Ingram House, Cannonball House (bearing scars from the War of 1812), Thompson Country Store, Rabbit's Ferry House, and a Plank House believed to have been built before 1700. All are open daily exc. Sun. 11-4, summer only, for sm adm.

NEWARK: University of Delaware houses the **Du Pont Mineral Collection** (Penny Hall, Academy St.) open Mon.-Fri. 10-4; closed hols; free. **Solar One** (190 S Chapel St.) is an experimental house in which heat and electricity are generated from the sun; open during academic year Fri. 4-6, Sat. 10-noon; in summer only Fri. afternoon; free.

NEW CASTLE: The flags of Holland, Sweden, Great Britain, and the U.S. fly from the balcony of the Old Court House here to honor the turbulent history of this now relaxed town. Colonial flavor survives near the waterfront, between Delaware and Harmony Sts.; many homes along The Strand were once inns. Brochures describing this area can be obtained at the **Old Court House** (on The Green at Delaware St.), Delaware's colonial capitol and meeting place of the State Assembly until 1777. The handsome cupola served as the center of the 12-m radial circle surveyed by Mason & Dixon that formed the Delaware-Pennsylvania boundary. Open summers Tues.-Sat. 10-5, Sun. 1-5; shorter hrs in winter; closed hols; free. The adjacent Green was laid out by Peter Stuyvesant.

Amstel House Museum (4th & Delaware Sts.), home of Gov. Nicholas Van Dyke, was built c. 1730; furnished in Dutch colonial style; George Washington was a wedding guest here in 1784; open Tues.-Sat. 11-4; closed hols; sm adm.

George Read II House (The Strand), an outstanding 1801 Georgian mansion, has gardens laid out in 1847 by Andrew Jackson Downing. **Old Dutch House Museum** (The Green), built before 1700, is open Apr.-Oct., Tues.-Sat. 11-4, Sun. noon-4; closed hols; sm adm. **Immanuel Church** (The Green) nave dates from 1703; some of the hangings and silver were gifts of Queen Anne in 1710; graveyard; open daily 9-5.

Buena Vista (4 m S on US 13): 1847 home of U.S. Sec. of State, is open Tues., Thurs., Sat. 11-4; free.

ODESSA: Once an important station on the Underground Railroad known as Cantwell's Bridge, this grain-shipping town later took the name of the Russian grain-shipping port. Today it is a quiet town with many restored 18th-19th-C homes; most are not open to the public, but their exteriors can be enjoyed on a short walk along the rectangle formed by 2nd and 4th Sts. and by High and Main Sts. These houses (as well as the Brick Hotel on 2nd St.) are administered by the Henry Francis du Pont Winterthur Museum and are open Tues.-Sat. 10-5, Sun. 2-5; closed Mon., hols; adm.

Corbit-Sharp House (Main & 2nd Sts.), a handsome Georgian home built 1772-74 by a tanner; beautiful furnishings by local craftsmen. **Wilson-Warner House** (next door), a 1740 merchant's home enlarged in 1769; fine paneling; 18th-C furnishings. **John Janvier Stable** (2nd St.), of unusual wood-and-brick construction, built in 1791 by a master cabinetmaker.

SMYRNA: Duck Creek Village (N, off US 13): buildings preserved by the Duck Creek Historical Society; a pamphlet is available at The Lindens, a miller's home built c.1725. Open daily, 11-5. Free.

Allee House (off SR 9 in the Bombay Hook Ntl. Wildlife Refuge, on Dutch Neck Rd.): brick house of the Queen Anne period built by a Huguenot refugee; carefully restored. Open Sat., Sun. 2-5. Free.

WILMINGTON: Fort Christina Historical Park (foot of E 7th St.), known as The Rocks, was the landing place of the 1638 Dutch-Swedish expedition; log cabin, introduced by Swedish colonists. Open 9-5 daily exc. Christmas. Free.

Old Town Hall (512 Market St.) has been restored to its 1798 appearance by the Historical Society of Delaware; china, silver,

weapons, furniture, portraits; superb library on state history. Open
Tues.-Fri. 10-4; closed Aug., hols. Free.

Delaware Art Museum (2301 Kentmere Pkwy at Woodlawn Ave.):
Bancroft collection of Pre-Raphaelite paintings; emphasis on American
artists—Wyeth family, Howard Pyle, John Sloan, Eakins, Homer,
Ryder. Open Mon.-Sat. 10-5, Sun. 2-6; closed hols. Free.

Holy Trinity (Old Swedes) Church and **Hendrickson House** (Church
& 7th Sts.): Consecrated in 1699; tower and ornate interior were later
embellishments. The stone house, built in Pennsylvania in 1690 and
moved here as a museum, has period furnishings. Open Tues.-Sun.
noon-4. Free.

Hagley Museum (3 m NW off SR 141 in Greenville): On this 185-
acre tract where E. I. du Pont's mills prospered, are indoor and outdoor exhibits on the evolution of industry in the U.S. An 1814 textile
mill houses models and dioramas; mid-19th-C machine shop models
demonstrate the manufacture of black powder when it was the world's
only explosive. Jitney buses carry visitors on tours of millraces and
other outdoor exhibits. Open Tues.-Sat. 9:30-4:30, Sun. 1-5; closed
Jan. 1, Thnks, Dec. 25; free. On grounds are a library of American
industrial history (open only to scholars) and **Eleutherian Mills,** built
by E. I. du Pont in 1803, with early American, Federal, and Empire
family pieces, open several weeks in spring and fall.

Henry Francis du Pont Winterthur Museum & Gardens (6 m NW on
SR 52): In a great country home du Pont amassed a superb collection
of 17th-19th-C American decorative arts in over 100 period rooms, each
complete to the finest detail. There are also special collections such as
the Hall of Statues, miniature furniture, and Chinese export porcelain.
Du Pont, also a noted horticulturist, landscaped the 60-acre gardens,
which can be seen on a self-guided 2½-mile trail; open for a moderate
fee from mid-Apr.-Oct., Tues.-Sun. 10-4 (in winter, by appointment).
The South Wing, 14 rooms arranged to show the chronological development of decorative arts between 1684-1840, may be visited without
appointment for a moderate fee from mid-Apr.-Oct., Tues.-Sun. 10-4;
Nov. 1-mid-Apr., Tues.-Sat. 10-4. Prior appointment is required for the
Main Museum (over 16 yrs only) exc. mid-Apr. to end-May, when a
selection of rooms is open without appointment Tues.-Sun. 10-4. Winterthur is closed Jan. 1, July 4, Thnks, Christmas. For details and fees,
write: Information, Winterthur, Del., 19735.

YORKLYN: Magic Age of Steam: Indoor and outdoor exhibits of steam
engines, cars, locomotives, popcorn machine; models and miniature
toys. Open mid-April-mid-Nov., Sat., Sun., hols, 1-4:30, and daily in
July & Aug. Adm.

DISTRICT OF COLUMBIA

U.S. Capitol (Capitol Hill) was designed by William Thornton, and Washington laid the cornerstone in 1793. The building had to be substantially rebuilt after the British burned it in 1814. The dome, surmounted by a bronze statue of Freedom, was added during the Civil War. Inside are murals of historic events and statues of presidents and other noted Americans. Exhibits in the Crypt explain architectural changes. Open daily 9-4:30; closed Jan. 1, Thnks, Dec. 25; tours given every 15 min; free. The park surrounding the Capitol was designed by Frederick Law Olmsted. Tickets to Senate and House visitors' galleries may be obtained from the office of your Senator or Congressman.

Supreme Court Building (facing the Capitol between Maryland Ave. & E. Capitol St.): designed by Cass Gilbert and completed in 1935; Corinthian columns; sculptures representing Liberty, Order, and Authority; door panels depicting historical scenes; marble-embellished courtroom. Open Mon.-Fri. 9:30-4; closed hols. Tours every ½ hr exc when court is in session (court meets on and off Oct.-June).

Library of Congress (10th St. SE & Independence Ave.) is the world's largest library, with more than 70 million items; created in 1800 to serve legislators, but open to the public. After its first collection was destroyed during the War of 1812, its present collection was begun with the purchase of Thomas Jefferson's library in 1815. The Renaissance-style building, erected 1889-97, is replete with symbolic statuary, paintings, murals, and embellished with Victorian taste. Guided tours weekdays exc hols 9-4; free. Concerts and other events frequently scheduled. Some treasures on display in the Exhibit Halls, open Mon.-Sat. 8:30 am-9:30 pm, Sun. & hols 11:30-9:30; closed Dec. 25; free.

National Archives (Pennsylvania Ave, 7th & 9th Sts. NW), on the former site of Center Market where slaves were auctioned until 1853, displays the original Declaration of Independence, Constitution, and Bill of Rights; other historic exhibits. Research rooms are open weekdays. Tours require advance arrangements. Exhibits open daily 9-6 (open to 10 pm spring-fall); closed Jan. 1, Dec. 25; free.

Folger Shakespeare Library (201 E Capitol St. SE), decorated with scenes from Shakespeare's plays in bas-relief and designed to resemble Elizabethan-age interiors, houses a scale model of the Globe Theatre and a full-size replica of an Elizabethan theater (performances Oct.-May); world's largest collection of Shakespeareana, including costumes and paintings, Folios and other literary items; rare works from the English Renaissance. Open Apr. 15-Labor Day daily, rest of year Mon.-Sat., 10-4:30; closed hols; free.

Public Library (9th & G Sts. NW), designed by Mies van der Rohe; materials on the District of Columbia; open Mon.-Sat. 9-5:30 (also open Sun. 1-5 in winter, and many evenings); closed hols; free.

Smithsonian Institution, housed in buildings along either side of The Mall, was founded in 1846 by James Smithson, an Englishman who had never been to the U.S., and in addition to an astonishing array of treasures on display it conducts research on a global scale. Many special events are scheduled throughout the year in its various buildings, which are open 10-5:30 (some are open later in spring, summer, or for special events); closed Dec. 25; free.

Air & Space Building (Independence Ave. & 10th St. SW) contains exhibits on the history of aviation and space.

Arts & Industries Building (Jefferson Dr. & 9th St. SW) has exhibits explaining aeronautical development from old planes such as *Kitty Hawk* and *Spirit of St. Louis* to space capsules and moon rocks.

Freer Gallery of Art (Independence Ave. & 12th St. SW) contains the lifetime collection of industrialist Charles L. Freer, who amassed a superb array of art works from the Near and Far East; 19th-C American paintings by Homer, Hassam, Sargent, and others; world's largest Whistler collection.

Hirshhorn Museum & Sculpture Garden (Independence Ave. at 8th St. SW) was donated by Joseph H. Hirshhorn, a Latvian whose widowed mother immigrated to the U.S. when he was 6, and who had to leave school at 12 to help support his sisters and brothers. His extraordinary collection grew with his career as a financier, and consists of more than 4000 paintings and 2000 sculptures tracing the development of modern art from the 19th C to the present.

National Collection of Fine Arts (8th & G Sts. NW) houses American paintings, sculpture, graphics, and decorative arts, including 18 oils by Albert Pinkham Ryder and 445 of George Catlin's Indian gallery. One of the finest Neoclassic buildings in the city, with vaulted ceilings and spiral stairs; during the Civil War it served as a hospital; the S wing contains the National Portrait Gallery.

National Portrait Gallery (7th & F Sts. NW) contains portraits and statues chosen for historical significance rather than artistic merit. Subjects include Pocahontas, Edwin Booth costumed as Iago, and modern presidents. Also here are the Archives of American Art, documentary records from colonial times to the present, and a research library, open to scholars.

Renwick Gallery (Pennsylvania Ave. & 17th St. NW), in an interesting 19th-C building restored to its Victorian appearance, specializes in American arts, crafts, and design. Exhibits include architecture, furnishings, and industrial design; a gem of a museum, with fine lectures, films, and other events.

National Museum of History & Technology (Constitution Ave. & 13th St. NW): vast array of Americana; the original Star Spangled Banner; folk art, glass, ceramics, costumes, toys; 19th-C general store; locomotive; musical history, postal history, coins, news reporting, ship models; nuclear energy.

National Museum of Natural History (Constitution Ave. & 10th St. NW): mounted animals in habitat settings, dinosaur skeletons, a stuffed elephant; American Indian culture and archaeology of the New World; early cultures of Asia, Africa, and the Pacific; superb gem and mineral collection; section explaining the interrelationships of all life forms; dozens of miscellaneous exhibits ranging from an Egyptian mummy to Oriental rugs.

Corcoran Gallery of Art (New York Ave. at 17th St. NW), one of the nation's finest art museums, has impressive 18th-20th-C American paintings: Copley, Stuart, Eakins, Sargent, Homer, Hudson River School, Ashcan School. Remington, Saint-Gaudens, and Daniel Chester French are included in the sculpture collection. Also English portraits, French Impressionist, 17th-C Dutch, and other paintings; furniture and decorative arts. Open Tues.-Sun. 11-5; closed Jan. 1, July 4, Thnks, Dec. 24, 25; adm Thurs.-Sun., free Tues.-Wed.

Dumbarton Oaks (1703 32nd St. NW), the 1801 Georgian-style mansion used for the UN conference, is maintained by Harvard University. Exquisite Byzantine collection, European and American paintings, tapestries. A wing designed by Philip Johnson houses a magnificent pre-Columbian collection. Stunningly landscaped grounds. Museums open Tues.-Sun. 2-5; gardens open daily 2-5; buildings and grounds closed July-Labor Day, & hols; free.

Howard University Gallery of Art (2455 6th St. NW) contains the Alain Locke African Collection and other exhibits; open during the academic year, Mon.-Fri. 9-5, Sat. noon-4; closed hols; free.

Museum of African Art (316 A St. NE) in the Frederick Douglass Town House, home of the 19th-C abolitionist and advisor to Lincoln, has a fine collection of art from almost every area of Africa; Douglass' study houses memorabilia. Open Mon.-Fri. 11-5, Sat. & Sun. 12:30-5; closed Thnks, Dec. 25; donation.

National Gallery of Art (Constitution Ave. & 6th St. NW) houses masterpieces from the 12th to present centuries from collections by Mellon, Kress, Widener, and others. The more than 2000 paintings include Rembrandt, Rafael, Titian, Van Gogh, Monet, Manet, Renoir, Whistler, Constable, Cezanne, Gauguin, Gainsborough, and Dali; well over 1500 sculptures. Concerts Sept.-June, Sun. 7 pm; guided tours; electronic narration. Open Mon.-Sat. 10-4 (to 7:30 in summer), Sun. 1-7; closed Jan. 1, Dec. 25; free.

Phillips Collection (1600-1612 21st St. NW), attractively displayed in the former Phillips home, has outstanding 19th-20th-C American and European paintings, including Renoir, El Greco, Picasso, Goya, Bonnard, Klee, Degas, and Daumier; concerts in winter. Open Tues.-Sat. 10-5, Sun. 2-7; closed July 4, Dec. 25; free.

Kennedy Center for the Performing Arts (New Hampshire Ave. & F St. NW) is dedicated to the late President; Italian marble structure by Edward Durell Stone has fine views from the upper terrace; concert halls, theater, American Film Institute archives. Tours daily 10-1:15; free.

Emancipation Statue (Lincoln Park on E. Capitol St. at 11th St.), honoring Lincoln on the 11th anniversary of his assassination, was paid for by voluntary contributions from emancipated slaves. **Ford's Theatre** (511 10th St. NW), where John Wilkes Booth shot Lincoln, was closed after the assassination. It reopened as a national shrine in 1968, rebuilt to be historically accurate, with the stage set for the 3rd act of *Our American Cousin.* A repertory company performs here, and a sound-and-light program is presented in summer. Open daily 9-5 exc when performances are scheduled, then 9-1; free. In the basement is the Lincoln Museum; exhibits on Lincoln's early years, family life, and career; items related to the assassination; Lincoln family mementos. Open daily 9-5; free. **House Where Lincoln Died** (516 10th St. NW), opposite Ford's Theatre, is where Lincoln was carried on Apr. 14, 1865. The 1849 brick home has been restored to its original appearance, including the room in which Mary Todd and her son Robert kept vigil, and the room in which Lincoln died early the next morning. From here Secretary of War Stanton issued the statement, "Now he belongs to the ages." Open daily 9-5; closed Dec. 25; free.

Lincoln Memorial (foot of 23rd St., NW) was conceived 2 years after the assassination but was not dedicated until 1922; 30 Doric columns represent the states in the Union at the time of Lincoln's death; on the walls are the names of the 48 states in the Union by 1922. Inside, Daniel Chester French's seated Lincoln faces the Capitol; on the walls are the Gettysburg Address, the 2nd Inaugural Address, and murals by Jules Guerin, one showing a slave being freed. Open 24 hrs daily; closed Dec. 25; free.

Jefferson Memorial (S edge of Tidal Basin), not authorized until 1934, is reminiscent of buildings Jefferson himself designed; statue by Rudulph Evans; quotations from Jefferson's writings engraved in the walls. Open 24 hrs daily; closed Dec. 25; free.

Washington Monument (The Mall, off 15th St. NW): completed in 1884 after a great deal of debate over the design; Robert Mills, the designer whose plans were radically changed, complained that the changes made it look like a stalk of asparagus. Observation room is reached by elevator. Open daily 9-5 (to midnight in summer); closed Dec. 25.

White House (1600 Pennsylvania Ave. NW), home to every President except George Washington, was built in 1800. When the British burned it during the War of 1812, Dolley Madison saved 2 portraits—the Gilbert Stuart one of George Washington, and her own. The building has been remodeled many times; detailed guide to its history, decoration, and many fine furnishings is available. Tours are given Tues.-Sat. 10-noon, Sat. to 2 in summer; closed Jan. 1, Dec. 25; free.

Blair House (1651 Pennsylvania Ave. NW), a guesthouse for important foreign visitors, is not open to the public.

Clara Barton House (5801 Oxford Rd., 6 m NW in Glen Echo, Md.), designed in Mississippi riverboat style, contains furnishings and belongings of the founder of the Red Cross. Open Tues.-Sun. 1-5; closed hols; donation.

Decatur House (Lafayette Sq., 748 Jackson Pl. NW), a Federal-style town house designed by Benjamin Latrobe in 1818-19 for Commodore Stephen Decatur, hero of the expeditions against the Barbary pirates, is maintained by the National Trust for Historic Preservation. Decatur, wounded in a duel, died here after only a year in the house, and later tenants included Henry Clay and Martin Van Buren. Open daily exc. Dec. 25, 10-4; sm adm.

Frederick Douglass Home, Cedar Hill (1411 W St. SE), home of the former slave who became a leading spokesman for human rights, has been restored with original furnishings and mementos. Douglass was born about 1817 in Maryland, and after rebelling was forced to change his name (originally Frederick Bailey) and flee to Great Britain, where friends raised money to buy his freedom so he could return in

1877; he lived here from then until his death in 1895. Open Mon.-Fri. 9-5, weekends 10-5; closed Dec. 25; free.

Georgetown, W of Rock Creek Park in the NW, was a thriving tobacco port on the Potomac, later incorporated into DC; now a wealthy residential area with many restored Georgian and Federal townhouses. A typical home is the 1733 **Yellow House** (1430 33rd St. NW); not open to the public. **Old Stone House** (3051 M St. NW), built about 1765, is a typical middle-class home of the British era; open daily 9:30-5; closed Dec. 25; free.

Heurich Memorial Mansion (1307 New Hampshire Ave. NW), housing the Columbia Historical Society, is an 1892 Renaissance-style building with ornate Victorian decor and furniture. Open daily; check hrs locally; closed hols; free.

Octagon (1799 New York Ave. at 18th St. NW) is an 8-sided Federal-style home built in 1800; beautifully restored with Chippendale, Sheraton, and Hepplewhite pieces. The Treaty of Ghent was signed here in 1815, and the Madisons lived here after the White House was burned. Open Tues.-Sat. 10-4, Sun. 1-4; closed Jan. 1, Thnks, Dec. 25; donation.

Woodrow Wilson House (2340 S St., NW), a National Trust Historic Property, was where the 28th President retired as a semi-invalid after leaving the White House. His widow, who lived here until 1961, preserved an extensive collection of mementos. Open daily exc. Dec. 25, 10-4; adm.

DAR Buildings (entrance at 1776 D St.) contain 50,000 items of American decorative arts from 1770-1830 selected for their associations with figures important in American history (many Presidential belongings among them). You can browse through a main gallery; 28 period rooms (music rooms, parlors, a replica of a 1680 Jacobean council chamber, dining rooms, children's attic, kitchen) are shown on guided tours. Also genealogy library (adm for nonmembers). Open Mon.-Fri. 10-3; closed hols; free.

Explorers Hall (17th & M Sts. NW), headquarters of the National Geographic Society, was designed by Edward Durrell Stone. Exhibits and earphone lectures explain the Society's work; oddities such as the stuffed body of Admiral Byrd's lead sled dog; a world globe 11 ft in diameter. Open Mon.-Fri. 9-6, Sat. & hols 9-5, Sun. noon-5; closed Dec. 25; free.

Klutznick Exhibit Hall (1640 Rhode Is. Ave. NW) in the B'nai B'rith Bldg., has exhibits on Jewish history, religion, and art; open Mon.-Fri. 1:30-5, Sun. 10-5; closed Jewish holy days, hols; free.

Walter Reed Army Medical Center Medical Museum (Alaska Ave. & 16th St. NW in Armed Forces Institute of Pathology): exhibits on the history of medicine and pathology, medical instrumentation. Library. Open daily 9-5; closed Dec. 25; free.

East Potomac Park (S of Jefferson Memorial) offers displays aboard the lightship *Chesapeake;* open June-Aug., Tues., Thurs., Sat., Sun. 1-5; Sept.-May weekends only 1-5; closed Jan. 1, Dec. 25; free. **U.S. Navy Memorial Museum** (bldg. 76 at the Navy Yard, 8th & M Sts. SE): exhibits depict the history of the Navy from 1775 to the present; open Mon.-Fri. 9-4, weekends & hols 10-5; closed Jan. 1, Thnks, Dec. 25; free. **Truxton-Decatur Naval Museum** (1610 H St. NW): ship models, naval instruments, other exhibits; open daily 10:30-4; closed hols; free. **U.S. Naval Observatory** (Massachusetts Ave. & 34th St. NW) is open Mon.-Fri.; guided tour at 2; evening tours can be arranged; closed hols; free.

Fort Washington (8½ m S on Maryland 210): museum depicting the history of the city's earliest defense; open daily 9-8 in summer, daily 9-5 in spring and fall, weekends 9-5 in winter. Free.

National Colonial Farm (20 m S on Potomac River at Brian Point Rd.) is an 18th-C working farm where old equipment and methods are demonstrated. Open June 15-Labor Day, daily 10-5; adm.

Christ Episcopal Church (N Washington St.) has George Washington's inscribed pew; old tombstones in the cemetery. **Friends Meeting House** (2111 Florida Ave. NW), unmarked, retains Herbert Hoover's pew. **Holy Land of America** (1400 Quincy St. NE), maintained by the Franciscan Monastery, contains replicas of Christian shrines in the church and on the landscaped grounds; also icons and other ecclesiastical art. Open daily 9-5; closed hols; donation. **Islamic Center & Mosque** (2551 Massachusetts Ave. NW), the cultural, religious, and educational center of Islam in the U.S., is attractive and interesting, with people on hand to answer questions. Open daily 10-4; closed during services Fri. 12:30-2:30; donation. **Metropolitan Memorial Methodist Church** (Nebraska & New Mexico Aves.), used by Presidents Grant and McKinley, has a pulpit with wood from the Garden of Gethsemane; chancel marble is from the tomb of King Solomon. **National Presbyterian Church & Center** (4101 Nebraska Ave. NW) was completed in 1969 but contains presidential pews dating back to Andrew Jackson. Several presidents are depicted in stained glass windows. Open daily; guided tours daily exc hols; free. **National Shrine of the Immaculate Conception** (4th St. & Michigan Ave. NE): built in the form of a Latin cross; combines Byzantine, Romanesque, and contemporary styles; huge exterior dome, 7 interior domes; much exterior sculpture; 10 exterior mosaics. Interior upper church has fine mosaics, plus 56 chapels symbolizing ways in which the Virgin is honored in many cultures. The crypt, also with mosaics, has low vaulted ceilings and the Lourdes chapel. Also carillon concerts (Sun. 3:30), organ concerts (Wed. & Fri. at noon, summer Sundays at 7 pm); tours Mon.-Sat. 9-5, Sun. 2-5:15. Open daily 7 am-8 pm. **New York Avenue Presbyterian Church** (New York Ave. & H St. NW), in a 1950's building, has preserved Lincoln's pew and other mementos. Open Tues.-Fri. 9-5, weekends 9-1; closed hols. **St. John's Episcopal Church** (16th & H Sts. NW) is so convenient to the White House that almost every President has worshiped here, earning it the nickname "Church of Presidents." Designed in 1815 by Benjamin Latrobe, it has handsome stained glass windows from Chartres. Open daily 9-5. **Washington Cathedral** (Wisconsin & Massachusetts Ave. NW), in 14th-C Gothic style, has been under construction since 1907; a chapel scaled for children. Open daily 8:30-5; tours available daily.

Agriculture Dept. (Independence Ave. between 12th & 14th Sts. SW) has a Visitor Information Center with exhibits and films; open Mon.-Fri. 9-5; closed hols; free. **Bureau of Engraving and Printing** (14th & C Sts. SW), where paper money, stamps, and certificates are made, offers booklets for self-guiding tours. Open Mon.-Fri. 8-2:30; closed hols; free. **Commerce Dept.** (14th St. NW between Constitution Ave. & E St. NW) has changing displays in the lobby and an aquarium in the basement. Open Mon.-Fri. 8:30-5, Sat. & Sun. 9-5; free. **FBI Building** (E St. between 9th & 10th Sts. NW) contains exhibits on the work of the FBI and the history of famous crimes; film; firearms demonstration; tours. Open Mon.-Fri. 9:15-4:15; closed hols; free. **Federal Trade Commission** (6th St. & Pennsylvania Ave. NW) is open Mon.-Fri. 8:30-5; closed hols; free. **Government Printing Office** (N. Capitol & G Sts.) issues the *Congressional Record* and other government publications. These are for sale in the bookstore (710 N Capitol St.), open Mon.-Fri. 8-4, Sat. 9-1; closed hols. **Internal Revenue Building** (Pennsylvania Ave., 10th & 12th Sts. NW) has exhibits on taxation, including a still; film. Open June-Aug. daily, Sept.-May Mon.-Fri. 9-4:30; closed hols; free. **Health, Education, & Welfare Building** (Independence Ave. between 3rd & 4th Sts. SW) has a Visitor Center in the lobby; library; free weekday tours of Voice of America. Open Mon.-Fri. 9-5:30; closed hols; free. **Interior Dept.** (between C & E Sts, 18th & 19th Sts. NW) has displays on the department's activities; library; open Mon.-Fri. 8-4; closed hols; free. **Organization of American States** (Constitution Ave. & 17th St. NW) has a flowered patio, Hall of the Americas, Hall of Heroes; open Mon.-Sat. 8:30-4; closed hols; sm adm. **Postal Service** (Pennsylvania Ave. at 12th St. NW) has a philatelic exhibit and salesroom in room 1315; open Mon.-Sat. 9-5; closed hols; free.

FLORIDA

APALACHICOLA: Trinity Church (Gorrie Sq.) was brought from New York by sailing ship in the early 1800's and assembled here. **John Gorrie State Museum** (6th St. & Ave. D) honors the inventor of the first ice-making machine. Dr. Gorrie produced his first ice accidentally in 1844 while inventing devices that would cool malaria patients; Open daily 9-noon, 1-5; sm adm.

BILL BAGGS STATE RECREATION AREA (off I-95, US 1 at Miami Beach): **Cape Florida Lighthouse,** replica of the keeper's living quarters; taped narration of the colorful history.

BRADENTON: South Florida Museum & Bishop Planetarium (201 10th St. W) features Indian relics, fossils, shells, and minerals; mounted birds; guns and weapons; 6 period rooms showing lifestyles from Spanish days to the present; Civil War display; open Tues.-Sat. 10-5, Sun. 1-5; closed Thnks; adm. Planetarium shows Tues.-Sat. at 3, Fri. & Sat. at 8 pm.

BULOW PLANTATION STATE HISTORIC SITE (8 m N of Ormond Beach off Old Dixie Hwy.): One of the most fabulous plantations in the area; exhibits and artifacts of plantation life; trails to the ruins; sm adm.

CEDAR KEY: Cedar Key State Museum (on W side of Cedar Key) houses a huge shell collection and exhibits on the history of this tiny island. Open daily 9-5; sm adm.

CORAL GABLES: Chamber of Commerce (Galiano & Aragon Aves.) or **City Hall** (Miracle Mile & Le Jeune Rd.) offer maps for a self-guiding auto tour marked with green signs. This community, planned in the 1920's, is built around landscaped plazas; most homes are patterned on Spanish and Mediterranean styles, but some sections incorporate Dutch, Chinese, and French styles. You can also tour the city by bicycle (20 m marked route starts at Cartagena Plaza). Cartagena Plaza (Sunset & Old Cutler Rds.) honors Coral Gables' sister city, Cartagena, Colombia, with a duplicate of the latter's statue of a pair of old shoes. City Hall duplicates a tower in Seville, Spain, and 3rd-floor murals depict Coral Gables' early days.

University of Miami's Lowe Art Museum (1301 Miller Dr.) features the Samuel H. Kress Collection of European painting, the Alfred I. Barton Collection of Indian and Pre-Columbian art, the Virgil Barker Memorial Collection of American Art, Oriental works, prints and drawings, and decorative arts; library. Open Mon.-Fri. noon-5, Sat. 10-5, Sun. 2-5; closed hols; free.

CRYSTAL RIVER STATE ARCHAEOLOGICAL SITE (W off US 19, 98 at sign N of town of Crystal River) offers a museum (open daily 9-5) with exhibits and a glass wall through which you can see the adjacent temple, burial and refuse mounds. A self-guiding trail leads through the mounds. Grounds open 8-sundown; sm adm.

DADE BATTLEFIELD STATE HISTORIC SITE (on US 301 near Bushnell) was site of the Dec. 28, 1835 Dade Massacre that touched off the Second Seminole War. The Seminole had refused to be moved to reservations in the West; to reinforce Fort King near the Ocala Indian agency, Maj. Francis L. Dade set out from Tampa with 100 men, oxen, cannon, and supplies. The first Seminole volley cut down Dade and half his men; only 3 badly wounded whites survived. A museum (open daily 8-noon, 1-5; sm adm) contains artifacts, and monuments and exhibits mark the battlefield.

DAYTONA BEACH: Museum of Arts & Sciences (1040 Museum Blvd. in Tuscawilla Pk.) contains 18th-20th-C Cuban paintings from the collection of former Pres. F. Batista; Latin American fine and decorative arts; historical and natural history displays; open Mon.-Sat. 9-5, Sun. 1-5, closed hols; free.

Museum of Speed (US 1 in S Daytona) displays land, air, and water vehicles noted for speed; open daily 9-5; adm.

DEBARY HALL STATE MUSEUM (1 m W of Deltona-DeBary Exit from I-4) preserves a showplace mansion built in 1871 by Baron Frederick deBary, who had come to the U.S. in 1840 as an agent for Mumm's champagne and was soon entertaining Pres. Cleveland, Pres. Grant, and Astors, Goulds, Vanderbilts, and European royalty. Furnishings of the 1800-1900 era, the baron's collection of hermetically sealed rare birds, paintings, sculpture, and other fine arts. Building open Tues.-Sun. 1-5; sm adm. The landscaped grounds are open daily 8-5; sm adm.

DELAND: DeLand Museum (449 E New York Ave.): Indian artifacts, shells, and toys. Open Mon.-Fri. 1-5, Sun. 2-4; closed hols & Aug.; free. **Gillespie Museum of Minerals** (Stetson University campus); open daily during academic year; free.

DESOTO NATIONAL MEMORIAL (on Tampa Bay, 5 m W of Bradenton off SR 64): Spurred by finds of gold in Mexico and Peru, the Spanish crown granted Hernando de Soto the right to explore North America for similar treasures. In 1539 he landed in this area with some 600 men and 220 horses. The Visitor Center offers an audiovisual program (daily 9-4) and exhibits of Spanish arms, armor, and other artifacts that help to interpret DeSoto's expedition; crossbow demonstrations too. An annual festival and pageant dramatize the history every March. Open daily 8-5; closed Dec. 25; free.

FORT CAROLINE NATIONAL MEMORIAL (10 m E of Jacksonville via SR 10, then N on Monument Rd.): In 1564 the first European colony north of Mexico, a short-lived one, was established here by 300 French sailors, soldiers, artisans, and servants. Most were Huguenots, and they were led by Rene de Laudonniere. Within a year a Spanish armada was sailing against the colony. At dawn on Sept. 20, 1565, the Spanish surprised the 240 or so French remaining at the fort, killing 142 men and capturing about 50 women and children. Laudonniere and some 40 others escaped to France on two ships. The outraged French sent an avenging fleet in 1568 to destroy Fort Caroline (renamed San Mateo by the Spanish); most of the Spanish were killed and the fort was burned.

The fort has been authentically reconstructed, based on early drawings and descriptions, and a Visitor Center tells the story of the French settlers through exhibits and pictures. Open Mon.-Fri. 8-5, Sat. & Sun. 8-6; closed Dec. 25; free.

FORT CLINCH STATE PARK (on SR A1A, 3 m from Fernandina Beach, Amelia Island): Well-preserved 1847 fort over which 8 flags have flown.

FORT GADSDEN STATE HISTORIC SITE (16 m SW of Sumatra): Remains of earthworks and trenches belonging to an 1814 British fort taken over by Indians and blacks who used it as a base for hijacking river traffic and aiding runaway slaves. Although the U.S. had no jurisdiction here at the time, Col. Duncan L. Clinch was sent to smash the fort. At dawn on July 27, 1816, the fort was blown apart with hot shot, killing almost 300 men, women, and children there; the Indian and black commanders were executed. Interpretive exhibits; open daily; free.

FORT GEORGE ISLAND STATE HISTORIC SITES (from Jacksonville on SR 105 or via ferry from Mayport to SR A1A, then N from village of Ft. George): **Huguenot State Historic Site** commemorates the French Huguenot landing in search of religious freedom. Explorer Jean Ribault is believed to have landed here in 1562. The oldest surviving structure is the tabby-brick house Anna Jai's, believed built after the island reverted to Spain.

Kingsley Plantation State Historic Site is the oldest surviving plantation home in Florida. In 1813, Zephaniah Kingsley developed the plantation to train slaves for resale. Booklets for self-guiding tours; period furnishings; historical exhibits; slave artifacts; open Mon.-Fri. 10-noon, 2-4; Sat., Sun., hols 10-5; sm adm.

Yellow Bluff Fort State Historic Site: Earthworks erected by Confederates in 1862 to protect the St. Johns River; open daily.

FORT JEFFERSON NATIONAL MONUMENT (in the Dry Tortugas, reached by boat or seaplane from Key West): Impressive fort begun in 1846, labored on for almost 30 years, yet never completed; it served military duty only sporadically. After the Civil War it was a prison, and several of the Lincoln conspirators were sent here (including Dr. Samuel A. Mudd, later pardoned for fighting the yellow fever epidemic here in 1867). Interpretive program; self-guiding tours; open daily in daylight; free.

FORT MYERS: Thomas A. Edison Home (2350 McGregor Blvd.) and guesthouse, built to his design in Maine in 1866, were brought by schooner to Florida, where he wintered until his death in 1931. The inventor's home and laboratory are as he left them. In the garden are plants he collected from all over the world, and a huge orchid collection begun by Mrs. Edison. Tours given every ½ hr, Mon.-Sat. 9-4, Sun. 12:30-4:30; closed Dec. 25; adm.

FORT WALTON BEACH: Temple Mound & Museum (on US 98, center of town) is hemmed in by commercial buildings so that the mound doesn't look like much. But the museum is unusually handsome, with intelligent, well-designed exhibits demonstrating 10,000 years of Indian occupation, a display of tools at which you can try your skill, and a striking funerary urn. Mound open daily in daylight, free. Museum open Tues.-Sat. 11-4, Sun. 1-4; closed Jan. 1, Dec. 25; sm adm.

GAINESVILLE: University of Florida (US 441 & University Ave.): **Florida State Museum,** designed to resemble an Indian mound, has anthropological displays; open Mon.-Sat. 9-5, Sun. 1-5; closed Dec. 25; free. **University Gallery** has historic and contemporary prints, paintings from India, small sculptures; open Mon.-Fri. 9-5, Sun. 1-5; closed hols & Sept.; free.

GAMBLE MANSION CONFEDERATE MUSEUM (on US 301 in Ellenton) is one of the oldest (1845-50) antebellum mansions on Florida's West

Coast; fine period furnishings; Confederate memorabilia (including Jefferson Davis' wedding bed). Open Mon.-Sat. 9-5, Sun. 1-5; sm adm.

GULF ISLANDS NATIONAL SEASHORE—FT. PICKENS AREA (W from Pensacola Beach via SR 399A): remains of the 1834 Fort Pickens and the Santa Rosa Island battlefield; tours available. For information write P.O. Box 100, Gulf Breeze 32561.

HOMESTEAD: Florida Pioneer Museum (826 N Krome Ave., 1 m S in Florida City) displays pioneer and Indian artifacts; open Oct.-May, Tues.-Sun. 2-5; rest of yr, Sun. 2-5; closed Easter, Dec. 25; donation. **Coral Castle** (28655 S Federal Hwy, 2 m N on US 1) was built by a Latvian hermit in 1920 as a dream castle for a girl who had jilted him in Latvia; the building and some of its fancifully carved furnishings are of coral; open daily 9-5:30; adm.

JACKSONVILLE: Cummer Gallery of Art (829 Riverside Ave.) is built around the collection of Mrs. Arthur Gerrish Cummer and includes a room from the Cummer mansion. Works range from the 6th cent BC to the present, with a noted collection of Meissen porcelain, medieval illuminated manuscripts, Renaissance portraits, rare tapestries and furnishings. Paintings range from Titian and Goya to Whistler and Eakins. Beautiful gardens overlook the St. Johns River. Open Tues.-Fri. 10-4, Sat. noon-5, Sun. 2-5; closed hols; free. **Jacksonville Art Museum** (4160 Boulevard Center Dr.) features Pre-Columbian and contemporary works; open daily 10-5; closed hols & Aug.; free.

    Jacksonville University (University Blvd, E of the St. Johns River) offers an art gallery in the Phillips Fine Arts Bldg. with changing exhibits of arts and crafts; open during the academic yr, Mon.-Fri. 9-4; closed hols; free. Also on campus is **Delius Cottage**, the restored home of the British composer, open during the annual Delius Festival (late Jan.-early Feb.); free.

    Riverside Baptist Church (2650 Park St.), a 1925 Addison Mizner design incorporating Spanish and Byzantine elements, is noted for the light cast by blue-glass windows and chandelier. Open Sun.-Fri.; free.

KEY WEST: Conch Tour Trains (depart from 303 Front St. & 3850 N Roosevelt Blvd.) offer 1½-hr narrated tours of this island, whose name is a corruption of the Spanish Cayo Hueso (Bone Key), so-called because of stories of human bones found in the mangroves here. Shrimping, sponge gathering, turtle hunting, and salvaging wrecked ships were the chief industries before modern tourism; tours daily 9-4, reasonable.

    Ernest Hemingway Home & Museum (907 Whitehead St.), a Spanish Colonial style mansion bought by the novelist in 1931; original furnishings and personal possessions. Hemingway owned this home until his death in 1961 and wrote many of his novels here. Open daily 9-5; adm.

Audubon House (205 Whitehead St.), restored with period furnishings, was where John James Audubon lived as a guest in 1832 while painting Keys wildlife; complete Double Elephant folio *Birds of America* is displayed. Open daily 9-noon, 1-5; adm.

Martello Gallery & Museum (S Roosevelt Blvd., E end of island) is housed in a fort begun in 1861 but never completed; contains observation platform, art gallery, and items of local historical interest. Open daily 9:30-5; closed Dec. 25; adm.

Lighthouse Museum (938 Whitehead St.) has Armed Forces and NASA exhibits, including a Japanese sub captured at Pearl Harbor on Dec. 8, 1941. Open daily 9:30-5; closed Dec. 25; adm includes lighthouse tower.

Pirate Treasure Ship (100 Margaret St.) displays treasure in a full-size replica of a Spanish galleon; narration on pirate life; open daily 9:30-5:30; adm.

KISSIMMEE: SST Aviation Exhibit Center (5 m E on US 192, 441) has aeronautical displays, planes, space capsule; open daily 10-sunset; closed Dec. 25; adm.

KORESHAN STATE RECREATION AREA (on US 41 at Estero) was the site of a unique 1893 settlement of people who call themselves Koreshans. Followers of Dr. Cyrus Reed Tweed, president of the Koreshan University of Chicago, who named himself Koresh for the biblical translation of Cyrus, they believe that the earth is the universe and that the sun (along with moon, planets, and stars) is *inside* the globe. Tours of buildings and large organic gardens are offered regularly in winter (about Oct.-May; other times by request) for a small fee.

LAKE JACKSON MOUNDS STATE ARCHAEOLOGICAL SITE (off US 27, N of Tallahassee at S end of Lake Jackson), the largest known ceremonial center of the Ft. Walton period, contains 3 mounds on some 12 acres of a 40-acre mound site. Excavation is still in progress, but it is believed that these were a well-organized people with powerful leaders who farmed but supplemented their diet by hunting and fishing. Open daily 8-sundown; free.

LAKELAND: Florida Southern College (McDonald St. & Ingraham Ave.) has the largest complex of buildings designed by Frank Lloyd Wright, created over a 20-yr period beginning in 1936. The Annie Pfeiffer Chapel, with glass wall inserts, is particularly interesting. At the Administration Bldg., you can obtain a map for a self-guiding tour. **Polk Public Museum** (800 E Palmetto) houses natural history, history, astronomy, and other scientific displays; open Mon.-Fri. 9-5, Sun. 1-4; closed Thnks, Dec. 25, Aug.; free.

LAKE WALES: Masterpiece Gardens (8 m NE off US 27) highlights a mosaic reproduction of Leonardo da Vinci's *The Last Supper*, made by artisans in Germany in 1930; it is unveiled every ½ hr, with a narration of its history. Miniature train tours through gardens; sky ride; monkeys, deer, birds, and other animals; bird shows. Open daily 9-6 (longer in summer); adm includes all attractions.

MARJORIE KINNAN RAWLINGS STATE MUSEUM (at Cross Creek on SR 325): author's home from 1928 until she moved to St. Augustine after her marriage to Norton Baskin. Works she wrote in this house made her a success. Many of her furnishings and books are here. Open Tues.-Sun. 9-5; sm adm.

MIAMI: Vizcaya (3251 S Miami Ave.) is a marvelous, 71-room, Italian Renaissance palace begun in 1912 and completed after 5 yrs of work by nearly 1000 artisans for James Deering, co-founder of the International Harvester Co. The rooms range from a sedate neoclassic Adam library to a rococo music room, Renaissance Hall, to a frescoed ceiling over a subterranean swimming pool. Many antique treasures—marble gates from Verona, sculpture, ceramics, wall panels from Italian palaces—were imported to complete and furnish it. Outdoors there are 10 acres of stunning gardens with reflecting pools, grottos, and a teahouse on Biscayne Bay; in the bay is a breakwater in the shape of a barge. Open daily 9:30-5:30; closed Dec. 25; adm (sm adm for gardens only).

Historical Museum of Southern Florida & the Caribbean (3290 S Miami Ave.) includes exhibits of marine life and exploration. Open Mon.-Sat. 9-5, Sun. 12:30-5; closed Jan. 1, Dec. 25; free.

Museum of Science & Space Transit Planetarium (3280 S Miami Ave.) highlights Florida archaeology, wildlife, and natural history. Open Mon.-Sat. 9-5, Sun. 12:30-10; closed Dec. 25; free. The observatory is open Fri.-Mon. evenings 7:30-10, plus Sun. 2-5. Free; planetarium shows are usually given daily; adm.

Holbrook Arms Museum (12953 Biscayne Blvd. in N Miami) features arms and armor from around the world; all items on display are for sale; ½-hr guided tours Tues.-Sat. 10-5:30; closed hols; adm.

Miami Art Center (7867 N Kendall Dr.) has sculpture from Africa, China, India, Japan, and France, plus changing exhibits. Open Mon.-Fri. 10-4:30, Sat. & Sun. 1-7; closed Aug. & hols; adm.

St. Bernard Monastery & Cloisters (16711 W Dixie Hwy. in N Miami Beach), owned by the Episcopal church, is an engaging monastery built in Segovia, Spain, in 1141. William Randolph Hearst bought it; had it taken apart and crated for shipment to the U.S., and it was reassembled here; medieval art works; cloistered walkways; gardens. Guided tours are given Mon.-Sat. 10-4, Sun. noon-4; closed Jan. 1, Good Friday, Easter, Thnks, Dec. 25; adm.

Plymouth Congregational Church, United Church of Christ (3429 Devon Rd.), modeled after a church in Mexico City, was built of coral rock by a single stonemason 1915-17. Open daily; free.

MIAMI BEACH: Bass Museum of Art (2100 Collins Ave.): paintings from old masters to the Impressionists, plus contemporary works; bronzes from Tibet and Nepal, sculpture, tapestries, medieval and baroque vestments, and miscellaneous collections such as coins and stamps. Open Tues.-Sat. 10-5; closed hols; free.

OLUSTEE BATTLEFIELD STATE HISTORIC SITE (on US 90, 2 m E of Olustee in Osceola National Forest) commemorates the 1864 Civil War battle over control of Jacksonville. A museum interprets the battle and houses artifacts. Open daily 8-sundown; sm adm.

ORLANDO: Orange County Historical Museum (27 E Central Blvd.) houses antique furnishings and implements, and displays on the county's history; open Mon., Wed., Fri. 2-5; closed hols; free.

Loch Haven Park (Mills Ave. & Princeton Blvd.) has the **Loch Haven Art Center,** with a small permanent collection of contemporary paintings and graphics, plus changing exhibits; reference library; open Tues.-Sun. 10-5; closed hols; free. **John Young Museum & Planetarium** has scientific and historical displays; open Mon.-Fri. 10-5; closed Dec. 25; free. Daily planetarium shows in afternoon or evenings; adm.

PALM BEACH: Henry Morrison Flagler Museum (Whitehall Way off Cocoanut Row) was built in 1901 as a home for Florida's pioneer developer and later served as a hotel; it has been restored to its original opulence, with many original furnishings; paintings, decorative arts, dolls, laces are among the collections; exhibits on the history of the state; on grounds is Mr. Flagler's private railroad car. Open Tues.-Sun. 10-5; closed Dec. 25; adm.

Society of the Four Arts (Four Arts Plaza, off Royal Palm Way) has art galleries open Dec.-mid-Apr., Mon.-Sat. 10-5, Sun. 2-5; closed hols. Library and botanic gardens open Mon.-Fri. 10-5, plus Sat. from Nov.-Apr.; closed hols; free.

Bethesda-by-the-Sea (S Country Rd. & Barton Ave.), an Episcopal church, is of Gothic design and contains many fine ecclesiastical paintings and carvings. The adjacent Cluett Memorial Garden is beautifully land-scaped. Open daily 8-5; free.

PENSACOLA: Pensacola Historical Museum (405 S Adams St. at Zaragoza St.), in Florida's oldest church (1832), houses historical exhibits, library, and genealogy library; open Tues.-Sun. 10:30-4:30; closed hols; free. Here you can obtain a brochure for a self-guiding walking tour of the historic **Seville Square** district. The first Spanish attempt to start a colony here in 1559 was a failure, but a permanent settlement arose in 1698; French, English, and Confederate flags also flew here before it became part of the U.S. Among the interesting houses in this area are: Walton House (221 E Zaragoza St.) of French West Indian Architecture; open May 15-Sept., Mon.-Sat. 10-4, Sun. 2-4; sm adm. The 1810 Charles Lavalle House (203 E Church St.) with a plastered interior; open Mon.-Fri. 8-5, Sat. 10-4:30, Sun. 1-4:30; closed Jan. 1, Dec. 25; free. The 1871 Dorr House (311 S Adams at Church St.), in Classic Revival style with period furnishings; open daily 10-2; closed Jan. 1, Thnks, Dec. 25; donation.

West Florida Museum of History (200 E Zaragoza St.), with historical exhibits including relics from the Spanish era, contains a transportation museum with a 1920's gas station, a turn-of-the-century fire station, and a replica of an 1890 railway station; open Mon.-Fri. 8-5, Sat. 10-4, Sun. 1-4; closed Jan. 1, Thnks, Dec. 25; free.

Piney Woods Sawmill (Barracks & Main St.) is open daily 8-5; closed Jan. 1, Dec. 25; free.

Buccaneer (at Municipal Pier) is a turn-of-the-century, two-masted fishing schooner, last of a 35-ship fleet that used to fish for snapper off the coast of Yucatan; open mid-May-Sept., daily 10-4; free.

US Naval Air Station, a navy base since 1825, offers self-guiding tour booklets; open Mon.-Fri. 9-2:30, weekends & hols 8-4; free. Included in the tour are the Naval Aviation Museum (Turner St. & Fisher Ave.), which depicts the history of aviation; open Tues.-Sat. 8:30-4:30, Sun. 12:30-4:30; closed Jan. 1, Thnks, Dec. 25; free. The Survival Exhibit explains techniques for surviving in extreme conditions such as the arctic; open Tues.-Sat. 8-4, Sun. noon-4; free. If the USS *Lexington* is in port, you may also board this carrier (daily 9-3; free).

Pensacola Art Center (407 S Jefferson St.), in what was once the city jail, has a permanent collection of regional paintings and graphics; temporary exhibitions; open Tues.-Sat. 9-5, Sun. 2-5; closed hols & 2 wks in Aug.; free.

T.T. Wentworth Jr. Museum (8382 Phalafox Hwy., 8 m N in Ensley) is a private collection of some 35,000 items of early Americana, with emphasis on Florida. Open Sat., Sun., hols, 2-6; free.

PEPPER PARK STATE RECREATION AREA (on SR A1A, N of Ft. Pierce): **St. Lucie Museum,** designed like the chambered nautilus, has exhibits on local Indians and Spanish treasure; 60-ft mural of historical events; open daily; sm adm.

PORT CHARLOTTE: National Police Hall of Fame & Museum (14600 S Tamiami Trail, 11 m NW on US 41 in N Port Charlotte) exhibits lie detectors, guns, and other police equipment, murder weapons, and criminology displays; open daily 9:30-4:30; adm.

PORT ST. JOE: Constitution Convention State Museum (on US 98) features dioramas and exhibits of Florida's first state Constitution Convention (1838-9), as well as of the vanished city of St. Joseph, a cotton boom town doomed by a yellow fever epidemic and two devastating hurricanes. Open daily 9-5; sm adm.

ST AUGUSTINE: Visitor Information Center (10 Castillo Dr. near the old city gate) shows a movie on the history of this city, the oldest in the U.S. St. Augustine was established in 1565 by the Spanish as a base for destroying the colony established by the French at Ft. Caroline. Sir Francis Drake destroyed the city in 1586, and after it was rebuilt pirates leveled it in 1668. In 1672, Spain began to build the massive Castillo de San Marcos. A long-term restoration program has been returning the city to its Old World charm. *Cross and Sword,* a musical drama about the city's founding, is presented in summer, and other special events are held throughout the year. Within the historic district there are tours by train and horse-drawn carriage. The Visitor Information Center provides maps, brochures, and information; open daily 8-5:30; closed Dec. 25; free.

   Restoration Complex, restored by the St. Augustine Preservation Board, is centered on St. George St. The complex includes silversmith, pottery, print, and other shops where many crafts are demonstrated. Buildings are open daily 9-5:15; closed Dec. 25; most charge a sm adm, or you can buy combination tickets. Among the houses you can enter on St. George St. are: **Gallegos** (#21), an early tabby house with a walled garden; **Ribera House** (#22), an early mansion with period furnishings; **Salcedo House** (#42), with a bakery in the rear; **Old Spanish Inn** (#43), originally a one-story coquina home later remodeled and furnished as an inn; **Arrivas House** (#46), a coquina house with a later wooden addition furnished to show both periods of its use; **Pan American Center** (#97), a typical upper-class home built of coquina and housing Latin American cultural displays; and the lovely **Government House** (at Cathedral St.), with historical displays and a research library. The nearby reconstructed **Spanish Military Hospital** (8 Aviles St.) houses displays on early medicines and pharmaceuticals.

   Casa del Hidalgo (St. George & Hypolita Sts.), the Spanish National Tourist Office, offers a museum of early Spanish life in the city and

Spanish handcrafts; open Tues.-Sat. 10-5; closed hols; free. **Fernandez-Llambias House** (31 St. Francis St.), from the first Spanish period, has coquina walls and interesting floors; antique furnishings include English, Spanish, and American; some interesting pieces from Minorcans who were early occupants. Open daily exc first Sun. of each month, 2-5; free. **Dr. Peck House** (143 St. George St.) was built 1690-95 with a lower story of coquina and upper story of wood, and served as the Treasury. Exquisitely furnished; many paintings, coins, and other collections of antiques. Open Mon.-Sat. 9-5; closed Jan. 1, Labor Day, Thnks, Dec. 25; amd. **Sanchez House** (105 St. George St.), a restored 1816 home with period furnishings, is open Mon.-Wed., Fri., Sat. 9:30-5, Sun. 1-5:30 (longer hrs in summer); closed hols; free. **Ximenez-Fatio House** (20 Aviles St.), built about 1797, is one of the few original buildings remaining in the city. Constructed of coquina and cedar, it is furnished with Spanish period pieces; operated as a museum by the Florida Colonial Dames. Open Jan.-May, Mon., Wed. 10-4; closed hols; sm adm.

Oldest House (14 St. Francis St.), maintained by the St. Augustine Historical Society to demonstrate the history of city life, is partly housed in a coquina home with tabby floors built in the early 1700's. Its rooms are furnished to represent various periods of the city's history. Adjacent **Tovar House,** also called Cannonball House for the shot embedded in one wall during Oglethorpe's attack, offers displays of architectural history and decorative arts. Open daily 9-5:40; sm adm includes both buildings.

Oldest Store Museum (4 Artillery Lane): replica of a general store that supplied St. Augustine during the last part of the 19th C; 100,000 items displayed; replicas of a gun shop, ship candlery, and other services. Open Mon.-Sat. 9-5:30, Sun. 12:30-5:30; closed Dec. 25; adm. **Oldest Wooden Schoolhouse** (14 St. George St.) was constructed during the first Spanish period (1565-1763). Open daily 9-5 (longer hrs in summer); sm adm. **Castle Armory** (62 Spanish St.) exhibits armor and ancient weapons from around the world; open daily 9-5 (later hrs in summer); closed Dec. 25; adm. **Museum of Yesterday's Toys** (52 St. George St.), in a 1702 building, exhibits puppets, dolls, and toys dating back to the 17th C. Open daily 10-5; closed Dec. 25; adm.

Cathedral of St. Augustine (north side of plaza) was established in 1565, and its register lists weddings and other events dating back to 1594. The present building, reconstructed after an 1887 fire, is still in use. The floor is of Spanish tile, and murals depict the life of St. Augustine.

Mission of Nombre de Dios (San Marco Ave., 5 blocks N of city gate) contains the shrine of Our Lady of La Leche. A 200-ft-high cross marks the site of America's first Indian mission and first parish Mass (1565). Open daily 7:30-dark; closed Dec. 25; donation.

Old Spanish Cemetery (Cordova St. between Orange & Saragossa) has many above-ground crypts.

Castillo de San Marcos National Monument (on Matanzas Bay in St. Augustine, opposite the City Gate on Castillo Dr.): Since its settlement in 1565, St. Augustine had successfully survived attacks by the French and by pirates. But when the British challenged, the Spanish, with Indian workers, began construction of this impressive coquina-stone fortress in 1672. Within the battle-scarred walls are guardrooms, detention cells, a chapel, and exhibits. Good views of St. Augustine; guided tour of the fort; frequent cannon firing demonstrations. Open daily 8:30-5:30 (8:30-7 in summer); closed Dec. 25; sm adm or GEP.

Fort Matanzas National Monument (14 m S of St. Augustine via SR A1A on the Matanzas River): Matanzas is Spanish for "slaughters" and the area got its name after French Huguenots in 1564 challenged Spain's claim to Florida by building Ft. Caroline at the St. Johns River and then sending a fleet south to attack St. Augustine. When a storm wrecked the fleet, some 500 survivors tried to return overland to Ft. Caroline; the Spanish intercepted them here and massacred the 334 who surrendered. The Visitor Center (open daily 8:30-5:30; closed Dec. 25; free) has interpretive exhibits and a view of the fort, but the fort is on Rattlesnake Island and must be reached by boat (these leave daily exc Tues., 9-4:30; sm adm.).

Lightner Museum (Cordova & King Sts.), in a restored 300-room building that once served as the Alcazar Hotel, features a columned bath area where toga-clad guests of the late 1800's enjoyed the first steam baths in Florida. "Streets of Yesterday" showcases products of 19th-C life in 15 stores; porcelain dating back to the late 1700's, Oriental art works, Victorian art glass (many pieces by Tiffany), statuary, paintings, and archaeological displays. Open daily 9:30-9; closed Dec. 25; adm.

Zorayda Castle (83 King St.), a copy of part of the Alhambra Palace in Spain, was built as a private home in 1883; mosaics; furnished with ancient treasures from the Mid East and the Orient; Open daily 9-6 (longer hrs in summer); closed Dec. 25; adm.

Flagler College (King St.) is in a Moorish-inspired building once the Ponce de Leon Hotel. **Flagler Memorial Church** (36 Sevilla St. behind the College) is an ornate Venetian Renaissance-style church that Flagler built in 1890 as a memorial to his daughter; carved woodwork, a copper dome inlaid with marble, fine Aeolian-Skinner organ. Open weekdays 8-5.

Fountain of Youth (155 Magnolia Ave., E of San Marco Ave.) claims to be the site of Ponce de Leon's landing in 1513; the spring; a museum; hourly shows of early Spanish exploration; hourly planetarium shows of early celestial navigation; Indian burial ground. Open daily 8-5 (longer hrs in summer); adm.

ST. PETERSBURG: St. Petersburg Historical Museum (335 2nd Ave. NE): natural history, science, history, and Americana; life and death masks of famous people. Open Mon.-Sat. 11-5, Sun. 1-5; closed Thnks, Dec. 25; sm adm.

Grace S. Turner House (3501 2nd Ave. S) is furnished with pieces from early St. Petersburg, including a small-scale children's room and a table that belonged to the pirate Jean Lafitte. **Haas Museum** (3511 2nd Ave. S) contains shops (barber, cobbler, blacksmith), a dentist's office, an early kitchen, a miniature railway. **Lowe House** (3537 2nd Ave. S), built in the early 1850's and later moved here, contains many original furnishings. All 3 are maintained by the St. Petersburg Historical Society and are open Tues.-Sun. 1-5; closed Dec. 25; Sept.; sm adm covers all 3 buildings.

Museum of Fine Arts (255 Beach Dr. N) exhibits include European and American painting from the 17th-20th C; Oriental and Pre-Columbian works; decorative arts; French and English period rooms; special exhibits, films, lectures, and concerts. Open Tues.-Sat. 10-5, Sun. 1-5; closed Jan. 1, Dec. 25; sm adm.

Bounty (345 2nd Ave. NE, adj to Municipal Pier) is a full-size replica of Capt. William Bligh's ship built for the MGM film of the mutiny. Adjacent Tahitian village. Open daily 9 am-10 pm; adm.

SAN MARCOS DE APALACHE STATE MUSEUM (at confluence of the Wakulla & St. Marks Rivers; follow signs from SR 363 in St. Marks) was where Panfilo de Narvaez arrived with 300 men overland from Tampa to build the first ships made by white men in the U.S. DeSoto came in 1539. A log fort was built in 1679, but was looted and burned by pirates in 1682. A stone fort, begun in 1739, was passed back and forth between the Spanish and English until Florida was ceded to the U.S. in 1821. The fort was promptly abandoned, but later served as a military post during the Civil War. In May 1800, the fort was captured by William Augustus Bowles, a disgraced British officer who married a Creek woman and declared himself King of Florida (his reign lasted only 5 weeks). Museum houses exhibits of its history. Open daily 9-5; sm adm.

SARASOTA: Ringling Museums (3 m N on US 41) are on the 68-acre estate left to the people of Florida by John Ringling at his death in 1936. He had selected Sarasota as winter headquarters for his circus in 1927 (many circus people still live here), and devoted much of his time to this estate and to civic improvement. The buildings are open Mon.-Fri. 9 am-10 pm, Sat. 9-5, Sun. 1-5; combination ticket to all buildings (Museum of Art is free on Sat). **John and Mable Ringling Museum of Art,** in a huge replica of a 15th-C Italian villa, is of local stone embellished with columns, sculptures, and other decorative features collected by Ringling on his travels. The courtyard sculpture garden, with fountains, is climaxed with a copy of Michelangelo's *David*. The collection of baroque paintings is believed by many to be the finest in the Western Hemisphere; fine Rubens collection includes his series of designs for tapestries. Tintoretto, Veronese, Murillo, Velazquez, El Greco, Titian, Rembrandt, Hals, Gainsborough, and Reynolds are represented. Also here are rooms from the Astor mansion in New York; reference library; shop. **Asolo Theater** is a modern building in which the 1798 theater from the castle of Queen Catherine Cornaro in Asolo, Italy, has been reassembled. This horseshoe-shape theater, with ornate boxes, is now the State Theater of Florida; programs are presented regularly. **Ringling Residence,** called Ca'd'Zan (house of John in the Venetian dialect), is a sumptuous Venetian-Gothic palace set on Sarasota Bay with terraces looking over the water reminiscent of those in Venice. Changing views of the water from inside the building are through windows of many colors made of Venetian glass. Some 30 rooms surround a Great Hall; Flemish and English tapestries, a 4000-pipe organ, 19th-C European and American paintings, and many priceless antiques. **Circus Museum** is a huge collection of circus wagons, posters, equipment, costumes, calliopes, and memorabilia tracing the history of circuses from ancient Rome to the present. Exhibits—of blacksmith and other shops, dining area, dressing tents—gives a vivid picture of circus life.

New College (on US 41 adj to Ringling Museums) contains the Charles Ringling Mansion and buildings designed by I. M. Pei.

Circus Hall of Fame (6255 N Tamiami Trail) is a large collection of circus memorabilia, including a coach Queen Victoria gave Tom Thumb; puppet shows given frequently, and circus acts performed late Dec.-after Easter, June-Labor Day, daily at 10, 12, 2. Open daily 9-3:30; adm (higher when circus acts are presented).

Bellm's Cars & Music of Yesterday (5500 N Tamiami Trail) houses more than 150 restored antique cars, a bicycle collection, and more than 1000 antique mechanical music machines dating from 1790. Open Mon.-Sat. 8:30-6, Sun. 9:30-6; adm.

SEBASTIAN INLET STATE RECREATION AREA (on SR A1A midway between Vero Beach & Melbourne): the star-shape McLarty State Museum, devoted to lost Spanish treasure, on the site of Spanish salvage operations of the 1715 silver fleet disaster; exhibits show Spanish trade routes, salvage operations, and Indian artifacts. Open daily 9-5; sm adm.

STUART: Elliot Museum (Hutchinson Island) has exhibits on the evolution of wheeled vehicles, art gallery and Americana shops, and a general store with post office; open daily 1-5; adm. **House of Refuge** (Hutchinson Island), last of a series of lifesaving stations built in 1875 to rescue shipwrecked sailors, houses a maritime museum with relics from shipwrecks and a sea turtle hatchery. Open Tues.-Sun. 1-5; closed Dec. 25; sm adm.

TALLAHASSEE: State Capitol (Monroe St. & Apalachee Pkwy.), on the highest hill, contains part of the 1845 original building; open Mon.-Fri. 8-5, Sat. 10-5, Sun. & hols 1-5; free. **Governor's Mansion** (700 N Adams St.), built in 1957, was modeled on Andrew Jackson's home, The Hermitage; open only on special occasions.

The Columns (100 N Duval St.), a restored 1830 brick mansion furnished with period antiques, houses the Chamber of Commerce; open Mon.-Fri. 8:30-5; free.

LeMoyne Art Foundation (125 N Gadsden St.) has exhibits of works by regional artists; sculpture garden. Open Tues.-Sat. 11-5, Sun. 2-5; closed hols; free.

Florida State University (on US 90), well-known for its circus (performances in spring only), has maps for self-guiding campus tours (Information Services, room 324, Physical Science & Admin Bldg.). **Art gallery** (Fine Arts Bldg.) has a good collection of American graphics, Baroque paintings, and changing exhibits. Open Mon.-Fri. 10-4, Sun. 1-4; closed academic hols; free.

TAMPA: University of Tampa (401 W Kennedy Blvd.), in Plant Park, occupies the old Tampa Bay Hotel built by railroad tycoon Henry B. Plant. Copied from the Alhambra in Spain; 13 minarets; 500 rooms; decorative themes based on a variety of periods, such as Elizabethan or Florentine. The Plant collection of Oriental and Italian antiques, and furnishings that once belonged to European royalty, is also here. Teddy Roosevelt used the hotel as his headquarters when he trained his Rough Riders for their Cuban campaign here. Part of the collection may be seen Tues.-Sat. 10-4; a full tour requires special arrangement; closed Aug.; free.

Hillsborough County Historical Commission Museum (room 250 in the County Courthouse on Pierce St. & Kennedy Blvd.) has exhibits of Indian artifacts and historical relics; also library. Open Mon.-Fri. 9:30-4:30; closed hols; free.

Hillsborough County Museum of Science & Natural History (5 m N at 1101 E River Cove) contains a large collection of minerals, Indian artifacts, bird eggs, marine life; open Tues.-Sat. 9:30-4, Sun. 2-4:30; closed hols; free.

Tampa Bay Art Center (320 North Blvd.) is open Oct.-May for special exhibits, June-July for permanent collection of visual arts, Tues.-Sat. 10-4:30; free.

University of South Florida (on SR 582) offers the **Florida Center for the Arts,** with library, exhibits of visual arts, performing arts. Open during the academic year, Mon.-Sat. 8-5, Sun. 1-5; closed hols; free. By reservation, you can also see a planetarium show (Physics Bldg.).

USS Requin (Doyle Carlton Dr.), docked on the Hillsborough River, is a WW II sub open for tours daily 11-6; closed Easter, Dec. 25; adm.

TARPON SPRINGS: Dodecanese Blvd. is the center of this colorful and attractive town to which Greek sponge fishermen migrated in the early 1900's. Sponge boats tie up here, and you can watch sponges being cleaned and sorted or auctions at the Exchange (Tues. & Fri. mornings). From the Sponge Docks (810 Dodecanese Blvd.), sponge gathering is demonstrated on cruises. **Spongeorama** (510 Dodecanese Blvd.) offers exhibits on the history of the sponge industry from ancient times, explanations of sponges, life of the fishermen; also film and sponge-diving exhibitions; open daily 10-6; adm.

Inness Paintings (in the Universalist Church (Grand Blvd. & Read St.) are 11 symbolic paintings by George Inness, Jr. (1854-1926) done especially for this church. Open Oct.-May, Tues.-Sun. 2-5; closed hols; sm adm.

St. Nicholas Greek Orthodox Church (36 N Pinellas Ave.), in wonderfully ornate Byzantine style, has a painting of St. Nicholas that is said to shed real tears. Open daily 9-5; donation.

TITUSVILLE: Kennedy Space Center Visitor Information (6 m S on US 1, then 6 m E on NASA Causeway) offers films, lectures, and exhibits on space technology. Open daily 8-dark; closed Dec. 25; free. From here you can take a 2-hr guided bus tour of NASA installations, including the rocket assembly plant in the Vehicle Assembly Building, launch sites at Cape Canaveral, and the Air Force Space Museum; tours daily 8-2 hrs before sunset; closed during launches and Dec. 25; adm. **Air Force Space Museum** (Complex 26) has audiovisual and other displays on the history and development of space flight; free. Driving through Kennedy Space Center and Cape Canaveral Air Force Station (reachable also via Gate 1, off SR A1A at Cape Canaveral) is permitted Sun. only, 9-3. **Patrick AFB** has an outdoor display of missiles. **Port Canaveral** (SR 401 at Cape Canaveral) often has nuclear submarines and missile ships in addition to a shrimp fleet.

Museum of Sunken Treasure (8625 Astronaut Blvd. in Cape Canaveral) has audiovisual exhibits on treasure recovered from a 1715 fleet of Spanish ships returning from the Orient and wrecked in a hurricane off Florida; ship models, recovered gold, and other treasures. Open daily 9:30-5:15; closed Jan. 1, Dec. 25; adm.

TOMOKA STATE PARK (N Beach St. in Ormond Beach): **Marsh Museum** displays works by Fred Dana Marsh and Indian history of the area; open daily; sm adm.

TORREYA STATE PARK (off SR 12, 13 m NE of Bristol): Greek Revival-style **Gregory House** (1834) is open Mon.-Fri. 10-noon, 2-4; weekends & hols 10-5; adm. A foot trail leads to Confederate gun pits and an old riverboat landing.

WEST PALM BEACH: Norton Gallery & School of Art (1415 S Olive Ave. in Pioneer Park) has a permanent collection of European and American paintings dating from Italian Renaissance works to Pollack and Motherwell; outstanding sculpture includes Maillol and Brancusi; Chinese bronzes, jades, pottery, and sculpture; changing exhibits. Open Tues.-Fri. 10-5; Sat., Sun., hols 1-5; closed July 4, Thnks, Dec. 25; free.

Science Museum & Planetarium (1141 W Lakewood Rd.): natural history and space exhibits; planetarium shows Wed.-Sun. aft. (adm); open Tues.-Sat. 10-5, Sun. 1-5; closed July 4, Thnks, Dec. 25; sm adm.

WHITE SPRINGS: Stephen Foster Memorial (on US 41) has a 200-ft carillon tower with antique furniture; more than 500 rare bells; carillon concerts daily. Museum with dioramas of the composer's life, Foster memorabilia, antique instruments and dolls. Open daily 9-5:30; closed Dec. 25; adm.

WINTER PARK: Rollins College, on a lovely campus on the NW shore of Lake Virginia, is housed in Mediterranean-style buildings. The Walk of Fame features inscribed stones from the birthplaces of famous people. On campus are: **Beal-Maltbie Shell Museum** (Park & Holt Sts.), with one of the world's finest displays; almost every known species of shellfish; also shell carvings and objects made of shells. Open early Sept.-May, Wed.-Sat. 10-5, Tues. & Sun. 1-5; adm. **Morse Gallery of Art** houses paintings, decorative art, and furniture by Louis Comfort Tiffany and skilled contemporaries. Open early Sept.-May, Wed.-Fri. 8:30-5, weekends 1-5, Tues. 1-9; closed hols; free.

Albin Polasek Home (633 Osceola Ave.), with studio, chapel, galleries, and many of the sculptor's works, is open Wed.-Sat. 2-4; tours given Tues. & Sun. aft; adm.

YULEE SUGAR MILL HISTORIC MEMORIAL (at Old Homosassa on SR 490): Here is part of a 5100-acre sugar plantation established 1851 by a West Indian family with an interesting history; the mansion was burned during the Civil War but the mill was spared; open daily; sm adm.

GEORGIA

ALBANY: Thronateeska Heritage Foundation (516 Flint Ave), in an 1860 building, houses Indian artifacts, minerals; open Mon.-Fri. 9-noon, 2-5, Sun. 3-5; closed major hols; free.

ALEXANDER H. STEPHENS MEMORIAL STATE PARK (½ m N of Crawfordville) contains **Liberty Hall,** the homey, unpretentious frame house of the Vice President of the Confederacy, restored with many original furnishings. **Confederate Museum** houses Civil War documents and relics belonging to Stephens and others. Open Tues.-Sat. 9-5, Sun. 1-5; closed Thnks, Dec. 25; sm adm.

ANDERSONVILLE NATIONAL HISTORIC SITE (9 m NE of Americus on SR 49) is site of the most notorious military prison of the Civil War. In 1864-5, more than 45,000 Union soldiers were confined in quarters built for 10,000; more than 12,000 died. When the war ended, the commandant was tried by a military tribunal and hanged, the only Confederate executed for war crime. Earthworks, escape tunnels, holes dug in a desperate search for water, and several monuments, including one to Clara Barton, are on the grounds. Also Andersonville National Cemetery. Open daily 8-5 (8-7 in summer); free.

ATHENS: Chamber of Commerce (155 E Washington St.) has a booklet describing auto and walking tours through this lovely old town called Georgia's Classic City. Some of the showplace homes are on Milledge Ave., and the most impressive block is at Prince & Grady Sts. Among the many old homes are the 1835 Howell Cobb House (698 N Pope St.), said to be haunted, 1828 Erwin Home (126 Dearing St.), 1830 Masonic Temple (279 Meigs St.), 1842 Sigma Alpha Epsilon House (247 Pulaski St.) considered to be one of the finest examples of Southern architecture. Annual tours are given by the Athens-Clarke Heritage Foundation (280 E Dougherty St.).

    Church-Waddel-Brumby House (280 E Dougherty St.), restored 1820 building, houses the Athens Welcome Center; open Mon.-Fri. 9-5, Sat. 9-noon, Sun. 2-5; closed Thnks, Dec. 25; free.

    Taylor-Grady Home (634 Prince Ave.) is a Greek Revival mansion built in 1839 by a planter and later owned by editor Woodfin Grady. The portico is supported by 13 Doric columns said to represent the original colonies. Open Mon., Wed., Fri. 10-2, Sun. 2-5; adm. **University of Georgia,** chartered in 1785, has many historic buildings dating from the early 1800's. **Georgia Museum of Art** (Jackson St.) features the Eva Underhill Holbrook Collection of American paintings from 1845-1945, and a large collection of European and American prints from the 17th-19th C. Open Mon.-Fri. 9-5, Sat. noon-5; closed late Aug.-early Sept. and Dec. recess; free. **Founders Memorial Garden & House** (325 Lumpkin St.) is a memorial to the nation's oldest garden club; sunken formal garden; smokehouse and other outbuildings. House open Mon.-Fri. 9-noon, 1-4; closed hols. Garden open daily 7-5:30. Both free. **President's Home** (570 Prince Ave.) is an 1856 mansion worth seeing from the outside (open only on special occasions); 14 Corinthian columns extend around 3 sides; Doric columns at rear.

Double-barreled Cannon (City Hall lawn), cast at Athens Foundry in 1863, was supposed to kill two Yankees at a time by firing simultaneously 2 balls; but it didn't work.

Eagle Tavern (8 m S via US 129, 441 to Watkinsville), built about 1800, was a tavern, stage stop, and store. Open Tues.-Sat. 9-5:30, Sun. 2-5:30; closed Thnks, Dec. 25; free.

ATLANTA: The original settlement was Standing Peachtree, a Creek village that became a trading post and fort. In 1864, when the city surrendered to Gen. Sherman, residents were evacuated and the city burned, leaving only 400 of its 4500 structures standing; about the only remnant of the past is the Eternal Flame of the Confederacy, an old gas lamp that still burns day and night at the corner of Alabama and Whitehall Sts. Information is available from the **Chamber of Commerce** (1300 Commerce Bldg. 30303) or the **Convention & Visitors Bureau** (229 Peachtree St.).

State Capitol (Capitol Sq.), modeled on the U.S. Capitol in 1884-9 as a symbol of rejoining the Union, is capped with gold from Dahlonega. **Georgia State Museum of Science & Industry** (4th floor) has exhibits on minerals, wildlife, and industry; open Mon.-Sat. 8:30-4:30, Sun. 1-5; closed hols; free. **Governor's Mansion** (391 W Paces Ferry Rd.), a 1968 pink Greek Revival building; outstanding American-made furnishings; antiques from England and the Orient; books about the state and by local authors; open Tues.-Thurs. 10-noon, Sun. 3-5; free.

Georgia Dept. of Archives & History (330 Capitol Ave. SE) features stained-glass windows depicting the rise and fall of the confederacy; rare manuscript collection; open Mon.-Fri. 8-4:30, Sat. 9:30-3:30; closed hols; free. **Rhodes Memorial Hall** (1516 Peachtree St. NW) is a copy of a Bavarian castle housing exhibits and collections of the State Dept. of Archives & History; open Mon.-Fri. 8:30-4:30; closed hols; free.

Atlanta Historical Society (3099 Andres Dr. NW) is in the magnificent, Palladian-inspired Swan House, built in 1928. Interior features include fine woodwork, wrought iron, free-standing circular staircase; 18th-C furnishings; exhibits on the city's history; some Margaret Mitchell mementos. Open Mon.-Sat. 10:30-3:30, Sun. 1:30-3:30; closed hols; free. Guided tours of period rooms are available for a charge. On the grounds is the **Tullie Smith House Restoration** of an 1840 farmhouse with gardens and outbuildings including a slave cabin; open same hours as above, exc closed Jan.; adm.

Memorial Arts Center (1280 Peachtree St., NE), a huge complex dedicated to 122 art patrons who died in a 1962 air crash in Paris, contains the **High Museum of Art,** with Italian Renaissance painting and 19th-20th-C European and American works; Samuel H. Kress, Ralph K. Uhry, and J. J. Haverty collections; open Mon.-Sat. 10-5, Sun. noon-5; closed hols; free.

Grave of Martin Luther King, Jr. is beside Ebenezer Baptist Church (413 Auburn Ave., NE).

Wren's Nest (1050 Gordon St., SW) was the home of Joel Chandler Harris from 1880; original furnishings, books, photographs. Open Mon.-Sat. 9:30-5 (last tour at 4:15), Sun. 2-5; closed Jan. 1, Thnks, Dec. 25; adm.

Underground Atlanta (Central Ave. viaduct at Hunter St.) was the commercial center of the city, abandoned when viaducts were built over it early in this century; restored to its Gay 90's appearance, with cobblestone streets, gas lamps (the sun doesn't reach here), and stained-glass windows; boutiques, restaurants, galleries, nightclubs, historic displays.

Cyclorama (Grant Park) re-creates the Battle of Atlanta in a 50-ft-high, 400-ft-round circular painting made by German artists in 1885-6; in 1936 the painting was made three-dimensional by setting into the foreground blended to seem part of the painting clay figures and fragments of war paraphernalia. Painting must be seen on guided tour that includes sound effects. Building also houses Civil War exhibits. Open daily 9:30-5:30 (last tour at 4:30); closed Jan. 1, Dec. 25; adm.

Fernbank Science Center (156 Heaton Park Dr. NE) is a 65-acre forest with self-guiding trails (open Sun.-Fri. 2-5, Sat. 10-5) containing a splendid planetarium (shows daily exc Mon.), observatory (Fri. eve after dark), exhibit hall with see-and-touch displays (Mon.-Sat. 8:30-5, Sun. 1:30-5, plus some eve hrs), and a science library (Mon.-Sat. 9-5 plus some eve hrs). Closed hols. Free exc for planetarium shows.

Emory University (1380 S Oxford Rd. in Druid Hills): **Emory Museum** collections of Far East, Near East, African arts; American Indian artifacts; local birds, fish, reptiles, insects; open Mon.-Fri. 10-noon, 2-4, Sat. 10-noon; closed hols and during academic recesses; free.

Stone Mountain Park (16 m E on US 78), a 3200-acre historic-recreational park, surrounds a huge relief carving of Robert E. Lee, Stonewall Jackson, and Jefferson Davis on horseback; observation tower is accessible by foot or cable car. Also in the park area: Memorial Hall (a Civil War Museum; free), Confederate Hall (sound-and-light program on the Civil War; sm adm), Antebellum Plantation (restored and furnished complex; adm), Antique Auto & Music Museum (adm), Industries of the Old South (working mills, cider press, still; free). Most attractions are open daily mid-June-Labor Day 10-9, rest of yr 10-5:30; closed Dec. 24-25. Park is open 6 am-midnight; parking fee plus individual or combination tickets.

Bulloch Hall (180 Bulloch Ave., 20 m N via US 19 in Roswell): Greek Revival mansion, home of Pres. Theodore Roosevelt's parents; escaped destruction during the Civil War; restored with period furnishings. Open Mon.-Sat. 9:30-5, Sun. 1-5; adm. **Barrington Hall** (also on US 19 in Roswell) likewise escaped destruction. Built in 1842 by the family who founded Roswell; exterior Doric columns are repeated in the stately hallway; elaborate mantels, many original antiques, Civil War documents. This and several other lovely homes in Roswell are open only on special tours.

AUGUSTA: Site of Fort Augusta, founded in 1735 by James Oglethorpe, is marked by a Celtic cross between St. Paul's Church and the river; this was the first city Oglethorpe founded after Savannah, and it served as state capital during the Revolution. **Augusta-Richmond County Museum** (540 Telfair St.): historic, natural science exhibits; open Tues.-Sat. 2-6, Sun. 2-5; closed Jan. 1, Dec. 25; free.

Gertrude Herbert Memorial Art Institute (506 Telfair St.) is in an attractive frame home built in 1818; paintings dating from the Renaissance to the present, works by local artists; open Tues.-Fri. 10-noon, 2-5, Sat. 3-5; closed Jan. 1, Dec. 25; free.

Mackay House (1822 Broad St.), built about 1760 and named for a Scots trader, was once an Indian trading post; said to be haunted by the ghosts of 13 patriots hanged in the stairwell by the British during the Revolution. Restored, with Revolutionary museum and Indian trade displays. Open Tues.-Sat. 9-5:30, Sun. 2-5:30; closed Thnks, Dec. 25; free.

Meadow Garden (1320 Nelson St.): cottage that was home to George Walton, a signer of the Declaration of Independence; now a DAR museum; portraits of George Washington and many Walton family heirlooms; open Wed., Sat. 1-4; closed Thnks, Dec. 25; sm adm.

CALHOUN: New Echota (4 m NE off SR 225), a restoration of the Cherokee capital (1825-38), depicts the story of the Cherokee attempt to establish a republican form of government modeled on that of the U.S.; unfortunately for the Cherokee, gold was discovered on their land, and they were forced to leave it and move to Oklahoma over the Trail of Tears.

Facing the Memorial Arch at the city limits is a statue of the great Sequoyah, who invented a written form for the Cherokee language. Reconstructed **Print Shop** contains typecases, printing press, other displays of the *Cherokee Phoenix*, printed here 1828-34 in both English and Cherokee.

Also reconstructed is the **Supreme Court** of the Cherokee Nation, which served as school and mission part of the year; **Vann Tavern**, erected by James Vann (see Chatsworth) in Buford, Georgia, in 1805, and moved here; **Worcester House**, home of a Congregational missionary. All are authentically furnished and open Tues.-Sat. 9-5:30, Sun. 2-5:30; closed Thnks, Dec. 25; free.

CARTERSVILLE: Etowah Mounds Archaeological Area (3 m S off SR 113), an important settlement occupied 1000-1500 AD, was a community of several thousand people. Seven mounds are grouped about 2 plazas; the largest mound covers several acres. A museum has artifacts from the excavations, including 2 extraordinary human figures and articles indicating extensive trade routes. Open Tues.-Sat. 9-5:30, Sun. 2-5:30; closed Jan. 1, Thnks, Dec. 25; free.

CHATSWORTH: Vann House (3 m W on US 76 at jct SR 225), once showplace of the Cherokee nation; elaborate interior carvings feature traditional Cherokee roses. Vann, son of a Scots trader and a Cherokee woman, was a wealthy chief who helped establish a Moravian Mission to educate Cherokee children. Open Tues.-Sat. 10-5:30, Sun. 2-5:30; closed Thnks, Dec. 25; free.

CHICKAMAUGA & CHATTANOOGA NATIONAL MILITARY PARK (9 m S of Chattanooga, Tennessee, on US 27): The railroads from Chattanooga, vital to Southern defense, drew Union forces under Gen. William S. Rosecrans here in June 1863. The **Visitor Center** explains the battle through exhibits and audiovisual programs, and also houses a collection of American weapons. From here there is a 7-m self-guiding auto tour of the major battlefield sites. Open daily 8-5 (8-6 in summer); closed Dec. 25; free.

COLUMBUS: Chamber of Commerce (1344 13th Ave.) or **Georgia Welcome Center** (Victory Dr. & 10th Ave.) can provide maps and other information; the latter operates Heritage Tours (Wed. at 10, Sun. at 3; adm) to: **Springer Opera House** (103 10th St. at 1st Ave.), an elegant 1871 theater where virtually every important stage personality in the U.S. appeared at the turn of the century; memorabilia of Edwin Booth, Otis Skinner, Oscar Wilde, William Jennings Bryan, and others; performances year round. **Rankin House** (1440 2nd Ave.), built 1850-70; iron grillwork; walnut double stairs; period furnishings. **Pemberton House** (11 7th St.), a memorial to the inventor of Coca-Cola, and **Walker-Peters-Langdon House** (716 Broadway), an 1828 clapboard, oldest structure in the city, with period furnishings, are also open for individual tours Mon.-Fri. 10-4; closed hols; adm.

Octagon House (527 1st Ave.) was once a double octagon house, the only one in Georgia and possibly in the U.S.; only one house remains; it is a private residence occasionally open; inquire locally.

Columbus Museum of Arts & Crafts (1251 Wynnton Rd.) exhibits toys, guns, some wonderful 16th-19th-C paintings, Yuchi and other Indian artifacts, antique jewelry. Open Tues.-Sat. 10-5, Sun. 2-5; closed Jan. 1, July 4, Thnks, Dec. 25; free.

Confederate Naval Museum (101 4th St. at US 27): displays the iron-clad gunboat *Muscogee,* under construction when the city was lost; it was set afire and sunk. Also salvaged were the remains of the wooden gunboat *Chattahoochee.* Also, Ladies' Defender Cannon made from brass beds, cooking utensils, and doorknobs. Open Tues.-Sat. 9-5:30, Sun. 2-5:30; closed Thnks, Dec. 25; free.

Fort Benning (5 m S on US 27) offers the U.S. Army Infantry Museum, with exhibits from the Revolution to the present; more than 14,000 objects trace the history of the enemy too, from Indians to Vietnamese; library. Open Tues.-Fri. 10-4:30, Sat. & Sun. 12:30-4:30; closed Jan. 1, Thnks, Dec. 25; free.

Hamilton (23 m N off US 27) has restored the area surrounding its square; 19th-C general store, apothecary, and other shops; antique automobile museum. Open Mon.-Sat. 10-6, Sun. noon-6; adm to each or combination tickets.

DAHLONEGA: Site of America's first major gold rush (1828), this town produced so much gold that the U.S. built a mint here in 1837. Although the mint closed in Feb. 1861 some people claim that the Confederate government managed to mint coins for at least a month after that. **Dahlonega Courthouse Gold Museum** (on the square) is in the 1838 Greek Revival county courthouse; exhibits of the gold rush, displays of local gold, and coins minted in town. Open Tues.-Sat. 9-5:30, Sun. 2-5; closed Thnks, Dec. 25; free. The museum personnel can direct you to the ghost town of Auraria (6 m S on SR 9E) and other sites where panning is still carried out.

DARIEN: Fort King George (1 m E on Ft. King George Dr.) was built to protect the first settlers against the Spanish and French. The Visitor Center has historical displays; open Tues.-Sat. 9-5:30, Sun. 2-5:30; closed Thnks, Dec. 25; free.

EATONTON: This antebellum town was the birthplace of Joel Chandler

Harris (1848) and the courthouse lawn has a statue of Br'er Rabbit. **Uncle Remus Museum** (3 blocks S of courthouse in Turner Park), in two connected slave cabins, has carved animal figures illustrating a dozen Harris stories; also Harris mementos and books. Open Apr.-Sept. Mon.-Sat. 9-noon, 1-5, Sun. 2-5; Oct.-Mar., Mon., Wed.-Sat. 9-noon, 1-5, Sun. 2-5; sm adm.

FITZGERALD: Blue & Gray Museum (N Hooker St.), dedicated to friendship between North and South, as is the city (streets are named for Union and Confederate generals), houses Civil War relics; open Mon.-Fri. 9-5; closed hols; sm adm.

FORT FREDERICA NATIONAL MONUMENT (N end St. Simons Island) preserves the most impressive British fortification in the U.S., established in 1736 by Gen. James Oglethorpe for operations against the Spanish in Florida. A town of English settlers prospered here until Oglethorpe's defeat of a Spanish invasion in 1742 put an end to hostilities. Oglethorpe's regiment was disbanded in 1749, destroying Frederica's economy, and a 1758 fire destroyed most of the buildings. The Visitor Center describes life in the town, and enough ruins remain to visualize it. Open daily 8-5 (8-6 in summer); closed Dec. 25; free.

FORT MCALLISTER (17 m S of Savannah off US 17), built on the Great Ogeechee River for the defense of Savannah, kept Union gunboats from pursuing the blockade-running *Nashville* in 1862 and resisted attacks from Union ironclads in 1863. But Sherman sent a division overland which took the fort in a 15-minute battle on Dec. 13, 1864. Restored earthworks and bombproofs; museum. Open Tues.-Sat. 9-5, Sun. 2-5; closed Thnks, Dec. 25; free.

FORT PULASKI NATIONAL MONUMENT (15 m E of Savannah off US 80): The fort, named for the Polish nobleman Casimir Pulaski (who died in the unsuccessful siege of Savannah in 1779), was begun in 1829; it took 18 yrs and $1-million to build—but when Confederates tried to hold it against the Union in 1862, it was surrendered unconditionally in 30 hours. This was the first demonstration that the old masonry forts were useless against modern rifled cannons. The Visitor Center provides information for a self-guided walking tour; the fort is in very good shape and has two drawbridges. On the grounds is a memorial to John Wesley, who gave thanks here for a safe Atlantic crossing in 1736. Open daily 8:30-5:30 (to 6 in summer); closed Dec. 25; adm or GEP.

JEFFERSON: Crawford W. Long Medical Museum (on US 129, SR 11) honors him as the first physician to perform a painless operation by using

sulphuric ether in 1842; memorabilia of Dr. Long; diorama of this operation; the history of anaesthetics. Open Tues.-Sat. 9-5:30, Sun. 2-5:30;
closed Thnks, Dec. 25; free.

JEFFERSON DAVIS MEMORIAL STATE PARK (SR 32 between Fitzgerald and Tifton at Irwinville) contains a small Confederate Museum with
Civil War displays and mementos of Jefferson Davis. Here Davis was
captured on his flight to Mexico after Lee's surrender at Appomattox.
Open Tues.-Sat. 9-5, Sun. 1-5; closed Thnks, Dec. 25; sm adm.

JEKYLL ISLAND: This lovely island was chosen as a winter resort by
60 millionaires who controlled it 1886-1946. J. P. Morgan, the Vanderbilts, Goulds, Rockefellers, and others built mansions, many of which still
stand (most are not open to the public) along the W side of the island.
At the exclusive Jekyll Island Club, built in 1888, a chef from Delmonico's
prepared elaborate menus. Here Morgan and his associates formed the
Federal Reserve Bank in 1913. **Jekyll Island Museum** (329 Riverview Dr.)
was a Rockefeller cottage built in 1892 with Tiffany windows; it contains
the original Edwardian furnishings; open Mon.-Sat. 9-5, Sun. noon-5;
adm (in summer this includes a guided tour of the area). **Faith Chapel,**
with stained-glass windows by Tiffany, is open daily 9-5; free.

KENNESAW MOUNTAIN NATIONAL BATTLEFIELD PARK (2 m N
of Marietta, off US 41): In May 1864, Gen. William T. Sherman threatened
to cut Gen. Joseph E. Johnston's Confederate forces away from their
Atlanta base. By June, Johnston began turning the Kennesaw Mountain
area into a fortress, and Sherman's attack here on June 27 failed. However, on July 2, Johnston was forced to abandon the mountain to protect
Atlanta. A **Visitor Center** depicts the battle through exhibits and a slide
program, and through the battlefield are wayside exhibits; open Mon.-
Fri. 8:30-5, Sat. & Sun. 8:30-6; the roads close earlier in winter and stay
open later in summer; closed Jan. 1, Dec. 25; free.

LA GRANGE: Bellevue (204 Ben Hill St.), built 1853-55, is a Victorian
baroque interpretation of Greek Revival, with massive Ionic columns on
three sides; this exceptionally impressive home has had many distinguished
visitors, including Jefferson Davis; period furnishings; open daily 10-5;
closed thnks, Dec. 25; adm.

LUMPKIN: The **Stagecoach Trail** is a route of some 30 pre-1850 houses
marked with stagecoach signs in this old town. **Bedingfield Inn** (US 27),
a frame residence built by a physician, became Lumpkin's stagecoach
stop in 1836; many Empire pieces; open May-Aug., daily 1-5; Sept.-Apr.,
Sat. 10-5 & Sun. 1-5; adm.

Westville Village (US 27) is a reconstructed village to which many authentic buildings have been moved to demonstrate a farming community of the 1850's; quilting and other crafts demonstrations; jousting and other special events throughout the year; open June-mid-Oct. 10-6; mid-Oct.-May 10-5; closed Jan. 1, Thnks, Dec. 25; adm.

MACON: Chamber of Commerce (640 1st St.) or Tourist Center (15 m N on I-75) can give you self-guiding maps and, for a fee, arrange tours.

City.Hall (Cotton Ave. at Poplar St.) served as state capitol 1864-5; on either side of the entrance the history of the area is depicted; open Mon.-Fri. 9-5:30; closed hols; free.

Hay House (934 Georgia Ave.), a resplendent 24-room Italian Renaissance villa, was built 1855-60; elaborate interior with vaulted, ornamented ceilings, wonderful plaster work, a 50-ft ballroom with sky-lighted ceiling, a secret room where Confederate money was stored; fabulous furnishings. The superstitious owner, who believed he'd die if the house were finished, left the last piece of iron fencing unhung. Open Tues.-Sat. 10:30-12:30, 2:30-4:30, Sun. 2-4; closed hols & Dec. 25; adm.

Cannon Ball House & Macon Museum (856 Mulberry St.) is a Greek Revival building showing Civil War scars, with war relics and period furnishings; the museum houses displays on Macon's history. Open Tues.-Fri. 10:30-1, 2:30-5; Sat. & Sun. 1-4; closed Jan. 1, Thnks, Dec. 24-5; adm.

Grand Opera House (651 Mulberry St.), restored to its 1884 appearance, has a stage so huge that Ben Hur was once performed here with live horses; Sarah Bernhardt, the Gish sisters, and the Lunts appeared here; inquire locally for tours.

Sidney Lanier Cottage (935 High St.) is birthplace of the state's most famous poet; inquire locally for hrs.

Historic Fort Hawkins (Maynard St.) site has displays on the history of the city and state in a reconstructed blockhouse; open Apr.-Nov., Sun. 2-6; sm adm.

MADISON: Madison-Morgan County Chamber of Commerce will give you a map for a walking tour of this old town which Sherman spared; with advance notice, they will provide guides and open some of the homes.

MIDWAY: Midway Museum (US 17) has exhibits on the history of the Midway Society, descendants of Massachusetts Puritans who settled here to be missionaries to the Indians in 1752; period furnishings; fine historical library. Open Tues.-Sat. 9-5:30, Sun. 2-5:30; closed Thnks, Dec. 25; free. Midway Church (adj to Midway Museum) became a center not only for Puritans but also for the rice planters of the area; one of its pastors was the father of Oliver Wendell Holmes, and another the father of Samuel Morse; cemetery; open daily.

Fort Morris Historic Site (in Sunbury, 12 m E on SR 38): a restored fortification originally built in 1776; audiovisual programs on its history; open Tues.-Sun. 9-5; closed Thnks, Dec. 25; free.

MILLEDGEVILLE: This city with many old homes was Georgia's capital 1807-68, and when Sherman's men entered in 1864 they held a mock legislative session to repeal the secession ordinance. **Old Governor's Mansion** (120 S Clark St. on Georgia College campus) is a model Greek Revival building of pink stucco. Designer Charles B. McCluskey created round, square, and octagonal rooms and a central rotunda rising 50-ft to a gilded, domed ceiling. Fine period furnishings. Since 1890 it has been the home of the college's presidents. Guided tours Tues.-Sat. 1-5, Sun. 2-6; closed hols; adm.

OCMULGEE NATIONAL MONUMENT (2 m E of Macon on US 80, 129): Human habitation here dates back at least 11,000 years, but the ruins date from the Macon Plateau culture, 900-1100. The **Visitor Center** houses an excellent archaeological museum and gives tours of a painted, circular earthlodge with a clay ceremonial platform in the shape of a bird. Information is available for self-guiding tours to the rest of the grounds, which include several mounds. Also a Creek trading post and summer living history programs. Open daily 9-5, closed Jan. 1, Dec. 25; free.

ROME: This town chose its name because it is built on 7 hills. On one hill stands the 1871 **Old Clock Tower,** which originally held the city's water. **Berry College & Academy** offers a Visitor Service (Krannert Center, open Mon.-Fri. 8-5, weekends 1-5) and the Martha Berry Museum & Art Gallery (Mon.-Fri. 10-5, weekends 2-5); free. **Chieftains Museum** (100 Chatillon Rd.) is an Indian cabin with Cherokee artifacts; open Feb.-mid Nov., Wed. 11-3, Sun. 2-5; closed hols; free.

SAVANNAH: The **Chamber of Commerce Visitor Center** (W Broad St.) presents an audiovisual program on this gracious, historic city and can give you maps, folders, and tape cassettes for self-guiding walking (you'll want to walk here) and driving tours.

This city was designed by Gen. James Oglethorpe, who brought 120 settlers from England in 1733. He laid out 24 green squares to enhance the streets stretching away from the harbor, and these are still, with their palms and moss-draped live oaks, some of the most charming corners of Savannah: On **Washington Square** (Houston & Congress Sts.), 18th-19th-C homes have been restored. **Johnson Square** (Bull & Congress Sts.) has the grave of Revolutionary hero Nathanael Greene. **Wright Square** (Bull & President Sts.) has a monument to the Yamacraw chief who befriended Oglethorpe's colonists. **Chippewa Square** (Bull & McDonough

Sts.) sports a Daniel Chester French memorial to Oglethorpe. **Monterrey Square** (Bull & Wayne Sts.) honors the Polish nobleman Casimir Pulaski. **Forsyth Park** (Bull & Gaston Sts.), with a lovely 1858 fountain, is spectacular in spring when the azaleas bloom.

The **waterfront** was once a lusty seamen's hangout, with River Street serving as the city's main street. **Ships of the Sea Museum** (503 E River St.) is unusually appealing, with beautifully crafted ship models, scrimshaw, figureheads, ship's library and shops, and other displays; open daily 10-6; adm.

From the early 1800's until the Civil War, Savannah was a leading cotton market. To save the city, residents were evacuated so that Sherman encountered no resistance when he entered in 1864; Savannah was not burned, and within 20 years was again a prosperous cotton center. **Factors Walk** (along the river bluff between Bull & E Broad St.), named for the cotton factors, is reached via iron bridges; antique street lamps; cobblestones (used as ballast in ships from England). **Factors Walk Military Museum** (222 Factors Walk) houses Civil War uniforms, weapons, and artifacts in a 1755 cotton warehouse; open Mon.-Sat. 10-5, Sun. 2-5; closed 2 wks during Christmas & New Year; adm. Here, too, is **Emmet Park**, named for Irish patriot Robert Emmet; the Old Harbor Light (E Bay & E Broad Sts.) was erected in 1852.

City Hall (Bull & Bay Sts.), topped with a copper dome, has historical markers honoring one of the ships named after the city and the first iron-sided American vessel; a model of the SS *Savannah* is exhibited in the Council Chamber. Open Mon.-Fri. 8:15-5; free. **U.S. Customs House** (Bull & E Bay Sts.), an 1852 Greek Revival building, has huge columns along the facade topped with tobacco leaves; inside are import displays; open Mon.-Fri. during business hrs; closed hols.

Georgia Historical Society (501 Whitaker St.) houses a genealogy and historical library; open Mon.-Fri. 10-6, Sat. 9:30-1; closed hols; free.

Owens-Thomas House (124 Abercorn St.), a William Jay masterpiece that he designed at age 19, is a Regency style home completed in 1819 with indirect lighting and other features unusual for the time. Beautiful Regency and Federal furnishings. Lafayette stayed here in 1825. Walled garden in back. Open Tues.-Sat. 10-5, Sun.-Mon. 2-5; closed hols & Sept.; adm.

Davenport House (324 E State St.) is a sedate mansion created in 1815 by master builder Isaiah Davenport. Historic Savannah Foundation has restored it; one of the finest Georgian houses in the nation. Open Mon.-Sat. 10-5; closed hols; adm.

William Scarbrough House (41 W Broad St.), a Regency townhouse designed by William Jay and completed in 1819 for Pres. Monroe's reception, has a particularly grand hall and mezzanine. Being restored by the Historic Savannah Foundation.

Olde Pink House (23 Abercorn St.), a pink-stucco Georgian home that once sheltered Georgia's first state bank, is now a restaurant. **Juliette Gordon Low Birthplace** (142 Bull St.), the Regency-style home of the founder of the Girl Scouts, is the Girl Scout National Center. Mrs. Low became famous at age 4 for making impudent remarks to Gen. Sherman and went on to become a member of the Victorian international set. Her childhood home, designed by William Jay and built 1818-21, displays her paintings, poems, and sculptures, and is furnished with many family pieces. Open Mon., Tues., Thurs.-Sat. 10-4, Sun. 2-4:30; closed Jan. 1, Thnks, Dec. 25; adm. **Colonial Dames House** (329 Abercorn St.), a Victorian stucco house built in 1848 was also lived in by Mrs. Low; some of her sculpture is in the back garden. Among famous guests were William Makepeace Thackeray and Robert E. Lee. Open Mon.-Sat. 10:30-5; closed hols & Sept.; adm.

Gen. Sherman's Headquarters (W side of Madison Sq.) was in the Green Meldrim House, an antebellum home now the parish house of St. John's Church; open Feb.-Nov., Tues., Thurs., 10-3; donation.

Trustees' Garden Site (E Broad St.) is site of America's first experimental garden, founded in 1733 by colonists who hoped to produce pharmaceuticals, wine, and silk. Fort Wayne was also here in 1762. **Pirates' House,** a 1754 inn for seamen mentioned in Robert Louis Stevenson's *Treasure Island,* is now a restaurant; legend says that Blackbeard died here, calling for his rum.

Colonial Park Cemetery (E Oglethorpe & Abercorn Sts.), the colony's first burial ground, used 1750-1853, contains the graves of many city founders. **Cathedral of St. John the Baptist** (222 E Harris St.) is a lovely white French Gothic structure with brown trim; many stained-glass windows from Austria; Italian white-marble altar; hand-carved Stations of the Cross from Germany. Open daily. **Christ Church** (Johnson Sq.), founded in 1733, is the third church on this site; the present 1838 Greek Revival building is noted foɪ its ceiling cast from Christopher Wren's molds for St. Paul's Cathedral in London, Revere bell, and balcony. John Wesley was an early minister here. Open daily 9-5; free. The church sponsors annual (usually Apr.) historic tours. **Congregation Mickve Israel** (20 E Gordon St.), consecrated in 1878, is the oldest Reform temple in the nation. Founded to serve Sephardic Jews who came here in 1733, it contains a museum with the Sefer Torah they brought with them and letters to George Washington; open Mon.-Fri. 9-5; free. **Evangelical Lutheran Church of the Ascension** (Bull & State Sts.), was built 1876-79 in Norman and Gothic style by the congregation; fine baptismal font and stained-glass window. In the auditorium the history of the congregation is depicted in hand-made miniature scenes. Open daily. **Independent Presbyterian Church** (Bull St. & Oglethorpe Ave.), built in the 1890's, is modeled after St. Martin-in-the-Fields in London. Woodrow Wilson was married here. Open Sun.-Fri. **Wesley Monumental United Methodist Church** (429 Abercorn St.) is a Gothic-style memorial, based on Queen's Kirk in Amsterdam, Holland, to John and Charles Wesley, the founders of Methodism; Tiffany stained-glass windows; open daily; free.

Telfair Academy of Arts & Sciences (121 Barnard St.) is partly housed in an 1818 mansion by William Jay. American graphics and paintings; 18th-20th-C European paintings; textiles, furniture; good Colonial and Federal portraits; rare-book library. Tues.-Sat. 10-5, Sun. 2-5; closed hols; adm. **Savannah Science Museum** (4405 Paulsen St.) exhibits animal habitat groups, aquariums, Indian artifacts, and other scientific material. Open Mon.-Sat. 10-5, Sun. 2-5; closed hols; free. **Fort Jackson Maritime Museum** (Islands Expwy, 3 m E) is on the Savannah River and surrounded by a moat; maritime displays; open Tues.-Sat. 9-5:30, Sun. 2-5:30; closed Thnks, Dec. 25; free.

SAVANNAH BEACH: Tybee Museum (US 80, opp lighthouse) depicts the history of Georgia through dioramas, pictures, documents, and other exhibits. Open May-Sept. daily 10-6; Oct.-Apr., Mon., Wed.-Sat. 1-5, Sun. 1-6; closed Jan. 1, Thnks, Dec. 24, 25, 31; sm adm.

THOMASVILLE: Lapham-Patterson House (626 N Dawson St.), a restored Victorian mansion, is open Tues.-Sat. 9-5:30, Sun. 2-5:30; closed Thnks, Dec. 25; free. **Chamber of Commerce** (401 S Broad St.) arranges plantation tours daily exc. Sun.

TOCCOA: Traveler's Rest (6 m NE off US 123), probably built 1816-25 as a home, was expanded by Devereaux Jarret (who bought it in 1838) for use as a tavern, trading post, and post office; original furnishings; register and account books; outbuildings. Open Tues.-Sat. 9-5:30, Sun. 2-5:30; closed Thnks, Dec. 25; free.

WARM SPRINGS: Little White House (US 27A, SR 85W): In 1924, 3 yrs after contracting polio, Franklin D. Roosevelt came here and found the warm spring waters beneficial. In 1932, on a beautiful site where he liked to picnic, he built this snug little house, with a feeling of a ship's cabin about it. Inside are ship models, Fala's dog chain, and other mementos, as well as the unfinished portrait on which Elizabeth Shoumatoff was working when FDR suffered a cerebral hemorrhage on April 12, 1945. The museum shows a film of his life at the spring. Open daily 9-5 (9-6 on summer weekends); adm.

WASHINGTON: Chamber of Commerce (on the square) offers maps for self-guiding driving and walking tours through this lovely town of old gardens and 40 white-columned antebellum homes (30 predate 1850); some of these are splendid examples of Greek Revival, with Doric, Ionic, or Corinthian pillars, and were spared because no Civil War battles took place here. Among those open during semiannual home and garden tours are: **Cooley-Wickersham House**, once home of a descendant of Pocahontas; **Robert Toombs House**, home of the Confederate general; **Sarah Hillhouse House**, home of the first woman newspaper editor in the United States; **Ficklen-Lyndon-Johnson House**, where Jefferson Davis took refuge; **Charles Saunders House**, built in 1780; and the **Tupper-Barnett House**, typical of the early Federal homes that prospering cotton men converted to neoclassical mansions by the addition of colonnades. **Courthouse Square** has historic markers, one noting that Pres. Jefferson Davis convened the final Confederate Cabinet meeting here on May 5, 1865. On June 4, Union soldiers were able to find only a fifth of the Confederate Treasury, and legend says that the rest is still buried in or near Washington.

Washington-Wilkes Historical Museum (308 E Robert Toombs Ave.) is a rambling 18-room house, with 13 doors to the outside, built in 1835. It contains a restored kitchen, Ku Klux Klan regalia, Civil War memorabilia, Jefferson Davis keepsakes, Indian artifacts, and other miscellaneous items. Open Tues.-Sat. 9-5:30, Sun. 2-5:30; closed Thnks, Dec. 25; free.

Callaway Plantation (5 m W on US 78) is a complex of Greek Revival and Federal style homes, with period furnishings, a 1785 kitchen, and outbuildings on a working farm; craft demonstrations; displays of old tools and farm equipment. Open Apr. 15-Oct. 15, Mon.-Sat. 10-5:30, Sun. 2-5:30; free.

WAYNESBORO: Waynesboro Historical Museum (US 25, 1 block S of courthouse) offers artifacts of early history in an antebellum home; open Tues.-Sat. 9-5:30, Sun. 1-5:30; free.

HAWAII

HAWAII: City of Refuge National Historic Park (Honaunau) preserves one of the religious sanctuaries where people (including defeated warriors) could claim asylum during war or escape punishment after breaking a kapu (taboo). A Visitor Center (open daily 7:30-5:30) provides orientation and cultural demonstrations; restored Hale-o-Keawe, a temple where the bones of deified kings were kept; reconstructed dwellings, royal sledding chutes, burial and shelter caves, tikis, a konane-playing area.

Puukohola Heiau National Historic Site (near Kawaihae off SR 26): stone-constructed Hill of the Whale Temple, built in 1791 by Kamehameha the Great; two other heiaus; petroglyphs. Open daily exc Dec. 25.

Hikiau Heiau Historic Site State Monument (Napoopoo): partially restored ancient ceremonial site; open daily.

Hulihee Palace (Alii Dr. in Kailua) was built in 1838 as the summer residence of Hawaiian royalty; Queen Kapiolani's carved four-poster bed, King Kamehameha II's feathered cloak; other royal memorabilia; portrait gallery of royalty. Open Mon.-Fri. 9-4, Sat. 9-noon; adm.

Kamuela Museum (jct SR 25, 26 Waimea): early Hawaiian relics and art objects; items from the collections of royal families; possessions brought to the island by early settlers from other countries. Open daily 8-5; sm adm.

Lyman House Memorial Museum (276 Haili St. Hilo), built by missionaries, is the oldest home on the island; period furnishings; tapa cloth, feather leis, other choice Hawaiian artifacts. Open Mon.-Sat. 10-4, Sun. 1-4, hols 10-4; sm adm.

Painted Church (Honaunau, just off Mamalahoa Hwy.), whose official name is St. Benedict's Catholic Church, is named for the murals and frescoes that completely cover the interior. The ceiling is painted to resemble the sky, palms top the columns, the walls sport murals of biblical scenes, and a trompe l'oeil painting behind the altar gives the illusion that the tiny church is part of a huge cathedral. Several other churches also have painted interiors, but this is the best; early priests apparently believed these paintings would encourage attendance by the outdoors-loving Hawaiians. Open daily 8:30-5. **Dai Fukuji Mission** (Keauhou, just off Mamalahoa Hwy.) is a frame Buddhist temple with elaborate altars. You must remove your shoes to enter. Open daily 9-4:30; free. **Mokuaikaua Church** (Alii Dr. in Kailua), built in 1837, is built of lava stone with a lovely koa wood interior. **St. Peter's Church** (Alii Dr. in Kailua), on the sea, is a tiny, picturesque church.

KAUAI: 88 Holy Places of Kobo Daishi (just N of Lawai) contains 88 miniature Buddhist shrines, representing the 88 sins; visitors are believed to be cleansed; open daily; free.

Holo-Holo-Ku Heiau (Wailua), one of the oldest temples, has been restored by the Kauai Historical Society & Bishop Museum; sacrificial stone; Royal Birthstones, which noblewomen had to reach before childbirth to insure the royal status of infants; priest's quarters.

Wailua River State Park and Reserve (Wailua): ruins of temples that once lined the banks of the river; boat trip to Fern Canyon, where kings were buried in caves; remains of a city of refuge in Lydgate area; temple ruins, bell, and other sacred stones in the Poliahu Area.

Menehune Ditch (Waimea): ruin of a great watercourse or aqueduct built before the Hawaiians came by the Menehune (legend says they were great engineers, building bridges and dams in a single night). **Menehune Fish Pond** (Niumalu, S of Lihue), enclosed by ancient stone walls, is still used for fish rearing.

Kauai Museum (Lihue Shopping Center): small museum depicting history of the island; open Mon.-Sat. 9:30-4:30; adm. **Kokee Natural History Museum** (Kokee State Park): botanical and geological exhibits; petroglyph displays; open daily 8-4; free.

St. Sylvester's Church (Kilauea): striking, 8-sided, lava rock church; altar is in the center; brilliant frescoes by Jean Charlot; open daily.

MAUI: Hale Hoikeike (2375 Main St., Wailuku) is the Maui Historical Society Museum; ancient artifacts, missionary memorabilia; open Mon.-Sat. 10-3:30; closed hols; adm.

Haleakala National Park (26 m from airport), where Maui snared the sun and made it promise to travel more slowly, has a Visitor Center with exhibits on geology, archaeology, ecology; open daily 6:30-5:30 in summer, 8:30-3:30 rest of yr.

Halekii-Pihana Heiaus State Monument (2 m W of Kahului off SR 341): partly restored temples of worship, sacrifice, and refuge, ordered destroyed by King Kamehameha II in 1819.

Lahaina: This was the royal capital 1802-45 and also the whaling capital (in 1859, 549 ships had been anchored here). Lahaina Restoration Foundation has preserved buildings from several periods of its history. **Baldwin Home** (Front St.), a restored missionary home built in 1834, is open daily 9:30-5; adm. **Hale Pa'i,** the missionary printing shop at the school, displays the old press on which Hawaii's first newspaper was printed in 1834; open daily 10-4; adm. **Hale Paahao** (Prison St.), the old jail, was built for the obstreperous whaling crews during the mid-1800's. **Old Waiola Church** graveyard contains graves of former queens. **Jodo Mission** (Ala Moana St.) is a Buddhist temple; open daily; free. **Lahaina Art Society Gallery** (Front St.) exhibits work of local artists; open Mon.-Sat. 9:30-5:30; free.

Whaler's Village Museum (Kahana) scatters whaling relics among shops and restaurants.

OAHU: Byodo-in-Temple (47-2000 Kahekili Hwy., Kaneohe), set against mountains in the Valley of the Temples Memorial Park, is a stunning replica of a 900-year-old temple in Uji, Japan; main hall shaped like a bird about to soar; golden Buddha inside; nearby teahouse, graveyard, brass bell cast in Japan; open daily 9-5; adm.

Polynesian Cultural Center (Laie), a nonprofit Mormon project, is an authentically re-created 15-acre complex of villages representing life on various Pacific islands; demonstrations of everyday life, formal shows, other events; tours. Open Mon.-Sat. at 10:45, with varying closing hrs; adm. Nearby Mormon Temple is open only to members; formal gardens open to public daily 10-4; free.

U.S.S. Arizona National Memorial (free Navy shuttle from landing at Halawa Gate, off Kamehameha Hwy. at Pearl Harbor) is a white concrete structure spanning the still-sunken vessel that sank under Japanese bombardment on Dec. 7, 1941. Most of the 1177 men who died aboard are still entombed in the hull, and the ship has never been decommissioned. Memorial with historical exhibits. Shuttle operates Tues.-Sun. 9-3:30; children under 6 not admitted. Boat tours of Pearl Harbor are available from Navy Public Information Service, Tues.-Sat., several times daily free. **Schofield Army Museum** (Trimble Rd., Wahiawa) offers historical military items; open Wed.-Sun. 10-4; free.

Honolulu has many buildings designed in blends of Eastern and Western architectural styles; especially interesting are the religious buildings, including Japanese **Honpa Hongwanji Temple** (1727 Pali Hwy.), with a magnificent 12th-C Buddha carved in Japan; the Indian-style **Jodo Temple** (1429 Makiki St.); **Korean Christian Church** (1832 Liliha St.); **Kwan Yin Temple** (170 S Vineyard St.); **Makiki Christian Church** (829 Pensacola St.), based on a Japanese castle, with many painted interior panels; the Chinese-style **St. Luke's Church** (45 Judd St.); the **First Church of Christ, Scientist** (1508 Punahou St.) with a unique design incorporating lava rock and native woods.); **Kawaiahao Church** (King & Punchbowl Sts.), built in 1841 of coral rock, is called the Westminster Abbey of Hawaii because it served as the royal chapel for more than 20 years and was the scene of coronations and other events. Open Mon.-Sat. 8:30-4; Sun. services in English and Hawaiian. The grave of King Lunalilo, who asked to be buried with the people rather than with kings, is in the courtyard. **Manoa Chinese Cemetery Pavilion** (3355 E Manoa Rd.) houses fine Tseng Yu-ho paintings; you must ask permission to see the cemetery; open daily. **Soto Zen Buddhist Temple** (1708 Nuuanu Ave.): delicate Italian-style building with ornate altar, rich accessories, and 800-year-old statue of Buddha; interpretive lectures in English given weekdays 9-11; open Mon.-Sat.; closed Jan. 1.

State Capitol (Hotel St.) represents the islands, with domes resembling volcanic cones, pools and columns representing ocean and palms; interior koa wood paneling; native crafts. A statue of Father Damien by Marisol is in front. Open daily, free. **Hawaii State Library** (478 S King at Punchbowl Sts.): materials on Hawaii and the Pacific; films; art exhibitions; open Mon.-Sat. 9-5, later some evenings; free.

Bishop Museum (1355 Kalihi St.) has splendid collections of Pacific and Hawaiian arts and artifacts; carved canoe prows, feather capes, helmets, kahĭlis; throne, crown, other memorabilia of the monarchy; miniature heiau depicting religious practices; other displays on Hawaiian culture. Open Mon.-Sat. 9-5, Sun. noon-5; closed Jan. 1, Easter, Thnks, Dec. 25; adm (combination tickets and bus service available to other Bishop Museum sites). **Hawaii Science Center,** adjacent, offers daily planetarium shows; adm. **Falls of Clyde,** a four-masted square-rigger built in 1878 and restored by the museum, is open daily 10-5 (later many evenings); adm. **Heritage Theater** (King's Alley, Waikiki), run by the Bishop Museum, documents Hawaiian royal history 1700-1900 through exhibitions and live performances; open 9 am-11 pm.

    Iolani Palace State Memorial (King & Richards Sts.), the U.S.'s only royal palace, is an 1881 ornate Italian Rennaissance style building; restored throne room; living and servants' quarters. Open Mon.-Fri. 8-noon, 1-4, Sat. 8-noon; free. Nearby are the reconstructed Iolani Barracks designed of coral block by a German craftsman. Also on the grounds are the Archives of Hawaii, with the most complete collection of Hawaiiana in the nation; open business hrs; closed hols; free. King Kamehameha's Statue (facing the palace).

    Queen Emma Summer Palace (2913 Pali Hwy., Nuuanu Valley): restored former home of the queen and Kamehameha IV; collection of Hawaiiana; open Mon.-Fri. 9-4, Sat. 9-noon; closed hols; adm. **Royal Mausoleum State Memorial** (2261 Nuuana Ave.): Sacred burial ground of Kamehameha and Kalakaua dynasties; open Mon.-Fri. 8-4, Sat. 8-noon; free. **Queen's Medical Center** (1301 Punchbowl St.): display of old Hawaiian medicinal plants on 1st floor; open Mon.-Fri. 8-5; free. **Mission Houses Museum** (533 S King St.): artifacts from the missionary era, including the islands' first printing press; open Mon.-Fri. 9-4, Sat. 9-1; closed Jan. 1, Thnks, Dec. 25; adm. On grounds is the Mission Historical Library, open Tues.-Fri. 9-4, Sat. 9-1. **Kamehameha Schools** (Kapalama Hts.), established for Hawaiian children, inherited the estate of the Kamehameha dynasty; visitors welcome. **Hawaii 1800 Museum** (grounds of Hilton Hawaii Village & Rainbow Bazaar): slides, pictures, Hawaiian royal artifacts; open daily 10-10; adm.

    Honolulu Academy of the Arts (900 S Beretania St.): excellent Oriental art; Kress Collection of Italian Renaissance painting; other Western works; local art; craft demonstrations, other activities. They can tell you about galleries showing work of contemporary Hawaiian artists. Open Tues.-Sat. 10-4:30, Sun. 2-5; free. The Academy maintains **Alice Cooke Spalding House** (2411 Makiki Hts. Dr.), with an impressive collection of Asian arts; open Tues.-Sun. 1-4:30; adm (free on Tues.).

    University of Hawaii: Office of University Relations (101 Bachman Hall) offers free guided tours (Mon.-Fri. at 1:30) or self-guiding maps. Bachman Hall has murals by Jean Charlot; murals by other island artists

are in Bilger Hall, Keller Hall, and the Music Building. Art Gallery
(George Hall) has changing exhibits. East-West Center has a Thai pavilion
donated by the king of Thailand.

Robert Louis Stevenson's Grass House (3016 Oahu Ave.), moved here
from Waikiki, contains mementos. It is maintained by the Salvation Army
along with the little chapel built for children; open Mon.-Sat. 9-4; free.

IDAHO

BOISE: State Capitol (8th & Jefferson Sts.) houses changing exhibits;
open daily 8-6; free.

Boise Gallery of Art (Julia Davis Park), with emphasis on Idaho
artists, includes European, American, and Oriental painting and sculpture;
open Tues.-Sun. 10-5; closed Thnks, Dec. 25-Jan. 2; free.

U.S. Assay Office (210 Main St.) built in 1871 soon after the gold rush
began in this area, was operated until the mid-1930's. The first floor
housed vaults, offices, and laboratories, and the second floor was used
as living quarters; open Mon.-Fri. 10-5; sm adm.

Idaho State Historical Society Museum (610 N Julia Davis Dr.) of
pioneer and Indian life is open Mon.-Fri. 9-5, Sat. & Sun. 1-5; closed
Jan. 1, Easter, Dec. 25; free. The society also maintains an outdoor display of early state architecture.

CHALLIS NATIONAL FOREST: Bonanza (8 m N of Sunbeam) is a
ghost town that boomed to 1500 people by 1889, with 9 saloons, 2 hotels,
2 general stores, and a newspaper; only a few cabins remain. Its cemetery
was shared with **Custer** (2 m beyond Bonanza), which boomed to 3500
people in the 1800's when gold and silver mines were opened. Custer Ghost
Town Museum is open daily, mid-June-early Sept., 10-6. A saloon and
cabins also survive.

FORT HALL: The Lander Cut-off of the Oregon Trail has been marked
from here to South Pass, Wyoming; booklets for a self-guiding tour can be
obtained from any BLM or Forest Service office adjacent to the trail.

FRANKLIN: This was Idaho's first settlement, begun in 1860 by
Mormons who thought they were in Utah. **Pioneer Relic Hall** contains
early artifacts, including the steam engine that Brigham Young had shipped

up the Missouri River, and then overland to Franklin. Open Mon.-Fri. 9-5; free.

HAILEY: Blaine County Historical Museum (N Main St.) is a small museum with an unusually large collection of arrowheads, mementos of poet Ezra Pound (born in Hailey), local historical items; memorabilia from political campaigns (badges, pennants, buttons) from the late 1800's. Open June 15-Sept. 15, Wed.-Mon. 10-5; sm adm.

IDAHO CITY: Now a tiny town, this was one of the most notorious of the gold rush cities in the early 1860's. Gold Hill (1 m N on Main St.) is rich placer country and gold flecks are found in much of the town's gravel today. **Boise Basin Museum** (Montgomery & Wall Sts.) records the gold rush days; open Memorial Day-Sept., Mon.-Fri. 2-4, Sat. & Sun. 1-5; sm adm. **Boot Hill,** the restored 40-acre cemetery, contains tombstones of many well-known outlaws; of 200 burials in 1863, only 23 of the deaths had been due to natural causes. **Masonic Hall** (Montgomery St.), erected in 1865, is open Apr.-Oct. daily 9-5, free; and **Pioneer Lodge #1, IOOF,** contains its original 1875 furnishings and is still in use (open on request). Nearby ghost towns (W beyond the airport) include Old Centerville, Pioneerville, and Placerville.

KELLOGG: Cataldo Mission (11 m W off US 10 in Cataldo), the Jesuit Mission of the Sacred Heart, was built between 1848-53 with the most primitive of tools by missionaries and Coeur d'Alene Indians. Indian murals depict heaven and hell, and behind the altar Indians left their hand-prints. The altar, statues, and other decorative elements are handcarved. Old cemetery. On Aug. 15 a special Indian mass is still given here. Open Apr. 15-Sept., daily 9-dark; rest of yr on request; sm adm.

LEWIS & CLARK TRAIL: Scenic US 12, called the **Lewis & Clark Highway,** parallels the path of the 1805 expedition and its return E in 1806.

The exact path of the expedition was on the **Lolo Trail,** used by Indian buffalo hunters from Idaho to Montana, which you can reach N off US 12 at Powell ranger station (where Lewis and Clark camped on Sept. 14, 1805 and were forced to kill one of their horses for food). Here you can get a map and information on road conditions; it's a rough road, usually open Mid-July-early Sept., depending on weather.

MASSACRE ROCKS STATE PARK (N along US 30, W of American Falls), on the Snake River, commemorates a narrow passage on the Oregon Trail where Shoshone ambushed a wagon train in 1862, killing about a dozen whites. **Visitor Center** (daily mid-May-mid-Sept. 9-6) has interpretive displays. At Rock Creek Camp, a favorite rest stop, travelers recorded their names and dates on rocks; the largest of these, Register Rock, is surrounded by a protective enclosure. Park open all yr.

MONTPELIER: Daughters of Utah Pioneers Historical Museum (430 Clay St.) is open June.-Aug., Mon.-Sat. 4-9; free.

MOSCOW: On the exceptionally handsome campus of the **University of Idaho,** the Administration Building (with a turreted clock tower) can give you information and a map. The university has one of the state's most complete historical archives, many Indian artifacts, historical displays, mineral displays at the Idaho Bureau of Mines, a Forest Sciences Laboratory, and Shattuck Arboretum.

Latah County Pioneer Museum (110 S Adams), in an 1880 Victorian mansion, houses dioramas and artifacts illustrating local history; open Wed., Sun. 2-5, Sat. 10-noon; adm. **Appaloosa Horse Museum** (Pullman Hwy.) exhibits saddles and cowboy gear, Nez Perce artifacts, and a history of the horse's development by the Nez Perce. Open Mon.-Fri. 8-5; closed hols; free.

NAMPA: Owyhee County Historical Museum (via SR 45 S, then SR 78 S to Murphy), a block behind the courthouse, includes gold rush material; open Thurs. 9-5, Sun. 1-5; free.

Silver City (23 m SW of Murphy on county road) is a picturesque ghost town, once the Owyhee County Seat (1866-1935). In the 1860's it served the 250 gold and silver mines in the area, and Idaho's first daily newspaper was printed here. Among many buildings still intact are shops, Masonic Hall, the gingerbread-trimmed Victorian hotel, and the schoolhouse (open in summer, daily 10-6; free). Gold Chariot Mine is on War Eagle Mountain. Hillside cemetery. Nearby are the traces of Ruby City and Dewey, and a few deserted buildings of what was once DeLamar.

NEZ PERCE NATIONAL HISTORICAL PARK (headquarters at Spalding, 15 m E of Lewiston via US 95), mostly on the Nez Perce reservation, consists of 23 historic sites that preserve the culture of the Nez Perce. Initially these Indians had good relations with whites and in 1855 signed a treaty defining their tribal boundaries. But when gold was discovered on their land in 1860, miners demanded that the treaty be renegotiated to remove 7 million acres from the Nez Perce. A group of Nez Perce led by Chief Joseph refused to renegotiate; hostilities broke out; the Nez Perce were defeated and sent to a reservation in Washington. A self-guiding auto trail (booklets available in Lewiston, Spalding, Lolo Pass) begins at

MacKenzie's Trading Post (in Clarkston, W of Lewiston, on US 12), established by fur traders working for Jacob Astor in 1812 but closed a year later when the Nez Perce explained they never trapped animals and had no desire to learn this skill. At **Spalding,** park headquarters, there's a museum open daily 8-4:30 (8-dusk in summer); closed Jan. 1, Thnks, Dec. 25, weekends in Dec. and Feb.; free.

OROFINO: Clearwater County Historical Museum (College Ave.) has exhibits of frontier days; open Tues.-Sat. 1:30-4:30; free. Nez Perce arts and crafts are displayed in the same building.

POCATELLO: Idaho State University offers a **Museum** (in Library Bldg.) of local anthropological and palaeontological materials; open Mon.-Fri. 8-5; free. The **Art Gallery** (Fine Arts Bldg.) houses changing exhibits; open Mon.-Fri. noon-5, Sat. & Sun. 2-4; free.
  Old Fort Hall Replica (Ross Park, 3 m S at S 2nd Ave.) houses historic displays in a blacksmith shop and other buildings. The fort had been an independent fur trading post that the Hudson's Bay Co. took over, and later was used by immigrants on the Oregon Trail. Open June-Sept. 15, daily 9-8; Apr.-May, Wed.-Sun. 9-1; free.
  Bannock County Historical Museum (Center St. & Garfield Ave.) contains many mementos of early railroad days, the fur trade, and Shoshone culture. Open Mon.-Sat. 2-5; closed hols; free.

SALMON: Lemhi County Historical Museum (W Main St.) is open Apr.-Oct., Mon.-Sat. 10-noon, 1-5; closed hols; free.

TWIN FALLS: Twin Falls County Historical Society Museum (3 m W on US 30) has exhibits of pioneer life; open Mon.-Fri. 10-5, Sun. 2-5; closed hols; sm adm. **Herrett Arts & Science Center** (1220 Kimberly Rd.) offers a museum open Mon.-Sat. 9-5:30; closed hols. Planetarium and observatory open on request.

WALLACE: Coeur d'Alene District Mining Museum (509 Bank St.) has fine displays; you can also get information here on nearby mine tours and ghost towns. Open Mon.-Fri. 10-4; June.-Aug. open Mon.-Sat. 9-6; closed hols; free.

WEISER: Historical Museum & National Fiddlers' Hall of Fame (44 W Commercial St.) contains local historic exhibits and memorabilia related to folk music. Open June-Labor Day, Thurs.-Sat. 10-noon, 1-4; closed hols; free.

ILLINOIS

ARLINGTON HEIGHTS: Historical Society Museum (500 N Vail Ave.) offers local historical exhibits in an 1882 home, reconstructed log cabin, and outbuildings; open Wed. 2-4, Sat. 1-4, Sun. 2-5; closed Jan. 1, Easter, Dec. 25; sm adm.

ATHENS: Long Nine Museum: reconstructed 1832 building where Lincoln and other members of the "Long Nine" celebrated their victory in moving Illinois' capital from Vandalia to Springfield. Dioramas and other displays portray Lincoln's life. Open Mon.-Sat. 10-5, Sun. noon-5; adm.

AURORA: Aurora Historical Museum (304 Oak Ave. at Cedar St.), in an 1857 house; period furnishings, portraits; 1905 astronomical clock by Blanford; Indian artifacts; fossils and minerals; Carriage House (open May-Oct., weather permitting); blacksmith shop. Open Wed., Sun. 2-4:30; closed hols; donation.

BEARDSTOWN: Beardstown City Hall (State St. & W 3rd St.) was the Cass County Courthouse; here Lincoln defended Duff Armstrong in the Almanac Trial; courtroom has been restored. Open daily 9-5; free.

BLOOMINGTON: Illinois State University (off I-55 in Normal) campus contains: **Historical Museum** (Milner Library, room 051) with early Americana; open Mon.-Fri. 10-5; Sun. 2-5; free. **Funk Gem & Mineral Museum** (Cook Hall) is open Sun.-Fri. 2-5; free. **Eyestone School Museum,** a restored and furnished one-room schoolhouse, and the **Hudelson Agriculture Museum,** with antique farm equipment, are open Tues., Thurs., Sun. 2-5; free. **Ewing Museum of Nations,** with art works from around the world, is open Tues., Thurs., Sun. 2-5; free. **Adlai E. Stevenson memorabilia** (Mon.-Fri. 2-5 or by appointment; free). Museums are closed national and school holidays.

    Clover Lawn (1000 E Monroe Dr.), 20-room mansion of Lincoln's friend David Davis, contains ornate Renaissance-style furnishings; open Tues.-Sun. 1-5; closed hols; free.

CAHOKIA: Historic Holy Family Mission Log Church (jct SR 3, 157), oldest church in the state, in continuous use since 1799; cemetery; open daily; donation. Adjacent Federal-style **Jarrot Mansion,** built about 1880, is open Sat. & Sun. 1-4; donation. **Cahokia Courthouse State Memorial** (214 W 1st St.), built about 1737 as a home, served as courthouse and jail 1793-1814; open daily in summer 9-5, in winter 8-4; closed Jan. 1, Thnks, Dec. 25; free.

CAHOKIA MOUNDS STATE PARK (5 m E of East St. Louis on US 40-Bus): remains of the largest prehistoric city N of Mexico, built by people of Mississippian culture about 850, and abandoned by 1500. The city covered some 6 sq m, had more than a hundred mounds and a population of tens of thousands. A museum displays artifacts. Open daily 9-5; free.

CAIRO: Magnolia Manor (2714 Washington Ave.) was built in 1869 by a wealthy merchant; Pres. & Mrs. Grant were entertained here in 1880; maintained in all its former splendor by the Cairo Historical Association; historical items from the city and surrounding area (known as "Little Egypt"). Open daily 9-5; closed Jan. 1, Dec. 25; adm.

CARMI: Ratcliff Inn (216 E Main St.), now a museum with historical exhibits, was where Lincoln stayed during an 1840 political rally. Open Mon.-Fri. 1-5, Sat. 10-noon; free. **Robinson-Stewart House Museum** (110 S Main Cross St.), built in 1814, served as a courthouse; early 18th-C furnishings; garden. Open Sept.-June, Mon.-Fri. 4-5, Sat. & Sun. 1-4; July-Aug., Sun.-Fri. 1-4, Sat. 10-5; closed Thnks, Dec. 25; sm adm.

CARTHAGE: Old Carthage Jail (307 Walnut St.), where Joseph Smith, founder of the Mormon Church, and his brother Hyrum were killed by a mob in 1844, offers a film and tour. Open daily 8-sunset; closed Dec. 25; free.

CHARLESTON: Chamber of Commerce will open on request: **Coles County Courthouse** (Charleston Sq.), where Lincoln practiced; scene of the Civil War Charleston Riot; museum of Lincoln memorabilia. **Lincoln-Douglas Debate House** (Fairgrounds), where the Sept. 18, 1858 debate took place.

CHICAGO: To remain a vigorous trade center after its devastating Great Fire of 1871, Chicago had to rebuild quickly. Engineers, working with great architects such as Louis Sullivan, developed concepts that led to skyscrapers and glass-wrapped buildings. Here, too, Sullivan's pupil Frank Lloyd Wright developed the "Prairie Houses" whose design elements have become standard. Architectural innovation continued with the arrival of Mies van der Rohe and other European masters, so that now the city is a living museum of urban architectural development. Tours sponsored by the **Chicago School of Architecture Foundation** (see Glessner House, below) cover the downtown Loop area, the 30 or so Frank Lloyd Wright houses in Oak Park and River Forest, and other landmarks; the Foundation can also supply you with maps and books for self-guiding tours. **Glessner House** (1800 S Prairie Ave.), built in 1886, is the last surviving work by Henry Hobson Richardson; restored by the Chicago School of Architecture Foundation; Frank Lloyd Wright furniture and other exhibits. Open Tues., Thurs., Sat. 10-4, Sun. 1-5; adm.

   Chicago Water Tower (800 N Michigan Ave.), a Gothic castle-like structure erected in 1869, survived the 1871 fire and is a landmark. **Monadnock Building** (53 W Jackson Blvd.), the world's largest office building at the time of construction (1891-93), is still the largest masonry building; designed by Burnham & Root and Holabird & Roche (each firm designed a half); open business hours. **The Rookery** (209 S LaSalle St.), completed in 1888, is the oldest remaining steel-skeleton "skyscraper" (11 stories) in the world; lobby remodeled by Frank Lloyd Wright in 1905; open business hours. **Auditorium Theater** (50 E Congress Pkwy.) was designed by Louis Sullivan and Dankmar Adler in 1889; tours can be arranged. **Holy Trinity Russian Orthodox Cathedral** (1121 N Leavitt) is a tiny and simple 1903 structure by Sullivan that incorporates traditional elements. **Chicago Civic Center** (66 W Washington St.) was designed by Skidmore, Owings & Merrill under the influence of Mies van der Rohe and completed in 1966. In the plaza is the 50-ft sculpture, made of the same steel as the building, that Pablo Picasso designed for this site and donated to the city.

   Old Town (roughly bounded by W North Ave., Ogden Ave., and N Clark St.) is called the Greenwich Village of the Midwest; its restored Victorian buildings now house boutiques, pubs, and restaurants, especially along N Wells St.; 1826-1834 Lincoln Park West are row houses designed by Sullivan in 1884. **The Gold Coast** (Lake Shore Dr. from North Ave. to Oak St.) once replete with mansions, is now lined with apartment houses; the twin towers at 860-880 Lake Shore Dr. were designed by Mies in 1951. **Marina City** (Dearborn at the Chicago River), designed by Bertrand Goldberg, is two cylindrical, 60-story towers housing living and commercial quarters.

   Pullman Community (104th to 115th St. at Calumet Expwy.) was established in 1880 by George Pullman (designer of the Pullman overnight railroad cars) and was the first planned company town in the nation; preserved as an outdoor museum of city planning and Chicago labor history.

   Riverside (between Harlem, Ogden, and 1st Aves., & 26th St.) was a planned community designed in 1869 by Frederick Law Olmsted and

Calvert Vaux. They also designed the Swiss cottage (100 Fairbank Rd.). Many homes designed by other major architects include a Gothic cottage by W. L. B. Jenney (124 Scottswood Rd.), two buildings by Louis Sullivan (277 and 281 Gatesby Rd.), and Frank Lloyd Wright's famous Coonley House (281 Bloomingbank Rd.).

Art Institute of Chicago (Michigan Ave. & Adams St.): one of the nation's foremost art museums; painting collection ranging from the 14th C to the present, with particularly fine Impressionist and Post-Impressionist work. Japanese print collection is outstanding. Also Chinese sculpture and bronzes, primitive art, textiles; Thorne collection of period rooms in miniature. Open Thurs. 10-8:30; free. Open Mon.-Wed., Fri., Sat. 10-5; Sun. & hols noon-5; adm. Closed Dec. 25.

Museum of Contemporary Art (237 E Ontario St.) has temporary exhibits only. Open Mon.-Wed., Fri., Sat., 10-5; Thurs. 10-8; Sun. noon-5; closed Jan. 1, Thnks, Dec. 25, between exhibits; adm. **Loyola University Martin D'Arcy Art Gallery** (6526 N Sheridan) features 16th-C and Renaissance art and sculpture; open Mon.-Fri. noon-4, Sun. 1-4; free. **Fountain of Time** (in Washington Park, W of Cottage Grove Ave.), designed by Lorado Taft (1860-1936), is a group of more than 100 figures representing humanity being observed by Father Time.

Chicago Historical Society (N Clark St. & North Ave.): outstanding displays on Lincoln and the Civil War; Great Chicago Fire; demonstrations of pioneer crafts; costumes; Pioneer, the city's first locomotive. Superb library of Americana. Open Mon.-Sat. 9:30-4:30, Sun. & hols 12:30-5:30; closed Jan. 1, Thnks, Dec. 25; sm adm.

Chicago Public Library (78 E Washington St.), built in 1897, has colored marbles, mosaics, Tiffany lamps, a 4th-floor room resembling the Doge's Palace in Venice, stained glass, and carved woodwork. The library houses more than 5 million volumes. Open Mon.-Fri. 9-9, Sat. 9-5:30; closed hols; free. **Crerar Library** (35 W 33rd St.), with outstanding medical and technical volumes among more than a million books, is open Mon.-Thurs. 8:30 am-10 pm, Fri. & Sat. 8:30-5; closed hols; free.

Hull House (Halsted at Polk Sts. on Univ. of Illinois Chicago Circle campus), built in 1856, is the famous social settlement founded by Jane Addams; restored and furnished; open daily 10-4; closed hols; free.

Du Sable Museum of African-American History (740 E 56th Pl.): displays of black history in America, African art objects; library; open Tues.-Fri. 10-5, Sat. & Sun. 1-5; sm adm. **Polish Museum** (984 Milwaukee Ave.): archives and artifacts collected by the Polish Roman Catholic Union; open Mon.-Fri. 1-4; free. **Balzekas Museum of Lithuanian Culture** (4012 S Archer Ave.): antiquities, artifacts, and literature spanning 800 yrs of Lithuanian history; open daily 1-4:30; closed Jan. 1, Dec. 25; free.

Chinatown (Cermak Rd. & Wentworth St.) has a **Chinese Temple** (2216 S Wentworth) open noon-10, and the **Ling Long Chinese Museum** (2238 S Wentworth) open daily 1-9.

Spertus Museum of Judaica (72 E 11 St.): large private collection of Jewish artifacts, manuscripts, and ceremonial objects; open Mon.-Thurs. 10-4, Sun. exc in Summer 10-3; free. **Morton B. Weiss Museum of Judaica** (1100 E. Hyde Park Blvd.): Unusual collection of Iranian Judaica; open after Fri. evening or Sat. morning services or by appointment.

Field Museum of Natural History (Roosevelt Rd. & Lake Shore Dr. in Grant Park), one of the world's finest museums, offers more than 10 acres of exhibits. Highlights include bird and mammal dioramas, primitive arts, American Indian cultures, civilizations of China and Tibet, halls of minerals. Open Fri. all year 9-9; free. Open mid-June-Labor Day, Mon.-Thurs. 9-6, weekends 9-9; Mar.-Apr., & after Labor Day-Oct., Sat.-Thurs. 9-5; Nov.-Feb., Mon.-Thurs. 9-4, weekends 9-5; May-mid-June, Sat.-Thurs. 9-6; closed Jan. 1, Dec. 25; adm.

Museum of Science & Industry (Jackson Park at 57th St.): 2000 displays in 75 halls (many can be animated) include a walkthrough coal mine, German sub, spacecraft, human heart model, chicken incubators, miniature circus; open daily 9:30-4 (to 5:30 spring-late fall, and to 6 Sun. & hols); free.

Adler Planetarium (1300 S Lake Shore Dr.): exhibits on astronomy, instrumentation, and space technology; open mid-June-Aug., daily 9:30-9; Sept.-mid-June, Mon., Wed., Thurs. 9:30-4:30, Tues. & Fri. 9:30-9:30, weekends & hols 9:30-5; closed Jan. 1, Thnks, Dec. 25; free. Double feature shows daily in Universe and Sky Theaters; adm; children under 6 not admitted.

John G. Shedd Aquarium (1200 S Lake Shore Dr.): more than 7000 fish; open Fri. all yr 9-9; free. Other days: May-Aug. 9-5; Mar.-Apr. & Sept.-Oct. 10-5; Nov.-Feb. 10-4; adm. Closed Jan. 1, Dec. 25.

Chicago Academy of Sciences (2001 N Clark St.) has exhibits on nature and ecology; open daily 10-5; closed Dec. 25; free.

International College of Surgeons Hall of Fame (1524 N Lake Shore Dr.): exhibits demonstrating the history of medicine; open daily 10-4; free. **American College of Surgeons** (55 E Erie St.): exhibits on pioneer instruments and books; open Mon.-Fri. 8:30-4:45; closed hols; free.

Chicago Board of Trade (141 W Jackson Blvd.), world's largest grain market; visitor center with films, talks, and viewing deck, open Mon.-Fri. 9:30-3; closed hols; free; no children under 16. **Midwest Stock Exchange** (120 S LaSalle St.) the largest outside of New York's; visitor gallery with explanation; open Mon.-Fri. 9-2:30; closed hols; free. **Chicago Mercantile Exchange** (444 W Jackson Blvd.), world's leading futures-trading market for perishables; visitor gallery open Mon.-Fri. 9-1; closed hols; free; tours only by appointment. Here also is the **International Monetary Market,** open same hrs; free.

University of Chicago (on the S Side flanking the Midway) offers tours of the campus (1212 E 59th St.) on Sat. at 10 am. Older buildings are Gothic, and modern structures are by Mies van der Rohe, Eero Saarinen, Edward Durell Stone, and others. **Robie House** (5757 S Woodlawn Ave.) is by Frank Lloyd Wright. **Rockefeller Memorial Chapel** (1156 E 59th St.), with a 72-bell carillon, is open daily and tours are given after Sun. services. **"Nuclear Energy"** (Ellis Ave. between E 56-57 Sts.) marks the site of Enrico Fermi's laboratory and the first controlled nuclear reaction. **Oriental Institute Museum** (1155 E 58th St.): handsome collections of arts and archaeological materials from Babylon, Thebes, Egypt, Palestine. Open Tues.-Sun. 10-5; closed hols; free.

Illinois Institute of Technology, on a campus designed by Mies van der Rohe, offers tours (10 W 33rd St.) Sept.-May on Sat. at 10. **Teller Brass & Copper Collection** (10 W 33rd St.) with more than 3000 items from around the world is open Mon.-Fri. 9-9, Sat. 9-4; free.

DANVILLE: Lincoln had a law office here. **Vermilion County Museum** (116 N Gilbert St.) is in an 1855 home that belonged to William Fithian, a physician with whom Lincoln used to stay; period furnishings; a small natural history museum, art gallery, and Dr. Fithian's office. Thurs.-Sat. 10-5, Wed. 10-9, Sun. & hols 1-5; closed Thnks, Dec. 25; sm adm.

DECATUR: Lincoln Log Cabin Courthouse replica (Fairview Park, jct US 36, SR 48), where Lincoln practiced law; open daily 8-sunset; free.

DE KALB: Ellwood House (509 N 1st St.) is a Victorian mansion, once home of Col. Isaac Ellwood, with family furnishings. De Kalb was known as Barb City because barbed wire was invented here, and Col. Ellwood was an early manufacturer; displays on barbed wire show its role in changing the West. Open spring-early Dec., Wed., Sun. 2-4:30; other time by appointment; adm.

DIXON: Lincoln Monument State Memorial (on N bank of Rock River between Galena & Peoria Aves.) is on the site of the Dixon Blockhouse, the southernmost point on the Black Hawk Trail, established as a trading post by John Dixon. The statue shows Lincoln in 1832, when he enlisted in the Black Hawk War and was unanimously elected captain of his company. Among others at the blockhouse in 1832 were Jefferson Davis, Zachary Taylor, and Robert Anderson. Open daily; free. **Old Settlers' Memorial Log Cabin** (Lincoln Statue Dr.), built in 1894, is a memorial to area pioneers; period furnishings; open May-late Oct., Sat., Sun., hols 1:30-5; donation.

DICKSON MOUNDS STATE MUSEUM (on SR 78, 97 between Lewistown & Havana), in the shape of a mound, is built over excavation of 237 graves; audiovisual program; handsome displays trace Indian life from the Paleo through Mississippian Periods; remains of 950-1200 village; open daily 8:30-5; closed Jan. 1, Easter, Thnks, Dec. 25; free.

EDWARDSVILLE: Madison County Historical Museum (715 N Main St.) is open Wed., Fri. 9-5, Sat. 1-5, Sun. 2-5; closed hols; free.

ELGIN: Laura Davison Sears Academy of Fine Arts has a museum with Peale and Stuart portraits of George Washington, 2 Corot pastoral scenes, Whistler's Ostend scene, and a few other works; open during the school year.

ELMHURST: Lizzadro Museum of Lapidary Art (220 Cottage Hill Ave. in Wilder Park) has brilliant displays of gems and art objects made from gemstones; prehistoric and Oriental carvings; dioramas with animals carved from semiprecious stones; fossils. Gem cutting and other programs. Open Tues.-Fri. & Sun. 1-5, Sat. 10-5; closed Jan. 1, Easter, July 4, Thnks, Dec. 25; sm adm (free Fri.).

EVANSTON: Northwestern University offers campus walking tours during academic year on weekday afternoons and Sat. morning by advance reservation; tours leave from 633 Clark St. **Dearborn Observatory** (2131 Sheridan Rd.) has public viewings on Fri. evening; free. **Lindheimer Astronomical Research Center** is open to the public Sat. 2-4; free. **Technological Institute** (2145 Sheridan Rd.) gives tours Sat. at 11 am; free. **Deering Library** has changing art exhibits and many rare books; open daily; free. **Shakespeare Garden** (E on Garret off Sheridan Rd.) contains plants mentioned in Shakespeare's works.

Evanston Historical Society (225 Greenwood Ave. at Sheridan Rd.) is in the 1894 home of Charles G. Dawes, Vice President under Calvin Coolidge. Displays on local history, period rooms, Indian artifacts. Open Mon., Tues., Thurs., Fri. 1-5, Sat. 9-noon; closed hols; sm adm.

National Women's Christian Temperance Union (1730 Chicago Ave.) maintains the 1865 Gothic-style Frances E. Willard Home; memorabilia of the WCTU founder; history of the organization; library in adj building. Open Mon.-Fri. 9-5, weekends and hols by appointment; free.

FORT DE CHARTRES STATE PARK (W of Prairie du Rocher via SR 155), on the Mississippi River, was site of successive forts built from

1719 onward to protect France's claim to the river. Some of the fort ruins have been reconstructed, and a museum houses historical displays. Interpretive programs in summer. Open daily 8-5; closed hols; free.

FORT KASKASKIA STATE PARK (9 m N of Chester, off SR 3 near Ellis Grove) is site of the historic 1733 wooden fort built to guard the old capital of Kaskaskia. The fort was rebuilt by the French in 1761 and then destroyed to prevent the British from taking it over after the Treaty of Paris. **Garrison Hill cemetery,** with 3800 pioneer graves removed from Old Kaskaskia, is nearby. **Pierre Menard Home,** fine French colonial architecture, was begun in 1802 by Menard (first lieutenant governor of Illinois); restored with many original furnishings; open daily 9-5; closed Jan. 1, Thnks, Dec. 25; free. **Kaskaskia Bell Memorial** (on Kaskaskia Island) houses the "Liberty Bell of the West" which rang on July 4, 1778 after George Rogers Clark captured Kaskaskia without a shot and convinced the inhabitants to support the American cause.

FORT MASSAC STATE PARK (off US 45 between Metropolis and Brookport), on the Ohio River: In 1757, the French built a fort here. After the French & Indian War, the fort was ceded to the British, and the Chickasaw promptly burned it down. In 1794, Pres. Washington ordered Mad Anthony Wayne to rebuild it to protect economic expansion; in 1805 it was scene of a plot by Aaron Burr and James Wilkinson to create a separate country W of the Alleghenies. Restored; interpretive programs.

FREEPORT: Stephenson County Historical Museum (1440 S Carroll Ave.): in an 1857 stone house; period furnishings; memorabilia of Jane Addams, born in nearby Cedarville; Lincoln-Douglas debate material. Open Fri.-Sun. 1:30-5; closed hols; donation. On the grounds is a typical Illinois farm with blacksmith shop and schoolhouse, open June-Oct., Fri.-Sun. 1:30-5; closed hols; free.

GALENA: Chamber of Commerce (221 S Main St.) offers a map for a self-guiding walking tour. Galena, the most important city of the Old Northwest Territory, retains many buildings constructed before the turn of the century; these are usually open for tours several times a year.

Galena Historical Society (211½ S Bench St.) maintains the adjacent Galena Historical Museum and Firehouse. Exhibits include clothing, toys, guns, Civil War memorabilia, Thomas Nast painting of surrender at Appomattox. Open May-Oct., daily 9-5; sm adm.

Old Market House State Memorial (at the river between Hill & Perry Sts.): outstanding architectural display. Open daily 10-5; closed Jan. 1, Thnks, Dec. 25; free.

Dowling House (N Main & Diagonal Sts.): oldest home in Galena, built in 1826 by a merchant; restored to original appearance as home and miner's trading post. Open late May-Oct., Mon.-Fri. 9-5, Sat. & Sun. 9-6; adm. **Orrin-Smith House** (600 Park Ave.): built by a riverboat captain in 1852; Italianate mansion typical of showplaces of the period; June-Oct. daily 9-5; adm.

Turney House (612 Spring St.): restored home and law offices; built about 1835; open late May-Oct., Mon.-Fri. 9-5, Sat. & Sun. 9-6; adm. **Stockade** (N Main & Perry Sts.) was a refuge for settlers during the 1832 Black Hawk War; Black Hawk Indian Museum, underground rooms. Open May-Oct., daily 9-5; sm adm. **Old General Store** (223 S Main St.) is open May-Oct. daily 9-5; sm adm. **The Belvedere** (1008 Park Ave.), now a hotel, was a mansion built in 1857 in Steamboat Gothic. **Grace Episcopal Church** (Hill & Prospect Sts.): early English Gothic style; lovely Belgian stained glass windows; hand-carved walnut altar; organ brought by steamboat from New Orleans in 1838. Open daily 10-4; donation.

Galena Gazette Museum & Printery (213 S Main St.) has historical newspaper displays and presses; open in summer, daily exc Tues. 10-5; in spring and fall, weekends only 10-5; closed Nov.-Apr.; donation.

Vinegar Hill Lead Mine & Museum (6 m N on SR 84), with displays of mining equipment and techniques, offers guided tours mid-Apr.-mid-Sept., daily 9-5; mid-Sept.-mid-Oct. weekends only 9-5; adm.

Ulysses S. Grant Home State Memorial (4th St. & Bouthillier St.): built in 1857 and presented by the people of Galena to Gen. Grant on his return from the Civil War in 1865. He lived here between official duties in Washington 1865-1880; personal possessions include souvenirs from world tour and the White House. Open daily 9-5; closed Jan. 1, Thnks, Dec. 25; free. Grant's pre-Civil War home is at 121 High St.

GALESBURG: Carl Sandburg Birthplace (331 E 3rd St.), a 3-room cottage, is a shrine to the poet born here in 1878, son of an immigrant railroad worker; Sandburg family pieces and furniture made at Bishop Hill. The Lincoln Room contains Lincoln memorabilia, some of it collected by Sandburg while working on the biography. Sandburg is buried on the grounds, under a granite boulder named Remembrance Rock for his historical novel. Open Mar.-Jan., Tues.-Sat. 9-noon, 1-5; Sun. 1-5; Feb., Tues.-Sun. 1-5; closed Jan. 1, Thnks, Dec. 25; free.

Knox College (S of Public Sq.) was originally housed in **Old Main,** and here, on Oct. 7, 1858, nearly 20,000 people gathered to hear the 5th Lincoln-Douglas debate; during this debate Lincoln first condemned slavery in public.

Bishop Hill (14 m N on I-74, then 15 m E on SR 17, then 2 m N) is a restored town founded in 1846 by Swedish religious dissenters whose leader, Erik Jansson, had been jailed in Sweden. The Janssonists walked 160 m across the prairie from Chicago and lived the first winter in caves; 96 died, but new immigrants arrived and the communal colony prospered until Jansson was murdered in 1850. Dissension then caused the colony to abandon collective ownership, and in 1861 the property was divided; descendants, many of whom still speak Swedish, have preserved and kept in use 13 of the original 16 buildings; these are either on the town square or nearby: **Colony Church,** the first permanent structure built. The sanctuary was on the 2nd floor and the building also housed a communal dining room and rooms in which 20 families lived, a family to a room. Housed here are primitive paintings by Olof Krans, who arrived in 1850; his attention to detail makes his paintings accurate portrayals of life then. **Steeple Building,** built in 1854 in Greek Revival style, with a clock with only one hand; replicas of 19th-C rooms and a doctor's office, a library, and the Henry County Historical Society Museum collections. Open May-Oct. daily 10-5; sm adm. Other buildings include the **Bjorkland Hotel,** once an important stagecoach stop, and the blacksmith shop where a huge forge enabled 4 blacksmiths to work at once; above the forge were assembled the carriages for which the colony was famous; craft demonstrations are given. Guided tours of the village are available Apr.-Oct. weekends for a pittance.

GENEVA: Fabyan Forest Preserve (S Batavia Ave.), covering 245 acres, contains the Fabyan house ("Riverbank") designed by Frank Lloyd Wright, a museum with antiques, a lighthouse, and a windmill. Open Memorial Day-Sept., Sun. & hols 1-5; free.

GLEN ELLYN: Cantigny War Memorial Museum of the First Division (5 m SW on US 30A): animated dioramas of the Omaha Beach landing; history of the First Infantry Division; military equipment; library. Open Tues.-Sun., May-Sept. 9-5, Oct.-Apr. 10-4; closed Jan. 1, Thnks, Dec. 25, and Tues. following Mon. hols; free. On the grounds: **Robert R. McCormick Museum,** the former publisher's residence, with a large collection of antiques. His nearby tomb is guarded by life-size statues of his dogs. Open Wed.-Sun., May-Sept. noon-5, Oct.-Apr. 1-4:30; closed Jan. 1, Thnks, Dec. 25; free.

GRAND DETOUR: John Deere Historic Site (off SR 2) honors the blacksmith who invented the "plow that broke the prairies." Pioneer farmers found that the prairie soil stuck to the plows they had brought from the east. By designing the first self-scouring plow in 1837, Deere helped open the West. Visitor Center; remains of his original shop; reconstructed blacksmith's shop with working forge; Deere's home furnished in 1830's style. Open daily 9-3 (9-5 Mar. 15-Nov. 15); closed Jan. 1, Thnks, Dec. 25; free.

HARRISBURG: Saline County Museum (1600 S Feazel St.) is a historical complex with general store and post office, farm home, other buildings; open daily in summer; sm adm.

HIGHLAND PARK: Chicago Historical Antique Auto Museum (3160 Skokie Valley Rd.): cars belonging to celebrities; classic and antique models. Open daily 9-6; closed Dec. 25; adm.

HINSDALE: Old Graue Mill & Museum (York Rd., ¼-m N of US 34): restored 1852 water-driven grist mill; barn, country store, Victorian parlor, child's room, and kitchen with period items. Open May-late Oct., daily 11-6; sm adm.

JOLIET: Old Canal Town Historic District (7 m NE via SR 171 in Lockport) preserves buildings from the days when Lockport was headquarters for the Illinois and Michigan Canal. **Illinois-Michigan Canal Museum** (803 S State St.), in the 1838 canal superintendent's home, contains historical exhibits; open daily 1:30-4:30; closed hols.

KANKAKEE: Kankakee County Historical Society Museum (8th Ave. & Water St. in Small Memorial Park) contains historical exhibits on this old French town; molds of 12 George Gray Barnard sculptures; open Sat., Sun. 2-5; closed June-Aug. & hols; free.

LINCOLN: Abraham Lincoln participated in the organization of this town and christened it in 1853 with watermelon juice. He practiced law here on and off during 1856-59 and owned a lot. **Lincoln College** (Keokuk & Ottawa Sts.) houses a Lincoln Collection of more than 2000 books, a table at which Lincoln worked, other historical items; the Museum of the Presidents contains pictures, medals, autographs, and documents of every U.S. President.

    Postville Courthouse State Memorial (5th St.): replica of the wooden courthouse (1840-48) in which Lincoln practiced law. The original courthouse, bought by Henry Ford in 1929, is in Greenfield Village in Dearborn, Michigan. The Postville records of cases tried here were lost in an 1857 fire, but some Lincoln documents are on display. Open daily 9-5; closed Jan. 1, Thnks, Dec. 25; free.

    Mt. Pulaski Courthouse State Memorial (12 m SE on SR 121 in Mt. Pulaski), restored Greek Revival building, served as county courthouse until 1853; Lincoln tried several cases here. Open daily 9-noon, 1-5; closed Jan. 1, Thnks, Dec. 25; free.

LINCOLN HOME NATIONAL HISTORIC SITE (S 8th St. & Capitol Ave., Springfield) preserves the only home Lincoln ever owned. He and Mary Todd Lincoln bought the 5-year-old building in 1844 when they tired of trying to raise their first son in a boardinghouse; after their other 3 sons were born (one also died here), they added a second story to the house, and lived here until they went to Washington in 1861. The carefully restored interior includes some of the children's toys and other family possessions. Open daily 8-5; closed Jan. 1, Dec. 25; free.

LINCOLN LOG CABIN STATE PARK (10 m S of Charleston on un-numbered road): reconstruction of cabin built by Thomas Lincoln in 1837. Abraham Lincoln's father lived here until his death in 1851 with his second wife, Sarah Bush Johnston Lincoln; both are buried in nearby Shiloh Cemetery (3 m). Free. At **Moore Home State Memorial** (1 m N), Lincoln ate his last meal with his stepmother before leaving for his inauguration in Washington in 1861.

LINCOLN'S NEW SALEM STATE PARK (20 m NW of Springfield off SR 97) is the authentically restored village where Lincoln spent 6 years (1831-37). From here, after clerking, enlisting in the Black Hawk War, serving as postmaster and surveyor, and failing in business, he was elected to serve in the Illinois General Assembly in 1834; the town therefore saw his transformation from an aimless youth to a dedicated politician. The only original building is the **Onstot Cooper Shop** where Lincoln studied law by the light of a fire made from the cooper's shavings. But faithfully re-created are **Rutledge Tavern,** where Lincoln slept in the loft and formed his friendship with Ann, **Denton Offut Shop** where he clerked, the first and second **Berry-Lincoln Stores,** and other buildings he knew. All are furnished with original pieces or items of the period, and even the flower and vegetable gardens have been planted for historical authenticity. Strangely, the town declined right after Lincoln left, because in 1839 Petersburg was made the county seat. New Salem was a decayed ghost town when William Randolph Hearst bought it for preservation.

A museum houses many artifacts of the period and offers guided tours (exc. Jan. 1, Thnks, Dec. 25). Picnic and camp sites; lodge; cafe. Open daily 9-5; free.

LINCOLN TOMB STATE MEMORIAL (Oak Ridge Cemetery, Springfield): Mrs. Lincoln requested that the President be buried here, and she and 3 of their 4 sons are also in this tomb. The monument, dedicated in 1874, contains a bronze version of Daniel Chester French's marble seated figure of Lincoln, statuettes reflecting his life, and texts from 4 of his speeches. Open daily 9-5; closed Jan. 1, Thnks, Dec. 25; free.

LINCOLN TRAIL HOMESTEAD STATE PARK (10 m W of Decatur via US 36, then S on local road) commemorates the site where Lincoln's father settled the family for a year after the trek from Kentucky. Most of the family moved on a year later, but Abe (and a cousin and a stepbrother) stayed to transport produce by flatboat on the Sangamon River—a job that led to Lincoln's only trip to the deep South (to New Orleans) and to his settling in New Salem. Open daily.

LINCOLN TRAIL STATE PARK (2 m S of Marshall off SR 1) has a historic marker noting that this is land through which the Lincoln family passed in 1830 after leaving Indiana; open daily.

MARENGO: Illinois Railway Museum (Olson Rd. in Union, 2 m SE via US 20 & unnumbered road): outdoor displays of antique railroad cars, trolleys, other vehicles; open daily 10-5 in summer, weekends 11-6 in spring and fall; closed Dec.-Feb. & hols; museum is free, charge for rides.

METAMORA COURTHOUSE STATE MEMORIAL (in Metamora, 14 m NE of Peoria via SR 116): This pleasing Greek Revival courthouse, constructed of native materials and home-baked bricks in 1845, was one of the buildings in which Lincoln practiced. He is accused of having advised a client, on trial for her husband's murder, to flee because the trial was going so badly. Courtroom contains many original furnishings; museum has displays of pioneer days. Open daily 9-5; closed Jan. 1, Thnks, Dec. 25; free.

MOLINE: Deere & Co. Administrative Center (7 m S on John Deere Rd.) is an award-winning complex designed by Eero Saarinen; 3-dimensional mural depicting rural life by Alexander Girard; displays of farm tools; company's products in a display building. Open daily 9-5, with tours weekdays at 10:30 & 1:30; free. No children under 12.

MOUNT VERNON: Abraham Lincoln practiced law in the old **Appellate Courthouse** here, now a repository for a large legal library boasting manuscripts and other materials dating back to Elizabethan England. **John R. & Eleanor R. Mitchell Art Museum** (Richview Rd.) has changing exhibits of historical and contemporary regional works; open Mon.-Fri. 10-noon, 2-4:30, Sat. 10-2, Sun. 2-4.

MUNDELEIN: Benedictine Sanctuary of Perpetual Adoration, small but unusually ornate, is embellished with enamels, mosaics, stained-glass windows, and marble colonnades. Open daily 10-5.

NAUVOO: This history-rich town on the Mississippi was once a Fox Indian village. In 1839, when the Mormons were driven out of Missouri, Joseph Smith led them here; they named the town Nauvoo (Hebrew for "beautiful place"). As more Mormons arrived and the city grew rapidly to 27,000 people, it became lawless and a rendezvous for criminals. Schisms developed among the Mormons, and clashes continued with non-Mormons, until 1846, when Brigham Young led the largest faction west, eventually to Utah, and splinter groups went to other states. Nauvoo became almost a ghost town. In 1849, the French Icarians, led by Etienne Cabet, took over the empty buildings and tried to set up a utopian society based on communal ownership. They founded a cheese and wine industry. But the colony failed and by 1856 the Icarians had also broken up and moved on. German settlers arrived next, taking over the Icarian fruit, wine, and blue cheese industries that still prosper today.

Nauvoo Restoration, Inc. Visitor Center (Young & Partridge Sts.) has historical exhibits, a film, and a map for self-guiding tour; free guided tours are also provided for some buildings. Open June-Oct., daily 8 am-9 pm, Nov.-May daily 9-6. Following a revelation in 1841, Joseph Smith began to construct a great limestone temple and a grand inn in which the prophet and his family were to live. Both were incomplete at his death in 1844. The inn, **Nauvoo House,** was completed in 1869 and is still in use. The **Temple,** into which a million dollars was said to have been poured, was complete enough to be used for services in 1844; but construction was halted by Smith's death, and vandals burned it in 1848; many pieces from it were incorporated in Nauvoo buildings and a pilaster is on display in Nauvoo State Park. Among the restored buildings are **Times and Seasons Buildings,** offices of the Mormon newspaper and post office; **Brigham Young Home; Heber C. Kimball Home** and **Wilford Woodruff Home,** dwellings of 2 of Smith's 12 apostles; a blacksmith shop; and many other landmarks.

Joseph Smith Historic Center (Main & Water Sts.) offers a tour and slide program. Open daily 8-5 (8-8 in summer); closed Jan. 1, Thnks, Dec. 25; free. Included are: **Joseph Smith Homestead,** the town's oldest building, an 1803 log cabin Smith moved into on his arival in 1839, with period furnishings. **Smith's Mansion,** built in 1843, with period furnishings. Graves of Joseph Smith, his wife Emma (who continued to live in Nauvoo until her death in 1879), and his brother Hyrum.

Nauvoo State Park (on SR 96, S of Nauvoo) contains the restored **Rheinberger Home,** built by Mormons with additions made during Icarian days (see Nauvoo); maintained as a museum; period furnishings in 4 rooms appropriate to Indian, Mormon, Icarian, and early pioneer periods of Nauvoo's history; wine cellar; adjoining vineyards were planted in the mid-1800's. House open May-Sept; park open all year.

OREGON: Oregon Public Library (300 Jefferson St.): work of past and contemporary local artists, some from the former artists' colony founded here in 1898 by Lorado Taft and others. Open Mon.-Thurs., Sat. 2-6, 7-9; closed hols & 2 weeks in Aug.; free. On the courthouse lawn is Soldiers Monument by Lorado Taft.

PEORIA: Peoria Historical Society has restored the 1837 Flanagan House (942 NE Glen Oak Ave.) with period antiques including Lincoln memorabilia, and the 1868 Morron House (1212 W Moss Ave.) with Victorian furnishings. Open Sun. 2-5; closed Dec. 25; donation. **Lakeview Center for the Arts & Sciences** (1125 W Lake Ave.): museum, planetarium, art gallery; open Tues.-Sat. 9-5, Sun. 1-6; closed Jan. 1, July 4, Dec. 25; free.

PERE MARQUETTE STATE PARK (5 m W of Grafton on SR 100): Here Jolliet first set foot on Illinois soil; Visitor Center with information on Marquette; dinosaur fossils; prehistoric finds; open all year.

PETERSBURG: Oakland Cemetery (Oakland Ave.) contains the graves of Ann Rutledge and Edgar Lee Masters, author of *Spoon River Anthology*. **Edgar Lee Masters Memorial Home** (Jackson & 8th Sts.), where the poet lived during his boyhood; period furnishings and family memorabilia. Open Memorial Day-Labor Day, Tues.-Sun. 1-5; closed hols; free. **Menard County Courthouse** (102 S 7th St.) contains documents pertaining to Lincoln; open Mon.-Fri. 9-5; closed hols; free. **New Salem Carriage Museum** (3 m S on SR 97): more than 130 horse-drawn vehicles; open May-Oct. daily 9-6; Sat. & Sun. in Apr.; sm adm.

QUINCY: Historical Society of Quincy & Adams County (425 S 12th St.): in an 1853 Greek Revival mansion; cigar store Indians, pioneer paintings, Civil War memorabilia, antique toys, reed organs, relics from the Mormon Temple at Nauvoo. Open Tues.-Fri. 11-5, Sat. & Sun. 1-5; closed hols; adm. **Washington Park** (5th & Maine Sts.) has a bronze bas relief by Lorado Taft commemorating the site of the 6th Lincoln-Douglas debate on Oct. 13, 1858.

ROCKFORD: Tinker Swiss Cottage (411 Kent St.), modeled on a Swiss chalet, was built in 1865 by a wealthy businessman; decorative arts and furnishings he collected around the world; octagonal library based on Sir Walter Scott's at Abbotsford, Scotland; American historical items. Open Wed., Thurs., Sat., Sun. 2-4; closed hols; sm adm. **Erlander Home Museum** (404 S 3rd St.): built in 1871 by an early settler and furniture manufacturer; Swedish antiques; displays of early Swedish settlers; inquire locally for hrs; adm.

Burpee Art Museum (737 N Main St.): contemporary American graphics, painting, and sculpture; library. Open Tues.-Sat. 9-5, Sun. 1-4; closed hols; free. **Burpee Museum of Natural History** (813 N Main St.): minerals, fossils, Indian artifacts, and wildlife. Open Tues.-Sat. 1-5, Sun. 2-5; closed hols; free. **Time Museum** (7801 E State St. on grounds of Clock Tower Inn): timepieces dating from 2000 BC, including sundials, complicated or unusual clocks. Open Tues.-Sun. 11-8; closed hols; adm.

ROCK ISLAND: Rock Island Arsenal (on Rock Island in the Mississippi Riv.): reconstruction of 1816 Ft. Armstrong Blockhouse; Confederate cemetery, National Cemetery; self-guiding booklet available; open daily 9-4; closed hols; free. On grounds is the **John M. Browning Museum,** with rifles developed by Browning and other firearms; open Wed.-Sun. 11-4; closed hols; free.

SPRINGFIELD: Convention & Tourism Commission (500 E Capitol Ave., 62701) can supply maps for the Lincoln Heritage Trail and a walking tour of Springfield (which became the state capital in 1837 because of a campaign led by Lincoln). Here Lincoln practiced law, married, raised his sons, and is buried. In addition to historic buildings, the town has many markers indicating the sites of his Farewell Address and former buildings associated with him.

State Capitol (2nd St. & Capitol Ave.), built 1868-87 in Renaissance style, has a 361-ft dome that can be seen for miles. Outside are statues of Lincoln (delivering his Farewell Address) and Douglas. Open Mon.-Fri. 8-4:30, Sat. & Sun. 8-4; closed Jan. 1, Thnks, Dec. 25; free. The **Archives Bldg.** (Spring St.) and the **Centennial Bldg.** (2nd & Edwards Sts.) housing the Illinois State Library are open Mon.-Fri. 8:30-4, Sat. 8:30-noon; closed hols; free.

Old State Capitol (on the square between 5th & 6th St., Adams & Washington Sts.), restored Greek Revival building, served as capitol from 1839 until it proved too small. Here Lincoln argued cases, researched in the law library, made his famous 1858 "House Divided" speech, and received visitors after his nomination for the Presidency; his body lay in state in the Hall of Representatives. Ulysses S. Grant also worked in this building briefly. Original furnishings; Lincoln memorabilia; Illinois State Historical Library. Open daily 9-5; closed Jan. 1, Thnks, Dec. 25; free.

Illinois State Museum (Spring & Edwards Sts.) has a totem pole outside topped with a figure of Lincoln; this was dedicated to him by Alaskan Tlingit groups who welcomed the end of slavery when Alaska was purchased in 1867. Inside are animal habitat groups, a Hall of Developing Life, dioramas illustrating the history of Illinois, anthropological displays, fine

Indian crafts, minerals and fossils, firearms, decorative arts, art gallery, library. Open Mon.-Sat. 8:30-5, Sun. 2-5; closed Jan. 1, Easter, Thnks, Dec. 25; free.

Lincoln Marriage Home & Museum (406 S 8th St.): replica of the 1836 home of Ninian Edwards, brother-in-law of Mary Todd, where the Lincolns met, courted, and were married. Following the assassination, Mrs. Lincoln stayed here often, and she died here in 1882. Dioramas depict Lincoln's life. Open Apr.-Oct. daily 9-5; closed Easter; sm adm. **Abraham Lincoln Museum** (421 S 8th St. opposite Lincoln Home) contains a lifesize wax figure of Lincoln made from molds of his face and hands; Brady photographs of the Civil War; many Lincoln personal effects and documents; open daily 9-5 (longer hrs in summer); closed Jan. 1, Thnks, Dec. 25; sm adm. **Lincoln-Herndon Bldg.** (6th & Adams Sts.): Lincoln had law offices here; period furnishings and documents; Federal courtroom in which Lincoln presented cases for some 15 years. Open daily 9:30-5; closed Easter, Thnks, Dec. 25; sm adm. **Lincoln Depot Museum** (10th & Monroe Sts.): site of Lincoln's Farewell Address. The depot, built in 1861, houses Lincoln and railroad memorabilia. Open Apr.-Nov. daily 9-5; sm adm.

Vachel Lindsay Home (603 S 5th St.) is an unassuming clapboard house in which the poet spent most of his life; drawings, paintings, manuscripts, letters; guided tours June-Aug., daily 9-4:30; rest of year by appointment; sm adm.

Thomas Rees Memorial Carillon (in Washington Park, W Fayette Ave. & Chatham Rd.) has 3 observation decks from which you can see the 66 Dutch bells. Open Memorial Day-early Sept. daily 2-8; rest of year, weather permitting, Sat. 2-4:30, Sun. 2-6; sm adm.

Clayville Stagecoach Stop (14 m W on SR 125 in Pleasant Plains) is a restored inn that may have been built as early as 1824. Named for Henry Clay, it was a rallying point for the Whig party, flourishing until the Civil War. Restored with antiques from the area. Summer demonstrations given by resident artisans. Open May-Oct., Tues.-Sun. 10-5; rest of yr by appointment; sm adm.

URBANA: University of Illinois has an extensive campus in Urbana and adjacent Champaign. **Illini Union** (Green & Wright Sts.) has self-guiding maps and also sponsors tours. **Kannert Art Museum** collections of ancient, medieval, European, and American art include paintings, sculpture, prints, and drawings; Oriental and Pre-Columbian works; American decorative arts; open Mon.-Sat. 9-5, Sun. 2-5; free. **Museum of Natural History** displays anthropology, botany, geology, and zoology; special collection on Gregor Mendel. Open Mon.-Sat. 8-5; free. **World Heritage Museum:** history of man from cave dwellers to modern times; handsome exhibits with many interesting artifacts; open during academic year, Mon.-Fri. 9-noon, 1-5, Sat. 9-noon, Sun. 2-5; free.

VANDALIA: **Visitor Information Center** (1408 N 5th St.) has information on historic sites, including Deer Spring, where Lincoln was said to have liked to sit and think, the old State Cemetery, and the Lincoln relics in the city library.

Vandalia Statehouse State Memorial (315 W Gallatin St.) was built by citizens in 1836 in an attempt to keep the state capital from being moved, but Springfield was chosen capital in 1837. Lincoln and Stephen Douglas served in the legislature here; period artifacts. Open daily 9-5; closed Jan. 1, Thnks, Dec. 25; free. On the grounds is a Madonna of the Trail Monument.

Little Brick House (621 St. Clair St.): pioneer home; period furnishings; doll collection. Open daily in summer, 11-5; rest of yr by appointment; adm.

WILMETTE: **Baha'i House of Worship** (Sheridan Rd. & Linden Ave.): set in lovely gardens on Lake Michigan; 9-sided building incorporating symbols from the world's major religions to emphasize the unity of man; Foundation Hall exhibits on the Baha'i faith. Open daily 10-5 (10-10 in summer); free.

INDIANA

ANDERSON: This city has many fine old homes, particularly along 8th St. **James Whitcomb Riley House** (8th & Morton) and 2 homes by **Frank Lloyd Wright** (422 W 9th St. and opposite Trinity Espiscopal Church, 1030 Delaware St.) are not open to the public. **Anderson Fine Arts Center** (226 W 8th St.), with Midwest works, is open Tues.-Sat. 10-5, Sun. 2-5; closed hols & Aug.; free. **Anderson College** (E 5th St. & College Dr.) has a museum of the Bible and Near Eastern studies, with Holy Land artifacts; open during academic yr, Mon.-Fri. 8-5, Sat. 9-5; closed hols; free.

ANGEL MOUNDS STATE MEMORIAL (on SR 662, 7 m E of Evansville) contains ruins of a prehistoric town occupied 1300-1500 by Mississippian culture; 10 mounds; temple and huts reconstructed and furnished; Interpretive Center provides orientation. Open daily 9-noon, 1-5; sm adm.

AURORA: **Hillforest** (213 5th St.), built in 1852 in Steamboat Gothic, has period furnishings; open Apr.-Dec., Tues.-Sun. 1-5; sm adm.

BERNE: Amishville (3 m SE) provides guided tours of an authentic Amish home; Amish life and beliefs are explained; open Apr.-Dec., Mon.-Sat. 9-5, Sun. noon-5; closed Dec. 25; adm.

BLOOMINGTON: Indiana University Museum of Art (Fine Arts Bldg.) has a good collection of Greek and Roman art, a variety of other works, and especially fine 20th-C painting and sculpture; open Mon.-Sat. 9-5, Sun. 1-5. Thomas Hart Benton's murals of the state's cultural and industrial progress are in the **Auditorium;** open Mon.-Fri. 8-5; guided tours available. A Calder stabile is in front of the **Musical Arts Building** (open Mon.-Sat. 9-5, Sun. 1-5). **Lilly Library of Rare Books,** open Mon.-Fri. 9-5, Sat. 9-noon, 2-5, Sun. 2-5.

CENTERVILLE: Mansion House (214 E Main St.), an 1841 Federal-style tavern once a stage stop on the National Road (US 40), is maintained by Historic Centerville, Inc., which is restoring other buildings in the area; open Apr.-Oct., Sat. & Sun. 1-5; sm adm. Among the many privately owned old homes in the area are the Greek Revival style 1848 **Morton Home** (111 S Morton Ave.) and the 1840 **Rawson-Vaile House** (111 W Walnut St.), the Federal-style **Lantz-Mulligan-Boyd House** (214 W Main St.) and the 1857 **Jacob Julian House** (116 E Plum St.), with interesting cast-iron exterior trim.

COLUMBUS: Visitor Center (506 5th Ave.) arranges architectural tours that include some dozen schools of superior design; **North Christian Church** (Tipton Lane), designed by Eero Saarinen; **First Baptist Church** (3300 Fairlawn Dr.), of natural materials, designed by Harry Weese; **Cleo Rogers Memorial Library** (536 5th St.), designed by I. M. Pei, with a Henry Moore sculpture; and the Victorian **Bartholomew County Courthouse** (Washington & 3rd Sts.).

CORYDON: Corydon Capitol State Memorial (Old Capitol Ave.), erected in 1812, served as seat of government of the Indiana Territory 1813-16 and as state capitol until 1825; museum; replicas of original furnishings; open daily 9-4; sm adm. **Posey House** (Walnut & Oak Sts.), 1817 home of the Territorial Governor, is a DAR museum; inquire locally for hrs.

CRAWFORDSVILLE: Gen. Lew Wallace Study (E Pike St. & Wallace Ave.) is a city museum containing paintings and memorabilia of the author of *Ben-Hur.* Open mid-Apr.-Nov., Mon., Wed.-Sat. 10:30-noon, 1:30-5, Sun. 1:30-5; closed hols; sm adm. **Lane Place** (212 S Water St.), home of former Governor, is a museum of the Civil War era; open Tues.-Sat. 1-4; closed hols; sm adm.

ELKHART: Elkhart County Historical Museum (Vistula St., 8 m E in Bristol): 1890 cottage, nineteen twenty Victorian-style house, other buildings; exhibits on the Amish, Indians, pioneers; library; cemetery; open Sat. 1-4, Sun. 1-5; closed Jan. 1, Dec. 25; free. **Ruthmere** (302 E Beardsley Ave.): elegant 1910 mansion; period furnishings; murals; open Tues.-Thurs. 11-4; closed hols; adm.

EVANSVILLE: Convention & Visitors Bureau (329 Main St.) has brochures for walking tours of Old Evansville (Riverside Dr. & 1st St.), where homes range from Federal to Victorian Gothic; included are a ballroom papered in gold leaf where Jenny Lind sang and P. T. Barnum danced, and a Gothic chapel copied from one in England; some have fine woodwork by early German settlers; most not open to the public.

Museum of Arts & Science (411 SE Riverside Dr.): designed by Victor Gruen; American archaeology; Oriental and Near East art works; Gobelin and Flemish tapestries; paintings by Titian, Murillo, others; historic and scientific displays; planetarium (Sun. 2:30); open Tues.-Sat. 10-5, Sun. noon-5; closed Jan. 1, Dec. 25; free.

Willard Library (21 1st Ave.), in an 1884 Victorian Gothic building, has superb materials on state history; open Tues.-Sat. 9-5; closed hols; free.

FORT WAYNE: Swinney Park: Allen County-Fort Wayne Historical Society (1424 W Jefferson St.) depicts the city's history from the time it was a French trading post (about 1690); open Tues.-Fri. 10-noon, 1-5, Sat. & Sun. 1-5; closed hols; donation. Near the Coliseum is a memorial to **John Chapman** (Johnny Appleseed).

Jack D. Diehm Memorial Museum of Natural History (1336 Franke Park Dr.): mounted animals in habitat settings; more than 300 species of mounted fish and insects; taxidermy, mineral, and coin exhibits. Open June 15-Labor Day, Tues.-Sun. noon-9; rest of yr, Tues.-Sat. 11-5, Sun. noon-6; closed Dec. 25; sm adm.

Lincoln Library & Museum (Lincoln National Ins. Co., 1301 S Harrison St.): literature, busts, portraits, personal possessions; open Mon.-Thurs. 8-4:30, Fri. 8-12:30; closed hols; free.

Concordia Senior College (6600 N Clinton St.) consists of 31 buildings designed by Eero Saarinen, modeled on a northern European village.

FRENCH LICK: House of Clocks Museum (225 College St.): more than 250 restored clocks and watches dating from the early 1800's; Eli Terry's "Pilar and Scroll" clock with wooden gears. Open Mon.-Tues., Thurs.-Sat. 9-5, Sun. 1-5; closed Jan. 1, Memorial Day, Thnks, Dec. 25; adm.

Northwood Institute (1 m N via SR 145 in W Baden) is in an extraordinary circular building, once a luxury hotel, surrounding a domed court; living museum is being created; open daily 9-5 in summer; by appointment rest of yr; free.

GENEVA: Limberlost State Memorial (off US 27), home of author Gene Stratton Porter for 20 years; original furnishings; open July-Oct. 9-noon, 1-5 daily; Nov.-June, Tues.-Sun. 9-noon, 1-5; closed Thnks, Dec. 25; sm adm. See also Kendallville.

GREENFIELD: Riley Home incorporates the log cabin in which poet James Whitcomb Riley was born in 1849; personal effects; open May.-Oct., Mon.-Sat. 10-5, Sun. 1-5; sm adm. **Old Log Jail,** with cells and historical exhibits, is open Mar.-Nov. Sat. & Sun. 1-5; sm adm.

GREENTOWN: Greentown Glass Museum (114 N Meridian St.) displays rare old chocolate and amber glassware; open Memorial Day-Labor Day, Tues.-Fri. 10-noon, 1-5, Sat. & Sun. 1-5; rest of yr, Sat. & Sun. 1-5:30; free.

HAGERSTOWN: Historic Hagerstown, terminal of the Whitewater Canal in the 1840's has marked historic houses with water wheels. Many are along SR 38 W to New Castle; others are in town along Sycamore and Perry Sts.

HUNTINGTON: Huntington County Historical Museum (in County Courthouse on Jefferson St., 4th floor) open Sept.-June, Mon.-Sat. 1-4; closed hols; free.

INDIANAPOLIS: State Capitol (Capitol & Senate Aves., Washington & Ohio Sts.), built of Indiana limestone in 1878, is open Mon.-Fri. 8:30-4:30; closed hols; free. **State Library & Historical Building** (140 N Senate Ave.) is open Mon.-Fri. 8:15-5; also Sat. 8:15-noon, Sept.-May; closed hols; free. **Indiana State Museum** (202 N Alabama St.): mounted animals and birds; exhibits on state history; works by state artists; open Mon.-Sat. 9-5, Sun. 2-5; closed hols; free.

World War Memorial Plaza (a 5-block area along N Meridian from E New York to E St. Clair) contains a massive limestone memorial modeled on the mausoleum at Halicarnassus; military museum and portraits. Open daily 9-4:30; closed hols; free. **Soldiers & Sailors Monument** (Monument Circle), an ornate 1902 structure, has Civil War exhibits; observation platform; open daily 9-4; closed hols; sm adm.

Indianapolis Museum of Art (1200 W 38th St.) has outstanding collections: **Krannert Pavilion** (primitive art; major Impressionist and American works; graphics; 19th-C British and American portraits; fine Oriental collection; sculpture court) and **Clowes Pavilion** (masters from the 12th C through the Renaissance; Turner watercolors) are open Tues. 11 am-9 pm, Wed.-Sun. 11-5; closed Dec. 25; free. **Lilly Pavilion of Decorative Arts,** built in the style of an 18th-C French Chateau, houses French, English, and Italian furnishings; Georgian library with molded plaster ceiling; open Tues.-Sun. 1-4; closed Dec. 25; adm.

Morris-Butler Museum (1204 N Park Ave.): mansion of hand-molded brick, with tower and carriage house; opulent interior with fine furnishings; pieces from Helena Rubenstein's John Henry Belter collection. Open Thurs., Sun. 1-5, or by appointment; closed hols, Aug.; adm.

Benjamin Harrison Memorial Home (1230 N Delaware St.), home of the 23rd President, contains his desk and exercise equipment; Mrs. Harrisons's gowns; original, elegant Victorian furnishings. Open Mon.-Sat. 10-4, Sun. 12:30-4; closed Dec. 25-Jan. 1; adm.

James Whitcomb Riley Home (528 Lockerbie St.): home of the poet for 23 years, restored with his possessions. Open Tues.-Sat. 10-4, Sun. noon-4; closed Jan. 1, Easter, Thnks, Dec. 25; sm adm. Around the house the Lockerbie Sq. village complex is being developed.

Scottish Rite Cathedral (650 N Meridian St.), of Tudor Gothic design with a carillon tower; Scottish rite symbols are depicted in bronze on the floor. Elaborate interior; 7000-pipe organ. Open Mon.-Fri. 10-3, Sat. 10-2; closed hols; free. **Carmelite Monastery** (2402 Cold Spring Rd.), a cloistered convent, patterned on the walls and towers of Avila, Spain. The lobby and chapel are open to the public. **St. John's Church** (126 W Georgia St.), in 13th-C French Gothic style, elaborate interior. Open daily 6-6. **Tabernacle United Presbyterian Church** (418 E 34th St.), in Gothic style, has outstanding stained-glass windows. Open daily in daylight.

Museum of Indian Heritage (6040 De Long Rd. in Eagle Creek Park) depicts most North American Indian cultural areas from pre-Columbian to the present. Open in summer Tues.-Sun. 10-5, weekends only the rest of the yr; closed Dec. 25; adm.

Conner Prairie Pioneer Settlement & Museum (Allisonville Rd., 18 m NE in Noblesville) is a living museum of the state's pioneer days, including an 1810 trading post, 1823 mansion, 1850 schoolhouse, and other authentically restored buildings; craft demonstrations, other activities. Open early Apr.-late Oct., Tues.-Sat. 9:30-5, Sun. 1-5; adm.

Indianapolis Motor Speedway & Museum (4790 W 16th St.): racing cars and displays of innovations tested at the track. Open daily 9-5; closed Dec. 25 & during races; free. Bus rides around track; sm charge.

Fort Benjamin Harrison Museum (Ft. Harrison, 14 m NE off SR 67) contains U.S. and foreign military memorabilia; open Tues.-Sat. 10-4; free.

JEFFERSONVILLE: Built on plans created by Thomas Jefferson, this town has long been a shipbuilding center; with advance notice, boatyards may be toured. **Howard Steamboat Museum** (1101 E Market St.) is in a 22-room Victorian mansion constructed by shipyard craftsmen; the hand-carved woodwork was done by a German artisan who spent 2 years at the work. Howard Shipyards (1834-1941), renowned for fine workmanship, was a prime builder of riverboats. The museum contains steamboat models and other artifacts. Open Mon.-Sat. 10-4, Sun. 1-4; closed hols; adm.

KENDALLVILLE: Gene Stratton Porter State Memorial (5.8 m W via US 6, then N on SR 9): log cabin home of the author 1913-18; Aztec stone carvings; open May-Oct., Mon.-Sat. and Nov.-Apr., Tues.-Sat., 9-noon, 1-5; Sun. all yr 1-5; closed hols; sm adm. See also Geneva.

KOKOMO: Howard County Historical Museum (1200 W Sycamore St.), in the Romanesque-style Seiberling Mansion, features murals and hand-carved woodwork; Indian, pioneer, and Civil War artifacts. Open Mon., Wed., Fri. 1-4, Sun. 2-4; closed hols; free. **Elwood Haynes Museum** (1915 S Webster St.): memorabilia of one of the developers of the automobile; open Tues.-Sat. 1-4, Sun. 1-5; closed hols; free. Memorial to Haynes' first successful road test is on Pumpkin Vine Pike at US 31 Bypass.

LAFAYETTE: Marquis de Lafayette statue by Lorado Taft (1886) stands on the lawn of the marvelously elaborate courthouse (many old buildings here reflect French influence). **Tippecanoe County Historical Museum** (South & 10th Sts.) is in an ornate 1852 residence; historic displays; Tippecanoe battlefield and Fort Ouiatenon artifacts; European and American paintings; weapons; porcelain; open Feb.-Dec., Tues.-Sun. 1-5; closed hols; free.

    Fort Ouiatenon (S River Rd., 4 m SW): Rebuilt 1717 French block-house and trading post; museum of French and English periods (from 1763). After the Revolution, Indians used the fort for raids as far S as Kentucky until George Washington ordered it destroyed in 1791. Open mid-Apr.-mid-Nov., Tues.-Sun. 1-5; closed hols; sm adm.

    Purdue University (in W Lafayette) offers self-guiding tour booklets. Amelia Earhart, a former instructor here, took off from the university's airport on her ill-fated round-the-world flight in 1937.

    Tippecanoe Battlefield State Memorial (on SR 43, 7 m N) com-memorates the 1811 defeat of the Shawnee, led by Tecumseh and The Prophet, in their last serious attempt to drive whites back across the Ohio River. Museum with exhibits, audiovisual program; open Tues.-Sat. 10-5, Sun. 1-5; sm adm. Self-guiding trail through battlefield.

LINCOLN BOYHOOD NATIONAL MEMORIAL (on SR 162, S of Lincoln City) preserves a portion of the farm Thomas Lincoln purchased after leaving Kentucky in 1816, when Abraham was 7; authentically furnished cabin and outbuildings reconstructed as a living history farm. In Oct. 1818, Nancy Hanks Lincoln died here of milk sickness, and a trail leads to her grave. Slightly over a year later, Thomas married Sally Bush Johnson; the new family lived here until 1830, when they moved to Illinois. **Visitor Center** shows a film on Lincoln's early life, and exhibits in the memorial buildings help interpret the site; open daily 8-5 in winter, 9-6 in summer; closed Jan. 1, Dec. 25.

LOGANSPORT: Cass County Historical Society Museum (1004 E Market St.) open Tues.-Sat. 1-5; closed hols & last 2 weeks of Aug.; free.

MADISON: Shrewsbury House (301 W 1st St.), built 1846-49, is in Greek Revival style with a spiral staircase rising 3 floors. Restored, with period furnishings. Open Mar.-Dec. daily 9-5; sm adm. **Judge Jeremiah Sullivan House** (304 W 2nd St.), a restored and furnished Federal-style home built in 1818, has fine handcrafted woodwork; exhibits of china, glass, silver. Open May-Oct., Tues.-Sat. 10-4:30, Sun. & Mon. noon-4:30; sm adm. **Talbot-Hyatt Pioneer Garden** (between Shrewsbury & Sullivan houses) has been restored with carriage house and community well; open year round; free. **J.F.D. Lanier State Memorial** (Elm & W 1st St.): 1844 Greek Revival mansion; fine original furnishings; open daily 9-5 in summer, 9-4 in winter; sm adm. **Dr. William Hutchings Hospital** (120 W 3rd St.): office and living quarters, 19th-C surgical equipment, and library; open May-Oct. daily 12-4:30; sm adm. **Chamber of Commerce** (Vaughn & Mulberry Sts.) provides maps for historic walking tour.

MUNCIE: Ball State University (Riverside & University Aves.): **Art Gallery** (Fine Arts Bldg.) houses an excellent collection that includes Roman glass, notable Renaissance paintings, 19th-C American landscapes (by George Inness and others), and contemporary works. Open Mon.-Fri. 9-4:30, Sat. & Sun. 1:30-4; closed hols; free.

    Stradling Farm & Museum (N on Wheeling Rd.) is an old-time farm operated by Delaware County Historical Society. Open Tues.-Fri. 1:30-5; adm.

NAPPANEE: Amish Acres (1 m W on US 6) illustrates the homesteads of the Amish in this area; guided tours of house and farm; open May-Oct., Mon.-Sat. 9-9, Sun. 11-5; Nov.-Apr., Sat. 11-9, Sun. 11-5; closed Jan. 1,

Dec. 25; adm. **Pioneer Museum** (8 m E on US 6): Indian and pioneer displays in 4-room schoolhouse; open in summer Mon.-Sat. 10-5, Sun. 1-5; in spring and fall Sat. 10-5, Sun. 1-5; adm.

NASHVILLE: Brown County Art Colony was founded here in the early 1900's, and the town prides itself on galleries exhibiting works by Indiana artists. Tour booklets are available. **T. C. Steele State Memorial** (8 m W via SR 46 to Belmont, then 1 m S), home and studio of one of the colony founders, is open daily 9-noon, 1-5; sm adm.

NEW ALBANY: Main Street is nicknamed Mansion Row for the many fine homes built during the riverboat era. **Floyd County Museum** (Main St. between Bank & Pearl Sts.) houses historic displays and can provide information on the old homes and shipyards. **Scribner House** (State & Main Sts.) is the 1814 home of the founders of the city and contains original furnishings; maintained by the DAR, it is open only by appointment for a sm adm. **Culbertson Mansion** (914 E Main St.), built in 1868 for a cotton merchant, was the largest mansion built during the riverboat era; cantilevered staircase; hand-painted ballroom ceiling and opulent Victorian furnishings. Open Apr.-Nov., Tues.-Sun. 1-4:30; adm.

NEW CASTLE: Henry County Historical Museum (614 S 14th St.) houses pioneer relics, Wilbur Wright memorabilia, relics of several wars, and genealogical library. Open Mon.-Sat. 1-4:30; closed hols; donation.

NEW HARMONY: This was the site of 2 attempts to create utopian communities. In 1814, George Rapp and his following of Harmonists (Lutheran dissenters), who had come from Wurttemberg, Germany, and first settled at Harmony, Pa., arrived here. Their society, which practiced celibacy and common ownership of land, quickly built an impressive town and established prosperous farms. Yet unrest developed, and in 1825 they returned to Pennsylvania. They sold the land to the Welsh-born reformer Robert Owen, whose communal society became an important cultural and scientific center attracting many eminent scholars. But quarrels over leadership soon doomed this community also. Background of both communities and self-guiding tour booklets are available from the **Visitor Center** (E Church St.), open May.-Oct. daily 9-5.

Fauntleroy Home (411 West St.), built by Harmonists in 1815 (furnishings from the 1840's), was headquarters for the Minerva Society; open May-Oct. daily 9-5; Nov.-Apr., Tues.-Sun. 9-4; sm adm. **Dormitory No. 2,** built for unmarried Harmonist men, under Owen was a cultural center with printshop and school; open June-Oct. daily 9-5; sm adm. **Workingmen's Institute Library & Museum** (Tavern & West Sts.) houses

Harmonist artifacts, paintings, ornate furniture, scientific displays; open Tues.-Sat. 10-noon, 1-4; closed Jan. 1, July 4, Thnks, several days in late Dec.; sm adm. **Colonial Dames Harmonist House Museum** (324 North St.), a typical Harmonist home, is open May-Oct., Tues.-Sun. 10-noon, 1-5; sm adm. Other buildings include: **Old Rappite Fort Granary** (Granary St. between Main & West Sts.). **Barrett-Gate House** (500 North St.), built in 1814 and the oldest house in New Harmony. **Rapp-Maclure Mansion** (428 Church St.), built in 1814 for George Rapp. Later it was the home of William Maclure, Owen's closest associate. **Thrall Opera House** (Brewery & Church Sts.) was the 4th dormitory erected by the Rappites, but under Owen it became an opera house; restored to its concert hall appearance; performances given in summer.

Labyrinth, made of hedges, was a symbol of choices in life; open daily; free. **Tillich Park** (Main St.) has the grave of theologian Paul Tillich; open daily; free.

Roofless Church (North St. between Main & West Sts.) was designed by Philip Johnson after the words of the prophet Micah, "Unto thee shall come a Golden Rose." The church has walls but no roof, and the dome, shaped like an inverted rosebud, casts a shadow in the form of a full-blown rose. Inside is the Jacques Lipchitz memorial to the Harmonist and Owen movements. Open daily.

PERU: Miami County Historical Museum (4th floor of courthouse, jct US 24, 31-Bus): Indian and pioneer artifacts; mementos of Frances Slocum, kidnapped by Indians in 1778 at age 5, of Cole Porter, who lived here, and of the circus (Peru had been home to 7 winter circuses); open Mon.-Sat. 9-noon; closed hols; free.

Puterbaugh Museum (11 N Huntington at W Main Sts.) offers Indian and pioneer artifacts, circus mementos. Open Mon.-Tues., Thurs.-Sat. 1-5; closed hols; free.

PLYMOUTH: Marshall County Historical Museum (317 W Monroe St.) open Mon.-Fri. 9-noon, 1-5, Sun. 1-5; closed hols, early June, late Dec.; free.

RICHMOND: Wayne County Historical Museum (1150 N A St.): 1864 Friends' Meeting House (Richmond was established by Quakers) re-creates an 1860's street scene; Gaar Williams cartoons; local historical items; eclectic collection from around the world; open early June-Oct., Tues.-Sun. 1-5; mid-Feb.-early June & Nov.-mid-Dec., Tues.-Sun. noon-4; closed Easter, July 4; adm.

Art Association of Richmond (McGuire Memorial Hall, Whitewater Blvd.) specializes in American artists, with many Midwestern artists represented. Open during the academic year, Mon.-Fri. 9-4, Sun. 2-5; closed school hols; free.

Joseph Moore Museum (Earlham College campus on US 40) has mounted birds and animals; complete skeletons of prehistoric animals. Open Sun. 1-5, also Mon.-Fri. 8-5 during academic year; free.

Levi Coffin House (on US 27 N & Mill St., Fountain City) was a station on the underground railroad. The Coffins, who were Quakers, are believed to have aided more than 3000 slaves to escape. The house was built in 1839 with secret closets, passageways, and recesses for hiding over a dozen slaves at a time. Open June-Oct., Tues.-Sun. 1-4:30; adm.

ROCKPORT: Lincoln Pioneer Village (City Park) is a memorial to the 14 years Lincoln lived in Spencer County and consists of 16 log houses and a replica of Old Pigeon Baptist Church (which Lincoln helped build but which he didn't attend). Open 8-5; sm adm.

ROCKVILLE: Billie Creek Village re-creates a turn-of-the-century town; craft demonstrations. Open late May-late Oct. daily noon-5; adm.

RUSHVILLE: Rush County Historical Museum (619 N Perkins St.) is open Sun. 2-5; free. **Wendell Willkie's home** (601 N Harrison St.) is open by appointment; his grave is in East Hill Cemetery (½ m E via SR 44).

SALEM: John Hays Center (307 E Market St.): Indian and pioneer artifacts, early medical equipment; open Tues.-Sun. 1-5; closed hols; sm adm.

SOUTH BEND: Northern Indiana Historical Society Museum (112 S Lafayette Blvd.) is housed in a Greek Revival courthouse, one of the few remaining works of Chicago architect John Van Osdel. Exhibits depict the early exploration of the area by Marquette and Jolliet in 1673-75, and by La Salle in 1679; on a second visit in 1681, La Salle made a peace treaty with the Miami and Illinois Indian Confederations under an oak (known as Council Oak, it is in Highland Cemetery on Portage Ave.). Also displays on the Studebakers, who arrived in 1852 and built their farm wagon and prairie schooner industry into an important truck and car plant. Library. Open Tues.-Sat. 9-5; closed hols; free.

University of Notre Dame (N off US 31) offers tours through the Dept. of Public Information (daily 9-5 in summer, during the academic year by appointment; closed Easter, Thnks, Dec. 25); free. **Administration Building** contains murals by Luigi Gregori, who worked on them 1874-91. **Grotto of Lourdes** is a replica of the one in France. **Church of the Sacred Heart,** a fine Gothic structure with an ornate altar, contains a carillon and many art objects. **Memorial Library,** with an immense collection, is adorned with an 11-story mural. **Log Chapel** is a replica of the first campus building. **O'Shaughnessy Hall** houses a varied collection of paintings by Van Dyck, Veneto, Tintoretto, Veronese, Murillo, and modern masters; medieval furniture; decorative arts; open daily 1-5; free.

Convention & Visitors Bureau (320 W Jefferson Blvd., 46601) provides information on other attractions. **Southhold Restorations, Inc.** (228 W Colfax Ave., 46601) provides tours of historic or architecturally interesting buildings in the South Bend-Mishawaka area. Examples are the 22-room Beiger Home (517 Lincoln Way E in Mishawaka); Horatio Chapin House (407 W Navarre St.), a 20-room Gothic Revival home built with secret passages for use in case of an Indian attack; Bartlett House (720 W Washington Ave.), an 1850 Federal-style home; and Tippecanoe Place (620 W Washington Ave.), the 1886 Romanesque home of Clement Studebaker that was built large enough to host a meeting of the entire Pan American Congress. South Bend also contains Frank Lloyd Wright's 1906 prairie-house-style Avalon Grotto (705 W Washington Ave.) and 1951 Herman T. Mossberg House (1404 Ridgedale Rd.); neither is open to the public.

SPRING MILL STATE PARK (on SR 60, 3 m E of Mitchell): an abandoned, early 1800's village with homes, shops, grist and saw mills, restored with period furnishings and shop equipment; adm. Also here is a memorial to astronaut Virgil I. Grissom, with exhibits on space.

TELL CITY: Swiss immigrants named this town for their legendary hero, William Tell. **St. Meinrad Benedictine Archabbey** (17 m N on SR 545) began as a log cabin in 1854 when Swiss monks arrived; now a complex of medieval-style buildings; tours Sun. at 1, 2:30, 4. **Christ of the Ohio** (4 m N at Troy): 15-ft-high statue built by a German POW at Camp Breckenridge, Ky., during WW II.

TERRE HAUTE: Historical Museum of the Wabash Valley (1411 S 6th St.): Indian and pioneer artifacts, military items, Victorian furnishings, period costumes, and a country store. Open Sun.-Fri. 1-4; closed hols; free. **Early Wheels Museum** (817 Wabash Ave.) displays antique automobiles; open Mon.-Fri. 10-4; closed hols; free.

Sheldon Swope Art Gallery (25 S 7th St.) has primitive art from Africa and the Pacific; Oriental works; 19th-20th-C American paintings; print collection ranges from the Renaissance to contemporary examples. Open early Sept.-late July, Tues.-Sat. noon-5, Sun. 2-5; closed Jan. 1, Dec. 25; free.

Paul Dresser Birthplace State Shrine & Memorial (in Fairbanks Park at 1st & Farrington Sts.) was home of the composer of Indiana's state song "On the Banks of the Wabash," and his brother, novelist Theodore

Dreiser. Open Sun.-Fri. 1-4; closed some hols; free. **Eugene V. Debs Home** (451 N 8th St.), Victorian home of the labor and Socialist leader who founded the American Railway Union; memorabilia of his life and work. Open Tues.-Fri., Sun. 1-5, or by appointment; closed Jan. 1, Dec. 25; free.

VALPARAISO: Valparaiso University: modern chapel noted for its stained-glass windows; collection of 19th-20th-C American paintings, including many by Junius R. Sloan, displayed in several buildings; open daily during the academic year; free. **Valparaiso Technical Institute Museum of Electronics,** with exhibits from the early 1900's to the present, is on the site where Edison built the first generating station in the Midwest; open Mon.-Fri. 8-5, Sat. 8-noon; closed hols; free.

VINCENNES: This, the oldest town in Indiana, was established at the Buffalo Trace, where animals and Indians crossed the Wabash River. In the late 1600's, French fur traders were coming through here, and in 1732 the French built Fort Vincennes; this was renamed Fort Sackville when it was turned over to the British in 1763, and its capture by George Rogers Clark opened up the Northwest Territory. For years this was a wild and lawless area. Vincennes, capital of the Indiana Territory 1800-13, became a gateway to the West as pioneers (including Abraham Lincoln and his family) continud to cross the Wabash at this point. The town remained primarily French until the mid-1800's, when large numbers of German immigrants settled here. Information on historic sites is available from the **Indiana State Information Center** (adj to Old Cathedral; open Mon.-Sat. 9-5, Sun. 1-5) or from the **Log Cabin Tourist Center** (at Vincennes University, open daily 9-5; closed Jan. 1, Thnks, Dec. 25).

    George Rogers Clark National Historical Park (S of Lincoln Memorial Bridge, on the river) honors the man who won the Northwest Territory for the U.S. during the Revolution; rotunda with statue of Clark, murals of his 1778-9 campaign, recorded commentary; open daily June-Labor Day 9-6, rest of yr 8:30-5; closed Jan. 1, Dec. 25; free.

    Grouseland, William Henry Harrison Home (3 W Scott St.): Harrison, a Virginian, built this James River style home in 1803-4, while he was governor of the Indiana Territory (1800-12); family furnishings and portraits; open daily 9-5; closed Jan. 1, Thnks, Dec. 25; adm.

    Old Cathedral (2nd & Church Sts.), an 1826 brick building with a white spire, is built on the site of the Jesuit log chapel founded in the early 1730's to serve French settlers; open daily 9-8; sm adm. Adjacent Old French cemetery. **Brute Library** contains some 11,000 volumes, including rare illuminated manuscripts dating as early as 1200. The nucleus of the collection is the 5000 volumes brought from France by Father Brute, whose family had been printers for the French royal family. Open Mon.-Sat. 9-5, Sun. 1-5; sm adm.

Vincennes University (1st & College Sts.) may be toured by arrangement through the Log Cabin Tourist Center. On campus are the **Friendship Garden; Mariah Creek Baptist Church; Dunseth Planetarium & Museum;** the one-room birthplace of novelist Maurice Thompson, author of *Alice of Old Vincennes,* built in 1844; and the modest **Indiana Territorial Capitol** (1st & Harrison Sts.), a 2-story frame building from which the present states of Indiana, Illinois, Michigan, Wisconsin, and part of Minnesota were governed 1800-13. **Western Sun Office** is a replica of Elihu Stout's printshop, where he began publication of the *Indiana Gazette* (later renamed *Western Sun*) in 1804.

Old State Bank (2nd & Busseron Sts.), chartered in 1834, is now an art gallery; in the Trappers and Traders Room, furs and skins were traded for cash or land; third floor lookout for Indians and other raiders. Open Apr.-Nov., Tues.-Sun. 10:30-4:30; closed Thanksgiving; donation.

WABASH: Wabash County Historical Museum (in Memorial Hall, W Hill & Miami Sts.) contains Indian and pioneer artifacts, exhibits on the Wabash & Erie Canal, Civil War items. Open Mon.-Thurs. 9-noon, 1-4; Fri., Sat. 9-noon; closed hols; free.

WILBUR WRIGHT STATE MEMORIAL (off SR 38, E of New Castle) is a replica of the home in which the inventor was born in 1867.

ZIONSVILLE: Colonial Village is a reconstruction of a 19th-C Main Street shopping area, including the Town Hall. **Patrick H. Sullivan Museum** houses Boone County artifacts; open Tues.-Sat. 10-4, Sun. 1-5; free.

IOWA

AMANA COLONIES (7 villages within a few miles of each other at jct SR 149, SR 220): These villages, founded by Lutheran Separatists in 1855 as a cooperative community, have been reorganized as a corporation. **Amana** contains the Amana Society headquarters, information center, and Heritage House—a museum of the Society's history—as well as shops displaying community skills and products. In **Homestead** (on SR 149, 3 m

S of Amana) is the Amana Heim, a century-old house preserved as a museum, as well as many shops. Museums are open Apr.-Nov., Mon.-Sat. 10 am-5 pm plus Sun. aft.; sm adm.

BENTONSPORT: Once an important stop for steamboats on the Des Moines River; now a ghost town of preserved 19th-C buildings. The **Post Office** is of solid walnut. **Mason House,** once a plush hotel with a well-known bar for rivermen, still has most of its original furnishings. Open daily Apr.-Oct.

CEDAR RAPIDS: On May's Island (in Cedar River) is **Memorial Coliseum** with a stained-glass window by Grant Wood. **Cedar Rapids Art Center** (324 3rd St. SE) has a Wood collection; works by local artists; open Tues.-Fri. 10-5; closed hols. Free. **Seminole Valley Farm** (in Seminole Pk, NW of city beyond Edgewood Rd.) is a restored farmhouse of the 1880's. Open May-Oct., Sun. 1-4. **Masonic Library** (813 1st Ave, SE) contains Masonic relics, materials on Iowa history. Open Mon.-Fri.; closed hols; free.

CHARLES CITY: In 1896 this was the birthplace of the farm tractor, and a 1913 model is displayed under plexiglass in the town square. **Floyd County Historical Society Museum** (107 N. Main St.) is open May-Sept., Thurs.-Sun., 1:30-4; sm adm.

CHEROKEE: **Sanford Museum and Planetarium** (117 E Willow St.) has geological, archaeological, and historical exhibits. Open Mon.-Fri. 9-noon, 1-5, Sat. 9-noon, Sun. 2-5; closed hols; free.

CLERMONT: **Montauk,** built in 1874, was home of former Iowa Governor William Larrabee; family furnishings; tours daily, May 30-Nov. 1, 10-5; adm. **Clermont Museum** houses crystal, china, fossils, coins, and Indian artifacts.

CLINTON: **Showboat Museum** (moored in the Mississippi off Riverview Park, N of US 30): Steamboat, refitted as a museum of the showboat era and rechristened the *Rhododendron;* shows in summer. Open late May-late Oct., daily, 9-9; sm adm.

CORYDON: **Wayne County Historical Society Museum** (on SR 2): open Apr.-Oct. 14, Tues.-Sun. 1-5; Oct. 15-Nov. 31, Sun. 1-5; sm adm.

COUNCIL BLUFFS: On scenic Rainbow Drive is the **Lewis and Clark Memorial,** marking their council with Missouri and Oto Indians. **Historic**

General Dodge House (605 3rd St.): opulent Victorian home of the Union Pacific Railroad's chief construction engineer; many family furnishings. Open Feb.-Dec., Tues.-Sat. 10-5, Sun. 2-5; closed Thnks, Christmas; adm.

DAVENPORT: Davenport Municipal Art Gallery (1737 W 12th St.) contains Oriental decorative arts and some European works, but emphasis is on American (Grant Wood, Remington), Haitian, and Mexican painting. Free. **Putnam Museum** (1717 W 12th St.) features wildlife, steamboat, and Oriental exhibits, primitive art. Open Mon.-Sat. 9-5, Sun. 1-5; closed hols. Sm. adm. On the campus of Palmer College of Chiropractic is **Little Bit O'Heaven** (808 Brady St.) with Oriental art objects. Open daily in summer only, 10-5; adm.

DECORAH: Vesterheim, Norwegian-American Museum (W Water St.): housed in 3 historic buildings; comprehensive collection of Norwegian arts and crafts; objects illustrating Norwegian influence on pioneer America. Open daily May-Oct. 10-4; adm.

DES MOINES: Iowa State Capitol (Grand Ave. & E 9th St.) is called the Golden Dome because its large central dome is covered with gold leaf; 4 smaller domes are seamed and capped with gold. Elaborate interior boasts mosaics, murals, paintings, and sculpture; Law Library with iron grillwork balconies and circular staircases. Open Mon.-Fri. 8-4:30 exc hols; free.

   Iowa State Department of History & Archives (Grand Ave. & E 12th St.): historical exhibits; Indian artifacts; fossils, minerals, and the Van Allen satellite. Open Mon.-Fri. 8-4 exc. hols; free.

   Des Moines Art Center (Grand Ave. at Polk Blvd.), designed by Eliel Saarinen with a sculpture wing by I. M. Pei, offers a superb collection, including Goya, Daumier, Pissarro, Klee, Courbet, Bellows, Hopper, Rodin, Moore, Arp, and Calder. Open Tues.-Sat. 11-5, Sun. and hols 2-4; free.

   Salisbury House (4025 Tonawanda Dr.) is a replica of King's House in Salisbury, England; Elizabethan furnishings; valuable art objects; rare-book library; open Mon.-Fri. 8-4:30; closed hols; sm adm. **Terrace Hill** (2300 Grand Ave.), a fine Victorian mansion built 1865-69, is the Governor's home. **Living History Farm** (E off exit 32 of I-80, I-35) is a 500-acre working pioneer farm with an 1870 mansion; open daily mid-Apr.-end Oct. 9-5; adm.

   Des Moines Center of Science and Industry (Grand Ave. at Polk Blvd.): physical and natural sciences; planetarium. Open Mon.-Sat. 11-5, Sun. 1-5; closed Mon., July-Aug; free.

DUBUQUE: Julien Dubuque Monument (S end of Julien Dubuque Dr.) commemorates the French miner after whom this, Iowa's oldest city, was named. **Dubuque Historical Museum** (at Eagle Pt. Park, Lincoln & Shiras Sts.) is an 1857 mansion; geologic and Indian exhibits; 1827 log cabin; railway caboose. Open Memorial Day-Labor Day, Tues.-Sun., 1-4:30; adm.

EFFIGY MOUNDS NATIONAL MONUMENT (3 m N of Marquette on SR 76) contains 191 prehistoric mounds, 29 in the form of bear and bird effigies. The self-guiding Fire Point Trail leads to representative examples as well as to scenic overlooks; the longer Hanging Rock Trail runs the length of the site. The Visitor Center has exhibits and an audiovisual presentation; open daily exc. Christmas, 8-5 (8-7 in summer).

FORT ATKINSON MONUMENT STATE PARK (SR 24, ½ m N of Ft. Atkinson): This fort is unique in that its purpose was to protect Indian tribes from each other. The old barracks and hospital are now a museum; powder magazine and part of another barracks have been reconstructed. Open May 16-Oct. 30, Mon.-Fri. 1-5, weekends and hols, 10-5; free.

FORT DODGE: The site of the original fort built to protect settlers against the Sioux is marked only with a tablet, but an exact replica has been built at **Fort Dodge Historical Museum** (SW at jct SR 20, 169); pioneer exhibits, Indian artifacts, a one-room schoolhouse. Open mid-May-mid-Sept. 9-7 daily; adm.

IOWA CITY: On the campus of the **University of Iowa** is the **Old Capitol** (Clinton St. & Iowa Ave.) with a hanging spiral staircase; open Mon.-Sat. 9-5, Sun. 1-5; free. **Museum of Natural History** (Macbride Hall); mounted animals, birds, fish, and reptiles; archaeological and geological materials. Open Mon.-Sat. 8-4:30, Sun. 1-4, closed hols; free. **Museum of Art** (Riverside Dr.): modern art, sculpture, antique silver, primitive art, jade; open Mon.-Sat. 10:30-5, Sun. 1-5; closed hols; free. **Plum Grove State Historic Monument** (727 Switzer Ave.): 1844 home of the first territorial governor; period furnishings; open Apr. 15-Nov. 15, daily exc Tues. 1-5; free.

   Herbert Hoover National Historic Site (on Downey St. in West Branch, N off I-80): The Herbert Hoover Presidential Library; restorations of the 2-room cottage in which he was born and the Quaker Meetinghouse he attended; graves of President and Mrs. Hoover. Open daily exc. Jan. 1, Thnks, Dec. 25; sm adm.

KEOKUK; Keokuk River Museum (Victory Park), the stern-wheel towboat *George M. Verity,* depicts upper Mississippi River history; open mid-Apr.-Oct., Mon.-Sat. 9-5, Sun. & hols 10-6; sm adm.

LE CLAIRE: Buffalo Bill Museum (206 N River Rd.): artifacts related to William Cody, who was born here, and local history. Open May-Oct. 9-5, Nov.-Apr. Sat. and Sun. 10-5; sm adm. (See also McCausland.)

MARSHALLTOWN; Fisher Community Center (709 S Center St.): 19th-C and early 20th-C painting and sculpture, including Degas, Matisse, Monet, Cassatt; open daily; closed hols; free.

MASON CITY: Charles H. MacNider Museum (302 2nd St., SE) of painting and sculpture is open Tues.-Sat. 10-5, Sun. 2-5, closed hols; free.

McCAUSLAND: Buffalo Bill Homestead (3 m SW off US 61), built by Bill Cody's father in 1847, contains period artifacts. Open daily 9-7; donation. (See also Le Claire.)

MOUNT PLEASANT: Midwest Old Threshers Heritage Museum (Walnut St., S of US 34) displays antique agricultural machinery and kitchen appliances Memorial Day-Labor Day, daily 9-4; adm. **Harlan-Lincoln Museum** (Iowa Wesleyan College campus), home of Sen. James Harlan, can be seen by contacting the Public Relations Office.

MUSCATINE: Laura Musser Art Gallery & Museum (1314 Mulberry Ave.): 22-room Edwardian mansion built in 1908 by lumberman; 731-pipe Estey organ; African art; works by Midwest artists; historical items; Japanese garden; open Tues.-Sat. 10-noon, 2-5, Sun. 2-5; closed hols; free.

NASHUA: Little Brown Church in the Vale (2 m NE on SR 346), made famous by Dr. W. S. Pitts' hymn "The Church in the Wildwood," is now popular for weddings. Open daily.

OSKALOOSA: Nelson Pioneer Farm & Craft Museum (Glendale Rd., NE of Penn College campus), consisting of a house, barn, schoolhouse, and log cabin, houses period artifacts. Open mid-May-mid-Oct., Tues.-Sat. 10-5, Sun. 1-5; sm adm.

OTTUMWA: Wapello County Historical Museum (402 Chester Ave.) is open May-Oct. 2-5 daily. **Antique Airfield & Airpower Museum, Inc.** (10 m W at Antique Airfield) is open 9-5 daily, 1-5 Sun.; adm.

PELLA: Pella Historisch Museum Park (507 Franklin St.) consists of a dozen buildings, one of which was Wyatt Earp's boyhood home from 1850-64, housing items recalling Dutch settlement here in 1847—Delft collection, Dutch costumes, and library. A craft shop makes and sells pottery and wooden shoes. Open Mar.-Nov., daily exc. Sun. and hols, 9-11:30, 1-4:30; adm.

PERRY: Dallas County Forest Park & Museum (on Country Rd., E off SR 144): Several buildings house pioneer, Indian, Civil War artifacts; open May 1-Nov. 1, Tues.-Sun. 1-5; free.

SIOUX CITY: Sioux City Public Museum (2901 Jackson St.) highlights pioneer history, Indian arts, wildlife, geology; open Tues.-Sat. 9-5, Sun. 2-5; closed hols; free. **Floyd Monument** (US 75 & Glenn Ave.) marks the grave of Sgt. Charles Floyd, the only member of the Lewis & Clark Expedition to die on the trail.

SPILLVILLE: Antonin Dvorak spent a summer in this old-world Czech village. The house in which he lived now houses **Bily Clocks,** elaborately carved clocks by master craftsmen Frank and Joseph Bily. A clock in the shape of a violin is their memorial to Dvorak. Open May-Oct. daily 8:30-5:30; Mar.-Apr. & Nov., Sat., Sun. 10-4:30; sm adm.

STRAWBERRY POINT: Wilder Memorial Museum (1 blck W of jct SR 3, 13) includes more than 400 dolls, period furnishings, and Indian artifacts. Open Memorial Day-Labor Day daily 1-5; Sun. aft in spring and fall; sm adm.

WATERLOO: Museum of History & Science (Park Ave. & South St.) features pioneer, Indian, and space exhibits. Tues.-Fri. 1-5; Sat., Sun. 1-4; closed hols; free. Planetarium shows Sat. aft.

WAVERLY: Bremer County Historical Museum (near jct US 218, SR 3), once a stagecoach stop, displays local history. Open May-Oct., Tues.-Sat. 1:30-4, Sun. 2-4; closed hols; sm adm.

WEST BEND: Grotto of the Redemption (N of town, W of SR 15): Minerals, fossils, and shells have been embedded in concrete to construct grottos and Stations of the Cross. Open 24 hrs; hourly guided tours June 1-Oct. 15; donation.

WINTERSET: Madison County Court House, built in 1876, has solid walnut stairs and fine interior woodwork; open weekdays 9-5 exc hols.

KANSAS

ABILENE: Eisenhower Center (201 SE 4th St.): Home occupied by family 1898-1946; memorabilia of 34th President; research library; chapel with his grave and that of his 3-year-old son Doud; interpretive program in the museum; open daily 9-4:45; closed Jan. 1, Thnks, Dec. 25; sm adm to museum, other bldgs free.

Dickinson County Historical Museum (412 S Campbell St.): exhibits on pioneer and Chisholm Trail days; open Apr.-late Nov., Mon.-Sat. 10-4:30, Sun. 1-5; rest of yr, weekends only; closed Jan. 1, Thnks, Dec. 25; free.

Old Abilene Town (201 SE 6th St. at Kuney St.): replica of Abilene in cattle boom days; some original buildings restored. Open 8 am-9 pm in summer, 8:30-5 rest of year; closed Jan. 1, Thnks, Dec. 25. Free exc museum. **Greyhound Hall of Fame** (405 S Buckeye St.) details the history of this dog from 5000 BC; open daily 9-5; closed Jan. 1, Thnks, Dec. 25; sm adm. **MicroZoo** (Kuney & SE 6th Sts.): museum explaining microscopic life; genetics. Open daily in summer 10-6; fall and winter, Fri.-Tues. 10-6; closed Easter, Thnks, mid-Dec.-end Jan.; adm.

ALMA: Minnie Palenske Zwanziger Memorial Museum, with local historical items, is open Tues.-Sat. 10-noon, 1-4, Sun. 1-4; closed hols; donation.

ARKANSAS CITY: Cherokee Strip Living Museum (2 m S on US 77): exhibits on the Cherokee Strip Run, when 75,000 homesteaders ran for the Cherokee Strip at noon, Sept. 16, 1893; open Sun. 1:30-5 all yr; Mon.-Sat. 10-5 from mid-May-mid-Sept.; also Sat. 10-5 in spring & fall; closed most of Dec.-Jan.; adm.

ATCHISON: Benedictine College Abbey Church contains frescos by Jean Charlot; handsome altars; open daily in daylight. **Atchison County Museum** (409 Atchison St.): exhibit on Amelia Earhart (her birthplace at 223 N Terrace is privately owned); period rooms; open spring-fall, Sat. & Sun. 2-5, or by appointment; free.

BALDWIN CITY: Baker University, to which Lincoln donated $100, was founded in 1858. **Old Castle Museum:** Indian, pioneer, and Santa Fe

Trail relics; open Feb.-mid-Dec., Tues.-Sun. 2-5; free. **Quayle Bible Collection:** first editions, documents predating the Christian era, illuminated manuscripts in a 17th-C Jacobean room imported from Urishay Castle, England; open during academic yr, Mon.-Fri. 8-4; donation.

BELLEVILLE: Pawnee Indian Village Museum (15 m W on US 36, then 8 m N on SR 266) is built around an excavated Pawnee earth lodge from the early 1800's; artifacts; open Tues.-Sat. 10-5, Sun. 1:30-5; closed hols; free.

CHANUTE: Safari Museum (16 S Grant St.): collections from Africa and the South Seas of adventurers/authors Martin and Osa Johnson; open Mon.-Sat. 10-5, Sun. noon-6; sm adm.

COFFEYVILLE: Dalton Museum (113 E 8th St.): displays on the Dalton gang (3 are buried in the city cemetery), Wendell Willkie (who lived and taught school here), and Walter Johnson; open daily 8-8; sm adm. **Brown Mansion** (2019 Walnut St.): 1897 building designed by Stanford White; original furnishings; open Tues.-Sun. 10-4:30; closed July 4; adm.

COLBY: Sod Town Prairie Pioneer Museum (2 m E on US 24): reconstructed sod homes; period furnishings; open spring-fall 8-8; adm.

COUNCIL GROVE: This was the last outfitting depot before Santa Fe for travelers on the Santa Fe Trail. **Council Oak Shrine** (210 E Main St.) is site of the 1825 treaty the Osage signed, granting right-of-way for the trail. **Post Office Oak** (E Main St. at Union) was where pioneers left letters for the next wagon train to pick up. Nearby is a Madonna of the Trail Monument. **Hays Tavern** (112 W Main St.), an 1857 trading post, later served as saloon, hotel, and supply depot. **Pioneer Jail** (502 E Main St.), built in 1849, is open daily 9-5; free. **Kaw Methodist Mission** (500 N Mission St.), built in 1851 for Indians, is now a museum; open Tues.-Sat. 10-5, Sun. 1-5; closed Jan. 1, Thnks, Dec. 25; free.

DODGE CITY: During the late 1800's, this was one of the most notorious towns in the nation; buffalo hunters and cowboys congregated here, and pioneers passed through on the Santa Fe Trail. Among the many law officers who became famous trying to tame the town were Bat Masterson, Luke Short, and Wyatt Earp. **Historic Front Street** (500 W Wyatt Earp Blvd.) is a 2-block reconstruction of the main street as it appeared in the 1870's. You can enter **Beeson Museum** (medical and other exhibits; donation), the jail, many shops, **Hardesty House** (furnished home of a cattle baron), **Long Branch Saloon** (portraits of lawmen, variety shows); open daily 10-6 (longer in summer). **Home of Stone** (112 E Vine St.), furnished 1881 Victorian home, is open June-Labor Day, daily 9 am-8 pm; donation. **Boot Hill** (Spruce St. & 5th Ave.) has hangman's tree and museum; donation.

EMPORIA: This was home of William Allen White, whose *Emporia Gazette* gained nationwide renown; his home, **Red Rocks** (927 Exchange St.) is worth seeing from the outside. **Emporia Gazette** (517 Merchant St.) offers White memorabilia, tours; open Mon.-Fri. 8-5, Sat. 8-noon; closed hols; free. **Emporia Public Library** (118 E 6th St.) keeps a file of the *Gazette;* open Mon.-Sat. 9-6; closed hols; free.

FORT LARNED NATIONAL HISTORIC SITE (6 m W of Larned on US 156): Established 1859, the fort was important in 1868-9, when Cheyenne were attacking wagon trains and settlers. Although Gen. Custer crushed Indian resistance at the 1868 Battle of Washita and the Indians were forced onto reservations, the fort remained active until 1878 to protect railroad crews. Commissary, bakery, workshops, other buildings well preserved, with exhibits; open daily 8-5 (longer hrs in summer); closed Dec. 25; free.

FORT SCOTT: Carroll Plaza (Marmaton, Blair, Benton, & Lincoln Aves.) was the parade grounds for the fort, manned 1842-3 when the Cherokee were being moved west; the fort was reactivated during the "bloody Kansas" era; reconstructed officers' quarters and blockhouse.

HANOVER: Hollenberg Pony Express Station (1 m E on SR 243) is a state museum; open Tues.-Sat. 10-5, Sun. 1-5; closed Jan. 1, Thnks, Dec. 25; free.

HAYS: Fort Hays (Frontier Historical Park, SW edge of city), established 1865 to protect roads, mails, and railroad construction crews, was also used by Gen. Custer and the 7th Cavalry. Visitor Center; displays in guardhouse, officers' quarters, and blockhouse; open Mon.-Sat. 10-5, Sun. 1:30-5; closed hols; free.
  Sternberg Memorial Museum (campus of Ft. Hays Kansas State College, W of town) has geological, palaeontological, natural history, and historical displays; open during the academic year on weekdays 8-5 and during vacations 2-5; closed hols; free.

HIAWATHA: Mt. Hope Cemetery (SE edge of town): unusual John M. Davis memorial—11 life-size statues of Davis and his wife at various points in their lives.

HIGHLAND: Iowa, Sac & Fox Presbyterian Mission (2 m E via US 36, then N on SR 136), founded in 1837, is a museum housing pioneer and Indian relics. Open Tues.-Sat. 10-5, Sun. 1:30-5; closed hols; free.

INDEPENDENCE: Montgomery County Historical Museum (Riverside Park, Oak & 3rd Sts.): 1869 log cabin, pioneer displays; open daily in summer 2-5; fall-spring, Wed., Sat., Sun. 2-5; free. **Independence Museum** (8th & Myrtle Sts.): Plains Indians artifacts; decorative arts; open Wed., Sat., Sun. 1-5; closed Jan. 1, Dec. 25; sm adm.

IOLA: Funston Memorial (4 m N on US 169): boyhood home of Gen. Frederick Funston, hero of the Philippine insurrection of 1901; open Mon.-Sat. 10-5, Sun. & hols 1-5; closed Jan. 1, Thnks, Dec. 25; free. **Old Jail Museum** (201 N Jefferson St.) is open May-Sept., Mon.-Fri. 10-noon, 2-4; free.

KANSAS CITY: Indian Cemetery (Huron Park, Center City Plaza at 7th St.) contains some 400 graves of Wyandot Indians, who came from Ohio to settle the city in 1843. **Shawnee Methodist Mission** (53rd St. & Mission Rd.) was established in 1830; 3 buildings still stand; original furnishings and historical items. Open Mon.-Sat. 10-5, Sun. 1-5; closed Jan. 1, Thnks, Dec. 25; free. **Grinter House** (S 78th St. in Muncie, W via SR 32): home of county's first white settler; open Tues.-Sat. 10-5, Sun. 1-5; closed Jan. 1, Thnks, Dec. 25; free.

Agricultural Hall of Fame & National Center (630 N 126th St. in Bonner Springs): displays on the evolution of agriculture. Open daily 9-5; closed Jan. 1, Thnks, Dec. 25; adm.

Wyandotte County Museum (631 N 126th St. in Bonner Springs): open Tues.-Sun. 1-5; closed Thnks, Dec. 25; free.

LAWRENCE: University of Kansas museums are usually open Mon.-Sat. 9-4:45, Sun. & hols 1:30-4:45; free: **Museum of Natural History** (fossils, mounted birds and animals, prehistoric and recent Indian cultures); **Spooner Thayer Museum of Art** (medieval and Italian Renaissance; 17th-18th-C European paintings; 19th-20th-C American works; Oriental decorative arts; European and American sculpture; graphics); **Wilcox Museum** (Greek and Roman antiquities); **Snow Entomological Museum**; carillon (Wed. eve & Sun. aft).

Oak Hill Cemetery: memorial to 150 victims of a raid by Confederate guerrilla William Quantrill in 1863 during the conflict over slavery (Lawrence, a center for Free Staters, was sacked and burned twice by pro-slavery forces).

LEAVENWORTH: Fort Leavenworth (on US 73, N of town), established 1827 to protect wagon trains; museum with exhibits on the growth of Leavenworth, an important supply center; old vehicles. Booklets for self-guiding tours of fort, U.S. Army Command & General Staff College, historic houses, bronze statue of Ulysses S. Grant by Lorado Taft, Santa Fe and Oregon Trail markers, National Cemetery. Fort open all yr; museum open Mon.-Sat. 10-4, Sun. noon-4; closed Jan. 1, Easter, Thnks, Dec. 25; free.

Leavenworth County Historical Museum (334 5th Ave.): displays of the late 1800's; open Tues.-Sun. 1-4:30; closed Jan. 1, Easter, late Dec.; adm.

LIBERAL: Coronado Museum (567 E Cedar St.) traces the 1641 route of Coronado (who entered the state here and went as far as Lindsborg); pioneer life displays; open Tues.-Sat. 9-5, Sun. noon-5; closed hols; free.

LINDSBORG: Founded by Swedish settlers in 1868, this town retains a Swedish flavor; information on crafts and attractions from **Chamber of Commerce** (120 E Lincoln). **McPherson County Old Mill Museum & Park** (120 Mill St.) depicts the Midwest Scandinavian heritage; open May-Oct., Tues.-Sat. 9:30-5, Sun. 1-5; Nov.-Apr., Tues.-Sun. 1-5; closed Jan. 1, Thnks, Dec. 25; adm. **Birger Sandzen Memorial Gallery** (401 N 1st St.) has Sandzen paintings and graphics, other works, courtyard fountain by Carl Milles; open Tues.-Sun. 1-5; closed hols; sm adm.

MANHATTAN: Riley County Historical Museum (Polyntz Ave.) is open Tues.-Sat. 1-5, Sun. 2-4:40; closed hols, early Dec.; free. **Goodnow House** (2301 Claflin Rd.), restored home of educator Isaac T. Goodnow, and adjacent **Hartford House,** brought by riverboat by Free Staters in the 1850's, are open Wed. 9-noon, Thurs. & Fri. 1-4, Sat. 10-5, Sun. 1-5; closed Jan. 1, Thnks, Dec. 25; free.

Beecher Bible & Rifle Church (on SR 18, E at Wabaunsee) was organized in 1857 by abolitionist settlers for whom Henry Ward Beecher's congregation raised money.

Fort Riley (9 m SW on SR 18), established in 1853 to protect the Santa Fe and Oregon trails, was home to the famed 7th Cavalry. The fort is open daily; self-guiding tour includes: **U.S. Cavalry Museum;** open daily 10-4; closed Dec. 25; free. **Gen. Custer's Home,** built in 1855 and still in use. **First Territorial Capitol,** where the Kansas Territorial Legislature met in 1855; furnished with period pieces; open Tues.-Sat. 10-5, Sun. 1-5; closed Jan. 1, Thnks, Dec. 25; free.

MARYSVILLE: The Oregon and Mormon trails converged 5 m S of here on the Blue River, and many wagon trains (including the ill-fated Donner Party) camped here in the mid-1800's. **Koester House Museum** (919 Broadway): built 1876; Victorian era furnishings and displays. Open Thurs.-Tues. 2-5; closed Thnks, Dec. 25; adm.

MEDICINE LODGE: **Medicine Lodge Stockade** (US 160): Replica of stockade built 1874 against Indian raids; this ground, considered sacred by Plains Indians, was site of an 1867 peace settlement. Museum with pioneer artifacts; furnished 1877 log home; open June-Oct. daily 10-6, Apr.-May daily 1-5, Nov.-Mar. weekends only 1-5; closed Thnks, Dec. 25; sm adm.

Carry A. Nation Memorial Home (211 W Fowler Ave.) is maintained as a museum by the WCTU. Carry Nation smashed up her first saloon in nearby Kiowa in 1900. Open daily 7 am-10 pm; donation.

NEWTON: This is the largest Mennonite settlement in the U.S. In Athletic Park is a memorial to Mennonite settlers, who arrived from Russia in the 1870's; they brought with them the hardy Turkey Red winter wheat that turned Kansas into the "breadbasket of the nation." Bethel College campus has an art gallery (open Mon.-Fri. 10-5, Sun. 1:30-5) and the **Kauffman Museum of Mennonite Culture;** exhibits on Mennonite pioneers, open Mon.-Fri. 8:30-12:30, 1-5, Sat. 8:30-noon, Sun. 1-5; closed Thnks, Dec. 25; adm. **Warkentin House** (211 E 1st St.), a Victorian home, belonged to a Mennonite leader; original furnishings; open daily 1-4:30 in summer, weekends 1-4:30 rest of yr; adm.

Victorian House of Clocks (615 Columbus): open Tues.-Sun. 9-11, 1-4 in summer; rest of yr, Thurs.-Sun. 1-5; closed hols & Jan.; adm. **Kansas Health Museum** (309 Main St. in Halstead, 12 m SW) offers health education exhibits, including transparent body model; open Mon.-Fri. 10-4, Sun. 1-5; closed hols; adm. **King's Antique Car Museum** (220 S Streeter, 7 m NW in Hesston): open Tues.-Sat. 10-5:30, Sun. 12:30-5:30; adm.

OBERLIN: **Indian Raid Museum** (258 S Penn) was site of the last Indian raid in Kansas, in 1878, when Northern Cheyenne tried to regain their homeland; Indian artifacts, period shops and offices. Open Apr.-Dec., Mon.-Sat. 9-5 (longer hrs in summer), Sun. & hols 1-5; closed Thnks, Dec. 25; sm adm.

OSAWATOMIE: **John Brown Memorial Park** (10th & Main Sts.) contains statue of the abolitionist, log cabin he used during the 1856 battle of Osawatomie; open Tues.-Sat. 10-5, Sun. 1:30-5; closed hols; free.

PHILLIPSBURG: Old Fort Bissell (City Park, ½ m W on US 36): replica of fort; gun and pioneer displays; open spring-fall 9-5 (longer in summer); free.

PORTIS: Continental Sculpture Hall displays more than 450 carvings of animals and people in 3 types of rock; open daily 9-9; closed hols; adm.

SALINA: Indian Burial Site (4 m E on SR 140), with skeletons of some 140 Indians, dates back about 1000 yrs; artifacts; open daily 9-6; sm adm. **Smoky Hill Historical Museum** (Oakdale Park, Mulberry St. & S 2nd Ave.): prehistoric and recent Indian materials, period rooms, Oriental art; open Tues.-Sun. 1-5; closed Jan. 1, Thnks, Dec. 25; free.

SANTA FE TRAIL was cut across Kansas roughly paralleling US 56; at Dodge City it divided, with branches leaving the state at Coolidge and Elkhart; ruts can be seen in many prairie areas. **Santa Fe Trail Center** (3 m W of Larned) explains the history; open daily 9-5 (longer in summer); closed Dec. 25; adm. Near Fort Larned (4 m SE via SR 242) there is a parking lot where you can examine a portion of the trail.

SMITH CENTER: Home on the Range Cabin (17 m NW via US 36, SR 8): home of Brewster M. Higley, pioneer physician who wrote the words to "Home on the Range" in 1872. Open daily; free.

TOPEKA: State Capitol (Capitol Sq.) is noted for murals of Kansas history by David H. Overmyer and John Steuart Curry. On the grounds are statues of Lincoln and the Pioneer Woman by Merrill Gage. Open Mon.-Fri. 8-5, Sat., Sun., hols 9-4; free. **Kansas State Historical Society** (Memorial Bldg., 10th & Jackson Sts.): one of the largest collections of newspapers in the U.S.; state's history from prehistoric times; sod house, stagecoach, period rooms; state archives, genealogy library. Open Mon.-Sat. 8-5, Sun. 1-5; closed hols; free.

WICHITA: Wichita Historical Museum (3751 E Douglas Ave.) depicts the city's growth from Indian village, trading post, and cow town; period rooms; open Tues.-Sat. 11-5, Sun. 1-5; closed hols; sm adm.
    Cowtown (1717 Sim Park Dr.) is a 37-building complex depicting Wichita in the late 1800's; open Tues.-Sun., 9-7 in summer, 9-5 in spring and fall; closed in winter; adm.
    Wichita State University (1845 Fairmount St.) gives tours with advance notice. **Corbin Education Center,** one of Frank Lloyd Wright's last

designs. **Edwin A. Ulrich Museum of Art,** with contemporary American works (open Wed.-Sat. 11-5, Sun. 1-5; closed hols; free).

Wichita Art Assn. (9112 E Central): attractive setting encompassing studios and classrooms; exhibitions mid-Sept.-mid-July, Tues.-Sun. 1-5; closed hols; free.

Fellow-Reeve Museum (Friends Univ., University & Hiram Sts.): mounted birds and animals; fossils; Indian and African material; pioneer artifacts; open Mon.-Fri. noon-5, closed hols; sm adm.

KENTUCKY

ABRAHAM LINCOLN BIRTHPLACE NATIONAL HISTORIC SITE (3 m S of Hodgenville on US 31E, SR 61): Thomas Lincoln bought Sinking Spring Farm for $200, and here Abraham was born in 1809; but by 1811 the farm was lost because of a defective title, and the Lincolns had to move. The log cabin is enclosed in a granite and marble monument. Visitor Center with audiovisual programs, exhibits. Open daily, June-Aug. 8-6:45, Sept.-May 8-4:45; closed Dec. 25; free.

BARBOURVILLE: Dr. Thomas Walker State Shrine (6 m S on SR 459): replica of 1750 cabin, home of first white settler; open all year; free.

BARDSTOWN: My Old Kentucky Home State Park (1 m E on US 150): Stephen Foster is said to have been inspired to write "My Old Kentucky Home" while visiting cousins in this 1795 manor house, Federal Hill; many original furnishings. *Stephen Foster Story* presented in summer. Open daily Mar.-Nov. 9-5 (longer hrs in summer); Tues.-Sun. 9-5 in Dec.-Feb.; closed Jan. 1, Dec. 25; grounds free; adm to house.

Visitor Information Center (Court Sq.) runs free Tourmobile to local attractions; mid-June-Labor Day, Mon.-Sat. 9:30 & 1:30. **Barton Museum of Whiskey History** (Barton Brands, Barton Rd., 1 m SW): open daily 8-noon, 1-4; distillery tours, Mon.-Fri. 8-noon, 1-4, exc hols; free. **Wickland** (½ m E on US 62), lovely 1813 Georgian home; unusually fine woodwork; period furnishings; open May-Oct., Mon.-Sat. 9-sunset; Nov.-Apr., Mon., Wed., Fri., Sat. 9-sunset; Sun. all yr noon-sunset; closed Easter, Thnks, Dec. 25; adm. **St. Joseph's Cathedral** (W side of jct US 31E, 62), handmade by pioneers in 1819, contains works by Rubens, Van

Eyck, Murillo, and others, donated by the exiled King of France, Louis Philippe, who visited here in 1797; open Mon.-Sat. 9-5, Sun. 1-5; sm adm.

Bloomfield Cemetery (9 m E on US 62, then 3 m N on SR 55) has grave of Jeroboam and Anna Beauchamp, buried in a single coffin by request. A local politician, Col. Solomon Sharp, supposedly seduced Anna at his home (see Frankfort) in 1825. Jeroboam murdered him, and the couple was sentenced to hang. On execution day they attempted suicide by stabbing themselves; Anna died, but Jeroboam lived to be hanged (first legal hanging in the state) in 1826. The tragedy inspired Robert Penn Warren's novel *World Enough and Time* and works by E. A. Poe and others.

BEREA: Berea College tours start at **Boone Tavern** (containing campus-made furniture) Mon.-Fri. 9, 2; Sat. 9; free. **Art Galleries,** with Renaissance and local work, and **Science Building,** with geology and biology museums, are open during the academic yr, Mon.-Fri. 8-4:30; closed hols; free. **Craft Demonstration Center** offers demonstration of woodworking, needlecraft, and other campus industries; Mar.-mid-Dec. Mon.-Sat. 4-6; free. **Appalachian Museum** has smokehouse, blacksmith shop, country store; audiovisual programs; open Mon.-Sat. 9-6 (9-9 in summer), Sun. 1-6; closed Easter, Thnks, Dec. 25; sm adm. **Indian Fort Theatre** has a crafts fair in May, performances of the Civil War musical *Wilderness Road* in summer, other events. **Weatherford-Hammond Mountain Collection** consists of recordings and printed material on Appalachia.

BLUE LICKS BATTLEFIELD STATE PARK (26 m SW of Maysville on US 68): Site of the last battle of the Revolution (Aug. 19, 1782, a year after Cornwallis surrendered). Museum with prehistoric human and animal remains, gun and glass collections; open Apr.-Oct. daily 9-5; sm adm.

BOWLING GREEN: Kentucky Library & Museum (Western Kentucky Univ., off US 68), in a Georgian building, houses 1000 specimens of local birds, nests, eggs, insects, mammals; guns; historical relics; Indian artifacts; records of Kentucky history, including the South Union Shakers; open during academic yr, Mon.-Fri. 9-5, Sat. 9-4; museum only Sun. 2-4; closed hols; free. **Riverview** (Hobson Grove Park, W end of Main St.): Italian-style villa; many original furnishings; open Tues.-Sun. 1-4; closed hols; adm.

Shaker Museum (14 m SW on US 68 in S Union) contains exhibits of Shaker community that flourished here 1807-1922; open mid-May-Labor Day, Mon.-Sat. 9-5, Sun. 1-5; also fall weekends; adm. See also Harrodsburg.

BREAKS INTERSTATE PARK (5 m SE of Elkhorn City), called the Grand Canyon of the South, has a **Visitor Center** with museum on geology, wildlife; bird song recordings; information on folklore and history of the region; open Apr.-Oct. daily 9-5; sm adm.

CUMBERLAND GAP NATIONAL HISTORICAL PARK (½ m S of Middlesboro on US 25E): Discovery of this natural pass by Dr. Thomas Walker in 1750 opened the way West; Daniel Boone followed in 1769, and after Indians drove him back in a 1773 attempt to settle in Kentucky, Boone returned in 1775 with 30 axmen to blaze the Wilderness Road; by 1800 the trail had been used by 300,000 settlers. During the Civil War the gap changed hands 4 times, the fortifications remain in several areas of the park. **Visitor Center** (open daily 8-5, 8-7 in summer; closed Dec. 25) has historical exhibits; audiovisual program. **Hensley Settlement** (on Ridge Trail) is a reconstructed mountaineer community; open daily exc Dec. 25. Free.

CAVE CITY: Mammoth Cave Chair Lift & Guntown Mountain (1 m W at jct SR 70, I-65): lift to re-created frontier town with museums, other buildings; open Memorial Day-Labor Day daily; lift fee plus adm.

DANVILLE: Constitution Square State Shrine (US 127, 150): on the site where the state's first constitution was framed and adopted in 1792; original post office; reconstructed log courthouse, church, jail; open daily 9-5; free. **McDowell House & Apothecary Shop** (125 S 2nd St.), where Dr. Ephraim McDowell performed a landmark abdominal operation in 1809 (without anaesthesia), is restored with period furnishings by the Kentucky Medical Assn.; open Mon.-Sat. 10-4, Sun. 2-4; closed for lunch Sept.-June; closed Jan. 1, Easter, Thnks, Dec. 25; adm.

    Perryville Battlefield State Shrine (10 m W off US 150): The battle on Oct. 8, 1862 marked the second and last Confederate attempt to win Kentucky; museum with dioramas, Gen. Bragg's hq, other buildings, memorials to the war dead; open June-Aug. daily 9-5; spring & fall, Tues.-Sun. 9-5; sm adm.

    William Whitley House State Shrine (19 m SE on US 150): Built 1787-94 as home and fo.t by an Indian fighter and scout, this became a stopping place for travelers on the Wilderness Road; furnished in 1770-1810 style; panels over the parlor mantel represent the 13 colonies; open June-Aug. daily 9-5; rest of yr, Tues.-Sun. 9-5; sm adm.

    Lincoln Heritage House (Freeman Lake Park, 1 m N on US 31W): double log cabin, home of Abraham Lincoln's father, Thomas, with examples of his carpentry skills. Nancy Hanks Lincoln had her first child, Sarah, here; after Nancy died, Thomas returned to Elizabethtown to marry the widow Sarah Bush Johnston. Open June-Sept., Tues.-Sat. 10-4, Sun. 1:30-5; sm adm.

ELIZABETHTOWN: Brown-Pusey House (128 N Main St.): fine Georgian building, formerly a stagecoach inn; Gen. George Custer stayed here 1871-73; many original furnishings; library; open Mon.-Sat. 10-5; closed hols; free.

FORT BOONESBOROUGH STATE PARK (9 m SW of Winchester on the Kentucky River): reconstructed 1775 fort, site of Daniel Boone's settlement; furnished cabins and trading post re-create life at the fort; museum with Boone memorabilia, other historic items, audiovisual program on pioneers; open Memorial Day-Labor Day daily 10-8; weekends only spring and fall 10-6; adm.

FORT KNOX: Patton Museum of Cavalry & Armor (Bldg. 4554, Fayette Ave.), honoring Gen. George S. Patton Jr.,; huge collection of military equipment, American and foreign; open Mon.-Fri. 9-4:30; weekends & hols 10-4:30 (10-6 in summer); closed Jan. 1, Dec. 25; free. **U.S. Bullion Depository** (Gold Vault Rd.) is not open to the public.

FRANKFORT: State Capitol (S end of Capitol Ave.), one of the nation's most impressive state capitols, is set in landscaped grounds overlooking the Kentucky River. French influences include the rotunda copied from the Hotel des Invalides, stairways after those of the Paris Opera, and the State Reception Room duplicating Marie Antoinette's drawing room in the Grand Trianon Palace. Murals of Daniel Boone, statues of Jefferson Davis and Lincoln, are among many historic works of art. Open Mon.-Fri. 8-4:30, weekends & hols 9-4:30; closed Dec. 25; free. On the grounds is a working floral clock. **Governor's Mansion,** built in 1797, was modeled on Marie Antoinette's Petit Trianon; weather permitting, tours leave from the Capitol information desk on Tues. & Thurs. 9:30-11:30.
    Kentucky Historical Society & Museum (Broadway & St. Clair St.) is in the Old State House, a splendid Greek Revival structure designed by Gideon Shryock that served as the capitol 1830-1910; documents and manuscripts; Jefferson Davis papers; Civil War material; Daniel Boone's rifle; other artifacts; genealogical library.
    Liberty Hall (218 Wilkinson St. at Main St.), a 1796 Georgian brick home built for John Brown, one of the state's first 2 senators, has Federal interior elements. Thomas Jefferson is said to have participated in its design. Beautifully furnished with many Brown family heirlooms. **Orlando Brown House** (202 Wilkinson St.) is an 1835 Greek Revival home designed by Gideon Shryock for John Brown's son, Orlando. Furnished with

Duncan Phyfe and other family antiques; family portraits. Both houses open Tues.-Sat. 10-5, Sun. 2-5; closed Jan. 1, Dec. 25; adm to each or combination ticket.

Frankfort Cemetery (E Main St.), on a hill above the Kentucky River, has a monument to Daniel Boone and his wife Rebecca (Boone died in Missouri and his body was buried here in 1845). Open daily in daylight; free.

Kentucky Military History Museum (E Main St.) in the Old State Arsenal, includes firearms belonging to famous people. Open Mon.-Sat. 9-4, Sun. 1-5; closed Jan. 1, Dec. 25; free.

Chamber of Commerce (71 Fountain Place) provides maps and brochures for self-guiding tours. The old section, bounded by the Kentucky River, St. Clair St., and Broadway, has many homes—in styles ranging from Georgian to Italian Renaissance—that hosted Thomas Jefferson, James Madison, Lafayette, the Bourbon Prince Louis Philippe, Aaron Burr, Andrew Jackson, and others. Aaron Burr stood trial for treason here and was acquitted after a defense by Henry Clay. Here too are the homes of John B. Bibb (developer of Bibb lettuce) and of distillery families, and the Sharp House, where Col. Sharp was murdered (see Bloomfield). The Chamber of Commerce also has information on free distillery tours, usually available Mon.-Fri. 8:30-3:30; closed hols.

GENERAL BUTLER STATE RESORT PARK (on US 227 2 m S of Carrollton): Butler Home, with period furnishings, houses the Museum of Ohio River Lore; family graveyard; open June-Aug. daily 10-6, spring & fall Tues.-Sun. 10-6; sm adm.

HARRODSBURG: Old Fort Harrod State Park (on US 68, 127): replica of palisaded fort that was Kentucky's first settlement (1774); pioneer cemetery; Mansion Museum with displays on George Rogers Clark, Lincoln, the Confederacy; Lincoln Marriage Temple, erected over the cabin in which Lincoln's parents were married; open 9-5 Mar.-Nov. daily, weekends only Dec.-Feb.; sm adm. Map for self-guiding **Red Arrow Tour** of area attractions is available here.

Morgan Row House & Museum (220 S Chiles St., behind Courthouse), oldest row house in Kentucky, contains the library and exhibits of the Harrodsburg Historical Society; open June-Labor Day, Tues.-Sun. 10-5; adm. **Old Mud Meetinghouse** (5½ m S via US 68), an 1800 Dutch Reformed Church, has a glass-enclosed section showing the original mud thatch walls.

Pleasant Hill Shaker Village (7 m NE on US 68): More than 25 buildings remain of this 19th-C village whose last resident died in 1923; Centre

Family Dwelling House and other restored buildings demonstrate the Shaker way of life; open daily, 9-5 spring-fall, shorter hrs in winter; closed Dec. 24, 25; adm. See also South Union.

JEFFERSON DAVIS MONUMENT STATE SHRINE (on US 68, Fairview): 351-ft obelisk with observation deck; replica of log cabin birthplace; open 9-5:30 daily June-Aug., Tues.-Sun. in spring & fall, weekends only in winter; sm adm.

JOHN JAMES AUDUBON STATE PARK (2 m N of Henderson on US 41): Memorial Museum with displays of Audubon's life and work; Audubon came here in 1810, where he was co-owner of a general store and then ran a grist mill, and spent 9 yrs studying and drawing birds; original paintings and prints; stuffed birds; egg, butterfly, and insect collections; a portrait of Daniel Boone by Audubon; open daily June-Aug., Tues.-Sun. in spring & fall, weekends only in winter; sm adm.

LEVI JACKSON WILDERNESS ROAD STATE PARK (2 m S of London on US 25) contains part of Boone's Trace, the Wilderness Trail, site of a 1786 massacre by Indians of 24 settlers; reconstructed 1812 **McHargue's Mill** with large collection of millstones; and **Mountain Life Museum,** furnished cabins depicting Kentucky frontier life; open May-Aug. daily 9-5; weekends only in Sept.; sm adm.

LEXINGTON: Chamber of Commerce (239 N Broadway) provides information on guided and self-guiding tours of historic sites and horse farms.

    Kentucky State Horse Farm (N on Iron Works Pike), formerly Walnut Hall Stud Farm, is a wonderful model farm with horse barns and museum dedicated to Kentucky horses; grave and statue of Man O'War; events; open Apr.-Oct. daily 9-5; sm adm.

    American Saddle Horse Museum (Spindletop Farm, 7 m N on Ironworks Pike): oil paintings, trophies, saddles and other horse paraphernalia; library; open June-Aug. Tues.-Sat. 10-4, Sun. 1-3; spring & fall, Tues.-Sun. 1-4; closed Nov.-Mar.; adm.

    Lexington Cemetery (833 W Main St. on US 421) contains the graves of Henry Clay, Lincoln's maternal relatives, King Solomon (hero of the 1833 cholera plague), and others; Confederate and Union Soldiers; open daily 8-5; free.

    Hunt-Morgan House, Hopemont (201 N Mill St. at W 2nd St.): lovely 1814 Georgian-style home of John Wesley Hunt, his grandson John Hunt

Morgan ("Thunderbolt of the Confederacy"), and birthplace of Thomas Hunt Morgan (Nobel Prize winner in genetics); antique furnishings; Confederate memorabilia; carriage house. **Henry Clay's Law Office**, restored to its 1803 appearance, when the Great Commoner was first elected to the state legislature. Both open Tues.-Sat. 10-4, Sun. 2-5; closed Thnks, Dec. 24, 25, 31, Jan.; adm.

Ashland (E Main St. & Sycamore Rd. on US 25 S), home of Henry Clay (1811 until his death 1852); family furnishings and mementos; outbuildings; open daily 9:30-4:30; closed Dec. 25; adm.

Waveland State Shrine (Higbee Mill Pike, 6 m S off US 27), a plantation begun by a nephew of Daniel Boone, with an 1847 mansion, has been restored to illustrate Kentucky life from pioneer through antebellum days; slave quarters, still, other outbuildings; open Tues.-Sat. 9-4, Sun. 1:30-4:30; adm.

Headley Museum (Old Frankfort Pike, 6 m W): jeweled bibelots, many designed by George Headley and made by leading craftsmen around the world, housed in a lovely building; art library; open Wed., Sat., Sun., noon-5; closed Jan. 1, Easter, Dec. 25; adm.

LINCOLN HOMESTEAD STATE PARK (on SR 528 5 m N of Springfield): replica of cabin built here 1782 by Lincoln's grandfather, where Thomas Lincoln lived 25 years; replicas of shops in which Thomas Lincoln worked; Berry House, where Nancy Hanks lived while being courted by Thomas Lincoln; all furnished with pioneer relics and open May-Labor Day daily 8-6; sm adm.

LOUISVILLE: Visitors Bureau (Founders Sq., 5th & Walnut Sts.) provides list of distillery and tobacco tours; nearby horse farms; map for walking tour; schedule for sternwheeler, *Belle of Louisville,* cruises. Narrated bus tours leave from here. Founders Square honors the city's founder, George Rogers Clark.

Louisville Museum of Science & History (743 S 5th at York): mounted animals; Indian artifacts; fossils; Kentuckiana; open Mon.-Fri. 9-5; closed hols; free.

Jefferson County Courthouse (6th & Jefferson), a Greek Revival design by Gideon Shryock, has statues of Thomas Jefferson (outside) and Henry Clay (in rotunda).

Farmington (3033 Bardstown Rd. at jct Watterson Expwy.): Thomas Jefferson designed this Federal-style home completed in 1810; hidden stairway, octagonal rooms; fine antique furnishings; outbuildings; open Tues.-Sat. 10-4:30, Sun. 1:30-4:30; adm.

Filson Club (118 W Breckinridge St.): good Kentuckiana, library; open Mon.-Fri. 9-5, Sat. 9-noon; closed hols & Sat. in July-Sept.; free.

Locust Grove (6 m NE via River Rd, then 1 m SW at 561 Blankenbaker Lane): George Rogers Clark spent his last 9 years (1809-18) in this 1790 Georgian mansion; period furnishings; open Tues.-Sat. 10-4:30, Sun. 1:30-4:30; adm. Clark is buried in Cave Hill Cemetery (701 Baxter Ave.).

Southern Baptist Theological Seminary Library (2825 Lexington Rd.): archaeological specimens in **Nichol Museum of Biblical Archaeology** and **Eisenberg Museum of Egyptian & Near Eastern Antiquities**; Billy Graham collection; open Mon.-Fri. 8 am-10 pm, Sat. 9-5; closed Thnks, Dec. 25; free.

University of Louisville (3rd St. & Eastern Pkwy, 3 m S): **J. B. Speed Art Museum** (2035 3rd St.): superb collection; antiquities; Rubens, Monet, other masters; sculpture; Elizabethan room; decorative arts; open Tues.-Sat. 10-4, Sun. 2-6; free. **Rauch Memorial Planetarium** (shows Fri. 8, Sun. 3, 5; adm); **Art Library; Main Library** (Patterson rare book collection).

Kentucky Railway Museum (Upper River Rd., 2 m E at Eva Bandman Park): engines, cars, railroad artifacts; open Apr.-Oct., Sat., Sun., hols 1-5; donation.

Zachary Taylor National Cemetery (4701 Brownsboro Rd., 7 m E on US 42): grave of the 12th President; his nearby home (Springfield, 5608 Apache Rd., where he lived 1784-90) is not open to the public.

MAMMOTH CAVE NATIONAL PARK (on SR 70, 10 m W of Cave City): **Visitor Center** (open daily in summer 7:30 am-8 pm, in spring & fall 8-5:30, in winter 8-5) has exhibits and orientation programs on this cave with more than 150 m of passageways, human history that goes back at least 2500 years, and specially adapted animal life. Several tours available, including a 2-m, 2-hr Historic Tour, daily.

MAYFIELD: Maplewood Cemetery (on US 45): At the grave of horse breeder Henry C. Wooldridge are life-size statues of his favorite dogs and horse, relatives, a deer, and a fox; open daily 7 am-6 pm; free.

PADUCAH: Chamber of Commerce (417 Washington St.) offers maps for self-guiding tours that include: **City Hall** (5th & Washington Sts.), designed by Edward Durell Stone; resembles his U.S. Embassy in New Delhi. **Market House** (Broadway & S 2nd St.) containing an art gallery, theater, and the **William Clark Museum** of early Americana (open Tues.-Sat. noon-4, Sun. 1-5; closed Jan. 1, July 4, Thnks, Dec. 25; sm adm).

PARIS: Duncan Tavern Historic Shrine (323 High St.): Restored and furnished 1788 Duncan Tavern, where Daniel Boone and other frontiersmen gathered, and 1800 **Anne Duncan House**, home of the innkeeper;

open Mon.-Sat. 10-5, Sun. 1:30-5; closed Jan. 1, July 4, Thnks, Dec. 25; adm. **Old Cane Ridge Meeting House** (8 m E on SR 537) is a 1791 log structure protected by a $100,000 limestone shelter; here the Disciples of Christ were formed in 1804 and revival meetings attracted thousands; open daily in daylight; donation.

RICHMOND: White Hall State Shrine (5 m N off I-75): grand 1799 Georgian home with elegant ballroom, heating, and plumbing in an 1860's Italianate addition, was home of Cassius M. Clay, abolitionist, publisher of *The True American,* and founder of Berea College; he was born here in 1810 and died in the same bed in 1903; period furnishings; family memorabilia; one room devoted to his daughter Laura, an early activist for women's rights; open early Apr.-early Nov. daily 9-5, rest of yr Tues.-Sun. 9-5; closed Jan.; adm.

    Courthouse (Main St. at N 1st St.) is an 1849 building used as a hospital during the Civil War; a Wilderness Road marker is in the lobby.

TOMPKINSVILLE: Old Mulkey Meeting House State Shrine (3 m S on SR 1446): Built 1804 by Baptists at the height of a religious revival that swept through Kentucky, with meetings that could last weeks; 12 corners represent the Apostles, 3 doors the Trinity. Daniel Boone's sister Hannah and other pioneers are buried in the graveyard; open daily 9-5; free.

WASHINGTON, laid out in 1785, has preserved a historic district of more than 30 buildings; furnished 1795 **Albert S. Johnston Home;** 1787 **Mefford's Station; Cane Break Log house;** 1810 **Paxton Inn** with library and period displays; open spring-early fall, Mon.-Sat. 11:30-4:30, Sun. 1-4:30; weekends only in fall; sm adm or combination tickets.

LOUISIANA

BATON ROUGE: State Capitol (Riverside Mall & Boyd Ave.) is a monumental structure built during Huey P. Long's administration (1931-2); replete with symbolism; lavish interior; a fitting memorial to the "Kingfish," who is buried in a sunken garden before it; open daily 8-4; tours hourly; closed Jan. 1, Dec. 25; free. Observation tower is open same hrs but closed Mon.-Fri. 11:45-12:30; free. Also on the Mall are: **Old Arsenal Museum** with historic exhibits (open Tues.-Sat. 10-noon, 1-4:30, Sun.

11:30-4:30; closed Thnks, Dec. 25; free) and **State Library** (open Mon.-Fri. 8-4:30; closed Mardi Gras, Good Friday, Aug. 30, hols; free).

Old State Capitol (North Blvd & St. Phillips St.), rebuilt after an 1862 fire, resembles a Norman castle, but Mark Twain called it the Monstrosity of the Mississippi and said it should be dynamited; interesting stained glass, spiral staircase; art gallery; open Mon.-Fri. 9-4:30; Sat. & Sun. 1-5; closed hols; free.

Louisiana Arts & Science Center & Planetarium (502 North Blvd), built by Huey Long and used as the Governor's Mansion 1930-32; eclectic collections of rare miniature furniture, Tibetan art objects, cultural, historic, and scientific displays; open Tues.-Sat. 10-5, Sun. 1-5; closed hols, Mardi Gras; free.

Louisiana State University & Agricultural & Mechanical College (3 m S): **Memorial Tower** houses the information center and Anglo-American Art Museum (English and American period rooms and decorative arts; fine paintings and drawings); open Mon.-Sat. 8-4:30, Sun. noon-4:30; free. **Geoscience Museum** (Geology Bldg) is open daily 8-4:30. **Museum of Natural Science** (Foster Hall) is open Mon.-Fri. 8-4:30, Sat. 8-noon, Sun. 2-4:30. **Indian mounds** are between West Campus & Fieldhouse Dr. **Library,** with historical exhibits and archives, is open Mon.-Fri. 7:30 am-10 pm, Sat. 7:30-noon, Sun. eve; closed hols. **Rural Life Museum** (Burden Research Center): complex of overseer's house, worker cabins, workshops, commissary, and other buildings illustrates plantation life of 18th-19th-C; open by appointment; free.

St. Joseph's Cathedral (Main & 4th Sts.), erected in 1853, has notable stained glass windows, mosaic Stations of the Cross, and a crucifix by Ivan Mestrovic (other works of his are in the Arts & Science Center); open daily.

Chamber of Commerce (564 Laurel St.) provides information on touring the 1962 Governor's Mansion (1001 Baton Rouge Expwy) and can confirm hours for plantations (listed below) in the surrounding area; they also have brochures on fine old homes in the city not open to the public, such as: the 1823 **Charlet House** (721 North St.), one of the few remaining structures of Spanish Town; 1848 Classic Revival **Dougherty-Prescott House** (741 North St.); 1850 **Potts House** (831 North St.), built by a master brick mason; 1837-40 **Warden's House** (703 Laurel St.), once a receiving station for prisoners; 1762 Creole-style **Tessier House** (342-348 Lafayette St.), where Lafayette spoke from the balcony; 1791 **Magnolia Mound** (2161 Nicholson Dr.), a planter's home.

Of the plantations N of the City, most spectacular is 1835 **Rosedown** (St. Francisville), magnificently restored; the wealthy planter who built it shopped personally in Europe for its opulent furnishings; open daily, Mar.-Nov. 9-5, Dec.-Feb. 10-4; closed Dec. 24, 25; adm. The less ostentatious but engaging **Cottage** (just N on US 61) is a rambling home built 1795-1859, with slave cabins, school, other buildings intact; open daily 9-5; closed Dec. 25; adm. Also nearby are **The Myrtles** (N on US 61), reputed to have at least one ghost, not open; **Catalpa** (5 m N on US 61), open daily 9-5, closed Dec.-Jan., adm; and **Asphodel** (on SR 68, S off US 61), a restored Greek Revival mansion that can be seen by appointment (Mon.-Fri. 10-4; closed hols; adm) through the adjoining inn. Especially interesting is the modest **Oakley** in Audubon Memorial State Park (on SR 965 off US 61, S); built in 1799 with West Indian-style balconies, it has period furnishings; John James Audubon tutored the owner's daughter here and painted 32 illustrations for his *Birds of America;* house open Mon.-Sat. 9-4:45, Sun. 1-4:45; closed hols, Mardi Gras; sm adm; surrounding wildlife sanctuary open daily 7-7.

Plantations SE of the city include: **Ashland-Belle Helene Plantation** (on River Rd., SR 75 between Geismar and Darrow), classic-style home of a sugarcane planter; open daily 9-4; closed hols; adm. **Hermitage** (on SR 942, 1½ m S of Darrow), built in 1812 in a blend of Louisiana colonial and classic styles; period furnishings; by appointment; adm. **Parlange Plantation** (19 m W on US 190, then 10 m N on SR 1 to Mix) is one of the loveliest homes on the False River; built about 1750, it is a rare example of bousillage construction; hand-carved cypress decoration; family heirlooms; open daily 9-5; adm. **Houmas House** (22 m SE on US 1 to Gonzales, then 8 m S on SR 44 to River Rd. in Burnside), an 1840 Greek Revival building, is another sugarcane planter's showcase; many furnishings locally crafted; open daily 10-4; closed Dec. 25; adm. **Tezcuco Plantation Home** (2 m S of Burnside on SR 44) is an 1855 raised cottage with antebellum furnishings; open Mon.-Sat. 10-4; adm. **Manresa Retreat House** (10 m S of Burnside on SR 44 in Convent), built in 1831, is a plastered brick building fronted by Doric columns; Greek Revival gatehouses; it houses a religious order but may be seen from the grounds, open Mon.-Wed. 9-4. **San Francisco Plantation House** (on SR 44, 2 m N of Reserve) is a gem of the Steamboat Gothic era; 100 slaves worked 1849-52 to build it; paintings on wood ceilings and door panels are by Dominique Canova; ornate furnishings and decorative arts; open daily 9-5; adm. **Destrehan Manor** (on SR 48, 5 m N of St. Rose), built 1787-90, has a roof similar to those used in Santo Domingo plantations; open Tues.-Sun. 10-4; closed hols; adm.

BOGALUSA: Louisiana Museum of Indian History (in Cassidy Park, Willis Ave.), with artifacts from the state, is open Sat. & Sun. 1-6; free.

CLINTON: Splendid 1841 Greek Revival **East Feliciana Parish Courthouse** and harmonizing Lawyer's Row; open Mon.-Fri. 8-5, Sat. 8-12;

closed hols; free. **Marston House** was a bank, with the banker's residence upstairs; open Mon.-Sat. 10-4, Sun. 1-4; closed hols; adm.

HOMER: Claiborne Parish Courthouse (on the Sq.), a 2-story 1848 Greek Revival building, has plastered-brick Doric columns on all sides; still in use, open Mon.-Fri. 8-4:30; closed hols; free.

LAFAYETTE: Lafayette Museum (1122 Lafayette St.), built c.1800, was home of former governor Alexander Mouton and now houses the Lafayette Tourist Center; Civil War and other exhibits; carnival costumes; open Tues.-Sat. 9-noon, 2-5, Sun. 3-5; closed hols; donation. **Blue Rose Museum** (I-10 W to Crowley, then 5 m SW on SR 13), an 1848 Acadian cottage of cypress and handmade brick; antique furniture, cut glass, silver, china; check locally for hrs; closed hols & Jan.-Feb.; adm.

LAKE CHARLES: Historical Museum (204 W Sallier St.) is open Wed.-Fri. 10-noon, 2-5, Sat. 10-noon, Sun. 2-5; closed Dec. 25-Jan. 1; donation.

MARKSVILLE PREHISTORIC INDIAN STATE PARK (1 m W of Marksville on SR 1), Indian mound and low earthern wall; museum with artifacts; open Mon.-Sat. 10-4, Sun. 10-5; sm adm.

MONROE: Northeast Louisiana University (700 University Ave.): Hanna Hall exhibits Indian materials from the Americas; African artifacts; minerals; open Mon.-Fri. 8-5; free.

NATCHITOCHES: French settled here in 1714, making this the oldest town in the Louisiana Purchase Territory. Front street (700 block) buildings have iron-lace balconies; grillwork on the Lacoste Building was imported from France; the patio at 720 Front St. has an iron spiral staircase. Historic tours of the city and nearby plantations are given annually (usually Oct.; write Box 2654). Open by appointment most of the year are the 1830 **Lemee House** (310 Jefferson St.) and 1821 **Oakland** (on SR 119, halfway to Derry); the 1826 **St. Maurice Plantation** (8 m NE via US 6, then 6 m S off US 71), of brick and cypress, with Victorian furnishings, is usually open Tues.-Sat. 9-5, Sun. noon-5; adm. **Historic Roque House** (on Cane River, foot of Lafayette St.), built c.1790, is a rare example of bousillage (a mud-and-moss wall filling); antiques; regional paintings; open Mon.-Fri. 8-5; closed hols; free.
    American Cemetery (Jefferson St. & Cane River) dates back to the late 1700's and contains earthworks from a 1715 fort. **Catholic Cemetery** (5th St.) has some above-ground tombs.
    Bayou Folk Museum (20 m S via SR 1 in Cloutierville), former home of

Kate Chopin, author of Creole short stories; period artifacts and memorabilia depict history of the Cane River country; open Mar.-Nov., Sat. & Sun. 2-6, weekdays by appointment; adm.

El Camino Real (SR 6) is marked with historic sites SW of the city; included are **Los Adais Historical Park** (at Robeline), from where the Spanish ruled the Province of Texas for 50 years, and **Fort Jesup State Historic Monument** (6 m E of Many) where reconstructed buildings from the fort established by Zachary Taylor in 1822 house a museum (open Tues.-Sat. 8-4:30, Sun. 1-5; sm adm).

NEWELLTON: Winter Quarters (3 m S off US 65), originally a 3-room winter hunting lodge, was expanded into a comfortable planter's home (the only one in the area spared by Grant during his 1863 march to Vicksburg); open daily 9-5; closed hols; adm.

NEW IBERIA: Founded before 1800 by French, Spanish, and Acadians, this town is on the lovely Bayou Teche (from an Indian word meaning snake). **Shadows-on-the-Teche** (117 E Main St.) is a townhouse built for a planter family whose fortunes declined with the fall of the sugar and cotton markets after the Civil War; the owner sent the furnishings from New England; heirlooms of 4 generations; open daily 9-4:30; closed Dec. 25; adm. **Justine** (4 m E on SR 86), built in 1822 with later additions, was moved here by barge along the bayou; cypress paneling; Victorian furnishings; china and glass from earlier periods; adjoining bottle museum; open Wed.-Sun. 10:30-5; closed hols; adm. Open by appointment is **Dulcito** (6 m W on SR 182 off US 90), a 1788 frame home typical of Spanish period architecture.

Statue of Hadrian (Weeks & St. Peter Sts.) was carved by an unknown sculptor in Rome about 130 AD.

Loreauville Heritage Museum (9 m NE via SR 86 to 401 Main St. in Loreauville) is a complex of old buildings depicting the history of the area; open daily 8-6; adm.

Albania Plantation House (15 m SE on SR 182 to Jeanerette, then ¼ m E), 1837-42, has a 3-story spiral staircase; doll collection; furnishings are Victorian with many older French pieces; open Tues.-Sat. 9-4:30, Sun. 1-4:30; closed Jan. 1, Easter, Thnks, Dec. 25; adm. **Oaklawn Manor** (25 m SE off US 90 on Irish Bend Rd.), prototype of antebellum architecture, has hand-carved marble fireplaces; tapestries; fine antique furnishings; open daily 8:30-4:30; adm. **Grevemberg House** (29 m SE on US 90 to City Park on Sterling Rd., Franklin) is an 1853 frame home with Corinthian columns; open Tues. & Fri. 4:30-6:30, Sat. & Sun. 2-6; free. **Frances** (29 m SE on US 90 to Franklin, then 4 m E), one of the tiniest and oldest colonial homes, is now a giftshop; open Tues.-Sat. 9-5; adm.

NEW ORLEANS: Visitor Information Center (334 Royal St.), open daily 8:30-5, offers brochures for walking and driving tours of the colorful Vieux Carre, or French Quarter (the original settlement, bounded by Canal and Esplanade Sts., N Rampart St., and the Mississippi River) and other parts of the city.

Jackson Square (between Chartres & Decatur at St. Peter Sts.), heart of the Vieux Carre, was the military parade ground under French and Spanish rule; the Louisiana Purchase transfer was made here in 1803; in the center is an equestrian statute of Andrew Jackson by Clark Mills. At the foot of the square is the **Old French Market** with the Cafe du Monde, famous for 24-hr service of delicious French doughnuts and New Orleans coffee; SW of here stretch the levee and docks (with narrated bayou and river cruises leaving daily from the foot of Canal St.). Facing each other across the square are the **Pontalba Apartments,** the oldest apartment houses in the U.S., built in 1849 by the Baroness Pontalba and still in use. The **1850 House** (523 St. Ann St.), an apartment furnished in 1800's style, is a state museum; open Tues.-Sun. 9-5; closed hols; sm adm.

Bordering Jackson Square on the north is **St. Louis Cathedral,** built 1794, with wall and ceiling paintings by Dominique Canova; open Mon.-Sat. 9-5, Sun. 1-5; closed religious hols; free. Behind the cathedral is **St. Anthony's Garden,** an old dueling ground. Flanking the cathedral are 2 state museums of similar design, built in the 1790's, the **Presbytere** (with portraits, maps, Louisiana historical exhibits, a Mardi Gras display) and the **Cabildo** (exhibits on Louisiana under French, Spanish, and American rule; Mississippi River steamboats and plantations), open Tues.-Sun. 9-5; sm adm.

Among the many buildings with elaborate iron grillwork are **Labranche Home** (700 Royal), **Le Petit Salon** (620 St. Peter), **Gardette-Le Pretre House** (716 Dauphine), **Gauche House** (704 Esplanade), whose German-made balconies feature Cupid, and the inn at **915 Royal** with the fence in the shape of cornstalks. Other interesting buildings include **1140 Royal,** supposedly haunted by mistreated slaves; **1035 Chartres,** 3 charming, identical cottages; **516 Bourbon,** home of author Lafcadio Hearn; **941 Bourbon,** the blacksmith shop used as a front for illegal activities by pirates Jean and Pierre Lafitte; and **708 Toulouse,** Court of Two Lions, once Planters Bank. Old buildings open as commercial establishments include **Old Absinthe House** (240 Bourbon), where Andrew Jackson and Jean Lafitte supposedly planned the 1815 defense of the city, a tavern since 1826; **Court of the Two Sisters Restaurant** (613 Royal), with a patio; the famous **Antoine's** (713 St. Louis); **Brennan's** (417 Royal), once the Banque de la Louisiane; the former planters' coffee house at 440 Chartres. Lovely **patios** open to the public include those at **615 Chartres, 520 Royal, 631 Royal** (former home of prima donna Adelina Patti), and **718 St. Peter.**

Historic New Orleans Collection (533 Royal St.), in 1792 Merieult House and 1888 Williams Residence, houses fine paintings, artifacts, and documents tracing the history of New Orleans; street-level gallery open free, adm for guided tour of 10 other galleries and the residence; open Tues.-Sat. 10-5; closed hols, Mardi Gras, Good Friday.

Gallier House (1118-32 Royal St.), elegant home of architect James Gallier 1860-68; all rooms open to galleries or balconies; architectural drawings, other exhibits; open Tues.-Sat. 10-5, Sun. 1-5; closed hols, Mardi Gras; adm. **Gallier Hall** (545 St. Charles Ave.) is considered Gallier's finest remaining work; open Mon.-Fri. 9-12:30, 1:30-4:30.

Hermann-Grima House (820 St. Louis St.), built about 1831; "Golden Era" furnishings; slave quarters; outbuildings; open Mon., Tues., Thurs.-Sat. 9-4, Sun. 1-5; closed hols; adm. **Madame John's Legacy** (632 Dumaine St.), a French Colonial building, and **Casa Hove** (723 Toulouse St.) vie for being the oldest buildings in the Mississippi Valley. The latter is particularly handsome, with a replica of a Christopher Wren stairway; furnishings of the city's "Golden Era" (1830-61) include pieces by master craftsmen and outstanding prints; open Mon.-Fri. 10-4:30, Sat. 10-3:30; sm adm. **Beauregard House** (1113 Chartres St.) is an 1827 Federal-style house; chess champion Paul Morphy was born here 1837; Confederate Gen. Pierre Beauregard lived here in the late 1800's; restored by novelist Frances Parkinson Keyes; open daily 10-4; closed Jan. 1, Dec. 25; adm. **Ursuline Convent** (1114 Chartres St.), completed in 1750, is open Tues., Thurs., Fri., Sat. 11-2; adm. **Pitot House** (1440 Moss St.), built 1799 on the Bayou St. John, is restored to early 1800s style; open Thurs. 11-2; adm.

New Orleans Jazz Museum (833 Conti St. in Royal Sonesta Hotel) displays memorabilia of Louis Armstrong, Bix Beiderbecke, others, tracing history of jazz; recordings; open Mon.-Sat. 10-5; closed hols; sm adm. **Preservation Hall** (726 St. Peter St.) offers concerts of traditional New Orleans jazz 8:30 pm-12:30 am; adm.

Pharmacy Museum (514 Chartres St.): Louis Dufilho, first licensed pharmacist in the U.S., operated an apothecary here until 1855; pharmaceutical memorabilia on display; open Tues.-Sat. 10-5; closed hols; free. **Mardi Gras Museum** (912 Toulouse St.) features the history of Mardi Gras; costumes; open daily 10-5; closed hols, Mardi Gras; adm. **Confederate Memorial Museum** (929 Camp St., near Lee Circle) contains flags, uniforms, other Civil War memorabilia; open Mon.-Sat. 10-4; sm adm.

Cemeteries throughout SE Louisiana are interesting because crypts and tombs are built above ground and are often ornamented. Examples in the city are **St. Louis Cemeteries No. 1** (Basin St. between St. Louis & Toulouse St.), **No. 2** (N Claiborne Ave & Bienville St.), and **No. 3** (3421 Esplanade Ave.), with tombs of many prominent locals, and **Metairie Cemetery** (Pontchartrain Blvd. & Metairie Rd.), whose drives follow the track of the famous antebellum race course.

Garden District (Jackson to Louisiana Ave. & Prytania to Magazine Sts.) contains lovely Greek Revival and mid-Victorian homes built by the aristocracy in the 1800s; many are beautifully landscaped; notable lacy cast iron at 1239 1st St., 1331 1st St., 1331 3rd St., and cornstalk-and-morning-glory fence at 1448 4th St.

New Orleans Museum of Art (City Park) collections range from the pre-Christian era to contemporary works; Kress Collection of Italian masterpieces; arts of Africa and the Far East; Latin American works include pre-Columbian and Spanish Colonial painting, sculpture, and decorative arts; 19th-C Louisiana works; open Tues.-Sat. 10-5, Sun. 1-6; closed hols, Mardi Gras, Good Friday, Nov. 1; free.

Tulane University (6823 St. Charles Ave.): Howard-Tilton Memorial Library houses archives of New Orleans jazz. Middle American Research Institute (Dinwiddie Hall) displays pre-Columbian to recent ethnological materials.

St. Patrick's Church (724 Camp St.), noteworthy Gothic Revival designed by James Gallier; lovely frescos and other decorations. **St. Mary's Assumption Church** (2030 Constance St.), a 19th-C American expression of German Baroque; dedicated in 1860 for German Catholics of the city; rich plaster and wood ornamentation; stunning altar from Munich. **St. John the Baptist Catholic Church** (1139 Dryades St.), built 1871; finest brickwork in the city.

Fort Jackson (off SR 23, 4 m S of Buras), a star-shape brick fort built 1822-48 to protect the river approach to New Orleans, held off Admiral Farragut's Union forces for 9 days before the fleet finally sailed up to capture the city; museum; interpretive displays; open daily 10-sundown; closed Dec. 25; free.

Tchoupitoulas Plantation (on SR 18, 3¼ m W of Huey Long Bridge) is open daily 11 am-10 pm as a restaurant. **Elmwood Plantation** (5400 River Rd.), a 1719 grant from Louis XIV of France, is the oldest plantation in the Mississippi Valley; open daily as a restaurant. **Magnolia Lane** (River Rd., 1 m N of Huey Long Bridge), of West Indies design, was built in 1784 on the Old Spanish Trail; open Wed.-Sun. 9-5 by appointment; adm.

Chalmette National Historical Park (6 m E on SR 46 in Arabi) was scene of the 1815 Battle of New Orleans, the last encounter of the War of 1812, when Gen. Andrew Jackson, with a force that included Jean Lafitte and the Barataria pirates, defeated the British. Visitor Center in the restored 1840 Beauregard House; audio-visual program and exhibits on the battle; self-guiding auto tour; National Cemetery; open daily 8-5 (8-6 in summer); closed Mardi Gras, Dec. 25; sm adm.

OPELOUSAS: Jim Bowie Museum (153 W Landry St.): tiny, modest museum of Bowie memorabilia; open Tues.-Sat. 10-4; closed hols; sm adm.
Magnolia Ridge (N via SR 182 to Washington, just off SR 103 NW),

an 1830 plantation mansion, is open daily by appointment; adm. **Arlington** (on SR 103 E of Washington), an 1829 brick home, is open daily 10-5; adm. **Homeplace** (at Beggs, SR 182 & 10), an 1826 country home of cypress, is near one of the last steamboat landings in the state; open daily 10-4; adm.

ST. MARTINVILLE: From this quiet town on Bayou Teche came the story of the romance between Emmeline Labiche and Louis Arceneaux on which Longfellow based "Evangeline." In 1755, when the British banished Acadians from Nova Scotia and herded them onto ships with various destinations in New England and the South, Emmeline and Louis, like many families and lovers, were separated. Emmeline, after a long search, found Louis; but contrary to Longfellow's version, Louis had married another girl. Emmeline died of a broken heart; a statue of Evangeline (posed for by Dolores Del Rio, who played the role in the motion picture version) has been erected over the grave of Emmeline in the churchyard of **St. Martin of Tours Catholic Church** (133 S Main St.). This church, founded in 1765 (the present building was erected 1838), contains a baptismal font and other gifts from Louis XVI and Marie Antoinette, as well as the Musee de Petit Paris de l'Amerique, containing possessions of the barons, marquises, counts, and other Royalists who fled the French Revolution; they attempted to re-create court life here, and the town was nicknamed Le Petit Paris. Church open daily 6-6; museum open daily 9:30-5:30, closed Jan. 1, Easter, Dec. 25, sm adm. **Longfellow-Evangeline State Park** (on SR 31, N of town) contains a 1765 home said to have belonged to Louis Arceneaux and now the Acadian House Museum depicting Acadian life and culture; open daily 8:30-4:30; closed Dec. 25; sm adm.

SHREVEPORT: Louisiana State Exhibit Museum (3015 Greenwood Rd.): attractive, interesting dioramas of the state's resources; historical exhibits; art gallery; open Mon.-Sat. 9-5, Sun. 1-5; closed Dec. 25; free.

R. W. Norton Art Gallery (4700 Creswell Ave.) provides a historical perspective with fine 17th-20th-C American arts (Bierstadt, Inness, many works by Charles M. Russell and Frederic Remington) and crafts (pressed glass, Paul Revere silver). Also 16th-C Flemish tapestries, 19th-C European painting and sculpture; Piranesi etchings, prints, Wedgwood collection; library; open Tues.-Sun. 1-5; closed hols; free.

Land's End (17 m S via Linwood Rd. & Linwood Ext. to Red Bluff Rd.), an 1847 Greek Revival mansion, has many original furnishings; open by appointment; adm. **Hughes Home** (N via SR 3 to SR 160 in Rocky Mount), an 1840's dogtrot cottage, is open Sat. & Sun. 1-5; sm adm.

SPAR Planetarium (2820 Pershing Blvd., Fairgrounds) shows Wed.-Fri. 3:30, 7:30; Sat. & Sun. 1:30, 2:30, 3:30; closed hols; sm adm.

Mansfield Battle Park State Monument (40 m S via US 171, on SR 175, 4 m S of Mansfield) commemorates the 1864 Confederate victory that ended the Red River campaign by Union troops attempting to reach Shreveport; interpretive museum; open Tues.-Sat. 9-5, Sun. 1-5; sm adm.

THIBODAUX: Edward Douglas White State Park (5 m NW on SR 1): Museum, a 1790 raised cottage, is a memorial to the former Chief Justice of the U.S. Supreme Court; 19th-C furnishings; open Tues.-Sun. 9-5; closed Jan. 1, Dec. 25; sm adm.

Nearby plantations include: **Madewood** (on SR 308, 3 m S of Napoleonville), a handsome Greek Revival mansion built 1840-48; the many fine works of art include a 17th-C Italian altarpiece and original Hogarth etchings; open daily 10-5; adm. (The 1853 Christ Episcopal Church, on SR 1 in Napoleonville, has a stained glass window used for target practice by Union troops and an interesting cemetery.) **Oak Alley** (on SR 18, 3 m W of Vacherie), built 1830-39; open daily 9-5; closed Dec. 25; adm.

MAINE

ACADIA NATIONAL PARK: Visitor Center (3 m NW of Bar Harbor on Mt. Desert Island) provides information on narrated bus tours, narrated cruises to smaller park areas on neighboring islands, and tapes for self-guiding auto tours; open mid-June-Aug. daily 8-8; May-mid-June & Sept.-Oct., Mon.-Fri. 8-4:30, Sat. & Sun. 9-5; closed Nov.-Apr. At **Sieur de Monts Spring** are a Nature Center and the Abbe Museum, with prehistoric exhibits; open June-mid-Sept., daily 9-5; free. **Islesford Historical Museum** (on Little Cranberry Island) has maritime and historic displays; reached by boat daily in summer from Northeast or Southwest Harbor.

AUGUSTA: State House (State & Capitol Sts.), designed by Charles Bulfinch but later remodeled, is open Mon.-Fri. 9-5; closed hols; free. **State Museum** has mounted wildlife, geologic, historic, and archaeologic exhibits; open June-Sept., Mon.-Sat. 9-5, Sun. 1-5; Oct.-May, Mon.-Fri. 9-4; closed Jan. 1, Dec. 25; free. **Blaine House,** the executive mansion, was home of James G. Blaine, who ran unsuccessfully for the Presidency on a platform denouncing "Rum, Romanism, and Rebellion"; open Mon.-Fri. 2-4; closed hols; free. **Fort Western Museum** (Bowman St. opposite City Hall): Restored barracks built by the Plymouth Co. in 1754 to defend the Kennebec River during the French & Indian War; museum of colonial living; open mid-May-Labor Day, Mon.-Sat. 10-5, Sun. 1-5; adm.

BANGOR: Bangor Historical Society Museum (159 Union St.): local historical, Civil War, and Indian relics; open mid-June-mid-Sept., Mon.-Fri. 10-4; free. **Penobscot Heritage Museum** (City Hall, 73 Harlow St.) has local historical displays; open Mon.-Fri. 9-4:30; closed hols; free.

BATH: Many fine mansions here were built when the city was a prominent port. America's first ship, the *Virginia,* was launched in 1607 from Popham Colony (16 m S on SR 209 on Sabino Head). **Fort Popham Memorial** (15½ m S on SR 209 in Popham Beach), a semicircular fort begun in 1861 but never finished, was garrisoned for only a year; nearby boulder is said to have Viking inscriptions; interpretive displays; open Memorial Day-Labor Day, daily 10-6; sm adm.

   Bath Marine Museum (963 Washington St.) in the 32-room Sewall Mansion contains 10,000 artifacts; please-touch exhibits for children; additional exhibits, farther along the Kennebec River, are housed in a church, apprentice shop, and shipyard; open late May-late Oct. daily 10-5; adm. Ferries operate on the river in summer.

   Arnold Trail, followed by Benedict Arnold and his troops in 1775 on the march to Quebec, is marked at intervals with interpretive signs for 194 miles from Fort Popham to Coburn Gore at the Canadian border.

BETHEL: Moses Mason House (Broad St.), restored 1813 home with murals, period furnishings; open June-Oct., Tues.-Sat. 10:30-noon, 2-4, Sun. 2-4; adm.

BOOTHBAY HARBOR: Boothbay Region Historical Society Museum (Hyde House) is open mid-June-Labor Day daily 10-5; rest of yr, Sat. 10-5; sm adm. **Grand Banks Schooner Museum** (100 Commercial St.) houses displays on cod fishing on the *Sherman Zwicker;* open mid-June-Sept. daily 9-sunset; adm. **Boothbay Railway Museum** (1 m N on SR 27) houses a general store and historic exhibits in 2 restored railroad stations; open mid-June-Labor Day daily 9-sunset; also fall weekends 9-sunset; sm adm.

BRUNSWICK: Bowdoin College (Main & College Sts.): **Museum of Art** (Walker Art Bldg.) has 19th-20th-C American paintings (Stuart, Copley,

Innes, Sloan, Homer), Kress Collection of Renaissance and 17th-C painting; antiquities; master drawings; open July-Labor Day, Mon.-Sat. 10-5
(also Mon.-Fri. 7-8:30 pm), Sun. 2-5; rest of yr, Mon.-Sat. 10-4, Sun. 2-5;
closed hols; free. **Peary-MacMillan Arctic Museum** (Hubbard Hall), with
memorabilia of the Polar explorers and Eskimo artifacts, is open summers
Mon.-Sat. 10-5, 7-8:30, Sun. 2-5; closed hols; free.

   Pejepscot Historical Society Museum (12 School St.), an 1827 church
housing historical artifacts, is open mid-June-early Sept., Mon.-Fri. 1-5;
closed July 4; free.

   First Parish Congregational Church (Maine St. & Bath Rd.), where
Longfellow lectured, preserves the Harriet Beecher Stowe pew; free. **Harriet
Beecher Stowe House** (63 Federal St.), where she wrote *Uncle Tom's
Cabin,* is now a restaurant.

BUCKSPORT: Jed Prouty Tavern (52 Main St.), built 1798, was once a
stage stop; historic guest list; now a restaurant open Mon.-Sat. 6 am-10 pm,
Sun. 7 am-8 pm; closed Dec. 25. **Buck Cemetery** (Main & Hinks St.) contains the Accursed Tombstone over the grave of Jonathan Buck; the leg
outline on the stone is said to be proof that the nonconformist recluse he
hanged (for the murder of a woman found with one leg chopped off) was
innocent. **Fort Knox State Park** (W on US 1): 1846 fort built for the
bloodless Aroostook War; interpretive displays.

CAMDEN: Information Office (Town Landing) has maps for local
historic tours. **Old Conway House Complex** (Conway Rd. & US 1) consists of an 18th-C farmhouse, blacksmith shop, and other buildings, and
the Mary Meeker Cramer Museum with paintings, costumes, documents,
and other memorabilia; open July-Labor Day, Tues.-Sun. 1-5; adm.

CARIBOU: Nylander Museum (393 Main St.): collections of the Swedish-
born geologist and naturalist include Indian and pioneer relics; open Apr.-
Dec., Mon.-Fri. 1-4; closed hols; free.

DAMARISCOTTA: Chapman-Hall House (Main & Church Sts.): restored colonial farmhouse with historic displays; open mid-June-mid-
Sept., Tues.-Sun. 1-5; sm adm. **Fort William Henry Memorial** (4 m S on
SR 129, then 9 m S on SR 130, 1 m W): reconstructed 1692 fort with
museum of relics, portraits, documents; open Memorial Day-Labor Day,
daily 10-6; sm adm. **Ancient Pemaquid Restoration** (14 m S via SR 129,
130): excavations have thus far uncovered the foundations of homes, a
tavern, and a jail; museum; open Memorial Day-Sept., daily 9-9; sm adm.
Pemaquid Point Light has a small art gallery and maritime museum;
open Memorial Day-Labor Day, Mon.-Fri. 10-5, Sun. 11-5; sm adm.

DEER ISLE: Miniature Village (SR 15 in Stonington) has miniature New England buildings; open June-fall, daily; free.

DOVER-FOXCROFT: Blacksmith Shop Museum (Chandler Ave.) is restored with period tools; open May-Oct., daily 8-8; free.

ELLSWORTH: John Black House (W Main St.) is an 1802 Georgian mansion with furnishings from 3 generations of the same family; carriage house; open June-mid-Oct., Mon.-Sat. 10-5; adm. **Tisdale House** (46 State St.): Early Republic house, now the city library; open Tues.-Sat. 2-5; closed hols; free. **Stanwood Museum** (2 m S on Bar Harbor Rd.), home of pioneer ornithologist, is open mid-June-mid-Oct. daily 10-4; closed July 4; donation; trails through surrounding bird sanctuary open all yr.

    Parson Fisher House (13 m SE on SR 172 to SR 15 in Blue Hill), built about 1795, was designed by Fisher, who also made many of the furnishings and woodcuts; open July-mid-Sept., Tues., Fri. 1-5; sm adm.

FARMINGTON: Nordica Homestead Museum (N off SR 4, 27 on Holly Rd.), birthplace of diva Lillian Nordica; mementos of her career; open June-Labor Day, Tues.-Sun. 10-noon, 1-5; adm.

FORT KENT: Fort Kent Blockhouse (N end of town), built 1839 during the bloodless Aroostook War, was never used; lumbering and Indian artifacts; open May-Labor Day, daily 8-9; rest of yr, weekends only; sm adm.

HOULTON: Aroostook Historical & Art Museum (109 Main St.) is open Mon.-Sat. in summer, Tues. & Fri. the rest of the yr, 10-noon, 1-5; closed hols; sm adm. **Hancock Barracks** (Garrison Hill on US 2), active 1828-46, was named for John Hancock, signer of the Declaration of Independence; diorama can be seen through a window; open June-fall, daily in daylight; free.

KENNEBUNK: Brick Store Museum (117 Main St.), with local historical and maritime displays, is open Tues.-Sat. 10-4:30; closed hols; free. The 1774 **First Parish Church** (Main St. & Portland Rd.) has a Paul Revere bell; open Wed.-Sun. 10-4. **Taylor-Barry House** (24 Summer St.), 1803 Federal-style house, period furnishings; open mid-June-mid-Oct., Tues., Thurs. 1-4; closed hols; adm. **Seashore Trolley Museum** (3 m NE on US 1, then 1.7 m E on Log Cabin Rd. in Kennebunkport), with more than 100 cars from 1873-1943, some from abroad, is open mid-June-Labor Day daily 10-6; rest of yr, weekends & some hols noon-5; adm.

KITTERY: Lady Pepperrell House (2 m E on Pepperrell Rd.): ornate, 1760 Georgian home with period furnishings; open mid-June-mid-Sept.,

Tues.-Sat. 11-4; closed hols; adm. **Fort McClary Memorial** (Kittery Point, 3½ m E of US 1): reconstructed 1809 blockhouse with interpretive displays; open Memorial Day-mid-Oct., daily.

MACHIAS: Burnham Tavern (Main St.), built in 1770, houses memorabilia from that period; open mid-June-Labor Day, Mon.-Fri. 10-5, Sat. 10-3; closed July 4; adm. **Fort O'Brien State Memorial** (5 m E on SR 92): breastworks of 1775 fort commissioned by Washington; interpretive displays; open Memorial Day-Labor Day, daily 9-sunset; free. **Ruggles House** (16 m SW on US 1 in Columbia Falls), built 1818, fine flying staircase and woodwork; period furnishings; open June-mid-Oct. daily 10-4; sm adm.

PORTLAND: Chamber of Commerce (142 Free St.) has information on historic sites in this town, twice destroyed by Indians, once by British bombardment in 1775, and once by the great fire of 1866; the Portland History Trail includes the revitalized waterfront, called Old Port Exchange. **Wadsworth-Longfellow House** (487 Congress St.), home of Henry Wadsworth Longfellow, was built by his grandfather in 1785; family furnishings and possessions; open June-Sept., Mon.-Fri. 9:30-4:30; closed July 4, Labor Day; adm. Behind it is **Maine Historical Society Museum,** open Mon.-Fri. 10-5; closed hols; free. **Tate House** (1270 Westbrook St.), built 1755 for the mast agent of the British navy; period furnishings; open July-mid-Sept., Tues.-Sat. 11-5, Sun. 1:30-5; closed July 4; adm. **Victoria Mansion** (109 Danforth St. at Park St.), mid-Victorian version of an Italian villa, has ornate period furnishings and decorative arts; open mid-June-mid-Oct., Tues.-Sat. 10-4; closed hols; adm.

　　Portland Museum of Art (111 High St.) consists of Sweat Memorial (19th-20th-C American painting and sculpture) and McLellan-Sweat House (superb 1800 Federal-style home; period furnishings), open Tues.-Sat. 10-5, Sun. 2-5; closed hols; free.

　　Yarmouth Historical Society Museum (6 m N on US 1 in Merrill Memorial Library, Yarmouth): historical items include artifacts from shipbuilding industry; open Apr.-Jan., Wed., Sat. 2-4; closed hols; free.

　　Shaker Village (16 m N on SR 26 at Sabbathday Lake), founded 1783, is maintained as a living museum by a handful of adherents; 17 buildings demonstrate Shaker life; a short tour includes the 1794 Meeting House, still in use and housing antique furnishings, herb shop, and other buildings; longer tour also available; open late May-late Sept., Mon.-Sat. 10-4:30; adm.

PRESQUE ISLE: Norton Museum of Natural History (Univ. of Maine on US 1) is open Mon.-Sat. 8-4:30; closed hols; free.

ROCKLAND: William A. Farnsworth Library & Art Museum (19 Elm St., US 1): 19th-20th-C American art, including Wyeth family; open

Mon.-Sat. 10-5, Sun. 1-5; closed hols; free. Adjacent **Farnsworth Homestead,** Greek Revival home, Victorian furnishings, is open June-mid-Sept., Mon.-Sat. 10-5, Sun. 1-5; free. **Rockland Coast Guard Station Marine Exhibit** (Tillson Ave.): history and artifacts of lighthouses and Coast Guard; open daily 9-5; free.

Montpelier (5 m SW on US 1 in Thomaston): reproduction of 1795 mansion of Revolutionary hero Henry Knox; many original furnishings; personal possessions; open Memorial Day-mid-Sept., daily 10-5; sm adm.

Friendship Museum (10 m S of Thomaston on SR 220 in Friendship), an old schoolhouse, has historic displays; open late June-Labor Day, Mon.-Sat. 12:30-5:30, Sun. 2-5:30; free.

ROOSEVELT CAMPOBELLO INTERNATIONAL PARK (on Campobello Is., 1½ m E of Lubec via SR 189): Franklin D. Roosevelt's summer home, where he was stricken with polio, is owned by U.S. and Canadian governments; Visitor Center. Open mid-May-mid-Oct. daily 9-5; free.

SACO: York Institute Museum (375 Main St., US 1): minerals, shells, antique decorative arts; open Tues.-Sat. 1-4 (also Sun. 1-4 in June-Aug.); closed 2 weeks at end-June-early July; donation.

SEARSPORT: Penobscot Marine Museum (Church St.) consists of the 1845 Town Hall and several 19th-C homes; period furnishings; ship models; whaling memorabilia; pressed glass; shipmasters' possessions; open Memorial Day-mid-Oct., Mon.-Sat. 9-5, Sun. 1-5; adm.

SKOWHEGAN: History House (Elm St.), built on the Kennebec River in 1839, houses china, toys, furnishings, documents; open mid-June-mid-Sept., Tues.-Sat. 1-5; closed July 4, Labor Day; adm.

SOUTH BERWICK: Jewett Memorial (101 Portland St.), birthplace of Sarah Orne Jewett, with colonial furnishings and personal possessions; open June-Sept., Wed.-Sat. 1-5; closed hols; adm. **Hamilton House** (on SR 236), a 1770 Georgian mansion, was setting for Jewett's *The Tory Lover;* hrs same as above; adm.

WATERVILLE: Colby College (2 m W, ½ m E of I-95) has free weekday guide service; **Art Museum** (primitive art; 19th-20th-C American works; open Mon.-Sat. 10-noon, 1-4:30; also Sun. 2-5 in June-Aug; closed hols; free); **Miller Library** (papers of Edwin Arlington Robinson, other Maine authors; strong on modern Irish literature; open Mon.-Fri. 9-noon, 1-4:30; closed hols; free); **Rose Chapel** (organ designed by Albert Schweitzer).

Redington Museum (64 Silver St): Indian relics, Civil War relics, furnishings, and other collections of the Waterville Historical Society; open May 15-Oct., Tues.-Sat. 2-6; donation.

Old Fort Halifax (Bay St., Winslow): 1754 Blockhouse Bridge; interpretive displays; open Memorial Day-Labor Day; free.

WISCASSET: Lincoln County Museum & Old Jail (Federal St., SR 218), built 1809-11, was Maine's first prison; adjacent jailkeeper's house has historic exhibits; open late May-Oct., Mon.-Sat. 10-5, Sun. 12:30-5; adm. Lincoln County Courthouse (The Common), built in 1824, is open Mon.-Fri. 8:30-4:30; closed hols; free. Nickels-Sortwell Mansion (Main & Federal Sts.): 1807 Federal home; imposing facade; family furnishings; open June-Sept., Tues.-Sat. 11-5; closed hols; adm. Behind it is Lincoln County Fire Museum, with fire equipment dating from 1803; open July-Labor Day, Mon.-Sat. 10-5, Sun. noon-5; sm adm. There are many lovely private homes along Main St.

Musical Wonder House (18 High St.): museum of antique music boxes, player pianos, other musical machines in 1852 home with period furnishings; June-Labor Day, Mon.-Sat. 10-5, Sun. 1-5; adm.

Fort Edgecomb State Memorial (1 m E off US 1): 1808 blockhouse; open Memorial Day-Labor Day daily 10-6; sm adm.

YORK: York Village Information (York St. & Lindsay Rd.): self-guiding historic tours include: Old Gaol Museum (built 1720 and used until 1860; dungeon; early household items) and the 1740 Emerson-Wilcox House (served also as a tavern) are open mid-June-Sept., Mon.-Sat. 9:30-5, Sun. 1:30-5; adm. Jefferd's Tavern (restored pre-Revolutionary hostelry; sm adm), Old School House (free), John Hancock Warehouse (Lindsay Rd. at York River; ship models and antique tools; sm adm), and Elizabeth Perkins House (Sewell's Bridge on York River; Victorian furnishings; sm adm) are open Memorial Day-early Sept., Mon.-Sat. 9:30-5, Sun. 1:30-5. First Parish Congregational Church (on the Green), built in 1747, is open daily 9-5.

MARYLAND

ANNAPOLIS: Settled in 1649 by Puritan refugees from Virginia and named in honor of Queen Anne, Annapolis has been called the most perfect example of a Colonial city in the nation; capital of Maryland from 1694; first peacetime capital of the U.S. (Nov. 26, 1783-Aug. 13, 1784). The preserved and restored waterfront is the focal point. Maps for self-guiding tours are available at the Visitor Information Booth (City Dock), open daily in summer and weekends in spring and fall, as well as in shops and at historic sites. Narrated boat tours leave from City Dock. Walking tours are conducted by **Historic Annapolis, Inc.** (Old Treasury Bldg., State Circle).

State House (State Circle, town center), a lovely Georgian building (1772), is the oldest state house still in use in the U.S.; here George Washington resigned his commission at the end of the Revolutionary War and the Treaty of Paris was ratified in 1784; open daily 9-5; closed Thnks, Dec. 25; free. Just south is the Old Treasury, built 1735. **St. Anne's Episcopal Church** (Church Circle), built in 1859, was founded in 1692; Sands Memorial Window by Tiffany won first prize for ecclesiastical art at the 1893 World's Fair; silver communion service was a gift of King William III in 1695; open daily.

Chase-Lloyd House (22 Maryland Ave.), begun in 1769 by Samuel Chase, signer of the Declaration of Independence, was completed 2 years later by master builder William Buckland; Francis Scott Key was married here in 1802; beautifully detailed; now a home for the elderly; open Mon., Tues., Thurs.-Sat. 10-noon, 2-4; closed Thnks, Dec. 25; sm adm. **Hammond-Harwood House** (19 Maryland Ave. at King George St.): this beautiful 1774 Georgian home is considered William Buckland's masterpiece; beautifully detailed and furnished with period pieces; open Mar.-Oct., Tues.-Sat. 10-5, Sun. 2-5; Nov.-Feb., Tues.-Sat. 10-4, Sun. 1-4; closed Dec. 25; adm. **William Paca House & Garden** (186 Prince George St.), the 35-room Georgian mansion built in 1765 for Paca, a signer of the Declaration of Independence and Governor of Maryland during the Revolution; beautifully restored and furnished; check locally for hrs; adm. **McDowell Hall** (St. John's College campus), built 1742-84 as the Governor's Palace, is now used for classrooms; open mid-June-mid-Sept., Mon.-Fri. 9-4; rest of yr, 9-11; closed hols; free.

U.S. Naval Academy (main entrance at Hanover St. & Maryland Ave.) Visitor Center (Field House, Gate 1) provides information (Mon.-Sat. 9-5, Sun. noon-5) and conducts tours (10-4); closed Jan. 1, Dec. 25. In the crypt of the Chapel is the tomb of John Paul Jones. Naval Academy Museum is open Tues.-Sat. 9-5, Sun. noon-5; free.

London Town Public House (London Town Rd. in Edgewater, 8 m SE via SR 2, 253), a Georgian inn built about 1744, served as a poorhouse 1825-1965; Visitor Center with exhibits; open daily 10-4; closed Jan. 1, Dec. 25; adm.

ANTIETAM NATIONAL BATTLEFIELD SITE (SR 65, 1 m N of Sharpsburg): Here on Sept. 17, 1862, the bloodiest day of the Civil War, Lee failed in his first attempt to invade northern soil; 12,410 Union soldiers and 10,700 Confederates were killed or wounded. Among the many monuments on the battlefield is one to Clara Barton, who attended the wounded.

The **Visitor Center** houses a museum and provides maps of the battlefield; open daily, June-Labor Day 8-6, rest of yr 8:30-5; closed Jan. 1, Thnks, Dec. 25; free. Musket and other demonstrations, and historical talks are frequently given. **Antietam National Cemetery** is open daily until dark.

BALTIMORE: Visitor Information Center (102 St. Paul St.) provides maps and information; advance reservations are necessary for touring Johns Hopkins Medical Institutions (Broadway & Monument St.), McShane's Bell Foundry (201 E Federal St.), and many industrial plants. **Patterson Park** (Patterson Park Ave. between Baltimore St. & Eastern Ave.) has a Chinese pagoda and observation tower; open daily. **Lexington Market** (400 W Lexington at Eutaw St.), an indoor market in operation since 1782, is open Mon.-Sat. 7:30 am-6 pm; closed hols. **Fells Point** (foot of Broadway) has dozens of well-preserved, century-old buildings remaining from the days when this was Baltimore's seaport and ship-building center.

Baltimore City Hall (Fayette & Holliday Sts.), built 1867-75 of local white marble, has a cast-iron dome manufactured in the city. **Shot Tower** (Fayette & Front Sts.), built 1828 for the production of lead shot; in 1829, crowds gathered here in response to E. A. Poe's newspaper announcements that on April Fool's Day a man would fly out of the tower across town.

Mount Vernon Place (Charles & Monument Sts.) in the Gay 90's was the fanciest residential neighborhood; many monuments; observation tower; Historical Information Center; open Fri.-Tues. 10:30-4; closed Jan. 1, Dec. 25; sm adm.

Maryland Historical Society (201 W Monument St.) contains historical and maritime displays; library (adm); **Darnall Young People's Museum of Maryland History;** open Tues.-Sat. 11-4, Sun. 1-5; closed hols; free.

Peale Museum (225 Holliday St.), exhibits on the life and history of Baltimore with paintings by the Peales, work by local silversmiths, maps, prints, other exhibits; open Tues.-Fri. 10:30-4:30, Sat. & Sun. 1-5; closed hols; free.

Enoch Pratt Free Library (400 Cathedral St.), the city's public library, has special collections on Poe and Mencken; open Mon.-Sat. 9-5 plus some evenings, Sun. 1-5 in winter; closed hols; free.

Carroll Mansion (Lombard & Front Sts.), built about 1812, was home of Charles Carroll, last surviving signer of the Declaration of Independence, who died here in 1832; fine example of merchant home, with offices, furnished in styles popular 1820-40; open Wed.-Fri. 10:30-4:30, Sat. & Sun. 1-5; closed hols; free.

Star-Spangled Banner Flag House (844 E Pratt St.), restored 1793 house, home of Mary Pickersgill, who made (for $405.09) the flag that Key saw flying over Ft. McHenry in September 1814; adjacent 1812 War

Museum houses war equipment and memorabilia; open Tues.-Sat. 10-4, Sun. 2-4:30, hols. 2-4; closed Jan. 1, Easter, Thnks, Dec. 23-27; adm.

Walters Art Gallery (600 N Charles St.) offers superb Near East and Classical artifacts; Impressionist, Post-Impressionist, and Renaissance Italian paintings; sculpture; Byzantine works; armor; jewelry; open Sept.-June, Mon. 1-5, Tues.-Sat. 11-5, Sun. & hols 2-5; July-Aug., Mon.-Sat. 11-4, Sun. & hols 2-5; closed Jan. 1, July 4, Thnks, Dec. 24, 25; free.

Baltimore Museum of Art (on Art Museum Dr., end of Howard St., in Wyman Park) is especially strong on 19th-20th-C French painting; also graphic arts, old masters, contemporary works, paintings of famous race horses; decorative arts; extensive African, Oceanic, and pre-Columbian works; open Tues.-Fri. 11-5; Sat. 10:30-5, Sun. 1-5; closed hols; free. Changing exhibits are displayed in **Newseum** (1 Charles Center), Mon.-Fri. 10-4:30; free.

Maryland Institute, College of Art offers exhibits of contemporary work in remodeled Mount Royal Station (Cathedral St. & Mt. Royal Ave.); open Mon.-Sat. 10-3, Sun. 1-4, some evenings; closed hols; free.

Museum of Natural History (Maryland Bldg., Druid Hill Park) displays Indian artifacts, plant and animal life native to the state; open Wed.-Sun. 10-5 in winter, Sat.-Wed. 10-4 in summer; closed Jan. 1, Thnks, Dec. 25; free.

Maryland Academy of Sciences (119 S Howard St.) offers exhibits and planetarium; open Mon.-Fri. 9-4:30; Sat in winter 9-3; closed hols; free.

Johns Hopkins University (Charles & 34th Sts.): The 1803 **Homewood House,** one of the most elegant Federal-period homes, is an administration building, not open to the public. **John Work Garrett Library,** with rare books, strong on Marylandia, is open to scholars. **Lacrosse Hall of Fame** is open weekdays 9-5.

Mount Clare Museum (Monroe St. & Washington Blvd. in Carroll Park), built 1754, an elegant Georgian mansion, is the city's oldest house; former home of barrister Charles Carroll, it is beautifully furnished with family antiques and portraits; open Wed.-Sat. 10-4, Sun. 1-4; closed hols; adm.

Mount Clare Station (Pratt & Poppleton Sts.), America's first railroad station, built by the B&O in 1830; 1884 roundhouse; Baltimore & Ohio Transportation Museum with an extensive collection of locomotives, cars, and memorabilia; open Wed.-Sun. 10-4; closed hols; adm.

Edgar Allan Poe House (203 N Amity St.), where the author lived 1832-5, is open Sat. exc hols 1-4; sm adm. Poe died in 1849 at the **Church Home & Hospital** (Broadway & Fairmount Ave.) and is buried in the cemetery of **Westminster Presbyterian Church** (Fayette & Greene Sts.); This church's history includes several suicides of people who hung themselves from the bell rope and at least one person buried alive.

U.S. Frigate Constellation (Pier 1, Pratt St.), oldest ship in the world still afloat, was launched in Baltimore in 1797; she saw action against pirates in 1799 and was retired in 1945 after serving as flagship of the Atlantic Fleet in WW II; Navy relics on display; open May-Labor Day, Mon.-Sat. 10-5:45, Sun. noon-5:45; rest of yr, Mon.-Sat. 10-3:45, Sun. noon-4:45; closed Jan. 1, Dec. 25; adm.

Fort McHenry National Monument (E end of Fort Ave.): Successful defense of this 5-sided fort against British bombardment in 1814 inspired the national anthem; restored officers' quarters and other buildings contain historic and military displays; living history demonstrations in summer; Visitor Center with exhibits and film; open daily 9-5 (8-8 in summer); closed Dec. 25; free.

Lovely Lane Church Museum (2200 St. Paul St.), designed in 1882 by Stanford White, is Etruscan-style, with a night sky reproduced in the vault of the dome; exhibits on the history of the Methodist church; open Mon. & Fri. 10-4, Sun. noon-4; closed hols; free. **Old Otterbein Church** (Conway & Sharp Sts.), oldest church in the city, was built 1785-86 by German settlers. **First Unitarian Church** (Charles & Franklin Sts.), built 1818, was designed by Maximilian Godefroy; Tiffany-designed chancel window and mosaic of Last Supper; art gallery in parish hall; free. **Basilica of the Assumption** (Cathedral & Mulberry Sts.), first Roman Catholic cathedral in the U.S., was designed in 1806 by Benjamin Latrobe; cruciform, Romanesque style, it has a domed and vaulted interior; open 6:30-3:30. **Lloyd Street Synagogue** (Lloyd & Watson Sts.), built 1845, has been restored as a museum by the Jewish Historical Society; open Nov.-May 1st & 3rd Sun. 1:30-4 or by appointment; closed Jewish hols; free. **Greek Orthodox Church of the Annunciation** (Preston St. at Maryland Ave.), built in the late 1800s in Romanesque style, was later elaborately redecorated with icons and rich Byzantine ornamentation. **Mother Seton House** (600 N Paca St.), where the founder of the American Sisters of Charity lived 1808-9 and opened a school for girls, has period furnishings; Seton memorabilia; open daily. See also Emmitsburg.

Babe Ruth Birthplace Shrine & Museum (216 Emory St.), with Ruth memorabilia, is open Wed.-Sun. 10:30-5; closed Thnks, Dec. 25; adm.

BETHESDA: National Library of Medicine (8600 Rockville Pike), the world's largest medical library, is open Mon.-Sat. 8:30-5 plus some evenings; closed hols; guided tours available Mon.-Fri. at 1; free.

CATOCTIN MOUNTAIN PARK (3 m W of Thurmont on SR 77), part of the National Park system, has a **Visitor Center** with small museum; whiskey still; craft demonstrations; interpretive signs on Charcoal Trail here and at **Catoctin Furnace** (on US 15, S of Cunningham Falls State Park Office), which produced the cannon balls Washington used against

Cornwallis and the iron plates for the Union *USS Monitor* and the Confederate *Merrimac*.

CHESAPEAKE & OHIO CANAL NATIONAL MONUMENT: The canal stretches 185 m from Georgetown (D.C.) to Cumberland. Unfortunately, on July 4, 1828, as Pres. John Quincy Adams was breaking a shovel trying to turn the first spade for this project, the B&O Railroad was also beginning construction; when the canal reached Cumberland in 1850, the railroad had already been there 8 years, so the canal was instantly obsolete and never completed; it had limited traffic until a series of floods closed it in 1924. The canal is now used for recreation. Information on exhibits and points of interest along the canal is available from hq (on SR 65 in Sharpsburg); open daily 8:30-5; closed Jan. 1, Dec. 25; free.

CHURCH CREEK: Trinity Church, Dorchester Parish (on SR 16), built about 1675, is the nation's oldest church still in use; open Mar.-Dec., Wed.-Mon. 9-5; Jan.-Feb., Mon.-Fri. 10-4; free.

CLINTON: Surratt House, home of Mary Surratt, hung as a conspirator in Lincoln's assassination, is now a museum; inquire locally for hrs.

CUMBERLAND: Emmanuel Episcopal Church (Washington & Greene Sts.) is on the site of Fort Cumberland, which was headquarters for Gen. Braddock and George Washington during the French and Indian War. From here the historic **Cumberland Trail** (National Road) went West; the road's restored **Toll Gate House,** built 1833, is 8 m W on US 40 in La Vale; open June-Oct., Wed., Fri., Sun. 1-4; free. **George Washington's Headquarters** (Riverside Park, Greene St.) is a tiny cabin with outdoor taped narration; free.

EASTON: Third Haven Friends Meeting House (S Washington St.), built 1682-4, was center of the Quaker community from which this quaint town grew; open daily 9-5; free. **Old Wye Church** (12 m N on US 213 in Wye Oak State Park), built in 1721 in Flemish style has been restored; 1750 vestry house; open mid-Apr.-Oct. Tues.-Fri., Sun. 10-3; closed hols; free. **Chesapeake Bay Maritime Museum** (10 m W on SR 33 in St. Michaels) traces the history of Chesapeake Bay; ship models; 1882 oyster sloop; aquarium; other exhibits; open 10-4 daily; closed Dec. 25 & Mon. in winter; adm.

ELLICOTT CITY: Brochures for self-guiding tour of historic buildings is available from the **Convention-Visitors Bureau** (3450 Court House Dr.). In Patapsco State Park (SE via Hilton Ave.), the **Patapsco Valley Histori-**

cal Center offers displays, and bus tours to historic sites are available on summer weekends.

EMMITSBURG: Mount St. Mary's College and Seminary (3 m S on US 15) offers a Shrine Center for orientation; information for self-guided tours to sites associated with Elizabeth Ann Seton during the last 12 years of her life; casket beneath the saint's shrine altar; museum of Seton memorabilia; replica of the Grotto of Lourdes; grounds open daily in daylight.

FREDERICK: Barbara Fritchie Museum (154 W Patrick St.) contains memorabilia of Mrs. Fritchie, depicted in the Whittier poem and in legend as having defied Stonewall Jackson in his march through the city; open Apr.-Dec. daily 9-5 and by appointment; closed Jan. 1, Thnks, Dec. 25; sm adm. Roger Brooke Taney Home & Francis Scott Key Museum (123 S Bentz St.), built in 1799 and restored with furnishings and memorabilia of Chief Justice of the Supreme Court Taney (Dred Scott decision) and his brother-in-law Key; open in summer Tues.-Sun. 9-4 or by appointment; sm adm. Mt. Olivet Cemetery (S end of Market St.) contains the graves of Barbara Fritchie and Francis Scott Key. Trinity Chapel (8 W Church St.) is where Francis Scott Key was baptized. Opposite is the Evangelical Reformed Church, where Barbara Fritchie worshiped and where Stonewall Jackson slept through the sermon before the Battle of Antietam; open daily.
    Arabian Horse Owners Foundation Museum (SW via I-70S & SR 109 to Barnesville) contains domestic and imported saddles and equipment, pictures, books about Arabian horses; open Tues.-Fri. 9-5, Sat. & Sun. 1-5; free. Some of the horse farms in the area can be visited.

GATHLAND STATE PARK (SR 67 in Burkittsville): remains of a 20-building estate of George Alfred Townsend (whose pen name was Gath), who erected a memorial to his fellow Civil War journalists; Visitor Center and museum of Civil War relics.

HAGERSTOWN: Washington County Museum of Fine Arts (City Park) offers old masters, 18th-19th-C European paintings, American paintings, Far East art objects, sculpture; open Tues.-Sat. 10-5, Sun. & hols 1-6; closed Jan. 1, Thnks, Dec. 25; free.
    Jonathan Hager House & Museum (19 Key St.), built in 1739 over springs for a water supply, has period furnishings; open Apr.-Sept., Tues.-Sat. 10-5, Sun. 2-5, or by appointment; sm adm. Miller House (135 W Washington St.), a lovely Federal town house built about 1820, has period furnishings; exhibits on the C&O Canal; clocks; other historic items;

open Tues.-Sun. 1-4; closed Easter, Thnks, Dec. 25; free. Fully stocked **Valley Store** (City Park, 400 Virginia Ave.) is open June-Sept. weekends & hols 2-4:30; sm adm. Nearby is the 1912 Baldwin Steam Engine, "Old 202."

Fort Frederick State Park (S of I-70 near Big Pool on SR 56), beside the C&O Canal; fort built during the French and Indian War; museum; occasional historical programs; open daily 9-sunset.

LA PLATA: Port Tobacco (3 m SW), one of the nation's oldest English settlements, built on the site of an Indian village, was chartered 1727; courthouse, store, and homes have been reconstructed; material found during the continuing archaeological excavation is on display; open daily 9-5; free. **Smallwood State Park** (16 m W near Rison) preserves the restored home and the grave of Revolutionary Gen. William Smallwood; summer historical programs; home open late May-Labor Day daily 10-6, weekends in spring and fall; sm adm.

ROCKVILLE: Beall-Dawson House (103 W Montgomery Ave.), built 1815, has period furnishings; historical displays; library; open Tues.-Sat. noon-4, 1st Sun. of each month 2-5; closed Dec. 24-Jan. 1; sm adm. Zelda and F. Scott Fitzgerald are buried in the cemetery of **St. Mary's Roman Catholic Church.**

ST. MARY'S CITY: The historic port area is being restored, with a Visitor Center and a museum of archaeological displays. The **Old State House** is a replica, because bricks from the original were used to construct nearby Trinity Church. Open Apr.-Oct. daily 10-5; Nov.-Mar., Tues.-Sun. 10-4; closed Jan. 1, Dec. 25; free. **Freedom of Conscience Statue** commemorates the 1649 landmark law granting freedom of religion.

Sotterley Plantation (17 m NE via SR 5, 246, 235 to Hollywood, then 3 m E on SR 245) manor house, built in the 1750's, has a modest exterior, but the interior reflects gracious living (Chinese Chippendale staircase; Chinese, English, and American antiques); outbuildings with farm displays; open June-Sept. daily 11-5; spring and fall by appointment; adm.

SALISBURY: Chamber of Commerce (300 E Main St.) has information on historic tours of the area. **Princess Anne** (13 M SW via US 13) has especially interesting Colonial and Federal buildings and the 1801 **Teackle Mansion** (Mansion St.), designed after a Scottish castle; open Sun. 2-4 and by request.

SILVER SPRING: National Capital Trolley Museum (Northwest Branch Regional Park in Layhill, N off SR 182) depicts the history of trolleys with imported and American examples; open late June-Labor Day, Wed.-Fri.

noon-4; weekends & hols noon-5; rest of yr weekends only; closed Jan. 1, Dec. 25; free.

TOWSON: **Hampton National Historic Site** (535 Hampton Lane): Elegant Georgian mansion (built 1783-90) of an "iron plantation"; outbuildings; it was home of one of the state's largest landholders and contains family portraits, Federal and Empire furnishings, fine decorative pieces; many ghost stories are associated with the house; open Tues.-Sat. 11-5, Sun. 1-5; closed hols; sm adm.

Towson State College (York Rd): Asian Arts Center has a large collection, including jades, ivories, porcelain; also African works; open Mon.-Fri. 10-noon, 2-4, Sat. & Sun. noon-4; closed hols; free.

Fire Museum of Maryland (1 m N in Lutherville) has fire-fighting equipment and memorabilia dating from the early 1800s; open Apr.-Oct., Sat. & Sun. 1-4; adm.

WESTMINSTER: **Historical Society of Carroll County** (206 E Main St.), in an 1807 home, displays hobnail glass, dolls in period costume, historical items; open Tues.-Sun. 1-4; closed hols; free.

Union Mills Homestead (6 m N on US 140), a 23-room clapboard home built in 1797, has served as a stagecoach tavern, store, post office, school, and magistrate's quarters; many original furnishings from 6 generations of the family; adjacent mill displays antique farm and mill equipment; open May-Aug., Tues.-Sat. 10-5, Sun. noon-5, or by appointment; adm.

Carroll County Farm Museum (1½ m E off US 140) is a complex of furnished farm home and buildings, with displays of equipment and demonstrations of old skills; open July-Aug., Tues.-Fri. 10-4, Sat. & Sun. noon-5; spring and fall weekends and hols noon-5; adm.

MASSACHUSETTS

AMESBURY: **John Greenleaf Whittier Home** (86 Friend St.) was residence of the poet from 1836 until his death in 1892; manuscripts, personal possessions; open Tues.-Sat. 10-5; closed Thnks, Dec. 25; donation. **Rocky Hill Meetinghouse** (Elm St. & Portsmouth Rd.) is a well-preserved 1785 building with original pews and woodwork; open June-Oct., Wed.-Sat. 1-5; closed hols; adm.

AMHERST: Amherst College offers exhibits in **Mead Art Bldg.** (mid-June-July, Mon.-Fri. 10-noon, 1-4; academic yr, Mon.-Fri. 9-5, Sat. & Sun. noon-5; closed hols, Aug.). Through the Office of the Secretary, the home of **Emily Dickinson** (Main St.) may be seen Tues. at 3, and the rare minerals and fossils on Mon.-Fri. 9-5. **Jones Library** (43 Amity St.), with collections on Dickinson, Frost, and other authors is open Mon.-Fri. 9-5:30, Sat. 10-5:30, some evenings; closed hols.

Farm Museum (5 m SW in Hadley at 147 Russell St.), in restored 1782 barn, displays farm and domestic equipment from Colonial days through the Civil War; open May-Oct. 15, Tues.-Sat. 10-noon, 1-4:30, Sun. 1:30-4:30; free.

The 1827 **Stone House** (S via SR 9 in Belchertown), with period furnishings and a collection of Rogers groups, plus carriage shed donated by Henry Ford with old vehicles made here, is open mid-May-mid-Oct., Wed., Sat. 2-5; sm adm.

ANDOVER: Addison Gallery of American Art (Phillips Academy, Main St.) houses an outstanding collection of American painting, sculpture, and decorative arts from Colonial times to the present; history of sailing illustrated through scale ship models; open Mon.-Sat. 10-5, Sun. 2:30-5; closed hols; free.

Amos Blanchard House & Barn Museum (97 Main St.) displays 17th-20th-C furnishings in 1819 Federal home and farm equipment in 1818 barn; open Mon., Fri., 2-4, Wed. 7-9; closed hols; sm adm.

Peabody Foundation for Archaeology (Main & Phillips St.) features North American collections from Mexico to Canada; open Mon.-Sat. 9-4:15, Sun. 2-5; closed hols; free.

Merrimack Valley Textile Museum (Massachusetts Ave., N Andover) exhibits equipment used before and after the Industrial Revolution; demonstrations Sun. 1-5; open daily 1-5; closed Jan. 1, Easter, Thnks, Dec. 25; free.

BEVERLY: Chamber of Commerce (219 Cabot St.) offers a booklet for self-guiding tours of historic sites. **Cabot House** (117 Cabot St.), headquarters of the Beverly Historical Society, was built 1781; maritime and other historical exhibits; library; open July-Aug., Mon.-Sat. 10-4; Sept.-June, Mon., Wed., Fri., Sat. 10-4; closed hols; sm adm. **Balch House** (448 Cabot St.), built 1636, is one of the oldest frame homes in the U.S.; displays on early home industries; open mid-June-mid-Sept., Mon.-Sat. 10-4; closed hols; sm adm. **Hale House** (39 Hale St.), built 1694 by Nathan Hale's great-grandfather, has family furnishings from several generations; open mid-June-mid-Sept., Tues.-Sat. 10-4; closed hols; sm adm.

Wenham Historical Association & Museum (3½ m N via SR 1A to Main St., Wenham) has a fine doll and toy collection with examples dating to 1500 BC; also library, 1664 Claflin-Richards House with early domestic tools, and Shoe Shop with shoemaking tools; open Mon.-Fri. 1-4, Sun. 2-5; closed hols & Feb.); adm.

BOSTON: Booklets for the 1½-m "Freedom Trail" and other self-guiding tours are available in advance from **Convention & Visitors Bureau** (125 High St., 02110) or after arrival at information centers on **Boston Common** (Tremont St. side; open daily 9-4; closed Jan. 1, Thnks, Dec. 25) or in the **State House** (East Lobby; open Mon.-Fri. 9-3:30). A Freedom Trail shuttle bus operates in summer. **Boston Common,** set aside for public use in 1634, still honors old rights such as cattle grazing; witches, pirates, and Quakers were hung near Frog Pond, and there are also stocks and pillory sites; **Central Burying Ground** (Boylston St. side) contains the unmarked grave of painter Gilbert Stuart.

　　State House (Beacon & Park Sts.), a Charles Bulfinch masterpiece completed in 1798, overlooks the Common; the Archives Museum contains the Mayflower Compact and other documents; statues, paintings, flags, other displays; interesting statues on the grounds; open Mon.-Fri. 8:45-5; closed hols; free.

　　Park St. Church (Park & Tremont Sts.), designed by Peter Banner and built 1809, is on "Brimstone Corner," named for the gunpowder stored in the cellar during the War of 1812; in 1829, William Lloyd Garrison gave his first antislavery address here; open Sun. 9-12:30 & 6-9; also Mon.-Fri. 9-4 in summer; closed hols; free.

　　Granary Burying Ground (Tremont & Bromfield Sts.) contains the graves of John Hancock, Samuel Adams, Paul Revere, and victims of the 1770 Boston Massacre; open daily 8-4; free.

　　King's Chapel (Tremont & School Sts.), built 1749-54, was a royal favorite and has a fine interior; Gov. Winthrop is buried in the cemetery; open Mon.-Fri. 10-4, Sat. & Sun. 10-noon; closed Jan. 1, Thnks, Dec. 25; free. Nearby, a tablet marks the site of the nation's First Public School (1635).

　　Old Corner Book Store (School at Washington Sts.), built about 1712, was a meeting place for Longfellow, Emerson, Hawthorne, Holmes, Stowe, Whittier, and others; literary memorabilia; open Mon.-Fri. 8:30-6, Sat. 8:30-2; closed hols; free.

　　Old South Meeting House (Washington & Milk Sts.), built in 1729, was both a church and town meeting house, where Samuel Adams acted as deacon and town clerk; on Dec. 16, 1773, more than 4500 protesters gathered here for the meeting that triggered the Boston Tea Party; open June-Sept., Mon.-Fri. 9-5, Sat. 9-4; Oct.-May, Mon.-Sat. 10-4; closed Jan. 1, Thnks, Dec. 25; sm adm.

　　Old State House (Washington at State Sts.), a 1713 Georgian building used as the seat of British and later town government, was scene of many historic events; in 1776, when the Declaration of Independence was read from the eastern balcony, symbols of British rule were burned in Dock Sq.; historical and maritime museum; library; open Mon.-Sat. 9-4; closed Jan. 1, Thnks, Dec. 25; sm adm. **Boston Massacre Site** (30 State St.) is marked by a ring of cobblestones.

Faneuil Hall (Merchants Row) has had a market on the ground floor since it was given to the city by Peter Faneuil in 1742; it was named the "Cradle of Liberty" by John Adams because of the emotional meetings held before the Revolution in the upstairs hall; top floor houses a military museum of the Ancient & Honorable Artillery Co.; open Mon.-Fri. 10-4; closed hols & Oct. 1-15; free.

Paul Revere House (19 North Sq.), built about 1670, is the oldest frame house in Boston; restored to the period of Revere's residency (1770-1800); Revere memorabilia; open Mon.-Sat. 9-3:45; closed hols; sm adm. Paul Revere Mall (Hanover St.) has a statue of Revere, 13 tablets describing historical role of the people of the North End 1630-1918; opposite is Boston's only remaining Bulfinch church, **St. Stephens** (401 Hanover St.), designed in 1802.

Old North Church (193 Salem St.) was built 1723; on the night of Apr. 18, 1775 2 lanterns were hung in the steeple window to signal the British march to Lexington and Concord; open daily 9-4:30; free.

Copp's Hill Burying Ground (Hull & Snow Hill Sts.), with burials dating to 1660, contains the graves of Increase, Cotton, and Samuel Mather, among other notables.

Nichols House Museum (55 Mt. Vernon St.), the only private home on Beacon Hill that is open to the public, may have been designed by Bulfinch; graceful spiral staircase; fine antique furnishings; library; open Wed., Sat. 1-5; closed hols; adm. Nearby is charming **Louisburg Square** (between Mt. Vernon & Pinckney Sts.), home to famous Bostonians (Louisa May Alcott lived at #10, William Dean Howells at #4).

At **Copley Sq.** (jct. Huntington Ave. & Dartmouth St.) are: 1877 **Trinity Church**, a Henry Hobson Richardson Romanesque building with fine murals and windows by John La Farge; open daily 8-4; free. The magnificent 1895 **Boston Public Library** in Italian Renaissance style, with a profusion of murals, paintings, and sculpture by masters such as John Singer Sargent and Daniel Chester French; adjacent 1972 building is by Philip Johnson; open Mon.-Fri. 9-9, Sat. 9-6, Sun. 2-6; closed hols; free. **John Hancock Tower,** with an observation deck and historical exhibits; information at Visitor Center in lobby; open Mon.-Sat. 9 am-11 pm, Sun. noon-11 pm; closed Dec. 25; adm.

Mother Church, First Church of Christ, Scientist (Huntington & Massachusetts Ave.) offers tours Mon.-Fri. 10-5, weekends & hols noon-5; free; tours also available of adjacent publishing house. **Mapparium,** a glass globe you can walk through, is open Mon.-Sat. 8-4, Sun. noon-3; free. **Mary Baker Eddy Museum** (120 Seaver St. in Brookline) offers tours of the exhibits on the life of the founder of Christian Science, Tues.-Sat. 10-3, Sun. 1-3; closed hols; adm. Information is available here on visiting Mrs. Eddy's homes in Stoughton (133 Central St.) and Swampscott (SR 1A).

Harrison Gray Otis House (141 Cambridge St.), a 1796 Federal mansion designed by Bulfinch, houses the Society for the Preservation of New England Antiquities; adj museum offers superb textile and wallpaper collections, glass, pewter, toys, ceramics, furniture, other exhibits, and library; open Mon.-Fri. 10-4; closed hols; adm.

Royall House (15 George St., Medford, 2 m N off SR 38), a farmhouse built by Gov. Winthrop in 1637, was expanded in 1732-37 by Antigua merchant Isaac Royall; excellent Queen Anne, Chippendale, Hepplewhite furnishings; open May-mid-Oct., Tues.-Thurs., Sat., Sun. 2-5; adm.

John F. Kennedy National Historic Site (83 Beals St., Brookline), birthplace of Pres. Kennedy, has original furnishings, family memorabilia; map available for nearby sites associated with the Kennedys; open daily 9-4:45; closed Jan. 1, Dec. 25; sm adm or GEP.

USS Constitution (Boston Naval Shipyard, Charlestown), "Old Ironsides," launched in 1797, is a replica with materials from the original; she never lost any of her 40 battles; museum exhibits; open daily 9:30-4; free.

Museum of Science (Science Park on Charles River Dam Bridge) is remarkable, with many participatory and demonstration exhibits, live displays, and lectures covering all aspects of science from prehistoric life to modern environmental concerns; open Mon.-Sat. 10-5, Sun. 11-5; closed Jan. 1, Labor Day, Thnks, Dec. 25; adm. Shows in adjacent **Charles Hayden Planetarium** are a small extra charge.

Museum of Fine Arts (465 Huntington Ave.), one of the best in the nation, is too huge to be seen in one visit; magnificent Oriental and Egyptian displays; Greek and Roman art; European Old Masters; French Impressionists; 18th-19th-C American painters; tapestries, textiles, embroideries, lace; period rooms; silver; musical instruments; costumes; films and other programs; open daily 10-6; closed Jan. 1, July 4, Thnks, Dec. 24, 25; adm (exc Sun. 10-1).

Isabella Stewart Gardner Museum (280 The Fenway), modeled on a 15th-C Venetian villa with central court, provides a stunning setting for European Old Masters, 19th-C American and European paintings, sculpture, furnishings, textiles, and other outstanding exhibits; musical and other programs; open July-Labor Day, Tues.-Sat. 1-5:30; rest of yr, Wed.-Sun. 1-5:30, Tues. 1-9:30; closed hols; free.

Guild of Boston Artists (162 Newbury St.) offers works by New England artists in changing exhibits; open mid-Sept.-June, Tues.-Sat. 10:30-5; closed hols; free.

Gibson House Museum (137 Beacon St.), a Victorian townhouse with period furnishings, is open Tues.-Sun. 2-5; closed hols; adm.

Boston Tea Party Ship & Museum (anchored at Congress St. Bridge on Ft. Point Channel), a full-size replica of one of the ships involved in the Boston Tea Party, offers audiovisual program and museum exhibits; open daily 9 am-7 pm; closed Jan. 1, Thnks, Dec. 25; adm.

Museum of the America China Trade (215 Adams St. in Milton, 7 m SE), in the 1833 Greek Revival mansion of a China trader, displays Chinese porcelains, textiles, silver, and other imports; historical exhibits; open Tues.-Sat. 2-5; closed hols; adm.

Museum of Transportation (Larz Anderson Park, 15 Newton St., Brookline), in a coachhouse and stable designed after a French castle, displays antique cars, carriages, sleighs, bicycles, fire engines; movies and other programs; open Tues.-Sun. 10-5; closed Jan. 1, July 4, Thnks, Dec. 25; adm.

BRAINTREE: Gen. Sylvanus Thayer Birthplace (786 Washington St.), built 1720 and restored with period furnishings, exhibits historic and military artifacts; open mid-Apr.-mid-Oct., Tues., Thurs., Fri., Sun. 1:30-4, Sat. 10:30-4; rest of yr, Tues., Thurs., Sat. 1:30-4; closed Jan. 1, Thnks, Dec. 25; sm adm. **Abigail Adams House** (2 m E in Weymouth at North & Pearl Sts.), birthplace of the wife of Pres. John Adams, has period furnishings; open July 4-Labor Day, Tues.-Sat. 1-4; sm adm.

BROCKTON: Brockton Art Center (Oak St.) offers changing exhibitions; open Tues.-Sat. 10-5, Sun. 1:30-5:30; closed Jan. 1, July 4, Thnks, Dec. 25; adm.

Standish Museums (8 m SE in E Bridgewater) offer guided tours of 18th-C apothecary and other buildings with displays on early agriculture, Utopian communities, musical instruments, Revolutionary War, and other exhibits; museum in 18th-C church; open Mon.-Sat. 9-5, Sun. 1-5; adm.

CAMBRIDGE: Harvard University (Harvard Sq.), the nation's oldest, was founded 1636. **Information Center** (1350 Massachusetts Ave.) provides brochures for self-guided tours; also student guides in summer. **Massachusetts Hall,** Harvard's oldest building, dates from 1720. **University Hall,** designed by Bulfinch in 1813, is especially handsome. **Sever Hall,** designed by Henry Hobson Richardson in 1880, was widely copied on other campuses. **Carpenter Center for the Visual Arts** (19 Prescott St.) is the only design by Le Corbusier in the U.S. **Sail** (McDermott Ct., E Campus) is a stabile by Calder. **Widener Library,** one of the most important in the U.S., is on the S side of Harvard Yard. **Fogg Art Museum** (32 Quincy St.) traces the evolution of art from ancient to modern times;

especially fine Chinese collection, Romanesque sculpture, 19th-C French paintings, Greek decorative arts, Italian primitives; prints, drawings, photographs; open mid-Sept.-June, Mon.-Sat. 9-5, Sun. 2-5; July-mid-Sept., Mon.-Fri. 9-5; closed hols; free. **Busch-Reisinger Museum** (29 Kirkland St.), modeled on 18th-C German architecture, has the largest collection of German art outside of Germany; also large contemporary collection; examples of European art from Middle Ages to present; open Mon.-Fri. 9-4:45; closed hols; free. **University Museum** (Divinity Ave. & Oxford St.) is a complex of museums on mineralogy, botany (including Blaschka glass flowers collection), zoology, and the outstanding **Peabody Museum of Archaeology & Ethnology**; open Mon.-Sat. 9-4:30, Sun. 1-4:30; closed Jan. 1, July 4, Thnks, Dec. 25; free.

Christ Church (Garden St. at the common) was used as a barracks during the Revolution; Victorian interior; open daily 7:30-5; free.

Longfellow National Historic Site (105 Brattle St.), a 1759 Georgian-style house, was home to George and Martha Washington during the siege of Boston and to Longfellow 1837-82; furnished as it was at the time of the poet's death; open daily 9-5; closed Jan. 1, Dec. 25; sm adm or GEP. (The home of the village smithy immortalized in Longfellow's poem is now a restaurant at 56 Brattle St.)

Massachusetts Institute of Technology offers brochures and tours at the **Information Center** (77 Massachusetts Ave., lobby). **Kresge Auditorium** and the unusual **Chapel** were designed by Eero Saarinen in 1955. **Hart Nautical Museum,** with ship models and plans, traces the development of marine engineering; open daily 9-5; free. **Hayden Gallery,** with changing exhibits, is open daily in summer 1-5; during academic yr, Mon.-Fri. 10-5, Sat., Sun., hols 1-5; free.

Cooper-Frost-Austin House (21 Linnaean St.), built about 1657 and displaying early furniture, is open June-Oct., Tues., Thurs., Sat. 1-5; closed hols; sm adm.

CAPE COD: Bourne: Aptucxet Trading Post (cross Bourne Bridge, turn right to 24 Aptucxet Rd.), a replica of 1627 Pilgrim, Dutch, and Indian trading post with artifacts displayed; also operating replica of saltworks, a rune stone dated to 1000 AD, Dutch windmill, herb garden; open June-Aug. daily 10-5; Apr.-May, Sept.-Oct., Tues.-Sat. 10-5, Sun. 1-5; adm.

Sandwich: Sandwich Glass Museum (Town Hall Sq., SR 130) displays rare pressed and blown glass made here 1825-88; open Apr.-Nov. 15, daily 10-5; adm. **Hoxie House** (SR 130), a restored saltbox, is furnished in late-17th-C style; **Dexter's Gristmill,** built 1654, grinds corn in summer; open mid-June-Sept., Mon.-Sat. 10-5, Sun. 1-5; sm adm to each. **Heritage Plantation** (Grove & Pine Sts.), a landscaped 76-acre estate, displays superb Americana; **Round Stone Barn,** a duplicate of one built 1826 in

Hancock by Shakers, houses the Lilly collection of automobiles dating from the 1890's to 1930's; the **Military Museum,** in a replica of a 1783 building, contains miniature soldiers and antique firearms; **Arts & Crafts Bldg.** features early paintings, trade signs, hand tools, Boehm birds, Steuben glass, scrimshaw; also a windmill and 1912 carousel; open May-mid-Oct. daily 10-5; adm. **Mashpee Wampanoag Indian Museum** (on SR 130, S of US 6 in Mashpee) displays artifacts of people who lived here before the Pilgrims arrived; re-created Indian dwelling, exhibits on village life; open mid-Mar.-Nov., Tues.-Thurs. 10-4, Fri.-Sun. 11-5; sm adm. **Yesteryears Doll & Miniature Museum** (Main & River Sts.) houses antique costumed dolls, doll houses, and accessories from around the world in a 1638 Meetinghouse; the bell and clock tower were purchased by a slave in memory of the master who freed him; open Memorial Day-mid-Oct., Mon.-Sat. 10-5, Sun. 1-5; adm.

Falmouth: Falmouth Historical Society Museum (Village Green), in the 1790 Julia Wood House, a sea captain's home with widow's walk, contains whaling memorabilia, antique silver and glass, other exhibits; open mid-June-mid-Sept. daily 2-5; sm adm. The church next door has a bell cast by Paul Revere. **Saconesset Homestead Museum** (2 m N on SR 28A in W Falmouth), is a 15-acre restoration including Ship's Bottom Roof House, built 1678; open mid-June-mid-Oct., Mon.-Sat. 10-6; adm.

Osterville: Osterville Historical Society Museum houses ship models, antique dolls, library, in home with 18th-19th-C furnishings; open Thurs. & Sun. 3-5 in summer; sm adm. **Centerville Historical Society** (3 m NE in Centerville), with costume collections, is open June-Labor Day, Tues.-Sun. 2-4:30; spring & fall, Tues., Thurs. 2-4:30; free.

Barnstable: Donald G. Trayser Memorial Museum (SR 6A), in the 1856 Customs House, displays ship models, scrimshaw, local silver, and other maritime and historical items; open July-mid-Sept., Tues.-Sat. 1-5; mid-Sept.-Oct., Sat. 1-5; sm adm. **Sturgis Library** (SR 6A) contains maritime and genealogical records of Cape Cod; open Tues., Thurs. 2-5, 7-9, Sat. 9-12, 2-5, plus additional hrs in summer; closed hols; free. Opposite is the 1754 **Crocker Tavern,** a stagecoach stop on the road to Boston, with antique furnishings and historical exhibits; open mid-June-mid-Oct., Tues., Thurs., Sat. 1-5; sm adm.

Yarmouth: Captain Bangs Hallet House (Strawberry Lane, Yarmouth Port), a restored 18th-C sea captain's home, features furnishings from France and England; open mid-June-Labor Day, Mon.-Sat. 10-4; closed July 4; sm adm. **Winslow Crocker House** (US 6 in Yarmouth Port), built about 1780, and the adjacent **Col. John Thacher House,** built 1680, have period furnishings; open June-Sept., Tues.-Sat. 11-4; closed hols; sm adm.

Dennis: Josiah Dennis Manse (77 Nobscusset Rd.), built 1736, and the 1801 **Jericho House** (Dennis Rd. in W Dennis) are maintained with period furnishings by the Dennis Historical Society; also schoolhouse, barn with household and farm tools; open July-Labor Day, Wed., Fri. 2-4; donation.

Brewster: New England Fire & History Museum (½ m W on SR 6A) contains early firefighting equipment, apothecary, blacksmith shop, other exhibits; open Memorial Day-Labor Day, daily 10-6; spring and fall weekends noon-5; adm. **Drummer Boy Museum** (2 m W on SR 6A) has 21 lifesize scenes of the American Revolution; open late May-mid-Oct. daily 9:30-6; adm. **Cape Cod Museum of Natural History** (2 m W on SR 6A) offers live and mounted exhibits of flora and fauna; library, nature trails; open June-Sept., Mon.-Sat. 10-5, Sun. 12:30-5; Oct.-May, Tues.-Sat. 9:30-4:30, Sun. 1-4:30; closed Jan. 1, Thnks, Dec. 25; sm adm. **Stony Brook Mill** (2 m W off SR 6A on Stony Brook Rd.) has exhibits on corn grinding; open July-Aug., Wed., Fri., Sat. 2-5; free.

Harwich: Brooks Free Library (Main St.) houses the John Rogers collection of American figurines; open Mon.-Fri. 1-4, Sat. 10-4; closed hols; free. The nearby **Harwich Historical Society** collection is open July-Aug., Mon., Wed., Fri. 1:30-4:30; adm.

Chatham: Atwood House (Stage Harbor Rd., S off SR 28) features Sandwich glass and shells among 2000 exhibits of the Chatham Historical Society; open mid-June-mid-Sept., Mon., Wed., Fri. 2-5; sm adm. **Railroad Museum** (Depot Rd. off SR 28) houses railroad memorabilia in a restored depot; open summers Mon.-Fri. 2-5; donation. **Old Windmill** (Chase Park), built 1797, grinds corn in summer, Fri.-Wed. 10-5; free. **Chatham Murals** (off Stage Harbor Rd. near Bridge St., Stage Harbor) are of biblical scenes for which local residents posed; open July & Aug. daily 9-6.

Eastham: Eastham Historical Society (off US 6) is open July-Labor Day, Mon., Wed., Fri. 2-5; sm adm. The 1793 **Grist Mill** (Grist Mill Park) is open in summer Mon.-Sat. 1-5; free.

Wellfleet: Historical Society Museum (Main St.), with local historical displays and nearby restored early home, is open July-Labor Day, Tues.-Sat. 2-5; sm adm.

Truro: Highland Light (5 m N, E off US 6), dating from 1797, contains shipwreck and other historic exhibits; open late June-mid-Sept., daily 10-5; sm adm.

Provincetown: Pilgrim Memorial Monument (Town Hill), a 252-ft tower modeled after the Mangia Tower of Siena, Italy, commemorates the Pilgrim landing (the site, marked with a tablet, is at Commercial St. & Beach Hwy.); Historical Museum with maritime, pewter, Sandwich glass, and other historic exhibits, including display on Arctic explorer MacMillan; open daily 9-5 (9-9 in summer); closed Jan. 1, Dec. 25; sm adm. **Oldest House** (72 Commercial St.), built 1746 with material from wrecks by a ship's carpenter, is open June-Sept., daily 10-5; sm adm. **Provincetown**

Art Assn. (460 Commercial St.) is open daily, late May-early Sept.; sm adm.

CAPE COD NATIONAL SEASHORE: Covering most of the upper hook of Cape Cod off US 6, the seashore consists of 4 major areas, all with nature trails, swimming, and recreational facilities. **Salt Pond Visitor Center** (Eastham) is open daily all year 9-5 (8-6 in summer). **Province Lands Visitor Center** (Race Point Rd., Provincetown) is open June 15-Labor Day 9-6; mid-Apr.-June 15 & Labor Day-Oct. 9-5. Both offer exhibits and interpretive programs on the human and natural history of the area. **Pilgrim Heights** (just S of Province Lands) has an interpretive shelter with exhibits about Pilgrims and Indians. **Marconi Station** (between S Wellfleet & N Eastham) offers an interpretive shelter with exhibits on the first wireless station. Information is available from the Supt., S Wellfleet 02663.

COHASSET: At jct of Main & Elm Sts. are **Independence Gown Museum** (a 200-yr history of costume), **Maritime Museum** (in a ship chandlery built about 1760), and **Historic House** (with 18th-19th-C furnishings), open late June-Labor Day, Tues.-Sat. 1:30-4:30; sm adm.

CONCORD: Minute Man National Historical Park interprets Battle Road (SR 2A), between Meriam's Corner in Concord and Fiske Hill in Lexington, on which the famous running battle took place. Information is available at **Battle Road Visitor Center** (daily Apr.-Nov. 9-6; Dec.-Mar. 9-5), **North Bridge Visitor Center** (June-Aug. 8-6, Sept.-May 8-5), and **Fiske Hill Information Center** (daily, weather permitting, 8-sunset); closed Jan. 1, Dec. 25.

   Old Manse (Monument St. at Old North Bridge), where Ralph Waldo Emerson spent much of his youth, was built in 1769 by his grandfather the Rev. William Emerson; furnishings date from 1842-46, when Nathaniel Hawthorne lived here and wrote *Mosses from an Old Manse* in the same study where Emerson had penned *Nature;* open June-mid-Oct., Mon.-Sat. 10-4:30, Sun. 1-4:30; mid-Apr.-May & mid-Oct.-mid-Nov., Sat. & Sun. 10-4:30; adm.

   Sleepy Hollow Cemetery (Bedford St.) contains the graves of Emerson, Hawthorne, the Alcotts, Thoreau, Margaret Sidney, and Daniel Chester French.

   The Wayside (½ m E on SR 2A) was home to the Alcotts, the Hawthornes, and Margaret Sidney, among others; tours given June-July daily 10-5:30; Apr.-May, Sept.-Oct., Thurs.-Mon. 10-5:30; sm adm.

   Orchard House (399 Lexington Rd.) was for many years home to Louisa May Alcott; she wrote *Little Women* here; Alcott family furnishings, memorabilia; tours mid-Apr.-mid-Nov., Mon.-Sat. 10-4:30, Sun. 1-4:30; adm.

Antiquarian Museum (Lexington Rd. & Cambridge Tkpe): 15 interesting period rooms dating from 1690-1840 include Ralph Waldo Emerson's study and the interior of the cabin Thoreau used at Walden Pond; diorama of the 1775 battle at North Bridge; tours 10-4:30 mid-Mar.-Oct., Mon.-Sat.; rest of yr Sat. & Sun. 2-4:30; adm.

Emerson House (Lexington Rd. & Cambridge Tpke), home of Ralph Waldo Emerson from 1835 until his death in 1882; open mid-Apr.-Oct., Tues.-Sat. 10-11:30, 1:30-5:30, Sun. 2:30-5:30; adm.

Concord Art Association (15 Lexington Rd.) displays early American glass and paintings in 18th-C home; sculpture garden; open Feb.-mid-Dec., Tues.-Sat. 11-4:30, Sun. 2-4:30; closed Apr. 19, July 4, Thnks; sm adm.

Concord Free Public Library (129 Main St.), with manuscripts by Concord authors, displays paintings and other historic items; open Mon.-Fri. 9-9, Sat. 9-6; closed hols; free.

Thoreau Lyceum (156 Belknap St.) contains Thoreau memorabilia, other historic items, natural history exhibits; replica of Thoreau's Walden Pond cabin on grounds; open Mon.-Sat. 10-5, Sun. 2-5; closed Jan. 1, Apr. 19, July 4, Thnks, Dec. 25; free. **Walden Pond State Reservation** (S of town on Walden St.) has a cairn marking the site where Thoreau built his cabin in 1845; open all year in daylight; free.

DANVERS: Rebecca Nurse House (149 Pine St.), built 1678, was home of an elderly woman hanged as a witch; open June-Sept., Tues., Thurs., Sat. 1-5; closed hols; adm. **Glen Magna** (2 m N on US 1, then ½ m E on Centre St. to Forest St.), a 1692 farmhouse expanded into a mansion, has 18th-19th-C furnishings; Samuel McIntire gazebo; Olmsted gardens; art and historical exhibits; open June-Sept., Tues.-Fri. 1-4; closed hols; adm. **Samuel Fowler House** (166 High St.), a lovely, Federal brick mansion, was built 1810; fine French wallpaper, hand-carved woodwork, furnishings; open June-Sept., Tues., Thurs., Sat. 1-5; sm adm. **Parson Capen House** (1 Howlett St. in Topsfield, N via SR 35, 97), a 1683 clapboard with overhanging 2nd story, has early American furnishings; open mid-June-mid-Sept. daily 1-4:30; sm adm.

DEDHAM: Fairbanks House (511 East St at Eastern Ave.), built in 1636, is one of the oldest frame houses in the nation; chimney bricks were originally ship ballast; heirlooms from family that lived here until 1903; tours May-Oct., Tues.-Sun. 9-noon, 1-5; closed hols; adm. **Dedham Historical Society** (612 High St.) houses genealogic library and historic relics in 1886 house; open Mon.-Sat. 2-5 (closed Sat. in July-Aug.); free.

DEERFIELD: When this lovely town was first settled in the 1660s, it was the northwestern frontier of New England; the many French and Indian attacks included the 1675 Bloody Brook Massacre during the King Philip's War, after which the town was abandoned for 7 years; it was resettled, but during the 1704 Queen Anne's War attack, 49 residents were killed, more than 100 were taken prisoner to Canada, and the town was burned. **Hall Tavern Information Center** (Main St.) provides brochures on historic houses and sells combination tickets to the dozen buildings that can be visited (early May-mid-Nov., Mon.-Sat. 9:30-noon, 1-4:30, Sun. 1:30-4:30; rest of yr, Mon.-Sat. 10-4, Sun. 1:30-4; closed Jan. 1, Thnks, Dec. 25): 1717 **Wells-Thorn House** featuring a lawyer's office; 1743 **Sheldon-Hawks House** with a sewing room; 1754 **Dwight-Barnard House** with a doctor's office; the clapboard **Ashley House** with a handsome parlor; the 1824 **Wright House** with Sheraton and other fine furnishings and China trade porcelain; the brick **Asa Stebbins House** with fine decorative arts; **Flynt Fabric Hall** with early textiles; and 1814 silver shop; and an 1816 printshop.

    Indian House Memorial (Main St.) consists of a replica of a 1698 home and an early 18th-C home, both with period furnishings; open mid-May-mid Oct., Mon., Wed.-Sat. 9:30-noon, 1-5, Sun. 1:30-5; sm adm.

    Memorial Hall Museum (Memorial St.), a 1797 brick building designed by Asher Benjamin for Deerfield Academy, contains Colonial and Indian artifacts; open Apr.-Nov. 15, Mon.-Sat. 9:30-5, Sun. 1:30-5; adm.

DOVER: Dover Historical Society (Dedham St.) is open Sat. 1-5; closed July-Aug.; free. The 1777 **Benjamin Caryl** House (Dedham St.), with period furnishings, is open Sat. 10-5; closed Aug.; free. The **Art Complex** (189 Alden St.) displays Shaker furniture, glass, costumes, and paintings; open Tues., Thurs., Sun. 2-5; closed hols; free.

FALL RIVER: Fall River Historical Society (451 Rock St.) houses memorabilia of the Fall River Steamboat Line, Lizzie Borden trial, textile industries; china, glass, toys, other collections; open Tues.-Fri. 9-4:30, Sat. 9-noon, Sun. 2-4; closed hols; free.

    Battleship Cove (jct SR 138, I-195) features the WW II submarine *Lionfish,* the *Massachusetts,* and the destroyer USS *Joseph P. Kennedy;* all may be boarded Mon.-Sat. 9-4:30, Sun. 10:30-4:30; closed Thnks, Dec. 25; adm. **Marine Museum** (70 Water St. at Battleship Cove) features ship models depicting the development of steam-powered shipping; also relics from the Fall River Line that sailed to New York via fashionable Newport for more than 90 years until 1937; open Mon.-Sat. 9-5, Sun. 12:30-5; closed Jan. 1, Thnks, Dec. 25; adm.

FITCHBURG: Fitchburg Art Museum (25 Merriam Pkwy.) exhibits French provincial furniture, decorative arts, and American paintings, sculpture, and graphics; open early Sept.-June, Tues.-Sat. 9-5, Sun. 2-5; closed Jan. 1, Thnks, Dec. 25; free.

GLOUCESTER: Gloucester Fisherman Memorial (Western Ave. at the harbor) is a bronze statue commemorating the 10,000 Gloucestermen lost at sea. **Cape Ann Historical Association** (27 Pleasant St.), a sea captain's home, displays antique furniture, silver, nautical equipment, and marine paintings by Fitz Hugh Lane; open Tues.-Sat. 11-4; closed Jan. 1, July 4, Thnks, Dec. 25; adm.

Hammond Castle (80 Hesperus Ave., off SR 127 between Magnolia & Gloucester), overlooking the sea, is a magnificent medieval-style castle built 1926-28 by inventor John Hays Hammond; paintings, sculpture, furnishings, and many building elements were brought from Europe; concerts are often given in the domed Great Hall on the 10,000-pipe Hammond organ; guided tours given June-Sept., Mon.-Sat. 9:30-3:30, Sun. 1:30-4:30; Oct.-May, weather permitting, daily at 11 and 2; closed Jan. 1, Thnks, Dec. 25; adm.

Sargent-Murray-Gilman-Hough House (49 Middle St.), a fine Georgian home with interior carving built by Winthrop Sargent in 1768, was later home to his daughter and son-in-law, John Murray, leader of Universalism; John Singer Sargent paintings; early glass; antiques; open June-Oct. 15, Tues., Thurs., Sat. 1-5; adm.

Beauport (Eastern Point Blvd.), a showplace built 1903-4, contains a splendid collection of 17th-18th-C furniture and decorative arts in replicas of rooms from many parts of New England; open for guided tours June-Sept., Mon.-Fri. 2:30, 3:30, 4:30; closed hols; adm.

GREAT BARRINGTON: Colonel Ashley House (9 m S in Ashley Falls), an elegantly designed 1735 home with fine paneling, displays early American furnishings; open Memorial Day-Oct. 15, Wed.-Sun. 1-5; adm. At **Tyringham** (15 m NE), many buildings remain from the Shaker settlement that flourished here 1792-1894. **Tyringham Galleries** (Tyringham Rd.) displays contemporary arts and crafts in the Gingerbread House, a 19th-C farmhouse converted into a studio by Sir Henry Kitson (who designed the Minuteman statue at Lexington and the Puritan maiden in Plymouth); the roof boasts a built-in witch's face; some Kitson work on display, pre-Columbian, other exhibits; open May-Oct., Mon.-Fri. 10-5, Sat. & Sun. 10-6; Nov.-May, weekends only; closed Jan. 1, Dec. 25; sm adm.

HARVARD: Fruitlands Museums (on Prospect Hill off SR 110) includes Fruitlands, the early 18th-C farmhouse where Bronson Alcott and others of the Transcendental Movement attempted to found a new social order in 1843; memorabilia of Louisa May Alcott, Emerson, Thoreau. **Old Shaker House** exhibits Shaker furniture and handcrafts; you can get directions here for driving to the buildings (privately owned) remaining from the old Shaker community and cemetery. **Picture Gallery** contains interesting primitives by itinerant artists and landscapes of the Hudson River School. **American Indian Museum** has dioramas, prehistoric implements, and examples of Indian arts. All are open May-Sept., Tues.-Sun. 1-5; sm adm.

HAVERHILL: John Greenleaf Whittier Birthplace (305 Whittier Rd., 3 m E on SR 110), a 1688 farmhouse, is maintained as the poet described it in "Snowbound"; open Tues.-Sat. 10-5, Sun. 1-5; closed Jan. 1, Thnks, Dec. 25; sm adm.

Haverhill Historical Society (240 Water St., SR 97) maintains several buildings including pre-1645 and 1814 homes with period furnishings; many Indian artifacts; relics of Hannah Dustin, who was kidnapped by Indians in 1697 and escaped with the scalps of 10 of her captors; other displays; open June-mid-Sept., Tues.-Sat. 1-5; rest of yr, Tues., Thurs., Sat. 2-5; closed hols; sm adm.

Capt. Samuel Brocklebank Museum (E Main St., 6 m E on SR 133 in Georgetown), built in 1640 and used as a stop on the Underground Railroad, displays local historical items, including ironware; open Memorial Day-Labor Day, Wed. 2-5, Sat. 1:30-5, Sun. 1:30-5:30; donation.

HINGHAM: Old Ship Church (90 Main St.), erected 1681 with roof beams resembling a ship's hull, has a compass painted on the ceiling; still in use; cemetery with an ancestor of Lincoln; open July-Aug. Tues.-Sun. noon-5; free. The **Old Ordinary** (21 Lincoln St.), built in stages 1680-1760, displays old tools and wooden ware; restored tap room; open mid-June-mid-Sept., Tues.-Sat. 1-4; closed hols; adm.

HOLYOKE: Church of the Blessed Sacrament (1945 Northampton St., US 5) is a circular, contemporary church; open daily 6:30 am-7 pm. **Holyoke Museum-Wisteriahurst** (238 Cabot St.), in a Victorian mansion featuring hand carving, a room with leather-covered walls, and antiques, displays fine arts, dioramas of local history; adjacent natural history museum for children; open Mon.-Sat. 1-5, Sun. 2-5; closed hols & July; free.

Mt. Holyoke College (5 m NE on SR 116 in S Hadley) offers tours during the academic yr, Mon.-Sat. 9-noon, 1-4, Sun. 2-5; closed hols. **Art Museum** has small but good collections of Far East, Greek, Sienese art; 19th-C American painting; open during academic yr, Mon.-Fri. 11-5, Sat. 1-5, Sun. 2:30-4:30; free. **Joseph Allen Skinner Museum** houses Indian relics, early furnishings and vehicles in a church, schoolhouse, and carriage house; open May-Oct., Wed., Sun. 2-5; free.

Granby Dinosaur Museum (14 m NE in Granby at 194 W State St.) has indoor and outdoor exhibits of tracks of Triassic dinosaurs and other animals from adjacent slate quarry; field trips by appointment; open daily 9-6; closed Jan. 1, Easter, Thnks, Dec. 25; adm.

IPSWICH: Among the many early buildings in this former lacemaking and hosiery town, one of the first to rebel against British taxation, are: **John Whipple House** (53 S Main St.), built in 1640 and restored with period furnishings by the Ipswich Historical Society, and **Thomas F. Waters Memorial** (40 S Main St.), built 1795 by a family engaged in China trade, with costumes, toys, and many Far East treasures; both open mid-Apr.-Oct., Tues.-Sat. 10-5, Sun. 1-5; adm. **Lakeman-Johnson House** (16 East St.), the 1827 Greek Revival home of a sea captain, with period furnishings and Oriental pieces, and **Howard House** (41 Turkey Shore Rd.), built about 1680, are open June-Oct., Tues., Sat. 1-5; closed hols; sm adm.

LANCASTER: First Church of Christ (The Common), built of brick in 1816, with a handsome pulpit and a Paul Revere bell, is one of the finest designs by Bulfinch; open Sun.; free.

LENOX: Tanglewood (1½ m SW on SR 183), where Nathaniel Hawthorne lived and wrote, is now home to the Berkshire Music Festival (July-Aug.). The Chamber Music Hall and Theatre were designed by Eero Saarinen. Hawthorne's Cottage, used for music studios, is open before concerts. Grounds are open daily; free exc during the festival (when guided tours are available daily 9-5:30).

LEXINGTON: Chamber of Commerce Visitor Center (E of The Green) provides information and a diorama of the Battle of Lexington; open Apr.-Oct. daily 9-5; rest of yr, 10-4. (See also Concord, for Minute Man National Historic Park.) On **the Green**, the Minuteman Statue faces the line of approach of the Concord-bound British troops, an inscribed boulder marks the line of Minutemen, and a monument marks the graves of 7 Minutemen. **Buckman Tavern** (E of The Green), rendezvous of the Minutemen before the battle, has been restored to its 1775 appearance. **Hancock-Clarke House** (35 Hancock St.) is where John Hancock and Samuel Adams were sleeping when Paul Revere roused them. **Munroe Tavern** (1332 Massachusetts Ave.) was taken over as headquarters by the British for the battle; Washington was entertained here in 1789. All are open mid-Apr.-Oct., Mon.-Sat. 10-5, Sun. 1-5; adm to each or combination ticket.

Museum of Our National Heritage traces the growth and development of the U.S. through exhibits on glass, quilting, and other crafts; open Mon.-Sat. 9:30-4, Sun. noon-5:30; free.

LINCOLN: Codman House (Codman Rd.), built about 1730 and remodeled in the 1790s and 1860s, contains furnishings of the family that occupied it until 1969; open June-Oct., Tues., Thurs., Sat. 1-5; adm. **DeCordova Museum** (Sandy Point Rd.), an 1880 castlelike building, has changing art exhibits, sculpture; open Tues.-Sat. 10-5, Sun. 1:30-5; closed hols; adm.

LOWELL: Whistler House & Parker Gallery (243 Worthen St.), birthplace of James Abbott McNeill Whistler in 1834, displays several of his etchings as well as contemporary works; open Sept.-June, Tues.-Sun. 2-4:30; closed hols; sm adm.

LYNN: Lynn Historical Society Museum (125 Green St.) houses paintings, glass, china, shoe display, other local historic items in 1836 house; open Mon.-Fri. 1-4; closed hols; free.

MARBLEHEAD: Chamber of Commerce (62 Pleasant St.) offers booklets describing local historic sites, including the 1742 **Fort Sewall** (end of Front St.), 1755 circular **Powder House** (37 Green St.), 1714 **St. Michael's Church** (Summer St.), and **Old Burial Hill** (off Orne St.). **Abbott Hall** (Town Hall, Washington Sq.) displays the 1684 deed of purchase of the peninsula for 16 pounds from the Indians and the original of the painting "Spirit of '76"; open Mon.-Fri. 8 am-9 pm, Sat. 8-noon; also open Sun. 1-5 in summer; closed hols; free.
   Jeremiah Lee Mansion (161 Washington St.), a superb Georgian home built 1768, is of wood, but sand-treated paint makes it look of stone; handsome detailing inside and out; original hand-painted wallpaper; fine period furnishings, paintings, documents; open mid-May-mid-Oct., Mon.-Sat. 9:30-4; closed Memorial Day; adm. **King Hooper Mansion** (8 Hooper St.), a 1728 dwelling elaborated in 1747 by a merchant ship owner, has notable woodwork, early furniture; art exhibits; open Tues.-Sun. 2-5; sm adm.

MARTHA'S VINEYARD: Dukes County Historical Society (Cooke & School Sts. in Edgartown), with a museum of island memorabilia, library, boat shed with maritime exhibits, is partly housed in the Thomas Cooke House, built by ships' carpenters in 1765; period furnishings, scrimshaw, ship models, whaling and other historical exhibits; open June-Sept., Tues.-Sat. 10-4:30, Sun. 2-4:30; adm. **Vineyard Haven's Association Hall** has striking murals of island life by Stanley Murphy; open Mon.-Fri. In **Oak Bluffs,** colorful gingerbread cottages surround the Methodist open-air tabernacle; the Hansel & Gretel Doll Museum (off New York Ave.), with antique toys, is open summers daily 9-5; sm adm.

NANTUCKET ISLAND: Settled in 1659 after being bought for 30 pounds and 2 beaver hats, this popular beach resort owes much of its charm to beautifully preserved homes built during prosperous whaling days; some of the handsomest are on the cobblestoned Main Street of Nantucket Town. The Nantucket Historical Society publishes booklets for self-guiding walking tours, available at the **Information Office** (23 Federal St.) or at historic buildings. The following buildings are open early June-early Sept., Mon.-Sat. 10-5 for sm adm: **Jethro Coffin House** (Sunset Hill off W Chester St.), the island's oldest house (1686). **1800 House** (Mill St. off Pleasant St.), with a borning room and period furnishings. **Windmill** (Mill Hill off Prospect St.), built 1746 of materials salvaged from shipwrecks. **Old Gaol** (Vestal St.), built in 1805 and used until 1933. **Old Fire Hose Cart House** (Gardner St. off Main St.), with early firefighting equipment. **Nathaniel Macy House** (Walnut Lane & Liberty St.), built in the early 1700s, with period furnishings. **Hawden House-Satler Memorial** (Main & Pleasant Sts.), modeled on a Roman temple in 1845, with Empire and Victorian furnishings, contrasts with the Quaker restraint of many of Nantucket's buildings. Other homes are opened on open-house tours a couple of times a summer.

Other interesting buildings are **Nantucket Atheneum** (Lower Pearl & Federal St.), where Emerson, Thoreau, Audubon, Melville, and others lectured; **Unitarian Church** (Orange St.), whose tower served as a fire and ship lookout, with interesting interior decorations; **Pacific Club** (foot of Main St.), founded by whaling ship masters in 1854 and used as a counting house and whale-oil warehouse; the **Three Bricks,** identical brick houses at 93, 95, 97 Main St.; the splendid **Thomas Macy House** (99 Main St.), built in 1770 and enlarged 1830, which was frowned on as being too pretentious; and homes typical of Quaker austerity (such as those at 117 Main St., 33 Milk St., 53 Orange St.).

Whaling Museum (Broad St. near Steamboat Wharf), with splendid materials from whaling days, and the nearby **Peter Folger Museum,** with exhibits on life in Indian and Quaker days, both have libraries and are open late May-mid-Oct. daily 10-5; adm.

Maria Mitchell Association (1 Vestal St.) maintains Memorial House, birthplace of the first American woman astronomer, with authentic furnishings; a scientific library and observatory; **Loines Observatory,** open to the public some summer evenings; and a **Natural Science Museum** with local flora and fauna plus an **Aquarium** (Straight Wharf); all are open mid-June-mid-Sept., Mon.-Fri. 10-noon, 2-5, Sat. 10-noon; sm adm.

Lifesaving Museum (2½ m on Polpis Rd.), is a replica of the first lifesaving station, with exhibits; open Tues.-Sun. 10-5; adm.

NEW BEDFORD: New Bedford Whaling Museum (18 Johnny Cake Hill) offers wonderful collections of scrimshaw, glassware, whaling relics, ship models including a half-size replica of a whaling bark; library; open June-Sept., Mon.-Sat. 9-5, Sun. 1-5; Oct.-May, Tues.-Sat. 9-5, Sun. 1-5; closed Jan. 1, Thnks, Dec. 25; adm. **Seaman's Bethel** (15 Johnny Cake Hill), the chapel described in *Moby Dick,* has a pulpit shaped like the prow of a ship; tablets commemorate whalemen lost at sea; open June-Aug., Mon.-Sat. 9-5, Sun. 1-5; Apr.-May, Sat. 9-5, Sun. 1-5; donation. **New Bedford Free Public Library** (613 Pleasant St.) has ship models, whaling memorabilia in the Melville Room; large collection of books on whaling; open Mon.-Sat. 9-5; free. **Fort Taber** (Clark's Point), Civil War fort and military museum, is open mid-May-Sept., Sun. 11-4; free. **Mattapoisett Historical Museum** (E off US 6 at Church & Baptist Sts. in Mattapoisett) is open July-Aug., Tues.-Sat. 10-noon, 3-5; adm.

NEWBURYPORT: Chamber of Commerce (21 Pleasant St.) offers booklets for auto and walking tours; a highlight are the great Federalist mansions built along **High St.** by sea captains and ship owners. Homes open to the public include: the 1651 **Coffin House** (16 High Rd.), with elaborations and furnishings of 8 generations; the 1671 **Swett-Ilsley House** (4-6 High Rd.), with paneling, and **Short House** (39 High Rd.), built about 1732, with original woodwork and William and Mary period furnishings; all are open June-Sept., Tues., Thurs., Sat. 1-5; sm adm.

NEWTON: Jackson Homestead (527 Washington St.), built in 1809 and once a station on the Underground Railroad, offers period furnishings and exhibits on the history of Newton and New England; open Sept.-June, Mon.-Fri. 2-4; July-Aug., Wed. 2-4; closed hols; free.

NORTHAMPTON: Parsons House (58 Bridge St.), built 1658, with a period kitchen, furniture, and portraits, is headquarters of the Northampton Historical Society, which offers a brochure of historic sites in this town that was once home to Jonathan Edwards and Calvin Coolidge. The Society also maintains the 1792 **Pomeroy-Shepherd House** (66 Bridge St.) and the 1812 **Damon House** (46 Bridge St.). All open Wed., Fri., Sun. 2-4:30; closed Dec. 25; sm adm.

Smith College Museum of Art (Elm St. & Bedford Terr.) offers a small but fine collection of 19th-20th-C French and American painting; graphics from 1600s to the present; open Sept. 15-June, Mon.-Sat. 9-5, Sun. 2:30-4:30; closed hols; free.

Calvin Coolidge Memorial Room (Forbes Library, 20 West St.) displays the late President's papers, memorabilia; open Mon.-Sat. 9-8:30, Sun. & hols 2-6; closed Jan. 1, July 4, Thnks, Dec. 25; free.

PITTSFIELD: Berkshire Museum (39 South St., US 7) displays Old Masters; strong on Hudson River School and other American painting; Chinese art objects; 18th-C European and American silver; Greek and Roman sculpture; early cultures of the Near East; natural history exhibits; open Tues.-Sat. 10-5, Sun. 2-5; closed Jan. 1, July 4, Thnks, Dec. 25; free.

Headquarters House (113 E Housatonic St.), built 1855-58 in Italian villa-style, is hq of Berkshire County Historical Society; Federal and Empire furniture; historic displays; open Mon.-Fri. 2-5; closed hols; sm adm. The Society also maintains **Major Butler Goodrich House** (823 North St.), a Federal-period home with fine antiques; open July-Aug., Thurs.-Sun. 1-4; sm adm.

Crane Museum (5 m E off SR 9 in Dalton) displays the history of the firm's manufacture of currency and fine papers since Revolutionary days; open June-Sept., Mon.-Fri. 2-5; closed hols; free.

Hancock Shaker Village (5 m W on US 20), restoration of a community that flourished 1780-1960, offers a Visitor Center with interpretive displays; 1826 round stone barn; dwellings and other restored buildings; open June-Oct. daily 9:30-5; adm.

PLYMOUTH: Visitor Information Center (N Park Ave.) offers combination tickets to historic sites; open late-May-mid-Oct. daily 9-9; mid-Apr.-late May, & mid-Oct.-Thnks, weekends only 9-5; a booth is also open summers at State Pier. **Plymouth Rock** (harbor at Water St.) is protected by a Grecian temple.

Plimoth Plantation (2 m S on SR 3A), a carefully researched reconstruction by a nonprofit educational organization, re-creates life in the early settlement. Included is a complete **Pilgrim Village,** with homes and an Algonquin Indian camp, where people in period costumes demonstrate 17th-C skills; **First House,** similar to cottages the Pilgrims left behind in England, and **1627 House** (both at Water St, N of Plymouth Rock); all open July-Aug. 9 am-7 pm; June, Sept.-Oct. 9-5; Apr.-May & Nov. 10-5; adm. **Mayflower II** (State Pier, Water St.), built in England, is a replica of the original, amazingly small ship that carried 102 passengers and a crew of 25; exhibits show what life was like during the 66-day voyage, during which 50 died; open July-Aug. daily 9-8:30; spring & fall, Mon.-Fri. 9-5, Sat. & Sun. 9-6; adm.

The earliest Pilgrims were buried at **Cole's Hill** (S of Plymouth Rock). Gov. Bradford is buried at **Burial Hill** (W of Town Sq.). Miles Standish, Priscilla and John Alden are buried in the **Old Burying Ground** (Chestnut St. in S Duxbury).

Howland House (33 Sandwich St.), built in 1667 and the only house still standing in which Pilgrims were known to have lived, has period furnishings; open June-Sept. 15 daily 10-5; sm adm. **Harlow Old Fort**

House (119 Sandwich St.), built 1677 with timber taken from the first Pilgrim fort, offers demonstrations of domestic arts; open Memorial Day-mid-Sept., daily 10-5; also open Thnks; sm adm. **Richard Sparrow House** (42 Summer St.), built 1640, has an interesting history; open June-Sept. Mon.-Sat. 10-5; sm adm. **General Society of Mayflower Descendants, National Headquarters** (4 Winslow St.), built 1754 with the King's arms at the gables, exhibits 18th-19th-C period furnishings; open mid-June-mid-Sept., daily 10-5; adm. **Pilgrim Hall Museum** (75 Court St., SR 3A) exhibits possessions of the first Pilgrims, portraits, and early decorative arts; research and geneaological library; open daily 9-4:30; closed Jan. 1, Dec. 25; sm adm. **Antiquarian House** (126 Water St.), a Federal-style home where Daniel Webster was a frequent guest, was built 1809, antique toys; period clothing; open Memorial Day-mid-Sept. daily 10-5; sm adm. **Spooner House** (27 North St.), occupied by the Spooner family 1763-1954, is furnished with family heirlooms; open Memorial Day-mid-Sept., daily 10-5; sm adm. **Major John Bradford House** (3 m NW on SR 3A to Maple St. & Landing Rd. in Kingston), built by a grandson of Gov. Bradford in 1674, has period furnishings; open mid-June-Labor Day, Wed.-Sat. 10-5, Sun. 1-5; sm adm.

Plymouth National Wax Museum (16 Carver St.) has animated lifesize scenes, with narration, following the Pilgrims from their departure from England to the establishment of a colony; open July-Aug. 9-9:30; Mar.-June & Sept.-Nov. 9-5; adm.

Jenny Grist Mill Village (Spring Lane), a replica of John Jenny's 1636 mill, grinds corn with water power; craft shops; open May-Dec. 25 daily 9-6; sm adm.

Middleborough Historical Museum (Jackson St., 15 m W via US 44, SR 105 in Middleborough), with a Tom Thumb collection, is open in summer; sm adm. In Duxbury are **Jonathan Alden House,** last home of Priscilla and John Alden (open summers; sm adm), and **King Caesar House,** restored home of Ezra Weston, 19th-C czar of shipping (open July & Aug., Tues.-Sun. 2-5; adm).

QUINCY: Adams National Historic Site (135 Adams St.): built 1731 by a West Indian sugar planter, the house was bought by mail by John Adams (then Ambassador to England), and enlarged by Abigail; 4 generations of the family (including the 2 Presidents, the ambassador Charles Francis Adams, and the historian Henry Adams) lived here 1788-1927; family furnishings, papers, and library; open mid-Apr.-mid-Nov. daily 9-5; sm adm or GEP.

Quincy Homestead (34 Butler Rd. at Hancock St.), childhood home of Dorothy Quincy, wife of John Hancock, has a secret room where patriots were hidden; open mid-Apr.-Oct., Tues.-Sun. 10-5; closed hols; adm.

Birthplaces of **John Adams** (131 Franklin St.) and **John Quincy Adams** (141 Franklin St.) are similar saltboxes; the Constitution of the Commonwealth of Massachusetts, on which the U.S. Constitution was modeled, was written in the law office of the latter building; open mid-Apr.-Sept., Tues.-Sun. 10-5; sm adm.

Col. Josiah Quincy House (20 Muirhead St., Wollaston), built 1770, contains Quincy family furnishings; open June-Sept., Tues., Thurs., Sat. 1-5; sm adm.

First Parish Church (1306 Hancock St.), was built in 1828 in Greek Revival style with granite donated by John Quincy Adams; he and his wife, as well as John and Abigail Adams, are buried here. (Nearby Hancock Cemetery, adjoining City Hall, has graves dating from the early 1600s.)

ROCKPORT: Rockport Art Assn (12 Main St.), with changing exhibits, publishes a map of the many galleries in the area; open Mon.-Sat. 10-noon, 2-5, Sun. 2-5; closed Jan. 1, Thnks, Dec. 25; free. **Sandy Bay Historical Society & Museum** (40 King St.), in an 1832 home, displays antiques, maritime and other relics; open July-Labor Day, daily 2-5; donation. **Old Castle** (Granite & Curtis Sts.), built in the 18th-C, is open July & Aug., Sat. & Sun. 2-5; free. **Cooperage Shop** (2 m N on SR 127), built 1658, displays early tools and furniture; open July-Labor Day, Tues.-Sun. 2-5; free.

SALEM: Salem Maritime National Historic Site preserves the historic waterfront surrounding **Derby Wharf,** a base for privateering during the Revolution and one of America's most prosperous and sophisticated ports from the 1760's until the mid-19th-C. Opposite the wharf is the Visitor Center in the 1819 **Custom House,** mentioned in Nathaniel Hawthorne's *The Scarlet Letter;* offices, including that where the author worked as a surveyor 1846-49, have been restored; adjacent are the 1819 **Bonded Warehouse** and 1829 **Scale House. Derby House** (168 Derby St.), Salem's oldest brick house, completed 1762, was home to one of the foremost merchant and shipping families; fine paneling; family pieces and other antique furnishings. Open daily 8:30-5; closed Jan. 1, Thnks, Dec. 25; free exc sm adm for Derby House.

Essex Institute (132 Essex St.), a remarkable historical museum and fine library, is housed in several handsome buildings displaying fine early furnishings, glass, china, silver, and portraits by American masters; Institute open Tues.-Sat. 9-4:30, Sun. 2-5; closed Jan. 1, July 4, Thnks, Dec. 25; sm adm to each building or combination ticket: **John Ward House** (behind Institute), a 1684 home with displays illustrating 17th-C life, and the 1727 **Crowninshield-Bentley House** (Essex St. & Hawthorne Blvd.), with period furnishings, are open June-Oct. 15, Tues.-Sat. 10-4, Sun. 2-4:30. **Pingree House** (128 Essex St.), built 1804, and **Peirce-Nichols House** (80 Federal St.), built 1782, are outstanding designs by Samuel McIntire; handsome furnishings; open Tues.-Sat. 10-4. **Assembly House** (138 Federal St.), built as a hall for social gatherings in 1782 and remodeled as a home in 1796 by McIntire, features teakwood furniture; open Tues.-Sat. 2-4:30.

Peabody Museum (161 Essex St.), in an 1824 building erected as a meeting hall for the East India Marine Society, has wonderful collections of curiosities brought home from around the world by Salem's sea captains and merchants; fine ethnological material from the Far East, Pacific, Africa, and South America; ship models; scrimshaw; primitive paintings; Chinese export porcelain; Derby Wharf diorama; natural history displays' open Mon.-Sat. 9-5, Sun. & hols 1-5; closed Jan. 1, Thnks, Dec. 25; adm.

Chestnut Street (Summer to Flint Sts.) is one of the loveliest streets in America; here, away from the commercial atmosphere of the docks, prosperous China merchants and sea captains built handsome homes and furnished them with treasures from around the world; #9 and #12 were designed by master carver Samuel McIntire; Nathaniel Hawthorne lived for a short time at #18. **Essex St.** (between North & Flint Sts.) also has some fine old homes. **Ropes Mansion** (318 Essex St.) is typical of the homes of wealthy shipping families; fine Chinese porcelain; Irish glass; family furnishings; open early May-Oct., Mon.-Sat. 10-4:30; closed hols; adm. **Witch House** (310½ Essex St.), built 1642, was the home of Judge Corwin; accused witches were brought here for pre-trial examination; open Mar.-Labor Day, daily 10-6; Labor Day-Nov., weather permitting, 10-5; sm adm.

House of the Seven Gables (54 Turner St., off Derby St.), built 1668, inspired Hawthorne's novel; lovely paneling; secret staircase; period furnishings. Moved to the grounds are **Nathaniel Hawthorne's Birthplace,** built about 1740, with memorabilia of the author; the 1682 **Hathaway House,** once a bakery; and the 1655 **Retire Beckett House,** now a giftshop. Guided tours daily, July-Labor Day 9:30-7:30; rest of yr, 10-4:30; closed Jan. 1, Thnks, Dec. 25; adm.

Pioneer Village (Forest River Park) reproduces a primitive 1630 settlement; crude dwellings include dugouts, wigwams, thatched cottages; facilities for salt making and other early industries; open June-mid-Oct. 9:30-5 (longer hrs in summer); sm adm.

Salem State College (Lafayette St. & Loring Ave.) offers an observatory and art gallery plus Chronicle of Salem, a 60-ft-long mural depicting the history of the town (open Mon.-Fri. 8-5; closed hols); free.

Salem Witch Museum (Washington Sq. in N Salem), in an old church, features life-size scenes plus narration describing the witchcraft hysteria of 1692-3, during which 19 people were hanged and one pressed to death;

open June-Sept., daily 10-7:30; Oct.-May, daily 10-5:30; closed Jan. 1, Thnks, Dec. 25; adm.

Charter St. Burial Ground (Charter St. & Liberty St.), dating from 1637, was mentioned in Hawthorne's writings; interesting gravestones.

City Hall (93 Washington St.) houses historic documents and portraits, and the **Courthouse** (Washington & Federal Sts.) contains documents on the witch trials.

SAUGUS: Saugus Iron Works National Historic Site (244 Central St.) is a reconstruction of the plant that laid the foundations for the U.S. iron and steel industry. Operations began here in 1643, with English iron-workers; they were soon joined by indentured servants of a Scottish investor who bought young men Cromwell had captured in 1650. Although the works failed and shut down about 1670, the men moved on to produce iron elsewhere in the country. Restorations include the Ironmaster's House, with period furnishings, a museum of relics discovered during excavations, the blast furnace, forge, and slitting mill; tours given daily Apr.-Oct. 9-5; grounds open also Nov.-Mar. 9-4; closed Jan. 1, Dec. 25; free.

SCITUATE: Cudworth House (First Parish & Cudworth Rds.) was built 1797; period furnishings include a cauldron made by an ancestor of Lincoln. **Mann Farmhouse** (Greenfield Lane & Stockbridge Rd.) houses furnishings of 5 generations of the same family. Both open mid-June-mid-Sept., Wed.-Sat. 2-5; sm adm.

SPRINGFIELD: Museum Center (State & Chestnut Sts.) includes: **George Walter Vincent Smith Art Museum** with superb jade, ceramics, bronzes, laquer, porcelain, and other Oriental collections as well as European decorative arts. **Museum of Fine Arts** also offers fine Oriental works, plus Gothic, Renaissance, 17th-19th-C European and American paintings and sculpture; contemporary American art. **Connecticut Valley Historical Museum** offers period rooms and a library with emphasis on economic history. **Science Museum,** with habitat groups, includes an aquarium and a planetarium. All open Tues.-Sat. 1-5, Sun. (exc July-Aug.) 2-5; closed hols; free.

Storrowton Village (Eastern States Exposition Park, SR 147 in W Springfield), a reconstructed early-19th-C village, clusters around a green a tavern, blacksmith shop, meetinghouse, school, and other buildings moved here from nearby sites; open mid-June-Labor Day, Mon.-Sat. 1-5; adm.

National Basketball Hall of Fame (460 Alden St. on Springfield College campus), dedicated to Dr. James Naismith, who invented the game in 1891, displays memorabilia from the earliest games to contemporary players; library; films; open Mon.-Sat. 10-5, Sun. 1-5, with longer hrs July-Aug.; closed Jan. 1, Thnks, Dec. 25; adm.

Springfield Armory Museum (Federal St.), with the organ of guns made famous by Longfellow's poem, "The Arsenal at Springfield," houses large collections of toy soldiers, small arms, and weapons from the 14th-C to modern times; open Mon.-Sat. 10-5, Sun. & hols 1-5; closed Jan. 1, Thnks, Dec. 25; adm.

STOCKBRIDGE: Mission House (Main & Sargeant Sts., SR 102), built 1739 by the Rev. John Sargeant, missionary to Algonquin Indians (his work was continued by Jonathan Edwards), is a museum of Colonial life; open June-Sept., Tues.-Sat. 10-5, Sun. 11-4; adm. (An Indian Burial Ground is W on Main St.)

Chesterwood (1½ m S of jct SR 102, 183), studio of Daniel Chester French, contains casts of his Minute Man statue for Concord, the Seated Lincoln for the Memorial in Washington, D.C., and other works; a modeling table on a flatcar could be moved outdoors on railroad tracks; tools, equipment, and other works in the Barn Gallery; open June-Sept., daily 10-5; Oct. weekends, 10-5; adm.

Old Corner House (Main & Elm Sts.), a late-18th-C Georgian home, contains displays of local history and of paintings by Norman Rockwell; open Wed.-Mon., 10-5; closed Jan. 1, Thnks, Dec. 25; adm. **Merwin House** (39 Main St.), built about 1820, reflects 19th-C interest in culture and foreign travel; large Tiffany collection; open June-Oct., Tues.-Sat. 10-noon, 2-5; closed hols; sm adm. **Naumkeag** (Prospect Hill, 1 m N of jct US 7, SR 102), a Norman-style mansion designed in 1885 by Stanford White, is furnished with Chinese and other antiques; fine gardens with Chinese temple and statuary; usually open in summer, but check locally for hrs; adm.

STURBRIDGE: Old Sturbridge Village (on US 20, 1½ m W of jct with SR 15): 37 buildings (meetinghouses, shops, homes, tavern, offices) have been moved here to re-create a typical New England village of 1790-1840; continuous craft demonstrations; special exhibits (clocks, guns, lighting, etc.); working farm; open Apr.-Oct. daily 9:30-5:30; Mar., Nov. daily 9:30-4:30; Dec.-Feb. daily 10-4; closed Jan. 1, Dec. 25; adm.

Sturbridge Military Museum (W on US 20), with foreign and American displays, is open May 15-Oct. 15, Tues.-Sun. 1-8, also some weekends before and after these dates; adm. **Sturbridge Auto Museum** (2 m W on US 20) is open June-Aug. daily 10:30-9:30; Apr.-May, Sept.-Nov. daily 10:30-5:30; adm.

SUDBURY: Longfellow's Wayside Inn (5 m SW on US 20), built before 1700 and said to be the oldest inn in the U.S. ("Food, Drink, and

Lodging for Man and Beast"), was immortalized in Longfellow's *Tales of a Wayside Inn* (1863); restored by Ford Foundation, it contains period furnishings; chapel, school, coach house, and gristmill also on grounds; open daily 9-6; closed Dec. 25; sm adm.

TAUNTON: Old Colony Historical Society (66 Church Green) has good displays of silver objects made locally (Taunton was once called "Silver City" for its more than 20 silver firms) and other Americana; open Tues.-Sat. 10-4; closed hols; sm adm.

WALTHAM: Gore Place (Main & Gore Sts.), the extraordinarily fine Federal home of Christopher Gore, Gov. of Mass. 1809-10, contains magnificent period furnishings; open mid-Apr.-mid-Nov., Tues.-Sat. 10-5, Sun. 2-5; adm. **Lyman House** (Lyman & Beaver Sts.), designed by Samuel McIntire and built 1793, has especially handsome ballroom and parlor; some original furniture; stable; gardens and greenhouse; open July-Aug., Thurs., Fri. 11-2; closed hols; adm.

WILLIAMSTOWN: Williams College Museum of Art (Main St.) features Spanish paintings and furniture, early American furniture; Classical works; medieval to contemporary painting; open summer, Mon.-Sat. 10-noon, 2-4, Sun. 2-5; winters, Mon.-Sat. 10-5, Sun. 2-5; free. **Chapin Library,** with displays of rare books and prints, is open summers, Mon.-Fri. 9-12, 1-4; winter, Mon.-Fri. 9-12, 1-5, Sat. 9-12; free.

   Sterling & Francine Clark Art Institute (South St.) offers Italian, Flemish, Dutch, and French Old Masters plus French Impressionists and American paintings; sculpture; silver; open Tues.-Sun. 10-5; free.

WOBURN: Rumford House (90 Elm St., N Woburn), birthplace of Count Rumford, founder of Royal Institution of Great Britain, displays models of his experiments and inventions; antiques, portraits, library; open Tues.-Sun. 1:30-4:30; free.

WORCESTER: Worcester Art Museum (55 Salisbury St.) has excellent collections of 50 centuries, arranged chronologically, from the Near East, Persia, Far East (fine Japanese prints), Europe (paintings from the Renaissance to 20th-C), pre-Columbian and primitive works to contemporary American paintings; a highlight is a Romanesque chapter house from France; lectures, films, other activities; open Tues.-Sat. 10-5, Sun. 2-6; closed July 4, Thnks, Dec. 25; free.

   Worcester Historical Society Museum (39 Salisbury St.) displays Indian relics, tools, furniture, pewter, glass, toys, and thousands of other items; open Tues.-Sat. 1-4; closed hols, Aug.-Labor Day; free.

Worcester Science Center (222 Harrington Way) contains a museum with many exhibits that can be touched, multimedia and planetarium shows in the omnisphere, a hall of energy with a working power plant; also zoo, botanical garden; open Mon.-Sat. 1-5, Sun. noon-5; closed hols; adm.

Robert H. Goddard Library & Exhibit (Clark Univ. campus) houses exhibits on the life and work of this space pioneer; open Mon.-Fri. 9-4:30; closed hols; free.

John Woodman Higgins Armory (100 Barber Ave.), in a 1928 building whose interior is modeled on a 10th-C Austrian castle, highlights tools, armor (including outfits for children and animals), and weapons from the Stone Age to the present; also tapestries, paintings; open Tues.-Fri. 9-4, Sat. 10-3, Sun. 1-5; closed hols; sm adm.

American Antiquarian Society (185 Salisbury St.), founded by printer Isaiah Thomas in 1812, offers a large collection of materials printed prior to 1820 and other research facilities for scholars; open Mon.-Fri. 9-5.

Cathedral Church of St. Paul (38 High St.), built in Gothic style 1874, is open daily in daylight.

MICHIGAN

ALPENA: Jesse Besser Museum (491 Johnson St.): superb prehistoric and recent materials on Indian cultures from the Great Lakes area; lumbering and historic displays, planetarium shows (sm adm); open Mon.-Fri. 9-5, Sun. 1-5; closed hols; free.

ANN ARBOR: University of Michigan Visitor Relations Office (phone 764-7268) provides information and will arrange for tours. **Burton Memorial Tower,** with 53-bell Baird carillon, is open Wed. 4-5, Sat. 11-noon. **Museum of Art** (S State St. & S University Ave.), emphasis on 20th-C works; African, Asian, and Western art; open Mon.-Sat. 9-5, Sun. 2-5. **Kelsey Museum of Ancient & Medieval Archaeology** (434 S State St.), fine collections from the Near East including Roman glass; open Mon.-Fri. 9-1, Sat. & Sun. 1-4. **A. R. Ruthven Museum** (1109 Geddes Ave.) of natural history; prehistoric life; planetarium shows (weekends); open Mon.-Sat. 9-5, Sun. 1:30-5:30, closed hols. **Stearns Collection of Musical Instruments** (Baits St. & Broadway) is open Mon.-Fri. 11:30-4:30; closed hols. **William L. Clements Library,** with an extraordinary collection of Americana, is open Mon.-Fri. 9-noon, 1-5; closed hols. **Phoenix Memorial Laboratory** (N

Campus) for research on atomic energy, is open by appointment. **School of Music** (N Campus) was designed by Eero Saarinen.

Kempf House (312 S Division St.), built 1853, restored by the Ann Arbor Historic District Commission, has classical Greek detailing, cast iron grills; local historical exhibits; open Sat. & Sun. 2-5; closed Jan. 1, Dec. 25; donation.

BATTLE CREEK: Leila Arboretum (W Michigan Ave.) contains **Kingman Museum of Natural History**, with fine fossils and minerals; bird and animal, Indian, biological, and geological exhibits; planetarium (extra charge); open Tues.-Sat. 9-5, Sun. 1-5; closed Easter, Dec. 25; sm adm. **Oak Hill Cemetery** (South Ave. & Oak Hill Dr.) contains the grave of Sojourner Truth, the slave born in the 1790s who gained her own freedom in the 1820s and crusaded for civil rights until her death in 1883. **Kimball House Museum** (196 Capital Ave. NE), built 1886, was home to 3 generations of doctors; Victorian furnishings and medical equipment; open Tues., Thurs., Sun. 1-4:30; closed Jan. 1, Dec. 25; donation.

Charlton Park Village & Museum (23 m N via SR 37, then E on SR 79) consists of an 1850 stagecoach inn, 1885 church, shops, and museum of pioneer life in a park with recreational facilities; museum open in summer, Mon.-Fri. 9-5, Sat. & Sun. 1-5; park open 8-dark; adm.

BAY CITY: Museum of the Great Lakes (1700 Center Ave.): Indian, lumbering, and local historic exhibits; open Tues.-Fri. 1-5; Sat. & Sun. 2-5; closed hols; donation.

BEAVER ISLAND (reached by boat Apr.-Dec. from Charlevoix): **Mormon Print Shop** (Main & Forest Sts., St. James), an 1850 log building where one of the state's first newspapers was published, was built for James J. Strang, leader of a Mormon colony that settled here in 1847; Strang's followers crowned him king in 1850, but he was murdered 7 years later; houses local historic collection; open in summer; sm adm.

BLOOMFIELD HILLS: Cranbrook (Lone Pine Rd) is a cultural complex established at the turn of the century; early architecture was by Albert Kahn, with woodcarving by John Kirchmayer; Eliel Saarinen was responsible for later buildings; Swedish sculptor Carl Milles (1875-1955) was resident artist here for 21 years and made many of the sculptures on the grounds. **Christ Church Cranbrook**, in English Gothic style, contains ancient and modern works of art—paintings, sculpture, a fresco, tapestries, stained glass; open daily 8-5; carillon concerts in summer on Sun. at 4; free. **Cranbrook Academy of Art Museum**, with many works by Milles and changing exhibits, is open Tues.-Sun. 1-5; closed hols; adm. **Cran-**

brook Institute of Science, with exhibits on geology, physics, math, biology, anthropology, and natural history; planetarium and observatory; open Mon.-Fri. 10-5, Sat. 1-9, Sun. 1-5; closed hols; adm.

COLDWATER: This town, which grew up along the Chicago Road, first major road into the interior of Michigan, has many old homes (especially along Pearl and Chicago Sts.) and has preserved the 1882 **Tibbits Opera House** (S Hanchett St.), still in use and open daily for free tours.

DEARBORN: **Greenfield Village & Henry Ford Museum** (Oakwood Blvd., ½ m S of US 12) contain a vast and superb array of Americana collected by Henry Ford. Greenfield Village is a re-created community demonstrating early American home life and industries; oldest building is a limestone cottage from Gloucestershire, England, typical of the homes early settlers left; nearly 100 homes, shops, and other 17th-19th-C buildings have been moved here from around the country—a courthouse where Lincoln practiced law, Noah Webster's home, the Wright brothers' cycle shop, Edison's Menlo Park laboratory. The Henry Ford Museum consists of: **Fine Arts Galleries** (American decorative arts from the 17th-19th-C); **Street of Early American Shops** (re-creations of shops in which crafts were demonstrated); **Mechanical Arts Hall** (evolution of tools and machinery used in agriculture, transportation, manufacturing). Open in summer daily 9-6; rest of yr, Mon.-Fri. 9-5, weekends & hols 9-6; closed Jan. 1, Thnks, Dec. 25; adm.

DETROIT: First laid out like Washington, D.C., and later converted to the grid system, Detroit is confusing to newcomers; a map (essential) is available from **Detroit Dept. of Public Information,** 1008 City-County Bldg., in the modern **Civic Center** (Woodward St. at the river), from which the major avenues radiate. Inquire here too about industrial tours; visitor hours at the auto plants vary, and plants sometimes close for model changeover. **General Motors Technical Center** (Mound & Twelve Mile Rds. in Warren), usually open for tours June-Labor Day, was designed by Eero Saarinen, with a fountain by Alexander Calder and "Bird in Flight" by Antoine Pevsner. Information on auto plant tours is also available at Greenfield Village (see Dearborn).

 Detroit Institute of Arts (5200 Woodward Ave.): magnificent collection, representing virtually every significant culture—Oriental, Classical, African, European, American painting, sculpture, decorative arts; Diego Rivera's frescos of industry; open Tues.-Sun. 9:30-5:30; closed hols; donation. **International Institute** (111 E Kirby Ave.) exhibits arts and crafts from around the world; folk dancing and other activities; open Mon.-Fri. 9-5; closed hols; free. **Meadow Brook Art Gallery** (Oakland Univ., Rochester) exhibits masks, carvings, and other African works; open Tues.-Sun. during academic yr; free.

Detroit Historical Museum (5401 Woodward Ave.) traces city's history; reconstructed streets; period rooms; economic growth (including auto industry); open Tues.-Sat. 9-5, Sun. 1-5; closed Jan. 1, Thnks, Dec. 25; donation. **Dossin Great Lakes Museum** (Belle Isle, via MacArthur Bridge) traces the history of shipping on the Great Lakes; Gothic Salon from a 1912 lake steamer is a highlight; open Wed.-Sun. 10-5:45; closed Thnks, Dec. 25-Jan. 1; donation. **Detroit Public Library** (5201 Woodward Ave.): extensive collections on the Old Northwest, automobile industry; murals by Sheets, Coppin, Blashfield; open Mon., Wed., 9:30-9; Tues., Thurs.-Sat. 9:30-5:30; Sun., Oct.-May, 1-6; closed hols; free.

Fort Wayne Military Museum (6053 W Jefferson Ave.), built 1843-48; well-preserved barracks, casemates, powder magazine; exhibits on Indian and military history; open Wed.-Sun. 10-5:45; closed Thnks, Dec. 25-Jan. 1; donation.

Money Museum (mezzanine of National Bank of Detroit, Woodward & Fort Sts.) exhibits coins, paper currency, barter objects from prehistoric times to the present; open Mon.-Fri. 8:30-5; closed bank hols; free.

International Afro-American Museum (1553 W Grand Blvd.) traces the history of blacks in the New World; open Mon.-Fri. 9-5; closed hols; sm adm.

Wayne State University (Cass Ave. & 2nd Blvd.): McGregor Memorial Conference Center, De Roy Auditorium, and other buildings were designed by Minoru Yamasaki.

Mariners' Church (170 E Jefferson Ave.), in Gothic Revival style, built 1849 to serve sailors on the Great Lakes, has nautical elements in the interior; open Mon.-Sat. 10-4; tours available; free.

ESCANABA: Delta County Historical Museum (in Ludington Park on SR 35), with railroad, lumber, and other local exhibits, is open mid-May-Aug., daily 1-9; donation.

FLINT: Flint Institute of Arts (DeWaters Art Center, 1120 E Kearsley St.): fine decorative arts of the Italian Renaissance; Oriental carvings; 19th-20th-C French and American painting; French paperweights, European glassware, other collections; open Tues.-Sat. 10-5, Sun. 1-5; closed hols; free. **Sloan Museum** (1221 E Kearsley St.) displays locally made antique carriages and autos; historic exhibits; open Tues.-Fri. 10-5, Sat. & Sun. noon-5; closed hols; sm adm. **Robert T. Longway Planetarium** (1310 E Kearsley St.) is open for shows Sat., Sun., and some hols, noon-5; sm adm.

FRANKENMUTH: Settled in 1845 by Lutheran missionaries from Germany, this town prides itself on its Old World atmosphere. The **Chamber of Commerce** and **Historical Museum** are on Main St., next to the Bavarian Inn.

GAYLORD: Call of the Wild Museum (850 S Wisconsin Ave.): 150 lifelike North American wild animals and game birds in natural surroundings; sound effects; open May-Sept., daily 8-9; rest of yr, daily 9:30-6; closed Dec. 25; adm.

GRAND RAPIDS: Grand Rapids Art Museum (230 E Fulton St.), in the beautiful Greek Revival Pike House, has a superb collection of German Expressionism; also Renaissance, 18th-19th-C French, and contemporary American painting; open Mon.-Sat. 9-5, Sun. 2-5; closed hols & Mon. in July-Aug.; free.

Grand Rapids Public Museum (54 Jefferson Ave. SE) features late-19th-C Gaslight Village with re-created shops, Indian artifacts; planetarium (sm adm); Grand Rapids furniture; animal habitat groups; miniature houses; open Mon.-Fri. 10-5; Sat., Sun., hols 2-5; closed Dec. 25; free.

Heritage Hill (bounded by Michigan & Pleasant Sts. & Union & Lafayette Aves.) has many Victorian mansions and 2 early Frank Lloyd Wright homes; **Voigt House** (115 College Ave. SE) and **Friant House** (601 Cherry St.) are sumptuous Queen Anne style homes; **Thompson House** (32 Union Ave. SE) is early Gothic Revival with gingerbread trim; **Morris Manor** (434 Cherry St. SE) is Italian villa style; historic house tours are offered periodically.

HANCOCK-HOUGHTON: These sister cities are the gateway to the Keweenaw Peninsula, site of the great copper rush. In 1841, state surveyor Douglass Houghton stumbled on the thousand-odd prehistoric Indian mines dotting the Copper Range; within 2 years miners—especially Finnish (who founded Suomi College in Hancock in 1896) and Cornish—were pouring in from Europe. But most of the deposits gave out quickly, and today the boom towns—Gay, Phoenix, Delaware, Hebard, Lac La Belle, Mandan, Wyoming, Copper Harbor—are either ghost towns or quiet resorts. **A. E. Seaman Mineralogical Collection** (Electrical Engineering Bldg., Michigan Technological Univ. on US 41 in Houghton) has a superb collection of minerals; inquire for hrs; free.

Arcadian Copper Mine (1 m E of Hancock on SR 26) offers underground tours June-Sept., daily 8-6; adm. **Quincy Mine Steam Hoist** (1 m N of Hancock on US 41) is open June-Labor Day 9-5; adm. **Houghton County Historical Museum** (on SR 26, 11 m NE of Hancock at Lake Linden) gives a good picture of the life and hardships of miners; open daily in summer; sm adm.

Calumet (11 m N of Hancock off US 41), especially along 5th and 6th Streets, typifies efforts made to give raw mining communities an aura of stability and prosperity; **Calumet Theater** (340 6th St.), built 1900, still gives performances in summer; the 1898 **Calumet Fire Station** (across the street) is typical of the Romanesque style adopted for public buildings. Of the fabulous **Cliff Mine** (Cliff Dr., 10 m N of Calumet), the first great copper mine (1846-1870s), only foundations and rock piles remain. The best ghost town is **Central** (4 m N of Phoenix on US 41), where the mine operated 1854-98; the many original buildings include a church built 1869 by Cornish miners. **Eagle River** (2 m NW of Phoenix on SR 26), with many old buildings from its ore-shipping days, has a monument to Douglass Houghton, who drowned during offshore copper explorations in 1844.

Fort Wilkins State Park (1 m E of Copper Harbor on US 41) contains the restored stockade and buildings of a post established in 1844; displays on mining and natural history; interpretive programs; open May-Oct.; sm adm.

HARBOR SPRINGS: Chief Andrew J. Blackbird Museum (349 E Main St.), devoted to Ottawa Indians, is open July-Labor Day, daily 10-noon, 1-5; free.

HOLLAND: Netherlands Museum (8 E 12th St.) features rooms furnished in the manner of the Dutch settlers who arrived here in 1847, seeking religious freedom; local historical displays; open Mon.-Sat. 9-5; also Sun. May-mid-Sept., 11:30-5; closed Jan. 1, Thnks, Dec. 25; sm adm. **Windmill Island** (entry via Lincoln Ave. & 8th St.), a municipal park with canals, drawbridge, and Little Netherlands miniature village, features a 200-year-old working windmill from Holland; open May-Oct., Mon.-Sat. 9-6, Sun. 11:30-6; adm.

Baker Furniture Museum (E 6th St. & Columbia Ave.) traces the history of furniture design in the Western world; some examples of pre-Christian and Far Eastern items; cabinet-making displays; Georgian room imported from England; open May-Sept., Mon.-Sat. 10-5, Sun. 1-5; sm adm. (The Baker Furniture Co. has a smaller but similar museum at the lower level of the Exhibitors Bldg. in Grand Rapids.)

Poll Museum (5 m N on US 31), with fine antique and classic cars and other vehicles, is open May-Sept., Mon.-Sat. 8-5 (longer hrs in summer); sm adm.

S.S. Keewatin, Saugatuck Marine Museum (8 m S via I-196 to Foot of Hamilton Ave. in Douglas), a Great Lakes steamboat, is devoted to Great Lakes shipping; open May-Sept. daily 10-4:30; adm.

HURON NATIONAL FOREST (stretches W from Lake Huron at Au Sable River): **Lumberman's Monument Historic Site** interprets the history of log transport along the river 1870-90 to sawmills on the shore of Lake Huron; auto tour through forest plantations starts E of SR 65 on the S shore of the river; ranger information stations at Mio, E Tawas, and Harrisville.

IRON MOUNTAIN: Iron Mountain Iron Mine (9 m E on US 2) offers guided underground tours by rail; equipment demonstrations; museum; open late May-Oct. 15, daily 8-8; adm. Remains of the great **Chapin Mine,** which opened in 1879 at the start of the wild boom era, include Chapin Pit (where the mine caved in) and Miners' Hall (a boardinghouse for bachelor Cornish miners); open-pit mining of low-grade ore is carried on today.

House of Yesteryear Museum (3 m SE on US 2) displays vehicles and historical items May 15-Oct. 15, Mon.-Sat. 8-8; adm.

IRON RIVER: Iron County Museum (2 m S in Caspian) has dioramas and exhibits of mining and lumber industries; Indian and Pioneer relics; open June 15-Labor Day, Mon.-Sat. 9-5, Sun. 1-5; adm.

ISHPEMING: National Ski Hall of Fame & Ski Museum (Mather Ave. & Poplar St.) has exhibits tracing the history of skiing; open mid-June-Labor Day, daily 10-4; rest of yr, Wed.-Sun. 1-4; closed some hols; donation.

JACKSON: Ella Sharp Museum (3225 4th St.): 1855 farmhouse with period furnishings, arts and crafts; planetarium shows Sun. afternoons; open Tues.-Fri. 10-4 & weekends 12:30-4 (longer hrs in summer); in Jan., open Sun. only 12:30-4; closed hols; sm adm. **Mann House** (205 Hanover St., 14 m SW via SR 60 in Concord), a Victorian clapboard typical of small-town prosperity; original furnishings; shop and farm equipment; open Tues.-Sat. 10-5, Sun. 1-5; closed hols; free. **Waterloo Farm Museum** (15 M E via I-94, then N to 9998 Waterloo-Munith Rd.), a memorial to early farmers, is a pioneer homestead with authentic furnishings, outbuildings, windmill; open June-Sept., Tues.-Sun. 1-4, also during Pioneer Festival in Oct.; sm adm.

KALAMAZOO: Kalamazoo Public Museum (315 S Rose St.) features Egyptian tomb with mummy and tomb furnishings; pioneer displays; weekly planetarium shows; open Mon.-Sat. 9-5:30; closed hols; free. **Kalamazoo Institute of Arts** (314 S Park St.) specializes in 20th-C American art; sculpture and graphics; open early July-mid-Aug., Tues.-Sat. 10-4; after Labor Day-early July, Tues.-Fri. 11-4:30, Sat. 9-4, Sun. 1:30-4:30; closed hols & mid-Aug.-Labor Day; free.

Chamber of Commerce (500 W Crosstown Pkwy.) provides information on the city and surrounding area. In **Three Rivers** (20 m S), the **First Ward District** between Main and Hoffman Sts. and Portage Ave. has many old Victorian homes. In **Constantine** (30 m S), **John S. Barry House** (280 N Washington St.), built 1835-6, is operated as a museum by the St. Joseph County Historical Society, and there are many Greek Revival homes in the **South Washington St. District**. **Gilmore Car Museum** (15 m NE on SR 43 at Hickory Corners Rd.) displays more than 50 restored antique and classic cars; open mid-June-mid-Sept., Sun. 1-5; adm.

LAKE CITY: Guest's Country Store Museum (Houghton & John Sts.), in buildings once used for schools, is a display of late 19th-C shops; open May-mid-Oct., daily 10-5; sm adm.

LANSING: State Capitol (Capitol & Michigan Aves.), built 1878, displays historic items; open Mon.-Fri. 8:30-4:30, Sat. & Sun. 11-5; closed hols; free. **Michigan Historical Museum** (505 N Washington Ave.) in a building modeled on Mt. Vernon, is open Mon.-Fri. 9-4:30; Sat., Sun., hols noon-4; closed Jan. 1, Dec. 31; free.

Michigan State University (E Lansing): **Kresge Art Center Gallery** offers a small but wide-ranging collection; strong on pre-Columbian works; also African and 20th-C American art; open Mon.-Fri. 9-5, Sat. & Sun. 1-4; free. **Michigan State Museum**, with historic exhibits, is open Mon.-Fri. 9-5, Sat. & Sun. 1-5; closed hols; free. Also on campus are Abrams Planetarium (shows Fri.-Sun.) and Beaumont Tower (carillon concerts).

LUDINGTON: Mason County Historical Museum (305 E Filer St.) is open June-Aug., Mon.-Sat. 10-4:30; Apr.-May, Wed. & Fri. 1:30-4:30; closed hols; free.

MACKINAC ISLAND: A national historic landmark, this island has been an Indian shrine, a strategic stronghold for control of the Northwest, and a resort; automobiles are prohibited (carriages, bicycles, and horses are available), and access is via boat from Mackinaw City or St. Ignace. **Mackinac Island State Park Visitor Center** (Huron St.) provides information; open mid-June-Labor Day, daily 9-5.

Fort Mackinac, on a bluff above the harbor, begun by the British in 1780, was the most important military post on the Great Lakes; blockhouses, dungeon, and other original buildings contain historic exhibits and period settings; costumed guides; cannon and musket demonstrations; open late May-Labor Day, daily 9:30-6; after Labor Day-Sept. daily 10-4. Adm includes: **Indian Dormitory** (at base of fort), constructed 1838, with Indian artifacts and murals depicting scenes from Longfellow's "Hiawatha"; and **Benjamin Blacksmith Shop** (Market St.), a working replica of a late-19th-C forge; both open late May-Labor Day, daily 11-5.

American Fur Co. Trading Post (Mackinac Is. village) was established by John Jacob Astor in 1809; still standing are the warehouse and agent's house; **Stuart House Museum** contains records, artifacts, period furniture;

open June-Sept., Tues.-Sat. 10:30-4:30, Sun. & Mon. 1-4; sm adm. Nearby are a Mission Church, Ft. Holmes, and Biddle House (home of a fur trader; furnishings from 1820s), also open to the public.

Beaumont Memorial is dedicated to Dr. William Beaumont, Fort Mackinac's surgeon, who cared for a young voyageur who had been wounded in the stomach; although the voyageur survived, an opening to his stomach never healed, and through this Dr. Beaumont made important studies of the human digestive system; open mid-June-Labor Day, daily 11-5; free.

MACKINAW CITY: Fort Michilimackinac (Michilimackinac State Park, S end of Mackinac Bridge) was built about 1714 to protect a French trading post and was occupied by the British 1761-81; authentically reconstructed buildings contain historic displays and relics, period furnishings, dioramas, and murals; guided tours; musket and cannon demonstrations in summer; open Mid-June-Labor Day, daily 9-8; mid-May-mid-June & after Labor Day-mid-Oct., daily 9-5; adm includes Mackinac Maritime Museum (1892 lighthouse, replica of 1775 sloop, exhibits on Great Lakes shipping).

MANISTEE: Manistee County Historical Museum (425 River St. in Russell Memorial Bldg.) offers furnished 1870 drugstore and general store, pioneer and Civil War relics, photographs, antique dolls, costumes; open Mon.-Sat. 10-5; closed hols; donation. The Museum maintains **Old Water Works Bldg.** (W 1st St.), with lumbering exhibits, Victorian parlor, kitchen, barbershop; open July-Labor Day, Mon.-Sat. 10-5, Sun. 1:30-5; donation. The historic **Ramsdell Opera House** (1st & Maple Sts.), built by a lumber magnate at the turn of the century, has been preserved; performances in summer.

MANISTIQUE: Fayette State Park (15 m W via US 2, then 17 m S along the bay) preserves the ghost town of Fayette, founded in 1867 around iron smelting operations; self-guiding tour to homes, opera house (with museum), other buildings, charcoal kilns; open daily mid-May-Oct; sm adm. At **Burnt Bluff** (5 m S of Fayette State Park) are caves once used by Indians; artifacts displayed.

MARQUETTE: Marquette County Historical Society Museum (213 N Front St.) is open Mon.-Fri. 9-noon, 1-4:30; closed hols; sm adm. **John Burt House** (220 Craig St.), honoring a pioneer surveyor, is a stone cottage with mid-19th-C furnishings; open July-Aug., daily 9-5; sm adm.

MARSHALL: Honolulu House (Kalamazoo & Michigan Aves.), built 1860, is a replica of the Hawaiian home of a former U.S. Consul to the

Sandwich Islands; ornate ceilings; period furnishings; hq of Marshall Historical Society, open mid-May-Oct., Tues.-Fri. 2-5, Sat. & Sun. 2-6; closed hols; sm adm. The Society also maintains the 1839 Greek Revival **Governor's Mansion** (built in an effort to have Marshall declared the capital) and the charming 1860 Gothic Revival **Capitol Hill School;** both open mid-May-Oct., Sun. 2-5; sm adm. The Society offers a brochure on Marshall's many 19th-C buildings and sponsors house tours in fall.

MENOMINEE: Mystery Ship Seaport (13th St. in River Park, 2 blocks E of Interstate Bridge) is the 1846 Great Lakes schooner Alvin Clark, which sank in 1864 and was raised in 1969; artifacts on display; open May-Oct. daily 9-6 (longer hrs in summer); adm.

MIDLAND: Midland Center for the Arts (1801 W St. Andrews) offers historic and scientific exhibitions (many with films and operating devices) and art galleries; open Mon.-Fri. 9-5, Sat. & Sun. 1-5; closed hols; free.

MONROE: Monroe County Historical Museum (126 S Monroe St.): pioneer and Indian displays, exhibits on Gen. George Custer, trading post, and country store, is open Tues.-Sun. 1-5; closed Dec. 25; free.

MOUNT CLEMENS: Trinity Museum (47460 Sugar Bush Rd., 6 m N), turn-of-the-century farm and country store, is open Mon., Tues., Thurs 2-8, Fri. 2-5:30, Sat. noon-4, Sun. noon-5; closed hols; donation.

MOUNT PLEASANT: Central Michigan University: Clarke Historical Library (Park Library, 4th floor), with Northwest Territory documents and rare books, is open Mon.-Fri. 8-noon, 1-5; closed hols; free. **Center for Cultural & Natural History** (Ronan Hall, 3rd floor), with exhibits on history and science, is open academic yr, Mon.-Fri. 8-5, Sat. & Sun. 1-5; closed hols; free.

MUSKEGON: Muskegon County Museum (30 W Muskegon Ave.) contains lumbering, fur trading, Indian, and natural history displays; open Wed.-Sat. 1-5; closed hols; sm adm. **Hackley Art Gallery** (296 W Webster Ave.), in an 1889 Greek Revival frame home, owns a few fine works from Persia, Japan, and Europe, but John Steuart Curry's *Tornado Over Kansas* and other American works are a highlight; open Mon.-Sat. 9-5, Sun. 2-5; closed weekends in July-Aug. & hols; free.

PAW PAW: Free wine tours are offered by **Frontenac Wine Co.** (3418 W Michigan Ave.), **St. Julian Wine Co.** (716 S Kalamazoo St.), and **Bronte Winery & Vineyards** (14 m SW in Keeler) daily 9-4; closed hols. Recheck hrs locally and inquire for other winery tours.

PONTIAC: Governor Moses Wisner House (405 Oakland Ave.) is an 1845 Greek Revival home with original furnishings, outbuildings; open July-Aug., Tues.-Sat. 1-4; closed hols; sm adm.

PORT AUSTIN: Pioneer Huron City (8 m E on US 25) preserves lumbering era buildings (1850-90) including log cabin, chapel, store, inn, Coast Guard station; period furnishings; tours by costumed guides; open July-Labor Day weekend, Mon.-Sat. 10:30-5, Sun. noon-5; adm.

PORT HURON: Museum of Arts & History (1115 6th St.) traces local history through Indian artifacts, art and historical displays, marine exhibits; open Wed.-Sun. 1-4:30; closed hols; donation.

SAGINAW: Saginaw Art Museum (1126 N Michigan Ave.) offers Indian pottery, American works, and a few European paintings by old masters; open Tues.-Sat. 10-5, Sun. 1-5; closed hols & Aug.-mid-Sept.; free. **Saginaw Historical Museum** (1105 S Jefferson Ave.) displays Indian and pioneer items, lumbering and other historical exhibits, antique toys, furniture, musical instruments; open Tues., Thurs., Sun. 1:30-4:30; closed hols & Aug.; sm adm. **Federal Building** (Federal & Jefferson Sts.), opened in 1898 as a post office, is one of the most beautiful and ornate in the nation; design, taken from the de Tocqueville family chateau, incorporates elaborate materials, allegorical figures, elegant displays, and peepholes for postal inspectors; open Mon.-Fri. 9-5; closed hols; free.

SAULT STE. MARIE: Soo Locks are the big attraction here; rapids on the St. Mary's River, connecting Lakes Superior and Huron, necessitated the building of these locks, which raise or lower ships the 22 feet between the lakes. Parks paralleling the locks contain an Information Bldg., scale models, other exhibits, and observation towers. Boat tours of the locks leave daily in summer from **Dock 1** (1157 E Portage Ave.), where there are dioramas on the history of the locks, **Dock 2** (500 E Portage Ave.), and **Government Dock** (Canadian side). Train tours of the city are available at 337 W Portage Ave. **Tower of History** (326 E Portage Ave.) has an observation tower; historic exhibit in lobby; open July-Aug. daily 9 am-11 pm; May-June & Sept.-Oct. 9-5; adm. **Model City** (E Portage Ave.) is a 100-ft replica of the Soo and river during the last century. **S.S. Valley Camp Marine Museum** (1113 Kimball St., 5 blocks E of docks) is a 1917 Great Lakes freighter, still operational, with marine and historical exhibits; Great Lakes Marine Hall of Fame; open July-Aug. daily 9 am-8 pm; late May-June & Sept.-early Oct. 10-6; adm.

SOUTH HAVEN: Liberty Hyde Bailey Memorial Museum (903 S Bailey Ave.), 19th-C home of the horticulturist, has Indian artifacts, family furnishings; open May-Oct., Tues., Fri. 2-4:30; free.

TRAVERSE CITY: Con Foster Museum (Clinch Park, Grandview Pkwy.) has thousands of Indian and pioneer relics; open late May-Sept., daily 10-7; sm adm. **Benzie Area Historical Museum** (32 m S via US 31 to Benzonia) houses exhibits on shipping, lumbering, domestic and farm life; open July-Aug., Tues.-Sun. 1:30-5; June & Sept.-Oct., Sat. & Sun. 1:30-5; free.

MINNESOTA

ALBERT LEA: Freeborn County Historical Museum & Village (Fairgrounds, N Bridge St.) consists of restored homes, shops, school, general store, other buildings; museum of household and farm tools, toys, musical instruments; open June-Aug., Tues.-Thurs. & Sun. 2-5; Apr.-May & Sept.-Nov., Wed. & Sun. 2-5; free.

ALEXANDRIA: Runestone Museum (206 Broadway) displays a boulder dated 1362, with runic writing describing a Viking visit to North America; the stone's authenticity has been questioned; Viking and Indian relics; open June-Sept., Mon.-Sat. 9-9, Sun. 11-9; Oct.-May, Mon.-Fri. 9-5; closed Jan. 1, Thnks, Dec. 25; adm.

AUSTIN: Mower County Historical Society (12th St. & 4th Ave. SW, County Fairgrounds): Indian and pioneer artifacts in restored courthouse, homes, other buildings; antique vehicles; open May-Oct. daily 10-5; free.

BEMIDJI: Information Center (3rd St. & Bemidji Ave.), with Paul Bunyan artifacts (statues of Paul Bunyan and Blue Ox are in the adjacent amusement area) is free; adj **Historical & Wildlife Museum,** with pioneer and Indian artifacts, mounted animals, has sm adm; both open mid-May-mid-Sept., daily 8:30-8:30.

BRAINERD: Crow Wing County Historical Museum (4th St. & Laurel St., in basement of courthouse), with Indian and pioneer exhibits, is open Tues.-Fri. 1-5 in summer, Tues. & Thurs. 1-5 in winter; closed hols; free.

Lumbertown, USA (4 m N on SR 371, then 8 m W on Pine Beach Rd.) is a re-creation of an old lumber town with more than 30 buildings; replicas of a Northern Pacific train and a riverboat; open 10:30-6:30 in summer, 10:30-5 in spring and fall; adm.

DULUTH: Cultural Center (506 W Michigan St.) includes: **St. Louis County Historical Society Museum,** with furnishings, household items, jewelry, clothing, other displays; Eastman Johnson's paintings and drawings of Chippewa; archives; open Mon.-Fri. 10-5 plus weekend afternoons in summer; closed hols; free. **A. M. Chisholm Museum,** with natural history, Indian, and miscellaneous displays; open Mon.-Fri. 9-5, Sat. 9-noon; closed hols; free.

University of Minnesota (College St. & Oakland Ave.) offers free planetarium shows weekly during the academic year and **Tweed Museum of Art** with good 16th-20th-C paintings (open Mon.-Fri. 8-4:30, Sat. & Sun. 2-5; closed hols; free).

Bible House (715 W Superior St.) displays Bibles, ancient scrolls; pottery and oil lamps used at the time of Christ; open Apr.-Oct., Mon.-Fri. 8:30-4:30; closed hols; free.

Skyline Parkway, a 16-m scenic drive with best views from **Enger Tower** (18th Ave.), dedicated by the Crown Prince of Norway in 1939. Off the parkway, in **Leif Erikson Park** (11th Ave. & London Rd.) is a statue of the explorer and a replica of the boat he sailed to America in 997; open May-Sept. in daylight; free.

Lake Superior Marine Museum (Canal Park, Minnesota Point), with exhibits on the maritime history of the lake, is open May-Oct. daily 10 am-9 pm; Nov.-Apr., Mon.-Sat. 8-4:30; free.

ELK RIVER: Oliver H. Kelley Farmstead (2 m SE on US 10, 52), homesteaded by the founder of the National Grange; furnishings typical of the late 1800s; open May-Sept., Tues.-Sun. 10-5; also weekends in Oct.; adm.

ELY: Voyageur Visitor Center (¼ m E on SR 169) offers exhibits and narration on the life of voyageurs (early French-Canadian fur traders), Chippewas, lumberjacks, and miners; handcrafted canoe; dioramas; geologic and natural history displays; canoe demonstrations; open mid-May-Labor Day daily 6 am-10 pm; closed hols; free.

EVELETH: U.S. Hockey Hall of Fame (US 53), with exhibits on players and the game, films, is open Mon.-Sat. 9-5, Sun. noon-5; closed Jan. 1, Dec. 25; adm.

FERGUS FALLS: Otter Tail County Museum (1110 Lincoln Ave. W), with a trapper's cabin and other local historical exhibits, is open Mon.-Fri. 11-5, Sat. & Sun. 1-4; closed hols; donation.

GLENWOOD: Pope County Historical Museum (SR 104), with Indian arts and crafts, plus historic displays, is open Mon.-Fri. 9-5; Sat. & Sun. 1-5 from May-Oct.; closed Jan. 1, Dec. 25; sm adm.

GRAND PORTAGE NATIONAL MONUMENT (38 m NE of Grand Marais on US 61) preserves the 18th-19th-C center for fur traders of the North West Co., who paddled and portaged trade goods and furs over the 3000-m waterway from Montreal to Ft. Chipewyan on Lake Athabaska. Grand Portage (a 9-m trail) was not the largest nor the most difficult portage, but here voyageurs traded their big Great Lake canoes for smaller ones appropriate to the inland river and lake route. The stockade, Great Hall, and other buildings have been reconstructed; also here, on the site of an 1838 bark-and-deerskin chapel, is the state's first Catholic mission, built in 1865. Grounds open daily; building tours given Memorial Day-mid-Sept., daily 8:30-5; free.

HIBBING: Minnesota Museum of Mining (on W Lake St. in Chisholm, 6 m NE via US 169, SR 73), located in an area where more than 100 mines once operated, provides exhibits, models of equipment; underground mine tour; open Memorial Day-Labor Day, daily 8-5; adm.

INTERNATIONAL FALLS: Municipal Park (NW edge of town) offers the **Koochiching County Historical Museum** (open Memorial Day-Labor Day, Mon.-Sat. 10-7, Sun. & hols 2-5; sm adm). **Lloyd's Wildlife Museum** (416 3rd St.), with mounted animals and birds in habitat settings, is open June-Labor Day, Mon.-Sat. 9-6, Sun. noon-6; sm adm.

JACKSON: Fort Belmont (jct US 16, 71) museum consists of a sod house, log chapel, fort, and other buildings; open Memorial Day-Labor Day, daily 9-6; adm.

LE SUEUR: W. W. Mayo House (118 N Main St.), where Dr. Mayo, founder of the Mayo Clinic, practiced medicine 1859-64, has been restored with his office; open Memorial Day-Labor Day, Sat. & Sun. 1-4:30; sm adm.

LITTLE FALLS: Charles A. Lindbergh State Memorial Park (on W bank of Mississippi River, S of town): childhood home of the aviator; audio-visual program, exhibits; open May-Oct., Mon.-Sat. 10-5, Sun. 1-5; free.

MANKATO: Blue Earth County Historical Museum (606 S Broad St.), in a large 1871 home, includes pioneer displays, early shops, a restored 1873 log cabin; open Tues.-Sun. 1-5; free.

MINNEAPOLIS: Convention & Tourism Commission (15 S 5th St.) provides information; see also St. Paul. **IDS Center** (80 S 8th St.) provides a view from the 51st-floor observation deck; open daily 9-midnight; closed Easter, Thnks, Dec. 25; adm.

Minneapolis Institute of Arts (201 E 24th St.) has particularly good collections of American painting, European masterpieces, Greek and Roman sculpture, 15th-20th-C drawings and prints, and Chinese bronzes; silver; period rooms; American and European decorative arts; films and other programs; open daily°but hrs vary, check locally; closed hols; donation. **Walker Art Center** (Vineland Pl.) features contemporary painting and sculpture, European and American; porcelains and jades; prints; changing exhibits; open Tues., Thurs., 10 am-9 pm; Wed., Fri., Sat. 10-5; Sun. noon-6; closed hols; free.

Hennepin County Historical Society Museum (2303 3rd Ave. S) features a miniature re-creation of a small-town Main Street of the early 1900s; 1500 miniature items from around the world; large collection of pioneer relics; open Tues.-Fri. 9-4:30, Sun. 2-4:30; also Sept.-May, Sat. 2-4:30; closed hols; free.

American Swedish Institute (2600 Park Ave. S) is in a 33-room castle-like building with tile ovens from Europe; exterior sculpture and interior plaster ceilings by Herman Schlink; elaborate wood carvings by Ulrich Steiner; interesting displays on the Swedish heritage; open Tues.-Sat. 2-5, Sun. 1-5; closed hols; sm adm.

Minnesota Transportation Museum (in S Minneapolis at Queen Ave. & W 42nd St.) displays antique trains, trolleys, other vehicles; open mid-May-Labor Day, Wed., Fri. eve; weekend afternoons; also weekends in fall; sm adm.

Science Museum & Planetarium (300 Nicollet Mall) is open Mon.-Fri. 9-5; Sat. 2-5 in summer, 9-5 in winter; Sun. 2-5; closed hols; free.

University of Minnesota, Bell Museum of Natural History (17th Ave. SE & University Ave.), featuring local wildlife in habitat settings, is open Mon.-Sat. 9-5, Sun. 2-5; free. **Art Gallery** (Northrop Memorial Auditorium), with good 20th-C American works, is open Mon.-Fri. 11-4, Sun. 2-5; free.

St. John the Evangelist Church (6½ m W at 6 Interlachen Rd., Inter-lachen Park, Hopkins), completed in 1969, is an exceptional design that has won architectural awards; open daily.

Grain Exchange (400 4th St. S) visitor balcony is open daily 9:15-1:15 (tours are given by appointment Mon.-Fri.); closed hols; free.

Minnehaha Park (Minnehaha Pkwy. & Hiawatha Ave. S), along the

Mississippi River, provides tape tours; Minnehaha Falls were made famous by Longfellow's "The Song of Hiawatha"; statue of Minnehaha and Hiawatha above the falls; restored 1870's depot; first frame house W of the Mississippi. Open daily; free.

Minnesota Valley Restoration Project (at Shakopee, 23 m SW, between US 169 and the Minnesota River) depicts 19th-C life with a French trading post, German immigrant farm, other buildings; open May-Oct., Wed.-Sun. 10 am-8 pm; adm.

MONTEVIDEO: Pioneer Village (jct SR 7, US 59), a reconstructed town of the late 1800s, and **Swensson House** (11 m SE via SR 7, County 6), of hand-cut stone and with hand-carved woodwork, completed in 1901 by a Swedish farmer, are open in summer; inquire locally for hrs; sm adm.

MOORHEAD: Rourke Art Gallery & Museum (523 S 4th St.), in a pioneer home, exhibits American Indian, African, and regional art; open Wed.-Sun. noon-5; closed Dec. 25; free. **Red River Art Center** (521 Main Ave.) also displays regional art.

NEW ULM: Defender's Monument (Center St.) honors the 100-odd citizens (German immigrants who had settled here in 1854) who were killed or wounded on Aug. 23, 1862, after provoking a Sioux attack that almost destroyed the town. **Fort Ridgely State Park** (14 m W o US 14, SR 68, then 9 m N on SR 4) preserves the partially restored fort where the Sioux were defeated; interpretive museum; open May-mid-Sept. daily 10-5; sm adm. (See also Mankato.) **Hermann's Monument** (Hermann Heights Park), a 32-ft-high bronze statute of Hermann the Cheruscan (a warrior who united German tribes in AD 9 and drove the Romans from their lands), was erected 1897 as a symbol of unity and freedom; observation platform; open daily 9-4; sm adm. **Brown County Historical Museum** (27 N Broadway in Public Library) is open Mon.-Fri. 1-5, 7-8; closed hols & Dec. 15-Jan. 2; free.

ONAMIA: Mille Lacs Indian Museum (10 m NW on US 169) displays artifacts of prehistoric peoples but features the social and cultural history of the Chippewa and Sioux; open May-Labor Day, daily 10-5; adm. Indian mounds dot the countryside in and around the Mille Lacs Indian Reservation, and a historic marker has been erected at the site of the 1745 battle of Kathio. **Village Hall** (in Milaca, 22 m S via US 169), constructed during the Depression by WPA workers, contains murals of logging days.

OWATONNA: Village of Yesteryear (Steele County Fairgrounds), with restored and furnished log cabins and other buildings, is open May-mid-

Sept., Wed., Sat., Sun. 1-5; donation. **Northwestern National Bank** (Cedar St. & Broadway), completed in 1908, was designed by Louis Sullivan and features rich ornamentation; open banking hrs.

PINE CITY: Connor's Fur Post (1½ m W on County 7): reconstructed, furnished 1804 trading post; open May-Labor Day, daily 10-5; adm.

PIPESTONE NATIONAL MONUMENT (1 m N of Pipestone; follow markers from town): For at least 3 centuries, Indians have considered this sacred ground; ¾-m Circle Trail runs past the quarries so that you can watch miners at work. The **Visitor Center** (with exhibits, dioramas of Indian life, reproductions of Catlin paintings) and **Upper Midwest Indian Culture Center** (with craft displays) are open daily 8-5 (8 am-9 pm in summer); closed Dec. 25. Films on the history and legends of the area are often shown, and Indians demonstrate various crafts (many are on sale). Free.

REDWOOD FALLS: Lower Sioux Agency (9 m SE via SR 67, County 2) Interpretive Center traces the history of the Dakota Indians from the mid-19th-C attempt to turn them into farmers (which they labeled a "harvest of sorrow") to the present; open May-Oct., Mon.-Sat. 10-5, Sun. 1-5; closed hols & Nov.-Apr.; free. **Indian Petroglyphs** (S via US 71 at Jeffers), with interpretive display; open May-Oct., Mon.-Sat. 10-6, Sun. 1-6; free.

ROCHESTER: Mayo Institutions (200 1st St., SW), a world-famous medical complex founded by Dr. William Mayo and his sons William and Charles, provide tours Mon.-Fri. 10, 2; closed hols; free. **Mayo Medical Museum** (Damon Bldg., entrance at 1st St. & 3rd Ave. SW) with exhibits on human disease and treatment, is open Mon.-Fri. 9-9, Sat. 9-5, Sun. 1-5; closed hols; free.

    Olmsted County Historical Center & Museum (3103 Salem Rd. SW), with changing exhibits on local history, is open Mon.-Fri. 9-5, Sat. & Sun. noon-4; closed hols; free. By reservation, the center provides guided tours of **Mayowood,** built in 1911 by Dr. Charles H. Mayo; antiques collected by the family; mementos of Napoleon; tours at 1 & 3 pm, Tues.-Sun. in July-Aug., and less frequently in spring and fall; closed Dec.-Mar.; adm.

    The town of **Mantorville** (W via US 14 to Kasson, then N on SR 57) has been restored to its 1880s appearance; self-guiding tour maps are available.

ST. CLOUD: Stearns County Historical Society Museum (123 4th Ave. S) is open Tues., Thurs. 1-5; also Fri. 1-4 in summer, Sat. 9-noon in winter; closed hols; free. **St. John's University** (10 m W on US 52 in Collegeville), founded in 1856, has outstanding modern abbey, church, library, and other buildings designed by Marcel Breuer.

ST. PAUL: Convention & Visitors Bureau (300 Osborn Bldg.,) provides maps and information; see also Minneapolis.

State Capitol (University & Park Aves.), a Cass Gilbert design completed in 1905, has one of the largest self-supporting marble domes in the world; elaborate interior contains many sculptures, murals, paintings; open Mon.-Fri. 8-5, Sat. 9-4, Sun. 1-4; closed hols; tours available; free.

Minnesota Historical Society (690 Cedar St.), with exhibits on state history, is open Mon.-Fri. 8:30-5, Sat. 10-4, Sun. 2-5; closed hols; free. The Society maintains the following, open Tues.-Fri. 10-4, Sat. & Sun. 1-4:30; adm. **Alexander Ramsey House** (265 S Exchange St.), 1872 French Renaissance mansion of the first governor of the Minnesota Territory; fine interior carving; Victorian furnishings; carriage house. **Burbank-Livingston-Griggs House** (432 Summit Ave.), built 1862, incorporates complete 17th-18th-C French and Italian villa rooms; a wealth of European furnishings and decorative arts. (The nearby mansion of railroad czar James J. Hill, at 240 Summit Ave., is not open to the public but is worth seeing from the outside.)

City Hall & Court House (14 W Kellogg Blvd.): 44-ft-tall white-onyx "God of Peace" by Carl Milles; murals in council chamber; interior finished in rare woods; open daily; free.

Minnesota Museum of Art (305 St. Peter St.) houses Oriental, African, and American Indian arts and crafts; also contemporary painting, sculpture, drawing, and crafts; open Tues.-Fri. 11:30-4:30; closed hols & Aug.; sm adm. **St. Paul Arts & Crafts Center** (30 E 10th St.), a complex with theaters and other facilities, contains a gallery maintained by the Minnesota Museum of Art and a Science Museum (open Mon.-Wed. 9-5; Thurs.-Sat. 9-9:30; Sun. 11-9:30; closed Jan. 1, Dec. 25; free).

Gibbs Farm Museum (2097 W Larpenteur Ave.) began as a 1-room cabin in 1854 and was expanded as farmer Hemen Gibbs prospered; original furnishings; demonstrations of pioneer skills; barn with old vehicles and tools; restored 1878 schoolhouse; open May-Dec., Tues.-Fri. 10-5, Sun. 1-4; closed Jan.-Apr.; adm. **Sibley House Museum** (218 River St. in Mendota, near jct Sr 13, 55), built 1835 by state's first governor, has family furnishings; on grounds is 1836 home of fur trader Jean Baptiste Faribault; open May-Oct., Tues.-Sat. 10-5, Sun. & hols 1-6; also Mon. 10-5 in spring & fall; adm.

Fort Snelling State Park (6 m SW at jct SR 5, 55): The fort was a fur-trade center built 1820-25 at the confluence of the Mississippi and Minnesota Rivers to control British influence on the frontier; this self-contained community, with everything from gardens and hospital to school and fortifications, is restored to show frontier life in the 1820s; open mid-June-Labor Day, daily 10-6; spring & fall 9-5; closed Nov.-Apr.; adm.

W.H.C. Folsom House (Government Rd in Taylors Falls, 34 m NE via US 61, 8), built 1855 for a wealthy lumberman, with pegged and mortised timbers, has original furnishings; historic exhibit on St. Croix River valley; open Memorial Day-Labor Day, Sat. & Sun. 1-4:30; adm. Surrounding Angels Hill Historic District has many interesting 19th-C buildings.

ST. PETER: Nicollet County Historical Museum (400 S 3rd St., US 169) is open Mar.-Dec., Tues.-Sat. 1-4; closed hols; free. **E. St. Julien Cox House** (500 N Washington St.), an 1871 residence with period furnishings, is open June-Labor Day daily 1:30-4; inquire locally for occasional additional hrs; sm adm.

SAM BROWN MEMORIAL STATE PARK (Browns Valley) honors the frontier's Paul Revere; in 1866, Brown rode his horse an arduous 150 m to warn of an Indian attack (that turned out to be a false alarm); 1863 cabin with Sam Brown memorabilia; furnished schoolhouse; Indian hieroglyphics; open late May-mid-Sept., daily; sm adm.

SAUK CENTRE: Sinclair Lewis Interpretive Center (jct I-94, US 71) provides an audiovisual program on Lewis, who spent his boyhood in this town and called it Gopher Prairie on *Main Street:* manuscripts and papers on display; research library. **Sinclair Lewis Boyhood Home** (612 Sinclair Lewis Ave.), restored with family furnishings and Lewis memorabilia, looks much as it did in 1903 when Lewis left to go to Yale University. Both open Memorial Day-Labor Day, Mon.-Sat. 10-4, Sun. 1-5; check locally for spring and fall hrs; adm.

SPRING VALLEY: Pioneer Home Museum (Washington Ave. & Main St.), with period furnishings, schoolroom, and historic displays, and the 1878 **Methodist Church** (221 W Courtland St.) with 23 stained-glass windows, are open Memorial Day-Oct., Sun. 2-4; sm adm. **Forestville State Park** (about 11 m E via US 16) contains the abandoned townsite of the Civil War era; museum; open daily in summer; sm adm.

STILLWATER: Washington County Historical Museum (602 N Main St.): former home of a prison warden, contains pioneer artifacts and displays on the late-18th-C lumbering industry; open May-Oct., Tues., Thurs., Sat., Sun. 2-5; closed hols; sm adm.

TOWER: Tower Soudan State Park (2 m E on SR 169) offers a Visitor Center and tours of the state's first underground iron mine (1882-1962);

open June-Labor Day daily 9-4; inquire for less frequent tours in spring and fall; adm. **Duluth & Iron Range RR Locomotive & Coach** (W end of Main St.) at the tourist information center, houses displays of Indian artifacts and logging and mining industries; open Memorial Day-Labor Day, daily 1:30-5:30; sm adm.

TWO HARBORS: Lake County Historical & Railroad Museum (foot of 6th St.), in an old railroad depot, offers exhibits on railroading, mining, and lumbering; outside are 2 steam locomotives, including the ore-hauling Mallet, the most powerful ever built; open late May-early Sept., Mon.-Sat. 9-4, Sun. 1-4; free. The ore-shipping docks are visible from the lake-front park here.

UPPER SIOUX AGENCY STATE PARK (4 m SE of Granite Falls on SR 67) contains an interpretive center and exhibits; open May-Labor Day, 10-5; sm adm.

WINONA: Winona County Historical Society Museum (160 Johnson St.): general store, early shops, vehicles, lumbering displays, and Indian artifacts are among the exhibits; open Sun.-Fri. 12:30-4:30; adm. The Society also maintains: **Julius C. Wilkie Steamboat Museum** (Levee Park, foot of Main St.), an 1898 Mississippi steamboat, is a museum with steamboat models, papers of inventor Robert Fulton, and other displays; open May-Sept., Mon.-Sat. 9-5, Sun. & hols 10-6; adm. **Bunnell House** (7 m S via US 14, 61 to Homer), built in the 1850s for a fur trader, is unusually elaborate for a pioneer home; period furnishings; open Memorial Day-Labor Day, Mon.-Sat. 11-5, Sun. & hols noon-6; adm. **Arches Branch Museum** (on US 14, 11 m NW near Lewiston), a pioneer farm and 1862 school, displays antique farm equipment; open Mon.-Sat. 8-6, Sun. noon-6; closed Jan. 1, Easter, Dec. 25; sm adm.

MISSISSIPPI

BILOXI: Beauvoir (5 m W on US 90), a shrine to Jefferson Davis, overlooks the Gulf in an area that has been a popular resort since the 1840s; the estate remained his home for the last 12 years of his life; after his death in 1889 it became a home for Mississippi's Civil War veterans. The house, restored with family furnishings, looks as it did in his time, with interesting memorabilia (especially on his daughter); outbuildings include the library where he wrote; museums of Confederate artifacts; Confederate cemetery; open daily 8:30-5; closed Dec. 25; adm.

Spanish House (206 W Water St.), built at the beginning of Spanish rule (1780-1810), was a social, religious, and military center; open Tues.-Sat. 10:30-5; adm. **Jean Baptiste Carquotte House** (410 E Bay View Ave.), built 1790, is one of the oldest buildings on the Gulf; period furnishings; open Sept.-May; adm. **Old Biloxi Cemetery** (Carter & Father Ryan Aves.) contains the graves of early French settlers.

Biloxi Lighthouse (on US 90, foot of Porter Ave.), a landmark erected 1848; to prevent its use by the Union, a local citizen removed the lens during the Civil War; it was painted black after Lincoln's assassination and draped in mourning at Kennedy's; from here the 10-m, 50-min, narrated **Shrimp Tour Train** to historic sites runs several times daily in summer; reasonable charge.

Ship Island (reached by boats that leave daily in summer from Small Craft Harbor on Main St.), a center for French settlement and exploration in the late-17th-mid-18th-C, was also the British base for the 1814-15 campaign against New Orleans. **Fort Massachusetts,** begun by Confederates but completed and renamed by the Union, became a vital link in the blockade of the South during the Civil War; open daily in summer.

BRICES CROSS ROADS NATIONAL BATTLEFIELD SITE (on SR 370, 6 m W of US 45 in Baldwyn): On June 10, 1864, Confederate Gen. Nathan Bedford Forrest, with only 3500 men, defeated a Union force of more than 8000; small park with markers overlooks the battlefield; open daily; free.

CLARKSDALE: North Delta Museum (12 m NW in Friars Point on Friars Point-Clarksdale Rd.) displays Indian and pioneer artifacts from the Delta area; open Tues., Thurs., Sat., Sun. 2-6; sm adm.

COLUMBUS: Built as Possum Town, a stopping point on the Military Road, this prosperous cotton community became a showplace of antebellum homes, many in Greek Revival style; more than 100 of these still stand (exemplary blocks are between the river and 5th St., between 2nd-8th Ave. S; also along 7th-9th St. N, between 3rd-7th Aves.). Many are open during an annual historic home pilgrimage in spring; others are open all yr; contact the Chamber of Commerce (318 7th St. N).

Waverley Plantation (10 m NW off SR 50 near West Point), named after the Waverley novels of Sir Walter Scott, was built 1848-52; 2 circular, self-supporting staircases; cupola served as a lookout; open daily in daylight; adm.

GREENVILLE: Winterville Mounds Historic Site State Park (7 m N on SR 1) preserves a Mississippian ceremonial center consisting of a 55-ft mound surrounded by more than a dozen smaller ones; museum of artifacts; open Tues.-Sat. 9-6, Sun. 1-6; closed Dec. 25; sm adm.

GREENWOOD: Cottonlandia (Cotton & Washington Sts.), museum of the Delta area, is open Mon.-Fri. 1-5, Sat. & Sun. 2-5; closed hols; adm. **Carrollton** (14 m E via US 82) is a lovely town with more than 20 antebellum homes, an old jail, courthouse, and cemetery; for information on spring tours write Pilgrimage (J. Z. George Law Office Bldg., Carrollton 38917). **Florewood River Plantation** (2 m SW off I-55) with 2 dozen buildings, gardens, craft demonstrations, is a state-run living history park; adm.

HOLLY SPRINGS: Kate Freeman Clark Art Gallery (College Ave.) contains more than 1000 paintings by this Holly Springs artist who painted during a 30-year residence in New York; Bank of Holly Springs will give you the schedule for the gallery; free. **Holly Springs Garden Club,** headquartered in the beautiful Greek Revival mansion, Montrose, sponsors a spring pilgrimage to the fine antebellum houses in town.

JACKSON: State Capitol (Mississippi & High Sts.), modeled after the national capitol, has lavishly decorated legislative halls, rotunda, and governor's offices; open Mon.-Sat. 8-5, Sun. 1-5; closed hols; free.
  Chamber of Commerce (208 Lamar Life Bldg., 317 E Capitol St.) sponsors an annual spring tour of homes, including the **Governor's Mansion** (Capitol & N Congress Sts.), but little survived Gen. Sherman's burning in 1863.
  State Historical Museum (N State & Capitol Sts.) is in the restored Old Capitol (1839-1903); dioramas and other exhibits trace state history; Jefferson Davis memorabilia; on grounds is State Dept. of Archives & History; open Tues.-Sat. 9:30-4:30, Sun. 1-5; closed Jan. 1, July 4, Thnks, Dec. 25; free. **Museum of Natural Science** (111 N Jefferson St.), with habitat groups and other exhibits of Mississippi fish, birds, and animals, is open Mon.-Sat. 8-4:30; closed Thnks, Dec. 25; free.
  Mississippi Petrified Forest (19 m N via US 49 to Flora, then 2 m SW via SR 22) offers ½-m self-guiding trail past petrified logs and a **Visitor Center** with interpretive displays; open daily 9-5 (9-7 in summer); closed Dec. 25; adm.

LAUREL: Lauren Rogers Library & Museum of Art (5th Ave. & 7th St.) houses 19th-20th-C American and European paintings; sculpture; silver; Japanese prints; American Indian baskets, jewelry, clothing; fine library of

Mississippiana; open Tues.-Sat. 10-noon, 2-5, Sun. 2-5; closed Jan. 1, July 4, Thnks, Dec. 24-5; free.

MERIDIAN: Merrehope (905 31st Ave.), a stately Greek Revival mansion begun in 1858 and enlarged several times, has fine detailing, Empire furnishings; open Tues.-Sat. 10-noon, 2-4:30, Sun. 2-4:30; closed hols; adm.

NATCHEZ: Named for the Natchez Indians, and ruled by France, England, and Spain, this is a double city: **Natchez-Under-the-Hill,** renowned during steamboat days for lustiness and wickedness, and **Natchez-On-the-Hill,** with more than 30 antebellum mansions that reflect the opulent life of the wealthy from the late 1700s until the city's decline after the Civil War. Open all year (daily 9-5; closed Dec. 24-25; adm to each) are: **Connelly's Tavern** (Jefferson & Canal Sts.), a historic inn that hosted boatmen and stage travelers, restored and authentically furnished; **King's Tavern** (611 Jefferson St.), with slave quarters and original furnishings; magnificent **Stanton Hall,** built 1851-59, a lavish home with a 72-ft ballroom and period furnishings; and **Longwood** (Lower Woodville Rd.), an ornate octagon house begun by a Union sympathizer and left unfinished after its owner's plantation was devastated by both Union and Confederate troops.

In addition, **The Briars** (where Jefferson Davis married Varina Howell in 1845), **Rosalie** (headquarters of the state DAR), and a dozen other magnificent, privately owned homes are open year round; contact the **Natchez Garden Club** (Connelly's Tavern) or the **Pilgrimage Garden Club** (Stanton Hall) for hours and fees. **The Natchez-Adams County Chamber of Commerce** (300 N Commerce St.) provides a map for self-guiding tours and a complete list of historic homes. During the annual spring Natchez Pilgrimage, additional homes are opened for guided tours, and a Confederate Pageant and other events are scheduled; information and tickets available at **Natchez Pilgrimage Headquarters** (Gay 90s Bldg., on Stanton Hall grounds) or by writing P.O. Box 347, Natchez 39120.

Woodville (33 m S on US 61) has spring tours of 9 antebellum homes, including **Rosemont Plantation,** boyhood home of Jefferson Davis.

NATCHEZ TRACE PARKWAY parallels the Old Natchez Trace, a historical road between Natchez and Nashville; blazed by animals and Indians, the trace was used by the early French, English, and Spanish. Later, boatmen from the Kentucky-Ohio area floated their products down the Mississippi to markets at Natchez and New Orleans; the only way home was to walk or ride the 450-m back to Nashville. After the U.S. created the Mississippi Territory in 1798, the trace became an important road for Indians, postmen, soldiers, missionaries, and pioneer settlers, but its many dangers included wild animals, insects, illness, accidents, floods, swamps, hostile Indians, and robbers. In 1812, Gen. Andrew Jackson earned his nickname Old Hickory here, by sharing the hardship of the trail with his Tennessee militia during the march to New Orleans and back. In 1812 also, the introduction of steamboats that could make the return journey upriver began to make the arduous trace obsolete. **Tupelo Visitor Center** (5 m N of Tupelo, off US 45) provides information and a film on the trace's history; exhibits; open daily 8-5 (8-6 in summer); closed Dec. 25; free. Nearby are a working farm and site of an old Chickasaw village. Along the parkway are wayside exhibits interpreting the trace's colorful history and legend. In several places you can walk along sections of the original trace (occasionally worn so deep that the banks rise above your head). **Mount Locust** (15 m NE of Natchez), built about 1777, was one of the first of some 20 inns built along the trace by 1820; most of the inns were crude, but Mt. Locust was considered comfortable; restored with frontier furniture and utensils; bldg open Mar.-Nov. daily 9:30-6; grounds open daily all yr; free. Of several Indian mounds along the trace, the most impressive is the 8-acre **Emerald Mound** (12 m NE of Natchez), built about 1500; open daily 8-6; free. Also see Tennessee.

OXFORD: University of Mississippi, in Greek Revival buildings on an attractive campus, has an art gallery (Fine Arts Center), museums of anthropology (School of Education Bldg.) and Greek and Roman archaeology (Bondurant Hall); the Mississippi Room in the Library houses works by state authors including William Faulkner (who described Oxford, under the name Jefferson, in his novels); most buildings open 8:30-4:30 during the academic yr, but some close on weekends. Also on campus is **Rowan Oak** (Garfield St.), Faulkner's home.

Mary Buie Museum (510 University Ave.) houses local historical displays, paintings, antique toys, Faulkner exhibit; open Tues., Wed., Sat. 10-noon, 1:30-4:30; Thurs., Fri., Sun. 1:30-4:30; closed hols & Aug.; free.

PASCAGOULA: Old Spanish Fort (4602 Fort St., N off US 90), built as a carpentry shop by French settlers in 1718, was later fortified against Indian attack; from 1780-1810 it was a Spanish military outpost; thick tabby brick walls; Indian and pioneer relics; open daily 9-5; sm adm.

Old Place Plantation (3 m W via US 90 in Gautier), built by an early French settler, is on the Singing River (named for its sound, which has several scientific explanations but which legend says is made by the ghosts of the Pascagoula Indians who chose to walk to their deaths in the river, singing, rather than be captives of a neighboring tribe); original furnishings; tours Jan.-Nov., Mon.-Sat. 9-5, Sun. noon-5; some tours Dec.; adm.

PORT GIBSON: Grand Gulf State Military Park (7 m NW off US 61), site of the former town of Grand Gulf; most of the town was destroyed in mid-19th-C floods, and the remainder by shelling from Union ironclad ships and by burning during the Civil War; observation tower; fortifications; reconstructed cabin; antique vehicles; cemetery; Civil War artifacts in Visitor Center; open daily 7-6 (7-8 in summer); closed Jan. 1, Thnks, Dec. 25; donation.

First Presbyterian Church (Church & Walnut Sts.), with a slave gallery and chandeliers from the steamboat *Robert E. Lee,* has a steeple topped by a hand whose finger points toward heaven; open daily 8-6; free.

Ruins of Windsor (W on Old Rodney Rd.): only 22 Gothic columns remain of a 4-story mansion topped by an observatory that served as a landmark for Mississippi River pilots; built by 600 slaves in 1860, the mansion burned in 1890; used as setting for the movie *Raintree County.*

Rodney (marked road near Alcorn State University, 8 m S on Old Rodney Rd.) was a river port that became a ghost town when the Mississippi shifted its course, leaving the town inland; restoration is planned.

Old Country Store (11 m S on US 61 in Lorman) has been in continuous use since 1875; open Mon.-Sat. 8-6, Sun. & hols noon-5; closed some hols; free.

TUPELO NATIONAL BATTLEFIELD (on SR 6, 1 m W of Tupelo): commemorates the July 14, 1864 Battle of Tupelo, mounted to keep Confederate Gen. Nathan Bedford Forrest away from the railroad while Sherman attacked Atlanta; the 1-acre site has interpretive signs; open daily; free.

VICKSBURG: Vicksburg National Military Park, curving NE around the city, preserves 9 major Confederate forts, 12 Union approach trenches, parapets, and other remains of the Battle of Vicksburg. An important river port on a bluff commanding Mississippi River traffic, Vicksburg became, in Lincoln's words, "the key" to dividing the Confederacy and giving the Union control of the river. From the summer 1862-spring of 1863, federal troops and gunboats failed to take the city. Gen. Ulysses S. Grant then executed a series of land maneuvers that enabled him to take Jackson on May 14, 1863; but when two subsequent frontal attacks on Vicksburg failed, Grant laid siege to the city. On July 4, after 47 days of siege, with residents starving in cave hideouts, the city surrendered. **Visitor Center** (off US 80) offers exhibits and brochures; open daily 8-5 (7-7 in summer); closed Dec. 25; free. Park with 16-m self-guiding auto tour open daily. On grounds is **National Cemetery** with graves of 17,000 Union soldiers, of whom about 13,000 are unknown (Confederate dead were buried in Vicksburg City Cemetery); open daily; free.

Jefferson Davis Cruises (waterfront) are 1½-hr narrated trips past historic sites along the Yazoo and Mississippi rivers; daily mid-Apr.-Labor Day; adm.

Old Court House Museum (Court Sq.), built in 1858 with slave labor, has restored the 2nd-floor courtroom with period furnishings; period rooms; museum displays of antebellum Americana, riverboats, and the Civil War; open Mon.-Sat. 8:30-4:30, Sun. 1:30-4:30; closed Jan. 1, Thnks, Dec. 24, 25; adm. **McRaven** (end of Harrison St.), known as The Home of 3 Periods, began as a frontier cabin in 1797, became a Creole plantation home in 1836, and was converted to a Greek Revival townhouse in 1849; much interior detail intact; many original furnishings; tours mid-Feb.-mid-Nov., Mon.-Sat. 9-4:30, Sun. 2-4:30; adm. **Cedar Grove** (2200 Oak St.), an elegant antebellum mansion built 1840-58, contains a cannonball left in a parlor wall as a reminder of the Union siege of the city in 1863; lavish decor and furnishings; tours Mon.-Sat. 9-4:30, Sun. 1:30-5; closed Dec.-Jan.; adm. **Candon Hearth** (2530 S Confederate Ave.), the 1840 Newman House, survived despite being on the Confederate defense line; battle scars include cannonball and shrapnel; local memorabilia on display; open daily 9-5; adm.

U.S. Army Engineer Waterways Experiment Station (5 m S on Halls Ferry Rd.) uses some 60 working models to reproduce major waterways, harbors, dams and other features from around the nation to facilitate research into such fields as flood control, environmental problems, and military transportation; open Mon.-Fri. 8-4:30, with tours at 10 & 2; closed hols; free.

Hospitality House (Monroe & Clay Sts.) provides information, tapes, guide service; open daily 8-5; closed Jan. 1, Thnks, Dec. 25. They can provide a schedule of performances for the old-time melodrama, *Gold in the Hills,* presented spring-fall.

MISSOURI

ARROW ROCK: Arrow Rock State Historic Site preserves the heart of once-bustling frontier town strategically located on an Indian trail crossing, the Old Santa Fe Trail, and (by 1817) the first ferry across the Missouri River. **Old Tavern,** erected of brick in 1834, had a taproom (a store) and ballroom added in 1840's; historic relics; open Tues.-Sat. 10-4, Sun. noon-5; closed Jan. 1, Easter, Thnks, Dec. 25; sm adm. Other restored buildings include: **George Caleb Bingham House,** home of the Virginia-born frontier artist, furnished as it was during his residency 1837-45; **Dr. Matthew W. Hall House,** built 1846 by a pioneer physician, with period furnishings; **The Calaboose,** the jail built in 1871 that legend says was never used because the first person jailed raised such a racket he was released; chapel; gunshop. Guided tours (from Dr. Hall House) given Apr.-Oct. daily 9-5 or by appointment; sm adm charged to some bldgs.

BRANSON: School of the Ozarks (3 m S on US 65 at Pt. Lookout), a liberal arts college where students participate in campus work programs; mini-train tours from Friendship House, Apr. 15-Oct., several times daily; free. **Ralph Foster Museum:** artifacts from North and South American Indian cultures; Western memorabilia; 100,000-piece numismatic collection; Hall of Fame honoring Ozark natives such as Thomas Hart Benton and Rose O'Neill (who invented the Kewpie doll); open Mon.-Sat. 8-5, Sun. 1-5; closed Jan. 1, Thnks, Dec. 25; free.

Shepherd of the Hills Farm (7 m W on SR 76), established in 1884, is maintained as it appeared in the Harold B. Wright novel, *Shepherd of the Hills;* furnished Old Matt's Cabin; museum housing art and antiques from the Ozarks; charge for motorized tour; grounds open Apr.-Nov. daily 9-6; free. Novel is reenacted in a pageant May-Oct. **Silver Dollar City** (9 m W on SR 76), replica of a pioneer mining village; craft demonstrations, family attractions; optional cave tour; open Memorial Day-Labor Day daily 9:30-7; late Apr.-late May, and after Labor Day-late Oct., Wed.-Sun. 9:30-6; adm.

CAMDENTON: Camden County Historical Museum (2¼ m NE via US 54 in Linn Creek) displays arrowheads and antique tools; open May-Sept., daily 10-5; sm adm. **Kelsey's Antique Cars** (1 m NE on US 54), with Stanley Steamer and other models dating from 1899, is open daily 9-5 (8-8 Apr.-Oct.); closed Jan. 1, Dec. 25; adm.

COLUMBIA: University of Missouri (Elm & 8th Sts.) offers a map of the campus; highlights are: **Ellis Library** (Lowry St.), with large Midwest collections, open Mon.-Fri. 8 am-11 pm, Sat. 9-5, Sun. 2-11; closed hols; free. In East Wing are **State Historical Society collections;** works by George Caleb Bingham, Thomas Hart Benton, Karl Bodmer, Bill Mauldin (open Mon.-Fri. 8-4:30). **Museum of Anthropology** (Swallow Hall); Indian displays emphasize the Midwest; open Mon.-Fri. 9:30-noon, 1-4:30; closed hols; free. **Museum of Art & Archaeology** offers art objects from the Classical world, Middle and Far East; primitive works from South America, Africa, the Pacific; sculpture, painting, prints from the 15th-C to the present; open Mon.-Fri. 8-5; some exhibits open weekends 2-5; closed hols; free. **Max Mayer Memorial Museum** (McAlester Hall), displays on history of psychology; open Mon.-Fri. 8-5; closed hols; free.

Stephens College (E Broadway & College Ave.) offers tours from the

Office of Admissions (Hickman Hall); the Chapel, designed by Eero Saarinen, is open daily.

EXCELSIOR SPRINGS: Watkins Woolen Mill State Historic Site (6½ m N on US 69), Missouri's first factory, opened in 1861; machinery has been preserved and some still operates; other buildings are being restored; open daily 10-4; closed Easter, Thnks, Dec. 25; adm. **Jesse James Farm** (6 m NW via US 69, SR 92), birthplace of the outlaw; original furnishings; open daily 9:30-5:30; adm.

FULTON: Winston Churchill Memorial & Library (on campus of Westminster College) is housed in the Church of St. Mary, Aldermanbury, built in London in the 12th-C, gutted by the Great Fire of 1666, restored by Christopher Wren, and gutted during WW II; it was shipped in pieces and reconstructed here, where Churchill delivered the 1946 speech that made "Iron Curtain" part of the vocabulary; Churchill memorabilia; open Mon.-Sat. 10-4, Sun. 10:30-4:45; adm.

GEORGE WASHINGTON CARVER NATIONAL MONUMENT (3 m SW of Diamond): Farm on which Carver was born a slave about 1860 and from which he was kidnapped by Civil War guerrillas in 1861; the Carvers succeeded in recovering the baby and he lived with them until he was a teenager, taking their surname. **Visitor Center** exhibits tell of his life as a teacher, botanist, and pioneer conservationist; open daily 8:30-5; closed Dec. 25; free.

HANNIBAL: Boyhood home of Mark Twain, and setting for many scenes from his novels, Hannibal is now an industrial town but has preserved many reminders of Samuel Clemens. **Chamber of Commerce** (320 N Main St.) shows a documentary film on Twain (June-Labor Day; sm adm). Fence painting, frog jumping, and other contests in July. Narrated tour train rides (3rd & Hill Sts.) and river cruises (foot of Center St.) are offered in summer. **Riverview Park** has statue of Twain looking out over the Mississippi River (park open daily 6 am-10 pm; free); statue of Tom and Huck on Main St. (at North St.). **Mark Twain Cave** (2 m S off SR 79), where Injun Joe died and where Tom and Becky were lost, offers guided tours daily 8-5 (8-8 Apr.-Oct.); closed Dec. 25; adm.

    Mark Twain Boyhood Home & Museum (208 Hill St.): clapboard home in which the Clemens family lived 1840s-50s; family furnishings; Twain memorabilia. **Becky Thatcher House** (211 Hill St.) was home of Laura Hawkins, after whom Becky was modeled; period furnishings. **Pilaster House** (Hill & Main Sts.), where the Clemens family lived and Twain's father died, has period living quarters, doctor's office, and drugstore. All open daily, June-Aug. 8-8, rest of yr 8-5; closed Jan. 1, Thnks, Dec. 25; free.

Rockcliffe Mansion (1000 Bird St.), elegant river estate of a lumber tycoon, has art nouveau decor, a Moorish room, other pretensions of the time; family antiques; open daily 9:30-5:30; closed Jan. 1, Thnks, Dec. 25; adm.

Mark Twain Birthplace Memorial Shrine (37 m SW via US 61, SR 19, 154, then N on SR 107) is the 2-room cabin in which Twain was born in 1835; Twain mementos; open Mon.-Sat. 10-4, Sun. noon-5; closed Jan. 1, Easter, Thnks, Dec. 25; sm adm.

HERMANN: Settled by Germans from Philadelphia in 1837, and named for a German hero, this town is proud of its Old World heritage. **German School Building** (4th & Schiller Sts.) now a museum devoted to town history and early settlers; information is available here on the Maifest and house tours·(phone 486-2017); open mid-May-Oct., Mon.-Sat. 10-5, Sun. 1-5; sm adm. Open by appointment, May-Oct., are: **Pommer-Gentner House** (108 Market St.), built 1840's, period furnishings. **Strehly House** (131 W 2nd St.), built about 1842 by immigrants who published an abolitionist newspaper in the basement; remains of a wing-making industry. **Klenk House** (432 E 3rd St.) has a restored smokehouse. Sm adm to each.

Bottermuller House (205 E 8th St.), built about 1850; period furnishings; country store; pioneer exhibits; open Mon.-Sat. 10-5, Sun. & hols 1-5; sm adm.

Stone Hill Winery (Stone Hill Hwy) offers tours and winetasting, Mon.-Sat. 8-5 (longer hrs in summer); also some Suns. 1-5; closed Thnks, Dec. 25; adm.

Graham Cave State Park (21 m N via SR 19 at Montgomery City) is a rock shelter occupied as early as 7850 BC; excavation is still in progress; open daily.

INDEPENDENCE: Harry S. Truman Library & Museum (US 24 at Delaware St.) contains reproduction of his White House office, mural by Thomas Hart Benton, exhibits relating to Truman's career; audiovisual programs; Truman gravesite in courtyard; open daily 9-5; closed Jan. 1, Thnks, Dec. 25; sm adm. **Harry S. Truman Home** (219 N Delaware St.) is not open to the public.

Jackson County Jail & Marshal's Home (217 N Main St.) has restored cells of 1859 jail, furnished marshal's quarters, museum exhibits; open June-Aug., Mon.-Sat. 9-5, Sun. 1-5; Sept.-May, Tues.-Sat. 10-4, Sun. 1-5; closed Thnks, Dec. 25; sm adm.

Saints Auditorium (River & Walnut Sts.), world hq of Reorganized Church of Jesus Christ Latter-Day Saints, offers guided tours Mon.-Sat. 9-5, Sun. 1-5; closed hols; free.

Ft. Osage (11 m NE on US 24 to Buckner, then N to Sibley), restored 1808 trading post and fort, first post in the Louisiana Purchase; exhibits in blockhouses, barracks, other buildings; open daily 8-5; closed Jan. 1, Thnks, Dec. 25; free.

JEFFERSON CITY: State Capitol (High St.), on a cliff overlooking the Missouri River, is capped with a statue of Ceres, goddess of grain; murals (Thomas Hart Benton, N. C. Wyeth) and decorations illustrate state legends and history; archaeological relics, guns, other collections of the Missouri State Museum; open daily 8-5; closed Jan. 1, Dec. 25; free. **Cole County Historical Society Museum** (109 Madison St.) houses antique furniture and decorative arts, old maps and photographs, inaugural ball gowns of state first ladies; library; open Tues.-Sat. 1-5; closed mid-Dec.-early Jan., July 4, Thnks; sm adm.

Moniteau County Courthouse (20 m W on US 50 in California), an 1868 brick Greek Revival building, has a domed octagonal cupola; historic exhibits; open Mon.-Fri. 9-5; closed hols; free.

JOPLIN: Mineral Museum (Schifferdecker Park on US 66) displays minerals and scale models of mining operations; open Tues.-Sat. 10-noon, 1-5; Sun. 1-5; free. **Dorothea B. Hoover Museum** (110 Joplin St.) depicts the city's history in period rooms; open Wed.-Sat. noon-4, Sun. 1-4; closed hols; free. **Spiva Art Center** (Newman & Duquesne Rds. on campus of Missouri Southern College), with works by local artists, is open Mon.-Fri. 9-4, Sat. & Sun. noon-2; closed Aug. & hols; free. **Municipal Bldg.** (303 E 3rd St.), houses Thomas Hart Benton's last mural, depicting city history; open Mon.-Fri. 9-5; closed hols; free.

KANSAS CITY: Convention & Visitors Bureau (1221 Baltimore) will provide maps and information on the city's outstanding parks (such as Swope and Penn Valley) and renewed areas, such as **Country Club Plaza** (with Spanish-style architecture, fountains, and statuary) and the **Country Club residential district** (with homes planned to harmonize with their surroundings), **River Quay** (restored riverfront with boutiques), **Civic Center** (with the City Hall observation roof open Mon.-Fri. 8-4:30; closed hols; free). The **City Market,** between Main & Walnut Sts., 3rd to 5th Sts., opens daily at 7 (exc. Sun. & hols). The **Stockyards** between Genesee St. and the Kansas River (12-23 Sts.); auctions (1600 Genesee St.) Tues. 10, Wed. 9, Thurs. 10; free. **Liberty Memorial** (100 W 26th St.), a limestone shaft with an eternal flame and museum of WW I relics, has an observation tower; open Wed.-Sun. 9:30-4:30; closed hols; sm charge for elevator.

Nelson Gallery of Art & Atkins Museum (4525 Oak St. at 45th St.) houses one of the nation's foremost collections in an impressive building that includes re-created Indian and Chinese temples, French cloister,

Jacobean room; works range from Sumerian vases to contemporary art; outstanding Oriental galleries; European masters; French Impressionists; English and American portraiture; Starr Collection of miniatures; period rooms; English pottery; decorative arts; armor; on landscaped grounds is fountain by Carl Milles; open Tues.-Sat. 10-5, Sun. 2-6; closed Jan. 1, July 4, Thnks, Dec. 25; sm adm. **Kansas City Museum of History & Science** (3218 Gladstone Blvd. at Indiana Ave.), in a 72-room mansion built by a lumber king, offers fine anthropological exhibits that include full-size dioramas of villages; fossils and minerals; regional history; planetarium shows (adm); open Mon.-Sat. 9-5, Sun. noon-5; closed Jan. 1, Dec. 25; free.

John Wornall House (Wornall Rd. & 61st Terr), Greek Revival mansion served as military headquarters and hospital during the Civil War; period furnishings; open Tues.-Sat. 10-4:30, Sun. 1-4:30; closed hols; adm.

Union Cemetery (2801 Warwick Trafficway), with grave of artist George Caleb Bingham, is open daily 7-4:30; the Victorian Sexton's Cottage, restored, is open Sat. & Sun. 1-4; free.

Jesse James Bank Museum (15 m NE in Liberty, Old Town Sq.), site of 1866 holdup; 19th-C banking displays; open Mon.-Sat. 9:30-5, Sun. 1-5; closed Thurs in winter, Thnks, Dec. 25-Jan. 1; adm. Mormon prophet Joseph Smith was confined in the **Liberty Jail** (1 block N of Sq.) in 1838-39; open Mon.-Sat. 8-6; free.

KIRKSVILLE: Thousand Hills State Park (4 m W via SR 6, then 3 m S on SR 157), a prehistoric ceremonial ground, contains petroglyphs made 1000-1600.

LACLEDE: Gen. John J. Pershing Boyhood Home, an 11-room house built 1858, has period furnishings and exhibits on "Black Jack" Pershing's life; open Mon.-Sat. 10-4, Sun. noon-6; closed Jan. 1, Easter, Thnks, Dec. 25; sm adm. **Pershing State Park** (2 m W on US 36) commemorates Pershing's birthplace.

LAMAR: Harry S. Truman Birthplace Memorial Shrine (1009 Truman Ave.), restored with period furnishings; guided tours Tues.-Sat. 10-4, Sun. noon-5 (noon-6 in summer); closed Jan. 1, Easter, Thnks, Dec. 25; sm adm.

LEXINGTON: Battle of Lexington State Park (10th & Utah Sts.), site of the 1861 Battle of Hemp Bales, contains the 1853 home of a hemp manufacturer, Anderson House; guided tours through the restored home, with rafters broken by cannonballs and blood-stained floors from its service as a field hospital; open Mon.-Sat. 10-4, Sun. noon-5 (noon-6 in summer); closed Jan. 1, Easter, Thnks, Dec. 25; sm adm.

Museum of the Yesteryears (on SR 13, 1 block S of jct US 24) houses examples of early shops and offices, antique vehicles, early tools and household items, musical instruments; open Mar.-Nov. daily 9-5; adm.

Linwood Lawn (2 m SE off US 24), a Georgian mansion built about 1850 and noted for fine woodwork, is open spring-fall by appointment (phone 259-3835); sm adm.

Lafayette County Courthouse, oldest in the state still in use (built 1847-9), has a cannonball embedded in one of its columns.

MEXICO: Audrain County Historical Society Museum (501 S Muldrow St.), antebellum mansion furnished with period antiques; dolls, Currier & Ives prints, period clothing, glass; also here is American Saddle Horse Museum; open Mar.-Nov., Tues.-Sun. 2-5; Dec.-Feb., Tues.-Sat. 2-5; closed hols; sm adm.

NEVADA: Bushwacker Museum (231 N Main St.) once housed the sheriff's office and jail; cell blocks with prisoner's graffiti; antique medical equipment, tools, guns; Osage Indian artifacts; open May-Sept. daily 1-5; sm adm.

OZARK NATIONAL SCENIC RIVERWAYS, along the Current and Jacks Fork Rivers, offers interpretive programs on the people of the Ozarks at: **Powder Mill Visitor Center** (10 m W of Ellington on SR 106), with operating blacksmith shop (weekends, Apr.-Oct.) and sorghum mill (Fri.-Sun., mid-Sept.-end-Oct.); open Apr.-Oct. daily 8-5 (later in summer); free. **Alley Spring Visitor Center** (5 m W of Eminence on SR 106), with cornmeal grinding (daily in summer, weekends in spring & fall) and a whiskey still (Wed.-Sun. in summer, weekends in spring & fall); open daily 9-5 in summer, weekends in spring & fall; free. Special programs frequently held; for information write to Supt., Van Buren 63965.

POPLAR BLUFF: Call of the Wild Museum (10 m S at jct US 160, 67) has mounted displays of game animals from around the world; pottery making demonstrations; open daily 8-5 (7:30-7:30 in summer); closed Dec. 25; adm.

ROLLA: University of Missouri Mineral Museum (12th & Rolla Sts. in Norwood Hall) displays more than 4000 specimens from around the world; open Mon.-Fri. 8-5, weekends by appointment; free. **The UMR Nuclear Reactor** is open Sept.-July, Mon.-Fri. 8-5; free. **Ed Clark Museum of Missouri Geology** (in Missouri Geological Survey Bldg. in Buehler Park, W edge of town), exhibits on state geology; open Mon.-Fri. 8-noon, 1-5; closed hols; free.

ST. CHARLES: First Missouri State Capitol (208-14 Main St.), seat of government 1821-26; period furnishings; open Mon.-Sat. 10-4, Sun. noon-5; closed Jan. 1, Easter, Thnks, Dec. 25; sm adm. **St. Charles Historic District,** with restored homes, is just S of here. **Bushnell Pioneer Museum** (4 m W off I-70), with a reconstructed village street and good collections of early Americana, is open May-mid-Nov., Tues.-Sun. 10-4, sm adm.

Daniel Boone Home (20 m SW via SR 94 to Defiance), built 1803-10, is where he died in 1820; fortress-thick walls and gunports; Boone family furnishings and memorabilia; open Mar.-Dec. daily 8:30-sunset; Jan.-Feb., Sat. & Sun. 9-sunset; closed Dec. 25; adm.

SAINTE GENEVIEVE: Founded 1735, oldest permanent settlement in Missouri, this town preserves many reminders of its French heritage (including a festival in Aug.). **Amoureaux House** (½ m S on St. Marys Rd.), built about 1770, is one of the oldest Creole houses still standing; period furnishings; dolls, glass, china, silver; open daily 10-5; closed Dec. 25; sm adm. **Bolduc House** (123 Main St.), Creole house from the 1780s, has period furnishings; open Apr.-Oct. daily 10-4; sm adm. **Greentree** (224 St. Marys Rd.), once a tavern, and **Guibourd-Valle House** (1 N 4th St.), with family heirlooms, are open daily 10-5; closed Thnks, Dec. 25; sm adm. **Dr. Benjamin Shaw House** (2nd & Merchant Sts.), built 1780s, incorporating parts of a wrecked steamboat; fur trading post with slave quarters; open Apr.-Oct. daily 11:30-4; sm adm. **Church of Ste. Genevieve** (DuBourg Pl. near Merchant St.), with religious paintings dating from 1663, is open daily 6-6. **Memorial Cemetery** (W end of Merchant St.) has graves dated back to the 1780s. **Historical Museum** (DuBourg Pl. & Merchant St.) contains local artifacts; birds mounted by John J. Audubon, who was a merchant here; open Apr.-Oct. daily 9-4; Nov.-Mar., Thurs.-Tues. noon-4; closed Jan. 1, Dec. 25; sm adm.

ST. JOSEPH: Founded in 1800 as a French fur-trading post, this city became a great river port, the starting point for the Oregon Trail and western terminus of the first cross-state railroad. It was also eastern terminus of the Pony Express, commemorated in a statue of horse and rider, and in the **Pony Express Stables Museum** (914 Penn St.); from here riders started the 1966-m trip that carried mail to Sacramento from 1860 until the completion of telegraph lines in 1861; route maps; saddles and other mementos of riders; open May-mid-Sept., Mon.-Sat. 9-5, Sun. & hols 2-5; free.

St. Joseph Museum (11th & Charles Sts.), in 1879 Gothic-style mansion; large, fine collections of North American Indian ethnology; local and Western history, including pioneer trails, the Pony Express, and St. Joseph; also natural history displays; open May-mid-Sept., Mon.-Sat. 9-5, Sun. 2-5; rest of yr, Tues.-Sat. 1-5, Sun. 2-5; closed Jan. 1, Dec. 25; free.

Patee House Museum (12th & Penn Sts.), considered the finest hotel W of the Mississippi when it opened in 1858; reconstructed Pony Express and railroad offices; other historic displays; open late May-late Sept., Mon.-Sat. 10-5, Sun. & hols 1-5; may be open weekends other times; adm. **Albrecht Art Museum** (2818 Frederick Blvd.), in attractive Georgian-style home; contemporary art; children's section; open Tues.-Fri. 10-4, weekends & hols 1-5; closed Jan. 1, Thnks, Dec. 25; sm adm. **Doll Museum** (1501 Penn St.), with miniature rooms and antique dolls and toys, is open Memorial Day-Oct., Tues.-Sun. 1-5; sm adm. **Jesse James Home** (1 m N off US 36) is where the outlaw was living under the alias Mr. Howard when he was killed (Apr. 3, 1882) by his former friend Bob Ford for a $10,000 ransom; open Mar.-Nov., Thurs.-Tues. 9-5:30; adm.

ST. LOUIS: Founded by French fur traders in 1764 and named for the king of France, St. Louis became the Gateway City after the Lewis & Clark Expedition outfitted here in 1804 and opened trails for westward expansion. With the coming of railroads (1857), Germans and other Europeans arrived, and the city gained world prominence in 1904 with the 6-month-long Louisiana Purchase Exposition. **Convention & Visitors Bureau** (500 N Broadway) provides information and sells tickets for the St. Louis Shuttle, a bus that passes many attractions. **Tourist Board** (911 Locust St.) offers brochures for self-guiding walking tours. Either can give you information on the **Historic Preservation Pilgrimage** (fall) and other events and tours; some tours, such as the police dept. and *St. Louis Post-Dispatch,* require advance reservation. **Anheuser-Busch brewery tours** (610 Pestalozzi St.) are available May-Sept., Mon.-Sat. 9-3:30; Oct.-Apr., Mon.-Fri. 9:30-3:30; free. **St. Louis Chapter of the American Institute of Architects** in the Wainwright Bldg. (107 N 7th St.), designed by Adler and Sullivan in 1890, distributes free brochures on historic buildings and conducts frequent tours. **Aloe Plaza** (Market St., 18-20th Sts.) contains fountain by Carl Milles. **Soulard Farmers Market** (730 Carroll St., S to Julia St., between 7-9th Sts.) was started about 1779; open Tues.-Thurs. 6:30-6, Fri. & Sat. 5:30 am-10 pm.

Forest Park (between Lindell, Skinker, & Kingshighway Blvds.), site of the Louisiana Purchase Exposition, has many statues (including one of Louis IX) and fountains; municipal opera; zoo; conservatory; and recreational facilities; also here are: **St. Louis Art Museum,** with a comprehensive collection; pre-Columbian, African, Japanese, and Chinese works; European masters from Titian to Braque; American painting; sculpture; decorative arts; open Wed.-Sun. 10-5, Tues. 2:30-9:30; closed Jan. 1, Dec. 25; free. **Missouri Historical Society** in Jefferson Memorial; exhibits on growth of the West; river history; Lewis & Clark display; toys; costumes; Lindbergh memorabilia, library; open daily 9:30-4:45; closed Jan. 1, July 4, Thnks, Dec. 25; free. **McDonnell Planetarium,** in a striking modern building, has exhibit halls open Tues., Fri., Sat. 10-10, Wed. & Thurs. 10-5, Sun. & hols noon-6; shows daily; closed Jan. 1, Thnks, Dec. 24, 25, 31; adm.

At the riverfront is **Jefferson National Expansion Memorial,** on the site of the city's original settlement, with Eero Saarinen's Gateway Arch symbolizing westward expansion; gondolas to observation deck daily 9-4:30 (8 am-9:30 pm in summer; longer hrs some weekends in spring & fall); **Visitor Center** open daily 8-5 (longer in summer, spring & fall weekends); closed Jan. 1, Thnks, Dec. 25; adm. NPS hq is in **Old Courthouse** (11 N 4th St. at Market St.), site of the Dred Scott trial; films; exhibits; open daily 9-4:30; closed Jan. 1, Thnks, Dec. 25; free. **Old Cathedral** (209 Walnut at 3rd Sts.), built 1831-34 on the site of the city's first church (1770), is open 7 am-9 pm, free; museum open daily 10-5, sm adm.

Also at the riverfront are: **Eugene Field Museum** (634 S Broadway), the poet's boyhood home; memorabilia; antique toys and dolls; open Tues.-Sat. 10-4, Sun. noon-5; closed hols; sm adm. **St. Louis Sports Hall of Fame** (between gates 5 & 6, Busch Stadium, 100 Stadium Plaza), with mementos of many sports, Stan Musial trophies, films; open in summer daily 10-5; spring & fall, Tues.-Sun. 10-5; also open game nights; closed Jan.-Feb.; adm. **USS Inaugural** (Wharf St., S of Arch), a WW II minesweeper, now a naval museum; open June-Aug. daily 9-9; Sept.-May, Mon.-Fri. 10-4:30, Sat. & Sun. 9-7; adm. **Visitor Information Center,** housed on the sternwheeler *Becky Thatcher,* provides information on the riverfront, schedules for river sightseeing excursions and for melodramas on the *Goldenrod* Showboat. Riverfront Trolley, which lets you on and off at attractions in the area, operates in summer.

Grant's Farm (Grant & Gravois Rds.), maintained by Anheuser-Busch, Inc., contains cabin once owned by Ulysses S. Grant, Clydesdale stables and paddock; trophy room; horse-drawn vehicles; zoo; reservations required 1 month in advance (write Grant's Farm Tours, St. Louis 63123); tour is by trackless train hourly, Apr.-Oct., Tues.-Sat.; closed hols; free.

Chatillon-DeMenil House (3352 DeMenil Pl), an 1848 fur trader's home later expanded into a Greek Revival mansion, has 19th-C French furnishings; open Tues.-Sun. 10-4; adm. **Campbell House Museum** (1508 Locust St.), a fur trader's Victorian mansion, has historical displays, period furnishings, gowns; open Tues.-Sat. 10-4, Sun. noon-5; adm. **Tower Grove House** (Missouri Botanical Garden, 2101 Tower Grove Ave. & Flora Blvd.) is a restored Italianate brick house; Victorian furnishings; open daily May-Oct. 10-5, Nov.-Apr. 10-4; closed Jan. 1, Dec. 25; adm. **Sappington House** (1015 S Sappington Rd. in Crestwood) was built in Federal style of handmade brick by slave labor; period antiques; open Tues.-Fri. 10-3, Sat. & Sun. noon-3; sm adm. **Hanley House** (7600 Westmoreland in Clayton) is a typical Missouri farm of the period 1855-94 restored by the city; period furnishings; open Fri., Sat., Sun. 1-5; closed hols; sm adm. **Priory of St. Mary & St. Louis Church** (500 S Mason Rd.) is a beautiful modern building that has won many awards; open daily. **St. Louis Cathedral** (4431 Lindell Blvd. at Newstead Ave.), in Byzantine style; wonderful mosaics cover much of the interior, including dome; open daily Apr.-Oct. 7 am-8 pm, Nov.-Mar. 7-6; free. **Washington University Steinberg Art Gallery** (Steinberg Hall, Forsyth St. & Skinker Blvd.) has fine modern works; European masters; Greek vases; ancient coins; open Mon.-Fri. 9-5, Sat. 10-4, Sun. 1-5; closed hols; free. **Museum of Science & Natural History** (Oak Knoll Park, Clayton Rd. & Big Bend Blvd.), with collections from prehistoric times to space travel, is open Tues.-Sat. 9-5, Sun. 1-5; closed hols; free. **St. Louis Medical Museum & National Museum of Medical Quackery** (3839 Lindell Blvd.) chronicles the history of medicine; open Easter-Labor Day daily 11-4; early-Sept.-Easter, Mon.-Sat. 11-4; free. **National Museum of Transport** (20 m W at 3015 Barretts Station Rd at Dougherty Ferry Rd. in Kirkwood), with old vehicles and railroad equipment, is open daily 10-5; closed Jan. 1, Thnks, Dec. 25; adm.

Jefferson Barracks Historical Park (10 m S on SR 231 on the Mississippi Riv.) preserves an army post used 1826-1946; 1857 powder magazine, stables, other buildings; museum; open early June-Labor Day daily 8-5, Sun. 1-5; rest of yr, Wed.-Sat. 8-5, Sun. 1-5; closed Jan. 1, Dec. 25; free.

Florissant (10½ m NW on I-70, then 4½ m N on Florissant Rd.), a town with many historic buildings, has a **Visitor Center** (1060 Rue St. Catherine) that provides booklets for self-guiding tours; among buildings open to the public are **Old St. Ferdinand's Shrine** (18th-C French tabernacle, early altars, pressed-glass chandeliers) and **Taille de Noyer** (a 3-room log cabin built about 1790 and later expanded into a 22-room antebellum mansion).

Gen. Daniel Bissell House (10225 Bellefontaine Rd.), a Federal-style home with furnishings of Bissell family who lived here 1814-1961; open Wed.-Sat. 8-5, Sun. 1-5; closed Jan. 1, Dec. 25; sm adm.

Black Madonna Shrine (8 m SW via I-44 to Eureka) contains rock grottoes decorated with trinkets; built by a Franciscan monk over a period of 22 years; mosaic portrait of Our Lady of Czestochowa, the Black Madonna, a duplicate of the picture in Poland allegedly painted by St. Luke; open Apr.-Oct. daily 8-8; parking fee.

SPRINGFIELD: Springfield Art Museum (1111 E Brookside Dr.) features American works, including antiques; open Mon.-Sat. 9-5, Sun. 1-5; closed hols; free. **Drury College** (Benton Ave. & Calhoun St.) campus has the **Harwood Gallery** of Oriental, primitive, and American art (open June-Aug. daily 2-5; during academic yr, Mon.-Fri. 9-5, Sat. & Sun. 2-5; closed hols & school vacations; free) and the restored and furnished 1852 **Bentley House** (open Mon.-Fri. 9-5; closed hols; free).

Wilson's Creek National Battlefield (13 m SW via US 60, SR ZZ), site of Aug. 10, 1861 battle for control of Missouri that resulted in heavy casualties; Confederates, victorious, were unable to pursue their advantage, and the state eventually was secured for the Union; map for self-guiding auto tour; information booth open June-Labor Day, daily 8:30-5; park open all year; free.

WASHINGTON STATE PARK (on SR 21 about 12 m S of De Soto): 2 areas contain petroglyphs, probably made 1000-1600; interpretive booklet at the entrance; small museum; open daily.

MONTANA

BAKER: O'Fallon Historical Society Museum (1 block W of jct US 12, SR 7), with pioneer memorabilia, is open early June-Sept., Wed., Sat., Sun. 2-8; free. **Carter County Museum** (35 m S via SR 7 in Ekalaka) has paleontological specimens, relics of early man, pioneer artifacts; open in summer, Tues.-Sun; prehistoric exhibits are also at nearby Medicine Rocks State Park.

BIG HOLE NATIONAL BATTLEFIELD (62 m SW of Butte on SR 43, W of Wisdom): Here at dawn on Aug. 9, 1877, the U.S. Army launched a surprise attack on the Non-Treaty Nez Perce, whose resistance to accepting a reduction in their ancestral lands in Idaho led them in an epic retreat toward the Canadian border; despite heavy losses here, the Nez Perce pushed on to Chinook (see Havre) before surrendering; Visitor Center; self-guiding trail; open daily 8-5 (8-7 in summer); free.

BILLINGS: Yellowstone County Museum (on SR 3 at Logan Intl Airport) offers displays on pioneers and Indians; old vehicles; open Tues.-Sat. 10:30-noon, 1-5, Sun. 2-5; closed hols; free. Nearby are **Range Rider of the Yellowstone** (a memorial to settlers) and the beginning of **Chief Black Otter Trail** (runs above the city toward the river, passing Boothill Cemetery). **Western Heritage Center** (2822 Montana Ave.) is devoted to regional history; Stetson hat collection; displays on Calamity Jane, Will James, and others; open Tues.-Sat. 10-5 (10-7 in summer), Sun. 1-5; closed hols; free.

Indian Caves (5 m SE off US 87, 212), used as dwellings 4500 years ago, have remains of pictographs; open daily; free. **Crow Indian Reservation** stretches SE to the Wyoming border; Crow Agency (on I-90, 15 m S of Hardin) offers visitor facilities and Crow Indian Heritage Village, portraying culture of the Crow; rodeos, other events, including a reenactment of Custer's Last Stand. **Chief Plenty Coups State Monument** (35 m SE of Billings at Pryor) preserves the ranch home, store, and gravesite of the outstanding leader (1848-1932); open May-Oct. daily.

BOZEMAN: Museum of the Rockies (S 7th Ave. & Kagy Blvd. on Montana State Univ. campus) has exhibits on Indians, pioneers, natural history; open Mon.-Fri. 8-5, Sat. & Sun. 1-5; closed hols & school vacations; free. **Ketterer Art Center** (35 N Grand), in 1900 pioneer home, offers exhibits by local artists and artisans; open Tues.-Sun. 1-5:30 (9:30-5:30 in summer); closed Easter, Thnks, Dec. 25; free.

Gallatin National Forest (S via US 191) offers a Visitor Center (on US 287, 22 m W of US 191) with exhibits, interpretive programs, information on self-guiding tours (including Madison River Canyon Earthquake Area on US 287, 3 m W of US 191, where 1959 quake left slides, faults, and a lake); open Memorial Day-Labor Day, daily 9-6; free. **Interagency Fire Control Center** (on US 191, 2 m N of West Yellowstone) tours by smoke-jumpers late June-mid-Sept. daily 9-6; free.

BROWNING: This is hq of the Blackfeet Indian Reservation. **Museum of the Plains Indian & Crafts Center** (½ m W at jct US 2, 89) displays costumes, beadwork, carvings, other Blackfeet arts and crafts; crafts for sale; Blackfeet Archives are housed here; a booklet is available for a 70-m tour of Blackfeet historic sites; open June-Sept. 14, daily 8-8; Sept. 15-30, daily 8-5; rest of yr, weekdays by appointment (phone 338-2230); free. Nearby **Museum of Montana Wildlife** features mounted specimens, miniature dioramas, paintings, sculpture; open early May-late Sept. daily 7 am-9 pm; adm.

BUTTE: Settled in 1864 on "the richest hill on earth," Butte was a gold placer mining camp and then a silver boom town. After gold and silver gave out, even greater fortunes continued to be made in manganese, lead, zinc, and especially copper (leading to the War of the Copper Kings). Today, the Anaconda Co.'s operations are the major industry, and the **Chamber of Commerce** (Finlen Hotel, 100 E Broadway at Wyoming) will arrange free mine tours; open-pit mining can be seen from the **Berkeley Pit** (N edge of town) observation platform. **World Museum of Mining** (W Park St.) is an indoor-outdoor museum at the defunct zinc and silver Orphan Girl Mine; reconstructed mining camp with saloon, assay office, other buildings; mining equipment displays; open June-Sept. daily 9-9;

Oct.-May, Tues.-Sun. 10-5; free. **Mineral Museum** (Montana College of Mineral Science & Technology, W edge of town via Park St.) displays minerals from around the world; flourescent exhibit; mine models; relief map of Montana ores; open daily in summer, Mon.-Fri. fall-spring, 8-5; closed hols; free.

Copper King Mansion (219 W Granite St.), elegant Victorian home of W. A. Clark, sports a 62-ft-long ballroom, frescoed walls and ceilings, opulent furnishings; open daily 9-9; closed Jan. 1, Dec. 25; adm.

Grant-Kohrs Ranch National Historic Site (edge of Deer Lodge, N on US 10, I-90) was the ranch of John Grant, one of the founders of Montana's cattle industry in the 1850s, later purchased by Conrad Kohrs, cattle king; 1862 ranchhouse; site being developed by NPS as an interpretive center on Montana ranching; inquire locally for hrs.

Anaconda, almost a suburb, is a smelter town; a reminder of Copper King Marcus Daly's vain efforts to make this town a showplace (and the capital) is the **Daly Hotel,** with Gothic pepperpot towers and a mosaic head of Tammany (his racehorse) inlaid on the bar floor.

CUSTER BATTLEFIELD NATIONAL MONUMENT (on Crow Reservation, 2 m SE of Crow Agency on US 212): Headstones on the field mark where Lt. Col. George A. Custer and about 260 soldiers and attached personnel fell during the Last Stand in June 1876. The battle, a result of Sioux and Cheyenne resistance to white gold seekers (who invaded Indian lands in 1874 in violation of the 1868 Ft. Laramie treaty), was the last great victory for the Plains Indians, who were soon confined to reservations. A Visitor Center offers interpretive exhibits; open daily in summer 7 am-8 pm; spring & fall 8-6; winter 8-4:30; closed Jan. 1, Thnks, Dec. 25; free.

DILLON: Beaverhead County Museum (15 S Montana St.) displays Indian and pioneer artifacts, iron implements, gold-mining relics; open mid-June-Aug. daily 9-5; Sept.-mid-June, Mon.-Fri. 9-5; closed hols; sm adm. **Bannack State Monument** (in Beaverhead Ntl Forest, 5 m S on US 91, I-15, then 20 m W on SR 278, then S) is a ghost town, site of the first major gold discovery in Montana (1862) and first territorial capital (1864); many log and frame buildings remain; open daily; hq in Dillon (US 91 & Skihi St.).

DRUMMOND: Bearmouth (15 m W on US 10, 12, I-90) is a ghost town; more than a million dollars in gold and silver were mined here in 1866; legend of a buried treasure. **Garnet** (just N on a secondary road leading to Clearwater State Forest), and 1896 mining camp, stabilized and partially restored by the BLM. **Granite** (20 m S on US 10A to Philipsburg, then E) is another ghost silver town.

FORT BENTON: Capt. Clark camped here in 1805 before his rendezvous with Lewis, and later the American Fur Co. built a trading post and block-house (the ruins are on the riverfront near Main St.). When the first steam-boat out of St. Louis came up the Missouri in 1859, Ft. Benton boomed as a supply center. In 1868, a freight trail opened N to Canada became famous as the Whoop-Up Trail because of the liquor transported. **Fort Benton Museum** (1800 Front St.) offers historical displays and dioramas; open June-Aug. daily 10-noon, 1-6; also open 1-5 daily in late May and to mid-Sept.; free.

GLACIER NATIONAL PARK: Spectacular scenery, 60 living glaciers, lakes, and plentiful wildlife; much is accessible only by horseback and foot trails. Particularly grand is the 51-m-long **Going-to-the-Sun Road** between St. Mary (on US 89) and West Glacier (US 2) over Logan Pass; Logan Pass is usually closed by snow mid-Oct.-early June. **Visitor Centers** with exhibits are at **St. Mary** (open daily late June-mid-Aug. 8 am-10 pm; late May-late June & mid-Aug.-mid-Oct. 9-6) and **Logan Pass** (late June-mid-Aug. 9-7; also, depending on weather, mid-late June & mid-Aug.-mid-Sept. 9-5). Information by mail from Supt., at West Glacier 59936.

GLASGOW: Fort Peck Dam (20 m SE on SR 24), largest earthfill dam in the U.S., has information center and museum (dinosaur bones and other fossils, wildlife, geology displays); guided tours of powerplant June-early Sept. daily 9:30-5:30; free. **Pioneer Museum** (½ m W on US 2) offers Indian artifacts and pioneer displays; open mid-end May, Mon.-Fri. 1-5; June-Labor Day, Mon.-Sat. 9-9; free.

GREAT FALLS: Charles M. Russell Museum & Original Studio (1201 4th Ave. N), home of the renowned cowboy artist from 1900 until his death in 1926; log studio with painting equipment; Indian and cowboy artifacts; films and lectures; open mid-May-mid-Sept., Mon.-Sat. 10-5, Sun. 1-5; rest of yr, Tues.-Sat. 10-5, Sun. 1-5; closed Jan. 1-6, Thnks, Dec. 25; sm adm.

HAMILTON: St. Mary's Mission (20 m N on US 93 in Stevensville), oldest mission in the Pacific NW; log church; 19th-C pharmacy; pioneer relics; open daily 8-8; donation. **The Rocky Mountain Laboratory of the U.S. Public Health Service** (S 4th St.), research center for infectious diseases, is open only to professional visitors (Mon.-Fri. 8-4:30; closed hols; free), but exhibits on the Laboratory's work are offered to the public in Ricketts Memorial Museum (1 m NW off US 93), open mid-June-mid-Aug., Mon.-Sat. 10-4; free.

HAVRE: H. Earl Clack Memorial Museum (on US 2 in Hill County Fairgrounds) offers exhibits on Indians of the area; importance of the buffalo; archaeological and geological displays; frontier life; open Memorial Day-Labor Day, daily 9 am-10 pm; free.

Fort Assiniboine (6 m SW on US 87), with some of the original buildings, was built in 1878 for Indians but later used as an agricultural experiment station.

Chief Joseph Battleground State Monument (21 m E to Chinook via US 2, then 16 m S) is site of the final battle and surrender of Chief Joseph and the Nez Perce in 1877, after a journey of nearly 2000 m and only 30 m from their destination. Here Chief Joseph delivered his moving speech, "From where the sun now stands, I will fight no more forever," before the promise to allow him to return to his homeland was betrayed.

Landusky (47 m via US 2 to Harlem, then about 35 m S off SR 376) was a boom gold camp in the 1890s named for Pike Landusky, buried in the town cemetery; he was shot by Kid Curry.

HELENA: Capital of Montana since 1875, Helena was established in 1864 when a party of discouraged prospectors decided to explore a gulch (now Main St.) they dubbed Last Chance Gulch; when they struck gold, the town boomed and produced more than $20 million in gold, silver, and lead. **State Capitol** (6th Ave. between Montana and Roberts), a neoclassic structure with a copper dome; commemorative paintings and statues; Charles M. Russell murals; open Memorial Day-Labor Day, daily 9-5:30; rest of yr, Mon.-Fri. 9-5:30; closed hols; free. **Montana Historical Museum & C. M. Russell Gallery** (225 N Roberts St., across from Capitol) traces the history of Montana through dioramas; re-created 1880s street scene; antique autos; good collection of Russell work; excellent historical library; open Mon.-Fri. 8-5 (8-8 in summer), Sat., Sun. & hols noon-5; closed Jan. 1, Thnks, Dec. 25; free. From here a trackless train, **Last Chance Tour Train**, runs several times daily in summer to major points of interest; reasonable fare.

Governor's Old Mansion (304 N Ewing St.), designed by Cass Gilbert, was executive mansion 1913-59; ornate detailing; furnishings of the 1800s; open in summer, Tues.-Sun. 9-4; rest of yr, tours available through Chamber of Commerce (201 E Lyndale); adm.

Reeder's Alley, brick row buildings constructed in the 1860s by a stonemason from Pittsburgh, Louis Reeder, as homes for miners, later housed muleskinners and Chinese laundrymen; now restored as artists' studios. **Pioneer Cabin** (208 S Park Ave.), constructed of hand-hewn logs by 2 gold miners 1864-9; authentic furnishings; open June-Aug., Mon.-Fri. 11-4:30, 6-7:30; Apr.-May & Sept., Mon.-Fri. 1-4; Oct.-Mar. by appointment (caretaker is next door); donation. **St. Helena Cathedral** (551 N Warren at Lawrence), replica of Vienna's Votive Church; statues in exterior niches; stained-glass windows made in Munich; tape tours available; open daily 6-6; free.

Kluge House, a rare example of Fachwerkbau architecture found in Prussia in 17th-19th-C; **Benton Ave.** Cemetery with graves dating from gold rush days; and the display of nuggets and other gold in the **Northwestern Bank** (360 N Last Chance Gulch; open banking hrs; free) are other attractions in town. Nearby ghost towns are **Marysville** (7 m N via I-15, then W off SR 279), where $50,000,000 in gold was produced; **Elkhorn** (29 m S on US 91 to Boulder, then S on SR 281 about 4 m, then N), a silver town; others, some hard to reach without 4-wheel-drive, most poorly preserved, are marked on the Montana State Highway Commission map. **Canyon Ferry Arms Museum** (10 m E on US 12, then 9 m N on SR 284 to Canyon Ferry State Recreation Area), with Indian and military artifacts, is open May-mid-Oct. daily 9-9; free.

KALISPELL: Fort Kalispell (3 m E on US 2), replica of frontier town with Indian village, art gallery, melodramas in the opera house, rides; open mid-Apr.-mid Oct. daily 7 am-11 pm; adm. **Hockaday Art Center** (3rd St. & 2nd Ave. E) offers traveling exhibits; open Mon.-Sat. noon-5; closed hols; free. **Village Square Art Center** (20 m SE on SR 35 at Bigfork) has historical, art, and craft exhibits; also tourist information; open mid-May-mid-Sept. daily 10-8:30; free. **University of Montana Biological Station** (14 m S of Bigfork on SR 35) offers a museum open late June-mid-Aug., Mon.-Sat. 8-5; closed July 4; free. **Hungry Horse Dam** (22 m NE on US 2) offers displays, booklets for self-guiding tours; open mid-May-late Sept. daily 9 am-8 pm; free.

LEWIS & CLARK TRAIL: The Lewis & Clark Expedition traveled about 1940 m in Montana. The route has been designated with historic markers and is outlined on a map available from state tourist authorities or the Montana Highway Commission (Helena 59601).

LEWISTOWN: Ghost towns that boomed in the 1800s gold-rush era are: **Maiden** (10 m N on US 191, then 6 m E); **Kendall** (16 m N on US 191, then 6 m W); **Gilt Edge** (14 m E on US 87, then 6 m N). Near the latter are the ruins of Fort Maginnis, established during the same period.

LIVINGSTON: Park County Museum, with local historical artifacts, is open mid-May-mid-Sept., Mon.-Fri. 2-4, 7-9; Sat. 2-4; free. **Danforth Gallery** exhibits local arts and crafts; open Tues.-Sat. 10-5:30, Sun. 1-5:30; closed hols; free. **Chico** and **Yellowstone City** are ghost towns in Emigrant Gulch (37 m S off US 89), where there was a brief gold boom in the 1860s.

MILES CITY: Range Riders Museum (W on US 10, 12) is crammed with memorabilia on westward expansion and Montana ranching; open June-Aug. daily 8-8, Apr.-May & Sept.-Oct. 8-6; sm adm.

MISSOULA: County Courthouse (200 W Broadway) contains historical murals by Paxson; open Mon.-Fri. 8-5; closed hols; free. **City-County Library** (101 Adams St.) houses outstanding materials on Montana; open Mon.-Fri. 10-9, Sat. 10-6; closed hols; free. **Gallery of Visual Arts** (Turner Hall on Univ. of Montana campus) offers changing exhibits of local work; open Mon.-Fri. 10-5, Sat. & Sun. 2-5; free.

Aerial Fire Depot (7 m W on US 10, I-90) conducts research on forest fires and trains smokejumpers; exhibits at Visitor Center; smokejumpers offer guided tours of their parachute loft and hq; open July 5-Labor Day, daily 8-5; June 15-July 3, Mon.-Fri. 8-5; rest of yr by appointment (phone 549-6511); closed July 4; free.

St. Ignatius Mission (39 m N on US 93 at St. Ignatius) was established by Jesuits in 1854 to serve Flathead and Salish tribes; exceptional frescos by an Italian-born brother who had had no formal artistic training; historical artifacts; open daily. **St. Mary's Mission** (20 m S via US 93 in Stevensville), established by Jesuits in 1841, is of logs; adjacent log cabin served as the state's first pharmacy and hospital; historical artifacts on display; open daily.

RED LODGE: Big Sky Historical Museum (S of town on US 212) contains Indian and pioneer relics, guns; open June-Sept. 15, daily 8 am-9 pm; adm.

SIDNEY: J. K. Ralston Museum & Art Center (221 5th St. SW), with a scale model of Fort Union (see ND), offers Ralston paintings, historical exhibits; library; open June-Aug., Tues.-Sun. 1-8:30; Sept.-May, Tues.-Fri. & Sun. 1-5; closed Thnks, Dec. 25; free.

VIRGINIA CITY: Montana's second biggest gold strike was made here in Alder Gulch in 1863; within a year, some 35,000 people had rushed in, establishing Virginia City and Nevada City. Virginia City was declared capital of the territory in 1865, but by 1875 the boom was over and the capital was moved to Helena. Today, Virginia and Nevada cities have been restored, with false-front buildings, gold panning, other attractions. In Virginia City, the **Thompson Hickman Memorial Museum** (Wallace St.), with relics of the gold days, and the **Virginia City-Madison County Historical Museum** (Wallace St.), with exhibits on area history, are open May-Sept., daily 8-6; free. Restored buildings include: offices of the state's first newspaper, the Montana *Post*; Wells Fargo Express office; Damours Tonsorial Parlor, where 5 men were hanged at once; Gilbert Brewery; Virginia City Opera House, where old-time melodramas are still given in summer; Rank's Drug Store Museum, open all year, with museum section open spring-fall; saloons; and shops.

Nevada City (1½ m W on SR 287) has been reconstructed on its original site with 1864-1900 buildings brought from other parts of the state;

homes, shops, and offices; exhibits include a railroad museum in the Nevada City Depot and nickelodeons in the music hall.

Vigilante Trail, between Virginia City and Bannack (see Dillon), has been designated with historic markers. During the heyday of Virginia City, road agents committed countless robberies and 190 murders within one 7-month period, and vigilantes organized to hunt them down; desperado headquarters was at Robbers' Roost (15 m W on SR 287), where there was a stage station; leader of the road agents turned out to be the sheriff, Henry Plummer, who was hanged on his own scaffold with some of his gang.

WHITE SULPHUR SPRINGS: The Castle (on US 12, 89), a hilltop, chateau-style mansion built 1892 by a wealthy rancher, is furnished to show 1890s ostentation in Montana; open June-mid-Sept. daily 9-9; late May & mid-Sept.-Oct. daily 9-5:30; or by appointment; sm adm. **Castle Ghost Town** (6 m E on US 12, then 15 m S on Forest Rd.) was a silver camp where Calamity Jane once lived.

WOLF POINT: Wolf Point Historical Society Museum (220 S 2nd Ave.), with exhibits on Indians and ranching, is open mid-May-mid-Sept., Mon.-Fri. 10-6; closed hols; free. **Daniels County Museum & Pioneer Town** (7 m E via US 2, then 48 m N in Scobey) preserves more than 30 buildings from Scobey's pioneer days, including a homestead shack, church, school, and stores; antique vehicles and farm equipment; open mid-May-mid-Sept., daily; adm. **Poplar Museum** (about 21 m E on US 2 in Poplar) in a former jail, displays a Missouri River ferry, Sioux and Assiniboine artifacts, arts and crafts; open June-Aug. daily; sm adm.

NEBRASKA

BROWNVILLE: Founded in 1854 on the Missouri River, where goods from steamboats were transferred to wagons going west, this was an important trading center. Steamboat rides and many special events in summer; among preserved steamboat-era buildings are: **Brownville Museum** (pioneer clothing, furnishings, tools, art work) and **Carson House** (showplace home of a financier, original furnishings), open June-Aug., Tues.-Sun. 1-5; May & Sept.-Oct., Sun. 1-5; sm adm. **Muir House** (2nd & Atlanta Sts.), Italianate mansion built 1868-72; Victorian furnishings, dolls, clothing, arts and crafts, vehicles; open June-Oct. daily 10-5; sm adm.

CHADRON: Museum of the Fur Trade (3½ m E on US 20) traces the history of the American fur trade from 1625-1900; Indian artifacts; firearms; restored French trader's post; open June-Labor Day daily 8-6; sm adm. **Sheridan County Historical Society** (33 m E via US 20 at 408 E 2nd St. in Rushville) is open May-Aug., 9-4; free.

CHIMNEY ROCK NATIONAL HISTORIC SITE (16 m W of Bridgeport off US 26, SR 92): This natural landmark on the Oregon Trail, signaling that the difficult mountain passage was ahead, was an emigrant campground; many travelers carved their names on it; can be seen from parking area on SR 92; information trailer open in summer.

CRAWFORD: Fort Robinson State Park & Museum (4 m W on US 20) preserves the 1874 fort guardhouse (where Crazy Horse was killed after his surrender in 1877) and workshops; Indian and military displays; museum open Apr.-Nov. 15, daily 8-5 (longer hrs in summer) or by appointment; free. **Crazy Horse Museum** (Crawford City Park) contains pioneer and Indian relics; open Sat. & Sun. in summer; free.

DALTON: Mud Springs Station, former Pony Express and stage station, has historical exhibits; open June-Labor Day, Mon.-Fri. 9-5, Sun. 1-6; free.

FREMONT: Louis E. May Historical Museum (1643 N Nye Ave.), 25-room home built 1874; period rooms; open early Mar.-late Dec., Wed., Sat., Sun. 1:30-4:30; free.

GRAND ISLAND: Stuhr Museum of the Prairie Pioneer (S at jct US 34, 281), on an island in a manmade lake, was designed by Edward Durell Stone; exhibits depict pioneer life in Nebraska; re-created shops. More than 60 buildings, including homes, church, post office, and railroad station, have been moved here and furnished to depict 19th-C rural life; farm machinery and antique car exhibits; closed in winter. Open Memorial Day-Labor Day, Mon.-Sat. 9-7, Sun. 1-7; rest of yr, Mon.-Sat. 9-5, Sun. 1-5; closed Jan. 1, Thnks, Dec. 25; adm.

    Fort Hartsuff State Historical Park (70 m N of Grand Island, on SR 11, 2½ m E of Elyria) preserves guardhouse, officers quarters, other buildings of fort established 1874 to protect settlers from the Sioux; pioneer and military displays.

HASTINGS: Hastings Museum (1330 N Burlington Ave. on US 34, 281 at 14th St.), known as House of Yesterday, offers displays on the natural history of Nebraska; Indian and pioneer weapons, household articles, clothing, tools; sod home; country store; coin collection (open daily in summer, Sun. only in winter); planetarium; open June-Aug., Mon.-Sat. 8-8, Sun. 1-5; rest of yr, Mon.-Sat. 8-5, Sun. & hols 1-5; closed Jan. 1, Thnks, Dec. 25; sm adm.

Red Cloud Chamber of Commerce (38 m S on US 281) offers tour maps of town and surrounding Webster County, including places associated with Willa Cather; maps can also be obtained at **Webster County Historical Museum** (6 blocks W of jct 281, 136), open Wed. & Sun. 1-4 in summer; sm adm. **Willa Cather Pioneer Memorial & Museum** (Webster St.) houses exhibits and papers of Willa Cather; pioneer items; local art works; open May-Sept. daily 1-5 or by appointment; free; for a slight fee they will open Cather's childhood home (3rd & Cedar Aves.), described in *The Song of the Lark.*

HOMESTEAD NATIONAL MONUMENT (off SR 4, 4 m NW of Beatrice): Daniel Freeman, who settled here, was one of the first to file under the Homestead Act, signed by Lincoln in 1862; **Visitor Center** displays pioneer farm and household items; 1½-m self-guiding trail to homesteader's cabin and other structures; open daily 8-5 (8-7 in summer); closed Jan. 1, Thnks, Dec. 25; free.

KEARNEY: Fort Kearney Museum (311 S Central) offers an eclectic collection from around the world; fossils, archaeological artifacts, antique instruments, guns, armor; also glass-bottom boatrides on lake; open June-Labor Day daily 9-9; adm. **Fort Kearney State Historical Park** (8 m SE via SR 10) was established to protect emigration on the Oregon Trail; restored stockade and workshops; interpretive displays; open daily; free.

Harold Warp Pioneer Village (20 m SE via SR 44, US 6, 34): displays a large collection of Americana in a museum building and 25 furnished homes, shops, and other buildings; agricultural and transportation exhibits; open daily 8-sundown; adm. **Phelps County Historical Society Museum** (29 m SW via SR 44, US 6, at 512 East Ave. in Holdrege): Indian and pioneer items; period rooms; open Mon.-Wed., Fri.-Sat. 2-5, Thurs. 7-9 pm; closed hols; free. **Dawson County Historical Museum** (37 m W via I-80 at 805 N Taft St. in Lexington): old vehicles, local historical items; open mid-Apr.-Sept., Tues.-Sun. 2-4; free.

LINCOLN: State Capitol (14th & K Sts.), visible for miles, was erected 1922; symbolic murals and mosaics; open Mon.-Sat. 9-4, Sun. 2-4; closed Dec. 25; free. On grounds is 1912 **Lincoln Memorial** designed by Daniel Chester French. **Executive Mansion** (1425 H St.) is open on guided tours Apr.-Oct., Thurs. 10:30-3:30; free.

University of Nebraska (between 10-17th Sts., R-Vine Sts.) offers: **Nebraska State Historical Society Museum** (1500 R St.) traces the state's history from prehistoric times; period rooms; works by local artists; excellent reference library; open Mon.-Sat. 8-5, Sun. 2-5; closed Jan. 1, Thnks, Dec. 25; free. **Sheldon Memorial Art Gallery** (12th & R Sts.), designed by Philip Johnson, specializes in 19th-20th-C American works; sculpture garden; open Tues.-Sat. 10-5, Sun. & hols 2-5; closed Jan. 1, July 4, Thnks, Dec. 25; free. **University of Nebraska State Museum** (14th & U Sts.), with natural history exhibits, including prehistoric animals, is open Mon.-Sat. 8-5, Sun. & hols 1:30-5; closed Jan. 1, Thnks, Dec. 24, 25, 31; free. Transparent Woman is shown in **Mueller Health Galleries**, afternoons, June-mid-Sept. daily, rest of yr on weekends & hols; free. **Mueller Planetarium** shows are offered afternoons, June-mid-Sept. daily, rest of yr on weekends & hols; sm adm.

William Jennings Bryan Home (4900 Sumner St. on grounds of Bryan Memorial Hospital), Fairview, was his home 1902-17; original furnishings; memorabilia; open June-Aug., Thurs.-Sun. 1-4 or by appointment; closed hols; sm adm.

Nebraska Statehood Memorial (1627 H St.), in 1869 mansion, features period furnishings, art works, historical items; open Tues.-Sat. 9-4, Sun. 2-5; closed Jan. 1, Thnks, Dec. 25; free.

Saline County Historical Society (34 m SW via I-80, SR 15 in Dorchester), with occasional old-time craft demonstrations, is open Sun. & hols 1-5; free. **Wilber Czech Museum** (36 m SW via US 77, SR 33, 103 in Wilber) is open Sun. 2-5 or by appointment; closed hols; free. **Anna Palmer Museum,** with Civil War items, period rooms and costumes, and the **York County Courthouse** (48 m W off I-80), with symbolic exterior decoration, are open weekdays.

McCOOK: George W. Norris Home (706 Norris Ave.), home of the former senator 1899 until his death in 1944, has exhibits on his career; open June-Labor Day, Tues.-Sat. 9-6, Sun. 2-6; also weekends 2-6 in spring and fall; free. **Museum of the High Plains** (423 Norris Ave.) is open daily 1:30-4:30; closed Jan. 1, July 4, Thnks, Dec. 24, 25; adm.

NEBRASKA CITY: Arbor Lodge State Historical Park (NW edge of town on US 73, 75): 65-acre, wooded estate; garden designed by Frederick Law Olmsted; restored Greek Revival mansion of former Sec. of Agriculture J. Sterling Morton, originator of Arbor Day; park open daily; mansion open mid-June-mid-Sept., Mon.-Sat. 10-5:30, Sun. 1-5:30; sometimes also open spring & fall afternoons; sm adm. **Wildwood Period House** (1 m W on SR 2 & Steinhart Park Rd.) is an 1869 home restored with mid-Victorian furnishings; open mid-Apr.-mid-Oct., Tues.-Sun. 1-5; sm adm.

NORTH PLATTE: Buffalo Bill Ranch State Historical Park (1 m N on Buffalo Bill Ave.): ranch house and outbuildings where William F. Cody wintered with his Wild West Show; Cody memorabilia; open Memorial

Day-Labor Day, daily 8 am-9 pm; inquire locally for additional hrs. **Pony Express Station** (34 m SE via I-80, on SR 47 in city park in Gothenburg), also a stop on the Overland Stage, contains historical exhibits; open May-Sept. daily 8 am-9 pm; free.

OGALLALA: Front Street (519 E 1st St.), with cowboy and pioneer displays, is open late Apr.-Sept. daily 8-midnight; free; stagecoach rides and musical shows are frequently offered. **Boot Hill Cemetery** (11-12th Sts.) dates from the mid-19th-C.

  Ash Hollow State Historical Park (27½ m NW on US 26), on site of an Oregon Trail stop, offers excavations of a prehistoric cave dwelling believed to date back almost 2000 yrs; cave is enclosed in an interpretive building. Nearby, **Blue Water Battlefield,** where in 1855 Sioux families were roused from sleep, shot and clubbed to death, is being developed with interpretive exhibits.

OMAHA; Joslyn Art Museum (2200 Dodge St.) has very fine painting, sculpture, and decorative arts from many periods, including works by European masters; Catlin, Bodmer, and other painters of the early West; regional pioneer clothing, household items; Nebraska Indian arts; open Tues.-Sat. 10-5, Sun. 1-5; closed hols; sm adm. **Union Pacific Historical Museum** (in hq bldg at 1416 Dodge St. & 15th St.): displays on the railroad's history; Lincoln funeral car replica; open Mon.-Fri. 9-5, Sat. 9-1; closed hols; free. **Mormon Cemetery** (Northridge Dr. & State St.) contains the graves of hundreds of Mormons who died here in the winter of 1846-7.

  Boys Town (10 m W on Dedge St.), founded for homeless boys by Father Flanagan in 1917, welcomes visitors Mon.-Sat. 8-4, Sun. 9-5; closed Good Friday, Dec. 25; free.

  Aerospace Museum (12 m S on US 73 to 2510 Clay St., Bellevue) exhibits aircraft and missiles; open daily 8-5; closed Jan. 1, Easter, Dec. 25; adm. Also in Bellevue, several mid-19th-C buildings have been preserved; **Sarpy County Historical Society** (1805 Hancock St.) has furnished an 1830s cabin as a museum (open June-Aug., daily 10-5; sm adm).

  Fort Atkinson (N via US 73 to Ft. Calhoun, then 1 m E), established after the War of 1812 on a site chosen by Lewis and Clark, is being restored; interpretive center open daily Memorial Day-Labor Day; site open daily all yr; free. **Washington County Historical Museum** (on US 73 in Ft. Calhoun) is open spring-fall, Wed., Sat., Sun. 1:30-4:30; closed hols; free.

SCOTTSBLUFF: Scotts Bluff National Monument (3 m S on SR 71 to Gering, then 3 m W on SR 92): 800-ft promontory that became a landmark for pioneers; Overland Mail, Pony Express, and other stations were built near here; **Oregon Trail Museum** (open daily 8:30-4:30, with longer hrs in summer; closed Dec. 25) traces the history of westward migration; sm adm or GEP. **North Platte Valley Museum** (across Platte River at 1349 10th St. in Gering) consists of historic displays in sod and log house; open June-Aug., Mon.-Sat. 9-5, Sun. 1-5; Sept.-May, Tues. & Thurs. 9-5; closed hols; sm adm.

    Agate Fossil Beds National Monument (9 m NW on US 26 to Mitchell, then 30 m N on SR 29): Miocene fossil mammal bones exposed in situ; **Visitor Center** with exhibits open Memorial Day-Labor Day daily 8:30-4:30; rest of yr on weekends or by contacting ranger; closed hols in winter; free.

    Pioneer Trails Museum (37 m E via US 26 to 205 Railroad Ave. in Bridgeport) is open late May-early Sept., 8-8; free.

VALENTINE: Sawyer's Sandhills Museum (on US 20), with Indian and pioneer displays and antique autos, is open June-mid-Sept. daily 9-7; sm adm.

NEVADA

AUSTIN: A silver boom town of the 1860s that rivaled Virginia City; colorful history includes the Sazarac Lying Club (where everyone told lies); Gridley Sack of Flour Auctions (a man named Gridley auctioned the same sack of flour again and again to raise $275,000 for Civil War wounded); camel pack trains (that carried supplies and ore to and from outlying mining communities); the Reese River Navigation Co. swindle (shares were sold to Easterners who had no idea the river was hardly more than a creek); and the Pony Express (stations are marked along US 50—13 m NW at Mt. Airy, 30 m NW at New Pass, 49 m NW at Cold Springs; 5 m E at Jacobsville). Historic district includes the no-frills Lander County Courthouse, 3 brick churches, *Reese River Reveille* (published continuously since 1863), and Stokes Castle (stone building with a roof garden on a hill to the SW; a landmark for miles).

    Hickson Petroglyph Recreation Site (24 m E on US 50) has Indian rock art probably made 1000 BC-AD 1500; open Apr.-Oct. daily; free.

    Berlin-Ichthyosaur State Park (8 m SW via US 50, SR 2, then 58 m S on SR 21, then 4 m E), in Toiyabe National Forest, contains the remains of amphibious reptiles 2-60-ft long, similar to today's porpoises in body form and habits; **Fossil Shelter** provides literature; ranger talks, weather permitting, daily in summer and Thurs.-Mon. rest of yr; interpretive signs have also been placed by ruins and features in **Union Canyon.** Also here is **Berlin,** an 1897 mining town: population 300, general store, 3 saloons, school, stage station, boarding houses; maintained in a state of arrested decay; interpretive signs; cemetery.

Other ghost towns and mining camps can be found along SR 21 NE of town: **Mineral Hill** (50 m, then E), **Cortez** (58 m, then E), **Tenabo** (70 m, then W).

CARSON CITY: Started in 1858 as a trading post and later named for Kit Carson, Carson City thrived as a crossroads on the Pony Express, Overland Covered Wagon, and other trails during the silver boom; it's been state capital since 1864. **Chamber of Commerce Information Bureau** (1191 S Carson St.), in a Virginia & Truckee Railroad caboose, offers brochures for self-guiding city tours and nearby ghost towns. Most of the residences built during mining boom days are privately owned and open only during fall historic homes tours; most are between N Minnesota & Curry Sts., W Robinson & King Sts., and on Victorian Square (2nd & Curry): **Orion Clemens home** (NW corner Division & Spear),where Mark Twain lived for a time with his brother; **Bliss Mansion** (710 W Robinson), where window catches and other metal fixtures are made of Comstock silver; the home at **204 N Minnesota** created a scandal because it was built by a judge who used prison labor and sandstone from the prison quarry; **Curry House** (406 N Nevada) built by the operator of the prison quarry; the lovely home at **204 W Spear** with circular porch and curved windows. The Nevada Landmarks Society has restored the 1859 **J. D. Roberts Home** (in a city wayside park at 1217 N Carson). **Governor's Mansion** (Mountain & Robinson Sts.), a 1909 sandstone structure; fine stairway and antique furnishings; tours in summer, occasionally at other times.

State Capitol (N Carson St.) has a silver dome supported by hand-hewn rafters; portraits; open Mon.-Fri. 8-5; Sat., Sun., hols, lobby only is open 8-5; tours available in summer; free. Opposite are: **Supreme Court & State Library Bldg.** housing newspapers, books, and documents about the state; open Mon.-Fri. 8-5; closed hols; free. **Nevada State Museum,** in a former U.S. Mint, has wonderful displays of coins, Western weapons, local wildlife, Indian and pioneer history; underground mine tour is a highlight; open daily 8:30-4:30; closed Jan. 1, Thnks, Dec. 25; free.

Warren Engine Co. Museum (111 N Curry St.), above the city's first fire company, organized 1863 and still functioning, offers Currier & Ives firefighting prints and historical relics; open daily 1-4; free.

Lone Mountain Cemetery (N edge of town) has pioneer graves, including that of colorful stagecoach driver Henry James (Hank) Monk.

Bowers Mansion (10 m N on US 395), an 1864 mansion built by one of the first Comstock Lode millionaires, has ornate statuary, furnishings; but the family went broke and Mrs. Bowers ended up telling fortunes for a living; open mid-May-Oct. daily 11-12:30, 1:30-4:30; sm adm.

Virginia City National Historic Landmark (8 m E on US 50, then 8 m N on SR 17): The Queen of the Comstock Lode, with more than 30,000 people, was one of the wealthiest cities in the nation. Gold was discovered in the 1840s, but after the big strike of 1859 more than a billion dollars worth of gold and silver from the Comstock helped finance the Civil War; build San Francisco; create Hearst, MacKay, and other fortunes; and supply imported delicacies and culture to the city itself. (Mark Twain's *Roughing It* provides a good picture of these days; he wrote for the *Territorial Enterprise* here.) Among the mansions of the silver kings, one of the best is the spare-no-expense Castle (70 South B St.) of Norman design, with a black-walnut hanging staircase from Germany, handcut Bohemian rock-crystal chandeliers, Italian marble fireplaces, European furnishings. Mansions, St. Mary's in the Mountains Church (now an art gallery), Fourth Ward School, and other restored buildings are open daily during Easter Week and Memorial Day-Oct.; Piper's Opera House (where Jenny Lind sang) and the saloons are open daily all yr; Ophir Open Pit and Old Chollar Mine offer tours; maps and schedules of hours may be obtained at the Visitors Bureau (C St.), which shows a film on the city's history. Special events (such as a camel race commemorating the use of camels to carry salt to the mines) are frequently held.

Dayton (4 m E on US 50), a ghost town, started as a rough trading post in 1850 and became the 3rd largest city in the state, center of Gold Canyon fever; among many remaining buildings—1862 saloon and billiard parlor, Odeon Hall, 1865 school. Other ghost towns are the 1862 Washoe City (15 m N on US 395) and Gold Hill, Silver City, and Como (all S of Virginia City on SR 17).

Mormon Station Historic State Monument (11 m S on US 395, then 4 m W at Genoa) commemorates the oldest permanent white settlement in Nevada. A trading post was established here in 1849 to service emigrants on the California trail; although 60-70 Mormon families were sent to establish a colony in 1856, they were recalled in 1857 to defend Salt Lake City against the U.S. Army. The reconstructed trading post is a museum with historic artifacts, including a cradle that Snowshoe Thomson carved for his son. Area open daily all yr 9-5; museum open May-Sept. daily 9-7.

ELKO: Northeastern Nevada Museum (1515 Idaho St.) covers ghost town relics; Pony Express station; Elko's development on the most popular emigrant trail; open Mon.-Sat. 9-5, Sun. 1-5; closed Jan. 1, Thnks, Dec. 25; free.

Tuscarora (28 m N on SR 51, 18 m N on SR 11, then 8 m W on un-numbered road) ghost town began silver production in 1871; some 3-4,000 Chinese (brought in to build the Central Pacific Railroad and then laid off) moved in, building 2 Joss Houses and an irrigation system; mine, smelter, and cabin remains; mineral and historical displays in small museum (sm adm); open daily. **Midas** (40 m W along same road) and **Metropolis** (46 m E of Elko on I-80, then 4 m N) are other ghost towns.

ELY: Ward Charcoal Ovens Historic State Monument (5 m SE on US 6, 50, 93, then 10 m S) contains 6 handsome stone ovens used to make charcoal during the 1870 mining boom; remains of the old mining camp of Ward are nearby; open daily; free. **Kennecott Open-Pit Mine** (6 m W off US 50 at Ruth) has observation area open daily in daylight; free. **White Pine Public Museum** (2000 Aultman St.) displays minerals, early vehicles and relics, Pony Express mementos; open daily 8-5; closed hols; free. You can follow the route of the Pony Express on a road from the Utah border paralleling US 50, past magnificent scenery and ghost town remains, through Baker, Ely, and Eureka.

Ghost towns: Osceola (35 m E off US 6, 50). **Cherry Creek** (48 m N on US 93, then 9 m W on SR 35). **Hamilton** (35 m W on US 50, then 10 m S). **Eureka** (78 m W on US 50) boomed in the 1870s with 9000 people, 2 newspapers, and an opera house, and produced so much lead it affected the world market; it is so well preserved it resembles a movie set; many ghost camps are in the vicinity, and gold is still mined at Newmont to the N.

FALLON: Churchill County Museum (S Main St.) offers local relics, in-cluding those of the Pony Express that passed S of here (stations were in the Singing Sand Mountain area at Sand Springs, 10 m E of Salt Wells on US 50, and at Carson Sink, 25 m SE off US 95); open Mon.-Fri. 9-5; Sat., Sun., hols noon-5; free.

HAWTHORNE: Ghost towns here are: **Aurora** (35 m SW off SR 31) boomed in 1861 with 10,000 population; Mark Twain was among the hope-ful gold seekers; the town is on the California state line, and residents voted in both states and seated legislators in both states. **Candelaria** (42 m E on US 95, then 7 m SW on SR 10) was developed by Mexicans in 1863; nearby **Marietta**, established 1867, produced salt (taken out by camel) and borax, and so avoided the ups and downs of metal camps. **Rawhide** (42 m NE) boom was contrived by promoters to stimulate sales of mining stock; they brought in sensational journalist Eleanor Glynn to provide publicity, but the boom was short-lived.

LAKE MEAD NATIONAL RECREATION AREA (4 m E of Boulder City on US 93): **Boulder Beach Visitor Center** (provides information on this 2-million-acre area; open mid-Apr.-Sept., Mon.-Thurs. 8-5, Fri.-Sun. 7 am-8 pm; rest of yr, Mon.-Thurs. 8-5, Fri.-Sun. 7-6 (or write Supt., Box 127, Boulder City 89005). **Hoover Dam** offers tours of the dam and powerhouse, exhibits; Memorial Day-Labor Day, daily 7:30-7:15; rest of yr, daily 8:30-4:15; sm adm. (A film on the dam is shown at the Visitors Bureau of Boulder City, daily 8-5:15; free.)

LAS VEGAS: This city grew out of a rest stop at springs on the Old Spanish Trail that connected Santa Fe with the missions of California. In 1885 Mormons arrived but were unable to get along with the Indians and soon closed their mission; they found silver but mistook it for lead, so the city didn't boom until the arrival of the Salt Lake Railroad (later the Union Pacific) in 1905; within days a mammoth tent city—complete with hotel, post office, saloon and gambling house, all in tents—arose. **Chamber of Commerce** (2301 E Sahara Ave.) provides information on the city and nearby attractions. Biggest attraction is **The Strip** (Las Vegas Blvd. S of town), with gambling casinos, shows, and flamboyant hotels. A Behind-the-Scenes Tour of gambling operations, plus film, is offered by the **Mint Hotel** (100 Fremont St.); daily; free; adults (over 21) only.

   University of Nevada at Las Vegas (2 m E of Strip at 4505 Maryland Pkwy) offers: **Mineral Collection** (room 119, Chemistry Bldg.), with more than 1000 local specimens; open Mon.-Fri. 8-5; closed hols; free. **Museum of Natural History,** with prehistoric artifacts; Indian, pioneer, and mining relics; local fauna; open Mon.-Fri. 8-5, Sat. 10-5, Sun. 1-5; closed Dec. 25; free.

   Southern Nevada Museum (13 m SE on US 95 to 240 Water St. in Henderson) has Indian artifacts; geologic displays; mining, gambling, and other historical exhibits; open Mon.-Sat. 9-noon, 1-5, Sun. 1-5; closed hols; sm adm.

   Valley of Fire State Park (31 m NE on I-15, then 2 m SE on SR 40), named for the brilliant red and pink sandstone formations; **Visitor Center** with exhibits on geology, ecology, prehistory, history of the area; trails to Indian petroglyphs; open daily (museum 9-5); free. **Red Rock Recreation Area** (17 m W via Charleston Blvd.) has interpretive signs at ancient pueblo-like structures and petroglyphs; open daily; free.

LOVELOCK: Scene of many battles between Indians and pioneers, Lovelock was where wagon trains rested before the rigors of the 40-m Black Rock Desert; wagon ruts can be seen for miles along the highway. **Ghost camps** include: **Vernon** and **Seven Troughs** (about 30 m NW on SR 48); **Rabbit Hole** (NW of Seven Troughs); **Scossa** (E of Rabbit Hole), scene of Nevada's last gold rush in 1931. **Rochester** (15 m NE on US 40, I-80 to Oreana, then 7 m E), with nearby **American Canyon** and **Unionville,**

in the Buena Vista Valley; Mark Twain was here briefly; remnants of a Chinese settlement, other mining camps throughout this area.

OVERTON: Lost City Museum of Archaeology, with fossil, mineral, Basketmaker, and Pueblo displays, is highlighted by local finds from a people who settled for some 30 m along the Muddy River at least 1200 yrs ago; many of the sites were flooded by Hoover Dam and reconstructions of their pueblo-like dwellings are exhibited here; open daily 9-5; closed Jan. 1, Thnks, Dec. 25; free.

PIOCHE: This town grew in Pah-Ute country on the trail blazed by Jedediah Smith in 1826 and later traveled by Mormons, prospectors, and emigrants. By the 1870s, with 7000 people, Pioche was known for violence; more than half the murders in Nevada were said to take place here, citizens went armed, businesses hired guards, and mines hired little armies. Despite gunpowder explosions and fires, many old buildings remain— the most famous is the **Million Dollar Courthouse,** built in exuberant boom days. **Lincoln County Historical Society Museum,** with historic displays, is open Mon.-Sat. 9-5, Sun. 1-5; closed hols; free. **Bristol** and **Monarch mine ruins** (just N, W of US 93), **Bullionville** (W off US 93, just S of town), and other mining camp ruins dot the area.

RENO: Chamber of Commerce Hospitality Center (150 S Virginia St.) offers information on the city, escorted and self-guiding tours to Mother Lode Country (tapes available), other nearby attractions.
    University of Nevada at Reno (9th & N Virginia Sts.): **Fleischmann Atmospherium-Planetarium** provides superb programs on astronomy and space; shows June-Sept. daily, Oct.-May, Tues.-Sun.; adm. **Nevada Historical Society Museum** owns a huge collection of prehistoric and recent Indian artifacts; also pioneer relics, musical instruments, early portraits; library with large map and picture collections; open Mon.-Sat. 8-5; closed hols; free. **MacKay School of Mines Museum** offers mineral specimens, displays on mining; open Mon.-Fri. 8-5; closed July 4, Labor Day, Thnks, Dec. 25; free. **Church Fine Arts Bldg.** has shows of regional art (Mon.-Fri. 9-5; free) and **Library** has a good Nevada collection (inquire for hrs).
    Nevada Art Gallery (643 Ralston St.) has regional works; open Tues.-Sun. 1-4; closed hols & Aug.; free. **Harrah's Automobile Collection** (3½ m E on 2nd St.) offers more than 1000 antique and classic cars; restoration shops; also antique planes, boats, motorcycles; Pony Express display; open June-Sept. daily 9 am-10 pm; Oct.-May daily 9-6; adm.

TONOPAH: Prospectors searched the canyons and mountains here for gold in the 1860-80s, but the boom started in 1900 after a mule kicked loose a silver find; a year later the town had 32 saloons, several newspapers, churches, gambling halls; strikes at Goldfield, Bullfrog, and Rhyolite also stimulated the economy. Many boom-era buildings are still in use today (such as the Mizpah Hotel, 100 Main St.). **Nearby ghost towns** are: **Belmont** (5 m E on US 6, 13 m N on SR 8A, then 25 m N on SR 82), noted for English-Irish feuds, has courthouse, saloon, other buildings; **Manhattan** (24 m N on SR 8A, then 7 m E); **Round Mountain** (35 m N on SR 8A, then 3 m E); **Smoky Valley** (49 m N on SR 8A); **Silver Peak** (32 m W on US 95, then 21 m S on SR 47); **Goldfield** (26 m SE on US 95), developed by Bernard Baruch among others, was a fabulous gold and silver town with many satellite camps, and has many surviving buildings; **Goldpoint** (41 m SE on US 95, then 7 m W on US 3) and (19 m W) **Lida**. Even farther S (93 m on US 95) another center developed at **Beatty** in the early 1900s; at **Rhyolite** (4 m W of Beatty) an intense 11-yr boom produced banks, stock exchange, opera house, and remains of many buildings and the railroad station still stand; nearby **Bullfrog** (just W) had a similar high-living boom.

WINNEMUCCA: This town grew as a supply center on the emigrant trails; by 1849 wagon trains following the Humboldt River formed an unbroken line from horizon to horizon; nearby canyon walls bear the names and dates of people who passed; prospectors also came, and the area is full of mining camp remains and legends of lost treasure; **Paradise Valley** (22 m N on US 95, then 19 m N on SR 8B) is the best preserved ghost town, with an opal mine still operating.

YERINGTON: Capt. Fremont and Kit Carson camped here on their winter trip to find the nonexistent Buenaventura River to the sea, and the town later became a trading post and stage stop famous for its poor (but strong) whiskey. **Fort Churchill Historic State Monument** (25 m N on US 95A, then 1 m W on SR 2B): This post was established to control the Paiutes who objected to white invasion of their lands during the Comstock rush; it was garrisoned 1860-69 and became a Pony Express station. Wovoka, the Indian Messiah who began the Ghost Dance intended to make white men disappear, lived in this area, and when the dance failed to achieve its aims there was even greater bloodshed. Visitor Center; pioneer graves; open all yr; sm adm.

NEW HAMPSHIRE

CLAREMONT: Old Fort No. 4 (10 m S on SR 11), replica of 1744 fort, built to defend settlers against Indians, with barracks, church, Great Hall, homes, other furnished buildings; audiovisual program, military drills, craft exhibits; open mid-June-Labor Day, daily 11-5; mid-May-mid-June & Sept.-Oct., Sat. & Sun. 11-5; adm. **Church on the Hill** (10 m S on SR 11), then 8 m SE to Acworth), attractive 1821-24 building crowns a hill on the common; bell cast by Paul Revere foundry.

Saint-Gaudens National Historic Site (12 m N on SR 12A) was the sculptor's summer residence 1885-97 and permanent home 1900 until his death 1907. His arrival established the Cornish Colony that produced other well-known artists; Saint-Gaudens supposedly chose the site because he was told the area had many "Lincoln-shaped" men he could use as models for his Lincoln statue. His home, "Aspet," Little Studio; many of his works (including copies of the Adams Memorial and "Puritan") plus those of other artists; the Temple, with family graves; open late May-mid-Oct. daily 8:30-5; sm adm.

Clock Museum (10 m E on SR 11 to 43 Park St., Newport) houses sundials, clocks, watches, some ancient and some from the state's early clock industry; coins, fans, other collections; tours hourly, Mon.-Sat. 9-4, Sun. 1-4; adm. **South Congregational Church** (58 S Main St., Newport), built 1823 of Isaac Damon design; especially fine tower.

CONCORD: State House (Main St.), built 1816-19, contains statues, portraits, flags; open Mon.-Fri. 8-4:30; closed hols; free. **New Hampshire Historical Society** (30 Park St.), in a lovely building; changing exhibits of Revolution-era items; period rooms; Concord coach; library; open Mon.-Sat. 9-4:30; closed hols; free.

League of New Hampshire Craftsmen Headquarters (205 N Main St.), with gallery and library, is open Mon.-Fri. 11-5; **Concord Arts & Crafts Center** (36 N Main St.), its exhibit and salesroom, is open Mon.-Thurs. 10-5:30, Fri. 10-8, Sat. 9-5; closed hols; free. Branch shops and showrooms are in: Exeter, Franconia Notch, Hanover, Holderness, Meredith, Nashua, N Conway, Sharon, Wolfeboro.

Pierce Manse (1 m N at 14 Penacook St.), home of Pres. Franklin Pierce 1838-48; original and period furnishings; open mid-June-mid-Oct.,

Tues.-Sun. 10-4; closed hols; adm. **Pierce's grave** is in Old North Cemetery (off N State St.). **Franklin Pierce Homestead** (24 m W on US 202 to Hillsborough, then 5 m W on SR 9, 31), into which the family moved when he was 3 weeks old, has period pieces; open Memorial Day-mid-Oct., Tues.-Sun. 9-5; sm adm.

Center Meeting House (32 m W on SR 103 at jct SR 103A in Newbury) is an 1832 Bulfinch design rebuilt from timbers of an earlier structure. **Shaker Village** (11 m N on SR 3B to Canterbury) is the partially restored 1792 community of the religious sect founded by Ann Lee, an English-woman who arrived in New York in 1774 with 8 Believers (the other New Hampshire colony, Enfield, existed 1793-1918); tours of museum and furnished buildings late-May-mid-Oct., Tues.-Sat. 9-5; adm.

DOVER: Hale House (5 Hale St.) is a Federal-style 1806 mansion; William Hale entertained Lafayette and other famous people of the time here; open daily 10-5; free. **Woodman Institute** (½ m S on SR 16 at 182-192 Central Ave.): collections of colonial furnishings are displayed in 1682 house, 2 later houses; open Tues.-Sun. 2-5; closed Thnks, Dec. 25; free.

EXETER: Established 1638 by religious nonconformists exiled from Massachusetts (including Anne Hutchinson and the Rev. John Wheelwright), Exeter has a radical history and was capital of New Hampshire during the Revolution; 17th-18th-C homes are preserved in the Front St. Historic District: 1798 **Congregational Church** (21 Front St.), open Mon.-Fri. 8-4; 1650 **Gilman Garrison House** (12 Water St.) with period furnishings and 1721 **Cincinnati House** (Governor's Lane), that served as a jail and during the Revolution as the state treasury, open May-Oct., Tues., Thurs. 2-4; sm adm.

HANOVER: Dartmouth College (Main & Wheelock Sts.) offers guided tours from Information Booth (E side of Green) in summer, free. On campus are: **Old Dartmouth Row** (E side of Green), some of the earliest buildings. **Museum** (Wilson Hall) with anthropology, geology, and zoology displays; open academic yr, Mon.-Sat. 9-5, Sun. 2-5, shorter hrs in summer; free. **Hopkins Center for the Arts** (the Green), with changing exhibits; open academic yr, daily 7:30 am-11 pm; summer, daily 8:30-5; free. **Baker Memorial Library,** with more than a million volumes, has frescoes by Orozco; open academic yr, Mon.-Fri. 8-midnight, Sat. 8-5, Sun. 2-midnight; summer, by tour Mon.-Fri. 8-5; free.

Webster Cottage (N Main St.), where Daniel Webster lived while a student at Dartmouth, has Webster memorabilia, Shaker furniture; open June-mid-Oct., Tues., Thurs., Sat., Sun. 3-5; rest of yr, Sat. 2-4; closed Jan. 1, Easter, July 4, Dec. 25; free.

Bulfinch Row (19 m N on SR 10, near jct SR 25A in Orford), row of houses erected in the early 19th-C, show influence of Charles Bulfinch.

KEENE: Colony House Museum (104 West St.), built 1820, houses collections of Historical Soc. of Cheshire County; included is rare local glass, produced here 1814-53, in nearby Stoddard and Mill Village, and at the Temple factory in Sharon (where Hessian glassblowers were employed); open June-Oct. 15, Tues.-Sun. 10-5; adm. **Wyman Tavern** (399 Main St.) was built 1762 by a veteran of the Indian Wars who led 29 Minutemen to Lexington from here on Apr. 22, 1775; open mid-May-mid-Oct., Wed., Sat. 2-4; sm adm. **United Church of Christ** (Central Sq.), erected as a modest meeting house in 1760, was given Victorian embellishments in 1860. **Park Hill Meeting House** (9 m NW on SR 12 in Westmoreland), 1762, has bell cast by Paul Revere foundry; rare 1791 pewter Communion set. **Amos Fortune Forum** (18 m SE on SR 124 in Jaffrey), in an old meeting house, is named for an African-born slave who purchased his freedom, established a tannery, and left $1000 to the Jaffrey school and church when he died at age 91 in 1801; open for summer events, Fri. 8 pm; free. **Cathedral of the Pines** (20 m SE on SR 124, then 2 m S to Rindge), nondenominational shrine to American war dead; bell tower; open May-Oct. daily 9-4 (9-6 in summer); free. **Barrett House** (21 m E on SR 101, then 11 m SE on SR 123 to Main St., New Ipswich), built 1800 and grand for its time, has ballroom, outbuildings; period furnishings, weaving equipment; open June-Oct., Tues.-Sat. 11-5; closed hols; adm.

LACONIA: Schuller Medieval Arms & Armor Museum (S on SR 106), offers 35 suits of armor; 14 huge heraldic plaques; crossbows, helmets, swords, other armament from Europe and Japan; European palace furniture; clocks, saddles, other items; open spring-fall, daily 9-5; adm.

Daniel Webster Birthplace (9 m SW on US 3 to Franklin), home in which Webster was born 1782, has historic displays; open mid-May-mid-Oct., daily 9-6; sm adm. A bust of Webster by Daniel Chester French stands outside Congregational Christian Church (33 S Main St.), which Webster attended.

MANCHESTER: Manchester Historic Association (129 Amherst St.) houses local historic artifacts including cotton from the renowned **Amoskeag Mills** (the brick buildings erected 1838-1915 that along with worker homes still line the E bank of the Merrimack River) and early clocks by artisans such as Isaac Blasel (who settled in nearby Chester 1762); open Tues.-Fri. 9-4, Sat. 10-4; closed hols; free.

Gen. John Stark House (2000 Elm St.) is 1736 home of the hero of battles of Bunker Hill and Bennington; period furnishings; open mid-May-mid-Oct., Wed. & Sun. 1:30-4:30; sm adm. **Currier Gallery of Art** (192 Orange St.) houses excellent European and American paintings; New England decorative arts; open Tues.-Sat. 10-4, Sun. 2-5; closed Jan. 1, July 4, Thnks, Dec. 25; free.

Mystery Hill (14 m SE on I-93, then 4 m NE on SR 111 at N Salem) is a controversial archaeological site with stone structures some people estimate to be 4000 years old; others claim the ruins are from colonial times; open mid-June-mid-Nov. daily 9-dusk; open, weather permitting, some spring weekends; adm.

PORTSMOUTH: Historic Information Center (143 Pleasant St.) is in the Gov. John Langdon Memorial, a splendid Georgian mansion built 1784 by the first President of the U.S. Senate; George Washington, one of many noted guests, considered it the handsomest house in town; very grand for its time, it has scenic wallpaper, exceptional carving, historic exhibits; open mid-May-mid-Oct., Mon.-Sat. 10-5; closed hols. Information is available here on the many 17-19th-C buildings in this historic seafaring town, once capital of the state; combination tickets to buildings are sold here and at other historic homes. The following are open mid-May-mid-Oct., Mon.-Sat. 10-5, Sun. 2-5; adm: **John Paul Jones House** (43 Middle at State St.), a dignified house built 1758 by a sea captain, where Jones boarded while his ship was being outfitted on nearby Badger's Island; rare local china; silver; costumes; furnishings; portraits. **Warner House** (Daniel & Chapel Sts.), a 1716, handsome Georgian home, has murals, fine paintings. **Moffatt-Ladd House** (154 Market St.), another fine Georgian home, has lovely 18th-C furnishings, weaving room, cellar kitchen, secret underground passage to wharves. **Jackson House** (Northwest St., 2 blocks E of Maplewood Ave.), 1664 home of a shipbuilder, is well restored with period furnishings.

Strawberry Banke Restoration (Hancock at Marcy Sts.) of the 1630 settlement that became Portsmouth; 10-acre site contains more than 30 buildings (1695-1865), including: 1695 Sherburne House, built by a seaman, exposed beams and interesting structural details; 1750 Capt. John Clark House of Georgian design; 1762 Chase House, a merchant's home; 1796 Capt. Keyran Wash House, finely crafted; 1811 Gov. Goodwin Mansion of Federal design with Greek Revival modifications; 1758 Old State House; 1766 Pitt Tavern; general store. Architectural and other museum exhibits; demonstrations of boatbuilding, weaving, other crafts; special events. Open May-Oct. daily 9:30-5; adm.

St. John's Episcopal Church (101 Chapel St.), built 1808, has rare Brattle pipe organ, baptismal font said to be part of French booty at Senegal, a 1717 Vinegar Bible (1 of 12 named for a misprint of "vineyard"), other unusual items; open daily 8-5; free. **Thomas Bailey Aldrich House**

(386 Court St.), built 1790 and owned by the author's grandfather, was called Nutter House in Aldrich's *The Story of a Bad Boy* (1870); early Victorian interior; silver; manuscripts; open mid-June-mid-Sept., Mon.-Sat. 10-5; sm adm. **Wentworth-Coolidge Mansion** (foot of Little Harbor Rd.) is a rambling 42-room home reflecting the period 1650-1750; it was the official residence of the stte's first governor; open Memorial Day-mid-Oct. daily 10-5; sm adm. **Wentworth-Gardner House** (140 Mechanic at Gardner Sts.) is one of the finest examples of Georgian architecture in the nation; 3 master carvers worked 1½ years on the interior; 10 fireplaces, some with inlaid Dutch tile; dining room wallpaper is notable; spinning attic; open May-Oct., Tues.-Sun. 1-5; adm.

    Prescott Park (Marcy St.), on the Piscataqua River, offers the 1812 Shaw Warehouse and 1705 Sheafe Warehouse (where John Paul Jones' *Ranger* was outfitted), with large collection of local folk art, wood carvings, maritime relics (open May-Sept. daily; free); also here are a 1766 Liberty Pole and early burying ground.

    Tuck Memorial Museum (10 m S off I-95 at 40 Park Ave., Hampton) contains antiques made in Hampton, other historic relics; open July-Aug. daily 1-4; free.

RUMNEY: Mary Baker Eddy Historic House (Stinston Lake Rd.), home of the founder of Christian Science, is open Memorial Day-Oct., Tues.-Sat. 10-5, Sun. 2-5; sm adm. Information available on visiting Mrs. Eddy's home in North Groton and her birthplace in Bow Junction.

WHITE MOUNTAINS NATIONAL FOREST, a popular 700,000-acre recreation area, is highlighted by the scenic, 34-m Kancamagus Highway (between Lincoln & Conway). **Passaconaway Information Center** (12 m W of Conway), in house built by a settler in the early 1800s, offers exhibits and information; open late May-mid-Oct. daily 9-5. Other features are: historic exhibit at **Dolly Copp** (5 m S of Gorham on SR 16); **Stone Iron Furnace** (Franconia Village, on SR 18, 116, S of jct SR 117) produced pig iron and the famous Franconia stoves, state's only surviving 19th-C ironworks; **Crawford Notch State Park** (12 m N of Bartlett on US 302), with the Willey house that survived 1826 avalanche in which family and hired hands died attempting to escape (open late-May-mid-Oct. daily 9-5).

WOLFEBORO: Clark House (S Main St.), a 1778 homestead with adjacent 1805 school house; period rooms, local historical collections; open early June-Aug., Mon.-Sat. 1-5; sm adm. **Libby Museum** (4 m NW on N Main St.), Indian and natural history displays; open late June-Labor Day, Tues.-Sun. 10-5; closed hols; sm adm.

NEW JERSEY

ALLAIRE STATE PARK (SE of Farmingdale via SR 524): **Howell Works,** a bog-ore furnace established in 1822, employed some 500 workers; dwellings, workshops, church, bakery, and other buildings have been restored; narrow-gauge steam train rides (adm); buildings open Apr.-Oct. daily 10-5, Nov.-Mar. weekends 10-5; sm adm.

ATLANTIC CITY: Absecon Lighthouse State Historic Site (Rhode Island & Pacific Aves.), built 1857, has small museum; open Memorial Day-Sept., Mon.-Sat. 10-5, Sun. noon-5; sm adm. **Historic Towne of Smith-ville** (13 m NW on US 9), an early 19th-C village reconstructed around the 1781 Smithville Inn, once a stagecoach stop, houses restaurants and boutiques; open daily 11 am-10 pm; free. **Museum Village,** a separate section where homes and other buildings have period furnishings, charges adm. **Barnegat Lighthouse State Park** (33 m N on Garden State Pkwy, then 7 m E on SR 72, then N to tip of Long Beach Island), historic 1857 light and museum; open Memorial Day-Labor Day, daily 8-4:45; May, Sept.-Oct., Sat. & Sun. 2-5; sm adm.

BATSTO STATE HISTORIC SITE (7 m NE of Hammonton on Sr 542): This charming, restored village grew up around the Batsto bog-iron furnace established in 1766; it produced munitions for the Revolutionary Army and the War of 1812 but failed in 1848; when an attempt to start a glass industry failed in 1867, Batsto became a ghost town. Ironmasters home, blacksmith and other shops; workers' cottages; other buildings; displays include Batsto glass; craft demonstrations; open Memorial Day-Labor Day 10-6; rest of yr, 11-5; closed Jan. 1, Dec. 25; grounds free, adm to mansion.

BRIDGETON: Settled in 1686, Bridgeton has many Colonial homes and the 1792 **Old Broad St. Church** (W Broad St. & West Ave.), a fine Georgian structure (open mid-Apr.-mid-Oct., Mon.-Fri. 10-3; free). **Greenwich** (7 m SW), settled by Quakers in 1675, has more than a dozen colonial homes; information on self-guiding tours, guided tours (Apr.-Oct.), and historic lectures available from **Cumberland County Historical Society** in **Gibbon House** (Main St.), a 1730 merchant's home with period rooms; open Mon.-Fri. 9-4 in summer, plus weekends 2-5 in spring & fall; closed hols; sm adm.

BURLINGTON: Settled by Quakers in 1677, this was an important 18th-C port; historic sites (most open by appointment only) include 1784 **Friends Meeting House** (High St. near Broad St.); 1703 **Old St. Mary's Church;** 1834 **New St. Mary's Church** (W Broad & Wood Sts.), first cruciform church in the U.S., designed by Richard Upjohn; **Gen. Grant House** (309 Wood St.). A booklet for a historic walking tour is available from **Burlington County Historical Society** (457 High St.), which maintains **James Fenimore Cooper House** (former home of the author), **Pearson-How House** (built early 1700s; period furnishings), **Wolcott Museum** (Quaker and other historic exhibits); open Sun. 2-4 or by appointment; free. **James Lawrence House State Historic Site** (459 High St.), birthplace of the naval hero who cried "Don't give up the ship," when fatally wounded during the War of 1812; open Tues.-Sat. 10-noon, 1-5, Sun. 2-5; closed Jan. 1, Thnks, Dec. 25; free.

CAMDEN: Walt Whitman Home State Historic Site (330 Mickle St.), where the poet lived from 1873 until his death in 1892; modest furnishings are original; Whitman memorabilia; open Tues.-Sat. 10-noon, 1-5; Sun. 2-5; closed Jan. 1, Thnks, Dec. 25; sm adm. **Harleigh Cemetery** (Haddon Ave. & Vesper Blvd.) contains the tomb of the poet, which he designed himself.

   Pomona Hall (1900 Park Blvd.), hq of Camden County Historical Society, has local historical exhibits; open Tues.-Fri. 12:30-4:30, Sun. 2-4; closed Jan. 1, Easter, July 4, Thnks, Dec. 25; free. **Campbell Museum** (Campbell Pl.) houses dinnerware from many countries, dating from BC; open Mon.-Fri. 9:30-5; closed hols; free.

   Tours of historic houses in Pennsauken (2 m NE on US 130) may be arranged through **Pennsauken Historical Society** (6711 Grant Ave., Pennsauken 08109). **Haddonfield** (5 m SE via SR 561) was founded in 1713 by 23-year-old Elizabeth Haddon, a Quaker immortalized in Longfellow's *Tales of a Wayside Inn.* Many of her possessions are in **Greenfield Hall** (343 King's Hwy E), hq of Haddonfield Historical Society; on grounds is a 1742 house she once owned; open Tues., Thurs. 2-4:30 or by appointment; closed hols & July-Aug.; adm. Also here is **Indian King Tavern State Historic Site** (233 King's Hwy E), built 1750, where the New Jersey State Legislature met in 1777; colonial furnishings; historic exhibits; open Tues.-Sat. 10-noon, 1-5; Sun. 2-5; closed Jan. 1, Thnks, Dec. 25; sm adm.

   National Park (6 m SW off US 130) contains **Red Bank Battlefield** (open daily 9-6; free); the 1748 **Ann Whitall House** (Sat. & Sun. 2-4; sm adm), bearing battle scars and housing battle relics, used as hospital for Hessians and Americans; and the remains of Ft. Mercer, which prevented British ships from sailing up the Delaware during the Revolution.

CAPE MAY COURT HOUSE: Cape May County Historical Museum (center of town on US 9), in a former courthouse; relics of shipping and whaling; glass; Cape May diamonds (quartz polished by the sea, found on Delaware Bay shore); open Mon.-Sat. 9-4; closed hols; sm adm. **Chamber of Commerce** (Crest Haven Red. & Garden State Pkwy) provides information on the many Victorian resort hotels and homes restored in the area.

CLINTON: Clinton Historical Museum (56 Main St.), with a 1763 mill and operating waterwheel, offers displays on early home and farm tools and industry; open Apr.-Oct., Mon.-Fri. 1-5, Sat. & Sun. noon-6; adm.

FLEMINGTON: The 1828 **County Courthouse** (Main St.) is famous for the Lindbergh kidnapping trial, held here in 1935. **Fleming Castle** (5 Bonnell St.), inn and home of Samuel Fleming, for whom the town is named, is a Colonial building housing DAR hq, open by appointment; adjacent is **Kase Cemetery,** with graves of first settlers and Tuccamirgan, their Indian friend. **Liberty Village,** a re-created 18th-C village with Swan Museum of the American Revolution, exhibits, craft demonstrations; open Apr.-Oct. daily 10:30-5:30; Nov.-Mar., Tues.-Sun. 10:30-5:30; closed Jan. 1, Easter, Thnks, Dec. 25; adm.

FREEHOLD: Monmouth County Historical Museum (70 Court St.) offers period rooms; silver and china; paintings including Emanuel Leutze's of Washington at the Battle of Monmouth in 1778; open Tues.-Sat. 10-5, Sun. 2-5; closed mid-end July, Thnks, Dec. 15-Jan. 1; free. On Throckmorton St. is a marker at the site of **Molly Pitcher's well,** from where she carried water to the troops until she took over her husband's gun after he was wounded.

GLASSBORO: Hollybush (Glassboro State College), 1849 mansion of glassmaker Thomas Whitney, was site of Pres. Lyndon Johnson's meeting with Premier Alexei Kosygin; open Mon.-Fri. 9-4; free.

HACKENSACK: Church on the Green (42 Court St.), the First Reformed Dutch Church, was originally built in 1696 by Dutch who established a trading post here; open by request Mon.-Fri. **Von Steuben House State Historic Site** (on the river, 3 m N on New Bridge Rd.), a Colonial-style Dutch house built about 1695, was given to Gen. von Steuben in appreciation for his war service; von Steuben never lived here; antique furnishings, glass, handcrafts, Indian artifacts; open Tues.-Sat. 10-noon, 1-5, Sun. 2-5; closed Jan. 1, Thnks, Dec. 25; sm adm. **USS Ling** (Court & River Sts.), restored WW II submarine, is open, weather permitting, daily 10-6; adm.

LAMBERTVILLE: Marshall House (60 Bridge St.) was home 1817-34 to James Wilson Marshall, whose discovery of gold at Sutter's Mill in California started the Gold Rush; historic displays on Delaware Valley; open Thurs., Sat. 1-5, possibly additional hrs; closed Jan. 1, Thnks, Dec. 25; sm adm. **John Holcomb House** (Main St.), where Washington stayed before crossing the Delaware, is not open to the public. **Hopewell Museum** (10 m E on SR 518 at 28 E Broad St., Hopewell) displays Colonial, Federal, and Victorian household furnishings and equipment; open Mon., Wed., Sat. 1-5; closed hols; adm.

MORRISTOWN: Schuyler-Hamilton House (5 Olyphant Pl.), now DAR hq, is a 1760 house in which Alexander Hamilton courted Elizabeth Schuyler in 1779; period furnishings; open Tues., Sun. 2-5 or by appointment; closed Dec. 25; free. **Morris Museum of Arts & Sciences** (Normandy Heights & Columbia Rds.) is open July-Labor Day, Tues.-Sat. 10-4; rest of yr, Mon.-Sat. 10-5, Sun. 2-5; closed hols; free. **Speedwell Village** (333 Speedwell Ave.), home and factory of Stephen Vail; here Vail and Samuel B. Morse conducted the first successful experiments with the telegraph; Vail also built 1818 engine for the first transatlantic steamship, *Savannah;* exhibits on steamships, telegraph; open Apr.-Oct., Thurs., Sat. 10-4, Sun. 2-5 or by appointment; sm adm.

　　Morristown National Historical Park: During the Revolution, the little village of Morristown became an important military center after Washington established winter encampments here (1777, 1779-80); park consists of 3 sections: 1) **Ford Mansion** (230 Morris St.), built 1774 by Jacob Ford, whose mill produced gunpowder for the Continental Army; home to Martha and George Washington 1779-80; many original furnishings. Behind it is the **Historical Museum** with interpretive exhibits, Washington memorabilia. Both open daily 10-5; closed Jan. 1, Thnks, Dec. 25; sm adm. 2) **Fort Nonsense** (at Washington St. & Western Ave.), probably built to defend supplies, was named in the belief its construction was merely a way of keeping the soldiers busy; open daily. 3) **Jockey Hollow** (3 m SW on Jockey Hollow Rd.), the 1779-80 encampment; reconstructed huts; replica of the Continental Army Hospital; restored 1750 **Wick House** with period furnishings (open daily 1-5; closed Jan. 1, Thnks, Dec. 25; free); grounds open daily exc Jan. 1, Thnks, Dec. 25; living history demonstrations in summer.

　　Museum of Early Trades & Crafts (5 m SE on SR 24 on Main St. & Green Village Rd. in Madison): early tools and products of New Jersey; open July-Labor Day, Tues.-Sat. 10-4; rest of yr, Mon.-Sat. 10-5, Sun. 2-5; closed hols; free. **Waterloo Village Restoration** (22 m W via SR 10, I-80, off US 206) preserves pre-Revolutionary village whose forge supplied iron weaponry for the Continental Army; buildings furnished in colonial style; shops, church, gristmill, homes, inn; open Apr.-Dec., Tues.-Sun. 10-6; closed hols; adm.

MOUNT HOLLY: Founded by Quakers in 1676, Mount Holly has preserved the 1796 Georgian-style **Burlington County Court House** (High St. near Garden St.), flanked by 1807 administrative buildings; **Burlington County Prison** (128 High St.), designed by Robert Mills and built 1811, now a museum (open Tues.-Sat. 10-noon, 1-4; closed hols; free); **Mill Street Hotel** (67 Mill St.), incorporating 1720 brick walls of the original building, a tavern. The 1759 **Old School House** (35 Brainard St.), where John Woolman taught, and the 1725 home, **Peachfield** (Burr Rd.) have been authentically furnished by Society of Colonial Dames of America and are open May-Oct., Wed. 1-4, or by appointment; free. **John Woolman Memorial** (99 Branch St.) is a 1783 home built on land owned by Woolman (1720-72), a leading abolitionist; period furnishings; open daily 9-4; free.

NEWARK: New Jersey Historical Society (230 Broadway at Taylor St.) houses period rooms, paintings, furnishings, decorative arts; library; open Tues.-Sat. 10-4:30; closed hols; free. **Newark Museum** (49 Washington St.) offers American painting and sculpture, Tibetan religious art; superb antique glass; European clocks; early American decorative arts; exhibits on science and industry; planetarium; open Mon.-Sat. noon-5, Sun. & hols 1-5; closed Jan. 1, July 4, Thnks, Dec. 25; free. **Cathedral of the Sacred Heart** (89 Ridge St.), in French Gothic style resembling the basilica at Rheims; gold-vaulted Baptistry ceiling, hand-carved reredos, 200 stained-glass windows, 14 bells made in Padua, mosaic Stations of the Cross; open daily 9-9. **First Presbyterian Church** (SW at Morris Ave. & Church Mall in Springfield) was rebuilt 1781 as replica of the original, burned by the British during the advance on Morristown in 1780; Rev. James Caldwell, "the fighting parson," tore up hymnals for gun wadding when American supplies gave out; Minute Man statue on grounds; open daily; free.

    Boxwood Hall State Historic Site (4 m S at 1073 E Jersey St. in Elizabeth) was home of Elias Boudinot, President of the Continental Congress; Washington lunched here in 1789 on the way to his inauguration; open Tues.-Sat. 10-noon, 1-5, Sun. 2-5; closed Jan. 1, Thnks, Dec. 25; sm adm.

    Grover Cleveland Birthplace State Historic Site (8 m W on I-280, then 2½ m N on SR 527 to 207 Bloomfield Ave., Caldwell) has been restored; Cleveland memorabilia; open Tues.-Sat. 10-noon, 1-5; Sun. 2-5; closed Jan. 1, Thnks, Dec. 25; sm adm. **Montclair Art Museum** (2½ m N on Grove St., then 3 m NW on Bloomfield Ave. to 3 S Mountain Ave., Montclair) exhibits 18th-20th-C American painting (including works by George Inness, who lived here); silver; American Indian art; open Sept.-June, Tues.-Sat. 10-5, Sun. 2-5:30; closed hols; free. The 1796 Federal-style **Crane House** (110 Orange Rd., Montclair) has period furnishings; open Labor Day-mid-June, Sun. 2-5; free.

Edison National Historic Site (3 m W on I-280, then ½ m N on Main St. to Lakeside Ave., W Orange) is a complex of buildings in which Thomas Alva Edison worked for 44 years; chemical and physics laboratory, machine shop, library, and the Black Maria (motion picture studio); original models of many of his inventions; showings of some of his first movies; interesting guided tours. Nearby is **Glenmont** (Llewellyn Park, off Main St.), his home from 1886 until his death in 1931; original furnishings, memorabilia; tours arranged from laboratory. Both open Mon.-Fri. 8-4:30, Sat. & Sun. 8:45-5:15; closed Jan. 1, Thnks, Dec. 25; sm adm. **Edison State Park & Museum** (13½ m S of Newark on Garden State Pkwy to Exit 131, then ½ m SW to Christie St. off SR 27, Edison) contains a memorial tower whose design includes several Edison inventions, topped by a light bulb; open Tues.-Sat. 10-noon, 1-5, Sun. 1-5; closed Jan. 1, Thnks, Dec. 25; sm adm.

NEW BRUNSWICK: Buccleuch Mansion (Buccleuch Park, near College Ave. & George St.), built in the early 1700s by a British army officer, has period rooms; open late May-Oct., Sat. & Sun. 3-5; closed hols; free. **Rutgers University Library** (College Ave.) has good collections on Walt Whitman and state history; open Mon.-Fri. 9-5; free.

OCEAN CITY: Ocean City Historical Museum (409 Wesley Ave.), with Indian, natural history, and historic displays, is open June-Aug., Mon.-Sat. 10-4; rest of yr, Tues.-Sat. 1-4; closed hols; free. **Somers Mansion** (3 m NW on SR 52 at Mays Landing Rd., Somers Point), built in 1720s; Atlantic County Historical Society collections; open Tues.-Sat. 10-noon, 1-5, Sun. 2-5; closed Jan. 1, Thnks, Dec. 25; sm adm.

PATERSON: Paterson Museum (268 Summer St.), archaeological, natural history exhibits; hull of the first submarine, invented by J. P. Holland of Paterson in 1878; open Mon.-Fri. 1-5, Sat. 10-noon & 1-5; closed hols; free. **Lambert Castle** (5 Valley Rd. in Garret Mountain Reservation), built by a silk manufacturer in 1891; collections of Passaic County Historical Society; period furnishings; library; open Wed.-Fri. 1-4:45, Sat. & Sun. 11-4:45; closed Jan. 1, Thnks, Dec. 25; free.

Van Riper-Hopper House (2 m W at 533 Berdan Ave., Wayne), built 1786, has 18th-19th-C furnishings, local historic items; open Fri.-Tues. 1-5; closed Jan. 1, Dec. 25; free. **Dey Mansion** (2 m W in Preakness Valley Park, 199 Totowa Rd.), a 1740 stone-and-brick Georgian mansion, was hq for Washington in 1780; 18th-C furnishings; colonial artifacts; open Tues., Wed., Fri. 1-5, Sat. & Sun. 10-5; closed Jan. 1, Thnks, Dec. 25; sm adm.

PLAINFIELD: Friends Meeting House (225 Watchung Ave.) has been in use since 1788; cemetery; open Mon.-Fri. 11:30-1:30; closed hols; free. **Drake House Museum** (602 W Front St.), in 1746 dwelling probably used by Washington as hq in 1777, has period furnishings, diorama of Battle for the Watchungs; open Mon., Wed., Sat. 2-5; closed hols; sm adm.

Scotch Plains (4 m NE on US 28): For information on **Deserted Village, Glenside Park** (S off Glenside Ave., New Providence), a former mill village now part of the Watchung Reservation, write Union County Park Commission (Box 275, Elizabeth 07207). Information on the 30-odd pre-Revolutionary homes in the area available at Public Library (Bartle St.).

PRINCETON: Princeton University, founded in Elizabeth in 1746 and moved here in 1756, offers visitor information and guide service daily exc hols from Stanhope Hall. **Putnam Memorial Collection** of sculpture, including works by Calder, Lipschitz, and Picasso, is scattered throughout the campus. **Art Museum** exhibits ancient to modern works; medieval, early American, and Oriental collections; open Tues.-Sat. 10-4, Sun. 1-5; closed hols; free. **Firestone Library** collections range from papyri to the papers of F. Scott Fitzgerald, Bernard Baruch, other writers and political figures; open Mon.-Sat. 9-5, Sun. 2-5; free. Buildings include **Nassau Hall** (built 1756; used as Revolutionary War barracks and hospital; Continental Congress sat here in 1783, when Princeton was the capital); 1925 Gothic Revival **Chapel** (with ornate interior carving); **Woodrow Wilson School of Public & International Affairs** (designed by Minoru Yamasaki). **Princeton Cemetery** (Witherspoon & Wiggins Sts.) has graves of Aaron Burr, Grover Cleveland. **Morven** (55 Stockton St.), now the Governor's residence, was Cornwallis' hq in 1776.

Rockingham State Historic Site (4 m N on US 206, then 4 m E on SR 518 in Rocky Hill): 1730 farmhouse used by Martha and George Washington Aug. 23-Nov. 10, 1783, while Congress convened at Princeton; here Washington composed his Farewell Address to the Armies; fine period furnishings; open Tues.-Sat. 10-noon, 1-5; Sun. 2-5; closed Jan. 1, Thnks, Dec. 25; sm adm.

RED BANK: Hendrickson House (W on county rd 520 to Longstreet Rd., Holmdel) is a 1717 Dutch-Colonial home with period furnishings; open May-Oct., Tues., Thurs., Sat., Sun. 1-5; closed hols; free. **Monmouth Museum** (3½ m W on Newman Springs Rd., Brookdale Community College campus, Lincroft) has changing exhibits on local themes; open Tues.-Sat. 11-4:30, Sun. 1-4:30; closed hols; sm adm. **Maripit Hall** (N on SR 35 to 137 King Hwy in Middletown) is a 1684 Dutch-Colonial building with period furnishings; open Tues., Thurs., Sat. 11-5, Sun. 2-5; closed Thnks, Dec. 25; free. **Twin Lights State Historic Site** (5½ m E on SR 520, then 3½ m N & W on SR 36) are lights erected 1862 to guide ships into New

York harbor; exhibit on first US lifeguard station; maritime displays; open late-May-Labor Day, Tues.-Sun. 1-5; sm adm.

RINGWOOD STATE PARK (Sloatsburg Rd., Ringwood): **Ringwood Manor,** built 1810, is an attractive, 78-room Victorian mansion, home to several ironmasters; many original furnishings; lovely grounds; occasional art or other exhibits. Nearby **Skylands Manor,** built 1924 to resemble a Jacobean manor house, is also set in gardens. Both open May-Oct., Tues.-Fri. 10-4, Sat. & Sun. 10-5; sm adm.

SALEM: Alexander Grant House (79-83 Market St.) offers collections of Salem County Historical Society, including Wistarburg glass and Indian relics, in 20 period rooms; information available on the several dozen 18th-C homes in this town settled in 1675; open Sept.-June, Tues.-Fri. noon-4; closed hols; adm. **Friends Burying Ground** (W Broadway) contains the oak under which the treaty was signed with the Lenni-Lenape Indians allowing settlement. At **Hancock House** (4 m S at Hancocks Bridge), built 1734, some 30 patriots were bayoneted to death by 300 Tories as reprisal for the Quaker community's aid to Revolutionary forces; adj is **Swedish Plank Cabin,** typical of homes constructed by early Swedish settlers; open Tues.-Sat. 10-noon, 1-5, Sun. 2-5; closed Jan. 1, Thnks, Dec. 25; sm adm.

SOMERVILLE: Wallace House State Historic Site (38 Washington Pl.), a 1778 house with period furnishings where Gen. & Mrs. Washington spent the winter of 1778-9, and **Old Dutch Parsonage State Historic Site** (65 Washington Pl.), a furnished 1751 Dutch brick home, are open Tues.-Sat. 10-noon, 1-5, Sun. 2-5; closed Jan. 1, Thnks, Dec. 25; sm adm.

TRENTON: Trenton-Mercer County Chamber of Commerce (104 N Broad St.) offers brochures for self-guiding tours. **State House** (121 W State St.), built 1790 in Renaissance style, is open Mon.-Fri. 9-5; closed hols; free. **Cultural Center** consists of the **State Library; Auditorium** (frequent lectures and other programs); **Planetarium** (excellent programs daily in summer, weekends & hols rest of yr); and **State Museum** (good 20th-C art collection includes Ben Shahn graphics; fine 19th-C decorative arts of New Jersey, including Trenton porcelain; natural history and science displays; sculpture garden; open Mon.-Sat. 9-5, Sun. 2-5; closed Jan. 1, July 4, Thnks, Dec. 25; free.

Old Barracks (S Willow St. at W Front St.), built of native stone 1758-9, housed British, Hessian, and Continental troops during the Revolution; battle dioramas; reconstructed soldier's room; open May-Oct., Mon.-Sat. 10-5, Sun. 1-5; rest of yr, Mon.-Sat. 10-4:30, Sun. 1-4; closed Jan. 1, Thnks, Dec. 24, 25; sm adm. **William Trent House** (539 S Warren

St.), home of William Trent for whom the city was named, is a 1719 brick Georgian structure; exceptional antique furnishings; open Mon.-Sat. 10-4, Sun. 1-4; closed Jan. 1, Thnks, Dec. 25; sm adm.

Washington Crossing State Park (8 m NW on SR 29), commemorating the historic crossing prior to the Battle of Trenton; museum of flags; **McKonkey Ferry Museum State Historic Site,** where Washington is said to have spent Christmas night 1776 after the crossing, restored as an inn (open Tues.-Sat. 10-noon, 1-5, Sun. 2-5; closed Jan. 1, Thnks, Dec. 25; sm adm).

Bordentown (7 m S off US 206), once a busy port on the Delaware & Raritan Canal, is worth seeing even though its historic buildings are not open to the public. **Bonaparte Park** (E of 3rd St., N side of Park St.) is part of an estate bought in 1816 by Joseph Bonaparte (exiled king of Spain and brother of Napoleon), who settled here; only the gardener's lodge remains. **Murat Row** (49-61 E Park St.) are attached houses converted from the mansion of Prince Murat (Joseph Bonaparte's nephew). **1-5 E Park St.,** with an iron balcony, was once a tavern; now a residence. **Borden House** (32 Farnsworth Ave.) was rebuilt after the British burned the original in 1778 as reprisal for the "mechanical keg" invented by Bordentown citizens, who planned to blow up the British fleet in Philadelphia. **Hopkinson House** (101 Farnsworth Ave.) was home of Francis Hopkinson, signer of the Declaration of Independence. **Clara Barton Schoolhouse** (142 Crosswicks St.) was established by Clara Barton as one of the first free public schools in the nation. **Crosswicks** (3 m E), an old Quaker settlement, has a 1773 Meeting House with a Revolutionary cannonball embedded in it.

NEW MEXICO

ALAMOGORDO: Three Rivers Petroglyphs (29 m N on US 54 to Three Rivers, then 5 m E on gravel rd), more than 500 rock carvings by Mogollon people 900-1400; marked trail, interpretive shelter; open daily; free. **Mescalero Apache Indian Reservation** (13 m N on US 54 to Tularosa, then 16 m E on US 70) has a trading post where crafts may be bought; inquire for festival schedule.

ALBUQUERQUE: Chamber of Commerce (Civic Center, 401 2nd St. NW) provides information on attractions and festivals in the city and nearby pueblos; maps for beautiful drives, including loop to Sandia Crest (15 m E via US 66, then 6½ m N on SR 14, then follow signs), usually open, depending on snow, mid-May-mid-Oct. **Sandia Peak Tramway** (5 m N off I-25 on Tramway Rd.) to the peak runs all year; fare includes admission to **Sandia Peak Museum** (base of the tram), which traces history of trade in the SW; tramway is on land belonging to **Sandia Pueblo,** established about 1300 and one of the pueblos visited by Coronado in 1540-1. **Sandia Man Cave** (12½ m E off I-25 on SR 44), where many Stone Age finds were made, is open all year, but artifacts are in the Univ. of N.M. Museum of Anthropology.

University of New Mexico (2 m E on Central Ave.), on an attractive campus with many pueblo-style buildings, offers: **University Art Museum** (Rendondo & Cornell NE), with 19th-20th-C works and Spanish colonial silver; open academic yr, Tues.-Fri., Sun. 1-5; sm adm. **Jonson Gallery** (1909 Las Lomas NE), with modern works, open Tues.-Sun. noon-6; free. **Museum of Anthropology** (Roma Ave. NE & University) has splendid collections from the Southwest; artifacts from Sandia Cave; kachinas; representative material from other cultural areas of North America; crafts from Iran and Pakistan; open Mon.-Fri. 9-4, Sat. 10-4, Sun. 11:30-5; closed hols; free.

Old Town (1 block N of Central Ave. at Rio Grande Blvd.), with San Felipe de Neri Church, art and craft shops surrounding Old Town Plaza, retains flavor of the city's original Spanish settlement (1706). **Museum of Albuquerque** (Yale Blvd. SE), history of the area from prehistoric times to present; scientific displays; open Tues.-Fri. 10-5, Sat. & Sun. 1-5; closed hols; sm adm. **Albert K. Mitchell Collection of Western Art** (5200 Gibson Blvd. SE) displays Frederic Remington and Charles M. Russell paintings and bronzes; open Mon.-Fri. 8-5, Sat. noon-5; free. **Indian Pueblo Cultural Center** (Menaul Blvd & 12th St NW) interprets Pueblo culture through demonstrations, dance, guided pueblo tours, other programs; Indian specialties in restaurant; open Mon.-Sat. 10-6 (later in summer), Sun. Noon-6; adm.

Pueblos to the N are: **Santa Ana** (18 m N via I-25 to SR 44, then 10 m N), usually open only on feast days; no photography allowed. **Zia** (8 m NW of Santa Ana, off SR 44); women make good pottery. **Jemez** (6 m N of Zia via SR 44, then 5 m NE on SR 4), whose ancestors include survivors from the pueblo preserved in Pecos National Monument; fine dancers; famous for embroidery, basketry, weaving; no photography. **Jemez State Monument** (10 m N of Jemez Pueblo on SR 4) preserves ruins of mission at abandoned Giusewa Pueblo; museum and visitor center; open Wed.-Sun. 9-5; free.

Coronado State Monument (18 m N via I-25, then W on SR 44 about 2 m to sign) contains ruins of pueblo founded about 1300; when visited by Coronado in 1540-1, it had 1200 ground-level rooms, with many additional rooms rising in stories above these; painted kiva; museum; open Fri.-Tues. 9-5; sm adm.

Isleta Pueblo (13 m S off US 85), occupied at least by the 15th-C, abandoned during the Pueblo Revolt of 1680, reoccupied about 1709; the mission, which had been burned, was reconstructed and is still in use.

Indian Petroglyph State Park (9 m W on Atrisco Rd.) preserves birds, animals, kachinas, and human handprints made 1100-1600; open daily 9-5 (9-7 Apr.-Sept.); closed hols; sm adm.

Sandia Atomic Museum (Bldg. 358, Kirtland Air Force Base, 7 m SE) depicts the history of nuclear weapons with photographs, equipment, and film; open Mon.-Fri. 9-5; Sat., Sun., hols noon-5; closed Jan. 1, Thnks, Dec. 25; free.

ARTESIA: Historical Museum & Art Center (503-5 W Richardson Ave.) exhibits pioneer and Indian relics, local art; open Tues.-Sat. 2-5, Sun. 3-5; closed hols; free. **Underground School** (18th St. & Centre Ave.) was built as a shelter against fallout; tours Sept.-late-May, Mon.-Fri. 9-4; closed hols; free.

AZTEC: Aztec Ruins National Monument (1 m N off US 550): ruins of one of the largest prehistoric pueblos in the SW, occupied off-and-on 1100-1300; 500 rooms surrounded a great kiva, now restored; museum with artifacts; self-guiding trail; open daily 8-5 (8-6 in summer); closed Jan. 1, Memorial Day, Dec. 25; sm adm or GEP.

Aztec Community Museum (125 N Main St.) displays Indian relics, artifacts from pioneer period; open Mon.-Fri. 10-noon, 2-4; closed hols; sm adm.

Salmon Ruins (7 m S via SR 44 to Bloomfield, then 2 m W), excavated pueblo from 11th-C; more than 700 rooms; **San Juan County Museum,** attractive, pueblo-style, exhibits artifacts; panoramic view of the dig; open daily 9-5; closed Dec. 25; sm adm.

BANDELIER NATIONAL MONUMENT (12 m S of Los Alamos, off SR 4) preserves ruins inhabited 1100-1580 by ancestors of modern Pueblos of Cochiti and San Ildefonso; from **Frijoles Canyon Visitor Center,** a self-guiding trail gives you a good view of masonry structures built in front of caves for 2 m along the base of volcanic-ash cliffs; trail climbs to 400-room Tyuonyi pueblo with early kivas; many additional trails to cave dwellings, pueblo ruins, kivas, petroglyphs; guided tours; campfire programs; open daily 8-5 (8-7 in summer); closed Dec. 25; sm adm or GEP. A separate section is **Tsankawi** (11 m N on SR 4), a 35-room unexcavated ruin atop a mesa with views of Rio Grande Valley; 2-m self-guiding loop trail, past cave structures and petroglyphs, follows a centuries-old Indian trail worn as deep as 18 inches.

CARLSBAD: Carlsbad Municipal Museum (101 S Halagueno St.) exhibits minerals, potash, and prehistoric artifacts; open Mon.-Sat. 1-7:30; closed hols; free. **Million Dollar Museum** (20 m SW on US 62, 180, then W on SR 7) exhibits early Americana; open daily 6 am-10 pm; adm.

Carlsbad Caverns National Park (20 m SW of Carlsbad via US 62, 180, then 7 m W on SR 7): This cavern, not yet fully explored, is one of the largest in the world, extending more than 15 m and in places more than 1000-ft deep. **Visitor Center** offers exhibits, interpretive walks, cave tours; complete tour is strenuous 3-m, 3½-hr descent to 829 ft, with return by elevator; an easier, 1¼-hr tour uses elevators both ways; open mid-June-Labor Day 7 am-9 pm, mid-May-mid-June 8-6, rest of year 8-4:30. Special feature is naturalist talk during spectacular flight of bats from caverns every evening May-Oct. Adm or GEP.

CARRIZOZO: White Oaks (3 m N via US 54, then 9 m E on SR 349), a ghost town, boomed after gold was discovered in 1879; it had saloons and outlaws, but also an opera house and 2 newspapers. **My House of Old Things** (24 m N on US 54, then 2 m E to Ancho) is a pioneer home; restored railroad office; open May-Sept., daily 9-5; adm. **Fort Stanton** (24 m E via US 380, then 3 m S) was established 1855 to subdue the Mescalero Apache; now an Indian hospital. **Lincoln County Courthouse** (32 m E on US 380 at Lincoln) was built 1874 as L.G. Murphy & Co., a store involved in a struggle for local power known as the Lincoln County War; the war climaxed in 1878 with 5 months of bloodshed; among cowboy participants was Billy the Kid, gunned down by lawmen 2 years later, at age 21; museum of regional history; exhibits on the war and on the Kid; pioneer and Indian artifacts; open daily in summer 8:30-5:30, in winter 9-4:30; closed Dec. 25; sm adm.

CHACO CANYON NATIONAL MONUMENT (from Blanco Trading Post on SR 44, 23 m S via SR 57—check road condition before starting; from Thoreau on US 66, 64 m N via SR 57): 12 large ruins and more than 400 smaller ones inhabited by Anasazi people about 650-late 1200s; largest is 800-room **Pueblo Bonito,** which probably housed 1000 people in the 11th-C. **Visitor Center** (S entrance), with interpretive displays, is open daily 8-5 (8 am-9 pm in summer); closed Jan. 1, Dec. 25; free. From here an auto loop and self-guiding trails lead to a sampling of major ruins, including huge kiva at **Casa Rinconada.** Also conducted walks; evening programs; trails to other ruins.

CIMARRON: This historic town, in stunning country, grew up on the Santa Fe Trail on part of huge land-grant belonging to Lucien R. Maxwell; several historic buildings remain. **St. James Hotel** hosted Annie Oakley, Wyatt Earp, and others; scene of many gunfights; restored as museum; open June-Aug. daily 9-5:30; also open weekends in May & Sept.; adm.

Old Mill Museum, an 1864 gristmill, houses local historic items; open May-Sept., Fri.-Wed. 9-5; sm adm. **Philmont Scout Ranch & Explorer Base,** Boy Scout camp, has **Kit Carson Museum** and **Ernest Thompson Seton Memorial Library & Museum,** with thousands of Indian artifacts, paintings, drawings, and volumes; hq (6 m S on SR 21) is open June-Aug. daily 7-7; rest of yr, Mon.-Fri. 8-5; closed hols; free.

COLUMBUS: Pancho Villa State Park (on SR 11) commemorates Villa's famous raid into American territory in 1916; Gen. "Black Jack" Pershing, with 15,000 troops, pursued Villa for months in Mexico; Villa escaped; historical markers and relics; cactus garden; free.

DULCE: Jicarilla Apache Indian Reservation (on US 64) offers **Jicarilla Arts & Crafts Shop & Museum** and unrestored prehistoric ruins; information available from Jicarilla Tourist Dept., P.O. Box 147, Dulce 87528.

EL MORRO NATIONAL MONUMENT (58 m SE of Gallup via SR 32 & 53, or 43 m W of Grants via SR 53): Towering landmark named Inscription Rock for the graffiti left by many peoples: Atop the mesa are unexcavated ruins of 2 Zuni pueblos (reached via handholds and footholds pecked into the cliff), whose people left hundreds of petrogylphs; Conquistadores carved their names 1605-1774; beginning in 1849, US Army officers, emigrants, and other whites moving W also left their markings. **Visitor Center** has interpretive exhibits; open daily 8-5 (8-8 in summer); sm adm or GEP.

FORT SUMNER: Fort Sumner State Monument (4 m SE): site of 1862-70 military post and the infamous Bosque Redondo Reservation, where more than 400 Mescalero Apache and 8500 Navajo, burned out of their fields and homes, were sent by Col. Kit Carson; more than 400 Apache and 1500 Navajo escaped or died before the project to turn them into farmers was abandoned; **Visitor Center** with interpretive exhibits; open Wed.-Sun. 9-5; free. Nearby is grave of Billy the Kid.

GALLUP: This is the shopping center for native Americans from several nearby reservations. **Museum of Indian Arts & Crafts** (103 W 66th Ave.) displays prehistoric and contemporary works by Hopi, Navajo, Zuni, and other tribes; audiovisual programs in summer; open Mon.-Fri. 9-5, Sat. 9-noon; closed hols; free. In same building, is **Chamber of Commerce,** which can provide schedules of local festivals and activities.

Navajo Indian Reservation occupies the NW corner of the state along either side of US 666 N of Gallup; chief center is **Shiprock,** named for unusual rock formation that figures in Navajo legend, with annual fair in Oct.; information from tribal hq in Window Rock, Arizona.

Zuni Indian Reservation begins 17 m S of Gallup on SR 32. Chief center is **Zuni Pueblo** (on SR 53, 6 m W of jct SR 32), only surviving settlement of the "7 Cities of Cibola" sought by Coronado because Fray Marcos de Niza had reported they were built of gold; although this pueblo has been inhabited since the 17th-C, excavations have uncovered ruins dating to prehistoric times. **Governor's office** provides information (the famous Shalako dance is held in late Nov. or early Dec.) and issues permits for photography. Also here is **Zuni Craftsmen Cooperative Association,** with superb work.

GILA CLIFF DWELLINGS NATIONAL MONUMENT (47 m N of Silver City via SR 15): excavated ruins of dwellings constructed inside natural caves in the cliffside from AD 100-1400; **Visitor Center** (open daily 8-5; closed Dec. 25); steep trail to the dwellings, 180 ft above the canyon floor. Park open daily 9-5 (8-6 in summer); closed Dec. 25; sm adm or GEP.

GRAN QUIVIRA NATIONAL MONUMENT (26 m SE of Mountainair on SR 14) is a ruin that traces arrival of Mogollon people about 800 (when they lived in pithouses), the mingling of culture as they came under Anasazi influence about 1000, and 17th-C appearance of the Spanish; ruins of pueblo, largest in the region, and of 17th-C Franciscan church and mission can be explored on a short, self-guiding trail; **Visitor Center** contains artifacts, displays illustrating history of the area; open daily 8-5 (8-7 in summer); closed Dec. 25; free.

GRANTS: Chamber of Commerce (500 W Santa Fe Ave.) offers exhibits of Indian artifacts, minerals, and the uranium ore (discovered in 1950) that brought new life to the area; information on the interesting surrounding region—the **Malpais Lava Beds** (SE via I-40 or SR 53), **ice caves** (26 m SW via SR 53; open daily in daylight, weather permitting, adm), and many festivals at nearby Pueblo villages; open June-Aug., Mon.-Sat. 8-7; Sept.-May, Mon.-Fri. 8-5; closed hols; free.

Acoma Pueblo (26 m E via I-40, then 13 m S), the Sky City, shimmers atop a 350-ft mesa, giving rise to the Spanish belief it was made of gold; occupied continuously since 1075; some of the building materials had to be brought from miles away, and all had to be hauled up the mesa on ropes or on the backs of the people; its mission of San Esteban Rey was built in 1629. Adm is charged to the pueblo; extra fee required for photo privileges; certain sections are off bounds to visitors; occasionally the entire pueblo is closed to outsiders. Check locally for festivals. **Enchanted Mesa** (3 m N of Acoma Pueblo on SR 23) figures in Pueblo legend; visitors are not permitted to climb up. **Laguna Pueblo** (33 m E off US 66), established about 1450, expanded into several nearby communities such as Paguate;

inhabitants work in modern industries and live in modern homes, so there are few restrictions on visitors to the old pueblo; permission required for photos; inquire locally for dates of the many festivals.

LAS CRUCES: Chamber of Commerce (760 W Picacho Ave.) provides information on scenic drives to ghost towns and other points of interest in this town named for crosses marking the burials of pioneers killed by Indians. **Mesilla** (2 m SW), once the Confederate capital of the Arizona Territory, has preserved the buildings surrounding the old plaza. **New Mexico State University** (S in University Park) offers a museum with prehistoric artifacts and historical items, open daily June-Aug. 1-4, Sept.-May 9-noon, 1-4; closed hols; free. **White Sands Missile Range** (28 m E on US 70) has missile exhibits open Mon.-Fri. 7:45-4:15; closed hols; free. **Ft. Seldon State Park** and **Leasburg State Park** (14 m NW off I-25) contain ruins of army post established 1865 to control the Navajo and Apache; historic markers.

LAS VEGAS: Chamber of Commerce (721 Grand Ave.) provides maps for self-guiding historic tours. **Rough Riders' Memorial & City Museum** (Municipal Bldg., 720 Grand Ave.) is open Mon.-Sat. 9-4; closed hols; free.

   Fort Union National Monument (20 m NE via I-25, then 8 m NW on SR 477): ruins of fort established 1851 on the Santa Fe Trail (wagon ruts can still be seen here) to mount campaigns against nomadic Indians of the area; the fort played a role in the Civil War by securing New Mexico for the Union and helping to keep Confederates from Colorado's gold fields. Campaigns against Indians continued into the 1870s; with the end of the Indian Wars and with railroads replacing the Santa Fe Trail, the fort ceased to be useful and was abandoned in 1891. **Visitor Center** has historic displays and artifacts; living history programs in summer; open daily 8-4:30 (8-7 in summer); closed Dec. 25; sm adm or GEP.

MOUNTAINAIR: Abo State Monument (11 m SW off US 60) and **Quarai State Monument** (6 m N off SR 14): unexcavated ruins of pueblos; drought and raids by nomadic tribes drove the people out in 1673-4; both contain ruins of 17th-C Franciscan churches, remarkable for their kivas indicating continued practice of traditional religion. Abo is open daily 9-5; free. Quarai has a Visitor Center and is open Wed.-Sun. 9-5; free.

PORTALES: Eastern New Mexico University houses Indian artifacts from prehistoric times to the present in several buildings (inquire on campus for locations and hrs); **Roosevelt County Museum,** with pioneer exhibits, is open Mon.-Sat. 8-noon, 1-4, Sun. 1-4; closed hols; free. **Blackwater Draw Museum** (7 m N on US 70), named for archaeological site nearby, offers dioramas, Clovis points, fossils, other material dating back 12,000 years to explain life of early hunters; open daily 1-5; closed hols; free.

RATON: Capulin Mountain National Monument (29 m E via US 64, 87 to Capulin, then 3½ m N on SR 325), an extinct volcano that was active 7000 years ago; explanatory exhibits, audiovisual program at the **Visitor Center;** open daily 8-4:30 (7 am-9 pm from May-early Sept.); sm adm. **Folsom Man Site** (N from the Monument on SR 325 to Folsom, then 7 m W on SR 72), named for the projective point found in the skeleton of an extinct bison here, proved man had been in N America at least 10,000 years (later finds in New Mexico and elsewhere pushed the date even further back); explanatory markers.

ROSWELL: Roswell Museum & Art Center (11th & Main Sts.) exhibits works by Peter Hurd, his wife Henriette Wyeth, regional artists; Chinese art; sculpture; contemporary American art; SW Indian art; exhibits on space pioneer Dr. Robert H. Goddard; planetarium; open Mon.-Sat. 9-5, Sun. & hols 1-5; closed Jan. 1, Dec. 25; free.

SANTA FE: Best place to start is **The Plaza** (between Palace Ave. & San Francisco St. at Lincoln), hub of the city since it was laid out by the Spanish in 1609; except for the Pueblo revolt 1680-92, the Spanish ruled here until the Mexican Independence of 1821; the plaza was the marketplace (Indians still sell crafts here) and terminal of the Santa Fe Trail. The **Chamber of Commerce** (SE corner of plaza) is in La Fonda Hotel, the Inn at the End of the Trail, a meeting place since pioneer days; here you can get information and maps for walking tours of the city and for drives to Pueblo Indian centers; inquire for a schedule of Indian ceremonials that welcome visitors.

   Palace of the Governors (N side of plaza), oldest public building in the nation, was completed in 1610 as the Spanish capital; here territorial governor Lew Wallace wrote part of *Ben-Hur* in 1880; it contains archaeological and historical exhibits, and forms the **Museum of New Mexico** along with: **Hall of the Modern Indian** (across the patio), devoted to displays on contemporary Indians; **Fine Arts Bldg.** (across Lincoln Ave.), a mission-style building, traditional and modern arts of the SW; **International Folk Art Bldg.** (Old Santa Fe Trail), with good Spanish colonial art, folk art from around the world; all open May 15-Sept. 15, Mon.-Sat. 9-5, Sun. & hols 2-5; rest of yr, Tues.-Sat. 9-5, Sun. & hols 2-5; closed Jan. 1, Dec. 25; free.

   Cathedral of St. Francis of Assisi (Palace Ave. at Cathedral St.), built 1870-89 under Archbishop Lamy (subject of Willa Cather's novel *Death Comes for the Archbishop*), contains La Conquistadora Chapel, with the oldest Madonna in the nation; open daily 5 am-6pm. **Our Lady of Light Chapel** (219 Old Santa Fe Trail), built 1873 by the Sisters of Loretto, is noted for Miraculous Staircase; an itinerant carpenter built it with no visible means of support, and disappeared before he could be paid; open daily 9-noon, 1-4:30; closed Dec. 24, 25; sm adm. **San Miguel Mission** (Old Santa Fe Trail & De Vargas St.) was built in 1610 by Tlaxcalan Indians the Franciscans had brought with them from Mexico; open daily 8:30-11:30, 1-5:30; donation.

Old buildings include **Delgado House** (Palace Ave., W of plaza), 1890 adobe home of a trader; **Sena Plaza** and **Prince Plaza** (Palace Ave., E of plaza), housing shops; **Oldest House** (215 E De Vargas St.), pueblo adobe structure from about 1200 to which Spaniards added in the 17th-C, now a shop. **Scottish Rite Temple** (Washington Ave., 3 blocks N of plaza) is modeled on the Alhambra. **State Capitol** (De Vargas St., W of Old Santa Fe Trail, built 1966, resembles a ceremonial kiva.

Museum of Navajo Ceremonial Art (704 Camino Lejo), in the shape of the traditional octagonal hogan, exhibits sand paintings, rugs, other cultural and ceremonial displays; library, recorded chants; open Tues.-Sat. 10-5, Sun. & hols 2-5; closed Jan. 1, Thnks, Dec. 25; free. **Canyon Road**, in pre-Spanish times an Indian trail to Pecos Pueblo, now offers studios and shops. **Christo Rey Church** (Canyon Rd. & Camino Cabra), believed to be the largest adobe structure in the U.S.; handsome stone reredos carved in 1761; open daily 7-5. **Institute of American Indian Arts** (Cerillos Rd.) trains native Americans in art; occasional exhibitions.

Old Coal Mine Museum (27 m S via US 85, SR 14 in Madrid) displays mining equipment and old vehicles; open daily 8-5; closed Dec. 25; sm adm.

Pueblos N of the city include: **Tesuque** (8 m N on US 84), where photography is sometimes prohibited; **Nambe** (20 m NE via US 84, SR 4); **San Ildefonso** (22 m NW via US 84, SR 4), known for black pottery developed by Maria Martinez, open 9-5, photo permit required; **Santa Clara** (27 m NW via US 84, SR 5), with the Puye Cliff Ruins (adm); **San Juan** (28 m N via US 84, 285), known for pottery and wood carving.

Pueblos S of the city were settled by people driven by enemies from the Pajarito Plateau (now part of Bandelier National Monument): **Cochiti** (30 m SW off US 85), known for double-headed drums, pottery, other crafts; **Santo Domingo** (31 m SW off US 85 on SR 22), known for pottery and jewelry; **San Felipe** (34 m SW off US 85), where the plaza has been worn into a bowl shape by dancing and the church has a painted portico.

Pecos National Monument (25 m SE off I-25): ruins of one of the largest Anasazi settlements in the SW, established about 1100; more than 650 rooms and 22 kivas; by the early 1620s, Franciscans established a huge, self-supporting mission with a large church, burned during the Pueblo Revolt of 1680; a smaller church was built after the Spanish reconquest, but war and disease so ravaged the population of more than 2500, that in 1838 the 17 survivors moved to Jemez; open daily 8-5 (8-7 in summer); closed Jan. 1, Dec. 25; free.

Villanueva (42 m S via I-25, SR 3) was established under a Spanish land grant in the 1790s on a high bluff over the Pecos River to prevent Indian attacks; the houses face plazas, so that their back walls served as part of the fortifications; mission church dates from 1818; retains much colonial atmosphere; structures in the state park here are made to harmonize.

At Los Alamos (42 m NW via US 84, SR 4): **Bradbury Science Hall of Los Alamos Scientific Laboratory** (Diamond Dr.) offers space exhibits open Mon.-Fri. 8-noon, 1-5; Sat. & Sun. 1-5; closed hols; free. **County Historical Museum** (1921 Juniper) is open July-Aug., Tues.-Sun. noon-5; Sept.-June, Wed.-Fri. noon-5, Sat. & Sun. 1-5; free.

SILVER CITY: Kwilleylekia Ruins (30 m NW via US 180 to Cliff, then 1 m N), a great Salado Pueblo established about 1415, was abandoned after severe floods in 1575; you can watch excavation in progress; guided tours; **Visitor Center** with fine displays of materials found on the site; open Apr.-Nov. daily 8-6; sm adm.

SOCORRO: San Miguel Mission (403 El Camino Real) dates from 1598, with carved beams, corbels, new walls constructed in 1626; relics on display; open daily 6-6; free. New Mexico Institute of Mining & Technology offers a **Mineral Museum** (daily 8-5) and the atmospheric research center at **Langmuir Laboratory** (16 m W on US 60, then 14 m W on Water Canyon Rd.; usually open weekends in summer); free.

TAOS: One of the most colorful towns in the nation, Taos has 3 sections: 1) **Don Fernando de Taos,** the chief settlement, built around a central plaza by Spanish colonists about 1615; Indian slaves were traded here; it was famous for corn whiskey (Taos lightning); now a center for handcrafts and paintings. **Stables Gallery** (N Pueblo Rd.) features work of local artists in attractive pueblo-style building; open daily 10-5 (longer in summer); free. 2) **Ranchos de Taos** (4 m S on US 64), founded by ranchers and farmers, has many adobe homes and the stunning **St. Francis of Assisi Mission Church,** erected early 1700s—fortress-thick walls, magnificent twin belfries capped with crosses, campo santo (graveyard), beautiful interior with ancient silver and paintings. 3) **Taos Pueblo** (2½ m N on Pueblo Rd.) has existed here since prehistoric times; inhabitants are conservative and often aloof, but open the pueblo to visitors (adm; photos are an extra fee) and welcome outsiders to their beautiful dances (inquire locally; dates are often on short notice).

Harwood Foundation, University of New Mexico (Ledoux St.), restored adobe complex; santos, Spanish colonial furniture and decorative arts,

Indian arts, Persian Miniatures; library of works on the SW, D. H. Lawrence collection; open Mon.-Sat. 10-5; closed hols; free.

Kit Carson Home & Museum (E Kit Carson Rd on US 64) is an 1825 adobe house he purchased in 1843; he lived here 25 years with his wife and children; family memorabilia; Indian and Spanish colonial artifacts, chapel, library; open June-Sept. daily 7:30-7:30; spring & fall daily 8-6; winter daily 8-5; closed Jan. 1, Thnks, Dec. 25; sm adm. Carson's grave is in nearby **Kit Carson Memorial State Park.**

Gov. Bent House Museum & Gallery (Bent St., 1 block N of plaza), where Bent was scalped, has exhibits of Western Americana; open Mar.-Dec. daily 9-5; sm adm.

Millicent A. Rogers Memorial Museum (4 m N on SR 3), pueblo-style house; Indian and Spanish art; open mid-Mar.-mid-Oct., Mon.-Sat. 9-5, Sun. 1-5; rest of yr, Mon.-Sat. 10-4; adm. **D. H. Lawrence Ranch & Shrine** (15 m N on Sr 3, then 5 m E on gravel rd to San Cristobal; check rd condition before starting) is maintained by the Univ. of N Mexico; small adobe hut with cross on facade displays Lawrence's typewriter, hat, jacket; Lawrence's ashes; open daily during daylight; free.

Carson National Forest (hq on Cruz Alta Rd., S of town), covers more than a million acres of beautiful country E and W of Taos and Santa Fe. **Ghost Ranch Museum** (US 84, 17 m NW of Abiquiu) displays fossil dinosaurs, other geological material; Indian arts and culture; live local animals; small-scale forest.

A feature of Spanish-American communities in the surrounding area are moradas, little windowless churches built on hilltops. A fine example of Spanish colonial architecture is the **Church of San Jose de Gracia de las Trampas** (on SR 76, S of Taos in Las Trampas), built more than 200 years ago with 6-ft-thick adobe walls; early sculpture, paintings, and other artifacts; open daily. Chimayo (23 m S of Las Trampas on SR 76), known for blanket weaving, has the lovely **Santuario de Chimayo,** with primitive decorations. **Picuris Pueblo** (San Lorenzo, 16 m S via US 64), founded in the 13th-C, offers archaeological excavations.

TRUTH OR CONSEQUENCES: Geronimo Springs Museum (325 Main St.) displays minerals and local historical items; open Mon.-Sat. 9:30-4:30, Sun. 1-4:30; closed Jan. 1, Easter, Dec. 25; sm adm.

TUCUMCARI: Tucumcari Historical Museum (416 S Adams St.) displays minerals, fossils, Indian and Western historical items; open May 15-Sept. 15, daily 9-noon, 1-8; rest of yr, Tues.-Sun. 9-noon, 1-5; sm adm.

WHITE SANDS NATIONAL MONUMENT (15 m SW of Alamogordo on US 70, 82): rare desert of glistening gypsum sand, ever-shifting dunes rising as high as 40 ft.; attractive, adobe-brick **Visitor Center,** with Spanish,

Indian, and Mexican motifs and furnishings; orientation on the special adaptations of plants and animals; naturalist programs; open daily 8-5 (8-7 in spring-mid-Sept.); closed Dec. 25. Scenic, 16-m, round-trip drive. Park open 7 am-6 pm (to 10 pm in summer); sm adm or GEP.

NEW YORK

ADIRONDACK PARK: Dept. of Environmental Conservation (Albany 12201) will provide information on this 2½-million acre forest preserve. **Adirondack Museum** (1 m N of jct SR 28, 30, Blue Mountain Lake): Adirondack guide boats; logging, maple sugaring tools; other exhibits tracing the history of the region, housed in 20 buildings; open June 15-Oct. 15 daily 10-5; adm. **Piseco Lake Museum** (off SR 8 in Piseco), 19th-C tavern with Adirondack relics; open July-Aug. daily 10-5; spring & fall, Tues.-Sun. 10-5; sm adm. See also Glens Falls, Lake George Village, Lake Placid, Plattsburgh, Saranac Lake, Saratoga Springs, Ticonderoga.

ALBANY: State Capitol (State St.), imposing structure that took 32 years to build; famous for Million Dollar Staircase (with busts of political leaders, angels, imps) and beautiful senate chamber (designed by Henry Richardson); portraits; military museum; guided tours available; open Memorial Day-Labor Day, daily 9-4; May-Memorial Day & Labor Day-Oct., Mon.-Sat. 10-3; Nov.-Apr., Mon.-Fri. 10-3, Sat. 10-noon; closed Jan. 1, Thnks, Dec. 25; free. **Gov. Alfred E. Smith State Office Bldg.** (S Swan St., behind Capitol) observation platform is open, weather permitting, late-May-Aug., Mon.-Fri. 10-4; free.

New York State Museum (South Mall) traces history of man in the area; good displays on the Iroquois; gem, fossil, natural history exhibits; open daily 9-4:30; closed Jan. 1, Thnks, Dec. 25; free. **Albany Institute of History & Art** (125 Washington Ave.) traces history of the Hudson Valley; furniture, silver, pewter, china; portraits and Hudson River School paintings; Egyptian, Etruscan, Greek, Roman art objects; open Tues.-Sat. 10-4:45, Sun. 2-5; closed hols; free.

Schuyler Mansion (27 Clinton at Catherine St.), built 1762 by Philip Schuyler; fine paneling and period furnishings; Alexander Hamilton married Schuyler's daughter here in 1780; open Tues.-Sat. 9-5, Sun. noon-5; closed hols; free. **Ten Broeck Mansion** (9 Ten Broeck Pl), built 1798, is furnished in Federal period; open Tues.-Sun. 3-4; closed Jan. 1, Thnks, Dec. 25; free. **Historic Cherry Hill** (S Pearl St., between 1st & McCarty Aves.), built 1768 by Col. Philip Van Rensselaer; original furnishings, portraits, silver, glass, china, documents; open Tues.-Sat. 10-4, Sun. 1-4; closed Jan. 1, Thnks, Dec. 24, 25, 31; adm. **Fort Crailo** (across Dunn Memorial Bridge at 9½ Riverside Ave. in Rensselaer), Dutch manor house built 1704 by Hendrick Van Rensselaer; period furnishings; a British army surgeon is said to have written *Yankee Doodle* here in 1758; open Tues.-Sat. 9-5, Sun. noon-5; closed Jan. 1, Easter, Election Day, Thnks, Dec. 25; free.

State University of N.Y. at Albany (NW edge of town off Western Ave.), with a 15-building complex designed by Edward Durrell Stone; guided tours from Information Desk, Campus Center, Mon.-Fri. 10-2; free.

ALEXANDRIA BAY: Boldt Castle (Heart Island), replica of a Rhineland castle, was begun by the owner of New York's Waldorf-Astoria Hotel as a present for his wife and was left unfinished at her death in 1902; open mid-May-Oct., daily 9-7; adm; most sightseeing boat tours from the docks include a ½-hr stop here.

ALFRED: Binns-Merrill Hall (Alfred Univ. campus) houses the important Silverman and Carder collections of glass; Wesp porcelain; crested plates made for royal houses of Europe; open Mon.-Fri. 9-5; free. **Whitney-Halsey Home** (15 m W via SR 244 at 39 South St., Belmont) is a furnished Victorian mansion; open May-Oct., Tues.-Sun. 10-5; adm. **Allegany County Historian's Office** (5 m N of Belmont via SR 19, then 3½ m E to Old County Infirmary on county #2) has local historic display; open Mon.-Fri. 10-4:30; free.

AMSTERDAM: Guy Park House (366 W Main St.), a 1766 Georgian home rebuilt after a fire, is handsome; period furnishings; open Tues.-Sat. 9-5, Sun. 1-5; closed hols; free. **Old Fort Johnson** (3 m W on SR 5), built 1749 by the British Colonial Indian Commissioner, was fortified in 1755; in 1777 it was confiscated and its lead roof melted into bullets for the Continental Army; many original furnishings, Colonial and Indian artifacts; open July-Aug., Tues.-Sat. 10-5, Sun. & Mon. 1-5; May-June, Sept.-Oct. daily 1-5; adm. **Erie Canal** (6 m W on SR 5S at Fort Hunter), section of the original canal, built 1822.

National Shrine of North American Martyrs (7 m W on SR 5S in Auriesville) is on site of a 17th-C Mohawk village where missionaries were killed; Indian museum; open early May-late Oct. daily 8-8; free. Nearby **Mohawk-Caughnawaga Museum** (½ m W of Fonda on SR 5) houses artifacts from excavated Mohawk village; open June-mid-Sept. 10-dark; donation. **William W. Badgley Historical Complex** (24 m S on Sr 30 in Schoharie): a museum of early furnishings and tools; carriage house with antique vehicles; regional historical displays in **Old Stone Fort Museum,** a 1772 church that was fortified during the Revolution; open June-Aug. daily 10-5; spring & fall, Tues.-Sat. 10-5, Sun. noon-5; closed hols; adm.

ARCADE: Arcade & Attica Railroad (278 Main St.) offers a railroad museum, Grover Cleveland's private car, steam train trips; open late May-late Oct., Sat., Sun., & hols noon-4; also Wed. in July-Aug.; adm. **Griffis Sculpture Park** (20 m SE off US 219 on Ahrens Rd. in Ashford Hollow) displays work of sculptor Larry W. Griffis; open June-Oct., daily 9-7; sm adm.

AUBURN: Seward House (33 South St.), home of William H. Seward, Lincoln's Sec. of State who was influential in the Alaska purchase; many original furnishings; paintings, Lincoln letters, Seward memorabilia including a Mongolian armored coat; open May-Dec., Mon.-Sat. 1-5; closed hols; adm. **Cayuga Museum of History & Art** (203 Genesee St.) has Indian and historic exhibits; open Tues.-Fri. 1-5, Sat. 9-5, Sun. 2-5 (exc Jan.-Feb.); closed hols; free. **Owasco Stockaded Indian Village** (3 m S on SR 38A in Emerson County Park), on site of 1150 village, offers cultural and craft exhibits; demonstrations; open July-Aug., Sun.-Fri. 1-5, Sat. 10-6; sm adm. **Sherwood Library & Museum** (15 m S on SR 34B in Sherwood) houses memorabilia of Emily Howland, early abolitionist and suffragette; open mid-June-mid-Sept., Tues., Thurs. 1-5; free. **Moravia** (18 m SE on SR 38), birthplace of Millard Fillmore, offers a replica of his log cabin in **Fillmore Glen State Park;** open mid-May-mid-Sept., daily 8 am-10 pm; sm adm. **St. Matthew's Church** (16 Church St., Moravia) has wonderful Oberammergau carvings; open daily.

BATAVIA: Holland Land Office Museum (131 W Main St.), where deeds for freeholds in western New York were issued, is a museum of the area's pioneer settlement; library; open Mon.-Sat. 10-5, Sun. 2-5; closed hols; free. **Cobblestone Society Museum** (19 m N via SR 98 at Childs), with 1834 church, 1849 school, has museum on cobblestone masonry and 19th-C life; open early July-early Sept., Tues.-Sat. 11-5, Sun. 1-5; sm adm.

BEACON: Madam Brett Homestead (50 Van Nydeck Ave.), built 1709 and visited by Washington, Lafayette; period furnishings; open mid-Apr.-mid-Nov., Wed.-Sat. 1-4; adm. **Foundry School Museum** (6 m S on SR 9D at 63 Chestnut St., Cold Spring) offers local foundry and Hudson River exhibits; open Wed. 9:30-4, Sun. 2-5; closed Jan. 1, Dec. 25; free.

  Boscobel (6 m S on SR 9D, S of Cold Spring), restored 1805 mansion in style of Scottish architect Robert Adam, has fine British and American period furnishings, below-ground kitchen; garden; tours Apr.-Oct., Wed.-Mon. 9:30-5; Mar., Nov.-Dec., Wed.-Sun. 9:30-4; closed Thnks, Dec. 25, Jan.-Feb.; adm. **Van Wyck Homestead Museum** (4 m E at jct US 9, I-84), restored 1732 Dutch Colonial home, was officers' hq for Washington's forces 1776-83; mock trial of Enoch Crosby, counterspy for Colonial forces, was held here; open Apr.-Oct., Wed. & Sun. 1-5, Sat. 10-5; sm adm.

BELMONT: Americana Manse (39 South St.), the Whitney-Halsey mansion, has Victorian furnishings; open May-Oct., Tues.-Sun. 10-5; adm.

BINGHAMTON: City Hall is a fine example of Hotel de Ville style; open Mon.-Fri. 9-4:30; free. **Roberson Center for the Arts & Sciences** (30 Front St.): archaeological and Indian displays, Royal Worcester birds, historical exhibits, arts and crafts, and planetarium in 1906 mansion with period furnishings, carriage house; addition designed by Richard J. Neutra; open Mon.-Fri. 10-5, Sat. & Sun. noon-5; closed hols; free.

Tioga County Historical Society Museum (23 m W via SR 17C at 110 Front St., Owego) offers Indian and pioneer artifacts, paintings, pewter, newspaper files; open Tues.-Fri. 10-noon, 1:30-4:30, Sat. & Sun. 1:30-4:30; closed hols; free.

BUFFALO: City Hall (McKinley Circle) 28th-floor observation deck is open Mon.-Fri. 9-3:30; free. In front is a memorial to Pres. William McKinley, assassinated while attending the 1901 Pan-American Exposition. N from here along Delaware Ave. are most of the major sights: **Buffalo Club** (388 Delaware Ave.), where U.S. Cabinet met while the President lay moribund Sept. 6-14, 1901; private. **Theodore Roosevelt Inaugural National Historic Site** (641 Delaware Ave.), Greek Revival Wilcox House in which Roosevelt took the oath of office on Sept. 14; audiovisual program; open Mon.-Fri. 10-5, Sat. & Sun. noon-5; closed hols; sm adm. **Forest Lawn Cemetery,** graves of Millard Fillmore and Seneca chief Red Jacket. **Delaware Park** (Lincoln Pkwy) was designed in 1870 by Frederick Law Olmstead. **Albright-Knox Art Gallery** (1285 Elmwood Ave.) is strong on 19th-20th-C American works (Harnett, Inness, Ryder, Sargent, Homer, Pollock, Kline, Rothko); also 19th-C French painting, 18th-C English painting; sculpture; open Tues.-Sat. 10-5, Sun. noon-5; closed Jan. 1, Thnks, Dec. 25; adm. **Buffalo & Erie County Historical Society** (25 Nottingham Ct & Elmwood Ave.), in a Doric structure, only building remaining from the 1901 Pan-American Exposition; exhibits on Niagara area from frontier days to present; reconstructed 1870 street; library; open Mon.-Fri. 10-5, Sat. & Sun. noon-5; closed hols; free. **Buffalo Museum of Science** (Humboldt Park), natural and physical sciences, archaeology;

Chinese and African art objects; children's museum; planetarium; library; open Mon.-Sat. 10-5, Sun. & hols 1:30-5:30; closed Dec. 25; free.

CANAJOHARIE: Canajoharie Library & Art Gallery (Erie Blvd.) offers large collection of Winslow Homer oils, watercolors; representative works from Colonial times to the present include Stuart, Hopper, Andrew Wyeth, Hudson River school, Ashcan school; sculpture; open Mon.-Fri. 10-5:15 (9-4 in July-Labor Day), Sat. 10-2; closed hols; free.

Fort Klock (9 m NW on SR 5 in St. Johnsville), a 1750 farmhouse and trading post fortified during the Revolution; carriage house, workshops; open Memorial Day-Labor Day, Tues.-Sun. 9-5; sm adm. **Golden Age Auto Museum** (1 m N on SR 5 to W. Grand St. in Palatine Bridge), more than 40 antique autos 1890-1940; open mid-June-mid-Sept. daily 10-5; spring & fall, Sun. 10-5; adm. **Fort Plain Museum** (4 m W on SR 5S in Fort Plain), on site of a Revolutionary fort; local historical artifacts; open June-Sept., Tues.-Sun. 10-5; sm adm.

CANANDAIGUA: Granger Homestead (295 N Main St.), a fine Federal home, was built 1816 by Gideon Granger, who served in the Jefferson and Madison administrations; carved woodwork, antique furnishings, silver, china; Carriage Museum with horse-drawn hearse, sleighs, peddlar's wagon; open Tues.-Sun. 10:30-5:30; closed Jan. 1, Easter, Thnks, Dec. 25; adm. **Ontario County Historical Society Museum** (55 N Main St.), with maps, documents, musical instruments, is open Tues.-Sat. 1-5; closed hols; free.

CLAYTON: Thousand Islands Museum (401 Riverside Dr.) houses exhibits on area history; open late May-late Sept., daily 9-9; sm adm. **Thousand Islands Shipyard Museum** (750 Mary St.) offers antique power boats and nautical exhibits; open late May-late Sept., daily 9-9; sm adm.

COOPERSTOWN: Fenimore House (1 m N on SR 80), built 1932 on the site of a cottage once owned by James Fenimore Cooper, has some Cooper mementos but the body of exhibits is a superb collection of American folkart; works by famous, trained artists; charming, intriguing works by lesser known or anonymous artists; also contemporary folk art; hall of life masks; hq of State Historical Assoc.; library adjacent; open daily 9-5; closed Jan. 1, Thnks., Dec. 25; adm. The Association also maintains the **Farmers' Museum** (opposite, on SR 80), a complex illustrating rural life 1783-1840 in shops, offices, tavern, and other buildings brought here from the surrounding area; craft demonstrations; exhibit on the Cardiff Giant hoax of 1869; open May-Oct. daily 9-5; Nov.-Apr., Tues.-Sat. 9-5, Sun. noon-5; closed Jan. 1, Thnks, Dec. 25; adm.

National Baseball Hall of Fame & Museum (Main St.): Abner Doubleday is believed to have invented the game here in 1839; open May-Oct. daily 9-9, Nov.-Apr. daily 9-5; closed Jan. 1, Thnks, Dec. 25; adm. **Carriage & Harness Museum** (Elk St.) houses vehicles and equipment used in sport driving in 1903 coach house and stables of a fancier; open May-Oct. daily 9-5; Nov.-Apr., Mon.-Fri. 9-5, Sat. 9-noon; closed Jan. 1, Thnks, Dec. 25; adm. **Cooperstown & Charlotte Valley Railway** (1 Railroad St.) offers 16-m trips in old coaches drawn by steam locomotive (daily in summer, weekends in spring & fall; adm) and the **National Railroad Museum** (May-Oct. daily 9-5; free). **Dennys Toy Museum** (9 m N on SR 80 in Springfield Center) offers antique toy displays mid-May-mid-Oct. daily 9:30-6; sm adm. **Cherry Valley Museum** (11 m NE on SR 166 on Main St., Cherry Valley), built 1832 on the Great Western Turnpike, has period furnishings, guns, relics of Cherry Valley Massacre, musical instruments; open late May-Sept., daily 10-5:30; adm.

CORNING: Corning Glass Center (Centerway) is an impressive showcase of glassmaking from Egyptian times to the present; Hall of Science push-button displays and films; glassmaking can be watched in the Steuben Factory; open July-Aug. daily 8:30-5; June, Sept.-Oct. daily 9:30-5; Nov.-May, Tues.-Sun. 9:30-5; closed Jan. 1, Thnks, Dec. 25; free, but parking fee in summer.

Rockwell-Corning Museum (Market St.) offers bronzes, paintings, drawings of the American West by Remington, Bierstadt, Russell, Sharp, others; displays of Steuben glass traces career of designer Frederick Carder; antique toys, guns, Navajo rugs; open Mon.-Sat., 10-5:30; closed hols; free.

Erwin Museum (3 m SW on US 15 in Town Hall, Water St., Painted Post) offers Indian relics, replica of the Painted Post, local historical material; open July-Aug., Mon.-Sat. 9:30-noon; rest of yr, Tues., Thurs. 2-4; free.

COXSACKIE: Bronck House Museum (4 m S on US 9W), a 1663 homestead, has stone and brick houses, 13-sided barn, Dutch barn, family cemetery, artifacts on display; open late June-early Sept., Tues.-Sat. 10-5, Sun. 2-6; adm.

ELMIRA: Arnot Art Museum (235 Lake St.), Greek Revival home of 19th-C industrialist Matthias Arnot, exhibits European painting from Old Masters to contemporary; American painting and sculpture; open Tues.-Fri. 10-5, Sat. & Sun. 2-5; closed hols; free. **Chemung County Historical Center** (304 William St.) offers displays on the Civil War, Mark Twain, area Indians, Eskimo, local history; open Tues., Wed., Fri. 1-4:30; also May-Oct., Sun. 2-5; free. **Mark Twain Study** (Park Pl., Elmira College campus), octagonal study designed 1874 to resemble the pilothouse of a steamboat, was where Samuel Clemens wrote *Tom Sawyer;* inquire locally for schedule; free. **Woodlawn Cemetery** (N end of Walnut St.) contains grave of Mark Twain.

GENEVA: Geneva Historical Society Museum (543 S Main St.), in 1825 Federal-style Prouty-Chew House, has period rooms, costumes, toys, art, local historical exhibits; open Tues.-Sat. 1:30-4:30; closed hols; sm adm. **Rose Hill Mansion** (3 m E on SR 96A), an 1839 Greek Revival house with spiral staircase; original furniture; open May-Oct., Mon.-Sat. 10-4, Sun. 1-4; adm. **Seneca Falls Historical Society Museum** (10 m E via US 20 to 55 Cayuga St., Seneca Falls), in 19th-C home; interesting displays on women's rights movement, textile industry; open Apr.-Nov., Mon., Tues., Thurs., Fri. 1-4; closed hols; adm.

HAMMONDSPORT: Glenn H. Curtiss Museum (Lake & Main Sts.) houses memorabilia of the town's aviation history and of native son Glenn H. Curtiss; open mid-May-Oct., Mon.-Sat. 10-3:30; adm. **Narcissa Prentiss Home** (NW via SR 53 in Prattsburg) was birthplace of first woman to cross the Rockies (1836); open late May-early Oct., Wed.-Sun. & hols 1-5; free.

   Greyton H. Taylor Wine Museum (2 m N on Bully Hill Rd.), housed in the old Taylor Winery (1883-1920), has exhibits on early winemaking; tours May-Oct., Mon.-Sat. 9-4:30, Sun. 1-4:30; Nov.-Apr., Mon.-Fri. by appointment; adm. Nearby wineries (**Pleasant Valley Wine Co.** and **Taylor Wine Co.**, 1½ m S on county #88, and **Gold Seal Vineyard**, 4 m N on SR 54A) usually offer free tours weekdays 9-3:30; inquire locally for exact hrs. **Widmer's Wine Cellars, Inc.** (NW via SR 53 to West St. in Naples) offers guided tours June-Oct., Mon.-Sat., 10-3; closed hols; free.

HERKIMER: Settled in 1725 by German Palatines, this town is named for Revolutionary War hero Gen. Nicholas Herkimer; county courthouse was site of Gillette trial on which Theodore Dreiser based his *An American Tragedy.* **Herkimer County Historical Society** (400 N Main St.) contains exhibits on local history; open June-Aug., Mon.-Fri. 1-5; Sept.-May, Tues. 9-5; free. **Remington Arms Museum** (4 m W in Ilion at 14 Hoefler Ave.) displays every type of firearm manufactured by the Remington Arms Co. since its formation near here in 1816; open daily 9-9; free.

   Herkimer Home (9 m E on SR 5S in Little Falls), 1764 Dutch Colonial mansion of Gen. Herkimer; original furnishings; open mid-Apr.-Oct., Mon.-Sat. 9-5, Sun. 1-5; free. Nearby (5 m E on SR 5S) is **Indian Castle Church**, a 1769 mission for the Mohawk; open May-Oct., daily 8-8; donation. **Holy Trinity Monastery** (9 m SE off SR 28 in Jordanville), founded 1930 by Russian monks, has typical onion-shape domes, ornate frescos and ceiling paintings, and icons; open daily. **Fort Klock** (17 m E via SR 5 to St. Johnsville, then 1 m E on SR 5), a fortified farmhouse built 1750 by Johannes Klock, is open June-Sept., Tues.-Sun. 9-6; sm adm.

HOOSICK FALLS: Bennington Battlefield State Historic Site (7 m NE on SR 67): During the British push toward Bennington, Vermont, American citizen-soldiers here defeated Indians and German mercenaries and mortally wounded their commander Lt. Col. Friedrich Baum on Aug. 16, 1777; this victory encouraged new American volunteers, and Burgoyne surrendered 2 months later; historic markers; open May-Oct., 9-dusk; free.

New Skete Monastery (11 m N via SR 22 to Cambridge, then 4 m E on Chestnut Hill Rd.) is an 8-domed Byzantine monastery operated by Brotherhood of St. Francis; arts and crafts; German Shepherd kennels; open Mon.-Fri. 8-3:30, Sat. & Sun. 9-4:30; free.

HUDSON: Shaker Museum (17 m NE on SR 66, then E on County #13 to Shaker Museum Rd., Old Chatham) is a complex housing furniture, tools, ironwork, other crafts and products from several Shaker colonies, including the nation's largest, established at nearby Mt. Lebanon in 1774; open May-Oct., daily 10-5:30; adm. **American Museum of Fire Fighting** (Harry Howard Ave.) houses antique fire-fighting equipment and memorabilia, folk art, paintings, photographs; open daily 9-5; free.

Olana (3 m S on SR 9G) is a Persian and Moorish influenced summer home built 1874 by Hudson River school painter Frederick E. Church; ornate, eclectic furnishings; paintings; open Memorial Day-early Nov., Wed.-Sun. 9-5; free.

House of History (15 m N on US 9 at 16 Broad St. in Kinderhook) is a Federal-period house with flying staircase and Hudson Valley furnishings from 1790-1845; memorabilia of Martin Van Buren, who was born and is buried in Kinderhook; open late May-mid-Sept., Tues.-Sat. 10:30-4:30, Sun. 1:30-4:30; adm includes **Van Alen House** (on SR 9H), a 1737 Dutch farmhouse, open same hrs.

Clermont State Park (16 m S on SR 9G, then W on County #6), with lovely river views; home of Robert R. Livingston, who administered oath of office to Washington; open mid-May-early-Sept., daily 9-5; sm adm.

Ancram Opera House & Gardens (18 m SE on SR 82 in Ancram), a restored early 20th-C opera house, and the **Johann Strauss Atheneum** (also known as the Operetta Museum), with programs, scores, sheet music from operettas on display, are open June-Aug., Thurs.-Sun. 1-5; Sept.-May, Sat. & Sun. 1-5; adm.

HYDE PARK: Franklin D. Roosevelt National Historic Site (1 m S on US 9), home built in the early 1800s and extensively remodeled after the 32nd

President was born here on Jan. 30, 1882; graves of Eleanor and Franklin Roosevelt; open daily 9-5; closed Jan. 1, Dec. 25; sm adm or GEP. Adjacent is **Franklin D. Roosevelt Library & Museum**, with personal memorabilia and research library; open daily 9-5; closed Dec. 25; sm adm.

Vanderbilt Mansion National Historic Site (1 m N on US 9), home built 1896-98 in Italian Renaissance style for Frederick W. Vanderbilt, grandson of Cornelius Vanderbilt; ornate dining room with Italian ceiling runs the length of the mansion; lavish furnishings typical of Gilded Age wealthy; open daily 9-5; closed Jan. 1, Dec. 25; sm adm or GEP.

Edwin A. Ulrich Art Museum (N on Albany Post Rd. to Wave Crest): 300 marine paintings and drawings by Frederick J. Waugh (1861-1940); open May-Oct., Thurs.-Mon. 10:30-4; adm. **Ogden Mills & Ruth Livingston Mills Memorial State Park** (4 m N on US 9 in Staatsburg), French Renaissance mansion built 1832; fine furnishings; art objects from Europe, Far East; open mid-Apr.-mid-Nov. daily 10:30-4; rest of yr, Sat., Sun., hols 10:30-4; closed mid-Dec.-Jan. 1; sm adm.

ITHACA: Cornell University, overlooking Cayuga Lake; campus maps at **Visitor Information Center** (Edmund Ezra Day Hall, East Ave.), open Mon.-Fri. 8:30-4:30; tours spring-fall, Mon.-Fri. 11 & 1, Sat. 11:30. Campus landmarks include **McGraw Tower** (concerts on the chimes daily, academic yr; visitors may watch chimemasters at work) and **Morrill Hall** (French Renaissance style, 1868, first campus building). **Herbert F. Johnson Museum of Art** (East Ave. & Tower Rd.), designed by I. M. Pei firm; 17th-C Dutch, 19th-C French, and 19th-20th-C American painting; sculpture; graphics; ceramics; Far East collection; open mid-June-late Aug., Tues.-Sat. 11-4:30, Sun. 1-4:30; rest of yr, Tues.-Sat. 11-5, Sun. 1-5; free. **Ornithology Laboratory** (3 m NE at 159 Sapsucker Wood Rd.) has fine library and observatory; open Mon.-Thurs. 8:30-5, Fri. 8:30-4, weekends & hols 10-5; free.

DeWitt Historical Society Museum (Clinton House, 116 N Cayuga St.), displays on Ithaca's history; Indian artifacts; glass, textiles, tools, toys; library; open Tues.-Sat. 12:30-5, Sun. 1-5; closed hols; free. **Payne Museum** (3 m SW via SR 13, then 18 m S on SR 34, 96, just before Spencer), Colonial, Indian, and Civil War displays; open May-Oct., Tues.-Sun. 8 am-9 pm; sm adm.

JAMESTOWN: Fenton Historical Center (68 S Main St.), local historical displays; open Mon.-Sat. 1-5; closed hols; free. **James Prendergast Library** (509 Cherry St.) exhibits paintings from 1870-90, local works; open Mon.-Fri. 9-9, Sat. 9-5, Sun. (Oct.-May) 2-5; closed hols; free.

Chautauqua Institution (17 m NW in Chautauqua) is a 700-acre, nonsectarian educational and recreational center; plays, concerts, art exhibits, courses, special events, boat cruises, outdoor model of the Holy Land; open July-Aug. daily for a general adm fee (some activities are an extra fee); for information, write Box 1095, Chautauqua 14722. **Lily Dale** (18 m NW off SR 60) claims to be world's largest center of Spiritualism; library, healing temple; seances, lectures in July-Aug.; write Lily Dale Assembly (5 Melrose Park, Lily Dale 14752). **Chautauqua County History Center & Museum** (27 m W via SR 17 in Village Park, Westfield) is in McClurg's Folly, 1820 mansion of Scots-Irish trader who had bricks transported to the wilderness from Pittsburgh; regional historic exhibits; library; open May-Oct., Tues.-Sat. 10-12, 1-5; also Sun. in July-Aug. 2-5; closed hols; sm adm.

JOHNSTOWN: Johnson Hall (Hall Ave.), splendid estate carved out of the wilderness by William Johnson, whose success in dealing with the Six Iroquois Nations helped end French influence in the NE and gained him the title of baronet; period furnishings, Johnson memorabilia, dioramas; stone blockhouse; open Tues.-Sat. 9-5, Sun. 1-5; closed some hols; free. Guided tours of historic landmarks in town leave Johnstown park June-Aug., Mon.-Sat. 10:30, 2; Sun. 2; free.

KATONAH: John Jay Homestead (Jay St.), handsome home of first Chief Justice of the U.S. 1801 until his death 1829; restored to 1780s appearance; personal possessions, portraits; open Wed.-Sun. 9-5; closed Jan. 1, Easter, Thnks, Dec. 25; free. **Yorktown Museum** (6 m W on SR 35, then S to 1886 Hanover Rd., Yorktown Heights), exhibits on folk life; library; open Wed., Thurs., Sun. 2-5; closed Easter, Thnks, Dec. 25; free. **Hammond Museum** (2 m N on I-684, then 7½ m E via SR 138, 121 to Deveau Rd., N Salem), changing exhibits on the humanities; open mid-May-late Dec., Wed.-Sun. & most hols 11-5; closed Thnks; adm.

KINGSTON: Established 1614 as a Dutch trading post, Kingston became New York's first capital in 1777; many colonial homes can be seen on free walking tours (leave Gov. Clinton Hotel, 1 Albany Ave.) May-Sept., 3rd Thurs. of month, 2 pm; tours also on Stone House Day in July. **Senate House** (312 Fair St.), built 1676, was meeting place of the state's first Senate in 1777; area furnishings; adjoining museum houses Hudson River marine art, portraits by John Vanderlyn, historic exhibits; open Wed.-Sat. 9-5, Sun. 1-5; closed Jan. 1, Easter, Thnks, Dec. 25; free. **Old Dutch Church** (Main & Wall Sts.) houses colonial records; grave of first N.Y. Governor, George Clinton; open daily 9-4:30; closed hols; free.

    Delaware & Hudson Canal Historical Society Museum (10 m S via SR 32, 213 to School Hill Rd., High Falls) houses canal memorabilia; open mid-May-late Oct., Fri., Sat., Sun. 2-5; free.

LAKE GEORGE VILLAGE: Fort William Henry (½ m S on US 9 at Canada St.), was built by the British in 1755 to defend Lake George-Hudson River portage, was burned by French in 1757; barracks and stockade reconstructed from original plans; museum of French & Indian War relics; military demonstrations; audiovisual program; adjacent Iroquois village; open daily, July-Aug. 9 am-10 pm; May-June & Sept.-Oct. 10-5; adm. **Historical Society of Bolton** (11 m N via 9N on Main St., Bolton Landing) displays items of local history; works by sculptor David Smith; open July-early Sept., Tues., Thurs., Sat. 7-9 pm; free. **Marcella Sembrich Memorial Studio** (on SR 9N, Bolton Landing) contains memorabilia of the singer; open July-early Sept. daily 10-12:30, 2-5:30; free.

LAKE PLACID: John Brown Farm State Historic Site (3 m S off SR 73 on John Brown Rd.), with some original furnishings; here the famous abolitionist moved with his family in 1855 and lived on-and-off until his execution in 1859; his grave is here; open Mon.-Sat. 9-5, Sun. 1-5; closed Jan. 1, Easter, Thnks, Dec. 25; free. **Uihlein-Cornell Sugar House** (Bear Cub Rd.), exhibits on maple sugaring; open July-Labor Day, Tues.-Sat. 1-5; also fall color season (about mid-Sept., mid-Oct., Fri. & Sat. 1-5); also sap boiling season (late Mar.-Apr.); free. **Lake Placid Historical Society Museum** (Averyville Rd.), displays on the Adirondack region; open July-mid-Sept., Tues.-Sun. 12:30-5; sm adm. **Adirondack Center Museum & Colonial Garden** (26 m E via SR 73, 9N at Elizabethtown) offers exhibits on Adirondack history; open May 15-Oct. 15, Mon.-Sat. 9-5, Sun. 1-5; sm adm.

LETCHWORTH STATE PARK (SW of Geneseo; entrances at Mt. Morris, Perry, Castile, & Portageville): **Museum of pioneer and Indian history** is open mid-May-Oct., Tues.-Sun. 10-5; free. Nearby memorial to Mary Jemison, White Woman of the Genesee; kidnapped by Indians in 1755, she refused to return to her people, and lived as a Seneca until her death in 1833.

LOCKPORT: Niagara County Historical Center (215 Niagara St.) is a complex including an 1860 home with period rooms; 1835 law office; Pioneer Bldg. with Indian, pioneer relics; Fire Co. Bldg. with early fire-fighting equipment; other exhibits; open Tues.-Fri. 10-5, Sat. & Sun. 1-5; closed hols; free.

LONG ISLAND: Attractions along the **North Shore,** from the New York City line eastward, include: **Saddle Rock Grist Mill** (1½ m W of Great Neck on Bayview Ave., Saddle Rock), gets its power from a tidal pond; display on milling; open Apr.-Oct., Wed.-Sun. 9-5; free. **Roslyn** has a number of historic sites not open to the public: **George Washington Manor**

(1305 Northern Blvd.), built 1753, tavern visited by Washington during his 1790 tour of L.I.; early-19th-C **Gerry House** (105 Main St.) and **Smith House** (106 Main St.); **Sycamore Lodge** (Bryant Ave. off Northern Blvd.), 1843 Greek Revival home, Flemish gable ends; **Cedarmere** (Bryant Ave. off Northern Blvd.), home of poet William Cullen Bryant, 1843 until his death in 1878, gardens designed by Frederick Law Olmstead. **Christopher Morley Park** (Searington Rd. off L.I. Expwy), named for the author, who lived here until his death in 1957, contains his writing studio; open Wed.-Sun. 1-5; closed hols; sm adm. Bryant and Morley are buried in Roslyn Cemetery (SR 25A & Wellington Rd.). **Garvies Point Museum & Preserve** (follow signs off Glen Cove Rd., Glen Cove), on site of an Indian camp; regional geology and archaeology museum open daily 10-5, closed Jan. 1, Thnks, Dec. 25; grounds open daily in daylight; sm adm. **Westbury House** (in Old Westbury Gardens on Old Westbury Rd. in Old Westbury), 1906 Georgian-style mansion of financier John S. Phipps; fine paneling, 18th-C furnishings; open early May-late Oct., Wed.-Sun. & hols 10-5; adm to house in addition to garden adm. **Old Bethpage Village Restoration** (on Round Swamp Rd., 1 m S of L.I. Expwy in Bethpage) has 2 dozen buildings (country stores, tavern, church, homes, shops, farm) moved here from other parts of the island to depict a pre-Civil War rural community; film; open Feb.-Nov. daily 10-5; Dec.-Jan. daily 9-4; closed Jan. 1, Thnks, Dec. 25; adm.

Raynham Hall (20 W Main St., Oyster Bay) was bought in 1738 by Samuel Townsend, a spy for Gen. Washington; the unsuspecting British used his home as hq; a conversation overheard here led to the capture of Major Andre and exposure of Benedict Arnold's plan to betray West Point; 18th-C and Victorian furnishings; open Mon., Wed.-Sat. 10-noon, 1-5, Sun. 1-5; closed Jan. 1, Thnks, Dec. 25; sm adm. **Sagamore Hill National Historic Site** (3 m NE of Oyster Bay on Cove Neck Rd.) contains the unpretentious Victorian home of the Theodore Roosevelt family, completed 1885 (TR worked on the plans himself); served as the summer White House 1901-09; original furnishings; TR's hunting trophies and gun collection; bronzes by Remington and Saint-Gaudens; interesting and charming; open July-Labor Day, daily 9-6; rest of yr, daily 9-5; closed Jan. 1, Thnks, Dec. 25; sm adm or GEP. **Theodore Roosevelt's Grave** is in Young's Cemetery (1 m E on E Main St., parking space on S side of road).

Whaling Museum (Main St., Cold Spring Harbor) records the history of this former whaling port; fully equipped whaleboat; ship models; figureheads; scrimshaw; portraits; library; open Sat., Sun. & some hols 11:30-5:30; also open in summer, Mon.-Fri. 11-4; sm adm.

In Huntington, the **Huntington Historical Society** (2 High St. at New York Ave.) in 1750 farmhouse, has 18th-19th-C period rooms, historic artifacts, library; costumes, pottery, other items in the **Quaker Thomas Powell House** (434 Park Ave.); both open Tues.-Fri. 1-4, Sun. 2-5; closed hols; sm adm. **Heckscher Museum** (in Heckscher Park at SR 25A & Prime Ave.) displays fine 19th-C American painting and a few European works; open Tues.-Sat. 10-5, Sun. 2-5; closed Jan. 1, Election Day, Thnks, Dec. 25; free. **Walt Whitman House** (246 Walt Whitman Rd., ½ m S of jct SR 110 & Jericho Tpke in Huntington Station), where the poet was born 1819 and spent much of his youth, has Whitman memorabilia; library; open daily 10-4; closed some hols; free.

Vanderbilt Museum—Eagles Nest (2 m N off SR 25A on Little Neck Rd., Centerport), rambling Spanish-Moroccan-style mansion; unusual furnishings, anthropological materials, other objects collected around the world by William K. Vanderbilt, Jr.; 17,000 marine and wildlife specimens in a separate building; antique car collection; planetarium; open May-Oct., Tues.-Sat. 10-4, Sun. & hols noon-5; sm adm.

Suffolk Museum (off SR 25A on Christian Ave., Stony Brook), in former village hall, exhibits paintings by William Sidney Mount (1807-68), cobbler shop, country store, local historical items (open daily 10-5; closed Jan. 1, Thnks, Dec. 25; sm adm); **Carriage House** (SR 25A) includes 2 carriages owned by King Ludwig of Bavaria, locomotives, 19th-C printshop, 1818 schoolhouse, harness maker's shop (open Apr.-Nov. daily 10-5; adm). **Thompson House** (SR 25A, 1 m N of Stony Brook railroad station in Setauket), a saltbox begun about 1700, is hq of Society for Preservation of L.I. Antiquities; period furnishings; open May-Oct., Fri.-Sun. 1-5; sm adm. **Presbyterian Church** (Village Green, Setauket) cemetery has graves of William Sidney Mount and Washington's spy, Abraham Woodhull. **Caroline Church** (Village Green, Setauket) steeple served as target for British ships during the Revolution; church is scarred from 1776 Battle of Setauket; open daily 9-6. **Sherwood-Jayne House** (Old Post Rd., E. Setauket), a 1730 saltbox with wall painting and period furnishings, is open May-mid-Oct., Fri.-Sun. 1-5; sm adm.

Suffolk County Historical Society (300 W Main St., Riverhead) displays early American glass, china, lusterware; toys; dioramas; country store; blacksmith shop; farm tools; vehicles; Indian relics; open May-Oct., Mon.-Sat. 1-5; Nov.-Apr., Mon.-Sat. noon-4; closed hols; free. **Chamber of Commerce** (313 W Main St., Riverhead) provides information on historic sites in the area. **Old House** (SR 25 on Village Green, Cutchogue), 1649, has 17th-C furnishings; open July-Aug. daily 2-5 plus June & Sept. weekends; sm adm. **Southold Historical Society Museum** (SR 25 & Maple Lane), homestead with antique furnishings; open mid-June-mid-Sept., Tues., Thurs., Sat. 2-5; sm adm. **Oysterponds Historical Society Museum** (Village Lane, Orient) exhibits Indian, colonial, and whaling relics in a

1790 tavern, 1740 Webb House, and other restored buildings; open July-Oct., Tues., Thurs., Sat., Sun. 2-5; sm adm. **Shelter Island** (reached via ferry from Greenport on the N Shore or from SR 114 N of Sag Harbor on the S Shore), settled by Quakers fleeing persecution by New England Puritans; several historic markers.

Attractions along the **South Shore,** from New York City Line eastward, include: **Rock Hall Museum** (199 Broadway, Lawrence), lovely 1767 Georgian dwelling with period furnishings, fine Chippendale; open Apr.-Nov., Mon., Wed.-Sat. 10-5, Sun. noon-5; free. **Black History Museum** (106A Main St., Hempstead) traces L.I. black history from colonial times; open Mon.-Sat. 9-5; closed Jan. 1, Dec. 25; free. **Sagtikos Manor** (on SR 27A, 3 m W of Bay Shore), 1692 home with 1890s addition, was hq for Gen. Henry Clinton; Washington visited in 1790; music room; original kitchen; open July-Aug., Wed., Thurs., Sun. 1-4; also Memorial Day, July 4, Labor Day, 1-4; adm. **Manor of St. George Museum** (S off SR 27 via William Floyd Pkwy to Neighborhood Rd., Smith Point), estate granted 1693 to Col. William Smith (Mayor of Tangiers, Africa), houses historic documents and prints; open mid-May-mid-Nov. daily 9-6; free.

Southampton, with many colonial homes, offers: **Southampton Historical Museum** (17 Meeting House Lane off Main St.), with Indian, colonial, and whaling exhibits; country store; schoolhouse; open mid-June-Sept., Tues.-Sat. 11-5, Sun. 2-5; closed July 4; adm. **Parrish Art Museum** (25 Job's Lane) has more than 1500 works, mostly Italian Renaissance and early Roman, plus modern American painting; sculpture; open Tues.-Sat. 10-5, Sun. 2-5; closed hols; free. **St. Andrew's Dune Church** (Dune Rd.), on the sea, has an 1851 nave originally a lifeboat station; biblical texts inscribed on windows and walls; shipwreck relics on grounds. **Halsey Homestead** (S Main St.), built 1648, has 17th-18th-C furnishings; Halsey's bride was scalped by Indians; the house became a refuge against Dutch or Indian attacks; open mid-June-mid-Sept., Tues-Sat. 11-4:30, Sun. 2-4:30; sm adm. **Long Island Automotive Museum** (1 m NW on SR 27) offers Henry Austin Clark collection of antique and classic cars, other vehicles, accessories; open June-Sept. daily 9-5; spring & fall, Sat. & Sun. 9-5; adm. **Old Water Mill Museum** (2½ m NE on Old Mill Rd., Water Mill), 1644 gristmill, operated until 1887; craft and farm tools, other relics; craft demonstrations; open mid-June-late Sept., Mon., Wed.-Sat. 11-5, Sun. 1-4; adm. **Bridgehampton Historical Museum** (SR 27 at jct Corwith Ave., Bridgehampton), in mid-18th-C home, has early regional and Victorian furnishings; open late-May-mid-Sept., Mon., Wed., Fri.-Sun. 1:30-5; sm adm. Nearby is **John E. Berwind Memorial** (S off SR 27 on Ocean Rd.), a Dutch windmill.

East Hampton: "Home Sweet Home" House (14 James Lane), built 1660, was birthplace in 1791 of John Howard Payne, who wrote "Home

Sweet Home"; colonial pewter; lusterware; early kitchen; antique furnishings; 1771 windmill on grounds; open July-Aug. daily 10-5; rest of yr,
Wed.-Mon. 10-5; closed Jan. 1, Thnks, Dec. 25; sm adm. **Historic
Mulford House** (James Lane), is a 1680 duplicate of the Payne house;
17th-C furnishings; open late June-mid-Sept. daily 1:30-5; sm
adm. **Clinton Academy** (151 Main St.), in 1784 building, displays Indian,
whaling, and other local historical relics; restored schoolhouse; open late-
June-mid-Sept. daily 1:30-5; sm adm. **Old Hook Mill** (36 N Main St. &
SR 27) is a restored windmill; open late June-mid-Sept. daily 10-5; sm
adm. Not open to the public are: **Thomas Moran House** (229 Main St.),
1884 English Tudor home of the painter; **Lyman Beecher Homestead**
(Main St. & Hunting Lane), where he lived about 1800 while pastor of
Presbyterian Church here. **Town Marine Museum** (1 m S of SR 27 on
Bluff Rd., Amagansett), fishing and whaling exhibits from settlement to
the present; open late June-mid-Sept. daily 1:30-5; sm adm. **Miss
Amelia's Cottage** (SR 27 & Windmill Lane, Amagansett), a 1730 Cape
Cod with period furnishings, is open June-Labor Day, daily; adm.

  Sag Harbor, a great whaling port, was drawn on for stories by James
Fenimore Cooper; here are: **Suffolk County Whaling Museum** (Garden &
Main Sts.), in whaler's home; whaling relics, scrimshaw, early guns and
toys; open mid-May-Sept., Mon.-Sat. 10-5, Sun. 2-5; adm. **Custom
House** (Garden St.) has historic documents and displays; open July-Sept.,
Mon.-Sat. 10-5, Sun. 1-5; sm adm. **Oakland Cemetery** (Suffolk St. & Jer-
main Ave.) monument in the form of a broken mast pays tribute to lost
whaling crews. Old homes not open to the public are: **Old Umbrella
House** (Division St. near Burke St.), cannon scars from War of 1812;
Cornelius Sleight House (Division & Burke Sts.), built 1790; **Howell
House** (Main St. near Howard St.), an 1833 whaler's home.

MASSENA: Bus tours of St. Lawrence Seaway leave **Chamber of
Commerce** (W Orvis St.) or **Eisenhower Lock** (NE via SR 37, 131 to W end
of Wiley-Dondero Ship Channel), late June-late Sept., Mon.-Sat., twice
daily. The latter has viewing platform open May-mid Nov. daily 9-9; sm
adm. A visitor center with working models, audiovisual program, observation deck is in **Robert Moses State Park** (NE on Barnhart Island); open
May 15-Nov. 15 daily 8-4:30 (8-8 in summer); rest of yr, Mon.-Fri. 8-4:30;
free. **Akwesasne Mohawk Indian Village** (12 m NE on SR 37 on St. Regis
Reservation) offers programs on Indian crafts and life; Iroquois
longhouses; open mid-June-early Sept. daily 10-8; weekends in Sept.-Oct.;
adm.

NARROWSBURG: Fort Delaware (on SR 97), replica of 1754 stockade,
blockhouses, other buildings; exhibits and demonstrations depict life

along Delaware River from French & Indian War through Revolution; open late June-Labor Day, daily 10-5:30; also Sat. & Sun. in June & Sept. 10-5:30; adm.

NEWBURGH: Washington's Headquarters (84 Liberty St.), overlooking the Hudson, was the handsome Hasbrouck house, built 1725 and later enlarged, where Martha and George lived Apr. 1782-Aug. 1783; period furnishings; adjacent is an interesting regional museum; open Wed.-Sat. 9-4:30, Sun. 1-4:30; closed Jan. 1, Easter, Thnks, Dec. 25; free. **New Windsor Cantonment** (4 m SW off SR 32, 1 m N of Vails Gate on Temple Hill Rd.), a military village planned by Gen. von Steuben to house 6000-8000 soldiers during 1782, has diorama of the army on the move, demonstrations of old skills, other exhibits; open mid-Apr.-Oct., Wed.-Sun. 9-4:30; free. Nearby is **Knox Headquarters**, a 1754 stone house built by the owner of a grist mill that supplied flour for American troops; the jolly, 300-lb Maj.-Gen. Henry Knox, von Steuben, and others occupied it during the Revolution; period furnishings; open Mon.-Sat. 9-4:30, Sun. 1-5; closed Jan. 1, Easter, Thnks, Dec. 25; free.

Storm King Art Center (7 m S off SR 32 on Old Pleasant Hill Rd., Mountainville) houses contemporary European and American paintings and drawings; sculpture garden includes works by David Smith; open Apr.-Oct., Tues.-Sun. 2-5:30; free. **Brotherhood Wine Cellars** (9 m S on SR 94 in Washingtonville) offers tours late June-early Sept., Mon.-Sat. 10-4; check locally for spring-fall hrs; closed Dec.-mid-Feb., Good Friday, Thnks; free but parking fee. **Museum Village of Smith's Cove** (16 m S on SR 32, 17M to Museum Village Rd., Monroe), complex of more than 30 buildings depicting 19th-C American technology; natural history museum; craft demonstrations; open mid-May-Oct. daily 10-5; adm. **Hall of Fame of the Trotter** (18 m SW via SR 207 at 240 Main St., Goshen), devoted to harness racing; open Mon.-Sat. 10-5, Sun. & hols 1:30-5; closed Jan. 1, Thnks, Dec. 25; free. **Historic Track** (Park Pl., Goshen) is a National Historic Landmark. **Antique Clock Collection** (20 m SW off I-84 in Middletown Savings Bank, 4 South St., Middletown) open Mon.-Thurs. 9-3, Fri. 9-5; closed hols; free.

NEW PALTZ: Huguenot Historical Society Old Stone Houses (Huguenot St.) are 7 attractive houses built by French Huguenots 1692-1712. Open all yr (closed hols), Wed.-Sun. 10-4, are the museum in Deyo House, 1717 French Church, 2 houses; sm adm to each. Open mid-May-mid-Oct. (closed July 4, Labor Day), Wed.-Sun. 10-4:30, are 3 additional houses; tours available; adm.

Col. Josiah Hasbrouck House (4 m S on SR 32) is a Federal-style dwelling with period furnishings; farm museum; open June-Sept., Tues.-Sun. 10-5; sm adm.

Hudson Valley Wine Co. (5 m E on SR 299, then 1 m S on US 9W to Blue Point Rd., Highland) offers tours late-May-early Sept., Mon.-Sat. 10-4; inquire locally for spring & fall hrs; free, but parking fee. **Mandia Champagne Cellars** (11 m SE via SR 32, US 44 on Bedell Ave., Clintondale) offers tours mid-Apr.-Oct., Mon.-Sat. 10-4; free. **Royal Winery** (11 m SE via SR 299, US 9W on Dock Rd., Milton) offers film, tasting, May- Nov., Mon-Fri. 10:30-5; free.

NEW YORK CITY—MANHATTAN: Convention & Visitors Bureau (90 E 42nd St.) provides maps, calendar of events, industrial tour information; open daily 9-6. **Information Center** on Times Square also provides maps and brochures. Narrated boat trips around Manhattan are given by the **Circle Line** (Pier 83, at W 43rd St. & the Hudson River), Apr.-mid-Nov., daily; adm. **Hudson River Day Line** (Pier 81 at W 41st St. & the Hudson River) offers trips up the Hudson to West Point and other sites in summer. **Staten Island Ferry** (between South Ferry at the tip of Manhattan and Staten Island), long famed as the cheapest sea voyage in the world, runs frequently daily; fine views of lower Manhattan and the Statue of Liberty. **Empire State Building** (350 5th Ave. at 34th St.) provides spectacular views from observation platforms on the 86th and 102nd floors; open daily 9:30-am-11:30 pm; adm. Other overviews are from the **RCA Building** (see Rockefeller Center, below), cafes in several midtown hotels, and downtown from the **World Trade Center** (W of Church St. between Vesey & Liberty Sts.). A view of the Times Square area is available from a 15-16th-floor cafe in **One Times Square** (1 Times Sq. at 42nd St., Broadway, & 7th Ave.). Walking tours in the city, street festivals, and other events are often listed in magazines such as *The New Yorker, New York,* or *Cue,* or in newspapers such as *The New York Times* and *The Village Voice.* **Landmarks Preservation Commission** (305 Broadway, NY 10007) will send you a free booklet on buildings of interest and historic districts in the 5 boroughs.

Statue of Liberty National Monument (Liberty Island; boats leave from Battery, on S tip of Manhattan Island, daily 9-4; adm); Statue, erected 1886, designed by Bartholdi, was gift of the French people to commemorate French-American alliance during the Revolutionary War; pedestal designed by Gustav Eiffel; book in left hand represents Declaration of Independence; top reached by stairs or elevator plus a spiral staircase; at base is American Museum of Immigration, with dioramas and exhibits on immigrants; open May-Oct. daily 9-6; Nov.-Apr. daily 9-5.

Castle Clinton National Monument (Battery Park, tip of Manhattan Island): Built 1811 during Napoleonic-era tensions, this fort was never tested; in 1824 it was converted to Castle Garden, a place of public entertainment famed for concerts (Jenny Lind sang here in 1850), fireworks, and promenades; from 1855-90, as an immigrant receiving station, it processed more than 8 million newcomers; now restored as a fort; open daily 9-4:30; closed Jan. 1, Dec. 25; free. **Old U.S. Customs House** (S side of Bowling Green, an old Dutch market, at foot of Broadway) is a 1907 neoclassic building designed by Cass Gilbert; replete with symbolic sculpture (4 groups by Daniel Chester French). **Fraunces Tavern Museum** (54 Pearl St.), oldest surviving building in Manhattan, was built 1719; Washington's Farewell to his Officers took place here 1783; relics of Revolution; still operates as restaurant; open Mon.-Fri. 10-4; closed hols; free.

   Federal Hall National Memorial (Wall & Nassau Sts.) is on site of former City Hall, where Stamp Act Congress met in 1765, Washington was inaugurated Apr. 30, 1789, and the first Congress met 1789-90. Present structure was erected 1842 as U.S. Customs House and became U.S. Subtreasury in 1862; historical exhibits and audiovisual program; display on John Peter Zenger, whose 1735 acquittal here on charges of "seditious libels" against the royal government was a victory for freedom of the press; open Memorial Day-Labor Day, daily 9-4:30; rest of yr, Mon.-Fri. 9-4:30; closed Jan. 1, Dec. 25; free. Also in the financial district are: **New York Stock Exchange** (20 Broad St.) offers visitor gallery, film, displays, explanations of trading, guided tours; open Mon.-Fri. 10-3:30; closed hols; free. **American Stock Exchange** (86 Trinity Pl.), tours by reservation Mon.-Fri. 9:45-3; closed hols; free. **Federal Reserve Bank of N.Y.** (33 Liberty St.), where gold bullion is stored in underground vaults; tours by reservation 1 week in advance (high school juniors or older) on Mon.-Fri. 10, 11, 1, 2; closed hols; free. **Trinity Church** (Broadway & Wall St.) has occupied this site since 1697; present Gothic building dates from 1846; graves of Robert Fulton, Alexander Hamilton, Albert Gallatin; open daily; free. **St. Paul's Chapel** (Broadway & Fulton St.), completed 1766, lovely Georgian structure modeled on London's St. Martin in the Fields; Waterford cut-glass chandeliers; ornamentation by Pierre L'Enfant; Washington's pew (used 1789-91); open daily 8-5:15; open hols 8-noon; free. **Fire Department Museum** (104 Duane St., between Broadway & Church St.) displays 18th-C equipment and memorabilia; open Mon.-Fri. 9:30-3, Sat. 9:30-12:30; closed hols; free.

   Just N of the financial district are: **City Hall** (E of Broadway between Chambers St. & Park Pl.), a beautiful French-influenced marble building completed 1811; Federal interiors. **Brooklyn Bridge** (E of City Hall Park across East River), an engineering feat when completed 1883; designed by John A. Roebling and his son Washington. **South Street Seaport & Museum** (Fulton St. & East River) is restoring several blocks in this area to illustrate the city's maritime history; 1891 Gloucester fishing schooner, 1907 lightship, other ships are tied up at Seaport Pier and some may be boarded (sm adm); Museum (16 Fulton St.) displays pictures and artifacts, and provides information on exhibits in other buildings; many special events; open daily noon-6; closed Thnks, Dec. 25; free. **Chinatown** (N of Worth St. on Mott, Pell, & Doyers Sts.) has Chinese shops and restaurants. **Chinese Museum** (7 Mott St.) displays of musical instruments, costumes, dragon (extra fee), food; open daily 10-10; closed Dec. 25; sm adm. **The Bowery** (runs N from Chinatown to Cooper Sq.), once a road to outlying farms, then a wealthy residential area and entertainment district, is now Skid Row. **Little Italy** runs N from Chinatown to Greenwich Village; its main artery is Mulberry St.; many restaurants, coffee and pastry shops; San Gennaro (Sept.) and San Antonio (June) festivals are held in the streets annually. **Soho** (South of Houston St., between Canal St., Broadway, Ave. of Americas) is a commercial warehouse district where artists have converted cast-iron-front bldgs into studios and living quarters; many galleries, shops, bars. **Cooper Union** (4th Ave. & E 8th St.), where Lincoln spoke in the Great Hall on Feb. 27, 1860 (open by appointment Mon.-Fri. 9-5), offers special events. **Greenwich Village** (stretches N from W Houston St. 10 13th St., and from Broadway W to the Hudson River), once a country retreat for wealthy New Yorkers, became famous as a center for artists and writers (Tom Paine, Walt Whitman, Henry James, Eugene O'Neill, Edna St. Vincent Millay, Franz Kline, Agnes de Mille, Martha Graham, Jack Kerouac were just a few of the famous residents); many boutiques, bars, cafes. **Washington Square** (S end of 5th Ave.), once a potter's field, contains an 1895 arch commemorating Washington's first inauguration; on the S side is **Judson Hall & Tower,** designed by Stanford White in Italian Renaissance style, where George Inness and John Sloan had studios; on the E is **New York University;** a block off the SE corner are apartment buildings designed by I. M. Pei surrounding an abstract woman's bust designed by Picasso and executed by Carl Nesjar; on the N are Greek Revival row houses (Edward Hopper died in the top-floor studio of one in 1967). Quaint streets are **Washington Mews** (runs between 5th Ave. & University Pl., between Washington Square N and W 8th St.), **MacDougal Alley** (off MacDougal St., between Washington Square N and W 8th St.), and **Patchin Place** (off W 10, between Greenwich Ave. & Ave. of the Americas).

Theodore Roosevelt Birthplace National Historic Site (28 E 20th St.), restored birthplace where the 26th President spent his first 15 years, has period furnishings, exhibits on Roosevelt's boyhood interests and career; open daily 9-4:30; closed hols; sm adm or GEP. **Police Academy & Museum** (235 E 20th St. between 2-3rd Aves.) has exhibits on crime, weapons, police work; firearms demonstration; open Mon.-Fri. 9-4:30; closed hols; free. **Astro Minerals Gallery of Gems** (155 E 34th St.) has exhibits of gems, fossils, minerals, shells; open Mon.-Sat. 10-6; closed Jan. 1, Dec. 25; free. **Pierpont Morgan Library** (29 E 36th St.), in a 1906

Renaissance-style marble building, is a reference library that mounts outstanding exhibits of manuscripts, art objects, master drawings, or other rare items; open Tues.-Sat. 10:30-5, Sun. 1-5; closed Sat. in July, hols, Aug.; free. **New York Public Library** (5th Ave. at W 42nd St.) has more than 5-million volumes, maps, photographs, engravings, documents, rare works; exhibits mounted throughout the building; many branches include the Schomburg Collection (103 W 135th St. near Lenox Ave.) tracing black history and culture, and Library & Museum of the Performing Arts (see Lincoln Center); information available on many special libraries in the city; open daily; closed hols; free. **United Nations** (1st Ave. between 42nd-48th Sts.) consists of Conference Bldg. (Marc Chagall stained-glass window), Library (open to scholars only), Secretariat, and General Assembly Bldg. (tickets to sessions are issued on a first-come basis before each meeting); doors open 9-5:20 daily. In General Assembly Bldg. is a lobby information desk that issues tickets and conducts frequent tours (daily 9-4:45; closed Jan. 1, Dec. 25; adm); in basement are book and gift shops, post office.

Rockefeller Center (W of 5th Ave. between 48th-51st Sts.), with extensive underground concourses, hundreds of shops and restaurants, ice rink, Channel Gardens, Radio City Music Hall; guided tours (concourse of the RCA Bldg., daily 9:30-5:30; closed hols; adm); observation roof (top of RCA Bldg., open Apr.-Sept. daily 9 am-11 pm, Oct.-Mar. daily 9-7; closed hols; adm); guided NBC studio tours (RCA Bldg., daily 9-5:30; closed Jan. 1, Dec. 25; adm).

Museum of Modern Art (11 W 53rd St.), one of the finest of its kind in the world; major works by Cezanne, Matisse, Pollock, other modern masters; *Guernica* among the Picasso masterpieces; large sculpture collection, some of it in garden; graphic arts; industrial arts; films; open Mon.-Sat. 11-6, Thurs. eve to 9, Sun. noon-6; closed Dec. 25; adm. **Museum of Contemporary Crafts** (29 W 53rd St.), with changing exhibits of American design, is open Tues.-Sat. 11-6, Sun. 1-6; closed Dec. 25; sm adm. **Museum of American Folk Art** (49 W 53rd St.) mounts engaging temporary exhibits devoted to special themes, periods, or areas; open mid-Sept.-early July, Tues.-Sun. 10:30-5:30; closed Jan. 1, Dec. 25 & between exhibits; sm adm. **Museum of Primitive Art** (15 W 54th St.) houses extensive collections from Africa, Oceania, pre-Columbian America; open Wed.-Fri. 11-5, Sat. noon-5, Sun. 1-5; closed between exhibits and Dec. 25; donation. **The Mill** (Burlington House, 1345 Ave. of the Americas at 54th St.) has a moving platform through simulated plant that processes raw materials into textiles; open Tues.-Sat. 10-7; free.

Central Park (5th-8th Aves., 59th-110th Sts.), begun 1857, is a masterwork laid out by Frederick Law Olmsted and Calvert Vaux. Attractive **vestpocket parks** include: Greenacre Park (217 E 51st St.), designed by

Hideo Sasaki, with water cascading over granite blocks, trees, flowers, benches. Paley Park (3 E 53rd St.), with 20-ft waterfall, plantings, tables and chairs.

Frick Collection (1 E 70th St. off 5th Ave.), exhibited in a private home (the mansion of steel czar Henry Clay Frick); outstanding 16-19th-C European painting (Titian, Goya, El Greco); 18-19th-C English painting (Gainsborough, Constable); Renaissance bronze; panels painted for **Mme du Barry** (Progress of Love) and Mme de Pompadour (Arts and Sciences); fine French furnishings, Sevres porcelain, sculpture; open June-Aug., Thurs.-Sat. 10-6, Wed. & Sun.-1-6; Sept.-May, Tues.-Sat. 10-6, Sun. & hols 1-6; closed Jan. 1, July 4, Thnks, Dec. 24-25; free; children under 10 not admitted. **Whitney Museum of American Art** (945 Madison Ave. at E 75th St.), in a building designed by Marcel Breuer, was begun by Gertrude Vanderbilt Whitney and has a comprehensive collection of 18th-20th-C American works; films; open Mon.-Sat. 11-6, Tues. eve to 10, Sun. & hols noon-6; closed Dec. 25; adm.

Metropolitan Museum of Art (5th Ave. at 82nd St.), one of the greatest in the world, houses outstanding Greek, Phoenician, Assyrian, and Egyptian antiquities; 34 galleries of European painting; 17th-18th-C American painting; contemporary works; European and American period rooms and decorative arts; ancient jewelry, period clothing, musical instruments, armor; exciting temporary exhibits; special events; open Tues. 10-8:45, Wed.-Sat. 10-4:45, Sun. & hols 11-4:45; adm.

Solomon R. Guggenheim Museum (1071 5th Ave. at E 88th St.), building designed by Frank Lloyd Wright; works displayed along a spiraling ramp; Impressionist and Post-Impressionist painting, 19-20th-C painting and sculpture, temporary exhibits; open Tues. 10-9, Wed.-Sat. 10-6, Sun. & hols noon-6; closed Dec. 25; adm. **Cooper-Hewitt Museum of Design** (9 E 90th St.), in Andrew Carnegie's 1901 mansion, is devoted to contemporary design (furniture, glass, metalwork, textiles); 16-20th-C drawings include 300 by Winslow Homer and 2000 by Frederick E. Church; open Tues.-Fri. noon-9, Sat. & Sun. 1-5; closed hols; adm. **Jewish Museum** (1109 5th Ave. at 92nd St.) displays ceremonial and ritual items, ceramics, paintings, coins, textiles; mounts temporary exhibits of contemporary art; special events; open Mon.-Thurs. noon-5, Sun. 11-6; closed hols & Jewish hols; adm. **Museum of the City of New York** (1220 5th Ave. at E 103rd St.) offers attractive displays on the city from Dutch days to the present; impressive collection of furniture, silver, costumes, and toys; sponsors city walking tours (spring-fall) and special events; open Tues.-Sat. 10-5, Sun. & hols 1-5; closed Dec. 25; free. **Studio Museum in Harlem** (2033 5th Ave. at 125th St.) offers changing exhibitions by black artists on Mon. & Wed. 10-9; Tues., Thurs., Fri. 10-6; Sat. & Sun. 1-6; free.

New York Jazz Museum (125 W 55 St.), in a former carriage house, traces jazz from its African origins with photos, instruments, audiovisual programs; special events; open Tues.-Sun. noon-7; closed hols; donation. **New York Cultural Center** (Broadway at W 59th St.), in building designed by Edward Durell Stone, houses changing exhibits of painting, sculpture, graphics, photography; special events; open Tues.-Sun. 11-6; closed Dec. 25; adm. **American Bible Society** (1865 Broadway at W 61st St.) displays rare domestic and foreign Bibles; open Mon.-Fri. 9-4:30; closed hols; free.

Lincoln Center for the Performing Arts (W of Broadway between W 62nd-66th Sts.) consists of New York State Theater, designed by Philip Johnson, 1964; Metropolitan Opera House, with 2 murals by Marc Chagall and *Die Kniende,* sculpted by Lehmbruck, a gift of the West German government; Philharmonic Hall, with sculpture by Lipton, Hadzi, and Lippold; Vivian Beaumont Theater, designed by Eero Saarinen, 1965; Juilliard School and Alice Tully Hall; Henry Moore sculpture in North Plaza. Also here is the New York Public Library's extensive collection of literature and recordings on music (Mon.-Sat. 10-6), theater and dance (Mon.-Sat. noon-6); exhibits; special events; open Mon.-Thurs. 10-9, Fri. & Sat. 10-6; closed hols; free. Guided tours of the complex leave Avery Fisher Hall daily 10-5; no tours Jan. 1, Dec. 25; adm.

American Museum of Natural History (Central Park W at 79th St.), too comprehensive to be seen in a day; development of life from invertebrates through man; bird and animal habitat groups; prehistoric and Indian cultures; attractive mineral and gem display; spectacular reconstructions of prehistoric animal life; countless other exhibits; films and special events; open Mon.-Fri. 10-4:45, Sat. 10-5, Sun. & hols 11-5; closed Thnks, Dec. 25; adm. Adjacent **Hayden Planetarium** offers display halls (open 1 hr before shows) that include a model of the solar system and a mural of the lunar surface; splendid shows Mon.-Fri. 2 & 3:30, Sat. 11 & hourly 1-5, Sun. hourly 1-5; additional performances in summer and crowded times; no shows Thnks, Dec. 25; adm.

New York Historical Society (170 Central Park W between 76-77th Sts.) offers 5 floors of early silver, weapons, 18th-19-C American paintings (including Hudson River school and Audubon watercolors), folk art, furniture, toys, vehicles, maps, needlework, and other rich stores; research library (adm); special events; open Tues.-Fri. 1-5, 10-5, Sun. 1-5; closed hols; free.

Yeshiva University (500 W 185th St.) provides tours by appointment; on campus are Mendel Gottesman Library with a splendid collection of Hebraica-Judaica (open Mon.-Fri. 9-5; closed hols & Jewish hols; free) and a museum of Jewish history and culture (open academic yr, Tues., Thurs. 11-5, Sun. noon-6; closed hols & Jewish hols; adm).

Columbia University (Broadway & 116th St.), founded 1754 as King's College, offers free guided tours during academic yr, Mon.-Fri. 3, exc. hols & exam periods, or by appointment, from Low Memorial Library (which houses administrative offices, Columbia archives, and Asian handcrafts). On campus are the 4-million-volume Butler Library with rare works, cuneiform tablets, papyri (open daily); Avery Hall with architectural library, paneled Lenygon Room, rare drawings and documents, bookcase designed by Samuel Pepys (open daily); St. Paul Chapel, with Italian Renaissance exterior, Byzantine interior (open Mon.-Fri.). **General Grant National Memorial** (Riverside Dr. & 122nd St.): tombs of Pres. & Mrs. Ulysses S. Grant; exhibits on Grant's career; mosaics and relics of Civil War battles; open June-Sept. daily 9-5; Oct.-May, Wed.-Sun. 9-5; free.

Hamilton Grange National Memorial (287 Convent Ave. at W 141st St.), home built by Alexander Hamilton 1801-2, first he had owned since his arrival from the British West Indies in 1772; the area (now Harlem) was then a healthy country environment in which to raise his 8 children; the family continued to live here after Hamilton was killed in the 1804 duel with Burr; open Mon.-Fri. 9-5; closed hols; free.

Museum of the American Indian (Broadway & 155th St.) has changing exhibits of outstanding quality, comprehensiveness; North, Central, and South American Indian material; open Tues.-Sun. 1-5; closed hols & Aug.; free. **Hispanic Society of America** (Broadway between W 155-156th Sts.) is an unusual collection of Spanish art from prehistoric times to the present; paintings, sculpture, ceramics, metalwork, textiles; library of rare volumes and Iberian culture; open Tues.-Sat. 10-4:30, Sun. 2-5; closed hols & Dec. 24, 31; free. Also in this complex are: **American Academy of Arts & Letters**, with frequent exhibits; **American Geographical Society**, with outstanding map collection (open Mon.-Fri. 9-4; closed hols); **American Numismatic Society**, with library and exhibit rooms (open Tues.-Sat. 9-5; exhibits also open Sun. 1-4).

Morris-Jumel Mansion (Edgecombe Ave. at 160th St.), handsome 1765 Georgian home of a British Loyalist, was bought by French merchant Stephen Jumel in 1810 (his widow married Aaron Burr here in 1833); during the Revolution it served as hq for George Washington and British General Sir Henry Clinton; Jefferson, Franklin, Hamilton, and Joseph and Louis Napoleon were among the guests here; late 18th-early 19th-C furnishings; open Wed.-Sun. 10-4; closed Jan. 1, Dec. 25; sm adm. **Dyckman House Park & Museum** (4881 Broadway at 204th St.) provides a picture of 18th-C Dutch life in New York; many original furnishings; replica of Hessian Officers' hut on grounds; open Tues.-Sun. 11-5; closed Jan. 1, Dec. 25; free.

The Cloister (in Fort Tryon Park, off Riverside Dr. just S of Dyckman St.), a division of the Metropolitan Museum of Art, is an extraordinary medieval enclave on a bluff above the Hudson River; chapels, cloisters, a chapter house, and halls from France and Spain have been reassembled into an interconnected complex housing magnificent medieval art; architecture and art works arranged chronologically; open Tues.-Sat. 10-5, Sun. & hols 1-5; adm. **St. Mark's In-the-Bowery Church** (2nd Ave. at 10th St.), built 1795, has Peter Stuyvesant grave; open Tues.-Fri. 9-3:30, Sun. 10:30-2. **Church of the Ascension** (5th Ave. & 10th St.), built in English Gothic style 1841; sculptured angels by Saint-Gaudens; John La Farge mural over altar; open daily noon-2, 5-7. **St. Mary's Catholic Church** (246 E 15th St.) is a Byzantine rite church; stained-glass walls; abstract bell tower; icons and mosaics; open Sat., Sun. & religious hols. **Church of the Transfiguration** (1 E 29th St.) was nicknamed The Little Church Around the Corner in the days when actors, considered disreputable, were refused services in the chic 5th Ave. churches but were welcome here; Victorian Gothic; stained-glass windows, carvings, paintings; garden; open daily. **St. Bartholomew's Episcopal Church** (Park Ave. at 50th St.), incorporating Byzantine and Romanesque elements, has portal with sculptured friezes designed by Stanford White; outstanding marble font in Baptistry; yellow Siena marble pulpit; 5 domes of the narthex lined with mosaics; open daily. **St. Patrick's Cathedral** (5th Ave. & 50th St.), with 330-ft twin gothic spires, has 15 side alters dedicated to various saints, domestic and imported stained-glass windows; open daily. **St. Thomas Church** (5th Ave. & 53rd St.) is noted for rich interior carvings in wood and stone, especially the stone reredos; open daily. **Central Synagogue** (123 E 55th St.) blends Moorish and Gothic elements in 1872 brownstone; minarets and onion domes; ceremonial silver in lobby; open Mon.-Fri. **Temple Emanu-El** (5th Ave. & 68th St.), basilica-style Reform tempie, has a wonderful rose window, side galleries with attractive marble columns, handsome Beth-El Chapel in Byzantine style with silver and enamel chandeliers, many mosaics, lovely Ark of the Testimony flanked by menorahs; open daily 10-5. **Cathedral Church of St. John the Divine** (Amsterdam Ave. at 112th St.) is still unfinished although the cornerstone was laid 1892; largest Gothic cathedral in the world; fine interior detailing; vivid stained-glass windows; chapels representing nationality groups; outstanding icons and other works of art (Mortlake tapestries, paintings by Veronese and Sabbatini); guided tours available daily exc. religious hols; open daily 7 am-6 pm; free. **Riverside Church** (490 Riverside Dr. & W 122nd St.), interdenominational, has carvings of philosophers, scientists, and world leaders from antiquity to the present at the West Portal and on the chancel screen; 4 of the stained-glass windows were made in the 16th-C for Bruges Cathedral; open daily; sm adm to carillon tower.

Just N of the city line, on the Hudson, is **Yonkers** (US 9) with: **Philipse Manor Hall** (Warburton Ave. & Dock St.), the lovely home of Dutch manor lords; fine antique furnishings and portraits; closed for restoraion; check for opening date and hrs. **Hudson River Museum** (511 Warburton Ave.), with attractive changing displays, art gallery, historic Trevor Mansion, period rooms; planetarium (adm); open Tues.-Sat. 10-5, Sun. 11-5; closed Jan. 1, Thnks, Dec. 25; sm adm weekends. **Sherwood House** (Tuckahoe Rd. & Sprain Brook Pkwy) is a restored 1740 farmhouse with period furnishings; open May-Sept., Thurs. & Sun. 2-5; sm adm. Also just N of the city boundary is **Mount Vernon** (via Bronx River Pkwy) with **St. Paul's Church** (S Columbus near S 3rd Ave.), National Shrine of Bill of Rights, where events leading to the 1735 trial of John Peter Zenger established freedom of the press; 1758 "sister" to the Liberty Bell; 1833 Erben organ; cemetery; tours July-early Sept., Sun. 1-4; donation. In **New Rochelle** (3½ m N via Hutchinson River Pkwy), is **Thomas Paine Memorial,** consisting of Paine Cottage (North & Paine Aves.) and **Paine Museum** with personal effects and memorabilia of the pamphleteer for Independence; open Tues.-Sun. 2-5; free. In **White Plains** (14 m N of the city via Bronx River Pkwy), **Washington's Headquarters** (off SR 22 in N White Plains) is a 1738 home used by Washington in 1776; old craft demonstrations; open Feb. 22-early Dec., Wed.-Fri. 10-4, Sat. & Sun. 1-4; free. Nearby is **Miller Hill Restoration,** restored earthworks of Washington's troops in Battle of White Plains, Oct. 28, 1776; plaque diagrams battle; marked trails of battle area; free.

NEW YORK CITY—BROOKLYN: Brooklyn Museum (188 Eastern Pkwy at Washington Ave.) has outstanding collections of primitive art from Africa, Oceania, the Americas; magnificent Egyptian works; representative works from India, Middle East, Far East, Islam; American and European decorative arts, plus 30 American interiors 1675-1930; excellent Colonial American painting; 14-20th-C prints and drawings; sculpture garden with architectrual ornaments salvaged from demolished New York buildings; crafts shop; open Wed.-Sat. 10-5, Sun. 11-5, hols 1-5; closed Dec. 25; adm. **Long Island Historical Society** (128 Pierrepont St.) contains costumes, paintings, graphics, large library; open Tues.-Sat. 9-5; closed Aug. & hols; free. **Green-Wood Cemetery** (5th Ave. & 25th St.) opened 1840 as N.Y.'s most fashionable burial ground; lush 478 acres with opulent Victorian statuary, mausoleums; among the famous buried here are Henry Ward Beecher, Peter Cooper, Currier and Ives, Horace Greeley, Duncan Phyfe, Samuel B. Morse, Lola Montez; open daily. **Lefferts Homestead** (in Prospect Park near Willink Gate), built

1776, contains period furnishings; open Wed., Fri.-Sun. 1-5; closed hols & Aug.; free.

NEW YORK CITY—THE BRONX: Van Cortlandt House Museum (Broadway & 246th St.), in Van Cortlandt Park, is a Georgian stone residence built 1748; Dutch-English furnishings; toys; Delftware; Washington hq several times during the Revolution; open in summer Tues.-Sat. 10-5, Sun. 2-5; in winter, Tues.-Sun. 10-4:30; closed Jan. 1, Thnks, Dec. 25; Feb.; sm adm. **Poe Cottage** (Grand Concourse & Kingsbridge Rd.), where E. A. Poe lived 1846-49 and composed "Ulalume" and "Annabel Lee," contains personal mementos; open Tues.-Sat. 10-1, 2-4; Sun. 1-4; free. **Valentine-Varian House Museum** (3266 Bainbridge Ave. at E 208th St.), a 1758 fieldstone farmhouse around which a Revolutionary War skirmish took place; historic exhibits on the Bronx; open Sun.-Wed. 10-4; sm adm. **Hall of Fame for Great American** (W 181st St. & University Ave.): busts in open-air colonnade; information at North Gate; open July-Aug. daily 9-4; Sept.-June daily 9-5; closed hols; free. **Bartow-Pell Mansion** (Shore Rd.), in Pelham Bay Park, attractive Greek Revival mansion built 1836-42; fine detailing; period furnishings; open Tues., Fri., Sun. noon-5; closed part of summer; sm adm.

NEW YORK CITY—QUEENS: Bowne House (37-01 Bowne St., Flushing), built 1661 and probably the oldest house in New York City, is a shrine to religious freedom; here John Bowne held Quaker meetings, for which he was imprisoned and finally banished by the Dutch; his plea before the Dutch West India Co. in Holland resulted in a letter from them to Gov. Peter Stuyvesant urging religious freedom; original furnishings; open Tues., Sat., Sun. 2:30-4:30; closed Jan. 1, Easter, Dec. 25; free. **Hall of Science** (111th St. & 48th Ave., Flushing), in Flushing Meadows- Corona Park; atomic power, weather, communications, chick hatching, transportation; space equipment on grounds; film; open Tues.-Fri. 10-4, Sat. 10-5, Sun. 1-5; closed Jan. 1, Thnks, Dec. 25; free but parking fee.

NEW YORK CITY—STATEN ISLAND: Staten Island Institute of Arts & Sciences (2 blocks from ferry at 75 Stuyvesant Pl. & Wall St.) has exhibits on Indians, island fauna and ecology, arts, crafts, decorative arts; open Tues.-Sat. 10-5 (10-4 in summer), Sun. 2-5; closed July 4, Dec. 25; free. **Billiou-Stillwell-Perine House** (1476 Richmond Rd., Dongan Hills) was begun in 1663, with additions through 1830; handsome; period furnishings; open Apr.-Oct., Sat. & Sun. 2-5; sm adm. **Jacques Marchais Center of Tibetan Art** (336 Lighthouse Ave., between Richmondtown & New Dorp) is devoted to Buddhist art objects; 20,000-volume library; gardens for meditation; open June-Aug., Tues., Thurs., Sat., Sun. 2-5; Apr.-May & Sept.-Nov., Sat. & Sun. 2-5; closed hols; sm adm.

Richmondtown (Richmond & Arthur Kill Rds.) is a restoration of the 1600s settlement, Cocclestown, the county seat until the island became part of New York City in 1898; several dozen buildings: **Staten Island Historical Society Museum** displays local historic items; library; open Tues.-Sat. 10-5, Sun. 2-5; closed Jan. 1, Thnks, Dec. 25; sm adm. **Voorlezer's House**, built 1695; **Treasure House** (named for $7000 in gold found in its walls, believed hidden by British during the Revolution) was built 1700 as residence of a Huguenot tanner; 1837 **Third County Courthouse** is an 1837 Greek Revival structure; 1740 **Lake-Tysen House** is a typical Dutch colonial farmstead; also shops, carriage house, saw mill; all open July-Aug., Wed.-Fri. 10-4, Sat. 11-5, Sun. 2-5; also Sun. 2-5 in spring & fall; grounds are free, but sm adm to some bldgs.

Conference House (7455 Hylan Blvd. at S tip of the island in Tottenville), built 1680 by a British sea captain; here on Sept. 11, 1776, delegates of the Continental Congress (including Benjamin Franklin and John Adams) rejected the peace terms offered by British General Lord Howe in the only peace conference attempted during the Revolutionary War; open Apr.-Sept., Tues.-Sun. 1-5; rest of yr, Tues.-Sun. 1-4; sm adm.

NIAGARA FALLS: Niagara Reservation State Park (foot of Falls St.) **information center** provides schedules on falls tours, boat rides, Viewmobile tours, other activities. **Schoelikopf Geological Museum** (Prospect Park), exhibits, audiovisual program on history of the falls; open Memorial Day-Labor Day, daily 10 am-8 pm, sm adm; rest of yr, Wed.-Sun. 10-6, free; closed Jan. 1, Thnks, Dec. 25. **Carborundum Museum of Ceramics** (3rd & Niagara Sts.) traces history of ceramics; exhibits from around the world, from prehistoric times to present; demonstrations; films; open Tues.-Sat. 10-5, Sun. 1-8; closed Dec. 25; adm. **Power Vista** (4½ m N on Robert Moses Pkwy), exhibits on hydroelectric power; observation deck; Thomas Hart Benton mural of Father Louis Hennepin; open late June-Labor Day 9-9; rest of yr, 9-5; closed Jan. 1, Dec. 25; free. **Fort Niagara State Park** (14 m N on Robert Moses Pkwy in Youngstown): restored 1726 stone fort built by the French; museum; French Castle, Indian trading center and fortification, restored with chapel and prison; other buildings; special events; opens daily at 9, closing hr varies with season; closed Jan. 1, Thnks, Dec. 25; adm.

OGDENSBURG: Remington Art Museum (303 Washington St.) has the world's largest collection of paintings, bronzes, and drawings by Frederick Remington, who grew up here; Indian artifacts, Belter furniture, early glass, other displays; library; open Mon.-Sat. 10-5; also Aun. 1-5 in June-Sept.; closed hols; sm adm.

OLEAN: St. Bonaventure University Library (3 m W on SR 17) exhibits paintings by Rembrandt, Rubens, Bellini, Velazquez, and 19-20th-C artists; china; rare books and manuscripts; 1368 Latin Vulgate Bible made by English Franciscans; open academic yr, daily 8-4; closed school hols; free.

ONEONTA: Hartwick College Library houses collections on James Fenimore Cooper and John Burroughs; **Hall of Science** comprehensive shell collection; **Yager Museum** American Indian collections, especially on the upper Susquehanna area; open Mon.-Fri. 10-3; free.

OSWEGO: Oswego County Historical Society (135 E 3rd St.), ornate 1850 home with hand-carved woodwork, Victorian furnishings; displays on the Civil War; antique toys and silver; costumes; open July- Labor Day, Tues.-Sun. 1-5; May 15-June & early-Sept.-Oct., Wed., Sat., Sun., 1-5; free.

Fort Ontario (foot of 7th St.), overlooking the lake, was built 1755 to protect British trade and military operations from the Oswego River to the Hudson Valley; restored to its 1860 appearance; **Visitor Center** has exhibits, audiovisual program, self-guiding tour booklets; demonstrations; open Apr.-Oct., Mon.-Sat. 9-5, Sun. 1-5; closed Easter; free.

PALMYRA: Mormon Historic Sites (4 m S on SR 21): On **Hill Cumorah** is a statue of the Angel Moroni; according to Mormons, in the 5th-C he buried gold plates discovered by Joseph Smith in 1827 and translated into the Book of Mormon; information center exhibits, guide service; open daily 8-6 (8 am-9 pm in summer); free. Annual pageant in July; free.

Hoffman Clock Museum (9 m E on SR 31 to Newark), in the public library, displays American and foreign models; open July-Aug., Mon.-Fri. 9-5; Sept.-June, Mon.-Sat. 9-5; closed hols; free. **Wayne County Historical Museum** (15 m E on SR 31 to 21 Butternut St., Lyons), in Victorian jail and sheriff's residence; exhibits on Erie Canal; local pottery and glass, weapons, tools; open daily 2-4; closed hols; free.

PLATTSBURGH: Kent-Delord House Museum (17 Cumberland Ave.), built 1797; British hq during War of 1812; regimental silver and other items; period furnishings; portraits; tours mid-Jan.-mid-Dec., Mon.-Sat. 10, 2, 4; donation. **Alice T. Miner Colonial Collection** (12 m N on SR 9 in Chazy), in 1824 home, consists of household furnishings and equipment; open Tues.-Sat. 11-5; closed Jan. 1, Dec. 25; free. **Ausable Chasm Antique Auto Museum** (12 m S on I-87 in Ausable Chasm) houses Walter H. Church collection of restored early cars; open mid-June-mid-Sept., daily 10-5; spring & fall, Sun. and some Sats. 10-5; adm.

POTSDAM: Potsdam Public Museum (Civic Center, Elm & Park Sts.), exhibits on local history; decorative arts; English pottery; open Tues.-Sat. 2-5; closed hols; free.

POUGHKEEPSIE: Vassar College Art Gallery (Taylor Hall, Raymond Ave., good collection of Baroque art, outstanding prints and sculpture, 19th-C French and 15-17th-C Italian works, Hudson River School, contemporary American works, Oriental art objects; open academic yr., Mon.-Fri. 9-5, Sun. 2-5; free. **Clinton House** (549 Main St.), 1765 stone house owned by the state; period furnishings; open Wed.-Sat. 9-5, Sun. 1-5; closed Jan. 1, Easter, Thnks, Dec. 25; free.

RHINEBECK: Old Rhinebeck Aerodrome (5 m NE off SR 308 on Stone Church Rd.) displays planes from 1900-37; air shows Sat. (July-Oct.) & Sun. (mid-May-Oct.) aft; open mid-May-Oct. daily 10-5; adm.

ROCHESTER: International Museum of Photography (900 East Ave.), in former home of George Eastman; 1840s daguerreotypes to modern cinematography; open Tues.-Sun. 10-5; closed Jan. 1, Dec. 25; sm adm. **Eastman Kodak Co.** (Kodak Park Div., 200 Ridge Rd. W, on SR 104) offers free tours (no children under 5), Mon.-Fri. 9:30, 1:30; tours at other plants also available.

Rochester Museum & Science Center (657 East Ave.): on natural sciences; archaeology and Indian cultures; reconstructed homes and shops from 19th-C Rochester; human biology and genetics; special events; open Mon.-Sat. 9-5, Sun. & hols 1-5; closed Dec. 25; sm adm. Adjacent **Strasenburgh Planetarium,** daily shows, open Mon.-Fri. 9-5, 7-9:30, Sat. & Sun. 1-9:30; closed Dec. 24-5; adm to shows.

Rochester Historical Society (485 East Ave.), in 1840 merchant's home with spiral staircase and a smoking room paneled in wood and leather, has 18-19th-C furnishings, 19th-C American paintings, guns, glass, costumes, muscial instruments; open Mon.-Fri. 10-4; closed hols; free. **Campbell-Whittlesey House** (123 S Fitzhugh St.), 1836 merchant's home in Greek Revival style, is handsomely appointed, with rare Empire pieces; open Tues.-Sat. 10-5, Sun. 1-4; closed hols & Dec.; adm. **Susan B. Anthony Memorial** (17 Madison St.), home of the Women's Suffrage leader 1866-1906; original furnishings; memorabilia; open Wed.-Sat. 11-4; closed hols; sm adm.

Memorial Art Gallery (490 University Ave.), part of the Univ. of Rochester; outstanding medieval art; paintings by European masters; 19-20th-C American painting; metalwork, pottery, sculpture; open Tues.-Sat. 10-5, Sun. 1-5; closed hols; sm adm. **Rush Rhees Library of University of Rochester** (Joseph C. Wilson Blvd.) houses 1½-million books, rare volumes, historical papers; open Mon.-Thurs., 8-midnight, Fri. 8 am-10 pm, Sat. 9-5, Sun. 1-midnight; free. **Sibley Music Library,** Eastman School of Music (44 Swann St.), scores and literature on music; open academic year, Mon.-Thurs. 8:30 am-10 pm, Fri. 8:30-6, Sat. 11-5, Sun. 1-8; shorter hrs in summer; closed hols; free. **Xerox Square Exhibit Center** (Xerox Sq.) offers changing art, cultural, scientific exhibits, open Mon.-Fri. 10-9, Sat. 10-7, Sun. 2-8; closed hols; free.

 Victorian Doll Museum (12 m W on SR 33 to 4332 Buffalo Rd., North Chili), with dolls and dollhouses, is open Tues.-Sat. 10-5, Sun. 1-5; closed hols; sm adm. **Valentown Museum** (12 m SE via I-490 to jct I-90, then 1 m W to Fishers), in 1879 community center; furnished shop displays; Mormon collection includes items made by Brigham Young; schoolroom; Indian and Civil War items; open May-Sept. daily 1-5; sm adm. **Brookwood Science Center** (18 m NE via SR 18) explains nuclear power with exhibits, films; open Sun.-Thurs. 10-4; closed Jan. 1, Thnks, Dec. 25; free.

ROME: Fort Stanwix National Monument (center of town) contains fort built during French & Indian War, later a trading post and Revolutionary military post; it burned in 1781 and has been reconstructed; **Visitor Center** and museum of the fort's history; audiovisual program; open Mon.-Sat. 9-4, Sun. 1-4; closed Jan. 1, Thnks, Dec. 25; free. **Oriskany Battlefield** (6 m E on SR 69), site of bloody 1777 battle where Continental Army stopped the British advance through the Mohawk Valley, offers a **Visitor Center** (mid-Apr.-Nov., Mon.-Sat. 9-5, Sun. 1-5); free.

 Erie Canal-Fort Bull Tourism Project (1½ m W off SR 49W), restored canal village of the 1840s, with shops, homes, craft demonstrations; train and boat rides along restored section of canal; open late May-Oct., Tues.-Sun. 9-5; adm. **Canal Town Museum** (20 m W via SR 365, I-90 to Canal St., Canastota) traces growth of Erie Canal; open mid-Apr.-mid-Sept., Wed.-Sun. noon-4:30; free. Sections of the canal can be seen in **Old Erie Canal State Park** (SR 5 & 46).

 Madison County Historical Society Museum (14 m SW via SR 365 to 435 Main St., Oneida), in early-19th-C home, displays local historical material; here in 1848, John Noyes founded a utopian community that collapsed in 1880; the community's silverware industry survives as a private corporation; also agricultural and Indian exhibits; open May-Oct., Tues.-Sun. 2-5; sm adm.

 Constable Hall (26 m N via SR 26 in Constableville) is an 1819 Georgian home built as copy of the Constable family's ancestral home in Ireland; fine period furnishings; tours late May-Oct., Tues.-Sat. 10-5, Sun. 1-5; adm.

SARANAC LAKE: Robert Louis Stevenson Memorial Cottage (11 Stevenson Lane), where the author lived 1887-8 while being treated for tuberculosis; memorabilia, orginal furnishings; open June 15-Sept. 15, Tues.-Sun. 9:30-noon, 1-4:40; sm adm. **Saranac Lake Free Library** (100 Main St.) exhibits mounted animals; Adirondackiana in Adirondack Room; open July-Aug., Mon.-Fri. 10-5:30, Sat. 10-1; rest of yr, Mon.-Sat. 10-5:30; closed hols; free. **Six Nations Indian Museum** (8 m N on SR 192A to Gabriels, then 6 m N via Rainbow Lake to Onchiota) displays arts, costumes, and artifacts; outdoor miniature Indian village; open May-Sept. daily 9-6; sm adm.

SARATOGA SPRINGS: Much of the opulence of the 19th-C Queen of the Spas is gone, and the original spring, High Rock Spring (Rock St. & High Rock Ave.), is inactive, but this is still a popular resort with mineral baths and pools at **Saratoga Spa State Park** (3 m S on US 9). **Casino** (Congress Park), a grand brownstone with fine Tiffany window, opened 1869 and hosted J. P. Morgan, Lillian Russell, and other personalities of the day; now it houses collections of Historical Society of Saratoga Springs; open July-Aug., daily 9:30-4:30; May-June & Sept.-Oct. daily 10-4; adm. **Saratoga County Historical Museum** (7 m S on SR 50 at Brookside, Ballston Spa) is open June-Sept., Sat. & Sun. 2-5; sm adm.

Saratoga National Historical Park (11 m SE, with entrances on SR 32 and US 4, N of Bemis Hts.) is scene of 1777 battles considered the turning point in the struggle for independence; here Gen. Horatio Gates defeated the British under Gen. John Burgoyne and gained control of the Hudson Valley. **Visitor Center** exhibits and audiovisual program; open daily 9-5 (9-6 in summer); closed Jan. 1, Thnks, Dec. 25; free. A 9-m tour road with interpretive signs is open Apr.-Nov., weather permitting; living history demonstrations in summer. **Neilson House, American staff headquarters,** and **Freeman House,** used by both Americans and British, are open June-Sept.; free. **Gen. Philip Schuyler House** (N on US 4 in Schuylerville), built 1777 to replace one burned by the British, offers demonstrations in Colonial crafts; open June 15-Labor Day daily 10-5; may be open additional weekends; sm adm.

National Museum of Racing (Union Ave. & Ludlow St.) traces history of thoroughbred racing through paintings, sculpture, memorabilia; films in racing season; open Mon.-Fri. 10-5, Sat. noon-5 (closed Sat. in Feb.); also open Sun. noon-5 from June 15-Sept. 15; closed Jan. 1, Thnks, Dec. 25; free.

Hathorn Gallery (Skidmore College campus) offers a small but good collection of paintings, sculpture, and prints; open daily academic yr; free.

Hyde Collection (17 m N off I-87 to 161 Warren St. in Glens Falls), in an Italian Renaissance-style home; fine collection of European masters (da Vinci, Rubens, Rembrandt, El Greco, Degas, Picasso) and American painters (Whistler, Homer, Eakins); furniture; sculpture; open Tues., Wed., Fri.-Sun. 2-5; closed July 4, Dec. 25; free.

SCHENECTADY: Stockade (bounded by State, Washington, Front & Ferry Sts.) is a 12-block area of privately owned, handsome examples of Dutch, Colonial, and Federal styles, dating from 1700-1840; once surrounded by a stockade built by the Dutch in 1662; during a 1690 massacre by French and Indians, the settlement was burned, but was rebuilt and fortified in 1704. Interiors of some buildings may be seen during the annual Walkabout (late Sept.). Tours of the area are conducted by the **YWCA** (44 Washington St.), daily in daylight. Booklets for self-guided tours are available from **Schenectady County Historical Society** (32 Washington Ave.), which also offers exhibits on local history and a library; open Mon.-Sat. 12:30-5, Sun. 2-5; closed hols; free.

Schenectady Museum (Nott Terrace Heights, off State St.) offers exhibits on anthropology, natural science, and contemporary art; planetarium; open Tues.-Fri. 10-4:30, Sat. & Sun. noon-5; closed hols; sm adm.

Old Stone Fort Museum (25 m SW on US 30 in Schoharie) was a 1772 church fortified against raids by Tories and Indians during the Revolution; exhibits on local history and the Revolution; open Memorial Day-Labor Day 10-5; May & Labor Day-Oct., Tues.-Sun. 10-5; adm.

STAMFORD: Lansing Manor (8 m SE on SR 23, then 7 m N on US 30), hydroelectric project hq, offers **Visitor Center** with exhibits, audiovisual program; open daily 9-5 (9 am-8 pm in July-Aug.); closed Jan. 1, Thnks, Dec. 25; free. **Burroughs Memorial** (8 m SE on SR 23, then 9 m S on SR 30 to Roxbury) contains grave and Boyhood Rock of naturalist John Burroughs, who was born here; open mid-Apr.-mid-Oct. daily 9-dusk; his summer cottage, Woodchuck Lodge, is open occasionally.

STONY POINT: Stony Point Battlefield Reservation (2 m N off US 9W), site of Gen. "Mad" Anthony Wayne's successful attack on the British, July 15-16, 1779; earthworks, museum, lighthouse; open May-Oct. daily 9-5; free.

SYRACUSE: Lowe Art Center, Syracuse University (309 University Pl.) features European and American 20th-C paintings and sculpture; Chinese bronzes; selected works from other periods; open Mon.-Fri. 9-4; closed hols; free. **Everson Museum of Art** (401 Harrison St.), in I. M. Pei building; superior collection of American art from Colonial times to the present; also fine Chinese art objects, contemporary ceramics, sculpture court; open Tues.-Fri., Sun. noon-5; Sat. 10-5; closed hols; free.

Onondaga Historical Association (311 Montgomery St.), exhibits on Indian and local history, including canals; library (Oct.-May daily 2-5); open Oct.-May, Sat. & Sun. 2-5; free. **Canal Museum** (Weighlock Bldg.,

Erie Blvd E & Montgomery St.), exhibits and audiovisual program on canal life; information on restored sections of canal; open Tues., Wed., Fri. noon-5; Thurs. noon-9; Sat. 10-5; Sun. 2-6; free. **Salt Museum** (4 m NW in Onondaga Lake Park at Liverpool) illustrates the extraction of salt from brine with models and pictures; salt spring; reproduction of 1656 French stockade and fort; open June-Aug. daily 9:30-8; mid-Apr.-May & Sept.-mid-Nov. daily 9:30-4; free. **Daniel Parrish Witter Agricultural Museum** (4 m N off I-690 at N. Y. State Fairgrounds), tools, vehicles; craft demonstrations (Sun. aft); open Tues.-Fri. 9-noon, Sat. 11-5, Sun. 2-5; closed hols; free exc during State Fair. **Lorenzo** (16 m SE via SR 92 to SR 13 in Cazenovia), Federal-style home of a Holland Land Co. officer; period furnishings; antique vehicles; open mid-Apr.-Oct. daily 9-5; free.

TARRYTOWN: Sunnyside (W off US 9, 1 m S of Tappan Zee Bridge) is the charming little stone mansion that was Washington Irving's home 1835-59; many personal effects; open daily 10-5; closed Jan. 1, Thnks, Dec. 25; adm. **Lyndhurst** (W off US 9, ½ m S of Tappan Zee Bridge) is the Gothic Revival manor built for William Paulding, a N.Y. City mayor, later owned by Jay Gould; opulent furnishings typical of Gilded Age; open May-Oct. daily 10-5, Nov.-Apr. daily 10-4; closed Jan. 1, Dec. 25; adm. **Philipsburg Manor** (W off US 9, 2 m N of Tappan Zee Bridge in N Tarrytown) was a 1680s trading center; manor house with period furnishings; operating gristmill; wooden dam; historical film; open daily 10-5; closed Jan. 1, Thnks, Dec. 25; adm. Also in N Tarrytown is the 1685 **Old Dutch Church of Sleepy Hollow**; its walls are made of bricks and rubblestone brought from Holland; adjacent cemetery contains graves of Washington Irving, William Rockefeller, Andrew Carnegie.

   Union Church (2 m NE via SR 448 on Lake Rd., Pocantico Hills) has stunning stained-glass panels by Marc Chagall, rose window by Henri Matisse; open weekdays 9-4, Sun. 1-4, but visitors must call in advance (631-2069). **Reader's Digest** (6 m NE via SR 448, 117 in Pleasantville), in a Georgian-style building with fine furnishings, displays Impressionist and Post-Impressionist paintings in its offices; open Mon.-Fri. 9-5; closed hols; free. **Van Cortlandt Manor** (9½ m N off US 9 in Croton-on-Hudson) is a handsome 18th-C Dutch-English manor house with period furnishings; also furnished Ferry House that hosted travelers on the Albany Post Rd.; open daily 10-5; closed Jan. 1, Thnks, Dec. 25; adm.

TICONDEROGA: Fort Ticonderoga (2 m E on SR 73), built to guard the waterway from Canada, was constructed 1755 by the French; captured by the British in 1759, it fell to Ethan Allen's Green Mountain Boys in 1775 and its weapons were shipped to the aid of besieged Boston; the British retook it in 1777, then burned it. Reconstructed to its French design, with barracks; fine collection of weapons; uniforms, documents, in summer; open July-Aug. daily 8-7, mid-May-June & Sept.-mid-Oct. daily 8-6; adm. **Fort Mount Hope** (½ m E on Burgoyne Rd.), restored hilltop fort that guarded the portage between the lakes; cannon and other relics; fine view; open late May-mid-Oct., daily 8-dark; sm adm. **Historic Mount Defiance** (1 m SE) toll road to summit follows the British military route of 1777; fine view; open Memorial Day-early Oct., daily 8-8; car toll.

Crown Point Public Reservation (13 m N off SR 9N, 22), ruins of 2 forts built by French and English; museum; nearby **Champlain Memorial Lighthouse** marks Champlain's 1609 discovery of the lake; open late May-mid-Sept., daily 9-5; auto fee.

Penfield Homestead (5 m W via SR 74, then N to Ironville), home of iron manufacturer who first applied electricity industrially to separate ores; period furnishings; exhibits of local history and iron industry; self-guiding tour through ironwork ruins; open May 15-Oct. 15, Tues.-Sun. 8-6; adm.

TROY: Rensselaer County Historical Society (59 2nd St.) is an 1827 Federal-style mansion with period furnishings, decorative arts, other exhibits; open Tues.-Sat. 10-4; closed hols; adm. **Uncle Sam's Grave** (Oakwood Cemetery, Oakwood Ave.) is grave of local meatpacker Samuel Wilson, who supplied beef to the U.S. Army during the War of 1812; soldiers interpreted the "U.S. Beef" stamp to mean Uncle Sam's Beef, and a caricature of Sam Wilson came to personify the U.S.; open daily 9-4:30; free.

UTICA: Munson-Williams-Proctor Institute (310 Genesee St.): Museum of Art, designed by Philip Johnson, with 18-20th-C American painting, 20th-C European painting; sunken sculpture court; Japanese woodcuts, prints, American decorative arts; library; adjacent is **Fountain Elms,** an 1850 Tuscan-style villa with Victorian furniture and decorative arts, exhibits on Mohawk Valley history, library; open Mon.-Sat. 10-5, Sun. 1-5; closed hols; free.

Musical Museum (16 m SW via SR 12B in Deansboro) displays melodeons, music boxes, other instruments; some may be played by visitors; concerts in summer; open Thurs.-Tues. 10-5 (daily 10-5 in May-Aug.); closed Jan. 1, Thnks, Dec. 25; adm. **Upstate Antique Auto Museum** (17 m S via SR 8 to jct US 20 in Bridgewater) displays more than 100 gas, steam, electric vehicles; bicycles; open Memorial Day-mid-Oct. daily 10-5; adm.

Baron von Steuben Memorial (15 m N on SR 12 to Remsen, then 3 m W on Starr Hill Rd.), on land granted the "drillmaster of the American

Revolution" in return for his services; his grave; replica of his log cabin with some original furnishings; memorabilia; open mid-May-mid-Oct., Tues.-Sat. 9-5, Sun. 1-5; free.

WATERTOWN: Jefferson County Historical Society Museum (228 Washington St.), in an 1870s home, displays Indian artifacts; local historic relics; open Tues.-Sat. 9-5; closed Jan. 1, Thnks, Dec. 25; free. **Roswell P. Flower Memorial Library** (229 Washington St.), in an 1890s neoclassic marble building; furnishings and other items of early French settlers here; dolls; miniature furniture; open July-Aug., Mon.-Fri. 9-6; Sept.-June, Mon.-Fri. 9-9, Sat. 9-5; closed hols; free.

   Sackets Harbor Battlefield (8 m W via SR 3 on the lakefront), where the British unsuccessfully attempted to destroy the shipyards during the War of 1812 offers a museum open June-Sept. daily 9-5; free. **Pickering-Beach Historical Museum** (503 W Main St., Sackets Harbor), 1817 house with period furnishings; memorabilia of the War of 1812; tours Memorial Day-Labor Day daily 10-5; sm adm.

WEST POINT: U.S. Military Academy, on a strategic Hudson River point chosen by Washington, was garrisoned during the Revolution; academy opened 1802. **Visitor Information Center** (Thayer Gate) is open mid-Apr.-mid-Nov., Mon.-Sat. 9-5, Sun. & hols 11-5. In winter, maps and information at **West Point Museum** (Cullum Rd.); displays on the history of warfare, dioramas of great battles, interesting paintings of war; open daily 10:30-4:15; closed Jan. 1, Dec. 25; free. Points of interest include **Cadet Chapel** (with blank plaque, intended for Benedict Arnold before his betrayal), **Catholic Chapel** (a replica of St. Ethelreda Carthusian Abbey in Essex, England), and many monuments.

WHITEHALL: Skenesborough Museum (US 4) commemorates birthplace of the U.S. Navy; first U.S. fleet built here 1775-6; model of 1776 harbor; canal locks; scale models of famous ships; hull of USS Ticonderoga (built 1814 and salvaged from Lake Champlain in 1958); dolls; local historical items; open mid-June-Labor Day daily 10-5; sm adm.

NORTH CAROLINA

ALBEMARLE: Town Creek Indian Mount State Historic Site (10 m S on US 52, then 5½ m E), with reconstructed stockade and temples of 15th-C ceremonial center, has museum exhibits and orientation in **Visitor Center;** open Tues.-Sat. 9-5, Sun. 1-4; closed Thnks, Dec. 25; free.

ASHEVILLE: Thomas Wolfe Memorial (48 Spruce St. between Woodin & Walnut Sts.), family residence and boardinghouse described as "Dixieland" in *Look Homeward, Angel,* was the author's boyhood home; family furnishings and memorabilia; open Tues.-Sat. 9-5, Sun. 1-5; closed Thnks, Dec. 25; adm. **Riverside Cemetery** (Birch St. off Pearson Dr.) contains graves of Thomas Wolfe and O. Henry (William Sydney Porter).

    Biltmore House & Gardens (2 m S on US 25 off I-40), built by some 1000 workmen laboring 1890-95, is the fabulous French Renaissance-style mansion of George W. Vanderbilt; woodwork, stonework, and other interior components were imported from Europe to create spectacular dining room, drawing room, library, and 200 other rooms furnished with the treasures of European royalty; many rare antiques, paintings, objets d'art; splendid gardens; open daily 9-5; closed Thnks, Dec. 16-Jan.; adm. **Biltmore Homespun Shops** (2 m NE via Charlotte St. on grounds of Grove Park Inn), established by Mrs. George Vanderbilt to preserve Old World methods of wool manufacture; demonstrations; open Mon.-Sat. 9-5; also Sun. 1-6 in summer; closed Jan. 1, Thnks, Dec. 25; free.

    St. Lawrence Church (97 Haywood St.), Baroque-style, completed 1920, was designed by Spanish architect Rafael Guastavino (buried in crypt); interesting tiles, statues, 17th-C Spanish Crucifixion tableau over altar; open daily.

    Colburn Mineral Museum (Civic Center, Haywood St.) offers displays and information on rockhounding sites in the state; open Mon.-Fri. 11-5; some weekends 11-5; closed Dec. 24-Jan. 1; free.

    Southern Highland Handicraft Guild (930 Tunnel Rd., 3 m E of tunnel on US 70) displays and sells quality mountain crafts; demonstrations of silver working at **Stuart Nye Silver Shop** (940 Tunnel Rd.); open Mon.-Fri. 8-4; closed July 4, Labor Day, Dec. 25-Jan. 1; free. The Guild sponsors annual handicraft fairs and maintains shops and showrooms at Allanstand and Blowing Rock, NC, and in Bristol, VA.

Zebulon B. Vance Birthplace State Historic Site (9 m N on US 23, then 6 m E on Reems Creek Rd to Weaverville): reconstructed 1795 home of North Carolina's colorful Civil War Governor; slavehouse, smokehouse, other buildings of this isolated frontier settlement; exhibits on Vance family and mountain life; **Visitor Center;** open Tues.-Sat. 9-5, Sun. 1-5; closed Thnks, Dec. 25; free.

BLUE RIDGE PARKWAY, a unit of the NPS, follows mountain crests 469 m from Shenandoah National Park (VA) to Great Smoky Mountains National Park. Mileposts (starting from Mile 0 at the N end) provide an easy reference to attractions listed in booklets available at **Visitor Centers** (at Miles 5.8, 60.9, 86, 176.1, 294.1, 364.6) or from Supt. (P.O. Box 7606, Asheville 28807). Attractions include: **Humpback Rocks** (Mile 5.8) reconstructed mountain farm homestead; **Otter Creek** (63.6) exhibit on James River and Kanawha Canal; **Peaks of Otter** (86) forestry display; **Mabry Mill** (176.1), featuring old-time mountain industry, water-powered grist mill, blacksmith shop; **Puckett Cabin** (189.8), home 1865-1939 of a midwife who claimed to have delivered 1000-odd babies but whose own 24 children died; **Doughton Park** (238.5), with weaving demonstrations, sales at Brinegar Cabin; **Northwest Trading Post** (258.6) displays of mountain crafts; **Parkway Craft Center** (294), in 1900 mansion of "Denim King" Moses H. Cone, craft demonstrations and sales; **Museum of North Carolina Minerals** (331), with displays, history of use from prehistoric times (open May-Oct., daily 9-5; free). Each Visitor Center features a different aspect of mountain history and provides information on visitor-use areas, naturalist programs, activities; all are open May-Oct., daily 9-5 (or longer). The parkway is open all year but snow may close some sections, especially from Mt. Mitchell southward, in winter. See also Virginia.

BOONE: Daniel Boone Native Gardens (¼ m E off US 421 on Horn in the West Dr.) contains Squire Boone Cabin Museum with frontier relics (open July-Aug., Tues.-Sun. 9-7; May-June & Sept.-Oct., Tues.-Sun. 9-5; sm adm); *Horn in the West,* drama of Boone's wilderness trek, is presented in summer.

BREVARD: NASA Tracking Station (9 m SW on US 64 to Rosman, then 10 m NW on SR 215) has an observation area open daily; explanations are given in Operations Building (open Mon.-Fri. 8-4; closed hols); free.

CHAPEL HILL: University of North Carolina at Chapel Hill: **Ackland Memorial Art Center** (S Columbia St.) exhibits representative painting, sculpture, and drawings from major historic periods and movements; open Tues.-Sat. 10-5, Sun. 2-6; closed hols & late Aug.; free. **Morehead**

Planetarium (E Franklin St.) offers exhibits, observatory, shows (Mon.-Fri. 8 pm, plus weekends in summer; adm); bldg open Mon.-Fri. 2-5, 7:30-10; Sat. 10-10, Sun. 1-10; free.

Chapel of the Cross (304 E Franklin St.) was built 1846-48 by slaves in Greek Revival style; open daily.

CHARLOTTE: Mint Museum of Art (E end of town at Hempstead Pl. & Eastover Rd.) is housed in the reconstructed U.S. Branch Mint that opened 1837, when this area was a major gold producer; Thomas Edison used the building 1900-03 for experiments in using electricity to extract gold from ore; now exhibits painting, sculpture, and decorative arts from Europe and America; pre-Columbian art; regional art; European and Oriental ceramics; open Tues.-Fri. 10-5, Sat. & Sun. 2-5; closed hols; free.

Charlotte Nature Museum (1658 Sterling Rd.) features a talking manikin, live and mounted animals, historical display, planetarium shows (weekends; sm adm); open Mon.-Sat. 9-5, Sun. 2-5; closed hols; free.

James K. Polk Birthplace State Historic Site (12 m S on US 521 at Pineville) contains reconstructed log cabin; **Visitor Center** with film, exhibits on Polk's life and career; open Tues.-Sat. 9-5, Sun. 1-5; closed Thnks, Dec. 25; free.

First Presbyterian Church (15 m NE via US 29 to 70 Union St., N. Concord), elegant interpretation of 18th-C English architecture; attractive garden; open daily. **Belmont Abbey Cathedral** (10 m W via I-85 on Belmont Abbey College campus), built in 13th-C Gothic style, is noted for stained-glass windows; open daily 6 am-10 pm.

Schiele Museum of Natural History (21 m W on I-85 to 1500 Garrison Blvd., Gastonia) displays Indian arts; minerals; more than 5000 mounted birds, reptiles, mammals; planetarium programs (weedends); open Tues.-Sun. 9-noon, 2-5; free.

CHEROKEE: This is the captial of the Eastern band of Cherokee, once a powerful tribe; most of the members were driven over the Trail of Tears to Oklahoma. **Museum of the Cherokee Indian** (½ m N on US 441 at Information Center) traces the history and culture; prehistoric and historic artifacts, including some rare works; open Apr.-Oct. daily 9-5 (longer hrs in summer); sm adm. **Oconaluftee Indian Village** (adj), replica of an 18th-C Cherokee village with homes and council house, offers demonstrations of skills and crafts on guided tours mid-May-mid-Oct., daily 9-5; adm. *Unto These Hils,* Cherokee historical drama, is presented here in summer.

DURHAM: Duke University, beneficiary of the Duke tobacco fortune, has handsome West Campus buildings in Gothic style dominated by

Chapel tower; on East Campus is **Museum of Art** (off W Main St.), especially strong on medieval sculpture and decorative art; North Carolina works; open Tues.-Fri. 9-5, Sat. & Sun. 2-5; free. The libraries are a rich source of material on the South.

Free guided tours of tobacco plants are offered by **American Tobacco Co.** (Pettigrew & Blackwell Sts.), Mon.-Fri. 9-2:30, and **Liggett & Myers Inc.** (W Main St.), Mon.-Fri. 8-11:15, 1-3; both closed hols & some hol weeks; check before going. Visitors welcome at warehouses for auctions (Sept.-Nov.). **Duke Homestead State Historic Site** (6 m N on Duke Homestead Rd.), 1852 home of the Duke family, has period furnishings and exhibits on pioneer tobacco industry; open Tues.-Sat. 9-5, Sun. 1-5; closed Thnks, Dec. 25; free.

Bennett Place State Historic Site (6 m NW off US 70, I-85), where Confederate Gen. Johnston surrendered to Gen. Sherman on Apr. 26, 1865; many original furnishings; museum displays; open Tues.-Sat. 9-5, Sun. 1-5; free.

Hillsborough (12 m W on US 70), founded 1754, capital of Revolutionary North Carolina for 5 years, preserves many fine 18-19th-C homes (all privately owned) between Queen & Wake Sts., Margaret Lane, Cameron Ave.; booklets for self-guiding walking tours are available; Hillsborough Historical Society sponsors open-house tours twice a year. **Orange County Courthouse** (E King & Church Sts.), an 1845 Greek Revival building with interior woodwork copied from the Asher Benjamin pattern books; clock donated by George III; museum exhibits on 2nd floor; open Tues.-Sun. 1:30-4:30; closed hols; free.

EDENTON: This old (1658) and charming town has many historic buildings (some not open, others by appointment only) described in literature available from **Chamber of Commerce** (E King St.); open business hrs. **Historic Edenton Visitor Center** (S Broad St.), in the pleasing 1782 Barker House, provides audiovisual program; museum; guided tours (fee) of historic buildings; open Tues.-Sat. 10-4:30, Sun. 2-5; closed Jan. 1, Easter, Thnks, Dec. 25. **Chowan County Courthouse** (18 E King St.) is a lovely Georgian-style building; open Mon.-Fri. 9-5, Sat. 10-4:30, Sun. 2-5; free. On Courthouse Green (W side) is a teapot marking the site where the town's women staged a Revolutionary tea party on Oct. 25, 1774. **St. Paul's Church** (W Church & Broad Sts.), a restored Georgian building, has Communion silver from 1725; colonial cemetery. The 1725 Jacobean-style **Cupola House** (408 S Broad St.) and 1778 **James Iredell House** (107 E Church St.) are open Tues.-Sat. 10-4:30, Sun. 2-5; closed Jan. 1, Easter, Thnks, Dec. 25; adm.

Somerset Place State Historic Site (18 m SE via SR 32, US 64 to Creswell, then 9 m S in Pettigrew State Park) preserves a plantation overlooking Lake Phelps; antebellum mansion; slave chapel, slave hospital, other outbuildings; period furnishings; open Tues.-Sat. 9-5, Sun. 1-5; closed Thnks, Dec. 25; free.

ELIZABETH CITY: This seafaring town on a landlocked freshwater harbor preserves many early-19th-C homes and the 1856 **Christ Episcopal Church** with beautiful stained-glass windows; booklets for walking tours from **Chamber of Commerce** (Main & Road Sts.); open business hrs. **Museum of the Albemarle** (2 m SW on US 17) has historic displays on the city and the surrounding coast, which was settled in the late 16th C; Indian artifacts, antique toys, decoys; open Tues.-Sat. 10-5, Sun. 2-5; closed Jan. 1, July 4, Thnks, Dec. 25; sm adm.

FAYETTEVILLE: Market House (Market Sq.), an 1838 farmers' market with Moorish arches, served as state capitol 1787-89; butchers left cleaver marks in the pillars; now houses art shows. **First Presbyterian Church** (Bow & Ann Sts.), a classic Colonial building with handwrought hardware and woodwork, crystal chandeliers, is open Mon.-Fri. 8:30-4, Sat. & Sun. 8:30-noon; closed hols; free.

    Fort Bragg & Pope AFB (10 m NW on SR 87) offers information on parachute jumps and other events at MP Visitors Booth (Randolph St. & SR 24); open daily, 24 hrs. U.S. Army John F. Kennedy Center for Military Assistance Museum (Gruber Rd.) has exhibits on guerrilla warfare; open Tues.-Fri. 11:30-4; Sat. & Sun. 1-4; free. 82nd Airborne Division Museum (Ardennes Rd. & Gela St.) displays memorabilia from WW I to present; open Tues.-Sun. 11:30-4; closed late Dec.-early Jan.; free.

GOLDSBORO: Bentonville Battleground State Historic Site (18 m W, follow signs, near Bentonville): Here, on March 19-21, 1865, less than a month before Lee's surrender, Confederates made a last, desperate attempt to halt Sherman's march from Atlanta to the sea; battlefield markers; restored Harper House used as hospital by both sides; **Visitor Center** with exhibits; open Tues.-Sat. 9-5, Sun. 1-5; closed Thnks, Dec. 25; free.

    Charles B. Aycock Birthplace State Historic Site (12 m N off US 117 near Fremont) consists of 19th-C farmhouse, outbuildings, school, and **Visitor Center** with exhibits tracing the life of the "educational governor"; open Tues.-Sat. 9-5, Sun. 1-5; closed Thnks, Dec. 25; free.

    Gov. Caswell Memorial—CSS Neuse State Historic Site (26 m E via US 70 to US 70A in Kinston) has a **Visitor Center** with exhibits on the life of the state's first governor; Caswell's grave; remains of Confederate ironclad sunk by her crew in 1865 to avoid capture and raised in 1963; open Tues.-Sat. 9-5, Sun. 1-5; closed Thnks, Dec. 25; free.

GREAT SMOKY MOUNTAINS NATIONAL PARK offers information at the **Oconaluftee Visitor Center** (2 m N of Cherokee on US 441); interesting Pioneer Museum in reconstructed log buildings tells the story of mountain settlers; open daily June-Oct., 8 am-7:30 pm; Nov.-Mar. 8-4:30; closed Dec. 25; free. Tapes for self-guiding auto tours of the park are advertised along US 411 in Cherokee. See also Tennessee.

GREENSBORO: University of North Carolina at Greensboro (1000 Spring Garden St.) offers **Weatherspoon Art Gallery** (McIver Bldg), with works by de Kooning, Calder, and other 20th-C artists; primitive and Oriental pieces; open academic yr, Mon.-Fri. 10-5, Sun. 2-5; free.

Guilford Courthouse National Military Park (6 m NW on US 220), where Cornwallis, with 2200 experienced men, met 4500 inexperienced Americans under Gen. Nathanael Greene on March 15, 1781, has marked self-guiding auto tour and foot trails; it was a Pyrrhic victory for Cornwallis, who lost 25% of his men and had to move into Virginia and surrender at Yorktown in Oct.; **Visitor Center** with interpretive material; open daily 8:30-5 (9-6 in summer); closed Jan. 1, Dec. 25; free.

Guilford College (5800 W Friendly Ave.), founded by Quakers in 1837, contains Quaker archives; open Mon.-Sat. 9-12:30; also Tues., Thurs. 2-4; free.

Greensboro Historical Museum (130 Summit Ave.), in a former church that served as a Civil War hospital, has exhibits (period rooms, glassware, china, military memorabilia) tracing history of Guilford County from prehistoric times to the present; Dolley Madison Room honors the First Lady born in the county in 1768; exhibits on William Sydney Porter (O. Henry), including reproduction of the drugstore where he worked and school he attended; restored 1761 log house; other displays; open Tues.-Sat. 10-5, Sun. 2-5; closed Jan. 1, Easter, Thnks, Dec. 25; free.

Chinqua-Penn Plantation (19 m N off US 29 to Reidsville, then 3 m NW off US 29 Bypass to Wentworth Rd.), maintained by the University of North Carolina, is a 1925 stone-and-log mansion with rare objects gathered around the world by the traveling owners; tours given Mar.-Dec. 15, Wed.-Sat. 10-4, Sun. 1-4; closed July 4, Thnks; adm.

Alamance Battleground State Historic Site (19 m E via I-85, then 5 m SW on SR 62), site of 1771 battle in which the Militia under Royal Gov. Tryon defeated some 2000 Colonial "regulators"; **Visitor Center** with exhibits, audiovisual program; restored log house and markers on grounds; open Tues.-Sat. 9-5, Sun. 1-5; closed Thnks, Dec. 25; free.

HENDERSONVILLE: Carl Sandburg Home National Historic Site (5 m S on US 25 to Little River Rd., Flat Rock), farmhouse and outbuildings, home of the poet 1945 until his death in 1967; **Visitor Center;** open Mon.,

Tues., Thurs., Fri., Sun. 9-5; Wed. & Sat. 9-noon; closed Jan. 1, Dec. 25; free. Sandburg's funeral service was held in nearby Church of St. John in the Wilderness, a simple building with exposed beams. **Oakdale Cemetery** (on US 64, W of Main St., Hendersonville) contains the angel believed described by Wolfe in *Look Homeward, Angel*.

HICKORY: Hickory Museum of Art (3rd St. & 1st Ave. NW) offers works by George Inness, Gilbert Stuart, and other Americans, plus a Tintoretto and other European paintings; open Mon.-Fri. 10-5, Sun. 3-5; closed hols & Aug.; free.

HIGH POINT: High Point Museum (1805 E Lexington Ave. at McGuinn Ave.), local history; city's furniture and hosiery industries; Quaker settlers; open Tues.-Fri. 9:30-4:30, Sun. 2-5; closed hols; free. Adjacent 1786 **John Haley House,** restored Quaker home with blacksmith shop, was once a stagecoach stop; open Tues. & Wed., 9-noon, Sun. 2-5; closed hols; sm adm.

NEW BERN: Preserved here, in this town settled 1710 by Germans and Swiss seeking religious and political freedom, are more than 50 houses of historic and architectural interest (especially on blocks between the Trent River & Johnson St., Neuse River & George St.); booklet and maps for self-guiding tours available from **Chamber of Commerce** (608 Broad St.). Tours of privately owned homes are conducted occasionally by **New Bern Historical Society** (511 Broad St.); open Tues.-Sat. 2:30-5; closed hols. Among interesting buildings are: pre-1800 **Wade-Boyd House** (214 Tryon Palace Dr.), of handmade brick; **Patterson-Duffy House** (226 E Front St.), designed after Morro Castle in Havana, Cuba, with figurehead of a woman and 2 lions on the Pollock St. side; **City Hall** (Craven & Pollock Sts.), with the figure of the Bern bear (Bern means bear); **James Davis House** (211 Broad St.), whose owner imported the first printing press and printed the town's first newspaper (open Mon.-Sat. 9-5; closed hols; adm); lovely **First Presbyterian Church** (Middle & New Sts.), from a Christopher Wren design; **Masonic Temple & Theater** (514-16 Hancock St.); **Cedar Grove Cemetery** (Queen St.), whose "weeping arch" of coquina is supposed to spell death to anyone touched by its drops of water.

New Bern Firemen's Museum (420 Broad St., behind fire station), houses antique fire-fighting equipment and memorabilia; open Tues.-Sat. 9:30-noon, 1-5; Sun. 1-5; closed Thnks, Dec. 25; sm adm.

Tryon Palace Restoration (S end of George St. at 613 Pollock St.) of an elegant palace built 1767-70 in Georgian style by the Royal Governor, William Tryon, and once considered the most beautiful building in the colonies; it served as the Colonial and first state capitol; exquisite furnishings; works of art; set in 18th-C English-style gardens; tours Tues.-Sat. 9:30-4, Sun. 1:30-4; closed Jan. 1, Thnks, Dec. 24-26; adm. Also here, open same hrs, adm, are: 1805 **Stevenson House,** reflecting New Bern's maritime history with roping in wood cornices and widow's walk, with Federal and Empire furnishings; 1780 **John Wright Stanly House,** typical 18th-C merchant's home, with 1750-80 American furnishings, English and Irish pieces.

Morehead City (35 m SE on US 70) offers the remains of fortifications built 1826-34, a fish and shellfish museum, and cruises. At nearby **Beaufort,** once a whaling center, the Beaufort Restoration to return the Turner St. area to its 18th-C appearance is in progress; here are 1767 **Joseph Bell House,** 1800s **Josiah Bell House,** 1836 **Jail,** a marine museum, and **Old Burying Ground** (where one English sailor insisted on being buried standing up); open June-mid-Sept., Mon.-Sat. 9-5, Sun. 2-5; tours of historic homes and other events in summer.

OUTER BANKS: Wright Brothers National Memorial (2 m S of Kitty Hawk on US 158 Bypass) is at Kill Devil Hill, site of the first successful, powered, man-carrying flight (Dec. 17, 1903) by Wilbur and Orville Wright; plane was aloft about 12 seconds and traveled 120 ft; takeoff and landing spots are marked; **Visitor Center** with reproduction of first plane, other exhibits; hangar-workshop and living quarters; open daily 8:30-4:30 (8-8 in summer); closed Dec. 25; free. Available here is a map to the Graveyard of the Atlantic; many of the vessels that wrecked along the Outer Banks are marked along the hwy and can be seen from the beaches.

Fort Raleigh National Historic Site (on Roanoke Island, 3 m N of Manteo off US 64) was site of the first English colony in America (1585); Virginia Dare was born here 1587, but a few days later Gov. John White returned to England for supplies. Queen Elizabeth, fearing a Spanish invasion, refused to allow ships to leave England, so White was unable to return until 1590. The colony had disappeared, leaving behind only the word "Croatoan" (the name of a friendly inland tribe of Indians) carved into a treetrunk; the fate of the colonists is unknown. **Visitor Center** with relics, exhibits, audiovisual program; excavated area, reconstructed fort; open daily 8-4:30 (9-8:15 in summer); closed Dec. 25; free. Nearby is the **Wayside Theater,** where the drama, *The Lost Colony,* is presented in summer. Also nearby is **Elizabethan Garden,** a memorial to the colonists; 16th-C portrait of Elizabeth I by Zucarro, period furnishings in the **Gate House Reception Center;** open daily 9-6; closed mid-Dec.-early Jan.; adm.

Cape Hatteras National Seashore extends southward from Whalebone Junction to Ocracoke Inlet (just S is the undeveloped Cape Lookout National Seashore); within its boundaries are 8 resort villages on private land; the hwy runs to Hatteras, and from there all-year ferries across Hatteras

Inlet (free) and from Ocracoke to Cedar Island (toll) make daily crossings (reservations advised in any season). At **Bodie Island, a Visitor Center** offers information and natural history exhibits; nearby is a lighthouse; open May-Sept. daily 9-6. At **Buxton, Cape Hatteras Lighthouse** with observation deck and Museum of the Sea (in the former keeper's residence) are open daily 9-5 (9-6 in summer), closed Dec. 25. At **Ocracoke,** the **Visitor Center** offers historic exhibits (including one on the death of Blackbeard the Pirate here in 1718); open daily 8-5; closed Dec. 25. For additional information, write Supt., Box 457, Manteo 27954.

RALEIGH: Chamber of Commerce (411 S Salisbury) provides maps and information for self-guiding auto and walking tours; industrial tours; and tours of the Governor's Mansion (Oct.-May), built by convicts who etched their initials into its bricks.

   State Capitol (Capitol Sq.), built 1833-40, is a dignified Greek Revival building with a colorful past (the stairs bear scars from the whiskey barrels once rolled in for its bar); legislative chambers have elaborate Greek ornamentation; park has many statues and monuments; open Mon.-Fri. 8:30-5:30 (8-5 in summer), Sat. 9-5, Sun. 1-5; free. Open same hrs is **State House** (Jones St. at Salisbury), a 5-dome marble structure designed by Edward Durell Stone; sessions may be viewed from visitor gallery; gardens; free. **State Museum of Natural History** (101 Halifax St., N of Capitol Sq.) offers exhibits on the state's flora, fauna, resources; open Mon.-Sat. 9-5, Sun. 2-5; closed Dec. 24-Jan. 1; free. **North Carolina Museum of History** (109 E Jones St.) houses exhibits on colonial times, Revolution and Civil War, clothing, silver, guns, armor, tools, crafts; open Mon.-Sat. 8:30-5:30, Sun. 2-5; closed Jan. 1, Thnks, Dec. 25; free. **North Carolina Museum of Art** (107 E Morgan St.) exhibits many European masterpieces, British and American painting, and sculpture; gallery for the blind; open Tues.-Sat. 10-5, Sun. 2-6; closed Jan. 1, Thnks, Dec. 24-26; free.

   Mordecai Square (Mimosa St.) contains restored **Mordecai House,** built 1785-1826, with many original furnishings, portraits; tours Oct.-May, Tues.-Thurs. 10-1; Sun. all yr 2-4; closed hols; free. **Andrew Johnson Birthplace,** in which the 17th President was born 1808; Johnson left Raleigh in 1824 and returned only occasionally; period furnishings; open Sun.-Fri. 2-5; sm adm.

   Christ Episcopal Church (120 E Edenton St.), designed by Richard Upjohn, was completed in 1849; the weathercock atop the spire was said to be the only chicken left in town after Sherman's troops departed; open daily.

   Dorton Arena (State Fair Grounds, New Bern Ave.) is an unusual, elliptical glass structure; open Mon.-Sat. 8-4:30; free.

   Country Doctor Museum (26 m E on US 64, 264 to Bailey) is a composite restoration of 2 doctors' offices; apothecary; operating table;

blood-letting and other equipment; reference materials used 1700-1900; medicinal garden; open Wed. 10-5, Sun. 2-5; sm adm.

ROANOKE RAPIDS: Historic Halifax State Historic Site (11 m SE off US 301), site of a 1723 settlement that thrived as a river port and became an important social and commercial center, was where the Halifax Resolves was signed; this was the first document in the colonies to propose independence from England, and some of its ideas were later incorporated into the Declaration of Independence. **Visitor Center** (Main St.) is in the handsome 1832 Clerk's Office; this and other buildings are open Tues.-Sat. 9-5, Sun. 1-5; closed Thnks, Dec. 25; free. Buildings open to the public include: 1770 **Constitution House,** with Revolutionary-period furnishings; 1760 **Owens House,** home of a wealthy merchant, with pre-Revolutionary furnishings; **Old Jail,** built of brick 1838 after prisoners burned the two previous ones; also spring, cemetery.

Historic Murfreesboro (33 m E via US 158) is a 12-block district with many fine 18-19th-C buildings; information available at **Roberts Village Center** (Main St.), consisting of an 18th-C home and other buildings housing the Historic Association, Chamber of Commerce, and Public Library. Restored buildings include: 1790 **William Rea Store Museum,** with exhibits on river trade and agriculture; 1851 **McDowell Columns Bldg.** (Chowan College campus) named for its massive white columns; **Wheeler House** (403 E Broad St.), a 19th-C merchant's home; and **Melrose,** a restored plantation.

SALISBURY: Livingstone College (701 W Monroe St.), established 1879 and named for African missionary David Livingstone, offers Heritage House, with artifacts on African and Afro-American culture, history of AME Zion Church; open academic yr, daily 9-5; free. **Rowan Museum** (114 S Jackson St.), in 1819 Maxwell Chambers House, has period rooms; county historic displays (Daniel Boone and Andrew Jackson lived here); locally crafted furniture; open June-Sept., Wed. & Sat. 2-5, Sun. 2-4; Oct.-May, Tues.-Sat. 2-5, Sun. 2-4; closed Thnks, Dec. 24-25; free. **Old Stone House** (4 m SE off US 52 in Granite Quarry) is a 1766 home with period furnishings; family cemetery; open Sat. & Sun. 2-5; closed Thnks, Dec. 24-25; sm adm.

SEAGROVE: Potters Museum (1 m N on US 220) traces the history of North Carolina pottery from the time the craft was imported from Staffordshire, England; toys, grave markers, foot warmers, and other unusual items from 1750-present; open Mon.-Sat. 10-4; closed hols; free. **Jugtown Pottery** (SR 705), replica of an early works, demonstrates methods; open Mon.-Sat. 8-5; closed Jan. 1, Dec. 25; free. Other potteries in the area are also open Mon.-Sat.

WASHINGTON: Historic Bath State Historic Site (20 m E on SR 92) preserves buildings from the oldest incorporated town in the state (1705), home for a time to Blackbeard, the pirate; **Visitor Center** shows a film on the town's history; 1734 **St. Thomas Church;** 1760s **Palmer-Marsh House;** 1825 **Bonner House;** 1825 **Van der Veer House;** 1827-32 **Glebe House;** open Tues.-Sat. 9-5, Sun. 1-5; closed Thnks, Dec. 24-26; adm to some bldgs.

WILMINGTON: North Carolina's chief port, made capital of the colony in 1743, Wilmington was a center of rebellion against England; in 1765 (8 years before the Boston Tea Party), local citizens burned Lord Bute in effigy, prevented the unloading of stamp paper from a British sloop-of-war, and forced the stamp master to resign. During the Revolution, Cornwallis had his hq here for a year. During the Civil War it was the chief port for the Confederacy, with much blockade-running past Union ships lying off Cape Fear, until Fort Fisher fell in 1865. Maps for self-guiding tours of the city and the Cape Fear Trail may be obtained from the **Chamber of Commerce** (P.O. Box 330). Among many gracious homes surviving in the old district is **Burgwin-Wright House** (224 Market St. at 3rd St.), which Cornwallis used as his hq in 1781; built 1771 on the foundations of a jail; dungeons in the cellar; underground tunnel to the Cape Fear River (probably for escape in case of pirate attack); 18th-C furnishings; open Mon.-Fri. 9-4; closed Easter Mon., July 4, Labor Day, Thnks; adm.

Moores Creek National Military Park (17 m N on SR 421 then 3 m W on SR 210) was scene of "the Lexington and Concord of the South," a Feb. 1776 battle in which patriots defeated loyalist militia, dashing British hopes of an easy sweep through the South and spurring Revolutionary fervor; loop drive past bridge greased by patriots to hamper loyalists; **Visitor Center** with exhibits; open daily 8-5; closed Jan. 1, Dec. 25; free.

Blockade Runner Museum (15 m S on US 421 near Carolina Beach) traces with dioramas, scale models, and displays the history of more than 2000 ships that attempted to run blockades during the Civil War; open daily 10-5 (9-6 in summer); closed Jan. 1, Dec. 24-25; adm. **Fort Fisher State Historic Site** (20 m S on US 421 beyond Carolina Beach) preserves large earthwork fort that kept Wilmington open to blockade runners during the Civil War until it was surrendered on Jan. 15, 1865; **Visitor Center** has audiovisual program, tours, museum with artifacts recovered from sunken ships, other exhibits; open Tues.-Sat. 9-5, Sun. 1-5; closed Thnks, Dec. 25; free.

USS North Carolina Battleship Memorial (W bank of Cape Fear River), only battleship to participate in all major Pacific offensives during WW II; memorial to North Carolinians who died in the war; you can tour most of the ship; small museum gives ship's history; open daily 8-sunset; adm.

Orton Plantation (18 m S off SR 133) is a showplace on the Cape Fear
River; 1725 manor house is not open but is worth seeing from the outside;
gardens are among the finest in the nation; seductive atmosphere; open
Feb.-Sept. daily 8-6; Oct.-Jan. daily 8-5; closed Dec. 24-27; adm. Just
outside the gates are signs to **Brunswick Town-Fort Anderson State
Historic Site,** about a mile S; Brunswick, founded 1725 as a real estate
venture, became a prosperous river port; Spanish privateers held it for 3
days in 1748; during the Revolution, its citizens fled before the British,
who burned it; it became a ghost town and was bought in 1842 by the
owner of Orton Plantation for $4.25; during the Civil War an earthworks
fort was built to aid blockade runners and remained in Southern hands a
full month after Fort Fisher fell; marked trail leads through excavated
foundations of town and fort; **Visitor Center** provides historical orientation; open Tues.-Sat. 9-5, Sun. 1-5; closed Thnks, Dec. 25; free.

WINSTON-SALEM: Old Salem (well marked, S off I-40, W off US 52) is
the inhabited restoration of a community established by German Moravians 1766; originally the people lived in groups according to age, sex, and
marital status, but today the Single Sisters House is a Salem College dorm
and many of the homes are private residences. Open to the public are:
1769 **Single Brothers House,** with demonstrations of early crafts; 1771
Miksch Tobacco Shop; 1784 **Salem Tavern** (serves lunch and dinner); 1794
Boys School; 1800 **Winkler Bakery** (sells delicious bread); 1819 **John
Vogler House.** Reception Center provides information on Salem and the
Moravians, museum exhibits, tours, combination tickets or single-
building tickets; open Mon.-Sat. 9:30-4:30, Sun. 1:30-4:30; closed Dec.
25. Also here are: **Museum of Early Southern Decorative Arts** (926 S
Main St.), displaying regional furnishings and decoration 1600s-1820 in 15
period rooms; fine research library; open Mon.-Sat. 11-6, Sun. 1:30-4:30;
closed Dec. 25; adm. **Gallery of Contemporary Art** (500 S Main St.),
dedicated to arts of the Southeast; paintings, sculpture, photography,
crafts; open Mon.-Sat. 10:30-4:30, also Sun. in Sept.-May 2-4:30; closed
hols; free.

Bethabara Park (2147 Bethabara Rd.) is site of the first Moravian settlement, founded 1753; by 1755 this was a center for trade and fine crafts
in 17 buildings (most moved to their new town, Salem, by 1772); remaining are foundations and reconstructed buildings; exceptional display of
18th-C American pottery; 1788 **Gemein Haus,** 1782 **Potter's House,** 1802
Brewer's House; open Easter-Nov., Mon.-Fri. 9:30-4:30, Sat. & Sun.
1:30-4:30; free.

Reynolda House (2 m NW on SR 67, Reynolda Rd.), home of Richard
J. Reynolds who founded the tobacco company, houses an important col-
lection of American art 1755-present (Copley, Stuart, Church, Eakins,
Hassam, Andrew Wyeth, Cassatt); family period clothing (1905-50s); fur-

nished with 18-19th-C pieces; Dorothy Doughty bird collection; open
Feb.-Jan. 1, Tues.-Sat. 9:30-4:30, Sun. 1:30-4:30; closed Dec. 25, Jan.
2-31; adm.

   Cooleemee Plantation House (13 m SW via US 158, then S on SR 801
to the Yadkin Riv.), a lovely antebellum mansion, usually offers tours in
summer; inquire locally for hrs; adm.

NORTH DAKOTA

BISMARCK: State Capitol (N 6th St.), called Skyscraper of the Prairies,
features a 19th-story observation tower; chandeliers in Memorial Hall
symbolize the importance of wheat to the economy; paintings by state artists; tours Mon.-Fri. 8-11, 1-4; also Memorial Day-Labor Day, Sat. 9-4 &
Sun. 1-4; closed hols; free. On grounds are: **State Historical Society
Museum** (Liberty Memorial Bldg) with relics of Indians, military posts,
pioneers; mounted wildlife; open Mon.-Fri. 8-5, Sat. 8-4; also in June-
Aug., Sun. 1-5; free. Statue of Pioneer family by Avard Fairbanks, of
Sakajawea, the Lewis and Clark guide.

   Camp Hancock Museum (Main & 1st Sts.) is at the original townsite,
established 1872 as a supply depot for the military (the name Bismarck was
not chosen until the coming of railroads, to encourage German capital in a
transcontinental line); restored buildings and church; steam locomotive;
museum of Indian and pioneer artifacts; open May 15-Sept. 15, Mon.-Fri.
9-noon, 1-5; closed hols; free.

   Mary College (7 m S on Airport Rd.) offers tours of its campus,
designed by Marcel Breuer.

   Fort Mandan Historic Site (40 m N on US 83, then W of Washburn) is
a reconstruction of the log fort erected by Lewis and Clark as a winter
camp in 1804; interpretive markers.

BOWMAN: Yellowstone Trail Museum, with homesteading items, is
open in summer, daily 10-5; sm adm. **Fort Dilts Historic Site** (20 m W off
SR 12) contains ruins of sod fort hurriedly built by members of a wagon
train who were attacked and besieged for 14 days by Indians in 1864.

DEVILS LAKE: Fort Totten Historic Site (15 m SW on SR 57) preserves
an 1867 fort built to protect the overland route to Montana; around the
parade ground stand barracks, surgeon's quarters, other buildings;
museum of pioneer relics; open May-Oct., daily 8-6; free.

FARGO: Founded 1872 as a supply and outfitting point, this city was named for William G. Fargo of Wells-Fargo Express Co. **Forsberg House** (815 3rd Ave. S) houses local historic items, folk art, musical instruments, dolls; open by appointment Tues.-Fri. 1-5; sm adm.

Bonanzaville, USA (on US 10 on Cass County Fairgrounds) re-creates farming in the Red River Valley in "bonanza" days (when huge tracts of land were worked as a single farm by hundreds of men); village buildings with period furnishings; **Red River & Northern Plains Regional Museum** with thousands of Indian and pioneer artifacts; demonstrations of frontier skills; other events; open June-Sept., Mon.-Fri. 9:30-5, Sat. & Sun. 1-5; spring & fall, Tues.-Fri. 9:30-4; adm.

GRAFTON: Pembina Historical State Park & Museum (50 m NE via US 81, I-29 in Pembina) is site of a series of fur trading posts, the earliest built 1797 for the Northwest Fur Co., that was settled by Scottish Highlanders in 1812; state's first settlement, with first church and school; museum; open May 15-Sept. 15, daily 9-5.

GRAND FORKS: University of North Dakota (University Ave.) offers art exhibits of regional, Oriental, and other works (open daily 1-5) and a zoology museum (open Mon.-Sat. 9-5) during the academic yr; free.

JAMESTOWN: Stutsman County Historical Museum (3rd Ave. SE & 4th St. SE) exhibits Indian artifacts, medical instruments, musical instruments, pioneer relics; open June-Sept., Wed. & Sun. 2-5, 7-9; sm adm. **Frontier Village** (SE of town on I-94) contains school, church, shops, homes moved here from the surrounding area; 19th-C furnishings; open late May-early Sept., daily 9-9; free. **Whitestone Battlefield State Historic Site** (37 m S on US 281, then 15 m W on SR 13 to Kulm, 15 m S on SR 56, then E) was site of last major battle between whites and the Sioux, 1863; cemetery and monument; museum; open mid-May-mid-Sept. daily 9-5; free.

MANDAN: Beck's Great Plains Museum (3 m S on county 1806) includes 1887 furnished log house, dental office, shops, firearms, antique vehicles, Indian artifacts, pioneer items; open June-mid-Oct., daily 9-dark; sm adm. **Fort Lincoln State Park** (3 m S on county 1806) commemorates 1872 fort built to protect construction of the Northern Pacific Railway; in 1876 this was Custer's hq; from here he set out with 265 men for the Battle of Little Big Horn which only the horse Comanche survived; fort foundations, reconstructed blockhouses; partially restored Mandan earthlodges of Slant Indian Village (1650-1750); museum; open May-Oct. 9-5 (longer in summer); sm adm.

Wrong Side Up Monument (on I-94) commemorates John Christiansen, who arrived in 1883 with German settlers to found New Salem; when he turned the sod to farm the land, an Indian warned, "wrong side up" and turned the sod back into place; after repeated crop failures, Christiansen decided the Indian might be right and turned to raising cattle; his portrait hangs in the N.D. Agricultural College Hall of Fame to honor his establishment of the prosperous cattle industry in the state.

Grant County Museum (42 m W on I-94, then 38 m S on SR 49 on Main St., Elgin), in a 1910 railroad depot, houses restored ticket office; replica of a sod house with period furnishings; schoolhouse; pioneer home and farm tools; open June-mid-Sept., daily 9-5; sm adm.

MEDORA: Chateau de Mores Historic Site (1 m SW off I-94) consists of a visitor center, chateau, and packing house ruins. Here in 1883 the colorful Marquis de Mores arrived, named the settlement for his wife, and intended to build a cattle empire to finance his claim to the French throne; the chateau, an unprepossessing frame building, was staffed with French servants and regally furnished for the lavish entertainment of European nobility; original furnishings include finely crafted French pieces, English Minton china, an enameled safe, guns, handcrafted armor, paintings, clothing and other personal possessions left when the Marquis failed and returned to Europe in 1886; tours daily (weather permitting) 9-5; sm adm. The Marquis (who was killed by North African tribes in 1896) also built an abattoir (it burned in 1907 and only the chimney survives), cold-storage facilities from Helena to Chicago, and operated a stagecoach line between Medora and the Black Hills. Still standing here are **St. Mary's Catholic Church** (built for his wife in 1884) and **Rough Riders Hotel** (whose name Theodore Roosevelt adopted for his Spanish- American War regiment).

Medora Museum has a fine collection of Plains Indian artifacts, pioneer relics, early weapons, mounted local wildlife; open mid-May-early Oct. daily 8-8; adm. **Medora Doll House** has antique dolls and toys from around the world; open mid-May-early Oct. daily 8-8; sm adm. **Western Gallery** exhibits regional art and pioneer quilts; open mid-May-early Oct. daily 8-8; free.

Theodore Roosevelt's National Memorial Park honors Roosevelt's contributions to conservation, an interest partly animated by his stay here; he came in 1883 to hunt big game and in 1884 to recuperate from the deaths of his wife and mother, buying interest in the Maltese Cross Ranch and establishing the Elkhorn Ranch. The **Visitor Center** in Medora provides information; behind it is Roosevelt's **Maltese Cross cabin;** audiovisual program, exhibits, ranger programs; open daily 8-4:30 (8-8 in summer). From here a 38-m scenic loop drive takes you through the South Unit. The North Unit (accessible on US 85 from Watford City) has a 13-m interpretive drive and ranger programs. Park open daily all year; sm adm or GEP.

Fort Houston Museum (21 m E off I-94 in Belfield) has a variety of frontier items, Badland artifacts; open Apr.-Oct. daily 7 am-9 pm; sm adm.

MINOT: Northwest Historical Society Museum & Pioneer Village (on State Fairgrounds) consists of the first county courthouse, a typical home, church, and other buildings; museum with historic relics; open May-Oct., Thurs.-Mon. 2-9 (open daily during State Fair); sm adm.

NEW TOWN: This is hq for the **Berthold Indian Reservation** and **Four Bears Memorial Park & Museum** is an Indian-owned modern complex maintained by Mandan, Arikara, and Hidatsa tribes; arts and crafts; historic displays; open Memorial Day-Oct., daily 9-9; adm. **Paul Broste Rock Museum** (15 m E off SR 23 in Parshall) is in an unusual building incorporating rocks and minerals designed by local farmer Paul Broste to showcase exotic specimens from all over the world; also paintings; on grounds is Homestead Shack, an early school, with original furnishings; open daily in daylight; sm adm.

RICHARDTON: Assumption Abbey, popularly known as the Cathedral of the Prairies, is a Benedictine monastery begun in 1899; early buildings were made by the monks of local clay made into bricks on the property; the twin steeples of the church have long been a prairie landmark; open daily.

RUGBY: Geographical Center of North America is marked with a monument, museum, reconstructed pioneer village; pioneer tools, dolls, guns, glass are on display; open May-Sept. daily 8-5; adm. **International Peace Garden** (46 m N on US 281), on the Canadian border, symbolizes friendship between the two nations.

TURTLE LAKE: Schlafmann Museum (2 m S, 2½ m W on SR 200) specializes in antique mechanical musical instruments—barrel organ, nickelodeons, player pianos, coin-operated machines, others; open Memorial Day-Sept., daily 8-sunset; adm.

VALLEY CITY: Barnes County Historical Museum (in courthouse on 4 St. NW) displays pioneer relics, Indian stone hearts, other artifacts; open Tues. 2-5; closed hols; free. **Steele County Historical Society Museum** (10 m E on I-94, then 28 m N on SR 32 in Hope) illustrates the history of prairie pioneers with furniture, farm machinery, other relics in a 19th-C home, school, and general store; open Memorial Day-Labor Day daily, rest of yr Sun. 2-5; sm adm.

Fort Ransom State Historic Site (2 m W on I-94, 33 m S on SR 1, 3½ m E on SR 27, 3½ m N) contains only earthwork remains of an 1867-72 military post on the Sheyenne River; settler cabin; there are many Indian burial mounds in this valley. Nearby is **Ransom County Museum,** with local historical items of this Scandinavian community (open Sun. & hols 2-5; free) and **Bjarne Ness Gallery,** with his paintings (open mid-May-mid-Oct., Tues.-Sun. 1-6; free).

WAHPETON: Richland County Historical Museum (2nd St. & 7th Ave. N) illustrates the history of the county with pioneer relics; open June-late Oct., Tues.-Sun. 2-5; rest of yr, Fri.-Sun. 2-5; closed hols; free.

Fort Abercrombie State Historic Site (20 m N on US 81, then E in Abercrombie) contains reconstructed blockhouses and stockade, original guardhouse of the first Federal military post in the state; one in a chain of forts extending from St. Paul to the Montana gold fields, it was occupied off-and-on 1857-77 to regulate fur trading, buffalo hunting, traffic through the Red River Valley, and to keep the peace; in 1862 it withstood a 60-day siege by the Sioux; interesting **museum** relates its history; museum open May-Sept. daily 9-5; site open all year, daily 9-5; sm adm.

Camp Buell Historic Site (34 m W on SR 13 at Milnor) has interpretive markers. **Ratherts Museum** (40 m W on SR 13, 9 m S on SR 32 in Forman) displays antique autos, dolls, musical instruments, other items; open daily in summer 9-5; sm adm.

WILLISTON: Frontier Museum & Pioneer Village (3 m N on US 2, 85) displays Indian and pioneer artifacts in 2 museums; village consists of church, school, log cabin, grocery, doctor and dentist offices; open Memorial Day-Labor Day, Mon.-Fri. 7 am-9 pm, Sun. & hols 2-5; adm. **Buffalo Trails Museum** (9 m N on US 2, 85, then 13 m E on county road to Epping) tells the history of the upper Missouri River area; interesting displays include interior of a homesteader's shack; a highlight is recordings of pioneers explaining what life was like; also regional paintings, diorama of Assiniboin life, fossils, other exhibits; open June-Sept., Mon.-Sat. 9-5; Oct., Sun. 1-5; adm. **Divide County Pioneer Village & Museum** (50 m N on US 85, then 14 m E on SR 5 in Crosby) displays local historical items in early church, school, other buildings; open spring-fall, Mon.-Sat. 2-5; closed hols; sm adm.

Fort Union Trading Post National Historic Site (5 m W on US 2, then follow signs) offers interpretive signs at foundations of 1828 fort (eventually to be reconstructed) that was the largest and most important on the Missouri; established 1828 by Kenneth McKenzie ("King of the Upper

Missouri"), an American Fur Co. executive; Indians from miles around camped on the plains surrounding the fort and often skirmished with each other; McKenzie lived regally in the wilderness, dressing for dinner at a table set with china and silver, and attracted prominent visitors such as Audubon; but by midcentury, white encroachment and attendant smallpox epidemics frightened the Indians—some fought back and others scattered—and the fort was abandoned; in 1868 its materials were used to build Ft. Buford; the site, being developed by the NPS, is open mid-May-Oct. daily 9-6; free.

Fort Buford Historic Site (5 m W on US 2, 17 m SW on county road) contains the officers' quarters and powder magazine of the fort established 1866 as part of a chain of military posts between Ft. Leavenworth and the Columbia River; its function was to quell Indian uprisings, and Sitting Bull surrendered here in 1881; museum with displays on military, Indian, and pioneer history; open Apr.-Sept. daily 9-5; sm adm. **Writing Rock Historic Site** (12 m W on US 2, then 40 m N to Alkabo) has pictographs; interpretive signs; open daily; free.

Lewis & Clark Trail Museum (19 m S on US 85 in Alexander) highlights exhibits on the explorers; diorama of Ft. Mandan, where they spent the winter of 1804-5; Catlin and Russell paintings of Indians; rooms furnished as pioneer shops and workshops; open Memorial Day-Labor Day, Mon.-Sat. 9-6, Sun. 1-6; adm. **Pioneer Museum** (41 m SE on US 85 at 109 Park Ave. W, Watford City) offers homestead interiors, school, country store; open Memorial Day-Labor Day, Tues.-Sun. 1-5:30, 7-9; adm.

OHIO

AKRON: Chamber of Commerce (137 S Main St.) provides maps and information, and can advise you on industrial tours of Goodyear, General Tire, and other plants. **Summit County Historical Society** (550 Copley Rd.) houses regional historical exhibits in 1837 Greek Revival **Perkins Mansion** (Perkins was a business partner of abolitionist John Brown) and in **John Brown Home** (514 Diagonal Rd. at Copley Rd.), where the abolitionist lived 1844-46; open Tues.-Sun. 1-5; closed hols; sm adm. **University of Akron** arranges tours through the Admissions Office (166 Fir Hill); features include a rare book collection and a rubber science hall of fame. **Akron Art Institute** (69 E Market St.) features contemporary painting (Picasso, Warhol, Stella, Robert Indiana); library; sculpture court; open Sun.-Fri. noon-5, Sat. 10-5; closed hols; free.

Stan Hywet Hall & Gardens (1½ m N of jct SR 18 at 714 N Portage Path), a Tudor Revival mansion built by F. A. Seiberling, founder of the Goodyear and Seiberling rubber companies, is magnificent; English craftsmen incorporated Elizabethan-style features; 14-18th-C furnishings; open Tues.-Sat. 10-4:15, Sun. 1-5; closed Jan. 1, Thnks, Dec. 25; adm. **Railways of America** (6 m N on SR 8 at 3656 Akron-Cleveland Rd., Cuyahoga Falls), in railroad station; huge display of operating model trains; open daily 11-8; closed Thnks, Dec. 25; adm. **Jonathan Hale Homestead & Western Reserve Village** (10 m N at 2686 Oak Hill Rd., Bath) preserves the 1826 Federal-style home built by pioneer from Connecticut (which claimed this area as its Western Reserve until 1800); many original furnishings. Other authentically furnished buildings moved to the green here include a saltbox, Greek Revival-style clapboard, log school, law office. Open May-Dec., Tues.-Sun. noon-5; closed Thnks, Dec. 25; adm. **American Indian Art Hall of Fame** (11 m N on SR 8, at jct SR 532 at 5000 Akron-Cleveland Rd., Peninsula), in an adobe-style building, offers Navajo rugs, Pueblo pottery and kachina dolls, Eskimo carvings, and other displays of work from 28 tribes; open Feb.-Dec., Tues.-Sat. 10-5, Sun. noon-5; closed Easter, Thnks, Dec. 25, Jan.; adm.

Hudson Library & Museum (10 m NE on SR 91 to 22 Aurora St., Hudson) has a room furnished as a Western Reserve parlor of 1830s, historical artifacts, documents; open Mon., Tues., Thurs.-Sat. 10-5; closed hols; free. **Presnick's Carnival Glass Museum** (23 m W on US 224 to Lodi, then 2 m N) is a private collection of Carnival Glass, or Ohio River Art Glass, produced 1890-1920; most of the factories were along the Ohio River between Grapevilla, Pennsylvania, and Williamstown, W Virginia; open May-Sept., Wed.-Sun. 1-6; adm.

ASHLAND: Ashland College Historical Center (414 Center St.) houses county Indian and pioneer relics, including an early printing press; open Apr.-Dec., Wed., Fri., Sun. 1-4:30; closed hols; free.

ASHTABULA: Settled by New Englanders, this was a center for abolitionists; one of the chief Underground Railroad stations was **Hubbard Homestead** (Lake Ave. & Walnut Blvd), now a community center. **Conneaut Historical Railroad Museum** (11 m NE on US 20 to 324 Depot St., Conneaut) houses memorabilia, model engines in a former New York Central depot; outdoor engine and caboose may be boarded; open Memorial Day-Labor Day, daily 10-6; free. **Shandy Hall** (12 m SW on SR 84 near Geneva), an 1815 Federal-style Western Reserve home features an ornate banquet hall with French wallpaper, law office, many original furnishings; open May-Oct., Tues.-Sat. 10-5; Sun. & hols 1-5; adm. Nearby **Old Tavern** (SR 84 & County Line Rd.), built 1805 and used by settlers and stagecoach drivers, was a station on the Underground Railroad.

BELLEFONTAINE: Piatt Castles (7 m S on US 68 to W Liberty, then 1 m E on SR 245), Norman-style chateaux, named for Mac-A-Cheek Indians. The 1864 **Mac-A-Cheek,** built by Gen. Abram Piatt, is of native materials; lavish woodwork; frescoed ceilings; Early American and French antiques; Mac-A-Cheek Indian and Piatt family relics. **Mac-O-Chee,** built 1879 by Col. Donn Piatt, charge d'affaires to the court of Louis Napoleon, features ornate woodwork; frescoes; rare tapestries; European and Asian antiques. Guided tours Memorial Day-Labor Day, daily 9-6:30; Apr.-late May & Labor Day-late Nov., daily 9:30-5:30; closed Thnks; adm.

CANTON: William McKinley, who opened his law office here in 1867 and conducted his Front Porch presidential campaign from here in 1896, is buried at **McKinley Memorial** (7th St., NW) with his wife and 2 children; open Tues.-Sun. 9-5; free. **Stark County Historical Center** (749 Hazlett Ave.), with scientific, industrial, and historical displays, includes McKinley Museum with memorabilia on his life and career; open Tues.-Sat. 10-5, Sun. 1:30-5; sm adm. **McKinley Room** (Hotel Onesto, Cleveland Ave. & 2nd St. NW) contains murals on McKinley's life.

    Cultural Center for the Arts (1001 Market Ave. N), a complex for artistic events, contains Canton Art Institute, with American and European painting and sculpture; open Tues.-Sat. 10-5, Sun. 2-5; closed hols; free.

    Pro Football Hall of Fame (2121 Harrison Ave.), N of Fawcett Stadium, is devoted to memorabilia of the game from 1895 to the present; library; film; open Memorial Day-Labor Day, daily 9-8, rest of yr, 9-5; adm.

CHILLICOTHE: Ross County Historical Society Museum (45 W 5th St.) is devoted to the history of the city (first capital of the Northwest Territory and of the state) and county; Mound Builder artifacts; pioneer displays; good presentation of regional folklore; crafts, riflemaking; toys; library; tours Feb.-Nov., Tues.-Sun. 1-4; adm. The Society also maintains **Franklin House** (80 S Paint St.), devoted to the role of women in county history.

    Ross County Courthouse (Paint & Main Sts.) is in the Greek Revival style affected by legislators who built their residences along Main St. **Chillicothe Gazette** (50 W Main St.), in a replica of the first statehouse that once stood on this site; Museum of Printing with examples from

Babylonian times, the Far East, Britain, and early America; open Mon.-Fri. 8:30-4:30; closed hols; free. **Adena State Memorial** (entry at W end of Allen Ave., off SR 104), the palatial 1807 home of a former governor, has 19th-C furnishings, lots of gadgetry, outbuildings; open Apr.-Oct., Tues.-Sun. 10-5; adm.

John Harris Memorial Dental Museum (24 m SW on US 50 in Bainbridge) is the tiny home and office of a dental pioneer, displaying antique instruments; open mid-Apr.-Oct., Fri.-Wed. 10-5; free.

Story Mound State Memorial (Delano Ave., 1 block S of Allen Ave.) is an Adena conical-shape mound, not yet developed for visitors. **Mound City Group National Monument** (4 m N on SR 104, on W bank of Scioto Riv.) consists of 23 burial mounds within an earthwall from Hopewellian culture; earthworks are in geometric patterns; walk-in burial mound; exhibits include elaborate copper offerings, death mask, stone pipes carved in shapes of animals; overlook from **Visitor Center;** open June-Labor Day, daily 8-8; rest of yr, daily 8-5; closed Jan. 1, Dec. 25; free. **Tarlton Cross Mound** (19 m N on SR 159 in Tarlton) is an earthwork in the form of a cross; open daily in daylight; free. **Seip Mound State Memorial** (17 m SW on US 50) is a group of ceremonial mounds and earthworks that has yielded a rich assortment of artifacts; museum open Apr.-Oct., Tues.-Sun. 9-5; area open daily in daylight; free. **Kilvert Mound** (20 m SW on US 50 to Bainbridge, then W) has not been excavated. **Fort Hill State Memorial** (20 m SW on US 50, then 10 m S on SR 41) is a prehistoric Indian hilltop earthworks; earthen wall is assumed to have enclosed a ceremonial center built by Hopewell people; museum of artifacts; (open Mar.-Nov., Tues.-Sun. 9:30-5; closed Thnks; sm adm); park open daily in daylight. **Serpent Mound State Memorial** (20 m S on US 50, then 20 m S on SR 41, then 3 m W on SR 73), an Adena site; extraordinary 1335-ft-long snake with an open mouth; constructed of stone, clay, and earth, it had religious or mystical importance; observation tower; museum displays on burial practices; open Apr.-Oct. daily 9-dark; free. **Leo Petroglyph State Memorial** (18 m SE off SR 35 on Co. Rd. 28), petroglyphs possibly carved as long ago as AD 1200; open daily in daylight; free.

Buckeye Furnace State Memorial (31 m S on US 35, then 5 m NE on SR 124, then county rd E), reconstruction of complex around stone stack of Hanging Rock charcoal iron furnace; ironmaster's home, company store, blacksmith shop; open Apr.-Oct., Tues.-Sun. 9:30-5; adm.

CINCINNATI: Convention & Visitors Bureau (208 W 5th St.) offers booklets for a 2-hr, self-guiding auto Queen City Tour that begins outside at Fountain Square and includes: **Elsinore Tower** (1720 Gilbert Ave. at Eden Park), built 1883 as a valve house for city waterworks; **Mt. Adams section,** with bars and boutiques lining the narrow, hilly streets and the

Tudor-inspired Rookwood Pottery building that produced art pottery 1892-1940s; **Capitoline Wolf** (Twin Lakes entrance to Eden Park), Etruscan statue donated by Italian government; **St. Francis de Sales Church** (Madison Rd.); **Clifton** (along upper Clifton & Lafayette Aves.), the city's oldest neighborhood, with gaslit streets, unusual Victorian houses (such as the Academy of the Sacred Heart occupying an 1867 home modeled after Kenilworth Castle in England and the castlelike, 19th-C iron merchant's home now part of Bethesda Home for the Aged); attractive horse watering fountain (Clifton & Woolper); **St. Monica Church** (328 W McMillan St.), with exterior statues and interior crucifix by a native sculptor, Byzantine-style saints and shrine by Carl Zimmerman; **Findlay Market** (Elder between Race & Elm Sts.) for produce, opens Wed. & Sat. at dawn; **Dayton Street,** called Millionaire's Row in the 1890s when the brewers lived here, with many restored townhouses including the 1870 **Hauck House** (812 Dayton St., open Thurs. 10-3); **Union Terminal** (1301 Western Ave.) with Winold Reiss murals of inlaid Italian mosaic; **St. Peter in Chains Cathedral** (Plum & 8th Sts.), a Greek Revival gem affectionately called The White Angel, interior warm with black marble, bronze statues, carved mahogany, and treasures such as a Cellini crucifix; **Isaac M. Wise Temple** (Plum & 8th Sts.), with minarets, Moorish interior glowing with gilding and stained glass. Overview of the city from **Carew Tower Observatory** (5th & Vine Sts.) daily 9-5; closed Jan. 1, Thnks, Dec. 25; sm adm.

Public Landing (foot of Broadway) is where the first settlers landed to establish a river port. Pioneer history is depicted in stained glass windows in City Hall (801 Plum St. at 8th St.), open daily 9-4:30; closed hols. **Fire Department Historical Museum** (329 E 9th St.) displays antique and modern equipment; open daily 1-4, 6-9; free.

Taft Museum (316 Pike St. at 4th St.), in 1820 Federal mansion; wonderful 17-18th-C Chinese porcelains; French Renaissance painted enamel portraits; portraits by European and American masters; atmosphere of a private home; furnishings include Duncan Phyfe, English Regency; open Mon.-Sat. 10-5, Sun. & hols 2-5; closed Thnks, Dec. 25; free.

Cincinnati Art Museum (Art Museum Dr. in Eden Park) houses a superb collection in a Greek Revival building; treasures from the Ancient World, Trans-Jordan, Far East, Europe; American portraits and paintings by Inness, Grant Wood, Cassatt, Hopper; 500 years of graphics; works in major 20th-C mediums; costumes, decorative arts of the U.S., Europe, Near and Far East; ancient musical instruments; sculpture; open Mon.-Sat. 10-5, Sun. & hols 1-5; closed Thnks, Dec. 25; free. **Museum of Natural History** (1720 Gilbert Ave. in Eden Park) features local flora and fauna; walk-through pre-historic exhibit; world-wide shell collection;

planetarium shows; films; open Tues.-Sat. 9-4:30, Sun. (exc July-Aug.) 1-5; closed hols & 3 weeks in Sept.; sm adm.

Stowe House State Memorial (2950 Gilbert at Foraker Aves.), where Harriet Beecher Stowe gathered material for *Uncle Tom's Cabin*; abolitionist materials; open June-Sept., Wed.-Sun. 10-5; sm adm.

William Howard Taft National Historic Site (2038 Auburn Ave.) was in a rural area when the 27th President was born in the first-floor bedroom in 1857; here he developed his interest in baseball (he began the presidential tradition of throwing out the first ball of the game season), got his law degree, and began to work up the political ladder; open Memorial Day-Labor Day, daily 8-5; rest of yr, Mon.-Fri. 8-5; closed Jan. 1, Dec. 25; free. Both sides of Auburn Avenue are lined with century-old homes.

Kemper Log House (in Cincinnati Zoo, 3400 Vine St.), built 1804 and oldest house in the Miami Purchase, has 18-19th-C furnishings; open Mother's Day-Labor Day, daily 10-5; sm adm.

Hebrew Union College (3101 Clifton Ave.) offers free guided tours Mon.-Fri. 9-5 (closed hols, academic hols, Jewish Holy Days); features include Dalsheimer Rare Book collection, Jewish Archives, Jewish Periodical Center, museum of Jewish ceremonial art.

Fort Ancient State Memorial (18 m NE on I-71, then 4 m E on SR 350) contains 3½ m of earthen walls enclosing 100 acres of burial mounds and other features believed built 300 BC-600 AD by Hopewellian people; good museum; life re-created in dioramas; open Mar.-Nov., Tues.-Sun. 9:30-5; closed Thnks; sm adm. **Christian Waldschmidt House** (18 m NE on SR 126 & US 50 Bypass to 7567 Glendale-Milford Rd., Camp Dennison) was built 1804 in Pennsylvania Dutch style by a Pennsylvanian; during the Civil War it was a training center for Union troops; 18-19th-C furnishings, museum of historic relics; open June-Aug. daily 1-5; Apr.-May & Sept.-Oct., Sun. 1-5; donation. **Clinton County Historical Society Museum** (47 m NE on US 22 to 149 E Locust St., Wilmington) exhibits pioneer relics, bronzes by Ohio Quaker Eli Harvey, photos and paintings of Indians of New Mexico by local artist Karl Moon; open Mar.-late Dec., Tues.-Fri. 1:30-5, Sun. 2-4; closed Easter, July 4, Thnks; sm adm. **Butler County Historical Museum** (22 m N on US 127 at 327 N 2nd St., Hamilton) in a charming old residence, displays early furnishings; open Tues.-Sun. 1-5; closed hols; free. **McGuffey Museum** (32 m NW on US 27 to Spring & Oak Sts., Oxford, on Miami Univ. campus), home of William Holmes McGuffey, compiler of the *McGuffey Eclectic Readers* while a faculty member here; open Tues. & Sat. 9-11, 2-4:30, Sun. 2-4:30; closed hols & Aug.; free. **Pioneer Farm Museum** (32 m NW on US 27, then 4 m N on SR 732 in Hueston Woods State Park), an 1835 farmhouse and barn, contains period furnishings, tools, glassware, toys; open Memorial Day-Oct., Wed., Sat., Sun., hols, 1-5; sm adm. **Glendower State Memorial** (32 m

NE on US 42 to Cincinnati Ave., Lebanon) is an 1836 Greek Revival mansion with the Empire and early Victorian furnishings that characterized the transition from pioneer simplicity to lavish living just before the Civil War in this area; open Apr.-Oct., Tues.-Sun. 9:30-5; sm adm. **Warren County Historical Society Museum** (32 m NE on US 42 to 105 S Broadway, Lebanon) has attractive displays of area life from prehistoric times to 19th-C; pioneer period rooms and shops; early arts and crafts; good Shaker exhibit; research library; open Tues.-Sat. 9-4, Sun. noon-4; closed hols; sm adm. Two doors N is the **Golden Lamb,** an 1803 log cabin that became an inn on the stagecoach route.

William Henry Harrison State Memorial (16 m W on US 50 to Loop Ave., North Bend), overlooking the Ohio River, is the tomb of the 9th President.

Ulysses S. Grant Birthplace (25 m SE on US 52 at jct SR 232), a 2-room cottage; period furnishings; Grant memorabilia, and **Ulysses S. Grant Schoolhouse** (20 m farther on US 52, then 7 m N on SR 221 to Water St., Georgetown), with adjacent museum on his life, are state sites open Apr.-Nov., Tues.-Sun. 9:30-5; sm adm. **John Rankin House** (53 m SE on US 52 to Liberty Hill, Ripley), built 1828 overlooking the Ohio River, was home of the abolitionist and a stop on the Underground Railroad; here Harriet Beecher Stowe heard the story of Eliza crossing the ice and other details she incorporated into *Uncle Tom's Cabin*; you can follow the path the slaves used in their escapes to freedom; open Apr.-Oct. Tues.-Sun. 9:30-5; sm adm.

CLEVELAND: Convention & Visitors Bureau (511 Terminal Tower, Public Sq.) is open Mon.-Fri. 9-5. The 42nd-floor observatory of **Terminal Tower** is open daily 8:45-4:45; closed Jan. 1, Dec. 25; adm. Sightseeing cruises on the Cuyahoga River leave from E. 9th St. pier from May-Sept. **Public Square** is the center of the shopping and business district, with **Soldiers' & Sailors' Monument** (open Mon.-Sat. 9-5; closed Jan. 1, Thnks, Dec. 25; free), statues of Gen. Moses Cleaveland and others; from this square the city's major avenues radiate and N and S streets are numbered, so it's easy to find your way around. Off the square is **The Mall,** with War Memorial Fountain, Cuyahoga County Court House with murals, and Public Library (open Mon.-Sat. 9-6; closed hols; free). Nearby are: **Cleveland Arcade** (401 Euclid Ave.), completed 1890, skylight-covered, shop-lined promenade; decorative iron grillwork; open daily. **Erie Street Cemetery** (Erie Ct. between E 9-14th Sts.) with mass grave of first settlers; shock of corn on tombstone of friendly Indian chief Joc-o-Sot. **Dunham Tavern Museum** (6709 Euclid Ave.) is a restored stagecoach stop; period furnishings; historic exhibits; open Tues.-Sun. 12:30-4:30; closed Jan. 1, Easter, July 4, Thnks, Dec. 25; sm adm.

Western Reserve Historical Society Museum (10825 East Blvd at University Circle), housed in a complex that includes two Italian Renaissance-style residences, emphasizes Ohio history; Indian artifacts, pioneer displays, decorative arts in period rooms; portraits; costumes 1790-present; Napoleon collection; toys and 1890 Bingham dollhouse; Shaker material; craft shops; antique cars and planes, with demonstrations in mechanics' shops; 1890s Ohio street scene; extensive libraries on the city, Western Reserve, and the state; open Tues.-Sat. 10-5, Sun. 2-5; closed hols; adm. **Cleveland Museum of Art** (11150 East Blvd at University Circle) has one of the nation's finest collections; wonderful Treasure Room of Coptic, early Christian, and Byzantine pieces; medieval material includes part of the 11th-C German Guelph Treasure; major artists from the Renaissance to the 20th-C are represented; outstanding Japanese art; choice examples of work from China, India, Africa, Oceania, pre- Columbian America; special events; 1971 wing designed by Marcel Breuer; open Tues., Thurs., Fri. 10-6; Wed. 10-10; Sat. 9-5; Sun. 1-6; closed Jan. 1, July 4, Thnks, Dec. 25; free. **Temple Museum of Religious Art & Music** (Silver Park at University Circle), Byzantine-style building with tiled domes; museum of ceremonial art; open Mon.-Fri. 9-5; free. **Cleveland Museum of Natural History** (Wade Oval Dr. at University Circle) features Ohio prehistory; mounted birds, fish, mammals; minerals and gems; fine vertebrate paleontology exhibits; planetarium shows; library; open Mon.-Sat. 10-5, Sun. 1-5:30; closed hols; adm.

Cleveland Health Museum & Education Center (8911 Euclid Ave.), talking transparent woman, mechanical brain, other body models; walk-in exhibits; films; open Tues.-Sat. 10-5, Sun. 1-5; closed Jan. 1, Thnks, Dec. 25; sm adm. **Howard Dittrick Museum of Historical Medicine** (11000 Euclid Ave. on 3rd floor of Allen Medical Library) traces history of medicine, dentistry, allied fields; pre-Civil War pharmacy; 1800 doctor's office; open July-Aug., Mon.-Sat. 10-5; rest of yr, Mon.-Sat. 1-5; closed hols; free.

Lakeview Cemetery (12316 Euclid Ave. at E. 123rd St.): elaborate monument (open Apr.-Oct. daily 9-4:30) to Pres. James A. Garfield; graves of John Hay and Mark Hanna; open daily 8-5:30; free. **Shakespeare & Cultural Gardens** (between East & Liberty Blvds in Rockefeller Park), sculpture display in gardens; open daily; free. **Park Synagogue** (3300 Mayfield Rd.), a striking modern building designed 1950 by Eric Mendelsohn, contains a wall of plastic panels by Yaakov Agam that a visitor can move to create abstract designs; open daily.

On the **West Side** of Cleveland are: **Oldest Stone House** (5 m W at 14710 Lake Ave., Lakewood), built 1838, with furniture brought by settlers or handmade by them; open Feb.-Nov., Wed. & Sun. 2-5; closed hols;

sm adm. **Romanian Folk Museum** (3256 Warren Rd. in St. Mary's Romanian Orthodox Church) with peasant costumes, ikons, Easter eggs, replica of peasant room; open Sun. noon-1 or by appointment; free. **Salvador Dali Museum** (24050 Commerce Park Rd. off Chagrin Blvd, Beachwood) is open by appointment (phone 464-0372) Tues.-Sat. 10-4; adm; may be moved. **Gates Mills Historical Museum** (Old Mill Rd. in Gates Mills) has rooms furnished in 1850-1900 styles; open Mon., Wed., Fri. 1-9; Tues. & Sat. 9-1; closed hols; free.

    Geodesic Dome (23 m E off SR 87, 2 m E of jct SR 306 in Metals Park) designed by R. Buckminster Fuller stretches 10-stories high over the American Society for Metals hq and covers a rock "garden" of minerals and ores from around the world; open daily 8:30 am-10 pm; tours available June-Sept.; free. **Lawnfield—James A. Garfield Home** (23 m E via I-90, SR 615 to 8095 Mentor Ave., Mentor), Garfield's home before the White House, has original furnishings, memorabilia; library; on grounds are his campaign office, replica of log cabin in which he was born; open May-Oct., Tues.-Sat. 9-5, Sun. & hols 1-5; adm. **Fairport Marine Museum** (27 m E on I-90, then 5 m N to 129 2nd St., Fairport Harbor), maritime relics; pilothouse; lighthouse; open Memorial Day-Labor Day, Sat., Sun., & hols 1-6; sm adm. **Century Village** (29 m E on SR 87 to Burton) is a reconstruction of a mid-19th-C Western Reserve town with homes, shops, church, school, other buildings reflecting the New England heritage; information in log cabin in park center; historic records and displays in **Geauga County Historical Museum** (SW corner of park); village open May-Oct., Tues.-Sat. 10-5, Sun. 1-5; closed Memorial Day; adm. Museum open additionally Mar.-Apr., Sun. 1-5; sm adm.

    Oberlin College (35 m W on SR 10 to jct SR 58 in Oberlin) offers campus tours in summer from Wilder Hall, in winter from Admissions Office; on campus are: **Conservatory of Music,** a complex designed 1964 by Minoru Yamasaki. **Allen Memorial Art Museum,** in Italian Renaissance-style building; art works from ancient Egypt to the present; European masterpieces, Japanese woodcuts; American pressed glass, costumes, Oriental rugs; open academic yr, Mon.-Fri. 10-noon, 1:30-4:30, 7-9; Sat. 10-noon, 2-5:30; open daily in summer, inquire for hrs; closed Jan. 1, July 4, Thnks, Dec. 25; free.

    Indian Ridge Museum (26 m W via SR 10, I-80 to West Ridge St at Fowls Rd., Elyria), with furnished log cabin, Indian and pioneer relics, is open Tues.-Sun. 1-5; adm. Nearby, the **Lorain County Historical Society Museum** (331 5th St.) exhibits early regional arts and crafts; open Tues.-Sat. 2-5; free.

COLUMBUS: State Capitol (park bounded by High, Broad, State, & 3rd Sts.), with huge Doric columns, 120-ft dome, and rotunda honoring 13 original colonies, took 22 years to complete; open daily 8-5; free. On grounds are a memorial to Pres. **McKinley** and **My Jewels Monument,** a bronze group in which the Roman matron Cornelia, who said that her sons were her jewels, calls attention to figures of Grant, Sheridan, Sherman, Garfield, Chase, Stanton, and Hayes. **Martha Kinney Cooper Ohioana Library** (11th floor of Ohio Dept. Bldg, 65 S Front St.), reference materials by Ohioans and on Ohio; open Mon.-Fri. 9-5; closed hols; free. **Center of Science & Industry** (280 E Broad St.), exhibits on medicine, electronics, communications, space, health, history; Foucault pendulum; planetarium shows; open Mon.-Sat. 10-5, Sun. 1-5:30; closed hols; adm. **Columbus Gallery of Fine Arts** (480 E Broad St. at Washington Ave.), in an Italian Renaissance-style building; Old Masters, 19-20th-C French and American painting; a room devoted to native son George Bellows; sculpture; decorative arts; Staffordshire china; open daily noon-5; closed hols; free.

Ohio Historical Center (off I-71 at 17th Ave.) is a modern complex attractively illustrating Ohio's archaeology, natural history, and history; Hall of Fame of Ohioans; special events; archives; open Mon.-Sat. 9-5, Sun. & hols 1-5; closed Jan. 1, Dec. 25; free. Adjacent is **Ohio Village,** reconstructed 19th-C town in which homes, shops, and offices demonstrate architectural styles of the state; artisans demonstrate old skills; open Wed.-Sun. 10-6; adm.

German Village (bounded by Livingston Ave., Blackberry Alley, Nursery Lane, Pearl Alley), settled by Germans in the mid-19th-C, is a 233-acre restored historic area with brick homes, cobblestone streets, Old World charm; crafts are sold; many special events; tours available; write German Village Society, Inc. (624 S 3rd St.).

Wagnalls Memorial (18 m SE off SR 674 in Lithopolis), built in memory of the co-founder of the Funk and Wagnalls publishing company, contains rare books, manuscripts; paintings; open Mon.-Sat. 1-5; closed hols; free.

Lancaster Area Chamber of Commerce (29 m SE on US 33 at 203 Kresge Bldg., Zane Sq., Lancaster 43130) provides tour maps for covered bridges, annual spring tour of historic homes, and **Square 13 Historic District** (bounded by Main, Broad, Wheeling, & High Sts.). Named for the first plot laid out by the town planner, Ebeneezer Zane, in 1800, Square 13 is surrounded with restored 19th-C homes, including the boyhood home of Albert Sidney Johnston, early log cabins, an 1810 inn; most of the buildings are open in summer and some house historic artifacts. Also here is **Sherman House State Memorial** (37 E Main St.), birthplace of Gen. William Tecumseh Sherman and his brother Senator John Sherman (Sherman Anti-Trust Act); many original furnishings, family memorabilia, Civil War material; open June-Oct., Tues.-Sun. 9:30-5; sm adm.

Hanby House (NE on US 3 to 160 W Main St., Westerville), home of composer Benjamin Hanby; original furnishings; open June-Sept., Wed.-Sun. 10-5; sm adm. Nearby **Usa Jinja-Kyoto Tea House** (State & Plum Sts., Westerville), replica of the 17th-C shrine at Usa with displays on Japanese life, is open by appointment; sm adm. **Ohio Railway Museum** (6 m N off I-71 at 990 Proprietors Rd., Worthington) has restored antique trolley cars, railway cars, other vehicles, railroad memorabilia; weekend train rides May-Oct.; open daily; closed Jan. 1, Easter, Thnks, Dec. 25; adm.

COSHOCTON: Johnson-Humrickhouse Memorial Museum (Sycamore & 3rd Sts.), pioneer guns, utensils, other relics; Indian artifacts; Oriental jade, porcelain, armor, temple bells; European lace; dolls, glass; locally made pottery; open Tues.-Sat. 1-4:30, Sun. 2-5; closed Jan. 1, Thnks, Dec. 25; free.

Roscoe Village (on SR 16, N of town), an 1816 settlement that became a thriving port on the Erie Canal, declined with the coming of the railroad; shops, homes, tavern, post office, and other buildings have been restored; costumed guides conduct tours of the 1836 **Williams House** with 1690-1840 furnishings (daily noon-5; closed hols; sm adm); horse-drawn barge trips on the canal are available daily in summer, weekends in spring and fall. **Visitor Center** provides guided tours (fee), information for self-guiding tours, exhibits, audiovisual program, tickets for many special events; open May-Sept., daily 10-6; Oct.-Apr. daily 11-5; closed Jan. 1, Thnks, Dec. 25; free.

DAYTON: Dayton Art Institute (405 W Riverview & Forest Aves.), examples from major periods, from classical and pre-Columbian times to 20th-C American painting; Oriental collection; prints, drawings; decorative arts; open Tues.-Fri., Sun. noon-5; Sat. 9-5; closed hols; free. **Dayton Museum of Natural History** (2629 Ridge Ave.), in building designed by Richard Neutra; Indian artifacts, Egyptian mummy, plant and animal displays (some live specimens); planetarium shows, observatory; open Mon.-Sat. 9-6 (Tues. & Fri. to 9), Sun. 2-6; closed hols; sm adm. **Paul Laurence Dunbar House State Memorial** (219 N Summit St.), home of the black poet and novelist 1903 until his death at 34 in 1906; memorabilia; open June-Sept., Wed.-Sun. 10-5; sm adm. **Masonic Temple** (525 W Riverview Ave.), an impressive building based on Greek Ionic style, is open Mon.-Fri. 8-4; closed hols; free. **Woodland Cemetery** (E end of Woodland Ave.), graves of Orville and Wilbur Wright, automobile pioneer Charles F. Kettering, other notables. **Aviation Hall of Fame** (6th & Main Sts. in Convention & Exhibition Center) mural of tiles depicts Wright brothers' experiments; portraits of aviation pioneers; open daily 8-5; free.

Carillon Park (2 m S off I-75 at 2001 S Patterson Blvd.) houses pioneer relics, wagons and coaches, a 1905 Wright brothers' plane, other exhibits in a complex that includes 1796 hewn-log Newcom Tavern, replica of the Wright Cycle Shop, replica of early railroad depot, other buildings; section of the Miami & Erie Canal with original lock, covered bridge; open May-Oct., Tues.-Sat. 10-8:30, Sun. 1-8:30; free. **U.S. Air Force Museum** (5 m NE on Springfield Pike on Wright-Patterson Air Force Base), one of the most comprehensive in the world; history of aircraft traced from early experiments by Da Vinci to the space age; open Mon.-Fri. 9-5, Sat. & Sun. 10-6; closed Dec. 25; free. **Miamisburg Mound State Memorial** (7 m S to Miamisburg, then 1 m SE on SR 725), largest conical mound in Ohio, 68-ft high; steps to top; unexcavated; open in daylight; free.

DEFIANCE: Au Glaize Village (5 m SW off US 24 on Krouse Rd.) consists of restored 1860-90 buildings and replicas, including doctor's office, cider mill, canal lockkeeper's house, railroad station; exhibits on archaeology, natural history, farming, the Civil War; adjacent 19th-C Black Swamp Farm; visitors encouraged to participate in craft demonstrations and other events; open Memorial Day-Labor Day, daily 10-6; May & Sept.-Oct., Sat. & Sun. 10-6; adm.

EAST LIVERPOOL: Chamber of Commerce (516 Market St.) provides information on pottery company tours and collections. **East Liverpool Historical Society** (Carnegie Public Library, 4th St. & Broadway) displays area pottery; open Mon.-Sat. 9-5; closed hols; free. **Old Stone House Museum** (16 m NW on US 30 to 100 E Washington St., Lisbon) was built 1805 as a tavern on the Pittsburgh-Canton stagecoach line; locally made household items on display; open mid-June-mid-Oct., Tues.-Sun. 1-4; closed hols; sm adm. **Ohio Hills Indian Museum** (4 m SW on SR 7, then 1 m N off SR 45 to 1127 Esther Ave.), Indian, pioneer, Wells Fargo artifacts; weapons; open spring-fall, daily 11-dark; sm adm.

FREMONT: Fort Stephenson Park (Groghan near High Sts.) was scene of War of 1812 battle in which Maj. George Groghan, with 150 soldiers and 1 cannon (Old Betsy) successfully defended Fort Stephenson against 400 English soldiers with 300 Indian allies; on grounds is Old Betsy; historical displays in **Birchard Public Library** (423 Groghan St.), open Mon.-Fri. 9:30-8, Sat. 9:30-6 (may close early in summer); closed hols, free; park open daily.

Rutherford B. Hayes State Memorial (1337 Hayes at Buckland Aves.), Spiegel Grove, where he lived until his death in 1893; Victorian manor house has family furnishings (tours Wed.-Sat. 9-5, Sun.-Tues. 2-5; adm); memorabilia and papers in Hayes Library & Museum; Pres. & Mrs. Hayes are buried on grounds; hardwoods in the grove are named for famous visitors; open Mon.-Sat. 9-5, Sun. & hols 1:30-5; closed Jan. 1, Thnks, Dec. 25; adm.

Clyde Museum (9 m E on US 20 in Clyde Public Library, 222 W Buckeye St., Clyde), dioramas of Indian life in Ohio; displays on Civil War Gen. James McPherson and of author Sherwood Anderson, who used Clyde as a model for *Winesburg, Ohio*; open Mon.-Fri. noon-9, Sat. 10-6; closed hols; free. **Interpace-Tiffin Glass** (20 m S on SR 53 to 4th Ave. & Vine St., Tiffin) tours of blowing and decorating lead crystal, June-Aug., Mon.-Fri. 8, 9:45, 1, 2:45; free.

GREENVILLE: Garst Museum (205 N Broadway), Indian and pioneer relics; exhibits on sharp-shooter Annie Oakley and news commentator Lowell Thomas, both natives; open Tues., Fri., Sun. 1-5; free. **Fort Jefferson State Memorial** (3 m S on SR 121), site of one of St. Clair's outposts in 1791; open daily in daylight; free. **Fort Recovery State Memorial** 23 m NW on SR 49 at Ft Recovery), partially reconstructed log fort on site where Chiefs Little Turtle and Blue Jacket defeated St. Clair in 1791; Gen. "Mad" Anthony Wayne ordered the fort built in 1793 in an effort to recover the area from Indians; museum with material on Indian Wars is open Mar.-Nov., Tues.-Sun. 9:30-5; sm adm.

GALLIPOLIS: Our House State Memorial (434 1st Ave.), an Ohio River tavern built 1819, hosted Lafayette, Louis Philippe, Jenny Lind; period furnishings; separate kitchen; open Apr.-Oct., Tues.-Sun. 9:30-5; sm adm.

LIMA: Allen County Historical Society maintains: Museum (620 W Market St.), Indian and pioneer artifacts, minerals, model of Miami-Erie canal locks, restored general store and doctor's office, dolls, china; open Tues.-Sun. 1:30-5; closed hols; free. **MacDonell House** (632 W Market St.), African and Alaskan trophies including albino mammals and birds; early-1800s Log House; open Tues.-Sun. 1:30-5; closed hols; sm adm. **Lincoln Park Railroad Exhibit** (Elm & Shawnee Sts.), 1882 caboose, last steam locomotive built by Lima railroad works, 1883 private Pullman car; open all year, daily, free. **Neil Armstrong Museum** (10 m SW off I-75 on Fisher Rd. in Wapakoneta), devoted to the astronaut and space; audiovisual program, exhibits; open Mon.-Sat. 9:30-5, Sun. & hols 1- closed Jan. 1, Thnks, Dec. 25; adm.

MANSFIELD: Kingwood Center & Gardens (1 m W on SR 430 to 900 Park Ave. W), French Provincial mansion of industrialist Charles Kelley King; original furnishings; open Tues.-Sat. 8-5; Easter-Oct., Sun.

1:30-4:30; closed hols; free; gardens open daily 8-sundown. **Louis Bromfield Malabar Farm** (12 m SE on SR 39, then S on SR 603 to Pleasant Valley Rd., Lucas), home of author and conservationist; tours of Gothic-style **Oak Hill Cottage,** an Underground Railroad stop, described as Shane's Castle in *The Green Bay Tree*; also, May-Sept., Sun., wagon tour of farm; open daily 9-5; closed Sun. in Dec.-Mar., Jan. 1, Thnks, Dec. 25; adm. **Old Town, USA** (7 m SW on US 42, then 3 m NW on Ontario Rd.) has replicas of old shops, school, fire station, other buildings; open June-mid-Nov. daily 1-5; adm. **Old Tool Crib Museum** (28½ m S off SR 13 at Beam's Lake, Mt. Vernon), hand tools used in crafts; clocks; steam and gas engines; open Mon.-Fri. 8-5; closed hols; free.

MARIETTA: Campus Martius State Museum (2nd & Washington Sts.) is on site of first permanent settlement in Ohio; Rufus Putnam, superintendent of the Ohio Co., built Campus Martius Fort in 1788 to house New England settlers while they laid out the town they named for Marie Antoinette; history of the settlement; furniture, glass, china, paintings, other pioneer items; Putnam's home, on grounds is Ohio Co. Land Office, from which Putnam administered the 1½-million-acre purchase; open Mon.-Sat. 9-5, Sun. 1-5; closed Jan. 1, Thnks, Dec. 25; adm.

Ohio River Museum State Memorial (Front & St. Clair Sts.) includes a restored 1918 steamboat (open weather permitting), audiovisual program, models, other exhibits on history of inland water transportation; open Mon.-Sat. 9-5, Sun. 1-5; adm. **Muskingum Park** (N of Putnam St., between Front St. & the River), Start Westward Monument, a memorial to expansion by Gutzon Borglum. **Mound Cemetery** (5th & Scammel Sts.), conical mound of Adena culture, believed to be a chieftain's burial place, surrounded by graves of Revolutionary soldiers. Sacra Via St. (from the river to Elevated Sq.) was sacred roadway to the mound. **Marietta College** (4th & Putnam Sts.) Library houses extensive collections of Americana, including Northwest Territory.

Chamber of Commerce (308 Front St.) offers maps for self-guiding tours of city and county, nearby covered bridges; attractions are: **Blennerhassett Island** (about 17 m S in the Ohio River), where Aaron Burr was said to have hatched his conspiracy for control of the Southwest. **Dexter City** (20 m N off I-77) monument to Johnny Appleseed, credited with starting apple orchards in this area of Ohio (other monuments to him are in Ashland and Mansfield). **St. Mary's Church** (24 m NE on SR 821, 145, 564, then NE on county rd to Fulda), built atop a hill by German settlers. **Monroe County Courthouse** (48 m NE on SR 26 in Woodsfield), with a stained-glass dome.

MARION: Harding Home & Museum (380 Mt. Vernon Ave.), from which Warren G. Harding launched his 1920 Front Porch campaign and where he lived 1891-1921; open June-Aug., Mon.-Sat. 10-5, Sun. 1-6; mid-Mar.-May & Sept.-mid-Nov., Tues.-Sat. 10-5, Sun. 1-6; sm adm. **Harding Memorial** (SR 423 & Vernon Heights Blvd.), tomb of the 29th President and his wife. **Wyandot County Historical Society Museum** (20 m N on US 23 to 130 S 7th St., Upper Sandusky), in Norman-style mansion, has local items; open Mon.-Fri. 9-11:30, 1-4; Sun. 1-5; closed hols; sm adm. **Indian Mill State Memorial** (22½ m NW beyond Upper Sandusky, off US 23), near site of mill built by the government in appreciation for the loyalty of Wyandot Indians during War of 1812; this 1861 successor is a museum of milling; open May-Oct., Wed.-Sun. 10-5; sm adm.

MASSILLON: Massillon Museum (212 Lincoln Way E), in 1835 home of the city's founder; local paintings, sculpture, crafts, furnishings, historic displays; open Mon.-Sat. 10-5, Sun. 2-5; closed hols & Sept.; free. **Spring Hill** (SR 241), 1821 home with original furnishings, secret staircase, outbuildings; open June-Aug., Thurs., Sat., Sun. 1-4; adm. **Canal Fulton** (6 m NW on US 21, then 1 m NE on SR 93), replica of 19th-C canal boat makes daily 1-hr trips in summer, weekends in spring & fall (fee); an 8-m stretch of the Ohio-Erie Canal is maintained as a public park here; canal days festival held annually; Old Canal Days Museum, with memorabilia of the canal, is open irregularly.

NEWARK: Newark Earthworks preserves 3 sites of what once was a huge social and religious center for Hopewell culture; **Mound Builders State Memorial** (S edge of city on SR 79), the Great Circle, earthen walls enclosing 26 acres and an eagle effigy mound. **Wright State Memorial** (James & Waldo Sts.), remains of walls that originally enclosed a large square linked by a walled corridor to the Great Circle. **Octagon State Memorial** (N 30th St. & Parkview), octagonal earthwork enclosing 50 acres, joined to a circular one enclosing 20 acres, with small mounds. All are open daily in daylight. **Museum of Ohio Indian Art** (SR 79) contains artifacts related to the Newark Earthworks and other areas of Ohio; open Mar.-Nov., Tues.-Sun. 9:30-5; sm adm.

    Licking County Historical Society Museum (in Sixth St. Park, between W Main & Church Sts.) displays unusual 19th-C antiques in the fine 1820 Federal-style Sherwood-Davidson House; on grounds is 1835 Buckingham House with temporary exhibits; tours Tues.-Sun. 1-4; closed hols & Jan.; sm adm.

    Flint Ridge State Memorial (5 m E on SR 16, then 5 m S), flint quarry bearing scars from prehistoric times; museum; open Mar.-Nov., Tues.-Sun. 9:30-5; sm adm. **Museum of Burmese Arts & Crafts** (6 m W on SR 16 to Burton Hall on Denison Univ. campus, Granville) has more than 900 pieces of lacquerware, wood carvings, textiles, other arts; open by applying to Visual Arts Dept.; free.

NEW PHILADELPHIA: Zoar Village State Memorial (3 m NW on SR 416, then 5 m NE on SR 800, then N on SR 212) is site of communal colony founded 1817 by German Separatists; with brick and rope making, sawmill, flour mill, brewery, even experiments in silk culture and a hotel, the community thrived; but failure to modernize agricultural and industrial methods, and death of the community leader, led the group to dissolve in 1898 and divide assets among the 222 residents. Private residences help create a living museum; blacksmith, tinsmith, wagon shop, bakery, and other buildings are open to the public; historical displays are in the museum (Main St.); open Apr.-Oct., Tues.-Sun. 9:30-5; adm.

Schoenbrunn Village State Memorial (3 m SE off US 250), reconstruction of village built by Indians in 1772 under Moravian missionaries (this was 1 of 6 such villages built 1772-98) and abandoned during the Revolutionary War; museum, craft demonstrations, many reconstructed buildings, cemetery; open May-Oct. daily 9-dark; Mar.-Apr. & Oct.-Nov. daily 9-5; adm.

Fort Laurens State Memorial (14 m N on SR 39, I-77, SR 212, then ¼ m S of Bolivar) is site of 1778 fort built as a defense against Indians and the British; museum; audiovisual program on the Revolution in Ohio; open Apr.-Oct., Tues.-Sun. 9:30-5; sm adm.

Amish Country extends W of town; members of this religious sect, who dress plainly and forego electricity, autos, and other modern conveniences, settled here in the 1820s; you can make a loop by going 10 m W on SR 39 to **Sugarcreek** (cheese factory, blacksmith shop); 4 m S on SR 93, then 10 m NW on SR 557 through **Charm** and then W to **Millersburg** (courthouse has hitching posts for Amish horses); then return E on SR 39 to **Berlin** (Aling Wool Mill sells braided rugs made by Amish women); 4 m E on SR 39 to **Walnut Creek** (the county library specializes in Amish materials); then SR 515 N to **Trail** (where bologna is made); then US 62 N through **Winesburg** to **Wilmot** (cheese factory); return 14 m E on US 25.

Warther Museum (331 Karl Ave. in Dover) displays 56 miniature working models of railroad locomotives carved of ebony, ivory, and wood; other items; open daily 9-5; closed Jan. 1, Dec. 25; adm.

Gnadenhutten Memorial (9½ m S on SR 416) marks graves of 96 Christian Indians massacred by American Militia in 1782. Gnadenhutten Historical Society Museum (on US 36) offers display on massacre; open in summer 9-5; free. **Custer Monument** (13 m E on SR 39, 5 m S on SR 212, 7 m SE on SR 151, 2½ m E on SR 646 in New Rumley) marks site of Gen. George A. Custer's birth; exhibit pavilion; open daily; free. **McCook House** (26 m E on SR 39 to Public Sq., Carrollton), dedicated to the

"Fighting McCooks" of the Civil War; open June-Sept., Wed.-Sun. & hols 10-5; sm adm.

PIQUA: Piqua Historical Area (3½ m NW on SR 66) is on crossroads where Indians and traders met in the 1700s; trading posts and forts, built along the Great Miami River, became stopping places for settlers and military expeditions; the Miami & Erie Canal is preserved (rides on 19th-C canal boat); **John Honston Home,** Dutch Colonial home built 1811 by an Ohio Indian agent, with cider house, other outbuildings; **Indian Museum,** artifacts of area Indians; open Apr.-Oct., Tues.-Sun. 10-5; adm.
     Peoples Federal Savings & Loan Association (10 m N on I-75 to Court St. & Ohio Ave., Sidney) is in a 1917 building designed by Louis H. Sullivan; mosaics above the entrance spell "thrift"; open banking hours.

PORTSMOUTH: Horseshoe Mound (Mound Park, 17th St. & Hutchins Ave.) is unexcavated. **Tremper Mound** (SR 73, NW of town) is a large unexcavated mound believed to represent a mammal. **Lake Vesuvius Recreation Area** (in Wayne National Forest, 29 m SE on US 52, then 7 m N off SR 93), named for Vesuvius iron furnace 1883-1906, contains ruins of furnace, interpretive signs, abandoned charcoal pits, whiskey still.

SANDUSKY: From here car ferries operate in summer to **Kelleys Island** (where state memorials preserve Indian petroglyphs and glacial grooves); from towns across the bay, ferries operate to other Lake Erie islands. **Perry's Victory & International Peace Memorial** (at Put-in-Bay on S Bass Island, reached by ferry from Port Clinton or Catawba Point) commemorates Commodore Oliver Hazard Perry's victory over the British in 1813 Battle of Lake Erie that put the lake under U.S. control; open Memorial Day-Labor Day, daily 9:30-6 or by appointment; free. Nearby **Perry's Cave** (where Perry stored ammunition, also served as a prison) and **Crystal Cave** (where tour includes Heineman Winery) offers tours Memorial Day-Labor Day, daily 11-5; adm. **Winery tours** are available at Meier's (1702 Campbell St., Sandusky), Mon.-Fri. 10-noon, 1-3, closed hols, free; also at Cooper's and Heineman's at Put-in-Bay (S Bass Island) or at Lonz (Middle Bass Island) in summer. **Ottawa County Historical Museum** (17 m NW on SR 2 to City Hall, Adams & 2nd Sts., Port Clinton), Indian and pioneer relics; memorabilia of 1813 Battle of Lake Erie; dolls, fossils, china, guns; open Thurs., Sat. 3-5; Wed. 6:30-8:30 pm; closed hols; free.
     Thomas A. Edison Birthplace Museum (14 m S on US 250 to 9 Edison Dr., Milan), brick cottage where Edison was born in 1847 and lived his first 7 years; family furnishings, Edison memorabilia; open Apr.-Nov.,

Tues.-Sat. 9-5, Sun. 1-5; mid-Feb.-Mar., Fri. & Sat. 9-5, Sun. 1-5; closed Thnks, Dec.; sm adm. Nearby Milan Historical Museum (10 Edison Dr.) consists of: **Dr. Lehman Galpin Home,** 1840s brick dwelling of Edison family doctor; early American pattern and art glass; flint; dolls; guns; blacksmith shop; country store. **Newton Memorial Arts Building,** paintings and decorative arts from around the world, native crafts. **Sayles House,** constructed and furnished in mid-19th-C style. All are open June-Aug., Tues.-Sun. 10-5; Apr.-May & Sept.-Oct., Tues.-Sun. 1-5; donation.

Firelands Museum (18 m S on US 250 to 4 Case Ave. at W Main St., Norwalk) is named for Firelands region (so-called because Connecticut awarded its Western lands to citizens whose villages had been burned by the British during the Revolution); antique guns, pioneer home and farm implements, lighting fixtures, costumes, other local relics; open July-Aug., Mon.-Sat. 9-6, Sun. noon-6; May-June & Sept.-Oct., Tues.-Sun. noon-6; Apr. & Nov., Sat. & Sun. noon-6; sm adm.

Great Lakes Historical Society Museum (21 m E on US 6 to 480 Main St., Vermilion), on the lake, is devoted to Great Lakes history; ship models; marine artifacts; paintings; photographs; library; open in summer daily 10:30-6; spring & fall, Tues.-Sun. 10:30-5; winter, Sat. & Sun. 11-5; sm adm.

SPRINGFIELD: This city grew after the National Pike came through here in 1839. A **Madonna of the Trail** monument (on US 40 at W edge of town) honors pioneer women on this road. **Pennsylvania House** (1311 W Main St.) served stagecoach travelers, cattle drovers, and pioneer families for half a century; period furnishings and artifacts in 1824 building; open first Sun. each month 1-4, or by appointment; sm adm. **Clark County Historical Society Museum** (300 W Main St.) also contains local artifacts; newspaper file; open Mon.-Thurs. 9-noon, 1-4; Sat. 9-noon; 2nd & 4th Sun. of each month 2-4; closed hols; free. **Westcott House** (E High St. & Greenmount Ave.), a 1905 Frank Lloyd Wright design, is an apartment building. Wittenberg University (N Wittenberg Ave.): Handsome **Weaver Chapel & Thomas Library,** with unusual stained-glass windows, statues of important Protestants, extensive material on Martin Luther.

George Rogers Clark State Memorial (3½ m W on I-70), site of 1780 Battle of Piqua; monument, historic marker; open daily in daylight; free.

STEUBENVILLE: Jefferson County Courthouse (3rd & Market Sts.), local records and portraits; open Mon.-Fri. 9-4:30; closed hols; free. **Federal Land Office** (1100 Stanton Blvd at jct US 22, SR 7), first in the Northwest Territory, was built 1800; period relics; open Memorial Day-Labor Day, Tues.-Sun. 1-5; free. **Friends Meeting House State**

Memorial (16 m S on SR 7, then 8 m W on SR 150 to Mt. Pleasant), 1814 meetinghouse, first W of the Alleghanies; a partition lowered from the ceiling separated the sexes; open May-Oct., Tues.-Sun. 10-5; sm adm.

TOLEDO: Toledo Museum of Art (Monroe St. & Scottwood Ave.), reconstructed 12-14th-C cloister houses medieval works; large Classical and Near East collection; extensive Oriental galleries; more than 700 paintings include 17-19th-C French, 19th-C English and American, and 20th-C works; sculpture; outstanding glass, from ancient Egyptian to contemporary examples; open Tues.-Sat. 9-5, Sun. & hols 1-5; closed Jan. 1, Thnks, Dec. 25; free. **Blair Museum of Lithopanes** (220 Columbus St.) displays some 2300 examples of this rare art in an Italian-style carriage house; appointment must be made at office (2243 Ashland Ave.). **Rosary Cathedral** (2561 Collingwood Blvd.), in unusual 16th-C Spanish plateresque style; painted ceilings, frescos, mosaics, paintings, statues are features of elaborate interior; open daily.

Toledo Zoological Gardens (4 m S on US 24 at 2700 Broadway), pioneer Peter Navarre Cabin, museum of natural history; open 10-7 in summer, 10-5 in winter; adm. **Fallen Timbers Monument** (10 m S on US 24), where "Mad" Anthony Wayne defeated Chief Turkeyfoot in 1794 to open region to white settlement; open daily in daylight; free. **Fort Meigs State Memorial** (across Maumee River, just SW of jct US 20, SR 65) is a restoration of a War of 1812 fort built by Gen. William Henry Harrison; this log outpost withstood 2 British-Indian sieges and held the territory; living history presentations; cemeteries; open Apr.-Oct., Tues.-Sun. 10-5; sm adm. **Columbian House** (14 m SW to River Rd. & jct. SR 64 in Waterville), constructed 1818 of handhewn beams with 23 black-walnut rooms, is now a restaurant (open spring-fall, Tues.-Sat.).

WOOSTER: Wayne County Historical Society Museum (546 E Bowman St.), Indian and pioneer relics; paintings; lusterware; natural history; log cabin, old school on grounds; open Tues.-Sun. 2-4:30; closed hols; free.

YOUNGSTOWN: Butler Institute of American Art (524 Wick Ave.) offers more than 3500 works by Homer, Inness, Audubon, Hopper, other American artists; paintings of American Indians, clipper ships; Ohio ceramics; early glass bells; open Tues.-Sat. 10-4:30, Sun. 1-5; closed Jan. 1, Easter, Thnks, Dec. 25; free. **Arms Museum** (648 Wick Ave.), in 1905 mansion designed by Mrs. Wilford Paddock Arms; Oriental rugs, portraits, silver, glass, armor, guns, pioneer and Indian relics; tours Wed.-Fri. 1-4, Sat. & Sun. 1:30-5; closed hols; sm adm.

McKinley Birthplace National Memorial (6 m NW at 40 N Main St., Niles), marble memorial marks site of 25th President's birth; museum on his life and career; open daily 9-5; closed hols; free. McKinley later lived at 210 Main St. in Poland (6 m S on SR 170), and in 1861 he enlisted in the Union army at the stagecoach stop, Sparrow Tavern. **John Stark Edwards House** (10 m N at 309 South St. SE, Warren), erected 1808, is oldest home in Western Reserve; restored to 1800-40 era; historical displays; open Tues., Thurs., Sun. 2-4:30; closed hols; sm adm. **Warren City Hall** (391 Mahoning Ave., Warren), in 1871 Tuscan-style villa; wood and stone carvings; period furnishings; open business hrs. **Pioneer Village** (7 m SW on US 62 on Canfield Fair Grounds, Canfield), law office, country store, other buildings typical of Western Reserve villages; grounds open all yr, buildings open in summer; free.

ZANESVILLE: Zanesville Art Center (1145 Maple Ave.) includes paintings by Rembrandt, Goya, Gainsborough; Oriental art objects; early Ohio glass; other exhibits; open Sept.-July, Mon.-Thurs. & Sat. 9:30-5; Sun. 2-5; closed hols; free. **Dr. Increase Mathews House** (304 Woodlawn Ave.), built 1805 and the oldest house in town; historic relics; early glass and ceramics; open May-Oct., Thurs., Sun. 2-5; sm adm. **Zane Grey Birthplace** (705 Convers Ave.), where the author was born 1872 and where he wrote his first story, is a private residence; the town was named for the author's great-great-grandfather, who surveyed Zane's Trace and selected the site.

National Road-Zane Grey Museum (10 m E on US 22, 40 in Norwich) traces history of the National Road from Cumberland (Md.) to Vandalia (Ill.) with models, dioramas; vehicles that traveled on the Road; Grey's California study reproduced, exhibits on his life as a dentist, baseball player, big-game hunter; ceramic and other exhibits; open Mon.-Sat. 9:30-5, Sun. & hols 1-5; closed Jan. 1, Thnks, Dec. 25; adm.

Ohio Ceramic Center (12 m S via US 22, SR 93 to SR 2 at Roseville), in several buildings, tells the story of the huge Ohio ceramic industry; functional ceramics, art pottery; potterymaking demonstrations; an information center will tell you about industrial tours; open Apr.-Oct., Tues.-Sun. 9:30-5; closed Easter; sm adm. Roseville firms that usually offer tours Mon.-Fri. 9:30-2:30 are Robinson-Ransbottom Pottery Co. and Nelson McCoy Pottery Co.; closed hols; free

OKLAHOMA

ALTUS: Museum of the Western Prairie (1100 N Hightower St.): attractive exhibits re-creating 18th-C life in SW Oklahoma; influences of French, English, Spanish, Indian, and cowboy culture; early vehicles; open Tues.-Fri. 10-5, Sat. & Sun. 2-5; closed Jan. 1, Thnks, Dec. 25; free. **Granite** (25 m N via US 283, SR 6) offers tours of the granite quarries; Boot Hill with old tombstones; small museum of antique automobiles and pioneer relics.

ALVA: Cherokee Strip Museum (508 7th St. in Public Library), displays on the Cherokee Strip; open Thurs., Fri. 2-5, Sat. 2-4; closed hols; free. **Northwestern State College** (jct US 64, 281), Natural History Museum with exhibits of prehistoric and recent Indians, good bird collection, fossils; open Mon.-Fri. 9-4; closed Jan. 1, July 4, Thnks, Dec. 25; free.

ANADARKO: Southern Plains Indian Museum & Crafts Center (on US 62, E of town), outstanding contemporary Indian painting, war dance costumes, other early and contemporary arts; open June-Sept. daily 9-5; Oct.-May, Tues.-Sun. 9-5; closed Jan. 1, Thnks, Dec. 25; free. Nearby is **National Hall of Fame for Famous American Indians,** a 10-acre park with busts of Sequoyah, Sacajawea, Osceola, and others; open daily in daylight; free. **Indian City USA** (2 m S on SR 8), authentic reconstruction of Apache, Caddo, Kiowa, Pawnee, Pueblo, Navajo, and Wichita villages; tours by Indian guides; dances and demonstrations; arts and crafts shop; open daily 9-5 (9-6 in summer); closed Thnks, Dec. 25; adm.

ARDMORE: 707 Ranch House (Fair Park), built before 1887, has been renovated as a museum; inquire locally for hrs. **Lake Murray State Park** (9 m SE on SR 77S) contains Tucker Tower, built in the 1930s as a summer retreat for state governors but never used for this purpose; today it is a museum of minerals, meteorites, fossils, Indian artifacts; open Tues.-Sun. 9-5; free. **Platt National Park** (25 m N on I-35, 10 m E on SR 7 to Sulphur, then S) offers Travertine Nature Center, with exhibits on ecology, cultural history of the area; audiovisual, interpretive programs; open mid-June-Labor Day daily 8-9; rest of yr, daily 8-5; closed Dec. 25; free.

BARTLESVILLE: Nellie Johnstone No. 1 (Johnstone Park on 300 block of N Cherokee) is a replica of the first commercial oil well (1897) in the state; open daily. **Phillips Exhibit Hall** (in Phillips Bldg., 5th & Keeler Sts., 2nd floor), history of petroleum (open Mon.-Fri. 8-5) and guided tour of facilities (Mon.-Fri. 5:30; Sat., Sun., hols 4:30); free. **Price Tower** (SE 6th St. & Dewey Ave.), designed by Frank Lloyd Wright and completed in 1956; open but no tours.

Woolaroc Museum (14 m SW on SR 123), on a 3500-acre ranch with wild animals roaming free, has an impressive mosaic entry; exhibits arranged chronologically trace the history of man in the New World; painting and sculpture by Remington, Russell, and others; on grounds is National Y Indian Guide Center with displays of arts and crafts and audiovisual programs; open daily 10-5; free.

BOISE CITY: Santa Fe Trail ruts are visible from the highway (8½ m N on US 287, 385). **Fort Nichols Site** (W to Wheeless, then 2½ m N), established 1865 by Kit Carson to protect wagons on the Santa Fe Trail; marked, scenic spot but undeveloped. **Black Mesa State Park** (22 m W, 8 m N on county roads), Indian pictographs, petrified wood, dinosaur excavation site; open daily; free.

CLAREMORE: J. M. Davis Gun Museum (333 N Lynn Riggs Blvd.) is state-owned; some 20,000 guns, swords, knives, and other weapons from all over the world; some were once owned by famous people; also steins, musical instruments, saddles, animal horns and trophy heads, WW I posters, and other curiosities; most complete John Riger's statuary collection in the world; fine research library; open Mon.-Sat. 8:30-5, Sun. & hols 1-5; closed Dec. 25; free.

Lynn Riggs Memorial (121 N Weenonah) honors playwright whose *Green Grow the Lilacs* was basis for musical, *Oklahoma!*; memorabilia; open Mon.-Fri. 9-1, 2-5, Sat. 9-noon; closed hols; free.

Will Rogers Memorial (1 m W on Will Rogers Blvd.), on land the cowboy-humorist had dreams of ranching, contains dioramas and murals of his life, taped excerpts of his broadcasts; saddle collection, personal possessions; Rogers is buried with his wife and son in the garden; open daily 8-5; free. **Will Rogers State Park** (10 m NW on SR 88, 2 m N on US 169) contains the 1879 cabin in which Rogers was born; open daily.

CLINTON: Western Trails Museum (2229 Gary Frwy) displays Indian points, flint, bone tools, beadwork; fossils; pioneer items; farm tools; pictures; open daily 9-5; free. **Thomas** (9 m N on US 183, 11 m E on SR 33) is Oklahoma's largest Amish colony.

DURANT: Fort Washita (13 m NW via SR 78, 199 on E shore of Lake Texoma) was built to protect the Chickasaw and Choctaw, removed here from the South, from the Plains Indians whose land this was; it was once commanded by Zachary Taylor; after gold was discovered in California, it became a busy center on the overland route; remains of 48 buildings, bake oven, blacksmith shop, stables; open Tues.-Fri. 9-5, Sat. & Sun. 2-5; closed hols; free.

White House of the Chickasaws (18 m NW on SR 78), home of Douglas H. Johnston, last Governor of the independent Chickasaw Nation; privately owned. **Tishomingo** (29 m NW on SR 78) was capital of the Chickasaw Nation from 1856 until statehood in 1907; former capitol is now Johnston County Courthouse; adjacent is Chickasaw Council House, a tiny, 1856 log building from which the Nation was first ruled; displays on tribal history; open Tues.-Fri. 8-5, Sat. & Sun. 2-5; closed Jan. 1, Easter, Dec. 25; free.

Boggy Depot State Recreation Area (25 m N on SR 48, then E on SR 7), campsite on the Texas Road and Shawnee Cattle Trail, later a stop on the Butterfield Overland Mail; buildings being restored; open daily; free.

ENID: Cherokee Strip Museum (Old Library of Phillips Univ., at E edge of city) has Indian and pioneer artifacts, display on the land rush that settled Enid in 1893; open Tues.-Fri. 10-5, Sat. & Sun. 2-5; closed hols; free. **Homesteader's Sod House** (30 m W on US 60, then 5 m N of Cleo Springs on SR 8), survivor of hundreds of thousands that once covered the state; restored with period furnishings by Oklahoma Historical Society; open Tues.-Fri. 9-5, Sat. & Sun. 2-5; closed hols; free.

ELK CITY: This town grew on the Dodge City or Western Trail (now SR 34) along which cattle were driven from Texas to railheads in Kansas 1874-93. **Old Town Museum** (US 66 & Pioneer Rd., W of town) is a gingerbread house; memorabilia of settlers; period rooms; doctor's office; Indian artifacts; open June-Aug., Tues.-Sat. 10-9, Sun. 10-5; Sept.-May, Tues.-Sat. 10-2; closed Jan. 1, July 4, Thnks, Dec. 25; adm.

Black Kettle Museum (11 m W on SR 6, then 21 m N on US 283 to Cheyenne) commemorates 1868 Battle of Washita, when Custer and the 7th Cavalry surprised Black Kettle's sleeping village in winter encampment on the Washita River; the Cheyenne, including Black Kettle, were massacred; battle artifacts; Indian, pioneer, cavalry relics; open Tues.-Sat. 9-5, Sun. 2-5; closed hols; free. **Washita Battlefield** (3 m W and N on SR 47 and 47A) is marked and has a memorial; open daily; free.

EL RENO: Canadian County Historical Society Museum (in Old Rock Island Passenger Station, Wade & Grand Sts.): Indian and pioneer artifacts; Fort Reno and the early Darlington settlement (named for a Quaker Indian agent who served the Cheyenne and Arapaho); railroad exhibit; on grounds is steam engine and log cabin; open Tues., Fri., Sat., Sun. 1:30-5; closed Easter, Dec. 25; free.

Old Fort Reno (5 m W on I-40, then 1½ m N) was established 1874 to quell Plains Indians who resented the arrival of eastern tribes and eastern tribes who wanted to return to their homelands; troops accompanied the 1876 buffalo hunt to keep peace, but within the next 3 years the buffalo disappeared and with it the Indians' ability to survive; Ft. Reno was reduced to a beef-issue station; Ft. Reno soldiers also manned the starting line of the Run of '89 to discourage sooners; the fort was also a post for horses and mules (Black Jack 2V56, the riderless horse at the funerals of Pres. Hoover, Kennedy, and Johnson, lived here); during WW II it housed German and Italian POWs, some of whom are buried beside the Indians, scouts, and early soldiers in the cemetery. Now the fort is a government livestock research station and prairie dog sanctuary; some 19th-C buildings; interpretive pamphlet; open daily.

Seay Mansion, restored 1892 home of the second Territorial Governor, and **Chisholm Trail Museum** (both 11 m N on US 81 to 11th & Overstreet, Kingfisher), with displays on Chisolm Trail, (which ran down Kingfisher's main street) and pioneer artifacts, are open Mon.-Sat. 9-5; sm adm. **Jesse Chisholm's Grave** (36 m NW on US 281, then 2 m E on SR 51A) is marked near Left Hand Spring.

GOODWELL: No Man's Land Historical Museum (on campus of Oklahoma Panhandle State University, Sewell St.), exhibits on history of the panhandle; geology, archaeology; Indian artifacts; open Sun.-Fri. 1-4; closed Aug. & hols; free.

GRAND LAKE: Also called Lake of the Cherokees, this is a popular resort area dotted with Cherokee historic sites. **Har-Ber Village** (3 m W of Grove on the E shore of the lake), reconstructed pioneer village with furnished printshop, stagecoach inn, other buildings; open mid-May-mid-Oct. daily 9-6; free. **Council House Weavers** (N Main St. in Grove) give demonstrations of rug weaving in summer. **Chouteau Museum** (at Salina on SE shore of lake) houses local historic items; open summers Tues.-Sat. 1-5, Sun. 1-4; sm adm. Studios of famous Cherokee wood sculptors are also here, Williard Stone at Locust Grove (S end of lake) and Calvin J. Berry at Vinita (3 m W on US 66 at jct US 69).

GUTHRIE: Oklahoma Territorial Museum (402 E Oklahoma Ave.) depicts territorial history from the city's settlement by 15,000 people on the first day of the Run of 1889 through Guthrie's role as Territorial

Capital (1890-1907) and state capital (1907-10); adjoining Carnegie Library, where the first territorial and state governors took oaths of office, houses reference materials; open Tues.-Fri. 9-5, Sat. & Sun. 2-5; closed hols; free.

Cooperative Press Museum was home of *The Oklahoma State Capital,* a newspaper that died when the state capital was switched to Oklahoma City; for nearly 75 years, the steam-driven presses, antique type faces, lay untouched; being developed as a museum of the press; inquire at Chamber of Commerce.

IDABEL: Memorial Indian Museum (12 m NE on US 70 at 2nd & Allen Sts.), Indian artifacts from prehistoric to modern times; Caddo pottery; early American glass; fossils and minerals; open May-Sept. daily 8 am-9 pm; rest of yr, daily 8-5; free. **Fort Towson** (19 m NW on US 70), established 1824 in the Choctaw Nation, never received word that the Civil War had ended; Gen. Stand Watie, commanding officer of the Cherokee Mounted Rifles, therefore did not surrender until 2 months after Appomattox; barracks, powder magazine, and other buildings have been partially reconstructed; interpretive signs; open Mon.-Fri. 9-5, Sat. & Sun. 2-5; closed hols; free.

LAWTON: Museum of the Great Plains (in Elmer Thomas Park, 601 Ferris Blvd) offers historic exhibits on Indians, fur traders, cowboys, settlers, buffalo hunters; archaeology of Great Plains; outdoor agricultural display; open Mon.-Fri. 8:30-5, Tues.-Thurs. also 7-10 pm; Sat. 10-6; Sun. 1:30-5:30; closed Jan. 1, Thnks, Dec. 25; free.

Fort Sill Military Reservation (4 m N on US 277), now U.S. Army Field Artillery Center, was established as a cavalry post in Indian Territory in 1869; most stone buildings of Old Post remain, with historic markers, and house exhibits of **U.S. Army Field Artillery Center Museum:** McLain and Hamilton Halls depict history of American field artillery from the Boxer Rebellion to the present; Hall of Flags has uniforms, weapons, paintings from the Revolution to the present; Old Guardhouse, called the Geronimo Hotel when Geronimo was imprisoned here, held many war chiefs of the SW and contains Geronimo's cell, animated display of Fort Sill, exhibits on Indians and soldiers; Cannon Walk is an outdoor display of U.S. and foreign weapons; Old Post Corral, built 1870 after a Kiowa horse-stealing raid, has replica of the old trading post, Indian tepees, pioneer vehicles, and smithing equipment used by Apache POWs. Also here are 1875 Old Post Chapel, 1870 Old Post HQ (not open but has historic markers); Sherman House, where the Kiowa almost killed Gen. William Tecumsah Sherman in 1871 (not open); Post Cemetery, with Chief's Knoll, where Quanah Parker and other chiefs are buried; the cemetery for Comanches, Apache POWs, and Geronimo's grave is 3 m N on the opposite side of the highway. Open daily 8-4:30; closed Jan. 1, 2 & Dec. 24, 25; free.

Medicine Park (8 m N on Pioneer Expy, then W on SR 49), an early and fashionable resort, provides historic markers for the nearby gold mining towns of Meers and Camp Doris, Frank James' Homestead, and Jessie James' cave hideout.

MCALESTER: This city grew from a tent store opened in 1870 by James McAlester at the crossroads of the Texas Road and the California Trail; McAlester, who married a Choctaw and became a member of the Choctaw Nation, was sentenced to death by a chief over rights to coal he mined but escaped and later became the state's lieutenant governor. **Old Tobusky County Courthouse** (200 E Krebs Ave.), used by the Choctaws before statehood, is still administrative center for tribal law; open June-Aug. for guided tours by Parks Dept.; adm. **McAlester Scottish Rite Temple** (Adams Ave. & 2nd St.), noted for multicolored dome, is open Mon.-Fri. 8-5; closed hols; free.

MUSKOGEE: Five Civilized Tribes Museum (3 m NW to Agency Hill, Honor Heights Park) chronicles cultural, artistic, and social history of the Cherokee, Chickasaw, Choctaw, Creek, and Seminole tribes; large collections of costumes, branding irons, photographs, documents; reference library; craft shop; open Mon.-Sat. 10-5, Sun. 1-5; closed Dec. 25; sm adm.

Thomas-Foreman Home (1419 W Okmulgee St.), where historians Grand and Carolyn Foreman wrote; original furnishings; Indian artifacts; open Tues.-Fri. 9-5, Sat. & Sun. 2-5; closed hols; free. **Horseless Carriages Unlimited** (2215 W Shawnee Ave.), antique and classic cars; some custom built for celebrities; open daily 10-6; closed Jan. 1, Thnks, Dec. 25; adm. **USS Batfish** (2 m NE via Muskogee Tpke, Hyde Park Rd.), a WW II submarine, is open Mar.-Oct., Tues.-Sat. 9-6, Sun. noon-6; adm.

Fort Gibson (9 m E on US 62 to Ft. Gibson, then ½ m N on SR 80), established 1824, was a lonely outpost in Indian territory; communication was via steamboat on the Arkansas River; French fur traders met here; in the 1830s, mounted rangers escorted Washington Irving on his tour of the prairies and George Catlin on his trip to the SW; Jefferson Davis, Robert E. Lee, Jeb Stuart, Zachary Taylor served here; reconstructed fort and stockade are open daily, 9-7 in summer, 9-5 rest of yr; closed Dec. 25; free. Fort Gibson National Cemetery, with grave of Sam Houston's Indian wife Talihina, is just E.

NORMAN: University of Oklahoma (University Blvd & W Boyd St.) offers information and tours from University Relations Office; on campus are: **Museum of Art,** European graphics; Oriental objets d'art; African textiles; American Indian paintings; contemporary works; open Tues.-Fri. 10-4, Sat. 10-1, Sun. 1-4; closed hols; free. **Stovall Museum,** devoted to American Indians; prehistoric material from Spiro Mound and other sites; extensive artifacts of 5 Civilized Tribes and Plains Indians; open Mon.-Fri. 9-5, Sat. & Sun. 1-5; closed hols; free.

Murray-Lindsay Mansion (35 m S on SR 76 in Lindsay), also called Erin Springs Mansion, was built by an Irish immigrant and his Choctaw wife to be the showplace of the Chickasaw Nation; lavish furnishings; open Tues.-Fri. 9-5, Sat. & Sun. 2-5; closed hols; free.

OKLAHOMA CITY: Chamber of Commerce (1 Santa Fe Plaza) provides information on this city that was settled in one day when 10,000 people converged here in the Apr. 22, 1889 land run; the city is undergoing renewal, and in Heritage Hills (NW 14th-21st Sts., between Walker & Robinson) homes built early in the city's history are being preserved.

State Capitol (NE 23rd St. & Lincoln Blvd.) is unique in that oil wells surrounding it have generated millions of dollars for the state treasury; murals; portraits; tours daily 9-4; closed hols; free. **Oklahoma Historical Society Museum** (opposite Capitol) is noted for large collection of American Indian material, especially from Plains cultures; archaeological material includes artifacts from Spiro Mounds; life-size paintings of Indian dances by Kiowa artists; other exhibits; library material on Five Civilized Tribes; open Mon.-Fri. 8 am-9 pm, Sat. 8-6, Sun. 1:30-4:30; closed hols; free.

First Christian Church (3700 N Walker Ave. at 36th St.) is of striking modern design; open daily 8-5; closed hols; free.

Fair Park (NW 10th St. & N May Ave.): **Oklahoma Art Center** (3113 Pershing Blvd.), few Old Masters; emphasis is on modern painting, drawing, and sculpture; also glass and decorative arts, Dorothy Doughty birds, regional exhibits; open Tues.-Sat. 10-5, Sun. 1-5; closed hols; free. **Oklahoma Science & Arts Foundation** (3000 Pershing Blvd.), especially fine material from ancient civilizations (Egyptian mummies include a cat) of the Near East and Central and South America; also ivories from Africa, the Orient, and Europe; Kirkpatrick Planetarium shows Tues.-Fri. in summer, weekends all year; open Mon.-Sat. 9-5, Sun. 1-5; closed hols; free.

Oklahoma Museum of Art at Red Ridge (5500 N Lincoln Blvd.) exhibits watercolors, drawings, antique furniture; open Tues.-Sat. 1-4, 1st Sun. each month 2-5; closed Aug. & Dec. 25; sm adm.

Oklahoma Firefighters Museum (2716 NE 50th St. in Lincoln Park) preserves the tiny, crude log shed that was the state's first fire station; antique equipment; open daily 10-5; closed Thnks, Dec. 25; adm.

National Cowboy Hall of Fame & Western Heritage Center (5 m NE on US 66 to 1700 NE 63rd St.) houses a magnificent collection of Western memorabilia colorfully displayed in life-size dioramas, a gun shop, an Indian village, a sod house, other re-creations; gallery of Western art; Fraser sculpture includes famous *End of the Trail*; Rodeo Hall of Fame; open daily 9:30-5:30 (8:30-6 in summer); closed Jan. 1, Thnks, Dec. 25; adm.

OKMULGEE: Creek Council House & Museum (Town Sq. on 6th St.), a handsome sandstone building erected 1878, contains 2 government chambers—House of Warriors (with murals, still used for tribal meetings) and House of Kings (with portraits and history of chiefs); prehistoric and recent Indian artifacts, pioneer-era relics; craft shop; open Mon.-Sat. 9-5, Sun. 1-5; donation.

PAWHUSKA: Osage Tribal Museum (Grandview Ave.) is devoted to Osage costumes, jewelry, beadwork, paintings, other Osage artifacts; documents; open daily 8-noon, 1-5; free. **Osage County Historical Society Museum** (700 N Lynn Ave): Indian and pioneer relics; oil; open daily in summer 9-6, in winter 9:30-4:30; closed Thnks, Dec. 25; free.

PAWNEE: Pawnee Bill Museum & Park (on US 64) was home of Gordon W. Lillie, who lived with the Pawnee and taught at their Indian Agency school before joining Buffalo Bill's Wild West Shop; he made this home a showplace, entertained lavishly, bred livestock and worked to preserve the pure-bred buffalo; on grounds is log cabin where his wife Mary retreated after an argument; memorabilia, frontier relics; open daily 9-5 (9-7 in summer); free.

PERRY: Cherokee Strip Museum (1208 W Fir Ave.) commemorates the land run of noon on Sept. 16, 1893 for the last refuge of the buffalo and Plains Indians, last great frontier to be opened to white settlement; despite many sooners, 100,000 people lined up at the border for the noon gun, and by nightfall Perry was a city of 25,000; photos of the run, the tent cities, pioneer relics; open daily 9-5 (9-7 in summer); closed Jan. 1, Thnks, Dec. 25; free. The original land office and turn-of-the-century buildings on Perry's square are also being preserved.

PONCA CITY: Pioneer Woman Museum (701 Monument Rd.), named for statue by Bryant Baker; relics of pioneers and of the famous 101 Ranch; open summer Mon.-Sat. 9-7, Sun. 1-5; rest of yr, Mon.-Sat. 9-5, Sun. 1-5; closed Dec. 25; free. **Ponca City Indian Museum** (1000 E Grand Ave. in Cultural Center), in former home of Gov. E. W. Marland, with hanging staircase, indoor pool; period furnishings, Indian artifacts, regional art, studio of Bryant Baker, old photographs; open Mon., Wed.-Sat. 10-5, Sun. & hols 1-5; closed Jan. 1, Dec. 25; free. **Yellow Bull Museum** (12 m W on US 64 on N Oklahoma Junior College campus) has natural history displays; large bird collection; documents and artifacts of 101 Ranch and pioneer days; open Mon.-Fri. 8-5; closed hols & school hols; free.

POTEAU: Kerr Museum (6 m SW on US 271, then 1 m E), in striking river-bluff mansion of former Sen. Robert S. Kerr, is devoted to the history of eastern Oklahoma; artifacts from Spiro Mounds and Fourche Maline culture; Choctaw relics; 11th-C rune stone said to be of Norse origin (ask about location of similar stones in Poteau and Heavener); weapons and pioneer relics; fossils, minerals; open daily 1-5; closed Jan. 1, Thnks, Dec. 25; sm adm.

Peter Conser House (12 m S on US 59 in Heavener), home of former senator in the Choctaw legislature, is a memorial to the Lighthorsemen, or the tribal police force that served the Choctaw Nation from its establishment in Indian Territory in 1834 to its close in 1906; Conser became captain of the Lighthorsemen after the Civil War; open Tues.-Fri. 9-5, Sat. & Sun. 2-5; closed hols; free.

Sequoyah's Home (39 m N on US 59 to Sallisaw, then 11 m NE on SR 101), log cabin built by the brilliant Cherokee who created the Cherokee alphabet; open Tues.-Fri. 9-5; Sat. & Sun. 2-5; closed hols; free.

TAHLEQUAH: In the fall and winter of 1838-9, 16,000 Cherokee were driven from their homes in Georgia and North Carolina along the Trail of Tears to Oklahoma; some 4000 died during the year's march; here they established the capital of the Cherokee Nation in 1839. **Cherokee Capitol** (Muskogee Ave.), erected 1867, is now the county courthouse; open Mon.-Sat. 8-5; closed hols. The 1844 **Cherokee Supreme Court Bldg** (Water Ave. & Keetowah St.) later housed the *Cherokee Advocate,* first newspaper published in Oklahoma, and now houses county offices. **Cherokee National Prison** (Water Ave. & Choctaw St.) is now the county jail. **Northeastern Oklahoma State University** (N on SR 82) uses the 1889 Cherokee Female Seminary as an administrative building; museum with displays of Cherokee culture is open on request Mon.-Fri. 9-5; free.

Tsa-La-Gi, Cherokee Cultural Center (3 m S on US 62, then E), re-created Cherokee village of about 1700; exhibits, demonstrations of crafts, dances; other events; open May-early Sept., Tues.-Sun. 10-5; adm. *Trail of Tears,* a portrayal in drama and dance of the Cherokee trek and struggle to begin anew, is presented here in summer. **George M. Murrell Home** (3 m S on SR 82, then E to Park Hill), built about 1844 by a white man who had married a Cherokee and who came West on the Trail

of Tears; original furnishings; open June-Sept. 9-7 daily; Mar.-May &
Oct.-Nov. daily 9-7; free. **Cherokee Arts & Crafts Center** (4 m S on US
62) displays and sells hand-made products; open June-Labor Day daily
10-6; rest of yr, Tues.-Sat. 10-5, Sun. 12:30-5; closed Thnks, Dec. 25-Jan.
5; free.

TULSA: Chamber of Commerce (616 S Boston Ave.) offers maps for a
self-guiding tour along a marked route.

Thomas Gilcrease Institute of American History & Art (2500 W
Newton St.) was founded by the Creek-descended Gilcrease, who made a
fortune in oil by age 21 and devoted the rest of his life to this collection;
5000 pieces of American art range from Colonial works to 20th-C artists
such as Willard Stone; included are West, Sully, Bierstadt,
Catlin. Gilcrease sponsored archaeological excavation in Arkansas and
Missouri; 200,000 artifacts come from these sites and from other parts of
the U.S. and Central America. Also 75,000 books and manuscripts on
American history. Open Mon.-Sat. 9-5, Sun. & hols 1-5; closed Dec. 25;
free.

Philbrook Art Center (2727 S Rockford Rd.), in ornate Italian villa of
a wealthy oil man; Italian Renaissance painting and sculpture; 19th-C
American and European landscapes; African sculpture; Chinese jade and
decorative arts; paintings of the oil industry; rare American Indian baskets
and pottery; outstanding Indian paintings; open Tues.-Sat. 10-5, Sun. 1-5;
closed hols; adm.

Rebecca and Gershon Fenster Gallery of Jewish Art (17th Pl. & Peoria
Ave.) displays ceremonial and art objects; open Sun. 2-4 or by appointment Mon.-Fri.; closed hols & Jewish hols; adm. **Boston Avenue
Methodist Church** (1301 S Boston Ave. at 13th St.), a 1925 design with a
skyscraper tower and circular sanctuary; glass-tile mosaic of Indians and
settlers; open daily 9-5; closed hols; free. **Frankoma Pottery** (14 m SW off
I-44 to 1200 Frankoma Rd. in Sapulpa) offers guided tours Mon.-Fri.
8-2:30; closed hols; free.

WOODWARD: Pioneer Museum (2009 Williams Ave., S of town)
stresses pioneer history on the Plains; Plains Indian artifacts, Western art;
open Tues.-Sat. noon-5, Sun. 2-5; closed hols; free.

OREGON

ASTORIA: Clatsop County Historical Museum (441 8th St.), 1883 mansion built by Capt. George Flavel, known for his skill and courage at sea and business acumen, at the height of his career; lavish interior with hand-carved woods, imported furnishings, marine paintings; Indian artifacts, relics from shipwrecks, other historical displays; open June-Sept., daily 10-5; rest of yr, Tues.-Sun. noon-5; closed Jan. 1, Thnks, Dec. 25; sm adm.

Astoria Column (marked route to Coxcomb Hill), 125-ft tower with a frieze depicting exploration of Pacific Northwest by Lewis & Clark and others, establishment of fur trading posts, other historic events; observation tower; nearby are pioneer cemetery, Indian burial canoe, monument to Chief Concomly, a Chinook who befriended settlers; open daily 8-8 (to 10 in summer); information booth open 9-5 in summer; free. **Fort Astoria** (Exchange St. at 14th St.), established 1811 by Astor's Pacific Fur Co., was first permanent American outpost W of the Mississippi; partially restored; museum open daily in summer, Tues.-Sun. in winter, 10:30-5; sm adm.

Columbia River Maritime Museum (Astoria Maritime Park, Exchange St. at 16th St.), outstanding displays on fishing, whaling, other maritime history of the NW Coast; models of many types of craft; figureheads, scrimshaw, marine paintings, early charts; relics from famous ships and from wrecks; riverboat pilot memorabilia; Coast Guard and Navy displays; moored outside is the lightship *Columbia* (named, like the river, for the vessel of Boston Capt. Robert Gray, first American ship to circumnavigate the globe and to claim the Pacific Northwest) that guided river shipping for 52 years; library; open May-Oct. daily 10:30-5; Nov.-Apr., Tues.-Sun. 10:30-4:30; closed Dec. 25; sm adm.

Fort Clatsop National Memorial (4½ m SW on US 101A): replica of fort, named for friendly Indians, erected by Lewis & Clark as winter quarters 1805-6; **Visitor Center** offers exhibits and audiovisual program; living history demonstrations in summer; open daily 8-5 (8-8 mid-June-Labor Day); closed Jan. 1, Thnks, Dec. 25; free. Information is available here on sites outside the park associated with Lewis & Clark, such as the **Salt Cairn Site** (11 m S on US 101 on Lewis & Clark Way, W of Beach Dr., Seaside), where salt was rendered from seawater, or **End of the Trail Monument** (end of Broadway in Seaside), commemorating success of the expedition.

Fort Stevens State Park (5 m W on US 101, then 5 m N), site of 1864 fort erected to guard the Columbia River against Confederate gunboats which never appeared; in 1942, it became only military post on the continental US to be fired on by foreign forces when a Japanese sub fired several shells here; concrete gun emplacements remain; cemetery; on Columbia Beach is the wreck of the British bark *Peter Iredale,* stranded during a 1906 storm; open all year.

Nearby ghost towns are **Brownsmead** (10 m E on US 30, then 5 m N); **Bradwood** and **Clifton** (14 m E on US 30, then 1 m N)—the latter, an 1870s cannery town, is sliding into the river; and **Mayger** (49 m E on US 30, then 7 m N), rotting wharves, church, cemetery.

BAKER: This town mushroomed after a gold find in 1861 set off a boom of nearby mining camps; people still prospect in this area. **First National Bank** offers a gold nugget display; open banking hrs; free. **Chamber of Commerce** (Box 69) has information about the many ghost towns in the area: **Auburn** was the largest mining town, with a population of 5000; hard-to-find cemetery remains. **Sumpter** (6 m S on SR 7, then 20 m W on SR 220) had 3000 residents, 3 newspapers, 6 churches, 12 saloons, a brewery, and an opera house; this, the best preserved town, still has a small population. **Bourne** (on a dirt road 6 m N of Sumpter) had 3 quartz mills and 250 residents. **Granite** (15 m W of Sumpter on a dirt road), settled 1862, had a Grand Hotel; many buildings remain. **Greenhorn** (via Forest Service road 6 m S from Granite) had 60 mines and more than 2500 people; only a few cabins remain. **Susanville** (SW on the John Day River) was another camp. (See John Day for other towns SW.) Ghost towns E of Baker are: **Sparta** (22 m E on SR 86, then 5 m N on gravel road), large placer mines, had a large Chinese population; 1870s store with fortlike walls, cemetery, few cabins remain. **Cornucopia** (54 m NE via SR 86 to Halfway, then 10 m N), a large gold producer, active until 1941.

Eastern Oregon Museum (11 m N on US 30 in Haines), pioneer artifacts either handmade locally or shipped around Cape Horn; blacksmith shop; saloon; open May-Oct., daily 9-5; donation.

CAVE JUNCTION: **Kerbyville Museum** (2 m N on US 199 in Kerby), in an 1871 merchant's home with period furnishings; gun collection; rocks and minerals; moonshining stills; 1898 log school, blacksmith shop; farm, logging, mining equipment; open May-Oct. daily 10-5; free.

COOS BAY: The drive along US 101 N from the California border to Florence offers spectacular coastal scenery: **Coos-Curry Museum** (3½ m N on US 101 at N edge of North Bend) traces local history with Indian artifacts and pioneer items; 1923 steam locomotive; military exhibits; open

June-Sept., Tues.-Sun. 11-5; Oct.-May, Tues.-Sun. 1-5; closed Dec. 25; free. **Dolly Wares Doll Museum** (49 m N on US 101 at 36th St., Florence), 2500 rare dolls; open Mar.-Oct., Wed.-Sun. 10-5; Nov.-Feb., Tues.-Sun. 10-5; closed hols; adm.

CORVALLIS: Horner Museum (Gill Coliseum, Oregon State Univ.) of Indian artifacts and pioneer items; fossils; open Tues.-Fri. 10-5, Sat. 10-2, Sun. 2-5; closed hols; free. **Sodaville** (11 m SE off US 20) is a ghost town. **Museum of Vanishing America** (11 m S on SR 99W to 5th & Orchard Sts., Monroe), 500 Winchesters, other guns and arms; open Mon.- Fri. 10-5; free. **Linn County Historical Museum** (17 m S on I-5, then 3 m E on SR 228 in Brownsville), pioneer-era rooms, doctor's office, blacksmith shop, country store, other exhibits; 1881 **Moyer House,** an Italian villa-style home with period furnishings; open mid-June-mid-Sept., Tues.-Sun. 2-5; rest of yr, Sat. & Sun. 2-5; closed hols; free.

CRATER LAKE NATIONAL PARK (47 m N of Klamath Falls on US 97, SR 62; the entry S from Diamond Lake is usually closed by snow late fall- July): This exquisite deep-blue lake, caldera of extinct Mt. Mazama, is circled by 33-m Rim Drive, accessible all year, weather permitting, from SR 62. **Rim Village** Exhibit Building with orientation, literature, exhibits; open mid-June-Labor Day daily 8-7; here too is **Sinnot Memorial Overlook Building,** lectures hourly; naturalist programs. **The Watchman** (on Rim Dr., beyond Discovery Point) natural history exhibits and overlook. Park open daily 8-5 (24 hrs mid-June-Labor Day); sm adm or GEP.

EUGENE: University of Oregon (bounded by 11th-18th, Alder, & Moss Sts.) offers: **Museum of Art,** extensive Oriental collection includes an 18th-C jade pagoda, Chinese ivory carvings, Japanese folding screens; Pacific Northwest art works; open Tues.-Sun. noon-5; closed hols; free. **Museum of Natural History,** Indians of the Northwest, fluorescent minerals; display on volcanism, local flora and fauna; open Mon.-Fri. 8-4:30; Sat. & Sun. 1-4:30; closed hols; free. Also on campus are the Library, with material on Oregon, and 2 attractive Victorian structures, Deady Hall and Villard Hall.

    Lane County Pioneer Museum (740 W 13th Ave.) depicts life of settlers; household furnishings, toys, farm tools, photographs; wagons; county archives; open Mon.-Thurs. 9-5, Sat. & Sun. 1-5; closed hols; free.

    Cottage Grove Historical Museum (10 m S via I-5 to Birch Ave. & H St., Cottage Grove), in a 19th-C church; displays on pioneer home, farm, industrial life; Indian artifacts; mining equipment; open mid-June-Aug., Wed.-Sun. 1-5; free. **Railtown, USA** (off I-5 at Village Green Station, Cottage Grove) displays antique steam locomotives and passenger cars, some with exhibits; adjacent steam-powered train excursions (mid-May-Sept.); open daily 10-5 (longer in summer); closed Jan. 1, Dec. 25; adm.

Bohemia Mining District (10 m S via I-5 to Cottage Grove, then 36 m SE on road paved only part way), where claims were staked in an 1860s boom around the ghost town of Bohemia City, has yielded gold, silver, lead, zinc, copper; many working, abandoned mines; self-guiding tour booklets available in Cottage Grove from Umpqua National Forest Service office or Chamber of Commerce (who can tell you about land rover tours into the area).

JOHN DAY: Oliver Historical Museum (2 m S on US 395 at 101 S Canyon City Blvd., Canyon City) depicts John Day and Canyon City gold rush era; gold, mineral specimens; mining equipment; settler artifacts (including relics of Indian and Chinese residents); on grounds is **Joaquin Miller Cabin,** where the Poet of the Sierras lived with his family while running a newspaper and composing his first poems; 1910 city jail also here; open Apr.-Oct., Tues.-Sat. 9-5, Sun. 1-5; sm adm. **Kam Wah Chung Co. Bldg.** (in Gleason Park), completed 1867, was a shopping center that provided an herb doctor, banking facilities, and a shrine for the many Chinese who worked the gold fields; being restored; inquire locally for hrs.

Grant County Chamber of Commerce (240 S Canyon Blvd.), fossil collection, information on fossil hunting, gold mining camps and ghost towns; map of **John Day Fossil Beds State Park** (41 m W on US 26), which has rich fossil beds and Indian pictographs in Picture Gorge. Within reach are Sheep Rock, Munro, and Force Fossil Beds. **Fossil** (38 m W on US 26, then 65 m N on SR 19) offers an old courthouse, city and private fossil and mineral collections, and leaf impressions in Wheeler Fossil Beds; **Lonerock** (25 m NE) is a ghost town; **Mayville** (8 m N on SR 19) has fossil beds, ancient cremation pits, ruts of stagecoach route from Fossil to Condon can be seen at **Thirtymile Creek.** Colorful fossil beds at **Blue Hills** (on SR 207 N of Mitchell); just N of these is ghost town of **Richmond,** with church, store, and other buildings still standing.

KLAMATH FALLS: Klamath County Museum (1451 Main St.), has extensive Indian displays on Klamath and Modoc; pioneer relics; natural history exhibits; open Tues.-Sat. 9-5, Sun. 1-5; closed hols; free. **Favell Museum of Western Art & Indian Artifacts** (125 W Main St.) also offers extensive Indian artifacts; regional art; open June-mid-Sept., Mon.-Sat. 9:30-5:30, Sun. 1-5:30; mid-Sept.-May, Tues., Sat. 9:30-5:30, Sun. 1-5; closed Jan. 1, Dec. 25; adm. **Klamath Indian Memorial Museum** (27 m N on US 97 in City Hall, Chiloquin) exhibits local history from Indian point of view; inquire locally for hrs.

Collier Memorial State Park (30 m N on US 97): Logging Museum with blacksmith shop, lumbering equipment, tools outdoors and in several log buildings; Pioneer Village, cabins built by trappers, miners, loggers, and homesteaders; pit houses occupied by Indians before Mt. Mazama erupted 7500 years ago; open daily in daylight; free.

LAKEVIEW: Schminck Memorial Museum (128 S E St.) houses glass, quilts, guns, china dolls, saddles, other early domestic items; open Mon., Wed.-Sat. 9-5, Tues. & Sun. 1:30-5; closed Jan. 1, Thnks, Dec. 25; sm adm.

MEDFORD: Chamber of Commerce (304 S Central Ave.) offers information on rockhounding, tours of lumber mills and fruit-packing plants. **Crater Rock Museum** (4 m N off SR 99 to 2002 Scenic Ave., Central Point), minerals, fossils, petrified wood, Indian artifacts; many minerals were found at famous early mines; tours daily 8-6; closed Dec. 25; donation.

Hilltop Doll Museum (S Stage Coach Rd.) is open spring-fall, Mon.-Sat. 9-6; adm.

Jacksonville (4 m W on SR 238), one of the best-preserved pioneer communities in the Northwest, boomed after gold was discovered in 1851; the railroad bypassed it in 1883; gold-era buildings still stand, and many are inhabited. Markers identify some 70 buildings: house whose plans and materials were bought through a mail order catalog; the 1881 **First Presbyterian Church,** stained-glass windows brought around Cape Horn from Italy; 1880 **U.S. Hotel,** inaugurated with a reception for Pres. & Mrs. Rutherford Hayes (the president complained of bedbugs, Mrs. Hayes earned her nickname Lemonade Lucy by turning her wineglass down at dinner, and their companion Gen. William Sherman complained the bill resembled the purchase price); 1862 **Beekman Bank,** established by a carpenter who gained a reputation for courage by freighting gold across the Siskiyous at night to avoid Indian attack. Many buildings are maintained by **Jacksonville Museum** (in Old County Courthouse, 206 N 5th St.); tours May-Aug.; brochures for self-guiding driving or walking tours; museum exhibits depict life during the gold rush, lawmen, gamblers, Chinese miners; Indian artifacts; work and personal belongings of pioneer photographer Peter Britt, a Swiss immigrant who arrived to mine gold in 1852; antique dolls, costumes, weapons; open May-Aug., Mon.-Sat. 9-5, Sun. noon-5; Sept.-Apr., Tues.-Sat. 9-5, Sun. noon-5; free.

Old Oregon Historical Museum (14 m NW off I-5 at 2335 Sardine Creek Rd., Gold Hill), Indian artifacts, relics of 1850-60 stagecoach and gold-mining era, guns, penny arcade machines, newspapers and documents; open Mar.-Oct., daily 10-5; sm adm. **Wolfcreek Tavern** (45 m

N off I-5, then W), a stagecoach stop built about 1857 on worked-out placer gold diggings; according to legend it has hosted Presidents Grant and Hayes, Gen. Sherman, Sinclair Lewis, Jack London (who may have written here); SW along Wolfcreek Rd. are played-out gold mines such as Alameda; **Golden** (4 m E on Coyote Creek Rd.), ghost mining town with remains of church, school, other buildings; Grave Creek Covered Bridge (4 m S at Sunny Vale) with 6 windows on each side.

NEWPORT: Oregon State University Marine Science Center (off US 101, S side of Yaquina Bay on Marine Science Dr.) conducts research in marine biology and oceanography; vessels sometimes open to the public; museum; aquarium; special programs in summer; open daily 10-4 (10-6 in summer); closed Dec. 25; free. **Lincoln County Historical Museum** (579 SW 9th St.), in a log building; artifacts from Siletz Indian Reservation; area historical relics; open June-Sept., Tues.-Sun. 11-5; Oct.-May, Tues.-Sun. 11-4; closed Jan. 1, Thnks, Dec. 25; free. **Sara** (325 SW Bay Blvd.), typical of the two-masted cargo vessels that plied the coast in the 19th-C; maritime exhibits; open daily, weather permitting, 11-5; adm. **Yaquina Bay State Park** (N end of bridge on US 101): 1871 Old Yaquina Bay Lighthouse; historical and maritime artifacts; also pioneer items, Indian costumes; open June-Sept., Tues.-Sun. 11-5; Oct.-May, Fri.-Sun. 11-5; free. **Cape Perpetua Visitor Center** (2 m S on US 101) of Siuslaw National Forest offers a film; dioramas of man's influence on the coast; natural history exhibits; 22-m self-guiding auto tour; trails with interpretive signs; Indian shell mounds; open May-Sept. daily 9-6; Oct.-Apr., Tues.-Sat. 10-4; free.

   Lacey's Doll House & Antique Museum (27 m N to 3400 N Hwy 101, Lincoln City) 4000 dolls from around the world, miniatures to life-size models; many in costume; also antique china, hurdygurdy, music boxes, other items; open daily 8-6; closed Thnks, Dec. 25; sm adm.

PORTLAND: Information on the "City of Roses" and its beautiful surroundings is available from **Visitor Information Center** (824 SW 5th Ave.); tours of the Univ. of Oregon Health Sciences Center and to most industrial plants require advance appointments. The city's interesting architectural history includes landmarks such as the Carpenter Gothic **Old Church** (1422 SW 11th Ave.), many examples of cast-iron facades (the 1872 **New Market Theater** is one), and elaborate eclectic styles (such as **Pittock Mansion,** or 1917-25 U.S. National Bank) at the turn of the century. Pietro Belluschi designed the 1932-39 Portland Art Museum, 1941 St. Thomas More, 1948 Equitable Bldg., 1951 Central Lutheran Church. More recent are **Lloyd Center** (on Broadway, 2 blocks E of Union Ave.), a complex of office and service buildings with landscaped pedestrian malls, and **Auditorium Forecourt** (SW 3rd Ave. & Clay St.), a 2-level garden with cascading water and pools.

Mount Hood Loop (marked drive starting at Visitor Information Center) offers spectacular scenery, recreational facilities; points of interest include; Lewis & Clark State Park (17.2 m), where the expedition paused on Nov. 3, 1805; Portland Women's Forum State Park (25.6 m) honoring railroad builder Sam Hill; Starvation Creek State Park (58.7 m), where railroad passengers were stranded in snowdrifts for 2 weeks in 1884; Pioneer Woman's Grave (110.2 m) honoring a woman who died just before reaching her destination in Willamette Valley; Laurel Hill (116.5), so steep that pioneers on the Barlow Road had to lower their wagons on ropes wound around tree trunks, with the pioneer trail worn as deep as 7 ft (see also The Dalles).

Portland Art Museum (1219 SW Park Ave. at Madison St.), art of Eskimos and Northwest Indians; Renaissance painting; 19-20th-C French and American painting; Japanese prints; Cameroon works; silver; open Tues.-Sun. noon-5; closed hols; sm adm.

Oregon Historical Society Museum (1230 SW Park Ave.), exhibits on state's Indians; Lewis and Clark memorabilia; tools of pioneer artisans; early rifles; horse-drawn vehicles; maritime relics; fine library; open Mon.- Sat. 10-5; closed hols; sm adm. The Society maintains 1856 **Bybee-Howell House** (12 m N via US 30 over Sauvie Island bridge, then follow signs); period furnishings; open about May-Oct. daily 10-5; closed hols; sm adm.

Pittock Mansion (off NW Irving Ave. in Pittock Acres Park), opulent 1914 home of founder of *Daily Oregonian*; French Renaissance style; fine plasterwork and woodwork; Turkish smoking room; unusual features such as a central vacuum cleaner; open Wed.-Sun. 1-5 (longer hrs in summer); closed hols & 2 wks in Jan.); adm. **Oregon Museum of Science & Industry** (4015 SW Canyon Rd.), fluid mechanics; ship's bridge; Eocene fossils; aerospace hall; walk-in heart; transparent woman; operating beehive; planetarium shows; open mid-June-mid-Sept., Mon.-Thurs. 9-6, Fri.-Sun. 9-9; rest of yr, Mon.-Thurs. 9-5, Fri. 9-9, Sat. & Sun. 9-6; closed Dec. 25; adm. **Western Forestry Center** (4033 SW Canyon Rd.), talking tree, displays on forest management and lumber industry; open daily 10-5; closed Dec. 25; sm adm. **Sanctuary of Our Sorrowful Mother** (NE 85th Ave. & Sandy Blvd), erected by Servite Fathers; grotto carved in 150-ft cliff; elevator (fee) to a higher level with religious art in gardens, panoramic views; impressive statues and wood carvings; open daily 8-sundown; free.

Caples House Museum (25 m N on US 30 in Columbia City), an 1870 saltbox; locally made furnishings; carriage house with period costumes; country store; tool shed; open Feb.-Dec., Tues.-Sun. 1-5; sm adm. **Trojan**

Nuclear Plant (42 m NW via US 30) Visitors Information Center (Belluschi participated in the design) exhibits on energy, multimedia presentation on ecology; Indian artifacts; open Mon.-Sat. 9-5:30, Sun. 1-5; closed Jan. 1, Easter, Thnks, Dec. 25; free. **Old College Hall** (23 m W on SR 8 on Pacific University campus, Forest Grove), built 1850, displays Indian and pioneer relics, Oriental artifacts; open academic yr, daily 9-noon; free.

Oregon City (just S on the Willamette River) was the end of the Oregon Trail and capital of the Oregon Territory 1845-52. **Municipal Free Elevator** (7th St. & Railroad Ave.) lifts you to observation platform; open Mon.-Sat. 6:30-12:30 am; Sun. 6:30 am-8:30 pm; closed July 4, Labor Day, Dec. 25; free. **McLoughlin House National Historic Site** (McLoughlin Park, 713 Center at 7th Sts.), retirement home built 1846 by Dr. John McLoughlin, who, as chief factor of the Hudson's Bay Co., ruled the Northwest Territory 1824-46; displays of his career as peacemaker with the Indians, overseer of the fur trade, and friend and advisor to settlers; family furnishings; open Tues.-Sun. 10-4 (10-5 in summer); closed hols; adm. **Barclay House** (719 Center St.), home of a Hudson's Bay Co. doctor; built 1850 of New England wood shipped around Cape Horn; period furnishings; historic displays; open Tues.-Sun. 10-4 (10-5 in summer); closed hols; free. Dr. Barclay, along with the Great Pathfinder, Peter Skene Ogden, is buried in Mountain View Cemetery. **Ainsworth House** (19195 S Leland Rd.), built 1850 by a Mississippi River pilot, was a showplace in its time; maritime relics; period furnishings; open Sat. & Sun.; closed hols; adm.

Aurora Colony Historical Society (23 m S on I-5, then 3 m S off SR 214 at 2nd & Liberty Sts.) preserves buildings of the communal Aurora Colony founded by Germans under the leadership of William Keil; Keil, a tailor who broke with the Methodists after his ordination, unsuccessfully attempted to establish a colony in Missouri in 1845; a decade later, carrying the body of his 19-year-old son in an alcohol-filled, lead-lined coffin (the son, dying of malaria, had asked to be buried in the "promised land"), Keil led his followers on 4-month trek to the Willamette Valley; here the new colony, named for his daughter, prospered with productive orchards and a large furniture factory, but disbanded after Keil's death in 1877; austere early cabin and more comfortable later homes; museum of settler relics and the handcrafted furniture they sold; open Wed.-Sun.; closed hols; adm.

Minthorn House (20 m SW on SR 99W at 2nd & S River St. in Newberg) is the restored Quaker home where Herbert Hoover came to live at age 10, after the death of his parents, with his uncle; many original furnishings; open Tues.-Sat. 10-noon, 2-4; Sun. 2-5; closed hols; sm adm. Nearby **Shambaugh Library** (414 N Meridian, on George Fox College campus) has exhibits and reference materials on Quakers; open June-Sept., Mon.-Sat. 8-5; Oct.-May, Mon.-Sat. 8 am-10 pm; closed hols; free. **Butteville** (E of Newberg on Wilsonville Rd.) was laid out in the early 19th-C as a retirement village for French Canadian trappers of the Hudson's Bay Co.; became a ghost town when the railroad passed it by; old buildings, the cemetery remain.

Champoeg State Park (7 m SE of Newberg off SR 219), on the site of a village destroyed by 1861 flood, was where trappers and settlers met in 1843 and voted to become part of the U.S. rather than be ruled by the Hudson's Bay Co.; open daily 8-5 (longer in summer). Here are: **Pioneer Mother's Home,** a DAR museum of pioneer life housed in a replica of an early cabin; **Robert Newell Residence & Museum,** only home to survive the flood, schoolhouse, other buildings, with Indian and pioneer relics, period furnishings, costumes; both open Feb.-Nov., Tues.-Sat. 11-5, Sun. 1-6; closed Thnks; sm adm. **Champoeg Historical Museum** houses relics of fur-trading era, early settlement, river life; open May-Sept. daily 11-5; Oct.- Apr. daily 11-4; closed Jan. 1, Thnks, Dec. 25; free.

Fort Yamhill Blockhouse (24 m SW on SR 99W, then 1 m SW on SR 233 to City Park, Dayton), blockhouse with gun slots, once part of 1856 fort; open daily; free.

ROSEBURG: Douglas County Museum (off I-5 on fairgrounds), Indian and pioneer displays, logging equipment; open daily 8:30-5; closed hols; free. **Lane House** (544 SE Douglas Ave.), 1850s residence of first territorial governor; Indian and pioneer relics, period furnishings; open Sat. & Sun.; closed hols; free.

SALEM: State Capitol (Court & Summer Sts.) sculpture honors Lewis and Clark, pioneers; tours in summer; open Mon.-Fri. 8-5, Sat. & Sun. 9-5; closed Jan. 1, Thnks, Dec. 25; free. At rear are outline maps of Oregon Trail, Lewis and Clark route. Nearby is State Library.

Bush Park (600 Mission St. SE) contains Bush House, Victorian mansion of Salem banker and newspaper publisher with period furnishings; open June-Aug., Tues.-Sat. noon-5, Sun. 2-5; rest of yr, Tues.-Sun. 2-5; closed hols; sm adm. Bush Barn Art Center exhibits works by Northwest artists; open Tues.-Fri. 9:30-5, Sat. & Sun. 1-5; closed hols; free.

Thomas Kay Historical Park (12th & Ferry Sts.) stresses white settlement of the Willamette Valley by Methodist missionary Jason Lee in 1830-40s, and the introduction of industry in the 1880-90s by Thomas Kay; 1841 Jason Lee House, home to several pioneer families, also served as store, post office, and territorial treasury; 1841 Parsonage; 1847 Boon House; 1896 Kay Woolen Mill and 1890s warehouse; exhibits on textile industry; open late May-early Sept.; inquire locally for hrs; sm adm.

THE DALLES: Fort Dalles Museum (16th & Garrison Sts.), in only remaining building of the 19th-C fort, the surgeon's quarters, features interesting pioneer relics; covered wagons, stagecoaches; open May-Sept.,
Tues.-Fri. 10:30-5; Sun. 10-5; Oct.-Apr., Wed.-Fri. noon-4, Sun. 10-4;
closed hols & 1st 2 weeks in Jan; free. **Winquatt Museum** (1 m E of I-80
tollgate), Columbia River archaeological artifacts, petroglyphs; open
same hrs; free.

Barlow Road: Covered wagons on the Oregon Trail at first came only
as far as The Dalles; here they had to be taken apart and floated
downstream on rafts. But in 1845, determined Kentuckian Samuel Barlow
cut a trail through the mountains around the cascades; it took 10 weeks of
enormous hardship, and he had to abandon his wagons before reaching
Oregon City; the following year he widened the trail and made it a toll
road. Though it remained a difficult passage, the Barlow Road section of
the Oregon Trail was used by thousands of immigrants. From The Dalles,
Barlow Road went S along what is now US 197; an 1863 farmhouse at
Dufur (14 m) became a rest stop for emigrants; at **Tygh Valley** (17 m) the
trail turned W to Wamic (6 m), the eastern toll gate. From here only a dirt
Forest Service road now follows the Barlow Trail (along slopes so steep
that wagons had to be lowered by ropes wound around trees, many of
which still bear ropeburns) to **Barlow Pass** (just N of jct SR 35, US 26),
where the road follows US 26W; at **Rhododendron** there's a replica of the
western toll gate.

Celilo Converter Station (4 m SE off US 197), N terminal for DC
transmission to California, welcomes visitors to control room; exhibits;
open daily in daylight; free. The **Dalles Dam & Reservoir** (3 m E off I-
80N) offers a 2-m train tour of locks, fish-counting station (May-Sept.,
Thurs.-Mon. 10-6); area open daily in daylight; free. **John Day Lock &
Dam** (30 m E on I-80N at Biggs), powerhouse observation area, fish ladders, lock; open daily in daylight; free. **Hood River Visitor Center** (20 m
W on I-80N to Port Marina Park, Hood River), historical displays on Columbia River area; open June-mid-Sept. daily 8-6; rest of yr, Mon.-Fri.
8-5; closed Jan. 1, Dec. 25; free. **Cascade Locks Park** (41 m W on I-80N),
museum in lock-tender's residence; exhibits on covered wagon days and
early fishing (including a fish wheel, now outlawed, that caught up to 3000
salmon a day); outside is the "Oregon Pony," first locomotive in Oregon;
open May-Oct., Tues.-Sun. 9-5; sm adm. **Bonneville Dam** (43 m W on I-
80N) offers powerhouse, lock, fish ladders, interpretive signs; guided
tours in summer; open daily in daylight; free.

TILLAMOOK: Tillamook County Pioneer Museum (2106 2nd St. at
Pacific Ave.), in former county courthouse; exhibits of wildlife that can be
found on the stunning Tillamook Loop Drive; minerals; old guns; early

vehicles; pioneer home replica with settler relics; salvage from an early 1700s Spanish shipwreck; other exhibits; open spring-fall, daily 9-5, Sun. 1-5; open in winter, Tues.-Sat. 9-5, Sun. 1-5; free.

PENNSYLVANIA

ALLEGHENY PORTAGE RAILROAD NATIONAL HISTORIC SITE (on US 22 between Duncansville & Cresson): Philadelphia, alarmed that New York's growth would accelerate with the Erie Canal, began to build a "Main Line" to Pittsburgh in 1826—a route of railroads (81 m Philadelphia-Columbia) and canals (276 m Columbia-Hollidaysburg and Johnstown-Pittsburgh); but engineers desperately sought a solution to covering the 36 m between Hollidaysburg and Johnstown over 2291-ft mountains; the solution, a portage railroad, was a sort of huge staircase, with locomotives pulling the cars along level areas, and mechanized inclined planes lifting or lowering cars from one level to another. But by 1854 the Pennsylvania Railroad completed service between the eastern seaboard and the Ohio Valley, making the Main Line and its portage obsolete. **Lemon House,** built about 1831 as a tavern and rest stop, is now the Visitor Center; explanations on the invention; interpretive signs at preserved or restored features of the railroad; summer guided tours, craft demonstrations; open mid-June-Labor Day, daily 8:30 am-7:30 pm; rest of yr, daily 8:30-5; closed Jan. 1, Thnks, Dec. 25; free.

ALLENTOWN: Zion's Reformed Church & Liberty Bell Shrine (622 Hamilton at Church Sts.), replica of the original bell, hidden here in 1777 as Philadelphia fell to the British; mural; historic exhibits; open mid-Apr.-mid-Oct., Mon.-Sat. 11-4, Sun. 2-4; rest of yr, Mon., Wed.-Sat. 11-4, Sun. 2-4; closed Jan. 1, Easter, Dec. 25; free. **Trout Hall** (414 Walnut at 4th St.), built 1770 by James Allen, son of the city's founders; period rooms; historical exhibits; library; open Tues.-Sun. 1-4; closed hols; free. **Allentown Art Museum** (5th & Court Sts.), Renaissance and Baroque works; European masters; wood carvings; Pennsylvania folk art; open Tues.-Sat. 10-5, Sun. 1-5; closed hols; free.

   George Taylor Mansion (4 m N off US 22 in Catasauqua), 1768 home of signer of Declaration of Independence, with period furnishings, and **Troxell-Steckel House** (6 m N on SR 145, then W on SR 329 in Egypt), a

1755 stone house in German medieval style, with museum exhibits, are open June-Sept., Tues.-Thurs. 1-4, Sat. & Sun. 2-4; free.

ALTOONA: Baker Mansion Museum (3501 Oak Lane), 19th-C stone home of an ironmaster; Greek Revival style; hand-carved Belgian furniture; historic displays; open June-Oct., Thurs.-Sat. 1:30-4:30; closed hols; adm. **Horseshoe Curve** (follow signs 6 m W), world-famous engineering feat completed in 1854 to link Penn Central track across the Alleghenies; overlook, monument, caboose; open daily; free.

BEDFORD: Fort Bedford Park & Museum (Ft. Bedford Dr., N end of Juliana St.), reconstruction of early blockhouse; Indian artifacts; settler relics; open mid-May-mid-Oct., daily 10-sunset; sm adm. Buildings from colonial days, still in use, include **Espy House** (123 Pitt St.), Washington hq during 1794 Whiskey Rebellion (it is now a bakery). **Bedford Historic Village** (2 m N on US 220-Bus), operating farm and a dozen structures dated 1771-1851; historic displays; craft demonstrations; open Apr.-Oct., daily 8-sunset; Nov.-Mar., Sat. & Sun. 9-sunset; closed Thnks, Dec. 25; adm.

BELLEFONTE: Centre County Historical Museum (203 N Allegheny St.), early furniture, clothing, dishes; library; open Tues.-Fri. 9 am-8 pm, Mon. & Sat. 9-5; closed hols; free.

BETHLEHEM: Moravians fleeing religious persecution in Germany established Bethlehem in 1741; preserved buildings cluster about **Central Moravian Church** (Church & Main Sts.), built 1806, noted for musical programs and elaborate creche (on display early Dec.-early Jan., daily 1-9; free); tours of Moravian buildings (fee) Mon.-Fri. (write Moravian Historical Tours Office at the church for schedule). Nearby: 1768 **Widow's House** (residence for widows of Moravian ministers); 1748 **Brethren's House** (residence for single men; used as hospital by Continental Army during Revolution); 1751 **Old Chapel**; 1746 **Bell House**. At the foot of Church St., a display of early industry is being developed in restored factory buildings. **Moravian Cemetery** (Heckewelder Pl.), headstones laid flat to illustrate equality in the sight of God, has graves dating from 1742. **Moravian Museum of Bethlehem** (Gemein Haus, 66 W Church St.), community house built 1741; exhibits on the community; Moravian furniture, clocks, silver, musical instruments, needlework; apothecary open by appointment; open Tues.-Sat. 1-4; closed Good Fri., Holy Sat., Memorial Day, July 4, Thnks, Dec. 24-26, all of Jan.); adm.

    Annie S. Kemerer Museum (427 N New St.): Venetian, Bohemian, American glass; Queen Anne, Chippendale, Hepplewhite, Belter furniture; clocks made locally; Moravian artifacts; fire-fighting equipment;

open Mon.-Fri. 1-4; 2nd & 4th Sun. of each month, 2-4; closed Good Fri., hols; donation.

BLOOMSBURG: Columbia County Historical Society (in Bakeless Center for the Humanities, Bloomsburg State College campus, Main & Penn Sts.), local historic displays, settler artifacts; library; open Mon.-Fri. 9-5; closed Easter, Dec. 25; free. **Magee Museums** (698 W Main St.), textile and carpeting, general historic section, usually open Sun. & hols; a transportation section (Millville Rd.) is open May-Nov. weekends; check locally for hrs, fees.

This mining area gained notoriety for the Molly Maguires, a violent miners' group seeking reforms; mine tours at: **Glen Burn Mine** (10 m SW on US 11 to Danville, then 16 m SE on SR 54, 61 to Shamokin), tunnel and above-ground tours, museum of mining memorabilia; early May-late Sept., Sat. & Sun. 10-6; adm. **Pioneer Coal Mine** (21 m S on SR 42 to 19th & Oak Sts., Ashland), tunnel tour and steam-train ride; open daily 10-7 in summer, weekends in spring & fall 10-5; adm.

BUTLER: Old Stone House (12 m N on SR 8 in Stone House), 1822 stagecoach stop on Pittsburgh-Erie road, once an outlaw hangout; blacksmith shop, craft displays; open Tues.-Sat. 9-4:30, Sun. 1-4:30; closed hol; sm adm. **Harmony Museum** (17 m SW via SR 68 to Evans City, then 4 m N to Main & Mercer Sts., Harmony) is noted for 1650 single-hand clock brought from Germany by George Rapp, who founded Harmony Society here in 1805 before migrating to Indiana (see New Harmony); more than 100 of Rapp's group are buried in Harmonists Cemetery (SE of town); museum depicts life in this and in Mennonite communities; open Memorial Day-Oct., Tues.-Fri. 1-4, Sat. & Sun. 1-5; closed Mon. in June & Sept.; sm adm.

McConnells Mill State Park (23 m W on US 422, then S on county rd), 1872 gristmill; open mid-May-mid-Sept., Mon.-Fri. 11-5; Sat., Sun., & hols 11-6; free.

CARLISLE: Carlisle Barracks (N on US 11), on site of 1750 frontier hq for campaigns during French and Indian War; troops marched from here to the Whiskey Rebellion; during the Civil War, Carlisle surrendered without resistance to Confederate cavalry in 1863, but the occupation lasted only 3 days. Carlisle Indian School, first nonreservation school for Indians, functioned here 1879-1918; Olympic star Jim Thorpe was a student. The 1777 **Hessian Guard House,** built by prisoners captured at the Battle of Trenton, serves as a museum of barracks, Indian School, and Jim Thorpe; open May- Sept., Sat. & Sun. 1-4; free. The post, with Army War College, is open daily in daylight.

Old West (on Dickinson College campus, W High St.) was designed by

Benjamin Latrobe; Jefferson, Madison, and Aaron Burr contributed to its construction; houses college offices. **Old Graveyard** (South St.) contains grave of Mary McCauley (Molly Pitcher). **Pine Grove Furnace State Park** (10 m SW on I-81, then 9 m SE on SR 233) contains ruins of 1764 iron furnace; interpretive signs; open daily.

CHAMBERSBURG: During the Civil War, Chambersburg, occupied 3 times by Confederates, was burned in 1864 after inhabitants refused to pay an indemnity of $100,000. Confederates also destroyed an arms-producing iron furnace in **Caledonia State Park** (10 m E on US 30); furnace remains, blacksmith shop, interpretive signs. Monument (10 m S on US 11) marks site of the first Union casualty on Northern Soil. **John Brown's Headquarters** (225 King St.), where the abolitionist posed as a prospector while collecting arms for his raid on Harper's Ferry, is a private home. **James Buchanan Birthplace** (14 m W on US 30, then 6 m S on SR 75 to Mercersburg), reconstructed on campus of Mercersburg Academy; open by appointment.

DOYLESTOWN: Mercer Mile is a route connecting the 3 castle-like concrete (Mercer feared fire) structures built by Dr. Henry Chapman Mercer (1856-1930), archaeologist, historian, ceramist, and collector of Americana; brochure available at Mercer Museum describes sites of interest; **Mercer Museum** (S Pine & E Ashland Sts.), begun in 1914 as last of the 3 "castles," houses Mercer's "Tools of the Nation Maker," more than 30,000 artifacts of trades and crafts before mass production; reconstructed workshops; products from handmade nails to iron stove plates to Conestoga wagons fill floor space, coves, and hang from the ceiling; furnished 1799 log cabin, horse sheds with antique vehicles, library. **Moravian Pottery & Tile Works** (Swamp Rd. & E Court St.), designed as a composite of Spanish mission churches in California, is decorated with the tiles it produced (the tiles are also in the Capitol at Harrisburg and Salem United Church of Christ in Doylestown); the name "Moravian" refers to the copying of early tile designs from Pennsylvania Dutch stove plates; original tiles are collectors' items, but copies may be bought here; guided or self-guided tours of tile making. **Fonthill** (behind the pottery on E Court St.), Mercer's home, was constructed 1908-10 around an 18th-C farmhouse; elaborately decorated with tiles; unusual antiques; carriage house, with a free-standing fireplace and vaulted, tiled ceiling, was Dr. Mercer's retreat; guided tours. All 3 buildings are open Mar.-Dec., Tues.-Sun. 10-5; closed Thnks, Dec. 25; adm.
  National Shrine of Our Lady of Czestochowa (1½ m N on US 611, 1½ m NW on SR 313, 2 m W on Ferry Rd.), striking stained-glass windows depict 1000 years of Christianity in Poland; copy of painting of Our Lady of Czestochowa; altar sculptures; open daily; free.

Newtown (4 m E on US 202, then 10 m S on SR 413) has many attractive pre-Revolutionary houses; self-guiding map from Historic Association in handsome 1733 Court Inn, well-known Revolutionary-era tavern; open house is held by many residents on 1st Sat. in June: 1690 Bird-in-Hand House (111 S State St.), named for sign painted by Edward Hicks; 1764 Brick Hotel (State & Washington Sts.); 1800 Milnor House (127 Sycamore St.); Temperance House (5 S State St.); Hicks House (122 Penn St.), 1821 stone house built by Edward Hicks.

Green Hills Farm (6 m N on SR 313 in Dublin), 60-acre estate and 1835 stone farmhouse was Pearl Buck's home until her death in 1973; memorabilia; porcelains and art objects from China; tours Mon.-Fri. 10:30-2; closed hols; adm.

EASTON: Hugh Moore Park (200 S Delaware Dr.), at the forks of the Delaware, preserves section of Lehigh Canal that operated 1829-31 to inland anthracite deposits; Canal Museum, tracing life of canal people, features of major canals, through photographs, film, exhibits (open Tues.-Fri. 10-4; Apr.-Oct., Sat. & Sun. 1-5; closed hols; sm adm); restored 1890s Lock Tender's House (open May-Sept., Sat. & Sun. 1-8 or by request; sm adm); park open daily, dawn-dusk; free.

ERIE: During the War of 1812, Commodore Oliver Hazard Perry took command of the 9-vessel American fleet, built here with materials from the forest, and defeated the British in the Battle of Lake Erie. In Presque Isle State Park, a 7-m peninsula curving around the harbor, is a monument to Perry; open daily all year. USS Niagara (foot of State St.), hull of Perry's flagship, sunk in Misery Bay in 1813 and raised in 1913; open Mon.-Sat. 9-4:30, Sun. 1-4:30; closed hols; sm adm. Perry Memorial House & Dickson Tavern (201 French St.), early-19th-C saltbox with secret passageways used by slaves on the Underground Railroad; Perry is believed to have stayed here while his fleet was being built; Lafayette was a guest in 1825; period furnishings and historic relics; open mid-June-mid-Sept. daily 1-4; rest of yr, Sat. & Sun. 1-4; closed some hols; sm adm. Wayne Blockhouse (560 E 3rd St., on grounds of Soldiers and Sailors' Home) is a replica of the one in which Gen. Anthony Wayne died on Dec. 15, 1793, erected over his grave (his remains were later removed to Radnor); open Memorial Day-Labor Day, daily 10-4; free. Old Custom House (407 State St.), an 1839 Doric-style building; exhibits on history of NW Pennsylvania; open May-Oct., Tues.-Fr. 1-4:30, Sat. 9-noon; closed hols; free. Erie Public Museum & Planetarium (356 W 6th St.), historical natural science displays; open Tues.-Sat. 10-5, Sun. 2-5; closed hols; free.

Fort Le Boeuf (16 m S on US 19), like the former Fort de la Presque Isle on present site of Erie, was occupied by the French 1753-59, rebuilt by the British 1760, burned by Indians 1763, and rebuilt by Americans 1794;

ruins of fort; 1820 **Judson House** is a museum of fort history; open Tues.-Sat. 9-4:30, Sun. 1-4:30; closed hols; sm adm.

GALETON: Pennsylvania Lumber Museum (12 m W on US 6), 19th-C lumbering techniques; reconstructed 1890s logging camp with bunk house, mess hall, shay locomotive, blacksmith shop; open May-Oct., Mon.-Sat. 9-4:30, Sun. noon-4:30; Nov.-Apr., Wed.-Sat. 9-4:30, Sun. noon-4:30; closed hols; sm adm.

GETTYSBURG: Gettysburg National Military Park (S on US 15-Bus), site of the 1863 battle that was the turning point of the Civil War, has an excellent **Visitor Center;** electric-map program (30 min; adm) gives step-by-step orientation on the battle; exhibit of Civil War relics (free); open late-June-Labor Day, daily 8 am-9 pm; May-late-June, daily 8-6; rest of yr, daily 8-5; closed Jan. 1, Dec. 25. Ranger-guided walks, living history programs, Children's Walk, other activities frequently available; free. Adjacent **Cyclorama Center** (open same hrs), with free film and exhibits, cyclorama of Pickett's Charge (adm). A 15-m self-guiding auto tour through the marked battlefield ends at National Cemetery, site of Lincoln's Gettysburg Address. Park roads are open 6 am-10 pm; free. **Eisenhower National Historic Site,** the late President's retirement farm, is not yet open to the public but may be seen from observation tower on W. Confederate Ave.

　　General Lee's Headquarters (401 Buford Ave.), where Lee planned his strategy for the battle; battle relics; open in summer daily 9-9; spring & fall daily 9-5; free. **Lincoln Room Museum** (Lincoln Sq.), bedroom in Wills House in which Lincoln completed the Gettysburg Address; audiovisual display; open in summer daily 9-9; spring & fall daily 9-5; adm. **Jennie Wade House** (Baltimore St.), home of only Gettysburg resident to be fatally shot during the battle; narration; open in summer daily 9 am-10 pm; spring & fall daily; adm. Other privately owned attractions (most open 9-9 in summer, 9-5 spring-fall, adm) are: **Hall of Presidents & First Ladies** (789 Baltimore St.), life-size wax figures; **National Civil War Wax Museum** (Steinwehr Ave. & Culp St.); **Gettysburg Battle Theatre** (571 Steinwehr Ave.), with miniature battlefield and film on strategy; **Charley Weaver's American Museum** (777 Baltimore St.) with sound-and-light dioramas of 10 Civil War battles; **Dobbin House & Diorama Museum** (89 Steinwehr Ave.), in 1776 home with secret slave tunnel, miniature diorama of the battle, Civil War photographs and relics.

HARRISBURG: Capitol Hill (3rd & State Sts.) is a 13-acre park with: Capitol, noted for dome modeled after St. Peter's Basilica in Rome, statuary, murals (open daily 9-4:30; closed Jan. 1, Election Day, Dec. 25;

free); ceiling murals by Maragliotti in Finance Building; murals in auditorium and Maragliotti ceiling in lobby of Education Building; murals in South Office Building. **William Penn Memorial Museum** (3rd & North Sts.) offers exhibits on Indian life, regional fauna and flora, religious life, other aspects of state history; period rooms; planetarium shows; open Mon.-Sat. 9-5, Sun. 1-5; closed hols; free.

John Harris Mansion (219 S Front St.), 1766 home of the city's founder, who refused to sell land to the legislature until the name was changed from Louisborg (for Louis XVI); maps; documents; furnishings; dolls; open Mon.-Fri. 1-4:30; Sat. in Sept.-June 1-4; closed hols & last 2 wks in Aug.; free.

Automobilorama (on US 15 at Tpke), history of cars from steam models to modern gas models; open Apr.-Oct. daily 9 am-10 pm; Nov.-Mar. daily 9-5; adm.

Fort Hunter Museum (6 m N on US 22, 322 at 5300 N River Rd.), 1787 house on site of frontier fort; exhibits on colonial domestic life; craft displays; toys; pewter; open May-mid-Oct., Tues.-Sun. 10-5; adm.

HERSHEY: Hershey Information Center (Airport Rd., entrance marked on US 322, 422) provides information on this community planned by the chocolate company; open daily 8-5. Here are: **Hershey Museum**, with American Indian, Pennsylvania Dutch collections; Apostolic Clock; antique china and glass, Stiegel pieces; open mid-May-Labor Day, daily 10-5; Feb.-mid-May & after Labor Day-Nov, Tues.-Sun. 10-5; closed hols; adm. **Hershey's Chocolate World**, where automated cars carry you past simulated scenes illustrating processing of chocolate; open Mon.-Sat. 9-5, Sun. noon-5; closed Jan. 1, Thnks, Dec. 25; free.

HONESDALE: Wayne County Historical Society Museum (810 Main St.) offers antique glass, displays on Delaware & Hudson Canal, other historic exhibits; open June-Sept., Mon.-Sat. 10-noon, 1-4; rest of yr, Tues., Wed., Fri., Sat. 10-noon, 1-4; closed Jan. 1, Thnks, Dec. 25; sm adm.

HUNTINGDON: Swigart Museum (E on US 22 in Museum Park) has antique and classic cars in operating condition; accessories; open June-Aug. daily 9-5; May & Sept.-Oct., Sat. & Sun. 9-5; adm. **Canterbury Guild** (317 Penn St.), regional art in Victorian home noted for fine woodwork; open Tues.-Sat. 1-6; closed hols; free.

JIM THORPE: Jim Thorpe Memorial (E on SR 903), mausoleum dedicated to 1912 Olympic champion for whom the town was named. **Asa Packer Mansion** (Packer Rd.), Victorian showplace of the founder of

Lehigh Valley Railroad and Lehigh University; lavish interior, ornate furnishings; open Memorial Day-Oct., Tues.-Sun. noon-5; adm. **Beltsville
State Park** (7 m E off US 209) has overlook rotunda at N end with fossils
and geologic displays, models of dam project.

JOHNSTOWN: Johnstown Flood National Memorial (10 m NE on US
219, SR 869 at South Fork Dam) marks devastation of May 31, 1889,
when the South Fork Dam broke; waves 30-40-ft high moved 40 mph
down the narrow valley, sweeping people, buildings, and a passenger train;
within about 10 minutes more than 2200 people were dead and almost
everyone in Johnstown and villages above it were homeless; Clara Barton
brought her newly organized Red Cross to stay for 5 months; **Visitor
Center** provides exhibits, audiovisual program, summer guided walks,
self-guiding walk booklets; open June-Labor Day daily 8:30-8; rest of yr,
daily 8:30-5; closed Jan. 1, Thnks, Dec. 25; free. **Grandview Cemetery** (1
m W via SR 271 to Westmont) contains graves of many victims, 663
unidentified. **Inclined Plane Railway** (Vine St. & Roosevelt Blvd.), connecting Johnstown and Westmont, has observation platform from which
flood area can be seen; operates Mon.-Sat. 7 am-11 pm, Sun. & hols 9
am-10 pm; closed Dec. 25; sm adm.
    Kinsey Museum (18 m SW on SR 271), log homestead with out-
buildings; pioneer relics; open Memorial Day-Labor Day, Sat. & Sun. 2-7;
adm. **Fort Ligonier** (22 m SW on SR 271 to jct US 30, SR 711 on S Market
St., Ligonier), reconstruction of 1758 fort built by the British during the
French & Indian War; officers' quarters and other buildings; museum
dioramas of frontier life; war relics; period rooms; open Mar.-Nov. daily
9- sunset; closed Thnks & day after; adm. **Forbes Road Gun Museum** (4 m
N of Ligonier on SR 711), emphasis on American models but also foreign
guns from 15th-C to present; open daily 9-9; adm. **Compass Inn** (3 m E of
Ligonier on US 30 in Laughlintown), log-and-stone building once a
stagecoach stop, has period furnishings; open early May-Oct., Tues.-Sat.
10-5, Sun. 1-5; Nov.-mid-Dec., Sat. & Sun. 1-5; adm.

LEBANON: Germans settled this area and many Hessian prisoners captured at the Battle of Trenton were confined here. **Weaver's Famous
Lebanon Bologna, Inc.** (15th Ave. & Weavertown Rd.) offers guided tours
Mon.-Thurs. 9-3:30; closed hols; free. **Cornwall Furnace** (5 m S on SR 72,
then 2 m E) produced iron 1742-1883 for tools and Revolutionary-era
munitions; the ore came from nearby mines still operated by Bethlehem
Steel Co.; stone houses of 1754 Miners Village are still occupied by
workers; museum in charcoal house explains production in 18th-19th-C;
open Mon.-Sat. 9-4:30, Sun. 1-4:30; closed hols; sm adm. **Historic
Schaefferstown** (5 m S on SR 72, then 7 m E on SR 419), established by

Swiss; village green with log and stone buildings; Thomas R. Brendle Memorial Library houses settler relics (open mid-June-mid-Oct., Sat. & Sun. 1-4 or by appointment; free); special events are often held here. **Fort Zeller** (11 m E on US 422, then S to Newmanstown), originally a log fort, rebuilt in stone 1745; descendants of builder still own it; open daily 9-4; donation.

LANCASTER: Pennsylvania Dutch Tourist Bureau Visitor Center (on US 30 at Hempstead Rd. Interchange, or write 1800 Hempstead Rd., Lancaster 17601) provides information, a film, exhibits, maps (including one showing buildings with hex signs), and counselors who will help you plan day or overnight trips; open May-Oct., Mon.-Sat. 9-6, Sun. 10-5; Nov.-Apr., Mon.-Sat. 8:30-5, Sun. 10-5; closed Jan. 1, Thnks, Dec. 25. Lancaster County was first settled by Mennonites from Switzerland in 1709; they were followed by Amish, French Huguenots, Quakers, Palatines, and others seeking religious freedom. The term "Dutch" is a corruption of Deutsch, and many settlers were German; a minority, such as Mennonites and Old Order Amish, are "plain" people who wear prescribed clothing and forego modern conveniences such as electricity and cars; the majority, who call themselves "fancy" or "gay" Pennsylvania Dutch, live and dress conventionally. Plain people accept guests and are happy to guide you, but they do not advertise; information is available at **Mennonite Information Center** (4 m E via US 30 to 2215 Mill Stream Rd.), with interpretive displays, open Mon.-Sat. 8-5, closed Thnks, Dec. 25, free. **Farmers markets** that sell home-grown and homemade products are: Central Market (Penn Sq.), on Tues., Fri. 6-5; closed hols. Southern Market (102 S Queen St.), Sat. 5:30-2; closed hols. Meadowbrook Market (5 m NE on SR 23), Fri. 10-9, Sat. 8-4.

Wheatland (1120 Marietta Ave.), brick home of Pres. James Buchanan 1848 until his death in 1868; original furnishings; personal possessions; tours Apr.-Nov. daily 10-4:30; adm. Buchanan is buried in Woodward Hill Cemetery (S. Queen St.). **Old City Hall** (Penn Sq.), built 1795, exemplifies Pennsylvania architecture in colonial days. **Trinity Lutheran Church** (S Duke St.), rebuilt in 1760s, has a 1794 steeple with statues of Matthew, Mark, Luke, and John. **Fulton Opera House** (12 N Prince St.), built 1852 on the foundations of a jail and renovated 1873, has served as a Civil War hospital and armory; tours June-Aug., Mon.-Sat. at noon; inquire for additional hrs; adm. **Amish Homestead** (3 m E on SR 462) uses old agricultural methods; 18th-C home; open Memorial Day-Labor Day daily 9-8; spring & fall, daily 9-5; late-Nov.-mid-Mar., Sat. 9-5; closed Dec. 25; adm. **Amish Farm & Home** (6 m E via SR 462, US 30), in early 19th-C stone buildings, provides view of the self-sufficient life of plain people; authentically furnished; windmill, Amish vehicles, farm animals; open in

summer daily 8:30-8; spring & fall daily 8:30-5; winter daily 8:30-4; closed
Jan. 1, Thnks, Dec. 24-26; adm. **Mill Bridge Craft Village** (7 m E off US
30 in Soudersburg), operating 1738 grist mill, blacksmith shop;
demonstrations of crafts made by plain people; Conestoga wagons, Steigel
glass; open Apr.-Oct., Mon.- Sat. 9:30-5; Nov., Sat. 9:30-5; adm. **Hex
Barn & Wagonland** (10 m E on SR 340 to Hollander Rd., Bird-in-Hand)
sells hex signs; horsedrawn vehicles on display; open Apr.-Oct. daily 8-6;
Nov.-Mar. daily 8-5; closed Dec. 24- Jan. 1; sm adm. **Railroad Museum
of Pennsylvania** (10 m SE via US 30, SR 896 in Strasburg), antique
locomotives, passenger cars, local railroad memorabilia; audiovisual exhibits; 4½-m trips in antique coaches daily in summer, weekends in spring
& fall; open Mon.-Sat. 9-5, Sun. noon-5; closed hols; adm. **Eagle
Americana Shop & Museum** (10 m SE via US 30, SR 896 to Strasburg,
then 2 m W on SR 741), in 1740 stone mill; outstanding weapons from
crossbow to modern models; finely crafted, locally made guns used by settlers during the French and Indian War and much prized during the
Revolution; antique toys, blown and pressed glass, iron, china; open
Apr.-Oct. Mon.-Fri. 10-5, Sat. & Sun. 10-7; adm. **Rock Ford** (3 m S at
881 Rock Ford Rd.), a 1793 Georgian-style home where Washington was
once a guest, belonged to Gen. Edward Hand, a physician and member of
the Continental Congress; most details, including window glass, are
original; open early Apr.-mid-Oct., Mon.-Sat. 10-4:30, Sun. noon-4:30;
adm.

Pennsylvania Farm Museum of Landis Valley (2 m N off US 222 at
2451 Kissel Hill Rd.) illustrates rural life through 25,000 items of everyday
use displayed in period buildings; spinning and other demonstrations;
open Mon.-Sat. 9-4:30, Sun. noon-4:30; closed hols; adm. **Zion
Evangelical Lutheran Church** (9 m N on SR 72 to E High & S Hazel Sts.,
Manheim), 1891 Victorian-Gothic church on land donated by Baron
William Stiegel, originator of the famous Stiegel glass, who owned the
town in 1770 and was in debtor's prison by 1774; rent for the land, a single
red rose, is still given to a Stiegel heir. **Pretzel House** (9 m N via SR 501,
772 to 219 E Main St., Lititz), established 1861; now a museum; early
pretzel-making equipment; demonstrations; open Apr.-Oct., Mon.-Sat.
9-5; sm adm.

Ephrata Cloister (13 m N off US 222 at 632 W Main St.) is a serene
enclave, site of a self-sufficient religious community of recluses founded
1732 by German Pietist mystic Conrad Beissel; members, who wore white
habits, belonged to celibate brotherhood or sisterhood or to a married
order. Self-denial and austerity are reflected in the buildings; "straight-
and-narrow" halls symbolize path of virtue; low doorways teach humility;
wooden benches for beds and wooden blocks for pillows. At its height in
the mid-1700s, the population numbered 300 and was known for fine

printed books, hand-illuminated songbooks, religious music (*Vorspiel,* a religious pageant incorporating the community's compositions, is presented in summer). The community declined after the Revolution, partly a result of typhus contracted while nursing soldiers after the Battle of Brandywine, and partly because of celibacy, but was not dissolved until 1934. Chapel, Almonry, Print Shop, residences, other buildings are restored; open May-Oct., Mon.-Sta. 8:30-5, Sun. 1-5; Nov.-Apr., Mon.-Sat. 9-4:30, Sun. 1-4:30; closed hols; sm adm.

LEWISBURG: Union County Historical Society Museum (in County Courthouse) has hand-drawn maps, antique dolls, local historic relics; open Mon.-Sat. 9-5; closed hols; free. **Fort Augusta** (9 m SE on SR 147 to 1150 N Front St., Sunbury) is a miniature replica of a frontier fort; open Tues.-Sat. 9-4:30, Sun. 1-4:30; closed hols; free. **Priestley House** (7 m S on US 15, then NE off US 11), built 1794, was last home of English clergyman Joseph Priestly who supported the Revolution; museum describes his discovery of oxygen; open Tues.-Sat. 9-4:30, Sun. 1-4:30; closed hols; sm adm. **Warrior Run Church** (13 m N on SR 147) is a lovely Greek Revival design; interesting cemetery.

MEADVILLE: Baldwin-Reynolds House Museum (639 Terrace St.), 1843 home of Supreme Court Justice Henry Baldwin; Indian artifacts, early medical equipment, other historic exhibits; open Memorial Day-Labor Day, Wed., Sat., Sun. 2-5; adm. **Bentley Hall** (Allegheny College campus, N Main St.), built 1824, is one of the finest Colonial-style buildings in the country; open academic yr, Tues.-Sat. 1:30-5, Sun. 2-4; free. **Venango County Museum** (32 m SE on US 322 to 415 12th St., Franklin) has models of frontier forts Venango and Machault; frontier weapons; memorabilia of John Wilkes Booth; open Apr.-Nov., Tues.-Sun. 1-5; closed Easter, Thnks; free. **Pioneer Cemetery** (Otter & 15th Sts.) graves date back to 1795. **Farmers Market** (12th St.) operates Wed. & Sat. mornings. **Drake Well Memorial Park** (27 m E on SR 27 to Titusville, then 1 m SE on SR 8), on site of first successful drilled oil well in the world (1859); full-size operating replica; museum of history of the state's oil boom; open Mon.-Sat. 9-4:30, Sun. 1-4:30; closed hols; sm adm. **Pithole City** (31 m E on SR 27, then 7 m S off SR 227, just N of Plumer), oil boom town of 1865, had 15,000 residents, was abandoned 2 years later.

NEW HOPE: Charming town, long an artist colony; mule-drawn barge trips (New St., S end of town) on the Delaware Canal (daily in summer, weekends in fall); excursions on steam train (32 W Bridge St.) in Victorian coaches (daily in summer, weekends rest of yr). Among many old buildings are: **Parry Mansion** (S Main & Ferry Sts.), an 1874 stone house built by the owner of New Hope Mills; restored to show evolution of upper-middle-class taste 1775-1900; open in summer, Wed.-Sun. 1-4; donation. **Parry Barn** (opposite) is open as a commercial art gallery. **Old Franklin Print Shop** (40 S Main St.) houses 1860 hand press; open daily 10-5; closed Thnks, Dec. 25; free.

PHILADELPHIA: Tourist Center (jct Franklin Pkwy, 16th St., JFK Blvd.) offers brochures for self-guided or guided walking tours of historic sites; the 150-m Liberty Trail auto loop; industrial tours (most require advance notice); commercial tours (several originate here); carriage tours (originate here or at Independence Hall); river cruises (in summer, from Penn's Landing); special events; open late May-early Sept., Mon.-Fri. 8:45 am-9 pm, Sat. & Sun. 8:45-5; rest of yr, daily 9-5; closed Dec. 25. Most attractions surround Independence Mall or are clustered along route of Culture Loop Bus that runs from Independence National Historic Park along tree-lined Benjamin Franklin Blvd. to the zoo (34th & Girard Ave.); buses run frequently, daily; for a small fee, you can get on and off all day. Good view of historic district from observation deck of **Penn Mutual Life Insurance Co.** (510 Walnut St. at 5th St.); check for schedule, but usually open mid-May-late Oct. daily 10 am-9 pm; rest of yr, Wed.-Sun. daily 10-5; closed Jan. 1, Dec. 25; adm.

    Independence National Historic Park covers the few blocks (2nd-6th Sts., Chestnut to Walnut Sts.) where the U.S. was created and from which it was governed in its formative years; here the First and Second Continental Congresses gathered, and the Declaration of Independence, Articles of Confederation, Constitution, and Bill of Rights were adopted. The **Visitor Center** (3rd & Chestnut Sts.) provides maps, information, audiovisual program, special events and activities; it is open daily 9 am-8 pm, free, as are the following except as noted: **Liberty Bell** (Independence Mall) in a glass pavilion. **Independence Hall** (Chestnut & 5th Sts.), Pennsylvania's State House; used by Second Continental Congress 1775-83 and Federal Constitutional Convention 1787; in restored Assembly Room are inkstand used in signing the Declaration of Independence and "rising sun" chair in which Washington sat while the Constitution was drafted. **Congress Hall** (Chestnut & 6th Sts.), restored with legislative rooms; where Congress met 1790-1800; Washington (second term) and Adams were inaugurated here. **Old City Hall** (Chestnut & 5th Sts.), where first Supreme Court met, 1791-1800. **American Philosophical Society Building** (rear of Independence Hall) is home of America's oldest (1743) learned society, founded by Benjamin Franklin; not open. **Second U.S. Bank** (420 Chestnut St. at 5th St.), used as U.S. Customs House 1845-1934; art exhibits. **New Hall** (Chestnut & 4th Sts.), reconstructed building housing U.S. Marine Corps Memorial Museum; open daily

9-5. **Pemberton House** (Chestnut & 4th Sts.), reconstruction of a Quaker merchant's home, houses Army-Navy Museum; open daily 9-5. **Carpenters' Hall** (320 Chestnut St. at 4th St.), originally a guildhall; site for First Continental Congress (1774); a hospital and army storehouse during the Revolution; historic exhibits. **First Bank of the U.S.** (3rd St. off Chestnut St.), organized by Alexander Hamilton; the nation's oldest bank building; museum exhibits. **Philadelphia Exchange** (313 Walnut St.), built 1832-34 to house the stock exchange, was designed by William Strickland in Greek Revival style. **Bishop White House** (309 Walnut St.), home of first Episcopal Bishop of Pennsylvania; furnished in late-18th-C style; open daily 9-5. **Todd House** (Walnut & 4th Sts.), where Dolley Madison lived with her first husband, John Todd, from 1791 until his death in 1793; open daily 9-5.

Christ Church (2nd St. between Market & Arch Sts.), 1744 classic Georgian Colonial structure; wineglass pulpit; bells cast by foundry that cast the Liberty Bell; Washington, Franklin, Adams, other patriots worshiped here; several signers of the Declaration of Independence are buried in the churchyard; open daily 9-5. Christ Church Burial Ground (5th & Arch Sts.), graves of Benjamin Franklin and his wife Deborah. **Arch St. Friends Meeting House** (4th & Arch Sts.) was built 1804; exhibits and a film on Quakers from their arrival in 1681, when they lived in caves dug into the banks of the Delaware; open daily 10-4; closed Jan. 1, Thnks, Dec. 25; free.

Also in this area: **Philadelphia Maritime Museum** (321 Chestnut St.); traces U.S. maritime history; ship models, paintings, scrimshaw; open Mon.-Sat. 10-5, Sun. 1-5; closed Jan. 1, Thnks, Dec. 25; donation. **U.S. Mint** (5th & Arch Sts.), produces coins for U.S. and foreign countries; exhibits; salesroom; self-guiding tours; open Mon.-Fri. 9-3:30; closed hols; free.

Near Penns' Landing, the renovated Delaware River waterfront, are: **Betsy Ross House** (239 Arch St.), where the seamstress is said to have made the first U.S. flag (adopted 1777); period furnishings; memorabilia; open daily 9-5 (longer in summer); closed Dec. 25; free. **Elfreth's Alley** (between 2nd & Front Sts.), with 33 houses believed built in 1722, is probably the nation's oldest continuously inhabited street; the homes are open on an annual (June) house tour; the little museum (No. 126) where blacksmith Jeremiah Elfreth once lived, is open by appointment only. **Fire Museum** (149 N 2nd St. at Quarry St.), in firehouse of first company (1736) in the nation; antique equipment, memorabilia; open Tues.-Sun. 10-4; closed hols; free. **USS Olympia** (Penn's Landing, Delaware St.), part of the fleet that helped launch U.S. sea power in the 1890's; flagship from which Comm. Dewey launched 1898 Battle of Manila Bay; her last mission (1921) was to bring home the body of the Unknown Soldier from France; self-guiding tour booklets; museum of naval relics; ship models; open Easter Mon.-day before Thanks., Mon.-Sat. 10-5, Sun. 11-6; rest of yr, Tues.-Sat. 10-4, Sun. 11-5; Closed Jan. 1, Easter, Thanks, Dec. 25, adm. **Gazela**

Primeiro (Penn's Landing, Delaware St.), last of the Portuguese square-rigged fishing fleet, was built 1883; small Portuguese fishing boat; open Memorial Day-Labor Day, daily noon-5; adm.

S of Independence National Historical Park is **Society Hill,** named for William Penn's land company, the Free Society of Traders. The area is also called Washington Square East because it is bordered by Washington Square (SW off Walnut & 6th Sts.), one of the city's 4 original squares— Unknown Soldier of the Revolutionary War, graves of Revolutionary war dead and yellow fever victims, statue of Washington. Among restored buildings open in this 25-block, 18th-C residential district are: **Man Full of Trouble Tavern** (127 Spruce St.), built 1759; last of the city's 18th-C taverns; pewter, English Delftware, homespun linens, other exhibits; open Apr.-Dec., Tues.-Sun. 1-4; Jan.-Mar., Sat. & Sun. 1-4; closed hols; sm adm. **Perelman Antique Toy Museum** (270 S 2nd St.) displays thousands of toys; many animated; early tin and iron examples; open daily 9:30-5; closed Jan. 1, Dec. 25; adm. **Powel House** (244 S 3rd St.), handsome Georgian mansion built before 1768, was one of the finest homes in the city; many original furnishings; tours Tues.-Sat. 10-4, Sun. 1-4; adm. **Hill-Physick-Keith House** (321 S 4th St.), built 1786, belonged to pioneer surgeon Dr. Philip Syng Physick; Federal furnishings; open Tues.-Sat. 10-4; adm. **St. Peter's Church** (Pine & 3rd Sts.), built 1761, is open daily 10-4. **Old Pine St. Presbyterian Church** (412 Pine at 4th Sts.), built 1768, is open Mon.-Fri. 10-5. **Old St. Mary's Church** (4th St. between Locust & Spruce), built 1763, has grave of John Barry ("father of the U.S. Navy"). **Athenaeum** (219 S 6th St.), founded 1814; library and museum emphasize 19th-C history; open Mon.-Fri. 9-4; closed hols; free. **Presbyterian Historical Society** (425 Lombard St.), displays and library; open Mon.-Fri. 9-5; closed hols; free.

Southwark (S of Society Hill), a Swedish settlement predating English arrival in the city; contains some of the oldest homes in Philadelphia and **Gloria Dei (Old Swedes) Church National Historic Site** (Delaware Ave. & Christian St.), dedicated 1700. **American-Swedish Historical Museum** (1900 Pattison Ave.), resembling a 17th-C Swedish manor house, traces history of Swedes in America from colonial times; jewelry; dolls; memorabilia; library; open Tues.-Fri. 10-5, Sat. & Sun. noon-5; closed hols; sm adm.

West of Independence National Historical Park are: **Atwater Kent Museum** (15 S 7th St.), hundreds of exhibits on the city's history from colonial days to the present; open Tues.-Sun. 8:30-4:30; closed Jan. 1, Good Fri., Thnks, Dec. 25; free. **Walnut Street Theatre** (Walnut & 9th Sts.), one of the oldest (1809) in U.S. still in continuous use; part of the ring barns where bareback circus riders practiced still stand. **Congregation Mikveh Israel Cemetery** (8th & Spruce Sts.) graves date back to 1751, including those of Revolutionary War financier Haym Salomon and Rebecca Gratz (believed to be Sir Walter Scott's model for Rebecca in *Ivanhoe*). **Pennsylvania Hospital** (8th & Spruce Sts.), first in the U.S., was founded 1751 by Benjamin Franklin; paintings by Sully, West, Eakins; tours on Mon. & Wed. by appointment.

Academy of Natural Sciences (19th St. & Franklin Pkwy), thousands of exhibits; rare gems; earth history; fossils; specimens collected by Lewis & Clark and by Audubon; underwater salvage finds; ecological dioramas; lectures with live animals; library; open Mon.-Sat. 10-4:30, Sun. 1-4:30; closed Jan. 1, Thnks, Dec. 25; adm. **Pennsylvania Academy of Fine Arts** (Broad & Cherry Sts.), good survey of American art from works of historic interest to fine paintings by Cassatt, Sargent, Sully, others; European painting; sculpture; open Tues.-Sat. 10-5, Sun. 1-5; closed hols; free. **Philadelphia Art Alliance** (251 S 18th St.), contemporary painting, sculpture, industrial design; open Mon.-Fri. 10:30-5, Sat. & Sun. 1-5; closed Jan. 1, July 4, Thnks, Dec. 25; free. **Print Club** (1614 Latimer), exhibits graphics; open Mon.-Fri. 10-5:30, Sat. 11-4; closed mid-June-early Sept.; free.

Free Library (19th & Vine Sts.) is one of the best in the country; millions of indexed items, rare books, special collections; special events; open Mon.- Wed. 9-9, Thurs. & Fri. 9-6, Sat. 9-5; closed hols. **Rosenback Museum** (2010 Delancey Pl.), collections of Philadelphia rare-book dealer and his brother's antique silver, paintings, furnishings; open Tues. 2-5; closed Aug.; adm.

Historical Society of Pennsylvania (1300 Locust St.) offers exhibits on William Penn, Washington, Jefferson, Lincoln, other statesmen; prints and paintings; documents; fine library (adm); open Apr.-Nov. daily 9-5; closed hols; free. **Edgar Allen Poe House** (530 N 7th at Spring Garden Sts.), where Poe lived with his child-bride and her mother for 3 years and wrote "The Tell-Tale Heart," "The Raven," other works; furnished as it might have been when he lived there; memorabilia, portraits, papers; open Mon.- Fri. 10-5, Sat. & Sun. 2-5; closed Jan. 1, Easter, Thnks, Dec. 25; adm. **Bartram's Mansion** (54th St. & Elmwood Ave.), 18th-C restored home of America's first botanist; open daily 8-4; closed hols; sm adm. **Chinese Cultural Center** (Chinatown YMCA Bldg., 125 N 10th St.) has art, musical instruments, other exhibits; open Mon.-Sat. noon-6; closed hols; adm. **Franklin Institute of Science Museum** (20th St. & Franklin Pkwy), founded 1824; exhibits on energy, mathematics, space, communications; many displays can be operated; planetarium shows daily; observatory tour Fri. at 8; Franklin Memorial Hall, with personal belongings and scientific equipment; James Earle Fraser's statue of Franklin in rotunda; open Mon.-Sat. 10-5, Sun. noon-5; closed Jan. 1, July 4, Labor Day, Thnks, Dec. 24, 25; adm (Franklin Hall is free). **Philadelphia Museum of Art** (26th St. & Franklin Pkwy), superb collections displayed in 11th-C Spanish cloister, Ming Dynasty palace reception room, other authentic settings; 13-20th-C European paintings; fine American collection with most major painters represented; tapestries from Palazzo Barberini in Rome; Indian works; European sculpture; Pennsylvania Dutch arts; Philadelphia furniture, silver, decorative arts; on grounds are Leif Ericson Memorial Fountain, statue of Joan of Arc on horseback; open Tues.-Sat. 9-5; closed hols; adm. **Rodin Museum** (22nd St. & Franklin Pkwy), largest collection of Rodin's works outside of Paris; sculpture, drawings; guided tours; open Tues.-Sun. 9-5; closed hols; sm adm. **Civic Center Museum** (34th St. below Spruce), primitive and folk art of the world; open Tues.-Sat. 9-5, Sun. 1-5; closed hols; free. **University of Pennsylvania Museum** (33rd & Spruce Sts.), superb collections on arts and culture of the American Indian; Chinese, Greek African displays; Egyptian mummies; open Tues.-Sat. 10-5, Sun. 1-5; closed hols; free. **Institute of Contemporary Art** (34th & Walnut Sts.) is open Mon.-Fri. 9-5, Sat. & Sun. noon-5; closed hols; free. **Drexel University Museum Collection** (32nd & Chestnut Sts.), 1773 astronomical clock by David Rittenhouse; 19th-C German and French painting; decorative arts; open academic yr, Mon.-Fri. **ILE-IFE Black Humanitarian Center Museum** (7th & Dauphin Sts.), displays on Afro-American heritage; artifacts from the Caribbean and Africa; open Mon.-Fri. 10-6 but phone (684-0352) for tour appointment; adm. **Heritage House** (1346 N Broad St.), exhibits on Afro-American culture; open Mon.-Fri. 9-5; closed hols; free. **New Year's Shooters & Mummers Museum** (2nd St. & Washington Ave.) traces history of the city's famous New Year's Day Parade; exhibits, recordings, audiovisual presentations; open Mon.-Sat. 9:30-6, Sun. noon-5; adm.

City Hall (Broad & Market Sts.), grand eclectic design influenced by the Louvre; topped with 37-ft-high statue of William Penn; lavish interior; statues, portraits; frescos, mosaics, intricate ceilings, 4 octagonal stairwells; observation tower; guided tours Mon.-Fri. at 10; open daily 9-4; free. **Philadelphia-Baltimore-Washington Stock Exchange** (17th & Sansom Sts. at Stock Exchange Pl.), built 1790; visitor gallery open by appointment Mon.-Fri. 10-4; closed hols; free. **St. George's United Methodist Church** (235 N 4th St.), oldest Methodist church in U.S.; site of ordination of first black Methodist minister in 1799; Methodist memorabilia; open daily 10-4; free. **Cathedral of SS. Peter and Paul** (18th St. & Franklin Pkwy) is based on Lombard Church of St. Charles in Rome; open daily. **Masonic Temple** (1 N Broad St.), built 1873 with lodge rooms in Corinthian, Norman, Gothic, Italian Renaissance, other styles; museum; guided tours Mon.-Fri., several times daily; closed hols. **Ukrainian Catholic Cathedral of the Immaculate Conception** (830 N

Franklin St.), impressive Byzantinestyle church; gold dome inset with stained-glass windows; icons, mosaics, wall painting; open daily. **Congregation Rodeph Shalom** (615 N Broad St.), built 1927 in Byzantine style; interesting painted walls; bronze doors of the Ark; archives of Philadelphia Jewish community; open Mon.-Fri. 9-4. **Chapel of Four Chaplains** (1855 N Broad at Berks Sts.), interfaith, honors 4 chaplains who went down off Greenland in 1943; murals; revolving altars; open early Sept.-July, Sun.-Fri. 9-4; closed hols; free. **Church of St. James the Less** (3227 W Clearfield St.), replica of 13th-C Gothic parish church in Cambridgeshire, England; fine stained-glass windows; open daily.

    Old Fort Mifflin (Ft. Mifflin Rd., near International Airport on Delaware River), begun 1772 by the British, was used by patriots in 1777 to protect the river from the British; military and craft displays on Sun.; open Memorial Day-Labor Day, daily, noon-4; rest of yr, Sun. 2-4; closed hols; adm.

    Fairmount Park (on banks of Schuylkill River, NW of Philadelphia Museum of Art) contains handsome mansions of wealthy Philadelphians abandoned during a late-19th-C typhoid fever scare; all restored, authentically furnished; most open daily 10-5, but may be closed hols or other days; brochures, schedule of hrs, and guided tours are available from Park Houses Office, Philadelphia Museum of Art; sm adm to each: **Cedar Grove** (Lansdowne Dr.), 1748 Quaker farmhouse enlarged in 1799; William and Mary, Queen Anne, Chippendale, other outstanding furnishings, some made in the city. **Sweetbriar** (Lansdowne Dr.), 1797 Adamesque estate built by a philanthropist who was patron of Audubon; elegant; many original furnishings. **Strawberry Mansion** (33rd & Dauphin Sts.), named for the strawberries that grew here; built 1797 in Federal style by a Quaker judge; a later owner added Greek Revival wings in 1820; fine woodwork; Federal, Regency, Empire furnishings; antique toys; early American Tucker porcelain. **Woodford Mansion** (33rd & Dauphin Sts.), 1756 dwelling where Benjamin Franklin was a frequent guest; enlarged by a Tory who entertained Lord Howe during the 1777 British occupation of the city; handsome painted rooms; exceptional furnishings include English Delftware, fine locally made pieces. **Lemon Hill** (E River Dr. at Boat House Row), named for lemon trees developed in the greenhouse; built 1799-1800 by Robert Morris, who helped finance the Revolutionary War; curved floating staircase and 3 oval rooms. **Mount Pleasant** (Mt. Pleasant Dr.), a 1762 Georgian home, was thought by John Adams to be the most elegant home in Pennsylvania; built during the height of Chippendale fashion in 1762 by a Scots sea captain; fine crafted woodwork; period furnishings; Benedict Arnold bought it as a wedding gift for his bride but was convicted of treason before they could move in. Also in Fairmount Park are: **Japanese Exhibition House** (Lansdowne Dr. & Belmont Ave.), authentically furnished Japanese home with garden; tea ceremony performed daily with explanation; open June-Aug. daily 10-5; Sept.-May, Wed.-Sat. 10-5, Sun. 1-5; sm adm. **Grant's Cabin** (E end of Girard Ave. bridge), a log hut occupied by Gen. Grant at City Point, Va., during the last days of the Civil War.

Germantown (E of Fairmount Park), settled 1683 by Germans seeking religious and political freedom, on land provided by William Penn; among historic buildings are: **Cliveden** (6401 Germantown Ave.), elegant Georgian home built 1767 for Supreme Court Chief Justice Benjamin Chew; when the British occupied it during the 1777 battle of Germantown, colonial forces were unable to breach its sturdy stone walls; Chew family furnishings created by 18th-early-19th-C local craftsmen; open daily 10-4; closed Dec. 25; adm. **Deshler-Morris House** (5442 Germantown Ave.), called the "Germantown White House," was occupied by Washington in the summers of 1793 and 1794, and by Gen. Howe in 1777; period furnishings; open Tues.-Sun. 9-5; closed hols; sm adm. **Stenton Mansion** (18th St. between Windrim & Courtland Sts.), built 1723-30 by William Penn's secretary, hosted Washington on Aug. 13, 1777 and Gen. Howe for the battle of Germantown; period furnishings; open Tues.-Sat. 1-5; closed hols; sm adm. **Germantown Historical Society** (5214 Germantown Ave.), in a 1772 dwelling, conducts annual tours of homes (June) and will arrange individual tours other times of yr; open Tues., Thurs., Sat. 1-5; closed hols; they can advise you on hours for 1801 **Loudoun House** (4650 Germantown Ave.), 1744 **Grumblethorpe** (5267 Germantown Ave.), costume displays in **Clarkson-Watson House** (5275 Germantown Ave.). **Germantown Mennonite Church** (6121 Germantown Ave.), founded 1690, is open Tues.-Fri. 10-12, 2-5. **German Society of Pennsylvania** (611 Spring Garden St.) has a library of material on the German heritage; open Wed., Sat. 1-5; Thurs. 5-7:30; closed July-Aug.

Andalusia (E on US 13 to just S or SR 63), imposing Greek Revival home of Nicholas Biddle on the Delaware River; open by appointment; write: Reservations, 6401 Germantown Ave., Philadelphia 19144. **Pennsbury Manor** (8 m E on US 13 to Bristol, then follow signs 5 m NE) is a re-creation of William Penn's 1683 estate on the Delaware; 17th-C furnishings; smokehouse, brewhouse, other outbuildings on 40-acre site; barge; livestock; open Mon.-Sat. 9-4:30; closed hols; sm adm. **Historic Fallsington** (9½ m E off US 1, then ½ m SE), a charming enclave in an industrial area, grew around a Friends Meeting House where William Penn worshiped; handsome stone houses include 1790 **Stage Coach Tavern**, a stop on the New York-Philadelphia line, with sign painted by Edward Hicks; 1789 **Burges-Lippincott House** with period furnishings; 1685 **Moon-Williamson House** is of logs, with traces of Swedish printed books, hand-illuminated songbooks, religious music (*Vorspiel,* a religious pageant incorporating the community's compositions, is presented in summer). The community declined after the Revolution, partly a result of typhus contracted while nursing soldiers after the Battle of Brandywine, and partly because of celibacy, but was not dissolved until 1934. Chapel, Almonry, Print Shop, residences, other buildings are restored; open May-Oct., Mon.-Sta. 8:30-5, Sun. 1-5; Nov.-Apr., Mon.-Sat. 9-4:30, Sun. 1-4:30; closed hols; sm adm.

LEWISBURG: Union County Historical Society Museum (in County Courthouse) has hand-drawn maps, antique dolls, local historic relics; open Mon.-Sat. 9-5; closed hols; free. **Fort Augusta** (9 m SE on SR 147 to 1150 N Front St., Sunbury) is a miniature replica of a frontier fort; open Tues.-Sat. 9-4:30, Sun. 1-4:30; closed hols; free. **Priestley House** (7 m S on US 15, then NE off US 11), built 1794, was last home of English clergyman Joseph Priestly who supported the Revolution; museum describes his discovery of oxygen; open Tues.-Sat. 9-4:30, Sun. 1-4:30; closed hols; sm adm. **Warrior Run Church** (13 m N on SR 147) is a lovely Greek Revival design; interesting cemetery.

MEADVILLE: Baldwin-Reynolds House Museum (639 Terrace St.), 1843 home of Supreme Court Justice Henry Baldwin; Indian artifacts, early medical equipment, other historic exhibits; open Memorial Day-Labor Day, Wed., Sat., Sun. 2-5; adm. **Bentley Hall** (Allegheny College campus, N Main St.), built 1824, is one of the finest Colonial-style buildings in the country; open academic yr, Tues.-Sat. 1:30-5, Sun. 2-4; free. **Venango County Museum** (32 m SE on US 322 to 415 12th St., Franklin) has models of frontier forts Venango and Machault; frontier weapons; memorabilia of John Wilkes Booth; open Apr.-Nov., Tues.-Sun. 1-5; closed Easter, Thnks; free. **Pioneer Cemetery** (Otter & 15th Sts.) graves date back to 1795. **Farmers Market** (12th St.) operates Wed. & Sat. mornings. **Drake Well Memorial Park** (27 m E on SR 27 to Titusville, then 1 m SE on SR 8), on site of first successful drilled oil well in the world (1859); full-size operating replica; museum of history of the state's oil boom; open Mon.-Sat. 9-4:30, Sun. 1-4:30; closed hols; sm adm. **Pithole City** (31 m E on SR 27, then 7 m S off SR 227, just N of Plumer), oil boom town of 1865, had 15,000 residents, was abandoned 2 years later.

NEW HOPE: Charming town, long an artist colony; mule-drawn barge trips (New St., S end of town) on the Delaware Canal (daily in summer, weekends in fall); excursions on steam train (32 W Bridge St.) in Victorian coaches (daily in summer, weekends rest of yr). Among many old buildings are: **Parry Mansion** (S Main & Ferry Sts.), an 1874 stone house built by the owner of New Hope Mills; restored to show evolution of upper-middle-class taste 1775-1900; open in summer, Wed.-Sun. 1-4; donation. **Parry Barn** (opposite) is open as a commercial art gallery. **Old Franklin Print Shop** (40 S Main St.) houses 1860 hand press; open daily 10-5; closed Thnks, Dec. 25; free.

PHILADELPHIA: Tourist Center (jct Franklin Pkwy, 16th St., JFK Blvd.) offers brochures for self-guided or guided walking tours of historic sites; the 150-m Liberty Trail auto loop; industrial tours (most require advance notice); commercial tours (several originate here); carriage tours (originate here or at Independence Hall); river cruises (in summer, from Penn's Landing); special events; open late May-early Sept., Mon.-Fri. 8:45 am-9 pm, Sat. & Sun. 8:45-5; rest of yr, daily 9-5; closed Dec. 25. Most attractions surround Independence Mall or are clustered along route of Culture Loop Bus that runs from Independence National Historic Park along tree-lined Benjamin Franklin Blvd. to the zoo (34th & Girard Ave.); buses run frequently, daily; for a small fee, you can get on and off all day. Good view of historic district from observation deck of **Penn Mutual Life Insurance Co.** (510 Walnut St. at 5th St.); check for schedule, but usually open mid-May-late Oct. daily 10 am-9 pm; rest of yr, Wed.-Sun. daily 10-5; closed Jan. 1, Dec. 25; adm.

Independence National Historic Park covers the few blocks (2nd-6th Sts., Chestnut to Walnut Sts.) where the U.S. was created and from which it was governed in its formative years; here the First and Second Continental Congresses gathered, and the Declaration of Independence, Articles of Confederation, Constitution, and Bill of Rights were adopted. The **Visitor Center** (3rd & Chestnut Sts.) provides maps, information, audiovisual program, special events and activities; it is open daily 9 am-8 pm, free, as are the following except as noted: **Liberty Bell** (Independence Mall) in a glass pavilion. **Independence Hall** (Chestnut & 5th Sts.), Pennsylvania's State House; used by Second Continental Congress 1775-83 and Federal Constitutional Convention 1787; in restored Assembly Room are inkstand used in signing the Declaration of Independence and "rising sun" chair in which Washington sat while the Constitution was drafted. **Congress Hall** (Chestnut & 6th Sts.), restored with legislative rooms; where Congress met 1790-1800; Washington (second term) and Adams were inaugurated here. **Old City Hall** (Chestnut & 5th Sts.), where first Supreme Court met, 1791-1800. **American Philosophical Society Building** (rear of Independence Hall) is home of America's oldest (1743) learned society, founded by Benjamin Franklin; not open. **Second U.S. Bank** (420 Chestnut St. at 5th St.), used as U.S. Customs House 1845-1934; art exhibits. **New Hall** (Chestnut & 4th Sts.), reconstructed building housing U.S. Marine Corps Memorial Museum; open daily influence; **Gillingham General Store** (on the square) has maps for self-guiding tours; guide available (sm fee) mid-Mar.-mid-Nov., Wed.-Sun. 1-5; free.

Bryn Athyn Cathedral (4½ m N on SR 232 in Bryn Athyn), outstanding Gothic church; fine stained-glass windows; open Sat.-Thurs. 9-noon, 2-5. **Beth Sholom Congregation** (½ m N on SR 611 to Old York & Foxcroft Rds., Elkins Park), only synagogue designed by Frank Lloyd Wright; triangular structure represents Mt. Sinai and the communion of God and man; triangle repeated in interior details; open Sun.-Thurs. **Alverthorpe Gallery** (2 m N on SR 611 to 511 Meetinghouse Rd., Jenkintown), miniatures, prints, drawings, illustrated books from 15th-C to present; open by appointment (phone 884-0466) Oct.-May, Mon.-Fri. 9-5. **Graeme Park** (8 m N on SR 611, just N of Horsham), unusual and charming home built 1722; originally a liquor mill; lovers' ghosts are said to dance over the pond at night; open Tues.-Sat. 9-4:30, Sun. 1-4:30; closed hols; sm adm. **Hope Lodge** (2½ m N at 555 Bethlehem Pike, Whitemarsh), stately Georgian manor believed built 1750 as a gift for a marriage that never took place; named for later owners (the family of Hope Diamond fame); during the Revolution it was a center of intrigue and hq for Gen. Nathanael Greene; open Tues.-Sat. 9-4:30, Sun. 1-5; closed hols; sm adm. **Fort Washington State Park** (3 m N off Bethlehem Pike), commemorating Washington's N defense line against the British in 1777, consists of 3 units: Fort Hill Historic Site (N of Turnpike); with earth reboubt, was the W anchor point of Washington's line; Clifton House (473 Bethlehem Pike), built 1801 as Sandy Run Tavern, houses a library, museum, and hq of Ft. Washington Historical Society (open Sun. 2-4); Militia Hill (S of Turnpike), defense line of the Pennsylvania Militia.

Mill Grove (13½ m NW on I-76 to SR 363, then 5½ m N to Egypt Rd., then 2 m W on Pawlings Rd.), former estate of John James Audubon; mementos, prints; open Tues.-Sun. 10-5; grounds open sunrise-sunset; closed Jan. 1, Thnks, Dec. 25; free. **Buten Museum of Wedgwood** (8 m NW on SR 23 & Montgomery Ave. to 246 N Bowman Ave., Merion), in a Tudor-style mansion; more than 10,000 pieces of Wedgwood pottery, porcelain, stoneware 1759-present; gallery talks; open Tues.-Thurs. 2-5, Sat. 10-1; adm. Also in Merion is **Barnes Foundation** (off Old Lancaster Rd. at 300 N Latch's Lane), in French-style chateau, the superb collection of crochety manufacturer of the patent cold remedy Argyrol, Dr. Albert C. Barnes; he once bought 50 Soutines in a day; works (mostly French but some 20th-C American) include 200 Renoirs, 60 Cezannes, 60 Matisses, 25 Picassos; Barnes' will prohibits the loan or reproduction of these works; admission is controlled: Sept.-June, Fri. & Sat. 9:30-4:30, 200 visitors are admitted, 100 by reservation; Sun. 1-4:30, 100 visitors are admitted, 50 by reservation; write for reservations or phone 667-0290; adm. **Haverford College** (8½ m NW off US 30 in Haverford) was founded 1833 by the Society of Friends; 1833 Founders Hall, typical of Quaker architecture; Magill Library, material on Quakers; Morris Cricket Library, displays and reference works on the game (open Mon., Wed., Fri. 2-4 during academic year; free).

Ridley Creek State Park (16 m W off SR 3) preserves several buildings of 18th-C village of Sycamore Mills; **Visitor Center,** 1789 stone farmhouse expanded into Hunting Hill Mansion in 1914, offers historical, natural history exhibits and programs. **Chester County Historical Society Museum** (27 m W on SR 3 to 225 N High St., W Chester), offers early pewter, glass, porcelain, furnishings; kitchen, shop, schoolroom; archives; open Mon.-Wed., 1-5, Thurs. & Fri. 10-5; closed hols & Aug.; free. The Society maintains: 1704 Brinton House (5 m S on US 202), a superb Colonial restoration, open May-Oct., Tues., Thurs., Fri. 1-4, adm; 1787 David Townsend House (225 N Matlack St.), open May-Oct. by appointment; free. **Brandywine Battlefield State Historical Park** (16 m W on US 1 to jct US 202, 322, near Chadds Ford) contains Lafayette and Washington's hq (open June-Sept., Tues.-Sun. 10-5; Oct.-May, Sat., Sun., hols noon-6:30); interpretive markers on site of Washington's defeat; park open daily in daylight; free. **Brandywine River Museum** (17 m W on US 1 to Hoffman's Mill Rd., Chadds Ford), in restored 1864 gristmill; large collection of works by the Wyeth family, Howard Pyle, Brandywine Valley artists, other American painters; open daily 9:30-4:30; closed Dec. 25; adm.

Morton Homestead (4 m SW on SR 291, then 1½ m N on SR 420 to Darby Creek) was built 1654 by the Swedish grandfather of John Morton; modeled on Finnish log cabins, introduced by Finns who accompanied Swedes to this area; 17th-C furnishings; open Tues.-Sat. 9-4:30, Sun. 1-5; closed hols; free. **Governor Printz Park** (4½ m SW off SR 291 in Essington, Tinicum Island) was site of the state's earliest settlement, Upland, in 1638, established by the Swedish Trading Co.; foundations of Printzenhof (residence and capitol); open daily in daylight; free. **Penn Memorial Landing Stone** (7½ m SW on SR 291 to Penn & Front Sts., Chester) marks the spot where William Penn landed 1682 to colonize the land granted him by King Charles II; he named the settlement after the English Quaker center of Chester; also in town are **Widener College** (library with good regional material) and **Old Swedish Burial Ground** (graves of John Morton, Swedish settlers); 1724 home of Quaker artist Benjamin West is on Swarthmore College campus (4 m N on SR 320. **Caleb Pusey House** (7½ m SW on SR 291 to Chester, then 2 m N to 15 Race St., Upland) was 1683 home of William Penn's good friend and mill manager; restored to reflect 17th-C way of life; 11 acres of the original plantation include 1790 log house, 1849 stone schoolhouse (now a museum), other buildings; open Tues.-Sun. 1-5; closed Jan. 1, Thnks, Dec. 25; sm adm.

PITTSBURGH: Visitor Information Center (3001 Jenkins Arcade in Gateway Center) provides maps, literature, and a film on cultural attractions and on the urban renaissance that resulted in the famed Golden Triangle; open Mon.-Fri. 9:30-5, Sat. & Sun. 9:30-3; closed hols. Sightseeing boat trips on Gateway Clippers leave from Monongahela Wharf, foot of Wood St. (Apr.-Oct. daily). Cable railways to the top of Mt. Washington offer panoramic views: 1870 **Monongahela Inclined Plane** (W Carson St., near Smithfield St. bridge), Mon.-Sat. 5:30-12:45 am, Sun. & hols 8:45 am-midnight; sm adm. **Duquesne Inclined Plane** (W Carson St., SW of Ft. Pitt bridge), Mon.-Sat. 5:30-1 am, Sun. 7-1 am; sm adm.

Point State Park (foot of Ft. Duquesne & Ft. Pitt Blvds.), where Allegheny and Monongahela rivers meet to form the Ohio, was site of 1758 British victory over the French that determined the Colonies would remain British; 1764 Fort Pitt Blockhouse (open Tues.-Sat. 9-5, Sun. 2-5); 2 of the original bastions, restored, house a museum devoted to local frontier history and the struggle for control of the Ohio Valley (open Mon.-Sat. 9:30-4:30, Sun. noon-4:30; closed Jan. 1, Election Day, Thnks, Dec. 25; sm adm); military drills on summer Sun. afternoons; riverfront promenade; fountain; area open daily.

Intriguing exhibits on the evolution of the city's architecture are offered by **Pittsburgh History and Landmarks Foundation** in the Old Post Office Museum (701 Allegheny Sq W), an 1897 building in Italian Renaissance style; also exhibits on toys, clothing, period styles; painting and sculpture; open Tues.-Fri. 10-4:30, Sat. & Sun. 1-4:30; closed hols; adm. They can provide you with information on the city's modern architecture and landmarks such as **Syria Mosque** (Bigelow Blvd., Oakland Civic Center), interesting Arabic architecture, and **Allegheny County Courthouse** (Grant St. & 5th Ave.), outstanding Norman Romanesque building by Henry Hobson Richardson, with murals in lobby (open Mon.-Fri. 8:30-4:30, Sat. noon-4:30; closed hols; free). **Historical Society of Western Pennsylvania** (4338 Bigelow Blvd.), Pittsburgh and other early glass, furnishings, paintings, books and documents; open Tues.-Fri. 9:30-4:30, Sat. 9:30-12:30; closed hols; free. **Allegheny County Soldiers & Sailors Memorial Hall** (Bigelow Blvd. & 5th Ave.) has Civil War relics, uniforms, weapons; open Mon.-Fri. 9-4; Sat., Sun., hols 1-4; free.

University of Pittsburgh (Bigelow Blvd. & 5th Ave.) features the 42-story Cathedral of Learning, with a 36th-floor overlook and 19 Nationality Classrooms representing the cultural heritage of the city's ethnic groups; **Visitor Center** in Commons Room provides campus maps, student guides, film; open Mon.-Fri. 9-5, Sat. 11-5; closed hols; free. Also on campus are: French Gothic Heinz Chapel, with stone carvings, stained-glass windows, and Stephen Foster Memorial with memorabilia of the composer (open Mon.-Fri. 9-4; closed hols; free). Henry Clay Frick Fine Arts Bldg. features a cloister; library; open Tues.-Sun. 1-5; closed July, hols; free.

Frick Art Museum (7227 Reynolds St. at Homewood Ave.), Italian Renaissance, French Rococo, other European works in intimate settings in Italian Renaissance building; Chinese porcelains, French decorative arts, tapestries, sculpture; open Wed.-Fri. 10-4, Sat. 10-5, Sun. 1-5; closed hols, Aug.; free. **Carnegie Institute** (4400 Forbes Ave.) offers: **Museum of Art,** with fine 19-20th-C French paintings, a few Old Masters, contemporary art, large collection of decorative arts. **Museum of Natural History,** dinosaur hall, wildlife and botany displays, marine exhibits; primitive works from around the world. Both open Tues.-Sun. 10-5; closed hols; adm. **Arts & Crafts Center** (5th & Shady Aves. in Mellon Park), changing exhibits; works of local artists; open Tues.-Sat. 10-5, Sun. 2-5; closed hols; free. **Buhl Planetarium & Institute of Popular Science** (Allegheny Sq. N) offers scientific exhibits, shows; spring science fair; open Mon.-Sat. 1-5, 7-10, Sun. 1-10; adm.

Old Economy Village (17 m NW on SR 65 to Great House Sq., NW of Ambridge), 3rd and final communal settlement attempted by the Harmony Society under the leadership of German-born George Rapp; after experiments at Harmony, Pa., and New Harmony, Ind., failed, Harmonists established a successful textile industry after moving here in 1825; they also had a winery, distillery, brick-making plant, lumber mill, flour mill, craft shops. Although the community was said to be worth a million dollars in its prime, it declined because of celibacy (Harmonists believed the world would end in their lifetime) and poor investments, and was dissolved in 1905. Among restored buildings, furnished with community artifacts, are: Baker House, one of some 100 austere communal residences built to the same floor plan; Great House, in which George Rapp lived more comfortably than did his followers; Feast Hall, where the entire community of 1000 could gather at meals; garden grotto for meditation; shops; wine cellars; granary. Open Mon.-Sat. 8:30-5, Sun. 1-5; closed hols; sm adm. Just N is **Logan Cemetery** (on SR 65), an Indian stronghold during the French and Indian War, with Revolutionary-era graves.

David Bradford House (23 m S on I-79 to 175 S Main St., Washington), 1788 home of a leader in the Whiskey Rebellion, which was centered in this town; open Tues.-Sat. 9-noon, 1-4:30, Sun. 1-4:30; closed hols; sm adm. **Meadowcroft Village** (40 m SW on SR 50 in Avella), settled 1795; log cabins, general store, other buildings moved here to recreate the village; exhibits of Americana; open May-Nov., Mon.-Sat. 9-5, Sun. 1-6;

adm. **Bushy Run Battlefield** (15 m SE via SR 130, 993) is site of Chief Pontiac's defeat in 1763; museum with interpretive displays; open Tues.-Sat. 9-4:30, Sun. 1-4:40; closed hols; sm adm. Park open daily, free. **Westmoreland County Museum of Art** (23 m SE on I-76, US 30 to 221 N Main St., Greensburg), period rooms with Reynolds, Gainsborough, Constable, other English paintings; American works by Whistler and others; open Wed.-Sat. 10-5, Tues. 1-9, Sun. 2-6; closed hols; free. Also in Greensburg is **St. Clair Monument** (in St. Clair Park on Maple Ave.), marking grave of Gen. St. Clair.

POTTSTOWN: Pottsgrove Mansion (W on US 422 on W High St.), home of ironmaster and town founder John Potts; when built 1752, it was considered so grand for the frontier that people walked miles to see it; Washington is believed to have stayed here in 1777; open Tues.-Sat. 9-4:30, Sun. 1-4:30; closed hols; sm adm. **Pollock Auto Showcase** (70 S Franklin St.), autos, motors, accessories; open Mon.-Fri. 9-4, Sat. 9-3; closed hols; adm. **Boyertown Museum of Historic Vehicles** (6 m NW via SR 100, 73 to Warwick St., Boyertown), autos, horse-drawn vehicles, fire trucks dating from late 1700s; open Mon.-Fri. 8-4; also June-Aug., Sat. & Sun. 1-4; closed hols; free. **Hopewell Village National Historic Site** (9 m W on SR 724, 5 m S on SR 345 in French Creek State Park) preserves an ironmaking community that produced pig iron 1770-1883. **Visitor Center** offers exhibits, slide talk; summer living history programs. Self-guiding trail shows you the entire iron-making operation plus authentically furnished company store, tenant houses, ironmaster's house; open daily 9-5; closed Jan. 1, Dec. 25; free.

QUAKERTOWN: Settled 1712, this was site of 1798 Hot Water Rebellion, when housewives went after Federal tax assessors with pots of hot water and troops had to be sent in. It was also a station on the Underground Railroad. **Liberty Hall,** small stone house with secret storage area where valuables were hidden from British troops; temporary hiding place for the Liberty Bell on its journey to Allentown in 1777. Here also are **Red Lion Inn** (4 S Main St.), built 1750; **Quakertown Historical Museum** (44 S Main St.); **Country Store** (1313 W Broad St.); inquire locally for hrs.

READING: The Pagoda (via Skyline Blvd to summit of Mt. Penn), a Japanese-style building erected as hotel in 1908; now an observation tower; open, weather permitting, Apr.-Nov. 9 am-11 pm; rest of yr, 11-11; free. **Historical Society of Berks County** (940 Centre Ave.), interesting products of early iron industry; old vehicles; decorative arts; open Tues.-

Sat. 9-4; also Oct.-May, Sun. 2-5; closed hols; free. **Reading Public Museum & Art Gallery** (500 Museum Rd.), American paintings, sculpture, Indian artifacts, science exhibits; open July-Aug., Mon.-Fri. . 9-4, Sun. 2-5; Sept.- June, Mon.-Fri. 9-5, Sat. 9-noon, Sun. 2-5; closed hols; free.

Daniel Boone Homestead (7 m E on US 422 to Baumstown, then N on Boone Rd.) was on the edge of wilderness when Boone was born here in 1734; he got his first rifle at age 10 and learned to hunt and trap; in 1750 the family moved to N Carolina; stone house restore to reflect 19th-C life; blacksmith shop, smokehouse, other buildings; open Mon.-Sat. 9-4:30, Sun. 1-4:30; closed hols; sm adm.

Pennsylvania Dutch Folk Culture Center (21 m NE on US 222, SR x43 to Lenhartsbille), local arts and crafts; schoolhouse on grounds; open June- Aug. daily 10-5; May & Sept.-Oct., Sat. & Sun. 10-5; adm. **Conrad Weiser State Historic Park** (15 m W on US 422), small stone house built 1729 by Pennsylvania's ambassador to the Indians; now a museum; open Tues.-Sun. 8:30-5 in summer, 9-4:30 rest of yr; closed hols; free.

SCRANTON: Iron Furnaces (291 Cedar Ave.), built by the Scranton family to employ anthracite coal instead of charcoal, revolutionized the industry and made the city prosperous; partially restored furnaces that operated 1840-1902 are open Wed.-Sun. 9-4:30, closed hols; free. **Nay Aug Park** (Arthur Ave. & Mulberry St. in E Scranton) offers Brooks Model Mine, demonstrating mining of anthracite coal; open mid-June-Aug., Tues.-Sun. 10-5. Also in park is Everhart Museum of Natural History, Science & Art, mounted birds and reptiles; American mammals; anthracite fossils; coal mining display; painting and sculpture; Oriental art objects; American Indian arts; American folk art; Dorflinger glass made 1852-1921; planetarium; open Tues.-Sat. 10-5, Sun. 2-5; closed hols & Good Fri.; free.

World Shrine (6 m S to Main St., Duryea), with stones from 32 foreign countries, is a memorial to Polish immigrants.

SOMERSET: Somerset Historical Center (5 m N on Old US 219), log cabin, sugar house, exhibits on history of Laurel Highlands region; open Apr.-Sept., Tues.-Sat. 9:30-4:30, Sun. 1-4:30; closed hols; sm adm.

STATE COLLEGE: Pennsylvania State University, attractive 4900-acre campus in University Park: Old Main (E of Mall), built 1863 and rebuilt 1931; beautiful frescos by Henry Varnum Poor; open Mon.-Fri. 8-5; closed hols. **Museum of Art** (Curtin Rd.), with changing exhibits; open Tues.- Sun. noon-5; closed hols; free. **Earth & Mineral Sciences Museum** (Pollock Rd.), fossils, gems, ores, art gallery; open daily 9-5; closed hols; free. **College of Agriculture** (Ag Hill), with dairy (daily 5 am-9:30 pm), creamery (salesroom Mon.-Sat. 7:30-5:30, Sun. 10-4:30; closed hols); flower gardens (July-Sept.); free.

Boal Mansion (4 m E on US 322 in Boalsburg), built 1789 and enlarged 1798, has European and early American furnishings; antique weapons, glass, porcelain, paintings, vehicles; Christopher Columbus Family Chapel, with 16th-C relics, vestments, paintings; open June-Labor Day daily 10-5; May & after Labor Day-Oct., daily 2-5; adm. Nearby is **Pennsylvania Military Museum,** dioramas of battles; equipment; 28th Division shrine; open Tues.-Sat. 9-4:30, Sun. 1-5; closed hols; sm adm.

STROUDSBURG: Quiet Valley Farm Museum (3 m SW on US 209-Bus, then follow signs), Pennsylvania German farm with 1765 log house, other buildings; family-guided tours; demonstrations of farm skills; open late June-Labor Day, Mon.-Sat. 9:30-5:30, Sun. 1-5:30; adm.

TOWANDA: French Azilum (2½ m E on US 6 to Wysox, then S on SR 187) was founded 1793 by refugees from the French Revolution and slave uprisings in Haiti, and lasted a decade (Napoleon's pardon of emigrants caused many to return home); about 50 log buildings were erected, the largest intended as a refuge for Marie Antoinette; 1836 Laporte-Hagerman House has period furnishings, historical library; cabins being restored; model of the village, displays; open May-Oct., Thurs.-Tues. 1-5; donation. **Tioga Point Museum** (15 m N on US 220 in Spaulding Memorial Bldg, 724 S Main St., Athens), displays on French Azilum, Stephen Foster (who wrote music as a child here); history of canals and railroads; open Mon. 7-9 pm, Wed. & Sat. 2-5; closed hols; donation.

UNIONTOWN: Fort Necessity National Battlefield (11 m SE on US 40), site of 1754 fort built by Washington and named for its strategic location; here Washington fought (and lost) his first major battle, the Battle of Great Meadows, that opened the French and Indian War; the French destroyed the fort; stockade, storehouse, entrenchments reconstructed; **Visitor Center** offers audiovisual program, exhibits on Great Meadows and 1755 Braddock Expedition; open mid-Apr.-mid-Oct. daily 8:30-5 (longer hrs in summer); rest of yr, Sat. & Sun. 8:30-5; closed hols; free. Nearby are: **Mt. Washington Tavern,** stage station built about 1827 on the National Pike (now US 40), the principal artery connecting Atlantic seaboard and Ohio Valley; period furnishings; open same hrs as Visitor Center; closed Jan. 1, Thnks, Dec. 25; free. **Braddock Park,** site of earlier skirmish in which Washington surprised the French; grave of British Gen. Edward Braddock.

Fallingwater (12 m SE on US 40, then 12 m NE on SR 381), dramatic residence designed 1936 by Frank Lloyd Wright; built over a waterfall;

tours Apr.-mid-Nov., Tues.-Sun. 10-4; adm; reservations advised (write Kaufmann Conservation on Bear Run, RD 1, Mill Run 15464). **Friendship Hill** (11 m SW on SR 21, then 7 m S on SR 166) was home of Albert Gallatin, Sect. of the Treasury under Jefferson; 35-room mansion with stunning interiors; open May or June-Oct. or Nov.; inquire locally for hrs. **Brownsville** (12 m NW on US 40) offers; **Nemacolin (Bowman's) Castle** (Front St.), with antique furnishings, historical displays; open Memorial Day-mid-Sept., Tues.-Sun. 1-5; spring & fall, Sat & Sun. 1-5; closed hols; adm. First Cast-Iron Bridge (Market St.) in U.S., built 1839 over Dunlap Creek.

VALLEY FORGE STATE PARK is a memorial to the 11,000 soldiers of the Continental Army, 3000 of whom died, who spent the bitter winter of 1777-78 here, starving and ill-clothed. **Reception Center** provides information and tapes for auto tours (Apr.-Oct. daily 9-2:30); narrated bus tours leave from here (Apr.-Oct. daily 9-3). **Observation Tower** (Mount Joy) offers a panoramic view. **Washington's Headquarters,** 1759 stone farmhouse; period furnishings. Valley Forge Park **Museum** houses encampment relics. Also here: Grand Parade Ground where Baron von Steuben drilled the troops; reproduction of field hospital; 1705 schoolhouse that served as a hospital; National Memorial Arch; reconstructed soldiers' huts. Park and most buildings open daily 9-5; closed Dec. 25; free. Museum open Mon.-Sat. 9-4:30, Sun. 1-5; closed Dec. 25; free. **Washington Memorial Chapel** (on SR 363 outside the park), outstanding Gothic chapel; stained-glass windows depict the nation's history; ornate woodwork; museum with relics of Valley Forge (sm adm); open daily 9-4:30; closed Dec. 25; free.

WASHINGTON CROSSING STATE PARK commemorates Washington's crossing of the Delaware with 2400 soldiers in a blinding snowstorm on Christmas night 1776 to launch a surprise attack on the Hessians at Trenton; 1 section is in New Jersey; 2 sections here are: **Bowman's Hill** (2 m S on New Hope on SR 32) with observation tower (open daily 8- sunset); Memorial Flagstaff (near tower) marking graves of unknown Continental Army dead; Thompson-Neely House, 1702 fieldstone farmhouse where Washington is believed to have conferred with aides; period furnishings; grist mill (open Mon.-Sat. 10-5, Sun. 1-5; sm adm). **Washington Crossing** (7 m S of New Hope on SR 32), with park hq in 1757 Taylor House (open Sun.-Fri. 8:30-5, Sat. 8:30-11); a statue of Washington at the point of embarkation; Concentration Valley, where the troops assembled; Old Ferry Inn, where Washington dined; Memorial Building, with full-size copy of Leutze's painting, *Washington Crossing the Delaware,* and David Library of the American Revolution (open daily 9-5).

WILKES-BARRE: Named for John Wilkes and Isaac Barre, members of the British Parliament who were colonial sympathizers (a monument to them is on Public Sq.), this city was settled 1769 by pioneers from Connecticut; soon the entire Wyoming Valley was scene of the Pennamite-Yankee War between Connecticut and Pennsylvania, both of which claimed the land; although Congress ruled in favor of Pennsylvania in 1782, conflict continued until 1800.

Wyoming Historical & Geological Society Museum (69 S Franklin St.), historical exhibits; displays on prosperous era of anthracite coal-mining; open Wed., Fri., Sat. 10-5; closed hols; free.

Swetland Homestead (7 m NE on US 11 to 885 Wyoming Ave. in Wyoming), begun 1797, shows changing way of life of one family who lived here until 1864; open mid-June-Labor Day, Tues.-Sun. 1-5; sm adm. **Wyoming Massacre Site** (4th St. & Wyoming Ave., Wyoming) commemorates massacre of settlers by Iroquois in 1778 after the fall of Forty Fort; the fort, guarded by some 300 frontiersmen, was attacked by 1200 Indians and whites led by a Tory colonel who called himself Indian Butler and a Seneca called Queen Esther; the defeat of the frontiersmen left Wyoming Valley settlers unprotected, and Indians spread throughout the valley, killing and pillaging.

Frances Slocum State Park (10 m NW) was named for a Quaker girl kidnapped by Delaware Indians in 1778, when she was 5; when her brothers located her 50 years later, she was living with Indians in Indiana, had married and had 4 children, had adopted an Indian name and ways; she refused to return home and died in 1838 at New Reserve, Indiana, where her grave is marked and a state park is named for her.

WILLIAMSPORT: Lycoming County Historical Museum (858 W 4th St.), Indian and settler artifacts; grist mill and workshop displays; lumber industry; open Memorial Day-Labor Day, Tues.-Fri. 10-4, Sun. 2-5; rest of yr, Tues.-Sat. 10-4, Sun. 2-5; closed hols; sm adm.

YORK: This city was the national capital Sept. 30, 1777-June 27, 1778, during British occupation of Philadelphia; here Congress received news of Burgoyne's surrender, adopted Articles of Confederation, received Baron von Steuben and Lafayette. **Tourist Information Center** (jct US 30, SR 24, or write: 1455 Mt. Zion Rd., zip 17402) or **Chamber of Commerce** (13 E Market St.), both open Mon.-Fri. 8:30-5, provide maps for self-guiding tours of Colonial York (King to Philadelphia Sts., Pine St. to Pershing Ave.). **Museum of Historical Society of York County** (250 E Market St.) features reproductions of the early city; library; open Mon.-Sat. 9-5, Sun. 1-5; closed Jan. 1, Good Fri., Thnks, Dec. 25; sm adm. The Society maintains: **Bonham House** (152 E Market St.), built 1840, reflecting the changing taste of the Bonham family in the 19th-C; glass, silver, bronzes, Oriental pieces. At 157 W Market St. are **General Gates House,** where a conspiracy to overthrow Gen. Washington was thwarted by Lafayette; 1741 **Golden Plough Tavern,** Germanic half-timber structure of medieval appearance; 1812 **Log House,** typical of austere homes built by German settlers.

Currier & Ives Museum (43 W King at Beaver Sts.), in 19th-C mansion; 300 original prints; period furnishings; open Mon.-Fri. 8:30-5; also June-Aug., Sat. 9-2; closed hols; adm. **York Meeting House** (135 W Philadelphia St. at Pershing Ave.), completed 1776, has been in continuous use by the Society of Friends. **St. John's Episcopal Church** (140 N Beaver St.), the "Liberty Bell," a gift of Queen Caroline, is in the vestibule. **Codorus Furnace** (5 m N on SR 181 to Emigsville, then NE), built 1765, produced cannon and shot for Washington's troops at Valley Forge; restored furnace. **Warrington Friends Meeting House** (14 m NW on SR 74) is a charming stone building begun 1762, still in use. **Little Red Schoolhouse Museum** (12 m W on US 30), built about 1860, restored; open June-Labor Day daily 10-6; spring & fall, Sat. & Sun. 10-6; free. Nearby is Old Holtzschwamm Church; open daily. **Indian Steps Museum** (24 m SE via SR 74, 425), on the Susquehanna River; arrow and spear heads, other Indian artifacts, many imbedded as decorations in masonry and walls; open Apr.-Oct., Tues.-Sun. 10-6; donation.

RHODE ISLAND

BLOCK ISLAND: Block Island Historical Society (Old Town Rd. & Ocean Ave.), with exhibits on island history, is open July-Sept., Mon.-Sat. 11-4; adm. Either here or from Chamber of Commerce you can get a list of historic sites: Indian burial ground; **Settlers' Rock** (Cow Cove), where the first settlers landed 1661; **Palatine Graves** (SW side of island near Dickens Pt.), made famous by Whittier's poem "The Palatine Light." The Palatines had sailed from Rotterdam in 1732, but polluted drinking water killed 300 passengers and crew; only 114 survived the ocean crossing; off Block Island, the ship was wrecked and set afire; only 16 passengers survived the swim to shore. The blazing ship, including a screaming woman who refused to abandon it, is said to be seen as the "Palatine lights" when a storm is brewing.

BRISTOL: The swamp at the foot of Mt. Hope was stronghold of Indian leader King Philip during the 1675-76 King Philip's War that almost annihilated the Narragansett tribe. Although the British burned part of Bristol in 1778, the town emerged from the Revolution as one of the nation's busiest ports, and many America's Cup winners were built in Herreshoff Boatyard here. **Bristol Historical & Preservation Society** (Court St.), in a former jail built of stone from ship ballast; slave ship relics, local artifacts; displays on Gen. Ambrose Burnside and carbine rifle he developed; open Apr.-Dec., Wed. 2:30-5 or by appointment; free. Either here or from Chamber of Commerce (Town Hall), you can obtain a brochure for a walking tour of historic sites; many well-preserved 17-19th-C homes; those along Hope Street particularly notable. **Bristol Art Museum** (Wardwell St.), in building designed as ballroom for adjacent mansion; changing exhibits; open June-Oct., daily 1-5; free. **Haffenreffer Museum of Anthropology** (near jct Metacom Ave. & Tower Rd.), collections from the Americas, Africa, Arctic, Pacific; open June-Aug., Tues.-Sun. 1-4; Sept.-May, Sat. & Sun. 1-4; closed hols & Feb.; free. **Colt State Park** (2½ m NW of SR 114) has a chapel and Coggeshall Farm, restored 18th-C farmhouse and blacksmith shop, a working farm; special events; demonstrations; open July-Aug., Sat. & Sun.; sm adm.

EAST GREENWICH: Kent County Court House (Main & Court Sts.) was built 1750. **Gen. James Mitchell Varnum House & Museum** (57 Pierce St.), home of Revolutionary War officer; period furnishings, museum exhibits; open early June-mid-Sept., Wed., Sun. 1-5; adm.

JAMESTOWN: Capt. Kidd was a visitor and stories of pirate treasure are part of the heritage. **Jamestown Historical Society Museum** (Narragansett Ave.), exhibits on island ferries and domestic life; usually open June-early Sept., Wed.-Sun. 1-4; sm adm. **Fire Museum** (Narragansett Ave.) with antique equipment, open Wed.-Sun. 9-4; 1787 **Windmill** in working order (1½ m N on North Rd.); **Sydney L. Wright Museum of Jamestown Philomenian Society Library** (North Rd.), local Indian artifacts from prehistoric and early settlements (open Mon., Wed., Fri. 10-noon, 1-5, 7-9; Tues. & Thurs. 7-9 pm).

KINGSTON: Main Street retains much 18th-C charm. **Kingston Free Library** (SR 138 & College Rd.) is in 1775 county courthouse; open Mon.-Fri. 10-noon, 1-5; Sat. 9-noon-1-5; closed hols. **Pettaquamscutt Historical Society** (Kingstown Rd.), in 1856 county jail; jail cells, period rooms, historic displays; open Tues., Thurs., Sat. 1-4; closed hols; sm adm. **Helme House** (1319 Kingstown Rd.), art exhibits in 1802 residence; open Tues.- Sun. 2-5; closed hols; sm adm. **Fayerweather House** (SR 138) was built 1820 by a black as his home and smithy; open Tues.-Sat. 11-4; closed hols; sm adm. **University of Rhode Island** (NW of town off SR 138) offers guided campus tours in summer; Watson House (Mon.-Fri. 9-noon,

1-4; open some weekends), restored 1790 farmhouse, and Geology Collection (Green Hall), usually open weekdays 8:30-4:30.

Museum of Primitive Culture (2 m SE off Kingstown Rd. in Peace Dale), utensils, weapons, other artifacts from Africa, South Seas, American Indian tribes; open on request at library (across the street) or post office (next door); free. Nearby is a Daniel Chester French statue of the Hazard family.

NEWPORT: Founded 1639 by victims of religious intolerance in Massachusetts who were shortly joined by Quakers and Jews, Newport became a prime shipbuilding center whose merchants prospered on the African slave run and West Indies trade. In 1779, the British occupied the town, severely damaging its economy, and Newport went into eclipse until after the Civil War, when wealthy families chose it for their lavish mansions and extravagant social life. Cliff Walk, a 3-m path between the mansions and the sea, is a wonderful way to get the feel of Newport in its heyday. Away from mansion row, the town retains much of its colonial seaport appearance; cobblestoned **Bowen's Wharf** (at the waterfront off Thames St.) has been restored; several hundred houses and public buildings built 1675-1820 are still in use. **Visitor Bureau** (93 Thames St.) provides maps for self-guiding tours, information on narrated bus tours and boat trips (from Goat Island Marine); open Memorial Day-Labor Day, daily 9-6. Information also available from: **Preservation Society of Newport County** (Washington Sq.), which sells combination tickets to mansions; open Mon.-Fri. 9-5; closed hols. **Newport Restoration Foundation** (39 Mill St.), which houses Doris Duke's fine collection of early Newport furniture in the Samuel Whitehorne House (Thames St.); inquire for hrs. Operation Clapboard encourages rehabilitation of old buildings, has marked more than 50 of these; most are not open.

Newport Historical Society Museum (82 Touro St.), in house built 1729; Newport silver, porcelain, furniture, Stiegel glass, costumes, paintings; open Tues.-Fri. 9:30-4:30, Sat. 9:30-noon; closed hols; free. **Touro Synagogue** (85 Touro St.), oldest synagogue in the U.S.; architectural gem built 1763; designed by Peter Harrison and considered his masterpiece; open late-June-Labor day, Mon.-Fri. 10-5, Sun. 10-6; rest of yr, Sun. 2-4; open Sat. for services; free.

Old Colony House (Washington Sq.) was the state's original capitol (pineapples, symbol of hospitality, are carved over the door), with the cellar rented out to a brewer; during the Revolution it was a hospital, barracks, and jail; Washington conferred with Rochambeau here on Yorktown strategy in 1781; as a courthouse, in 1842 it was the scene of the Thomas Dorr (Dorr Rebellion) trial for treason; open July-Aug. daily 9:30-noon, 1-4; Sept.-June, Mon.-Sat. 9-noon; closed hols; free.

Wanton-Lyman-Hazard House (17 Broadway), fine 1675 Jacobean house, oldest residence in Newport; period furnishings; open July-Labor Day, daily 10-5; adm. **Capt. John Mawdsley House** (228 Spring at John Sts.), tiny 1860 home, enlarged in mid-18th-C by wealthy merchant; some furnishings are connected with state history; open June-Sept., Tues., Thurs., Sat. 1-5; sm adm. **Newport Artillery Museum** (23 Clarke St.), in 1836 armory; domestic and foreign military costumes; open May-Sept., Tues.-Sun. 11:30-4:30; Oct.-Apr., Sat. 1-4; donation. **Naval & Underseas Museum** (Spring & Church Sts.), artifacts from underwater explorations around the world; open June-Sept., daily 9:30-5; sm adm. **Trinity Church** (Church & Spring Sts.), built 1726 and modeled on the London churches of Christopher Wren; gold bishop's mitre atop the spire; unusual 3-tier wineglass pulpit; open mid-June-mid-Sept. daily 10-5. **St. Mary's Church** (Spring St.), site of Jacqueline Bouvier-John F. Kennedy wedding. **Brick Market** (Washington Sq.), designed 1762 by Peter Harrison, houses Historic Newport Reproductions of furniture, silver, glass, other antiques; open Mon.-Sat. 10-5; closed hols; free. **Hunter House** (54 Washington St.), built 1748, is a superb illustration of pre-Revolutionary prosperity and culture in Newport; Admiral de Ternay, commander of French naval forces during the Revolution, used it for his hq; elegant interior detailing; Rhode Island-made furniture (Townsend, Goddard), silver, china, paintings; open Memorial Day-Sept., daily 10-5; adm. **H.M.S. Rose** (King's Dock, foot of America's Cup Ave.), reconstructed British frigate that blocked Rhode Island harbors during the Revolution; naval displays; open Apr.-Dec. daily 10-sunset; Jan.-Mar., weather permitting, Sat. & Sun. 10-sunset; adm.

Mt. Zion Black Museum (8 Bellevue Ave.), in foyer of a pre-Civil War church; exhibits on black history and culture; open Memorial Day-Labor Day 9-4; free. **Redwood Library & Athenaeum** (50 Bellevue Ave.), designed by Peter Harrison; early books and portraits; George Berkeley was one of the founders; open Mon.-Sat. 10-6; closed hols; free. **Art Association of Newport** (76 Bellevue Ave.), built 1863 in the style of English half-timbered homes; interesting interior detail; open for special shows Mon.- Sat. 10-5, Sun. & hols 2-5; free. **Old Stone Mill** (Touro Park at Bellevue Ave. & Mill St.) was believed to have been built by Norsemen, but excavation has dated it about 1673; free. **National Lawn Tennis Hall of Fame & Tennis Museum** (194 Bellevue Ave.), in 1880 Casino built to rival or surpass European counterparts; white-and-gold ballroom designed by Stanford White; in 1881 the first US tennis matches were played here; tennis memorabilia; open mid-May-late Oct., Mon.-Sat. 9:30-5, Sun. & hols 11-5; adm.

Kingscote (Bellevue Ave.), large Victorian cottage built 1839; outstanding paintings and portraits acquired by owner engaged in the China trade; Tiffany glass windows; Townsend and Goddard furniture; 1881 dining room with cork ceiling open Memorial Day-Oct. daily 10-5; mid-Apr.-late- May, Sat. & Sun. 10-5; adm. **The Elms** (Bellevue Ave.), built for a coal king in 1901; modeled on a French chateau; elegant furnishings; grounds with statues, gazebos, terraces, gardens; open Memorial Day-Oct., daily 10-5; rest of yr, Sat. & Sun. 10-5; special summer programs; adm. **Salve Regina College** (Ochre Point Ave.), modeled on a French chateau; designed 1890 by Hunt; elaborate interior wood and marble carving; fine furnishings; ironwork; now a school, inquire for hrs. **The Breakers** (Ochre Point Ave.), designed 1895 by Hunt for Cornelius Vanderbilt; modeled on 16th-C northern Italian palaces; original lavish furnishings; on grounds is small-scale Cottage, children's playhouse in Victorian style; open Memorial Day-Oct. daily 10-5; mid-Apr.-late-May, Sat. & Sun. 10-5; adm. **The Breakers Stable** (Coggeshall & Bateman Aves.) houses the family's large collection of carriages, other vehicles; open July-mid-Sept. daily 10-5; adm. **Chateau-sur-Mer** (Bellevue Ave.), lavish Victorian mansion built 1852 for William S. Wetmore who made his fortune in the China Trade; French ballroom; Italian dining room; Chinese moon gate; antique toys; open Memorial Day-Oct. daily 10-5; mid-Apr.-late-May, Sat. & Sun. 10-5; adm. **Rosecliff** (Bellevue Ave.), built 1902 for a Comstock Lode heiress; modeled on Petit Trianon of Marie Antoinette; Court of Love designed by Augustus Saint-Gaudens; huge ballroom; open Memorial Day- Oct. daily 10-5; mid-Apr.-late-May, Sat. & Sun. 10-5; adm. **Marble House** (Bellevue Ave.), built 1892 by Hunt for William K. Vanderbilt; styled after the palace of Versailles; named for lavish use of marble; highlight is elaborate gilded ballroom; original furnishings, many designed for the house; open Memorial Day-Oct., daily 10-5; mid-Apr.-late-May, Sat. & Sun. 10-5; adm. **Belcourt Castle** (Bellevue Ave.), designed 1891 by Hunt after the palace of Louis XIII; treasures from 32 countries; stained glass; Portuguese coronation coach; dolls and toys (extra charge); open late-Apr.-mid-Nov. daily 10-5; mid-Nov.-late Apr., Sat. & Sun. 11-5; adm.

Fort Adams (off Harrison Ave.), one of the largest fortifications ever built in the U.S., consumed 33 years of construction and $3-million but was outdated on completion; guided tours daily 10-6 in summer; sm adm.

Whitehall Museum House (3 m NE on Berkeley Ave., Middletown), built 1729 by philosopher George Berkeley and named for the royal house in London; he intended to establish a college, but when funds failed to materialize he gave his house to Yale and returned to England; outstanding English furnishings; mezzotints and engravings; open July-Labor Day, daily 10-5; adm.

Portsmouth (7½ m NE on SR 138) was settled by followers of Anne Hutchinson. Battle of Rhode Island was fought here in 1778 by patriots (including Gen. Sullivan, Gen. Greene, Lafayette, John Hancock, Paul Revere) against British and Hessian troops; at Lehigh State Picnic Grove (on SR 114), many Hessians were buried in Hessian Hole (their ghosts are said to march about smartly on foggy nights). **Prescott Farm & Windmill House** (W Main Rd.) was site of one of the most daring raids of the Revolution; on the night of July 9, 1777, 41 patriots in longboats rowed with muffled oars through the British fleet to Portsmouth and captured British Gen. William Prescott, who was sleeping here; museum exhibits in guardhouse; mill; country store; open May-Sept., Tues., Thurs., Sat., Sun. 10-4; sm adm. **St. Gregory's Chapel** (off SR 114 via Cory Lane, on grounds of Portsmouth Abbey), inspired by Chapel of San Vitale in Ravenna, Italy, was designed by Pietro Belluschi; open daily 2-5. **Memorial to Negroes** (jct. SR 24, 114) commemorates first black regiment to fight for the American flag, at Battle of Rhode Island, 1778.

PAWTUCKET: Old Slater Mill Historic Site (Slater Ave. off Roosevelt Ave.) contains restored buildings of 1793 Slater Mill built by Samuel Slater and his partners, who, working from memory, built machines to create U.S. textile industry with mass production methods; also 1810 Wilkinson Mill, 1758 Sylvanus Brown House, typical of its era and area; demonstrations of hand and machine methods on restored equipment; open Memorial Day-Sept., Mon.-Sat. 10-5, Sun. 1-5; rest of yr, Sat. & Sun. 1-5; closed Jan. 1, Thnks, Dec. 25; adm.

PROVIDENCE: Founded 1636 by Roger Williams after he was driven from Massachusetts for his religious views, and named for God's providence in granting the site, this city was dedicated to religious freedom where Quakers, Jews, Baptists, and other victims of persecution were welcome. Despite disfigurement by industry, the city preserves an intriguing historic district with reminders of its shipbuilding, slave and rum running, and China trade past. Booklets on the rich historic and architectural heritage are available from **Greater Providence Chamber of Commerce** (Howard Bldg., 10 Dorrance St.), open Mon.-Fri. 8:30-5; closed hols. The city's core has always been **Market Square** (on the river at Main St.); here in 1775 the citizens tossed British-taxed tea into a bonfire. The 1774 **Market House** (now part of R. I. School of Design) has historic markers; one commemorates the 1815 storm that swept ships right into the square.

W of Market Square is the business district: **Turk's Head** (jct Westminster & Weybosset St.) was named for a ship's figurehead of an Ottoman warrier that once adorned a house here (the head appears in the belt course ornamenting the office building now on the site); here (on Weybosset St. side) are the 1855 Italian-Renaissance-style **Merchant's**

Bank, 1856 **U.S. Customs House,** and the cast-iron-front **Equitable Bldg.** Slightly beyond is the **Arcade** (runs through between Westminster & Weybosset Sts.), a showplace when built 1827-8; massive Ionic columns, shops under a glass-covered passage. The 1901 **Union Trust Bldg.** (Dorrance & Westminster Sts.) is exaggeratedly opulent. **Grace Church** (Westminster & Mathewson), 1846 Richard Upjohn design with interior plaster scribed to resemble stone. **Providence Public Library** (150 Empire St.), resembling a Venetian palace, displays ship models and historic artifacts; collections include early children's books, Civil War, slavery, whaling, architecture materials; open Mon.-Thurs. 8:30-9, Fri. 8:30-6, Sat. (exc July-Aug.) 8:30-6; closed hols; free. The 1809 **Beneficent Congregational Meeting House** (Weybosset at Empire), known as Round Top because it has a dome (open daily) and graceful 1827 **Arnold Palmer House** (Empire & Pine) are noteworthy. To the N is Kennedy Plaza; lantern landmark atop the Industrial Trust Bldg. is visible for 40 m at night; Renaissance-style **Federal Bldg.** was built 1908 to balance the facing 1878 **City Hall** (bust of Roger Williams crowning the entrance, mansard roof). Farther N is **Rhode Island State House** (Smith St.), designed by Stanford White; enormous dome topped with statue of "Independent Man"; Gilbert Stuart portrait of Washington; open Mon.-Fri. 8:30-4:30; closed hols; free.

Just **N of Market Square** is **First Baptist Meeting House** (75 N Main St. at Waterman St.), established 1638 by Roger Williams; impressive 1775 Georgian building; open Apr.-Nov., Mon.-Fri. 9-3:30, Sat. 9-noon; closed hols; free.

E of Market Square is **College Hill,** where more than 200 well-preserved period homes surround Brown University; on campus are: **University Hall,** built 1770 as the first campus building; barracks and hospital for French and American forces during Revolution. **John Hay Library;** Lincoln, other collections; open Mon.-Fri. 9-5; Sept.-May, Sat. 8:30-noon. **John Carter Brown Library** (George St.), excellent Americana, especially of Colonial materials; open Mon.-Fri. 9-5; Sept.-May, Sat. 9-noon. **Rockefeller Library** (College & Prospect) houses scholarly Italian works, Gardner Ch'ing Dynasty collection; open daily. **Annmary Brown Memorial** (21 Brown St.), mausoleum, Hawkins Collection of Incunabula, American portraits; open Mon.-Fri. 9-5, Sept.-May, Sat. 8:30-noon. Bell Gallery (64 College St.), changing art exhibitions; designed by Philip Johnson; open Mon.-Fri. 11-4, Sat. & Sun. 1-4; free.

Also here is **Rhode Island School of Design** (2 College St.), with: Museum of Art exhibiting Latin American and modern U.S. works; English watercolors; European paintings, sculpture; selected primitive, African, Indian, Oriental and Classical works; also 18th-C English and

American decorative arts in Pendleton House; open Tues.-Sat. 11-5, Sun. & hols 2-5; adm. Woods-Gerry Gallery (62 Prospect St.), in a Richard Upjohn residence built 1860-64; changing exhibits; open academic yr, Tues.-Sat. 11-4, Sun. 2-4; closed hols; free.

Many 18-19th-C homes (some open only during special tours) can be seen on a walk along Benefit and nearby streets; interesting are: **John Brown House** (52 Power St. at Benefit), Georgian masterpiece built 1786 by wealthy merchant John Brown; R.I. Historical Society's fine collection of locally made furniture, silver, pewter, glass, paintings; Brown's 1782 chariot; open Tues.-Fri. 11-4, Sat. & Sun. 2-4; closed hols; adm. (The Society also maintains a library at 121 Hope St.; open Tues.-Sat. 9-5; closed hols.) **First Unitarian Church** (Benefit & Benevolent Sts.), built 1816 in Federal style; Adamesque interior, largest bell ever cast by Paul Revere's foundry; open Sept.-June, Mon.-Fri. 9-5, Sat. & Sun. 9-noon; closed hols. **Gov. Stephen Hopkins House** (Benefit & Hopkins Sts.), home of signer of Declaration of Independence and 10 times governor of the state; built 1707 with later additions; period furnishings; open Wed., Sat. 1-4; free. **Providence Athenaeum** (251 Benefit St. at College), small but excellent art collection, established 1753; open mid-June-mid-Sept., Mon.-Fri. 8:30-5:30; rest of yr, Mon.-Sat. 8:30-5:30; closed hols; free. **Providence Art Club** (11 Thomas St. at Benefit), 1787 and 1790 residences joined by an arch house studios; changing exhibits; open Mon.-Sat. 10-4, Sun. 3-5; closed hols, weekends in summer; free. **Shakespeare's Head** (21 Meeting St.), built 1772, housed a bookshop and post office, was a stop on the Underground Railroad. **Old State House** (150 Benefit St., just N of Meeting), built 1762 with an 1851 tower belfry; now a courthouse; Rhode Island was proclaimed the first free republic in the New World here, 2 months before the Declaration of Independence was signed in Philadelphia; open Mon.-Sat. 8:30-4:30. **Sullivan Dorr House** (109 Benefit St.), outstanding Federal building; facade copied from Pope's Villa at Twickenham, England; built 1810; Sullivan's son Thomas led Dorr Rebellion for suffrage in 1842. **Prospect Terrace** (a block E at Congdon & Cushing St.), site of Roger Williams Memorial; panoramic view. **Roger Williams Spring** (N Main at Alamo Lane) was site of the original settlement. **Sarah Helen Whitman House** (in a lovely row on Benefit St. between Church & Star Sts.) was home of Edgar Allen Poe's fiancee, the inspiration for "To Helen" and "Annabel Lee"; the 1848 engagement was broken when Poe failed to mend his ways. **North Burying Ground** (1 m N on N Main from Market Sq.), graves of first settlers.

S of Market Square are: **Joseph Brown House** (50 S Main), thrown open, as were so many homes in town, to Rochambeau's officers. **Dolphin House** (403 S Main), built about 1770 by a sea captain, was a tavern for China Trade sailors; nearby, the narrow old alleys (Guilder, Sovereign, Doubloon) run down to the waterfront. **De Fersen House** (312 S Main) was home of the Swedish nobleman, lover of Marie Antoinette, who in 1791 drove the carriage in which the queen had tried to escape to make her way to America. **Lightning Splitter House** (53 Transit St.), built 1781, has a steeply pitched gable added in 1850 in the belief it would split lightning so it would drop harmlessly on either side of the house.

Roger Williams Park (3 m S on Elmwood Ave.) contains recreation grounds; many statues; Museum of Natural History with mounted birds and animals, minerals, exhibits of South Seas, materials collected during the state's early trade (open Mon.-Sat. 8:30-4:30, Sun. & hols 2-5; closed Jan. 1, Dec. 25; free); Betsy Williams Cottage, home of a Roger Williams descendent, with family burial ground, Colonial furniture, historic relics (open Mon., Tues., Fri. 10-4, Sun. & hols 1-4; free).

Gov. Sprague Mansion (6 m S via Westminster & Cranston Sts. to 1351 Cranston St., Cranston), 1790 home with 1864 addition; Oriental art objects; carriage house, old vehicles; open early summer-early fall, Tues., Sun. 2-4; closed hols; adm. **Gen. Nathanael Greene Homestead** (11 m S on I-95, then 5 m W on SR 117 to Anthony), restored 1770 home; period furnishings; family memorabilia; open Mar.-Nov., Wed., Sat., Sun. 2-5; closed hols; adm.

Eleazar Arnold House (6 m N via SR 126 to jct SR 123, at 449 Great Rd., Lincoln) was stoutly built 1687 as a defense against Indian attack; inquire at house in rear for entry; sm adm. **Limerock** (8 m N on SR 146), where the limestone quarries are believed to have been worked since 1643, is a picturesque area with many old homes.

TIVERTON: The home of Capt. Robert Gray (Sakonnet Point), who gave the U.S. its chief claim to the Oregon Territory, is now a convalescent home. At **Tiverton Four Corners** (4 m S on SR 77) are: 1730 Chase-Cory House (May-Oct., Sun. 2-4:30; sm adm); 1760 Soule-Seabury House, owned by the China Trade captain whose voyages were described in Washington Irving's *Astoria,* has original furnishings (July-Sept. daily 1-5; May-June, Sat. & Sun. 11-5; adm). **Little Compton** (8 m S on SR 77), an offshoot of the Plymouth Colony, Historical Society has restored Wilbor House & Barn (W Main Rd.), a 1680s farmhouse and 1860 barn, furnished, with exhibits on settlers (open mid-June-mid-Sept., Tues.-Sun. 2-5; adm); 19th-C Friends Meeting House (open for special events); grave of Elizabeth Alden Pabodie, daughter of Priscilla and John Alden, the first white girl born in New England (Commons Burial Ground).

WESTERLY: Babcock-Smith House (124 Granite St.), 1730s Georgian home of a physician; open in summer, Sat. & Sun. 1-4; adm. **Watch Hill**

(6 m S on Beach St.) has many Victorian homes and an 1850 Carousel originally turned by draft horses but now mechanized.

WICKFORD (N KINGSTOWN): Main Street and its side streets preserve some 60 18th-C homes. **Old Narragansett Church** (Church Lane off Main St.), 1707, has Queen Anne silver, wineglass pulpit, slave gallery; open July- Aug., Fri. & Sat. 2-4, Sun. 8-noon. **Smith's Castle** (just N on US 1), built 1678 on site of a trading post, was a rendezvous for troops during Great Swamp Fight; mass grave for 40 soldiers killed in that battle; authentic furnishings; doll collection; open mid-Mar.-mid-Dec., Mon.-Wed., Fri.-Sat. 10-5, Sun. 2-5; sm adm. **South County Museum** (3 m NW off SR 2 on Scrabbletown Rd.), pioneer household equipment and farm tools; open Memorial Day-Sept., Tues.-Sun. 1-5; sm adm. **Silas Casey Farm** (3 m S on US 1 on Boston Neck Rd., Saunderstown), early 18th-C farm with 1725-50 home that bears scars from a Revolutionary War skirmish between patriots and sailors from British vessels blockading Narragansett Bay; period furnishings, demonstrations; open June-Oct., Tues., Thurs., Sat. 1-5; adm. **Gilbert Stuart Birthplace** (5 m S off SR 1A on Gilbert Stuart Rd., Saunderstown), where the portraitist was born 1755; period furnishings; his father's snuff mill also restored; open Sat.-Thurs. 11-5; closed Thnks, Dec. 25; sm adm.

SOUTH CAROLINA

ALLENDALE: Rivers Bridge State Park (15 m E off SR 641), site of Civil War skirmish; Confederate museum.

BEAUFORT: Chamber of Commerce (1006 Bay St.) offers pamphlets and tapes for self-guided tours of this gracious old port: **Hext House** (Pinckney & Hancock Sts.); **B. B. Sams House** (Short St.), built 1852; **Thomas Hepworth House** (214 New St.); **Beaufort Baptist Church** (600 Charles St.), built 1844, with lovely plaster ornamentation done by slaves; **St. Helena's Church** (507 Newcastle St.), built 1724, with a communion set donated by Capt. John Bull in memory of his wife who was captured by Indians and tombstones that were used as operating tables during the Civil War when the church was used as a hospital; **Bank of Beaufort** (1001 Bay at Charles Sts.), originally a dwelling, used as a Civil War hospital, with elaborate plasterwork and period furnishings (the bank is downstairs;

upstairs is open Mon.-Sat. 11-3, closed hols, adm); **Retreat Plantation** (Battery Creek); tabby ruins of 1731 **Ft. Frederick** (on grounds of U.S. Naval Hospital, 4 m S on SR 281); **John Mark Verdier House** (801 Bay St.), wealthy merchant's 1790 home used as Union hq during Civil War and where Lafayette was a guest in 1825 (open Mon., Wed., Fri. 9-1; closed hols; adm). **Beaufort Museum** (Craven & Scott Sts.), in a 1795 tabby home; Indian artifacts, antique glass, china, guns, historic relics; open Mon.-Fri. 10-5, Sat. 1-5, Sun. 2-5; closed hols; donation.

   Parris Island (10 m S via SR 281), Marine Corps base; Visitor Center (in Bldg 283); museum; monument to Jean Ribaut, French Huguenot who founded 1562 Charlesfort; open daily 8-8; free.

CAMDEN: Historic Camden (S Broad St.) is a restoration of the Colonial town burned by the British in 1781 and by Sherman in 1865; Visitor Center provides information and museum; log cabin, town house, the home Cornwallis made his hq during the Revolution, other buildings and fortifications; open June-Labor Day, Tues.-Sat. 10-6, Sun. 1-6; rest of yr, Tues.-Fri. 10-4, Sat. 10-5; closed Thnks, Dec. 25; adm. **Bethesda Presbyterian Church** (DeKalb & Little Sts.), built 1820; masterpiece by Robert Mills; on grounds is memorial to Johann de Kalb, German-born hero of Battle of Camden, who was mortally wounded in 1780. **Quaker Cemetery** (Campbell St.) has interesting tombstones. **Rectory Square** (Chestnut & Lyttleton Sts.) has a memorial to the 6 Confederate generals from Camden.

CHARLESTON: By the time of the Revolution, Charleston was widely acknowledged as the most gracious city in the Colonies; fashionable and prosperous, she was an outpost of English culture in the New World. Today, Old Charleston is one of the loveliest urban areas in the U.S. **Visitor Information Center** (Arch Bldg, 85 Calhoun St.) provides maps for walking and auto tours; information on bicycle rental, guides, tape rental, narrated horse-drawn carriage tours (leave daily exc Jan. 1, Dec. 25 from 96 N Market), narrated harbor tours (Gray Line Pier, foot of King St., daily Mar.-mid-Oct.), boats to Fort Sumter (Municipal Marina, Lockwood Dr., daily exc Dec. 25), house tours (usually in spring); open daily 8:30-5:30; closed Jan. 1, Thnks, Dec. 25.

   Old Charleston runs N from **White Point Gardens** (E Battery & Murray Blvd), at the tip of the peninsula; here settlers constructed a walled city with moats and bastions; views of harbor, Ft. Sumter, Ft. Moultrie; site of Ft. Mechanic (named for artisans who provided labor for this harbor defense during 1798 crisis with France, when funds for defense were insufficient) and of the gallows on which the Gentleman Pirate, Stede Bonnet, and 38 of his men were hanged in 1718.

Exchange Bldg & Provost Dungeon (E end of Broad St.) was erected 1771 with large cellars for customs storage; colonists hid seized tea here in 1773, and in 1774 met secretly to elect delegates to the Continental Congress; during the Revolution, Gen. Moultrie's forces hid their powder in these dungeons, where it lay undetected while the British occupied Charleston 1780-82; the British used the vaults as a prison for patriots; open Mar.-Sept. 10-5; Oct.-Nov. 10-2; closed Dec.-Feb.; adm.

Edmonston-Alston House (21 E Battery), built 1828 by a wealthy merchant and wharf owner, remained in the family for more than 100 years; family portraits, silver, furnishings; open Mon.-Sat. 10-5, Sun. 2-5; closed Dec. 25; adm. **Nathaniel Russell House** (51 Meeting St.), fine example of Adams style built by a Rhode Island merchant nicknamed King of the Yankees for his business acumen; free-flying staircase; unusual oval drawing room; elliptical rooms; French, English, and American period furnishings; open Mon.-Sat. 10-5, Sun. 2-5; closed Dec. 25; adm. **Sword Gates** (32 Legare St.), with spears joining to form a cross, are outstanding examples of wrought-iron. **Heyward-Washington House** (87 Church St.), built 1770, was owned by Thomas Heyward, signer of the Declaration of Independence; used by Washington in 1791; superb furnishings made in Charleston; carriage house; kitchen; open daily 10-5; closed hols; adm. **Cabbage Row** (89-91 Church St.), named for produce once sold on the street, was described as Catfish Row in DeBose Heyward's novel *Porgy,* later made into the operetta *Porgy and Bess.* **Dock St. Theatre** (135 Church St.) opened in 1736 as the first building used solely for theatrical purposes; inside are rooms from Planters Hotel, built in early 19th-C, and an auditorium still in use; open June-Sept., Mon., Wed., Fri. 10-1; Oct.-May, Mon.-Sat. 10-1, 2-5; closed hols; free. **Joseph Manigault House** (350 Meeting St.), designed for a rice planter; elegant 1803 home in Adams style; unsupported and secret staircases; outstanding plasterwork; French and Charleston-made furniture; Waterford glass, English porcelain, silver; open daily 10-5; closed hols; adm. **Old Slave Mart Museum** (6 Chalmers St.) has a balcony from which slaves were sold at public auction; in stalls where they waited their turn on the block are examples of handcrafts the blacks made on plantations, African crafts, historic displays on slavery; open Tues.-Sat. 10-5, Sun. & Mon. 2-5; closed Thnks, Dec. 25, Jan.); adm. **Old Powder Magazine** (79 Cumberland St.), part of the original fortification; built about 1712 of brick with oyster-shell mortar; local historic relics; open July-Aug. daily 9:30-4; Oct.-June, Mon., Wed.-Fri. 9:30-4; closed Dec. 25; sm adm. **Confederate Museum** (188 Meeting at Market Sts.) displays local Confederate relics; open mid-Mar.-mid-Oct., Mon.-Sat. 1-5; closed hols; sm adm. **City Market** (off E Bay St. along Market St.) is a public market for fresh produce.

Hunley Museum (Church & Broad Sts.) depicts naval history of

Charleston during the Civil War; full-scale replica of *Hunley,* Confederate submarine made from an old steam boiler that locals hoped would break the Federal blockade; on the first 4 tries it went under, killing its crew; on Feb. 17, 1864 it rammed a torpedo into the USS *Housatonic,* sinking her, but the *Hunley* crew went down too; open Mon.-Sat. 10-5, Sun. 1-5; closed hols; free. **City Hall Art Gallery** (80 Broad at Meeting St.), built 1801 as a bank, became City Hall in 1818; important collection of historical portraits; black-walnut furniture in the council chamber was made in Charleston for this room; open Mon.-Fri. 9-5; closed hols; free. **Thomas Elfe Workshop** (54 Queen St.), built about 1760; home of acclaimed Colonial cabinetmaker; furnishings, reproductions of his work, are typical of early Charleston; open Mon.-Fri. 10-5, Sat. 10-1; closed hols; adm. **Gibbes Art Gallery** (135 Meeting St.), fine 18-19th-C American portraits (including more than 250 miniatures), landscapes, genre paintings; historic lithographs and engravings, Far East works; contemporary paintings; open Tues.-Sat. 10-5, Sun. 2-5; closed hols; free. **Huguenot Church** (138 Church at Queen Sts.), 1845, is on site of 1681 church; lovely altar; rare 1845 Henry Erben tracker organ; tombstones inscribed in French; open Feb.-May, Mon.-Fri. 10-1, 3-5, Sat. 10-noon; June-Jan., Mon.-Fri. 9-1, Sat. 10-noon; closed part of Dec.; free. **St. Philip's Church** (144 Church St.), whose chimes were melted and recast for Confederate cannon during the Civil War, is an 1838 Georgian building with fine plasterwork; graves of John Calhoun and other notables; Gateway Walk leads from here to **St. John's Lutheran Church;** open daily 9-5. **St. Michael's Church** (Meeting & Broad Sts.), handsome colonial building erected 1762; 1764 tower clock; steeple bells were stolen by British troops during the Revolution but later returned; during the Civil War, the bells were taken to Columbia for safety, but Sherman's army broke and burned them there; they were returned to England and recast in the original molds in 1867; it is said that as long as they ring, all is well in the city; open Mon.-Sat. 9-5, Sun. 9-1; closed some hols. **Unitarian Church** (8 Archdale St.), begun 1772, used as a stable by the British during the Revolution, was completed 1787; interior detail modeled after Henry VII Chapel in Westminster Abbey; open daily 9-5. **Kahal Kadosh Beth Elohim** (90 Hasell St.), handsome 1840 structure in the style of a Greek Doric temple; historic documents; open Mon.-Fri. 10-1; free. **St. John's Lutheran Church** (Archdale & Clifford Sts.), built 1817; noted for steeple, wrought-iron gates, fence, and graveyard; open Fri.-Wed. 9-1; closed July 4, Labor Day.

    Charleston Museum (121 Rutledge Ave. at Calhoun St.), oldest museum in the U.S., was founded 1773; exhibit of Charleston ironwork; mounted animals; open Mon.-Sat. 9-5, Sun. 1-5; closed hols; adm. **Charleston Library Society** (164 King St.) houses rare historical documents on this city; open Mon.-Fri. 9:30-6, Sat. 9:30-6 in winter &

9:30-2 in summer; free. **J. I. Waring Historical Medical Library** (Ashley & Bee Sts.), part of Medical University of S. Carolina, is open Mon.-Fri. 9-1:30.

The Citadel (Moultrie St. & Elmwood Ave.), named for a fortress maintained in case of slave rebellion, is Military College of South Carolina; museum with exhibits on the Citadel and military memorabilia; open Mon.-Fri. 2-5, Sat. 9-5, Sun. 10-5; free.

Charles Towne Landing (1500 Old Town Rd., SR 171), a park on the site of the first permanent settlement in the state, re-creates 1670 setting; reconstructed fortifications; pavilion with exhibits that include recordings of Gullah dialect, spirituals, Indian war chants; replica of 17th-C trading ketch; open Apr.-Sept. daily 10-6; Oct.-Mar. daily 10-5; closed Dec. 25; adm.

Fort Sumter National Monument (on an island in the harbor, accessible by boat from Municipal Marina on Lockwood Blvd.): Although historians question whether the first shot of the Civil War was actually fired here, Fort Sumter, built as part of U.S. coastal fortifications after the War of 1812, became a symbol to North and South. South Carolina, the first state to secede (Dec. 20, 1860), refused to surrender the fort on demand on Apr. 11, 1861; on Apr. 12, Confederates opened fire, and after 34 hours of bombardment agreed to evacuate (but, technically, not surrender) the fort. Despite frequent Union bombardment, Fort Sumter never surrendered; it was evacuated along with Charleston in Feb. 1865 as Sherman approached the city. Parts of original walls remain; weaponry demonstrations; museum; guided tours; open daily in summer 8-6, in winter 8-5; closed Dec. 25; free.

Fort Moultrie (US 17 N, then SR 703 to W Middle St., Sullivan's Island) was originally commanded by William Moultrie, who won the first decisive victory of the Revolution in repelling a British naval attack in 1776. Edgar Allen Poe was once stationed here. Osceola, famous Seminole leader, died here 1838 after a month's imprisonment and is buried here; before his death he had become a celebrity in Charleston, delighting children with his war whoop. Cannon, guns, other weaponry on display; open daily in summer 8-6, in winter 8-5; closed Dec. 25; free. Nearby is Sullivan Island Lighthouse (Atlantic Ave.), open, weather permitting, Tues., Thurs. 3-4, Sat. & Sun. 2-4; free.

Boone Hall Plantation (8 m N off US 17 on Long Point Rd., Mt. Pleasant), reproduction of early-18th-C plantation home; period furnishings; original slave houses; 1750 ginhouse; open Mon.-Sat. 9-5, Sun. 1-5; closed Thnks, Dec. 25; adm.

Middleton Place Gardens & Plantation Stableyards (14 m NW on SR 61), one of the greatest, and perhaps oldest, gardens in U.S.; laid out by Henry Middleton, president of First Continental Congress, in 1741; 1751

Georgian home (open Mon.-Sat. 10-6, Sun. 2-6); 1741 springhouse; pre-Revolutionary rice mill; slave cemetery; displays of coopering, tanning, other skills in stableyards demonstrate rice plantation life; special events; open daily 9-5; adm.

Old Dorchester State Park (19 m NW on SR 61), site of village established 1696 by colonists from Massachusetts; the town declined in the late 18th-C and was burned by the British in 1781; only foundations and ruins of a fort and church are visible; being excavated; open daily; free.

Francis Marion National Forest was named for Revolutionary War hero called The Swamp Fox, considered by some to be the father of modern guerrilla warfare; he so harrassed the British that their supply lines from Charleston to the Carolinas were almost useless; historic markers indicate sites of Revolutionary or Civil War events, rice plantations: At **Huger** (on SR 41) is a pre-Revolutionary church and graveyard; also Quinby Bridge, site of a bitter Revolutionary battle, where bones of the war dead have been uncovered and where ghosts of horsemen are said to gallop. At **Tarpit Recreation Area** (on US 17A, E of Jamestown) is a pre-Revolutionary tar kiln and tar pit; the pitch was used to caulk wooden sailing ships. S of McClellanville is Sewee Indian shell mound (take SR 432S just after Awendaw). **St. James Santee Church** (W of McClellanville on SR 45, then N on Georgetown Rd.) was built 1768 from bricks shipped from England.

CLEMSON: Clemson University, founded during Reconstruction, taught scientific agricultural methods to aid the recovery of the South; on campus are: **Fort Hill,** 1803 plantation home enlarged when John C. Calhoun bought it during his first term as Vice President; his country home until his death in 1850; his daughter married Thomas Clemson here; sideboard of paneling from Old Ironsides was gift of Henry Clay; chair and sofa were George Washington's. **Hanover House,** built 1716 on the coast by a French Huguenot and named for George I of England (who had befriended Huguenots), was fortressed, with gun slots in the basement for use in Indian attacks; beautifully restored with rare furnishings. Both open Tues.-Sat. 10-noon, 1-5:30, Sun. 2-6; closed Jan. 1, July 4, Thnks, Dec. 25; free. **Rudolph Lee Gallery** (Lee Hall) exhibits 17-18th-C Dutch and Flemish paintings collected by Clemson in Europe; changing shows; open Mon.-Fri. 8-4:30; free.

COLUMBIA: Planned with unusually wide streets to discourage the spread of infectious diseases, Columbia was almost totally burned the night of Sherman's arrival in 1865. **State House** (Main & Gervais Sts.), begun 1855, one of the few buildings spared, was shelled; brass stars cover scars of Union cannon balls; handsome building in Italian Renaissance style, with huge dome and cupola, pleasing lobby; inside and on the grounds are many statues and memorials; Columbia Garden Trail starts here; open Mon.-Fri. 9-5; free. Opposite is **Trinity Church** (1100 Sumter St.), built 1846 after the Cathedral of St. Peter in York, England; austere interior with lovely stained-glass windows; prominent locals buried in the cemetery; open Mon.-Fri. 9-5, Sat. & Sun. 9-noon; free.

University of South Carolina (Sumter St., S from Pendleton St.) quadrangle has several 19th-C buildings, including the 1805 Rutledge College Bldg; on campus are: University Museum (War Memorial Bldg), splendid collection of gems, fine cutting; Bernard Baruch collection of English silver; open Mon.-Fri. 9-5, Sat. by appointment; free. South Caroliniana Library (Horseshoe Dr.), portraits, statues, relics; books and manuscripts; open Mon.-Fri. 9-5, Sat. 9-1; free.

Columbia Museum of Art & Science (1112 Bull St.): impressive Renaissance painting; excellent local furniture, silver, jewelry, historic paintings and miniatures, pottery; Spanish Colonial relics; contemporary painting, graphics, sculpture; dolls; mounted wildlife; displays on sciences; planetarium (adm); open Tues.-Sat. 10-5, Sun. 2-6; closed Jan. 1, July 4, Thnks, Dec. 25; free.

Hampton-Preston House (1615 Blanding St.), built 1818, reflects Hampton family's way of life before the Civil War; open Tues.-Sat. 10-4, Sun. 2-5; closed Thnks, Dec. 24, 25; sm adm.

Woodrow Wilson's Boyhood Home (1705 Hampton St.), built 1870 by the President's father; family furnishings, memorabilia; open Tues.-Sat. 10-4, Sun. 2-5; closed Thnks, Dec. 24, 25; sm adm. Wilson's parents are buried in graveyard of First Presbyterian Church (1324 Marion St.).

First Baptist Church (1306 Hampton St.) was site of the First Secession Convention (1860); open Mon.-Fri. 9-5, Sat. 9-noon; closed Jan. 1, July 4, Thnks, Dec. 25; free. **De Bruhl-Marshall House** (Laurel & Marion Sts.), handsome private residence, built 1820, one of the few homes to survive 1865 burning. **Governor's Mansion** (800 Richland St.), only remaining structure of a military school burned by the Union, has housed governors since 1879; artifacts of former governors, paintings by local artists, silver service of battleship USS *South Carolina;* ironwork trim is repeated on Lace House (801 Richland St.) used for official entertaining; tours Mon.-Fri. 9:30-11, 2:30-4:30 by appointment; closed hols; free. **South Carolina State Hospital & Archives** (2100 Bull St.), in 1828 building designed by Robert Mills, has antique furnishings, historic exhibits; tours Mon.-Fri. 10:30-noon, 3-5:30; closed hols; free. **South Carolina Archives Bldg** (1430 Senate St.), changing exhibits, research rooms; open Mon.-Sat. 9-9, Sun. 1-9; closed hols; free.

Robert Mills Historic House & Park (1616 Blanding St.) is preserved as a memorial to the first American-born professional architect, who designed it in 1823 for Ainsley Hall (Columbia's "Merchant Prince"); Hall died before it was completed, and outbuildings and interior detail called for in Mills' plans were added in this century; Mills (1781-1855) designed the Washington Monument, U.S. Treasury, other national buildings; elegant Empire, Regency, and Classic Revival furnishings; open Tues.-Sat. 10-4, Sun. 2-5; closed Thnks, Dec. 25; adm.

Lexington County Homestead Museum (12 m W on US 378 to Lexington) depicts way of life of Swiss-German settlers; domestic and farm tools in outbuildings; open Apr.-Dec., Tues.-Sat. 10-5, Sun. 2-5; sm adm. Nearby **Fox House** (Fox St., off SR 378) was constructed 1833-4 by volunteer labor as a Lutheran seminary; now a museum of the small 19th-C landowner; artifacts made before 1850; handmade furnishings; open in summer Tues.-Sat. 10-5, Sun. 2-5; in winter, Fri. & Sat. 10-4, Sun. 2-4; sm adm. **Church of the Holy Cross** (32 m E on US 76, 378 to Stateburg), Gothic Revival chapel of rammed earth completed 1852; German stained-glass windows; open Wed. & Sun. At **Winnsboro** (23 m N off US 321), the Fairfield County Courthouse (Congress St.) was designed by Robert Mills; town clock in Market Building (Washington St.) was imported from France in 1834; both open business hrs; free.

EDGEFIELD: Oakley Park (jct US 25, SR 23), a 40-acre park with 1835 Greek Revival clapboard home of Gen. Martin Gary (the Bald Eagle of the Confederacy), honors the Red Shirts, led by Gary, who arose in 1876 to wrest control of the state from blacks, scalawags, and carpetbaggers, and to elect Wade Hampton as governor; fine interior wood carving and plasterwork; period furnishings; museum room; shrine to men who fought in the Mexican War; open Tues., Fri. 9:30-11:30, 2-4:30; sm adm. **Magnolia Dale** (320 Norris St.), built 1837, houses collections of Edgefield County Historical Society; English furniture; possessions of Alamo heros Travis, Bonham, and Bowie; early portraits; newspapers; other displays; open Tues.-Fri. 2-4; closed hols; free.

FLORENCE: Florence Museum (558 Spruce St.), arts of Africa and American Southwest; Chinese bronzes; frescos, ceramics; Near East works; regional arts, historical displays; open Tues.-Sat. 10-5, Sun. 2-5; closed Jan. 1, Easter, Thnks, Dec. 25-31; free.

Timrod Park & Shrine (Timrod Park Dr. & S Coit St.) honors Henry Timrod, poet laureate of the Confederacy; one-room schoolhouse in which he taught in 1859; open daily; free.

GEORGETOWN: Spaniards who attempted to settle here in 1526 were driven out by disease and Indians; a city was laid out 1729, when fertile river bottoms lured rice and indigo planters; **Chamber of Commerce**

(Front St.) provides maps for self-guided tour of historic sites, information on historic train tours and annual plantation tours: 1824 **Court House,** Classic Revival style with 6-ft-thick walls, possibly designed by Robert Mills; 1857 **Winyah Indigo Society Hall; Pyatt-Doyle House** (630 Highmarket St.), on a Bermuda coral stone foundation (may be open weekdays); **Prince George Winyah Church** (Highmarket & Broad Sts.), built about 1750 (open daily 8-5); 1760 **Harold Kaminski House** (1003 Front St.) with family heirlooms (open Tues.-Fri. 10-4; closed hols; adm).

Rice Museum (Front & Screven Sts.) is in 1842 Market Bldg that has served as jail, town hall, with produce market at street level; plaque marks landing of Lafayette in 1775 to aid the American cause; museum uses dioramas to trace history of local rice culture (Georgetown was once the world's leading exporter of rice); open Mon.-Fri. 9-5, Sat. 10-1 (10-5 in Mar.-Sept.), Sun. 2-5; closed Jan. 1, Thnks, Dec. 25; adm.

Hopsewee Plantation (12 m S on US 17), on N Santee River, was home of Thomas Lynch, delegate to the Continental Congress, and birthplace of his son Thomas, signer of Declaration of Independence; house, built before 1740, is of black cypress; handsome staircase and carved moldings; outbuildings; open Tues.-Fri. 10-5; closed hols; adm; grounds open daily in daylight. **Thorntree** (36 m W on US 251, then 6 m N on SR 377, in Fluitt-Nelson Memorial Park, Kingstree), built 1749; furnished with pieces of 1749-1826, many made locally; open Sun. 2:30-5:30 or by appointment; adm. **Wedgefield Plantation** (2 m N off SR 701), a 618-acre estate on the Black River; beautiful Georgian Regency architecture; grounds said to be haunted by ghost of British sentry, beheaded by one of Gen. Francis Marion's cavalrymen, who cannot rest in his grave in the plantation garden until he locates his head; open Mon., Sun. 10-5; adm. **Brookgreen Gardens** (18 m N on US 17, 4 m S of Murrells Inlet) was created by Anna Hyatt Huntington as a stunning setting for her own sculpture and pieces she collected; large works scattered throughout gardens; appealing court for smaller works; small zoo; open daily 9:30-4:45; closed Dec. 25; adm. **Conway** (35 m N on US 701) offers a marked house-and-garden trail for motorists.

GREENVILLE: Bob Jones University Art Museum (3 m N on US 29), 27 galleries devoted to religious art; 15-19th-C icons; Botticelli, Veronese, Titian, Rubens, Rembrandt, other French, Italian, Flemish masters; open Sept.-May, Tues.-Sat. noon-5, Sun. 1:30-6; June-Aug. & Christmas season, Tues.-Sun. 2-4; closed Jan. 1, Dec. 24-25, 31; free.

Greenville City Hall (Main & Broad Sts.), completed 1892 on an Indian burial ground, is said to be haunted by ghosts of Indians during construction; wide Romanesque Revival, castellated towers, precast terracotta insets; ornate interior carving; open Mon.-Fri. 9-5; closed hols;

free. **Greenville County Museum of Art** (420 College St.) exhibits American arts and decorative arts; library; open Mon.-Sat. 10-4, Sun. 1-5; free.

GREENWOOD: Greenwood Museum (605 Phoenix St.), local historic exhibits; replica of old doctor's office; Indian artifacts; minerals; open Mon.-Fri. 9-5, Sun. 2-5; closed hols; free.

Star Fort & Ninety Six (11 m E on SR 34 to Ninety Six, then 2 m S on SR 248), ruins of star-shape earthen fort built by the British, site of the first Southern land battle of the Revolution (1776). **Cokesbury Historic District** (6 m N on SR 254) preserves 8 of 54 mansions of early-19th-C cotton village that collapsed during Civil War.

ROCK HILL: Andrew Jackson Historical State Park (14 m SE on SR 5), on site where Old Hickory was born; blockhouse and museum with exhibits on the 7th President; open Tues.-Sat. 9-5:30, Sun. 1-5:30; free. **Nature Museum of York County** (7 m NE off SR 161 on Mt. Gallant Rd.), African, Latin American Indian artifacts; mounted birds and animals; Thomas Edison exhibit; small zoo; open Mon.-Fri. 9-4, Sat. 1-5, Sun. 2-5; closed Jan. 1, Easter, Dec. 25; free.

SPARTANBURG: Spartanburg Regional Museum (501 Otis Blvd at Pine St.) exhibits history of Up-Country; dolls; Indian artifacts; maps; open Tues.-Sat. 10-noon, 3-5; mid-Sept.-May, Sun. 3-5; closed Jan. 1, Easter, Thnks, Dec. 25; free.

Kings Mountain National Military Park (29 m NE off I-85): here the British misjudged American frontiersmen; Maj. Patrick Ferguson sent out a message demanding allegiance to Britain, and waited confidently on Kings Mountain for the reply. On Oct. 7, 1780, untrained frontiersmen from the Carolinas, Georgia, and Virginia surrounded the mountain and swarmed up the slopes; losing only 28 men, they killed Ferguson and killed or captured his 1100 soldiers. Self-guiding trail through battlefield; Ferguson's grave, other monuments; museum with dioramas, battlefield map; open June-Labor Day, daily 8:30-6; rest of yr, daily 8:30-5; closed Dec. 25; free. **Cowpens National Battlefield Site** (9 m NE on I-85, then 6 m N on SR 110): Gen. Nathanael Greene set a successful trap for Cornwallis by sending a diversionary force of 600 men to this area; Cornwallis detached 1100 men, and the forces met at Cowpens (once a cow pasture) on Jan. 17, 1781; Americans finished the battle in 50 minutes, killing 110, wounding 200, and herding 550 off to prison, while losing only 12 men themselves. Although the battles of Kings Mountain and Cowpens did not end the campaign, they helped decimate Cornwallis' troops before Yorktown; open daily; free; interpretive material at Kings Mountain.

Walnut Grove Plantation (8 m SE off US 221), 1765 home of Kate Barry, Revolutionary heroine who acted as scout for Gen. Daniel Morgan, commander of Battle of Cowpens; period furnishings; outbuildings include a forge and school; family cemetery; open Apr.-Oct., Tues.-Sat. 11-5, Sun. 2-5; Nov.-Mar., Sun. 2-5; closed hols; adm. Rose Hill (26 m SE on US 176, then S on SR 16 in Sumter National Forest), in Rose Hill State Park; restored cotton plantation with 1832 Federal-style mansion named for extensive rose gardens; open daily in daylight.

SOUTH DAKOTA

ABERDEEN: Dacotah Prairie Museum (21 S Main St.), in 1888 bank building; Plains Indian, early settler relics; animal trophies from India, Africa, the Arctic; period rooms; 1890s barbershop; art gallery; open Mon.-Fri. 9-5, Sat. & Sun. 1-4; closed hols; free.

Prayer Rock Museum (34 m E on US 12, then 29 m N on SR 27 to Main St., Britton), Indian, pioneer artifacts; guns; glassware; open May-Sept., Mon.-Sat. 9-5, Sun. 1-5; free.

Fort Sisseton State Park (51 m E on US 12, then 11 m N on SR 25, 10 m N on unnumbered road) preserves 1864 fort built to protect settlers from Indians. From here Samuel Brown rode 55 m at night in a blizzard to warn Ruilliard's Trading Post of an impending Sioux attack; at the post, he learned that Pres. Andrew Johnson had just signed a peace treaty; the army therefore had to be warned not to move against the Sioux, so he rode back home the same night, a ride that left him paralyzed the rest of his life. Visitor Center displays give good picture of life on the frontier; restored hospital, officers' quarters, school, blacksmith shop, guardhouse, other structures; open mid-May-mid-Sept., Tues.-Sun. 10-6; sm adm.

BELLE FOURCHE: Tri-State Museum (831 State St.), displays of frontier history, Indian culture; fossils, mounted animal trophies; open June-Aug., Mon.-Sat. 8-8, Sun. 2-8; May 15-31 & Sept. 1-15, daily 2-8; closed Memorial Day, Labor Day; free. Buckskin Johnny Cabin (801 State St.) provides tourist information; open June-Aug., daily 9-11,, 1:30-5:30; free.

Black Hills State College (11 m S on US 85 to University Ave., Spearfish) offers wildlife art of Lyndle Dunn in student center lounge; open daily; free.

BROOKINGS: South Dakota Memorial Art Center (Medary Ave. at Harvey Dunn St.), oils of pioneers by Harvey Dunn (1884-1952), a South Dakotan; works by Reginal Marsh, Thomas Hart Benton, contemporary Sioux artists; Vera Marghab embroidered linens; open Mon.-Fri. 8-5, 7-9, Sat. 10-5, Sun. 1-5; closed hols; free.

South Dakota State University offers **Visitor Center** at Coughlin Campanile (panoramic view from the top) in summer 1-5 daily; rest of yr, information from Physical Plant Office (room 304, Admin. Bldg.), open Mon.-Fri. 8-noon, 1-5; on campus is a Museum & Heritage Center (basement of Wenona Hall), with Indian and settler artifacts; open Mon.-Fri. 9-noon, Sun. 1:30-4:30; free.

Brookings County Historical Society Museum (4 m W on US 14 to city park, W edge of Volga), local historical displays, pioneer pictures; open June-Sept. daily; rest of yr, Sun.; free.

CHAMBERLAIN: Old West Museum (3 m W on US 16) frontier items; covered wagons, 1898 army ambulance wagon, stagecoach; Indian artifacts; guns and powder horns; early toys; open June-Labor Day, daily 7 am-10 pm; mid-Apr.-May & after Labor Day-mid-Oct., daily 7:30 am-9 pm; sm adm. **Lewis & Clark Trail Museum** (6 m SE), Indian artifacts, local historic exhibits; open May-Labor Day, daily 8-8; sm adm.

Soper's Sod House (17 m W on I-90, then 46 m S on SR 47 to US 18 E of Gregory), replica of prairie home built of earth; plastered interior; pioneer furnishings; open Mar.-Oct. daily; sm adm. **Papineau Trading Post** (25 m E on I-90, 24 m S on SR 45, 7 m E on SR 44, 9 m S on SR 50 in Geddes), built 1857 for fur trading; open daily in summer. **Bijou Hills** (14 m S off SR 50 is a ghost town.

Big Bend Dam (20 m N off SR 47): museum and visitor center (open mid-May-mid-Sept., daily, free); nearby is a replica of Fort Thompson, the Crow Creek Indian agency; sites of early trails, trading posts, Lewis and Clark campsites have historic markers. **Fort Randall Dam** (25 m E on I-90, 24 m S on SR 45, 38 m SE on SR 44, 50, US 18) visitor center displays on history of Missouri River area; guided tours of powerhouse; Memorial Day-Labor Day, daily 9-5; rest of yr, Mon.-Fri. 9-4:30; site open all yr, daily 7 am-6 pm.

CUSTER: Chamber of Commerce (31 S 5th St.) offers brochure for self-guiding tours of historic sites; pageant of gold discovery days late July; melodramas in summer; Black Hills Central Railroad, 1880 Train, offers daily round trips in summer to Hill City. **Wiehe's Frontier Museum** (25 N 5th St.), Indian artifacts, guns, relics from ghost towns, gold from French Creek, other memorabilia; open mid-June-Labor Day, daily 8-6; sm adm. **Way Park Museum** (Way City Park, Mt. Rushmore Rd.), 1875 log cabin; relics of pioneer life, Custer's cavalry; open June-Aug., daily 8-8; sm adm.

Crazy Horse Memorial (5 m N off US 16, 385), carved on granite summit of Thunderhead Mountain, honors chief who defended Sioux rights to the Black Hills after 1868 treaty was broken by whites; Crazy Horse defeated Custer at Little Big Horn in 1876 and was killed a year later by a white soldier while under a flag of truce; 563-ft statue of the chief on horseback is the work of Korczak Ziolkowski; studio-home exhibits other examples of his work; Indian museum; open daily in daylight; adm.

Jewel Cave National Monument (14 m W on US 16), named for calcite crystals lining the walls; **Visitor Center** (Apr.-Oct. daily 8-5) offers moderately strenuous Scenic Tour and strenuous Historic Tour (Memorial Day-Labor Day, daily; fee).

Borglum Ranch & Studio (18 m E on US 16, SR 36), home of Gutzon Borglum, sculptor of Mt. Rushmore; works displayed; open mid-May-mid-Sept., daily 7:30-7:30; adm. **Custer State Park** (3 m E of US 16A) can be seen on an 18-m Wildlife Loop Trail (starts on SR 87, 10 m S on jct US 16A); here are: **Badger Clark Memorial** ½ m E of Legion Lake), rustic cabin built by hand by Charles Badger Clark (1883-1957), poet laureate of South Dakota; original furnishings, personal effects; open mid-May-Sept., daily 8-5. **Gordon Stockade** (on US 16A), replica of 1874 fort built by Gordon party (26 men 1 woman, 1 boy) who entered Sioux lands illegally to pan for gold; nearby monument to Black Hills pioneer Annie Tallent; open daily. **Museum** (on US 16A), of native stone; Indian and pioneer relics, geological and natural history displays; open mid-May-Sept. daily 8-5. Park open daily all year; adm. **Game Lodge Doll House** (14 m E on US 16A), 2000 costumed dolls from many countries; also miniature exhibits; open mid-May-Sept. daily 8-8; sm adm.

DEADWOOD: During height of 1876 gold rush, Deadwood had a population of 25,000 (most of whom shortly ran to the new strike at Lead), a roaring red-light district, and a possibly exaggerated reputation for wickedness. The main street runs through Deadwood Gulch, so narrow that the rest of the town had to built on steep canyon walls. **Adams Memorial Museum** (Sherman & Deadwood Sts.) displays pictures of famous characters, gold nuggets, guns, and relics of pioneers in the Black Hills; open mid-June-Labor Day, daily 9-6; rest of yr, Mon.-Sat. 9-5, Sun. 2-5; closed hols; donation. A wax museum and other small museums (most open mid-May-Sept.) also help give a picture of mining days in this picturesque town. While playing poker in 1876, Wild Bill Hickok was shot in the back by Jack (Crooked Nose) McCall; the trial, held in a saloon with a jury of miners and Calamity Jane as a witness, freed McCall (he was later hanged by a U.S. court for his crime); trial reenacted daily in summer at **Old Towne Hall** (Lee St.). Hickok's bust by Korczak Ziolkowski is on Sherman St. Hickok, along with Calamity Jane, Potato Creek Johnny, Preacher Smith (who arrived in 1876 to preach to gold miners and was killed by Indians 4 months later), others are buried in **Mt. Moriah Cemetery** (follow signs from town center). **Broken Boot Gold Mine** (1 m W on US 14A) gives underground tours mid-May-Sept., weather permitting, 7 am-6 pm; adm.

The 1876 gold strike at Lead (4 m S) resulted in development of largest producing gold mine in the Western Hemisphere, **Homestake Mine** (Main St.), operated continuously since 1877; daily tours through surface workings June-Aug., Mon.-Sat. 8-5; May & Sept.-Oct., Mon.-Fri. 8-4; closed hols; adm. **Rockford** (17 m S of Lead on forest road) and **Tinton** (8 m S on US 85, then 2 m N off US 14A) are ghost towns where gold was mined.

HOT SPRINGS: Fall River County Historical Museum (300 N Chicago Ave.), period rooms, Indian and pioneer artifacts; open June-mid-Sept., Mon.-Fri. 8-5; free. **Cascade** (9 m S on forest road), ghost town that aspired to be a hot-springs resort but lost out when the railroad was laid to Hot Springs.

Wounded Knee Battlefield (64 m SE on US 18 E of Pine Ridge, then 7 m N), site of last major confrontation between the Sioux and the U.S. On Dec. 29, 1890, more than 400 Sioux, who had surrendered to the 7th Cavalry, were being searched for weapons by the Army when a shot was fired; the Army let loose a barrage of gunfire that killed about 250 defenseless Indian men, women, and children; a monument marks the mass grave.

HURON: State Fair Pioneer Museum (on US 14 at State Fairgrounds) has Indian and pioneer exhibits, log cabin; open Memorial Day-Labor Day, Mon.-Fri. 6-9 pm, Sat. & Sun. 1-5; donation.

Laura Ingalls Wilder Memorial (33 m E off US 14 in De Smet) honors author of *The Little House on the Prairie* and other books set in De Smet; surveyor's shanty in which the family spent the winter of 1879-80; 1887 Ingalls Homestead; replica of period school; author's memorabilia; open May-Aug. daily 9-5 or by appointment; adm. Paintings by native son **Harvey Dunn,** are exhibited in City Library and in De Smet News office. **De Smet City Museum,** with local historic exhibits, is open free in summer.

KADOKA: Red Cloud Indian Museum (W off I-90) has a good collection of Sioux feather bonnets, beaded moccasins; weapons; utensils; open mid-May-mid-Sept. daily 7 am-8 pm; adm. **Badlands Petrified Gardens** (E Kadoka exit of I-90), 3 acres with petrified logs, indoor exhibit of fossils, minerals, dinosaur tracks; open May-late Oct., daily 7 am-8 pm; adm.

Two Strike (18 m E on I-90 at Exit 40) is a re-created 1880s village with Wells Fargo office, barbershop, saloon, other buildings once used for a movie set; open spring-fall, daily; adm. **Hill Top Museum** (46 m S on SR 73, then 14 m W on US 18), sod house with farm machinery; open mid-Apr.-mid-Oct., daily; free.

LEMMON: Petrified Wood Park was created by a local philanthropist to provide employment during Depression of 1930s; for 2 years, 40 men labored to transport to town 6½-million lbs of petrified wood—some in logs 5-ft in diameter, about 100 large spires, 400 smaller pieces, many with imprints of plants or sea life—and to construct of this petrified material: The Castle, a fortress-like structure; the Chamber of Commerce building; and a museum with pioneer and fossil displays; open daily; free.

MITCHELL: The Corn Palace (604 N Main St. at 7th Ave.), built 1892 of Moorish design, with turrets, domes, and minarets, is redecorated each year with 2000-3000 bushels of corn arranged to create murals on the outer walls; African trophy display, special events; open June-Labor Day, daily 8 am-9 pm; rest of yr, Mon.-Fri. 9-5, closed hols; free.

Museum of Pioneer Life (1311 S Duff St. on Dakota Wesleyan University campus) depicts the way Indians, pioneers, and soldiers lived in the Dakota Territory; weapons, clothes, vehicles, farm and home utensils; schoolroom, country store, railroad depot; works by Harvey Dunn, Oscar Howe, Childe Hassam, James Earl Fraser; library; lectures in summer; open June-Sept., Mon.-Sat. 8 am-9 pm, Sun. 1-9; adm. **Oscar Howe Cultural Center** (W 3rd St.) displays works by this and other regional artists; inquire locally for hrs.

Milltown (22 m S on SR 37, then 12 m E on SR 44), a thriving center that became a ghost town; picnic and recreational area.

MOBRIDGE: Municipal Auditorium (Main St.) has 10 colorful murals of Sioux ceremonies and history by Oscar Howe, a Dakota Sioux; open Mon.-Sat. 8-5; closed hols; free. **Land of the Sioux Museum** (511 N Main St.), beadwork, ghost shirts, costumes, other displays on Indian history and culture; Sitting Bull, Oscar Howe; open Memorial Day-Labor Day, daily 1-6; free. **Sitting Bull Memorial** (4 m W on US 12, then S on unnumbered rd), a bust by Korczak Ziolkowski, stands on a hill overlooking the Missouri River Valley; nearby is monument to Sakajawea, the Lewis and Clark guide. **Sioux Cultural Center** (41 m W on SR 20, then 31 m S on SR 63 to US 212 in Eagle Butte), displays showing transition from Plains life to the reservation; craft shop; open daily in summer; free.

MURDO: Pioneer Auto Museum & Old Western Town (jct I-90 & US 83), antique autos, tractors, farm machinery; horse-drawn vehicles; some 30 buildings, including jail, school, general store, blacksmith shop, homesteader cabin; open Memorial Day-Labor Day, daily 7 am-10 pm; spring and fall, daily 8-8; adm.

PIERRE: State Capitol (Capitol Ave. E), landscaped beside a lake; 2-story Ionic staircase; stained-glass panels in dome; guided tours weekdays 8-5; open daily; free. **Robinson Museum** (opposite Capitol in Soldiers' & Sailors' War Memorial) highlights the Verendrye Plate, a lead tablet buried in 1743 claiming the country for France and accidently discovered by children in 1913; Indian and pioneer displays; other historic exhibits open Mon.-Fri. 8-5, Sat. 10-5, Sun. 1-5, closed hols; free. **Verendry Museum** (across the river on Deadwood St., Ft. Pierre), ranching and homesteading items; open June-Labor Day, daily; sm adm. **Mentor Graham House** (20 m NE on US 14 on Commercial St., Blunt), small home of the man who taught Lincoln grammar, diction, and other skills; Graham was 84 when he moved in here in 1884; furnishings as they were at his death a year later; open Apr-Oct. daily; free.

RAPID CITY: South Dakota School of Mines & Technology (St. Joseph St.) offers: Museum of Geology (O'Hara Memorial Bldg.), finest collection of Badlands fossils in the world; rare examples include a female oredont with unborn young; reconstructed skeletons; rare minerals from around the world and the Black Hills; open June-Aug., Mon.-Sat. 8-6, Sun. 2-8; Sept.-May, Mon.-Fri. 8-5; closed hols; free. Surbeck Center Art Gallery features arts and crafts by regional artists; open May-Aug. daily 8-4; Sept.-Apr. daily 8 am-10 pm; closed hols; free.
    Sioux Indian Museum & Crafts Center (1002 St. Joseph St., Halley Park), historic exhibits of beadwork, costumes, other Sioux relics; contemporary arts and crafts; shop; open late May-Sept., Mon.-Sat. 8-5; Sun. 1-5; Oct.-late May, Tues.-Sat. 10-5, Sun. 1-5; closed hols; free. **Minnilusa Historical Museum** (West Blvd in Halley Park), exhibits on pioneers in Black Hills; mounted regional fauna; other displays; open June-Sept., Mon.-Sat. 8-5, Sun. 1-5; spring & fall, Mon.-Sat. 10-5, Sun. 1-5; free.
    Rockerville Ghost Town (8 m S on US 16 in Rockerville) boomed in 1878 and became more densely populated than Rapid City; museum, saloon, general stores, other buildings; summer melodramas (adm); open mid-May-Sept. daily 7-9; free. **Horseless Carriage Museum** (10 m S on US 16), development of the auto; music boxes, guns, pioneer shops; open May-Oct. daily 8-8; adm. **Big Thunder Gold Mine** (18 m S off US 16A at Keystone) guided tours mid-May-mid-Sept. daily 7:30-7:30; adm. **Hill City** (24 m SW on US 16), established 1876 after a gold find, became a

ghost town after the strike in Deadwood; some buildings were abandoned in mid-construction; the town boomed again and was abandoned again after successive discoveries of tin, gold quartz, and tungsten; the city maintains one of the original 13 saloons as a museum; the Black Hills Central Railroad runs excursions in summer.

Mount Rushmore National Memorial (22 m S off US 16A), the carved faces of Washington, Jefferson, Lincoln, and Theodore Roosevelt on a 6000-ft mountain, is the work of Gutzon Borglum, who began work in 1927 and had almost finished at his death in 1941; special lighting in summer; Visitor Center offers information and special programs; open daily 8-sundown (6 am-10 pm in summer); free.

Chapel in the Hills (5 m W on SR 40), built to honor Norwegian immigrants, is a copy of a winsome stave church built about 1150 in Borgund, Norway; elaborate exterior wood carving is by famed Norwegian carver Erik Fridstrom; altar and disciples at the top of each stave were carved by Helge Christiansen, a Danish immigrant; Christian and pagan themes are represented; Stabbur Reception Center is in a sod-roof stabbur imported from Norway; open May-Oct. daily 7 am-sunset; rest of yr, only sunken garden is open; free.

Badlands National Monument (62 m E via I-90, US 16A), with strange and colorful formations; **Visitor Center** audiovisual program, exhibits, summer ranger programs; open daily 8-5 (7-9 in summer); closed Jan. 1, Dec. 25; free. **Prairie Homestead Historic Site** (just S of the Monument in Interior) preserves original sod dugout; furnished; open mid-May-Oct., daily; sm adm.

SIOUX FALLS: Pettigrew Museum (131 N Duluth Ave.) has Sioux, Blackfoot, other Indian displays; rocks and fossils; mounted wildlife; guns; historic exhibits; open Mon.-Sat. 9-noon, 1:30-5, Sun. 2-5; closed hols; free. **Minnehaha Museum** (W 6th St.), in old county courthouse; exhibits on local history; open daily 8-5; closed hols; free. **Sioux Falls College** (22nd St. & Prairie Ave.), Indian and Chinese collections open daily 8-5; closed school hols; free. **Battleship South Dakota Memorial** (W 12th St. & Kiwanis Ave.), a circular brick building with the same dimensions as the ship, and paneled with material from the ship, displays a scale model, memorabilia; open Memorial Day-Labor Day, daily 10 am-8 pm; free.

Prairie Village (16 m W on I-90, then 28 m N on SR 19, then 2 m W on US 81, SR 34), reconstructed late-19th-C town of some 50 buildings moved from other parts of the state and furnished; sod house, opera house (productions given in summer), 1893 carousel with handcarved horses, steam- and gas-powered farm equipment; special events; open June-Aug. daily 8-8; May & Sept. daily 10-4; adm.

STURGIS: Old Fort Meade Cavalry & Pioneer Museum (1 m E on SR 34, 79), on site of the fort to which surviving members of the 7th Cavalry and the horse Comanche came after Little Big Horn; 1878-90 buildings; museum with memorabilia of Indian wars, cavalry days, pioneers; cemetery (tallest monument is to 2 soldiers who died from drinking wood alcohol); open Memorial Day-Labor Day, Mon.-Sat. 9-5, Sun. 1-6; donation.

Bear Butte State Park (6 m NE on SR 79) was land sacred to the Mandan Indians, trespassed by whites seeking gold in the Black Hills; Custer camped here 1874 during his Black Hills expedition. Visitor Center has Cheyenne Indian Shrine; displays of buffalo robes, skulls, arrowheads, other Indian artifacts; natural history exhibits; open Memorial Day-Labor Day, Mon.-Sat. 9-5, Sun. 10-8; free.

WATERTOWN: Mellette House Memorial & Museum (415 5th Ave. at 5th St. NW), restored home of last territorial and first state governor (who gave his entire fortune to the state during the 1894 financial crisis), is an 1883 brick Victorian dwelling; original furnishings and carved woodwork; open mid-May-Oct., Tues.-Sun. 2-5; free.

Blue Cloud Abbey (15 m W of Milbank on US 12), named for a prominent Sioux and dedicated 1967, maintains American Indian Culture Research Center, an advisory and research facility; visitors lounge has mural of early Benedictine work among Indians of Dakota Territory; small exhibit of beadwork, ceremonial pipes, dioramas.

YANKTON: Capital of the Dakota Territory 1861-83, Yankton was a major steamboat port; until the coming of railroads it was a major link in the Missouri River transcontinental transportation system; **Chamber of Commerce** (104 E 4th St.) provides maps of marked historic sites— steamboat landings, Indian agencies, military and trading posts, other sites including Custer's campsite (E of town); Brave Bear's hanging (Douglas near 5th); trial of Wild Bill Hickok's killer, Jack McCall (Capital St. between 3rd & 4th); McCall's public hanging (2 m N on state hospital grounds). **Dakota Territorial Museum** (in Westside Park, Summit Ave.), in 1860s building where Territorial legislative assembly met; office of first governor; rooms furnished in pioneer style; Indian and Territorial relics including items such as a buffalo overcoat and a sod-buster plow; open Memorial Day-Aug., Wed.-Mon. 1-4; free.

Yankton College (12th & Douglas Sts.) offers a Museum of Natural Sciences with mounted wildlife, fossils, Indian art; open academic yr, daily; free. **Mt. Marty College** (1100 W 5th St.) offers changing exhibits in Bede Hall Art Gallery and Indian artifacts at Chief Eagle Feather Museum Area (W end of campus); both open academic yr, daily; free.

Gavins Point Dam and Lewis & Clark State Recreation Area (5 m W on SR 52), tours of powerhouse (in summer, daily 10-6; free); museum in **Visitor Center** displaying Indian artifacts, mounted animals, and relics of cavalry, homesteading, trapping, and steamboat days (May-Sept., daily 9-5; sm adm); marker at Calumet Bluff, where Lewis and Clark smoked a peace pipe on their first meeting with the Sioux. **Bon Homme** (19 m W on SR 50, then 2 m S) has a replica of the first school in South Dakota; ½-m W is a cemetery with graves of 6 of Custer's men who died during the 7th Cavalry trek through here; ½-m S is the townsite. **Midway Museum** (23 m W on SR 50 in Tyndall), in log cabin; relics of local history; open all yr; inquire for hrs; free. At **Wagner** (54 m W on SR 50) or at **Fort Randall Dam** (12 m SW of Wagner on SR 46) you can get a map of historic sites in the area; Fort Randall, built in 1856, was where Sitting Bull was held captive—a chapel and cemetery remain. **Greenwood** (13 m S of Wagner), one of the earliest settlements, had the Territory's first Indian agency; 2 cemeteries; flagpole marks the site where Lewis & Clark wrapped an Indian infant (who grew up to be Sioux chief Struck-by-the-Ree) in an American flag. **Marty** (6 m W on SR 46, then 5 m S) has an Indian Mission Church and school, open to visitors.

W. H. Over Museum (26 m E on SR 50 to Clark St. on University of South Dakota campus, Vermillion), extensive material on the Sioux; studio and gallery of Sioux artist Oscar Howe; Territorial Days room; animal habitat displays; open most of yr, inquire for hrs; free. A map of historic sites in this former steamboat port is available from Chamber of Commerce.

Freeman Junior College (37 m N off US 81 in Freeman) offers a museum and historical library on this interesting area with many Mennonites; Swiss, who had first moved to Volhynia (a province of Poland and Russia) settled SE of town in 1874; Low Germans settled NE; Hutterites, who had also gone first to Russia, arrived in 1874 and settled W of town; inquire locally for hrs; free. Articles brought from Russia are sometimes displayed at area festivals.

TENNESSEE

CAMDEN: Nathan Bedford Forrest State Park (7 m NE via Eva Rd.) honors Civil War General who in 1864 set up hidden batteries here; catching the Union by surprise, he destroyed more than 30 vessels in the Tennessee River, rendering useless the Union supply base at Johnsonville; museum open daily 8-6 (7-10 in summer); sm adm.

CHATTANOOGA: Convention & Visitors Bureau (399 McCallie Ave.) offers information; boat and train tours, or maps for self-guiding auto tours, are offered during autumn color (Oct.). Overviews from Lookout Mountain Incline (3917 St. Elmo Ave.), daily 7-7:30 (to 9:30 in summer); adm. Views of Grand Canyon of the Tennessee River are available from Signal and James Points on Signal Mountain (9 m N on US 127). Visitor overlooks are open daily, free, at Chickamauga Dam (12 m NE via SR 58, 153), Sequoyah Nuclear Plant (20 m NE via US 27), and Nickajack Dam (15 m W on US 41).

    Lookout Mountain (S via Ochs Hwy & Scenic Hwy) was site of the Battle Above the Clouds, part of 1863 Battle of Chattanooga that resulted in Union control of Tennessee and a base in Chattanooga from which Sherman launched his march to the sea. **Point Park** (1101 E Brow Rd.), scene of one of the great Union charges of the war, is part of Chickamauga & Chattanooga National Military Park (see Georgia); **Ochs Museum** explains the battle and offers maps pinpointing Missionary Ridge, Signal Point Reservation, and other segments of the battleground (all with monuments and markers) in and near Chattanooga; open daily 8-5 (8-6 in summer); closed Dec. 25; free. Nearby is **Cravens House,** used as Confederate hq and badly damaged by Union fire; it was rebuilt after the war and is restored with period furnishings; open mid-Feb.-mid-Dec., Tues.-Sat. 9-5, Sun. 1-5; sm adm. **Lookout Mountain Museum** (1100 E Brow Rd.) exhibits dioramas and artifacts of prehistoric Indian life in the area; Civil War memorabilia; open daily 9-6; closed Dec. 25; sm adm. At foot of Lookout Mountain is **Confederama** (3742 Tennessee Ave.), a re-creation of the Battle of Chattanooga with figures, light and sound; open Mon.-Sat. 8-6 (to 9 in summer), Sun. 1-6; closed Dec. 25; adm.

    Hunter Gallery of Art (10 Bluff View), a former residence housing 18-20th-C American arts and decorative arts; open Tues.-Sat. 10-4:30, Sun. 1-4:30; closed hols; free. **Houston Antique Museum** (201 High St.), so packed that some displays hang from the ceiling; pitchers, Toby jugs, whale-oil lamps; art glass, Sandwich and Tiffany glass, pressed glass, lusterware; open Mon.-Sat. 10-4:30, Sun. 2-4:30; closed hols; adm. **Siskin Memorial Foundation** (526 Vine St.), a religious, civic, and educational center; religious and ceremonial art; library of rare books, Bibles; open Mon.-Fri. 9-5; closed hols; free.

Tennessee Valley Railroad Museum (2202 N Chamberlain Ave.), passenger cars, steam locomotives, railroad memorabilia; 3-m train ride; open late Apr.-mid-Sept., Sun. 1-6; closed hols; adm.

COLUMBIA: James K. Polk Ancestral Home (301 W 7th St.), built 1816 by the father of the 11th President, of hand-shaped bricks; fine woodwork; Polk was away at school when it was built but visited his parents here 1820-24; personal memorabilia, family furnishings and portraits; open Mon.-Sat. 9-5, Sun. 1-5; closed Dec. 25; adm.

Pinewood-Stasia Hall (31 m NW on SR 50, then 7 m NW on SR 48 in Nunnelly), lovely Italian Renaissance mansion; plaster friezes; staircase of Cuban mahogany; built 1866-68; Empire and other elegant furnishings; open daily 1-5; closed hols; adm.

David Crockett State Park (42 m S on US 43 to Lawrenceburg, then W on SR 64), grist mill reconstructed near site where Crockett operated a powder mill, grist mill, and distillery; Crockett lived in Lawrenceburg 1817-22, while serving in the state legislature; museum exhibits in mill; open daily; sm adm.

CUMBERLAND GAP: For Cumberland Gap National Historical Park, see Kentucky. **Lincoln Memorial University** (in Harrogate), one of the best collections of Lincolniana (in Duke Hall); personal effects, papers, statuary, photographs; Civil War collection; open Mon.-Fri. 8-noon, 1-5, Sat. 8-noon, Sun. 2-5; closed hols; free.

DAYTON: Rhea County Courthouse (N Market St.) preserves courtroom in which John T. Scopes was tried for teaching evolution in the "Monkey Trial" of 1925; his defense attorney, Clarence Darrow, argued unsuccessfully against the "silver-tongued" William Jennings Bryan, who died in Dayton 5 days after the verdict. **Robinson's Drugstore** (N Market St.), table at which Scopes decided to test the state law demanding that only the Biblical version of man's creation be taught; open Mon.-Sat. 8-7, Sun. 2-5; closed hols.

FORT DONELSON NATIONAL MILITARY PARK & CEMETERY (on US 79 W of Dover): Earthworks and river batteries remain on site of log-and-earth fort built by soldiers and slaves to protect the Cumberland River from inland attack. Here in 1862, when Northern morale was low after Manassas and other Confederate victories, Ulysses S. Grant propelled himself to national prominence by delivering the Union's first major victory of the Civil War; in taking the fort, he earned his nickname Unconditional Surrender Grant. **Visitor Center,** audiovisual program, museum exhibits; 8½-m self-guiding auto tour of battlefield; Dover Hotel, where Confederates surrendered; national cemetery; open daily 8-4:30 (to 5:30 in summer); closed Dec. 25; free.

GREAT SMOKY MOUNTAINS NATIONAL PARK (43 m SE of Knoxville via US 441): **Visitor Center** (2 m S of Gatlinburg on US 441 at Sugarlands) provides information on this beautiful park; open May-Oct. daily 8 am-9 pm; Nov.-Apr. daily 8-4:30; closed Dec. 25. Tapes for self-guiding auto tours detailing history and attractions are for rent along US 441 in Gatlinburg. Appealing **Cades Cove** (25 m W of Sugarlands), where an 11-m auto loop circles pioneer homesteads and a water-powered gristmill; this community, believed settled about 1818, remained isolated for a century, and is now maintained as a living museum by descendants of the settlers. See also North Carolina.

GREENEVILLE: Named for Revolutionary War hero Nathanael Greene, Greeneville was capital of an independent sovereign state called Franklin, established 1785 by John Sevier, Rev. Samuel Doak, Francis Ramsey, William Blount, James White, and others; the state of Franklin was dissolved in 1788 and became part of the Union with Tennessee in 1796. A log cabin and marker (off SR 70, NW of town) commemorates Franklin.

    Andrew Johnson National Historic Site honors the 17th President; at an early age he abandoned school and became a tailor to support his family; he educated himself by hiring people to read to him, and was elected to Greeneville's Board of Aldermen in 1829; the site is in 3 sections; **Visitor Center** (Depot & College St.), Johnson's little tailor shop with some original furnishings; exhibits on Johnson's career. **Johnson Homestead** (Main St.), Johnson's home 1851 until his death in 1875; simple furnishings are original. Both open daily 9-5; closed Dec. 25; sm adm. **Johnson Grave** (Monument Ave.), in national cemetery, marked with marble shaft with a carved eagle; open daily 8-dark; free.

    Davy Crockett Birthplace State Park (9 m E off US 11E), replica of log cabin in which Crockett was born 1786; visitor center; open Apr.-Nov. daily 7 am-10 pm; free.

JACKSON: Casey Jones Home & Railroad Museum (211 W Chester St.) honors John Luther Jones, hero of song and legend, who was at the throttle of "Old 382" on Apr. 30, 1900 when he saw a stalled train ahead;

although the fireman yelled at him to jump, Casey tried to slow the train and was killed in the wreck. The cottage, furnished as it was when he died, is a memorial to the average working man; railroad timetables, whistles, other memorabilia; open Mon.-Sat. 9-4, Sun. 1-4; closed hols; adm. Casey's grave is in Mt. Cavalry Cemetery. **Old Country Store** (514 Airways Blvd), 1840 interior, stocks old-time merchandise; open Mon.-Sat. 8 am-9 pm; closed Thnks, Dec. 25; free. **Pinson Mounds Park** (11 m S on US 45 to Pinson, then E), on Forked Deer River; 1000 acres with 30 mounds, earth walls, interpretive displays; open daily; free.

JAMESTOWN: Pickett State Park (2 m N on US 127, then 12 m NE on SR 154) contains Sergeant York Historic Area, home and gristmill of WW I hero Sgt. Alvin C. York; open daily. **Cordell Hull Birthplace** (23 m NW via US 127 just W of Byrdstown), rebuilt log cabin where Pres. F. D. Roosevelt's Secty of State and the 1945 Nobel Peace Prize winner was born; museum of personal effects; inquire locally for hrs; free.

JOHNSON CITY: Reece Museum (SW edge of town on E Tennessee State Univ campus), attractive displays of 18-19th-C regional art and artifacts; open daily 1-4:45; closed hols; free.

Tipton-Haynes Living Historical Farm (S edge of town) is at a spring used by Indians and colonials, where Daniel Boone built a hunting camp; Capt. James Tipton, who built a log house here after the Revolution, led a battle here against the faction who wanted to establish the independent state of Franklin (see Greeneville), and Tipton's victory helped seal the state's doom. During the Civil War, the property was owned by a state senator whose law office has been restored. Operated as a working farm with typical crops, equipment; open Apr.-Oct., Mon.-Fri. 10-6; Sat. & Sun. 2-6; adm.

Rocky Mount Historic Shrine (5 m NE on US 11E), log house built 1770 that served as capitol 1790-92, during William Blount's term as Governor of the Territory of the U.S. South of the River Ohio; Blount took pride in the glass windows, a rarity on the frontier; in 1838-47, the house served as post office and stopping place on Baltimore-Old Southwest stagecoach route; kitchen, blacksmith shop, country store, other outbuildings; museum with exhibits on frontier life and regional history; open Apr.-Oct., Mon.-Sat. 10-5, Sun. 2-6; adm.

Sycamore Shoals (7 m E toward Elizabethton) was site of an independent colony established 1772 on land leased from the Cherokee on the Watauga River; their government, the Watauga Association, bound itself to obey a body of laws considered the first constitution adopted by independent Americans. In 1780 this was the rendezvous point for frontiersmen marching against British and Loyalist forces at the Battle of Kings Mountain. Interpretive displays being developed.

Jonesboro Historic District (8 m W on US 411), a planned community chartered 1779, oldest town in the state; log courthouse was built the first year, and by 1800 more than 100 homes lined the single street; state of Franklin was organized here in 1784; Andrew Jackson was admitted to the bar and tried his first case; the first abolitionist periodicals in the U.S. were published here in the 1820s. Among the buildings are 1797 Chester Inn (where Andrew Jackson, James Polk, John Sevier stayed); 1820 Sisters Row; 1830s Hoss House; 1848 Presbyterian Church with slave gallery; 1840s Methodist Church.

KINGSPORT: Netherlands Inn Complex on the banks of Holston River opposite Long Island of the Holston, is site of an early river port that served travelers on the Great State Road (Washington, D.C. to New Orleans) during the 19th-C; restoration, continuing, includes homes, public buildings, and Boatyard Historic District with wharf and warehouse. **Allandale** (5 m W on US 11W), country mansion built of materials salvaged from an 1847 home, incorporates an 1861 home; lavish furnishings include Jacobean, Hepplewhite, Louis XIV; open Sun. 1:30-4:30; Apr.-Nov., Tues.-Sat. 9:30-4:30, Sun. 1:30-4:30; closed July 4; adm.

KNOXVILLE: This attractive city grew from a trading post that supplied wagons headed West on the Wilderness Road. It was capital of the Territory South of the River Ohio 1792-96, and state capital 1796-1811, 1817. During the Civil War, Confederates held the city until 1863, when the troops went to Chattanooga; they never regained it. **Gen. James White Home & Fort** (205 E Hill Ave.), built 1786 by the first settlers (White once owned all the land on which Knoxville was later built), was surrounded by a stockade in case of Indian attack; here Blount signed the peace treaty with the Cherokee; log house contains original furnishings; open Mon.-Sat. 9:30-5, Sun. 1-5; closed Dec. 25; adm. **Governor William Blount Mansion** (200 W Hill Ave.) was center of political and social activity after Washington appointed Blount in 1790 to oversee the Territory of the U.S. South of the River Ohio; Blount's treaty with 41 Cherokee chiefs freed the area from Indian attack and allowed it to develop rapidly; when Tennessee was admitted to the Union in 1796, Blount was elected one of the first U.S. Senators, but a year later he was expelled on an accusation he had conspired to seize the lower Mississippi area with the aid of Britain; later he was a state senator. The house, designed by an architect from Charleston, S.C., was unusually sophisticated for the frontier; fine furnishings; pewter; tin and sweetgum chandelier; Oriental rug with design of Aesop's fable of fox and the grapes; Blount memorabilia. Nearby **Craighead-Jackson House** (1000 State St.), brick home built 1818, is restored with woodwork from Knoxville houses of the same period; outstanding 18-19th-C furnishings; 1623-1820 silver; 19th-C glass. Both open Tues.-Sat. 9:30-5, Sun. in May-Oct. 2-5; closed Thnks, mid-Dec.-Jan. 1; adm.

Knox County Courthouse (Main & Gay Sts.) lawn has graves of first Knoxville governor, John Sevier, and his wife Catherine (Bonnie Kate). **First Presbyterian Church** (620 State St.) graveyard is burial place of William Blount. **McClung Historical Collection** (500 W Church Ave in McGhee Library), devoted to the history of Tennessee; open Mon.-Sat. 9-5; closed hols & Sat. in June-Aug; free. **Confederate Memorial Hall** (3148 Kingston Pike), antebellum mansion, Confederate hq during siege of Knoxville; Civil War relics; tours daily, Apr.-Sept. 2-5, Oct.-Mar. 1-4; closed Thnks, Dec. 25; adm. **Dulin Gallery of Art** (3100 Kingston Pike), residence designed by John Russell Pope in 1915; exhibits of art; miniature period rooms; open Tues.-Sun. 1-5; closed hols; sm adm.

University of Tennessee at Knoxville (W Cumberland Ave.), founded 1794 at the suggestion of William Blount: Frank H. McClung Museum (Circle Park), anthropological material; fine arts; natural history; historical displays on Knoxville; open Mon.-Fri. 9-5, Sat. & Sun. 2-5; free. Hoskins Library (1401 W Cumberland Ave.), papers and memorabilia of Sen. Estes Kefauver; open Mon.-Fri. 9-5:30; also Sat. in Oct.-May 9-noon; free.

Ramsey House (6 m NE on Thorngrove Pike), constructed 1797 of local marble and limestone, remained in the family until 1866; period furnishings; open Apr.-Oct., Tues.-Sat. 10-5, Sun. 1-5; adm. Nearby **Lebanon-in-the-Fork Presbyterian Church** (NW on Thorngrove Pike to Asbury Rd., then right on Tennessee River) contains family graves.

Marble Springs (5½ m S via US 441, SR 33 to Neubert Springs Rd.) log trading post built before 1792 by John Sevier, Indian fighter, Kings Mountain hero (he helped organize the Overmountain men), governor of the independent state of Franklin, first governor of Tennessee (he served 6 terms, 1796-1801, 1803-09); he died in 1815, serving on a U.S. Senate commission attempting to establish the boundary between Georgia and the Creek Nation. The trading post protected settlers going south on the French Broad River; Sevier spent weekends here and may have made it his home before his death; reconstructed with outbuildings; visitor center with exhibits; open mid-Mar.-mid-Nov., Mon.-Sat. 10-6, Sun. & hols 2-6; sm adm.

Sam Houston Schoolhouse (17 m S on US 129 to Maryville then 5 m NE off US 411 on Sam Houston Rd.), 1794 log building in which Houston, despite little formal education, taught at age 19 in 1812; tuition was $8 a term, paid ⅓ in cash, ⅓ in corn, ⅓ in calico for his shirts; **Visitor Center** has Houston memorabilia; open Mon.-Sat. 9-sunset, Sun. 1-sunset; closed Dec. 25; free.

Museum of Appalachia (18 m N on US 441, then SW on SR 61), cabins, blacksmith and other workshops, broom and rope factory, mule-powered molasses mill, other buildings depicting pioneer life in the area; museum exhibits; open mid-Feb.-mid-Nov., daily 8-8; adm.

McMINNVILLE: Cumberland Caverns Park (6 m SE off US 70S), guided tours of caverns include area where saltpeter was mined during War of 1812 and Civil War; *God of the Mountain,* drama, presented underground on every tour; open June-Aug. daily 9-5; May & Sept.-Oct., Sat. & Sun. 9-5; adm.

MEMPHIS: Named by Andrew Jackson because its location on the Mississippi brought to mind the Egyptian city on the Nile, this was a wild port in steamboat days; during the Civil War it was a Confederate supply depot until 1862, when Federal gunboats sank a Confederate fleet in the river, while the population watched from the bluffs, and the Union took the city; bankruptcy and yellow fever made postwar recovery slow, but Memphis has since thrived as a major cotton market (the Cotton Exchange, Front & Union Sts., can be visited Fri 9-4; free). Beale Street Historic District preserves the area where W. C. Handy gave birth to the blues with "Memphis Blues," "St. Louis Blues," and other songs; his statue is here in Handy Park. Sightseeing riverboat cruises leave from the foot of Monroe Ave. daily (exc Dec. 25), weather permitting.

Victorian Village is a downtown area (especially 600 block of Adams Ave. & surrounding streets) with preserved Victorian homes: **Mallory-Neely House** (652 Adams Ave.), built at mid-century and later remodeled by a wealthy cotton factor, has stained-glass windows, 1890s furnishings; open daily 1-4; closed hols; adm. **Fontaine House** (680 Adams Ave.), an industrialist's home built 1871, is in French Victorian style with furnishings from several periods; carriage house; playhouse; open daily 1-4; closed hols; adm. **Pillow-McIntyre House** (707 Adams Ave.) is a brick Greek Revival mansion restored with fine antiques; open Mon.-Fri. 9-5; closed hols. **Magevney House** (198 Adams Ave.) was built about 1832 and became a center for Catholic life in early Memphis; some original furnishings; open Tues.-Sat. 10-4, Sun. 1-4; closed Jan. 1, Thnks, Dec. 24, 25; free.

Brooks Memorial Art Gallery (Overton Park, East Pkwy & Poplar Ave.), excellent collection of Renaissance masterpieces, English landscapes, other European paintings; 18-19th-C American works; porcelain, glass; open Tues.-Sat. 10-5, Sun. 2-5; closed Jan. 1, Thnks, Dec. 25; free.

Southwestern At Memphis (University St. at N Pkwy) houses memorabilia and works of Richard Halliburton in Memorial Tower; Oriental arts exhibited in Clough Hanson Gallery; inquire for hrs; free.

Memphis Pink Palace Museum (232 Tilton Rd. & Central Ave.), a palatial home built for a financier, houses regional historic and natural history displays; hand-carved, miniature animated circus; open Tues.-Sat. 9-5, Sun. 2-5; closed Jan. 1, Thnks, Dec. 24, 25; free.

Joseph Schlitz Brewing Co. (5151 E Raines Rd.), guided tours several times daily, Mon.-Fri; closed hol; free. Visitor center is a riverboat with exhibits on steamboat days; free.

Chucalissa Indian Village & Museum (5 m S on US 61, 4½ m W on Mitchell Rd. in T. O. Fuller State Park), site of Indian village founded about AD 900, abandoned in 1600s, excavated by Memphis State Univ.; temple and grass-roof mud houses re-constructed; skeletons in situ at burial site; museum with audiovisual program, artifacts; Choctaw arts demonstrations; open Tues.-Sat. 9-5, Sun. 1-5; closed Jan. 1, Thnks, last 3 weeks Dec.; sm adm.

MORRISTOWN: Davy Crockett Tavern & Museum (2020 E Main St.) is a replica of a tavern David Crockett's father operated on the Abingdon-Knoxville road in the 1790s to provide food and shelter for drovers taking livestock to market in Virginia; Crockett spent his youth here; period furnishings; basement museum honors Crocketts and other pioneers; on grounds is a covered wagon; open May-Oct., Mon.-Sat. 9-5, Sun. 2-5; adm.

Jefferson County Courthouse (6 m S on US 25E, then 10 m SW on SR 113 in Dandridge) has been in use since 1845; museum exhibits include Cherokee relics, Civil War artifacts, documents including Davy Crockett's 1806 marriage license; open Mon.-Sat. 9-5; free.

Glenmore (11 m S on US 11E at Jefferson City), built 1869 for the president of the state's first railroad, is a choice Victorian mansion with fine carved woodwork, Dutch fireplace tiles, ballroom, 3-story staircase, original furnishings; the mansion was so hard to heat that in winter the family moved to a small replica of the house, attached to the rear; outbuildings; open Apr.-Oct., Sat. & Sun. 1-5; adm.

MURFREESBORO: Oaklands (end of N Maney Ave.), a 1798 home expanded 1820-50 was a showplace and social center to which visiting dignitaries (Gen. Braxton Bragg, Pres. Jefferson Davis, and others) were automatically invited; furnishings show a succession of styles; special events; open Tues.-Sun. 10-4:30; closed Thnks, Dec. 25; adm.

Stones River National Battlefield (3 m NW on US 41) preserves the ground on which 13,000 Federals and 10,000 Confederates were killed or wounded in a vain Confederate attempt to halt the Union march on Chattanooga Dec. 31, 1862-Jan. 2, 1863; **Visitor Center** with audiovisual program and exhibits; self-guiding auto tour; national cemetery with graves of 2562 unidentified Union dead; living history demonstrations in summer; open daily 8-4:45 (8-7 in summer); closed Dec. 25; free.

NASHVILLE: Chamber of Commerce (161 4th Ave. N) offers maps, calendar of events, information on guided and package tours to historic and musical sites. **Historical Commission of Metropolitan Nashville & Davidson Co.** (room 329, Stahlman Bldg., zip 37201) puts out brochures for walking tours; also available at hotels, major attractions, Chamber of Commerce. An overview is available from 31st floor of **L & C Tower** (4th Ave. & Church St.), open Mon.-Sat. 8-4:30 or longer, Sun. noon-6; closed hols; sm adm. Narrated cruises on the Cumberland River are offered spring-fall (from 1st Ave. N, near foot of Broadway, and 10 m NE via I-40 & Briley Pkwy to Pennington Rd.).

State Capitol (6th & Charlotte Aves.), imposing Greek Revival building designed by William Strickland (buried in the wall) in 1845, was damaged during the Civil War by Union troops who used it as a garrison; scars on the first-floor staircase are from bullets fired at legislators attempting to leave a forced session in 1866; historical portraits, murals, ceiling frescos; replica of Sir Walter Scott's study is used as a legislative lounge; tours daily 8-4:30; closed hols; free. State Library & Archives (7th & Charlotte Ave.) is open Mon.-Sat. 8-4:30; closed hols; free. **Tennessee State Museum** (Capitol Blvd & Union St. in War Memorial Bldg), relics related to state history; portraits; war memorabilia; natural history displays; open Mon.-Fri. 9-5; closed hols; free.

Fort Nashborough (170 1st Ave. N at Church St.), reconstructed palisade enclosing blockhouses and cabins on the Cumberland River, a memorial to the city's founding at Great Salt Lick in 1779; cabins are furnished with pioneer items; open Mon.-Sat. 9-4; Sun. noon-4 in June-Aug.; closed hols; free.

The Parthenon (Centennial Park, West End Ave. & 25th Ave. N) is an accurate replica of the Athens masterpiece; the illusion of perfect balance is created by avoiding straight lines, varying the spaces between elements, and varying the sizes of steps, columns, and other elements; inside are a reproduction of the Elgin marbles, pre-Columbian artifacts, 19-20th-C American works including paintings by Church and Homer; open Mon.-Sat. 9-4:30, Sun. 1-4:30; closed hols; free.

Fisk University (17th Ave. N) offers the Stieglitz Collection of modern art in the library and the Carl Van Vechten Gallery of Fine Arts; open academic yr, Mon.-Fri. 9-5, Sun. 2-5; closed hols; free. **Vanderbilt University** (West End Ave.) offers a Fine Arts Museum and prehistoric Indian artifacts in Kirkland Hall; open academic yr, Mon.-Fri. 9:30-noon, 1-5; Sat. & Sun. 1-5; closed hols; free. **George Peabody College for Teachers** (21st Ave. S) offers Renaissance and contemporary painting, prints, sculpture in Cohen Memorial Fine Art Bldg; open academic yr, Mon.-Fri. 9-5; free.

Tennessee Botanical Gardens & Fine Arts Center (7 m W off SR 100 on Cheek Rd.) houses 17-20th-C painting, sculpture, and art objects from Europe, the Far East, and America in Cheekwood, an impressive Georgian mansion built 1930; 18th-C English furnishings; gardens; open Tues.-Sat. 10-5, Sun. 1-5; closed Jan. 1, Thnks, Dec. 24, 25, 31; adm.

Cumberland Museum & Science Center (800 Ridley Ave. in Ft. Negley Park), natural history and environmental exhibits; live specimens; planetarium; open Tues.-Sat. 10-5, Sun. 1-5; closed hols; adm.

The **Upper Room** (1908 Grand Ave.) is a Georgian chapel; chancel is an adaptation of the upper room in da Vinci's "The Last Supper," which is reproduced as a polychrome wood carving on the rear wall; religious artifacts; library; open Mar.-Dec. daily 8-7:30; Jan.-Feb. daily 8-6; free. **Holy Trinity Episcopal Church** (615 6th Ave. S), an outstanding Gothic church built 1853 of limestone and cedar; interesting ceiling, hand-carved furnishings; Union troops stored supplies here during the Civil War and used the altar as a butcher block; open weekends. **First Presbyterian Church** (154 5th Ave. N), built 1851, was designed by William Strickland and is a rare example of Egyptian Revival style; Union troops used the church as a hospital and the basement as a stable; open daily. **Old City Cemetery** (1001 4th Ave. S at Oak St.) contains graves of many famous Tennesseans, including Capt. William Driver who named the U.S. flag "Old Glory"; open Mon.-Fri. 8-4, Sat. & Sun. 10-5.

Music Row (roughly bounded by Grand Ave. & Division St. between 16-18th Aves.), where music industry offices are located, gives Nashville its nickname, "Music City." A highlight of the area is **Country Music Hall of Fame & Museum** (700 16th Ave. S), with costumes, instruments, memorabilia of performers; portraits; film; demonstration of recording session; library; open June-Aug., Sun.-Tues. 8:30-5, Wed.-Sat. 8:30-8; Sept.-May, daily 9-5; closed Jan. 1, Thnks, Dec. 24, 25; adm. **Ryman Auditorium** (116 5th Ave.), home of Grand Ole Opry 1943-74, was built as a religious tabernacle by a riverboat captain; now a monument to the stars who performed there; open daily 8:30-4:30; closed Jan. 1, Dec. 25; adm. **Opryland USA** (4 m E on I-40, then 5 m N on Briley Pkwy) is a family entertainment park with American music as its theme (open daily 10-10 in summer; weekends in spring & fall; adm). Here is Grand Ole Opry House, with folk music shows Fri. & Sat., Gospel show on Sun. Grand Ole Opry Tours (write 2800 Opryland Dr.) of historic sites, stars' homes, other attractions are available by reservation.

The **Hermitage** (13 m E on US 70), beautiful home of Andrew Jackson, is furnished as it was on his death in 1845. After Jackson bought the land in 1804, the family lived in log cabins (Aaron Burr was entertained here in

1805) while Jackson rose to fame as an Indian fighter and hero of the Battle of New Orleans. The stately home with white pillars, wide verandas, and spiral staircase was erected 1819 and has been widely copied. Tomb of the President and Rachel (who died before the first inauguration) is in garden. Across the road is **Tulip Grove**, built 1836 by Rachel's nephew and the President's secretary, Andrew Jackson Donelson, whose wife served as White House hostess after Rachel's death. Nearby is **Old Hermitage Church** (also called Rachel's Church), built by the President for Rachel in 1823. Open daily 9-5; closed Dec. 25; adm.

Cragfont (29 m E on US 31E, then 5 m E on SR 25 in Castalian Springs) was built 1798 by Revolutionary hero Gen. James Winchester, who brought stone masons and ships' carpenters 700 m through the wilderness from his home state of Maryland to erect it; stone was quarried and woods hand-hewn on the property; Lafayette, Andrew Jackson, Sam Houston were said to have been guests; Federal furnishings include many family pieces; ballroom, weaving room, wine cellar, tool display in basement; open mid-Apr.-Oct., Tues.-Sat. 10-5, Sun. 1-6; adm. Nearby **Wynnewood** (4 m E of Cragfont on SR 25) is built at site of a mineral spring that attracted animals and therefore Indian and white hunters; log inn erected 1828 as a stagecoach stop became a spa; Andrew Jackson was a frequent visitor; open Mon.-Sat. 10-5, Sun. 1-5; closed hols; adm.

Travellers' Rest Historic House (5 m S off US 31 on Farrell Pkwy) was built 1799 by John Overton, friend and law partner of Andrew Jackson, and reflects the sophistication of his native Virginia; museum exhibits of period furniture, Indian artifacts, early records; open Mon.-Sat. 9-5, Sun. 1-5; closed Jan. 1, Dec. 25; adm.

Belle Meade (7 m SW at 110 Leake Ave. & Harding Rd.), an elegant mansion called Queen of Tennessee Plantations, was focus of a 5300-acre estate, a noted thoroughbred breeding farm, and was probably designed by William Strickland. The site was first settled as Dunham Station on the Natchez Trace, and the 1793 log cabin for travelers is still standing. Mansion is furnished with choice 19th-C antiques; outbuildings include an elaborate Victorian carriage house and Tudor-Gothic dairy; open Mon.-Sat. 9-5, Sun. 1-5; closed Jan. 1, Thnks, Dec. 25; adm.

Sam Davis Home (15 m SE on US 41, 70S, then 1½ m E on SR 102) is a shrine to the Boy Hero of the Confederacy, apprehended in 1863 carrying information on Union movements and convicted as a spy; he was hanged after refusing to betray his informer, and is buried in the family cemetery here. The 1810 frame house typifies middle-class attempts to add Greek Revival details to their homes; family furnishings; slave cabins, other outbuildings; open Mar.-Oct., Mon.-Sat. 9-5, Sun. 1-5; Nov.-Feb., Mon.-Sat. 10-4, Sun. 1-4; closed Jan. 1, Thnks, Dec. 25; adm.

Franklin Historic District (18 m S on US 31 or 431) preserves the area of the bloody Battle of Franklin, 1864, begun in anger rather than for strategic gain; Gen. Hood, trying to recapture Nashville, was so enraged when Union forces managed to slip through his lines that he ordered a suicidal frontal attack (accompanied by band music) late in the day; the Federal forces escaped during the night, leaving behind 2326 dead; the Confederates lost 6252 men, including 6 generals. **Visitor Information Center** (Public Sq.) will advise you on tours of historic homes and offers brochures for self-guiding auto tours of the area (tour includes historic sites, an Indian burial mound, and Forge Seat, which produced rifles used by Jackson at the Battle of New Orleans); open Mon.-Sat. 9-4, Sun. 1-4; closed hols. **Carter House** (1140 Columbia Ave.) was built 1830 by Fountain Branch Carter, a merchant, surveyor, and farmer, and became the Union command post during the Battle of Franklin; the Carter family hid in the basement, but a son was wounded and later died; the bullet-scarred, neat brick building typifies the simple but comfortable lifestyle in early Tennessee; many family furnishings; Civil War memorabilia in basement; outbuildings; open May-Oct., Mon.-Sat. 9-5, Sun. 2-5; Nov.-Apr., Mon.-Sat. 9-4, Sun. 2-4; closed Jan. 1, Thnks, Dec. 25; adm.

Rock Castle (10 m NE on US 31E at Hendersonville), built 1780s, is a fine Federal-style home with period furnishings; inquire locally for hrs; adm.

NATCHEZ TRACE PARKWAY enters Tennessee at Cypress Inn and runs NE to Gordonsburg; eventually it will be completed to Nashville. Sections of the original trace can be seen at **Old Trace** (NE of Cypress Inn) and on the 2½-m **Old Trace Loop Drive** (NE of jct US 64); exhibits of an early iron industry are at the open-pit Napier Mine and Metal Ford (both at Napier). **Meriwether Lewis Park** (Gordonsburg) contains the grave of the explorer (marked with a broken column to symbolize a broken career) who met a mysterious death at an inn on the trace in 1809. See also Mississippi.

OAK RIDGE: American Museum of Atomic Energy (Tulane & Illinois Aves.) explains atomic fusion, space exploration, and applications of atomic energy with exhibits, tours, demonstrations, films, visitor-operated consoles; open Mon.-Sat. 9-5, Sun. 12:30-6:30; closed Jan. 1, Thnks, Dec. 25; free. **Visitor overlooks** are open daily at Kingston Steam Plant (5 m SW on SR 58); Melton Hill Dam (9 m SW on Clinch River); Bull Run Steam Plant (5 m SE on Melton Hill Reservoir); Oak Ridge Gaseous Diffusion Plant (10 m W on SR 58). National Laboratory Graphite Reactor (10 m SW on Bethel Valley Rd.) offers interpretive exhibits Mon.-Sat. 9-4; closed hols; free.

Fort Loudon (8 m S on SR 95, 6 m SW on US 11, then follow signs on US 411 N from Vonore), erected 1756 by South Carolina to stop French advances into the Mississippi Valley, was a symbol of British friendship with the Cherokee (whose women, children, and old found protection here during tribal conflicts). But British relations with the Cherokee deteriorated, and in the winter of 1760 the Cherokee blockaded the fort; by August, the garrison's food supply was exhausted and it surrendered on promise of safe passage to Charleston. But about 15 m from the fort, the soldiers and their families were attacked and 23 were killed; survivors were captured and later ransomed; the fort was burned. Site is enclosed with palisade; reconstructed powder magazine; museum; self-guiding trail; open daily 9-5; closed Thnks, Dec. 25; sm adm.

Rugby Restoration (22 m NW on SR 62, 21 m N on US 27, 5 m W on SR 52 in Rugby) preserves buildings of a colony founded 1880 by Thomas Hughes and named for the English school that was the setting for his classic, *Tom Brown's Schooldays*; the colony, intended to provide manual training for the sons of English gentry unable to enter the crowded "acceptable" fields of medicine, law, or the clergy, declined after a typhoid epidemic and an 1884 fire. Of the original 65 buildings, 17 remain (some are examples of Carpenter Gothic), including several cottages; Kingston Lisle, the Hughes home, now a museum; Christ Episcopal Church, with 1849 rosewood organ made in London; and Hughes Public Library with Victorian literature; open spring-fall, Tues.-Sun.; sm adm.

SEWANEE: University of the South offers free guided tours and can arrange for you to see their art and library (material on the Confederacy) collections; Breslin Tower and All Saints Chapel were designed after structures at Oxford University, England.

SHELBYVILLE: Chamber of Commerce (100 N Cannon Blvd) provides a map of Tennessee walking horse farms and stables in the area; the annual walking horse celebration is in Sept.

SHILOH NATIONAL MILITARY PARK (10 m SW of Savannah on SR 22): Enormous casualties (23,746 killed, wounded, or missing) made Shiloh, first major battle of the Western Campaign, one of the bitterest encounters of the Civil War: In Apr., 1862, Grant camped his men at Shiloh Church near Pittsburg Landing to await the arrival of Buell's Army of the Ohio for a combined attack on Confederates massed 22 m S at Corinth, Mississippi. But Confederate Gen. Albert Sidney Johnston decided to attack first, before Buell's arrival, and took Grant by surprise on Apr. 6. Grant rushed to the battlefield to find his men in confusion and retreat. However, Johnston was wounded (and somehow allowed to bleed to death), and his replacement, Gen. P.G.T. Beauregard, rather than pressing the advantage, ordered a cease fire. This gave Buell time to join Grant, and on Apr. 7 their combined forces had Confederates in retreat toward Corinth. The battle is also known for having one of the first field hospitals established during the Civil War and for the later eminence of many participants (John Wesley Powell, later head of the U.S. Geological Survey, who lost an arm here; James A. Garfield; Henry Morton Stanley of "Dr. Livingstone, I presume" fame; Gen. Sherman). **Visitor Center** offers a film, maps, exhibits; open daily 8-5 (8-6 in summer); closed Dec. 25; free. Here booklets are available for a 10-m self-guiding auto tour of marked battlefield sites; rebuilt Shiloh Church; a log cabin that survived the battle; unexcavated Indian mounds; national cemetery.

TENNESSEE VALLEY AUTHORITY, created by Congress in 1933 to harness the Tennessee River, has provided one of the most popular water recreation centers in the nation. **Information Office** (New Sprankle Bldg, Knoxville 37902) issues data on TVA projects and lakes. Navigational charts, boat docks, campgrounds, and other public facilities are listed on maps obtainable from **TVA Maps** (Haney Bldg., Chattanooga 37401, or from Union Bldg, Knoxville 37902). Visitors are welcome at TVA dams and steam plants.

UNION CITY: Reelfoot Lake State Park (9 m S on US 51, then 19 m W on SR 21), museum with regional natural history displays, Indian relics, Civil War memorabilia; open Apr.-Oct. daily; free. **Crockett Cabin** (20 m S on US 45W, on grounds of high school in Rutherford) is a reproduction, using material from the original, of a cabin Davy Crockett built on the Rutherford Fork of the Obion River; he lived here 1823-35, leaving after losing his bid for reelection to Congress, and died at the Alamo; 19th-C furnishings include a rocking chair made by Crockett; on grounds is his mother's grave; inquire locally for hrs; sm adm.

TEXAS

ABILENE: Old Abilene Town (4 m NE on I-20) is a replica of a Western frontier town; amusements; historic displays; open daily 11-7 in summer, 8 am-9 pm rest of yr; closed Dec. 25; adm. **Burro Alley** (S 1st St. & Willis), re-created Mexican village with shops; open Mon.-Sat. 10-5:30; closed hols; free. **Fort Phantom Hill** (10 m N on FM 600) contains ruins of 1851 fort built to protect California-bound gold miners from Indian

attack; ruins of stone commissary, guardhouse, powder magazine; interpretive signs.

At **Albany** (33 m NE on SR 351, US 180) the *Albany News* maintains a
file of frontier-era newspapers. Ledbetter Picket House Museum (in
Webb Park, S. Jacobs St.), a dog-run cabin, houses artifacts from Ft.
Griffin, pioneers, and the 1860 Ledbetter Salt Works; open daily 8-5;
closed hols; free. Across the street the old jail, with 2-ft-thick walls, has
been reconstructed. **Fort Griffin State Park** (14 m N of Albany off US
283), contains ruins of an 1867 cavalry post established to escort government mail and to protect cattle drovers and settlers; the wild town that
grew around the fort counted many gunfights; buildings are marked with
interpretive signs; open daily.

ALPINE: Museum of the Big Bend (Sul Ross State Univ. E of town) offers chronological displays of local history, with Indian, Spanish, Mexican, and pioneer artifacts; reconstructed general store and workshops;
open Tues.-Fri. 1-5, Sat. 1-6, Sun. 2-6; closed some hols; sm adm.

Fort Davis National Historic Site (25 m NW on SR 118): impressive
ruins of 1854 frontier fort (named for Jefferson Davis) intended to guard
travelers on the El Paso road to California from Apache and Comanche
raids. The 8th Infantry, on foot or on mules (and, for a while, experimen-
tally, on camels) rarely succeeded in catching raiders, despite the erection
of new forts along the road; the forts were abandoned when Texas seceded
in 1861, and Confederate troops occupied Ft. Davis until the Apache
wrecked it. In 1867, Federal troops moved in, constructing 50 new
buildings, and remained until the Indians were defeated in 1891. Officers'
Row, the hospital, other buildings have been restored. **Visitors Center**
presents a movie and other interpretive materials and programs; open daily 8-5:30 (8-8 in summer); sm adm or GEP. (The town of Ft. Davis has
small Overland Trail Museum, open Sat. & Sun. 1-5, and Neill Museum,
an 1898 house with period furnishings, open daily in summer 9-6; adm to
each.)

McDonald Observatory (28 m NW on SR 118) on Mt. Locke; conducted tours daily; information for self-guiding tours; open Mon.-Fri.
8-5; closed Thnks, Dec. 25; free.

Santiago Mountain (40 m S on SR 118) was site of an early-1900s land
fraud, when a promoter sold lots in the nonexistent "Progress City" (said
to be on the summit) to out-of-state buyers. **Study Butte** (77 m S on SR
118) was a retreat for Apache and Comanche warriors, bandits, and smugglers; the town boomed after mercury deposits were discovered about 1900,
but faded as the mines proved unprofitable; today it is a ghost town, with
only a few families. **Terlingua** (77 m S on SR 118, then 5 m W on SR 170)
is another mercury ghost town; largest ruin was home of the mine owner,

whose Eastern bride spent only one night here before returning to civilization; Old Waldron Mine tours are offered (adm). **El Camino del Rio** (SR 170 W of Terlingua) parallels an old trail used by Spanish explorers, the Army, and smugglers; because gold and silver were transported along it, many legends of buried treasure have arisen.

Shafter (26 m W on US 90 to Marfa, then 39 m S on US 67), in an area that once produced some $18-million in silver, is almost a ghost town. **Fort Leaton State Historic Site** (20 m S on Shafter at Presidio) was site of 1683 Spanish mission; buildings were used for a trading post about 1846 but abandoned when frontier patrols were withdrawn during the Civil War; site being restored with interpretive signs; open daily; free.

AMARILLO: Helium Monument & Amarillo Tourist Center (I-40 at Nelson St.) displays items sealed into the time capsule; displays on helium industry; information on cattle auctions and other city attractions; open daily 10-6; closed Jan. 1, Thnks, Dec. 25. **Amarillo Art Center** (2200 Van Buren St.), with changing exhibits and programs, was designed by Edward Durell Stone. Books and documents on the Panhandle are housed in **Bivins Memorial Library** (10th & Polk Sts.). Weapons and pioneer items are displayed in **Nielsen Memorial Museum** (Police Dept., 609 S Pierce St.), open Mon.-Fri. 8-5; closed hols; free.

Panhandle-Plains Historical Museum (15 m S on I-27 to 2401 4th Ave. on W Texas State Univ. campus in Canyon), with entrance doors ornamented with historic brands, offers imaginative exhibits on prehistoric Indian life; the Kiowa and Comanche; pioneer and ranching life; full-size replicas of frontier homes and shops; guns; fossils; wildlife; wonderful Western paintings include works of Frank Reaugh; open Mon.-Sat. 9-5, Sun. & hols 2-6; closed Dec. 25; free.

Alibates National Monument (33 m N on SR 136) preserves flint quarries used since 10,000 BC; information and ranger-guided tours are available at **Bates Canyon Information Station;** open daily in summer; at other times, write to Lake Meredith Recreation Area (Box 325, Sanford 79078).

Square House, Carson County Historical Museum (31 m NE on US 60 to Pioneer Park, Elsie & 5th Sts., Panhandle) is an 1893 ranch dwelling housing attractive displays on Indians, ranching, buffalo hunters, oil boom; old tools and vehicles; on grounds is reconstructed half-dugout, authentically furnished; open daily; inquire for hrs; free.

AUSTIN: Established 1839 as capital of the new nation of Texas (which had won independence from Mexico 3 years before), this city was laid out in the middle of Indian territory so that the first construction workers had to be protected by armed guards. Historic markers along Congress Ave.

(6-8th Sts.) locate the sites of the former Republic's administrative
buildings; the unique mercury vapor lights were installed in 1895; Bre-
mond Block (7-8th Sts., San Antonio & Guadalupe Sts.) was begun in 1863
by a man whose children subsequently built adjacent homes reflecting
changing 19th-C tastes (privately owned). Information is available at the
Old Bakery (1006 Congress Ave.), built 1876 by a Swedish baker and
restored with antique ovens and cafe; open Mon.-Sat. 9-4; closed hols;
free.

   State Capitol (N end of Congress Ave.), built 1888 of granite from
Marble Falls (47 m NW) and covering 3 acres, has historic murals and
mosaics; statues include Stephen Austin, Sam Houston, a Texas cowboy, a
Texas Ranger; **Tourist Information Center;** open daily 8-5; closed Dec. 25;
free. On grounds are: **Archives & Library Bldg** (1201 Brazos St.), with a
mural and historic documents; open Mon.-Sat. 8-5; closed hols; free. **Old
Land Office** (112 E 11th St.), an imposing 1857 building housing Confederate memorabilia in the 1st-floor Texas Confederate Museum and
relics of early settlers and the Texas Republic in the 2nd-floor Daughters
of the Republic of Texas Museum; open Tues.-Sat. 9-noon, 1-5; closed
hols; free. **Governor's Mansion** (1010 Colorado, between 10-11th Sts.),
an elegant 1856 Greek Revival mansion, displays interesting portraits and
furnishings, including Sam Houston's four-poster and Stephen Austin's
desk; open Mon.-Sat. 10-noon, Sun. 2-4; closed Thnks, Dec. 25; free.

   University of Texas at Austin (between San Jacinto Blvd. & Guadalupe
St., 19-26th Sts.) has a **Visitor Information Center** (Sid Richardson Hall),
open daily 9-5; closed Dec. 25. Main Bldg has an observation tower open
Mon.-Sat. 10-4; free. Santa Rita No. 1, an oil rig, has a marker giving
history of first oil strike on campus. Library has an unusual collection of
mystery novels and books on crime, begun by donations from Ellery
Queen and Erle Stanley Gardner (whose interesting California office was
moved to the campus). **Lyndon Baines Johnson Presidential Library**
(2313 Red River St.) houses 31 million documents related to the 36th President's career; audiovisual program; exhibits; open daily 9-5; closed Dec.
25; free. **Art Museum** (23rd St. & San Jacinto Blvd) offers changing exhibits of major works; open Sept.-May, Mon.-Sat. 9-6, Sun. 1-5; June-
Aug., Mon.-Sat. 10-4, Sun. 1-5; closed hols; free. **Humanities Research
Center** (Guadalupe & 21st Sts.) houses 20th-C American art; open Mon.-
Sat. 10-5, Sun. 1-5; closed hols; free. **Texas Memorial Museum** (24th &
Trinity Sts.) offers exhibits on early Texana, petroleum dioramas,
dinosaur tracks, regional wildlife, Indians; open Tues.-Sat. 9-5, Sun. 2-5;
closed hols; free.

   Laguna Gloria Art Museum (3809 W 35th St.), in a former private
estate on Lake Austin; changing exhibits; open Tues.-Sat. 10-5, Sun. 1-5;
closed Jan. 1, Thnks, Dec. 25, 2 weeks in Aug.; free. **Elisabet Ney**

Museum (304 E 44th St. at Ave. H), former studio of sculptress and early feminist who died in 1907, houses her works; open Tues.-Fri. 9:30-4:30, Sat.-Mon. 2-4:30; closed hols; free. **O. Henry Museum** (409 E 5th St.), home of author William Sydney Porter, contains original furniture and memorabilia; open Tues.-Fri. 9:30-11:30, 1:30-4:30; Sat.-Mon. 1:30-4:30; closed hols; free. **Old French Legation** (802 San Marcos St.), a handsome 1840 house with Louisiana bayou influence, was built for the French charge d'affaires to the Republic of Texas; unusual furnishings include some brought from France; French Creole kitchen; open Tues.-Sun. 1-5; closed Dec. 25-Jan. 1; adm. **State Cemetery** (E 7th & Comal), known as the Arlington of Texas, has graves of Stephen Austin and other Texan heros. **Round Rock Cemetery** (10 m N on I-35 in Round Rock) contains grave of outlaw Sam Bass, who plagued stagecoaches, trains, and banks in the area until killed by Texas Rangers in 1878.

Fort Croghan Museum (20 m N on US 183, 23 m W on SR 29 at Burnet) is in original stone building and blacksmith shop of 1848 fort built to protect settlers; other buildings have been moved here to reconstruct the fort; historical exhibits; open Memorial Day-Labor Day, Wed.-Sun. 1-5; closed hols; donation. Also in Burnet are **Old Mormon Colony & Mill** (S Pierce St. to Mormon Mill Rd.), cemetery, marker, other remains of 1851-53 colony established by 200 Mormons; nearby are several Indian mounds.

Longhorn Cavern State Park (43 m W on SR 71, 13 m N on US 281, 5 m W on park rd) contains cavern used by prehistoric men, bandits, and Confederates; Robert E. Lee once drove Indians into it, hoping to trap them, not knowing of the many exits; museum of Indian, frontier, and Civil War artifacts; tours Apr.-Sept. daily 10-5; Oct.-Mar., Mon.-Sat. 10-3, Sun. 10-5; adm. **Pioneer Town** (20 m W on US 290, 13 m S on FM 12 to River Rd., Wimberley), reproduction of 1880s village; buildings with period furnishings; rides, melodrama, other entertainment; open late May-Labor Day, daily 8-8:30; some buildings open weekends rest of yr; sm adm plus fees for activities.

Bastrop (20 m SE on SR 71), settled 1829 on El Camino Real but almost abandoned in 1836 because of Indian attacks, has a marked Memorial Medallion Trail that includes: **Bastrop Museum** (702 Main St.), built 1850, with historic documents and artifacts; open Sat. 10-5, Sun. 1-5; adm. **C. Erhard & Sons Drug Store** (921 Main St.), established 1847 and still owned by the same family; old furnishings, old products. **Lock's Drug** (1003 Main St.), with antique medical and drug displays. Interpretive folder and map from **Chamber of Commerce** (Main & Pine Sts.).

Southwest Texas State University (29 m SW on I-35 to N Lyndon B. Johnson Dr., San Marcos), alma mater of Pres. Johnson, houses LBJ memorabilia in Alumni House; open Mon.-Fri. 8-5; closed hols; free.

BEAUMONT: Spindletop Park (3 m S) contains Lucas Gusher Monument, site of oil well that in 1901 blew in, turning Beaumont into a boom town. Spindletop Museum (8866 College St.) offers exhibits and film on the discovery; open Sun. 2-5; free. **Beaumont Art Museum** (1111 9th St.) has collections in many media; open Tues.-Sun. 10-5; closed hols; free. **French Trading Post Museum** (2995 French Dr.), opened by a Connecticut tanner, John French, in 1845 as a trading post; period clothing, furnishings, other relics; audiovisual program depicts Beaumont in the days before oil, when it was a trading center for French and Spanish fur trappers; open Tues.-Sat. 10-4, Sun. 2-5; hrs subject to change; closed hols; sm adm.

BIG BEND NATIONAL PARK (103 m S of Alpine on SR 118 or 68 m S of Marathon on US 385): **Administration Bldg** (Panther Junction) offers information on this 707,000-acre wilderness; exhibits; open daily 8-5 (8-8 in summer). Information is also available at Persimmon Gap and Chisos Basin; S of Persimmon Gap, before Panther Junction, is a fossil exhibit. Open all yr.

BROWNSVILLE: Fort Brown (S end of Elizabeth St.) was established 1846 by Gen. Zachary Taylor to maintain the U.S. claim that the Rio Grande was the boundary with Mexico; the historic buildings, marked with plaques, are now part of Texas Southmost College. **Stillman House Museum** (1305 E Washington), built about 1850 by the town's founder, depicts pre-Civil War living in Brownsville; Stillman family furnishings; open Mon.-Sat. 10-noon, 2-5, Sun. 1-5; closed hols; sm adm. **Palo Alto Battlefield** (5½ m N on FM 1847), historic marker on site where Gen. Zachary Taylor won 1846 artillery duel that began Mexican War. **Palmito Hill Battlefield** (12 m E on SR 4), last land battle of the Civil War was fought here May 12-13, 1865, more than a month after Lee's surrender at Appomattox. Port Isabel Lighthouse State Historic Site (21 m E on SR 48 to Port Isabel, off SR 100), at site of fort commanded by Zachary Taylor during the Mexican War, has historic markers, overview; open daily 10-5; sm adm.

    Confederate Air Force Flying Museum (25 m N on US 77, 83 to Rebel Field, NE of Harlingen), obsolete military aircraft from the U.S. and other countries; displays trace military flying 1939-present; open Mon.-Sat. 9-5, Sun. 1-6; closed Dec. 25; adm. Nearby **Lower Rio Grande Valley Museum** (also at Harlingen Industrial Air Park) traces growth of Indian, Spanish, Mexican, and American cultures in the area; displays on early Harlingen (known as Six-Shooter Junction in its wilder days); open Tues.-Fri. 9-5, Sun. 2-5; closed hols; sm adm.

BROWNWOOD: Douglas MacArthur Academy of Freedom (Austin Ave. & Coggin St.), part of Howard Payne College, resembles a medieval castle; 3-story-high mural; replica of Assembly Room in Philadelphia's Independence Hall; Mediterranean Room with exhibits on classic civilizations; exhibits interpret Western democracy; MacArthur mementos; open daily 9–5; closed hols; free. **Chamber of Commerce** (521 E Baker St.) provides information on other buildings, such as 1902 Old Jail with towers and ramparts.

BRYAN: Texas A & M University (S at College Station) visitor center offers audiovisual programs and information on touring buildings.

Calvert (30 m NW on US 190, SR 6) has a number of Victorian buildings marked with historic plaques. **Navasota** (26 m S on SR 6) has a monument to La Salle (on SR 90), murdered near here by one of his own men while exploring from his coastal colony, Fort St. Louis. **Chappel Hill** (26 m S on SR 6 to Navasota, 5 m SW on SR 90, 20 m S on FM 912, 1155) has a Historical Museum (Poplar St.), open Wed. & Sun. 1-4, and more than 25 structures with historic markers, including an 1847 Stagecoach Inn.

Washington-on-the-Brazos State Park (26 m S on SR 6 to Navasota, then 3 m SW off SR 90), reconstruction of pioneer homes and shops along the original streets of Washington; the town arose at a ferry crossing on the Brazos about 1822, had a population of about 300, and in 1836 was first capital of Texas and site of the signing of the Texas Declaration of Independence. **Independence Hall** has audiovisual program, guided tours; open daily 10-5; free. **Anson Jones Home,** with a doctor's office, was residence of last president of the Republic of Texas; original furnishings; open June-Aug. daily 10-5; Sept.-May, Wed.-Sun. 10-5; sm adm. The highlight is **Star of the Republic of Texas Museum,** a star-shape building housing exhibits on Washington and days of the Republic; audiovisual programs; library; open June-Aug. daily 10-6; Sept.-May, Wed.-Sun. 10-5; free.

Fort Tenoxtitlan (25 m W on SR 21 to Caldwell, then inquire for directions) was established 1830 by Mexican cavalry to be capital of Mexican Texas, to prevent Anglo settlement, and to encourage Mexican colonists; but the plan was dropped when Mexican settlers failed to arrive and when the commander, Jose Ruiz, refused to run out the Anglo settlers; Ruiz later cast his lot with the Anglos and signed the Texas Declaration of Independence. The state is restoring the site. Exhibits on the fort are in Burleson County Courthouse in Caldwell.

CORPUS CHRISTI: Corpus Christi Museum (1919 N Water St.) offers marine exhibits, earth sciences, hall of man; open Tues.-Sat. 10-5, Sun. 2-5; closed hols; free. **Art Museum of South Texas** (1902 N Shoreline Blvd), in building designed by Philip Johnson, offers changing exhibits; open Tues.-Sat. 10-5, Sun. 1-5; closed hols; free. **Centennial House** (411

480TEXAS

N Broadway), built 1849, has period furnishings; open Wed., Sun. 3-5; sm adm.

CORSICANA: Pioneer Village (900 W Park Ave. at 19th St.), 1850s homes and shops restored and furnished by Navarro County Historical Society; open Mon.-Sat. 9-noon, 1-5, Sun. 1-5; closed Thnks, Dec. 25; sm adm. **Navarro Junior College** (2 m SW on SR 31) offers a collection of Indian artifacts; open Mon.-Fri. 8-4; closed hols; free.

Fairfield (32 m S on I-45) offers the antebellum **Bradley House Museum** (Coleman St. off N Bateman Rd.) with antique china-doll collection (open June-Sept. daily; sm adm); **Freestone County Museum** (302 E Main St.) with local memorabilia in old jail (open Wed., Sat., Sun.; sm adm); **Stewards Mill Country Store** (7 m N at US 75, FM 833), more than 100 years old, with museum exhibits. **Burlington-Rock Island Railroad Museum** (32 m S on I-45, 9 m SW on US 84 in Teague), in original brick station; memorabilia of Trinity & Brazos Valley and Burlington & Rock Island lines; pioneer relics; open Sat. 10-5, Sun. 1-5; closed hols; sm adm.

DALLAS: Convention & Visitors Bureau (1507 Pacific Ave.) provides information. **Historic Preservation League, Inc.** (P.O. Box 9765, zip 75214) is engaged in preserving homes built 1890-1930 in Old East Dallas (between US 75 and White Rock Lake). **John Fitzgerald Kennedy Plaza** (bounded by Commerce, Market, & Main) has a memorial designed by Philip Johnson. A pleasant oasis is **Dallas Market Center International Sculpture Gardens** (2700 Stemmons Frwy) with contemporary sculpture in a landscaped setting. An overview is available at **First National Bank** (1401 Elm St.), with a 50th-floor, glass-enclosed observation terrace, open Mon.-Sat. 9-5; closed hols; sm adm.

State Fair Park (2 m E off I-20, I-30) is a permanent exposition, open year-round exc during preparation for annual state fair (Oct.); here are: **Dallas Museum of Fine Arts,** with 20th-C American paintings; some 19th-C European works; Congolese sculpture includes objects of ritual use; pre-Columbian works, Oriental screens, Greek sculpture, regional art; open Tues.-Sat. 10-5, Sun. 1-5; closed Dec. 25; free. **Texas Hall of State,** dedicated to Texan heros; dioramas of events in Texan history; murals; statues; exhibits drawn from Dallas Historical Society collections; open Mon.-Sat. 9-5, Sun. & hols 2-6; closed Easter, Dec. 25, mid-Sept.-opening of fair; free. **Dallas Museum of Natural History** has excellent habitat groups of regional wildlife; Boehm porcelain bird collection; geology; botany; open Mon.-Sat. 8-5, Sun. & hols noon-6; closed Dec. 25; free. **Health & Science Museum** offers unusually good exhibits, many animated, on human health and on science; transparent organs; a step-by-step appendectomy; rocks and minerals; planetarium shows (adm); open Mon.-Sat. 9-5, Sun. & hols 1-5; closed Dec. 24, 25; free. **Age of Steam Railroad Museum** exhibits plush passenger cars, engines, and other memorabilia; open June-Labor Day, Sat. & Sun. 11-5; daily 10-6:30 during State Fair; rest of yr, Sun. 11-5; adm. Also here are aquarium, wax museum, concert hall, Cotton Bowl, sports hall of fame, midway with rides, ice arena, attractive tropical garden.

Dallas Heritage Center (Old City Park, St. Paul & Ervay Sts.) traces history of Dallas with displays in 1898 Drummer's Hotel, 1875 railroad station, 1880 railroad section house, children's playhouse, 1847 Miller Log Cabin, and 1855 Greek Revival Millermore Museum with Victorian furnishings; open Tues.-Fri. 10:30-1:30, Sun. 1:30-4:30; closed Dec. 24, 31, Sept.; adm. **Dallas County Historical Plaza** (bounded by Main, Market, & Elm) contains John Neely Bryan Cabin, first house built in city (1841) by man who named Dallas; also terrazzo map of the county in 1846. **Dallas Public Library** (Harwood & Commerce), with more than a million volumes, has exhibits on 3rd-floor; open Mon.-Sat. 10-5, Sun. 1-5; free. **Dallas Firefighters Museum** (3801 Parry), in old firehouse, has antique equipment, photos, tools on display; open daily 10-4; donation. **Dallas Theater Center** (3636 Turtle Creek Blvd), only theater designed by Frank Lloyd Wright, offers tours Mon.-Fri. 1-1:30, Sat. 2-4, Sun. 2-4:30; closed hols; sm adm.

Southern Methodist University (5 m N off US 75 to Hillcrest Ave.): Owens Fine Arts Center exhibits 15-19th-C Spanish paintings; prints; Italian works in sculpture court; open Mon.-Sat. 10-5, Sun. 1-5; free. Museum of Archaeology features Egyptian and Babylonian antiquities; Bridwell Library owns rare early books.

Heard Natural Science Museum & Wildlife Sanctuary (28 m N on SR 5 at McKinney), exhibits on regional flora, fauna, geology; nature prints and paintings; nature trails; open Tues.-Sat. 9-5, Sun. 1-5; closed Jan. 1, July 4, Dec. 25; free.

DEL RIO: Whitehead Memorial Museum (1308 S Main St.), in a former trading post, contains relics of the SW frontier; on grounds are graves of Judge Roy Bean and his son; open Mon.-Sat. 9-5; sm adm.

Amistad Recreation Area (12 m NW on US 90), at international dam project; bronze eagles symbolizing U.S.-Mexican cooperation; statue of Aztec rain god Tlaloc at Mexican end of dam; prehistoric pictographs; open daily.

Judge Roy Bean Visitor Center (60 m NW on US 90 in Langtry): tourist information center dioramas and recordings tell the life of the colorful Roy Bean; Bean's preserved saloon, "The Jersey Lilly"; cactus garden. Bean, a saloon keeper, was named Justice of the Peace in 1882 (when the closest legal authority was 100 m away at Ft. Stockton); he held court in his saloon, choosing juries from its patrons, basing rulings on his single law book, keeping a six-shooter on the table next to him, and earning the nickname "Law West of the Pecos." His bar was named for British actress Lillie Langtry (known as the Jersey Lily but misspelled by the sign painter as Jersey Lilly), whom he had never met but to whom he wrote; after he told her he had named a town for her, she did visit, in 1904, but Bean had died several months before. Open daily 8-5 (longer in summer); closed Dec. 24-26; free.

At **Brackettville** (31 m SE on US 90), the Chamber of Commerce provides information on historic sites; **Alamo Village** (6 m N on RM 674), with replica of the Alamo built by Mexican adobe craftsmen as the set for the movie "The Alamo," is a family entertainment complex (open daily 9-6, longer in summer, adm).

DENISON: Eisenhower Birthplace State Historic Park (208 E Day St.) is the modest clapboard house in which the 34th President was born Oct. 14, 1890; period furnishings, personal effects; open daily 10-5; sm adm.

Bonham (12 m SE on US 69, 15 m E on US 82) is named for James Butler Bonham, called the bravest man at the Alamo; he left the besieged fort to get reinforcements, then fought his way back in, dragging his wounded mount the last few yards; **Sam Rayburn Library** (US 82) preserves Rayburn papers, duplicate of his Capitol office (open Mon.-Fri. 10-5, Sat. 1-5; closed Thnks, Dec. 25; free); Sam Rayburn House (½ m W on US 82) offers audiovisual program on his life and tour (open Tues.-Sat. 9-5, Sun. 1-5; closed Thnks, Dec. 25; free).

DENTON: North Texas State University Historical Collection (W. Mulberry & Ave. A.) houses dolls from many countries, guns, other frontier items; open Mon.-Sat. 2-5; closed hols & school hols; free. **State Museum of DAR** (1103 Bell St. on Texas Woman's Univ. campus) displays inaugural gowns of wives of state governors and presidents of the Texas Republic. **City-County Library Museum** (on Oakland near Congress) has mementos of outlaw Sam Bass (a trail driver who took up robbery after losing his wages gambling in Deadwood and who was killed during an attempted robbery in Round Rock; his hideout cave was at Pilot Knob, 4 m S on US 377), also Civil War weapons, other local memorabilia; open Mon.-Sat. 9-5; free.

EAGLE PASS: Fort Duncan Park (Adams St.) preserves 10 buildings of an 1849 infantry post that remained active until 1916; open daily 1-5; sm adm.

EL PASO: Named El Paso del Norte in 1598, this remained a Mexican city until after the Mexican War, when the border was set through the middle of the Rio Grande, dividing the city into U.S. and Mexican sections; the Mexican section was later renamed Juarez; English and Spanish are spoken on both sides of the boundary, and border regulations are minimal; information from **Chamber of Commerce** (1 Civic Center Plaza). Overlooking the city is **Sierra de Cristo Rey** (3 m W), topped with a statue of Christ; accessible via 4-m trail lined with 14 stations of the Cross. **Aerial Tramway** (Alabama & McKinley Ave.) goes to an observation deck on Ranger Peak; open June-Labor Day daily noon-9; rest of yr, noon-6; adm. **Chamizal National Memorial** (via Delta Dr.), on the border, commemorates the peaceful settlement of the international boundary; film, exhibits in museum; bilingual programs; on Mexican side are monuments to each of Mexico's 28 states; open daily 10 am-8 pm; free.

El Paso Museum of Art (1211 Montana Ave.) features 13-19th-C European works, including Old Masters; Mexican pre-Columbian and Colonial art; graphics; 19-20th-C American painting; sculpture; open Tues.-Sat. 10-5, Sun. 1-5; closed hols; free. **University of Texas at El Paso** (NW end of town) buildings are of unusual Bhutanese design; Centennial Museum offers Indian, Spanish, Colonial, and natural history exhibits; open Mon.-Fri. 10-5, Sat. & Sun. 1-5; closed some hols; free.

Fort Bliss Replica Museum (N of Montana Ave. on Pleasanton Rd. at Ft. Bliss), cavalry, infantry, artillery relics from post established 1848; from here troops went out against Geronimo and protected prospectors headed for California Gold Rush; 4 adobe buildings house displays of SW history and the post; open daily 9-4:45; closed Jan. 1, Easter, Thnks, Dec. 25; free. **Cavalry Museum** (10 m SE off I-10 at 12901 Gateway Blvd W) has fine historical paintings of the SW, relics of cavalry and Mexican Revolution; open daily 10-8; closed hols; free.

Ysleta Mission (11 m SE on I-10, then 2 m SW on FM 659) was founded in 1682 by Tigua Indians from New Mexico who were removed here by the Spanish during the Pueblo Revolt of 1680; mission building is of adobe with Moorish bell tower; Tigua Indian museum offers crafts and folk dances; open in summer, Tues.-Sat. 10-5, Sun. noon-6; adm. **Socorro Mission** (3 m SE on FM 258), founded about the same time, has hand-carved wooden beams. **San Elizario Presidio Chapel** (5 m S on FM 258) was built 1843 to replace one founded in 1777 to serve the military garrison at the seat of government for the Spanish viceroy; nearby is Los Portales, an arcade that may be the oldest building in Texas. **San Elizario** was site of the Salt War of the 1860-70s over the salt flats (86 m E on US 62, 180); Mexicans considered the salt public property, and in 1877 a mob executed the district judge and 2 other officials at San Elizario over the issue.

Hueco Tanks State Historic Park (28 m E on US 62, 180, then 7 m N) is an unusual rock formation that held water in natural hollows; pictographs show a long history of use by Indians; wagon trains and the Butterfield line used a route closely paralleling US 62, 180, and also stopped here; open daily; sm adm.

FORT STOCKTON: Old Fort Stockton was established in 1859 at Comanche Springs, long a popular spot with Indians and the crossing point of Comanche War Trail and Old San Antonio Road; later, California travelers and the Butterfield Overland Mail also came through here, and a town grew around the fort; the adobe officers' quarters, old guardhouse, and cemetery (with tombstones indicated that no one lived beyond 40) remain on Rooney St., Williams St., Water St. (2-8th Sts.). **Chamber of Commerce** (Dickinson & Jackson Sts.) provides a map of area sites, including: 1899 **Riggs Hotel** (301 S Main St.), a popular stop on the Butterfield line, now a museum with area relics (open Mon., Tues., Thurs.-Sat. 9:30-11:30, 2:30-5:30, Sun. 3-6.) **Grey Mule Saloon** (Main & Callaghan Sts.), famous for its red-eye. **Tunis Creek Stagecoach Stop** (20 m E in roadside park on US 290), a Butterfield station. **Dinosaur Park** (22 m NE on US 67, 385) with preserved footprints.

FORT WORTH: The city's motto, "Where the West Begins," refers to a treaty Indian leaders made to remain W of this point; with the beginning of the great cattle drives from Texas to the Kansas railhead, Ft. Worth became a major stop for cowboys on the Chisholm Trail, but population dropped in the 1870s as it became evident that the city was doomed unless it got a railroad. When an attempt to build a railroad failed, private citizens pitched in to lay the track themselves in 1876. The Cattlemen's Exchange and stockyards are on the North Side, where Western-style shops and restaurants line traditional boardwalks on Exchange Ave. Information from **Chamber of Commerce** (700 Throckmorton at 6th St.), open Mon.-Fri. 8:30-5; closed hols.

    Will Rogers Memorial Center (Lancaster St. & University Dr.), an exposition center where rodeos and other events are held, offers: **Amon Carter Museum of Western Art** (3501 Camp Bowie Blvd.), in a handsome building designed by Philip Johnson; works by Frederic Remington and Charles Russell; historical prints; works by Grant Wood, Bierstadt, Georgia O'Keeffe, Leonard Baskin on Western themes; open Tues.-Sat. 10-5, Sun. & hols 1-5; closed Dec. 24, 25; free. **Kimbell Art Museum** (Will Rogers Rd. W), in an interesting building designed by Louis I. Kahn; 18th-C English portraits and Old Masters; 12th-C French frescos; Asian art; pre-Columbian works; open Tues.-Sat. 10-5, Sun. 1-5; closed hols; free. **Fort Worth Art Museum** (1309 Montgomery St.) is devoted to 20th-C works; many impressive paintings; sculpture court; open Tues.-Sat. 10-5, Sun. 1-5; closed hols; free. **Fort Worth Museum of Science & History** (1501 Montgomery St.), exhibits on history of medicine and physiology; history of Texas in re-created rooms; mounted wildlife, minerals; primitive arts and culture; planetarium shows; open Mon.-Sat. 9-5, Sun. 2-5; closed hols; free.

Log Cabin Village (2121 Colonial Pkwy in Forest Park) consists of 7 authentic homes built during the 1850s; period furnishings; open Mon.-Fri. 8-5, Sat. 9-5, Sun. 1-5; closed Dec. 25; sm adm.

Pate Museum of Transportation (15 m SW on US 377 near Cresson) has antique and classic cars, horse-drawn vehicles, saddles, aircraft; open Tues.-Sun. 9-5; closed Thnks, Dec. 25; free. At **Cleburne** (31 m S on US 81, SR 174), Layland's Museum (201 N Caddo) displays local historic relics, Indian artifacts, fossils (Wed.-Fri. 3-5, Sun. 2-5), and the 1860s Little Old House (409 N Buffalo) has period furnishings (open through City Manager's office). **Texas Railroad Museum** (21 m W on I-20 to E. Fort Worth St., Weatherford), in 1906 Santa Fe Depot; early railroad memorabilia, streetcars, steam locomotive, other equipment; open June-Aug., Mon.-Sat. 9-5, Sun. 1-5; Sept.-May, Sat. 10-5, Sun. 1:30-5; sm adm.

Fort Richardson State Park (60 m NW on SR 199, US 281 at SW edge of Jacksboro) preserves cavalry post active 1867-78 to guard settlers from Indians; original buildings include the stone hospital (housing Western artifacts and library of Western lore), morgue, guardhouse, commissary, powder magazine, officers' quarters, bakery; open June-Aug. daily 10-5; inqure for hrs rest of yr; sm adm.

FREDERICKSBURG: Germans from New Braunfels settled here in 1846, when it was Comanche country; a charming story of the Easter rabbit who lit bonfires in the hills to boil the children's Easter eggs was invented to explain the bonfires of watchful Indians surrounding the settlement; reenacted annually in a pageant the Sat. before Easter. Many inhabitants were killed when they refused to join the Confederate Army during the Civil War because they disapproved of slavery; others fled to Mexico. **Chamber of Commerce** is in Vereins Kirche (Pioneer Plaza off Main St.), reproduction of 1847 octagonal building that served as church, school, and meeting hall; open Mon.-Fri.; free. Here you can obtain brochures for self-guided tours of historic sites, including the charming Sunday Houses, mini-homes used only on weekends when the farmers came to town for Sat. market and Sun. services. **Old Gillespie County Courthouse** (across Main St.) contains a library with a prized German collection; open Mon.-Fri. 9-5, Sat. 9-2; closed hols; free. **Pioneer Museum** (309 W Main St.) displays relics of German settlers; open May-Oct., Mon.-Sat. 10-5, Sun. 1-5; Nov.-Apr., Sat. 10-5, Sun. 1-5; closed Jan. 1, Dec. 25; sm adm. **Admiral Nimitz Center** (340 E Main St.) is an area of restored 19th-C buildings, including 1847 Nimitz Hotel, one of the most famous hostelries in the region, which hosted Rutherford B. Hayes, Robert E. Lee, other notables; historic displays; exhibits honoring Chester Nimitz, grandson of the hotel's founder; open daily 8-5; closed Thnks, Dec. 25; free.

Comfort (23 m S off US 87), also settled by Germans, has a history similar to Fredericksburg's; exhibits in the Comfort Historical Museum (838 High St.) are open Sat. 1-5 or by appointment; donation.

Fort Mason (43 m NW on US 87 at Mason), active 1851-69, was a cavalry post where Robert E. Lee and John Bell Hood served; only foundations remain; interpretive markers on Mason Courthouse square, Post Hill (5 blocks S of courthouse); fort's colorful history is detailed in a museum in the Library (300 Moody St.), built 1887 of stones removed from the fort.

GAINESVILLE: Founded in 1850 as a stop on the Butterfield Overland Stage Line, this city has many old brick homes with intricate masonry, iron columns, and a courthouse with a stained-glass cupola; information from **Chamber of Commerce** (Culberson & California St.). Nearby **Saint Jo** (24 m W on US 82), a watering stop at the crossroads of the Chisholm Trail and California Road, was supposedly named for its founder, Joe Howell, who was opposed to the sale of liquor, but local historic relics are displayed in the restored **Stonewall Saloon Museum** (N side of town square), open daily 8-6; closed hols.

GALVESTON: This island-city has always been sea-oriented and today boasts 32 m of beaches, a 10-m seawall against hurricanes, a Mosquito Fleet of shrimp trawlers, and busy wharves (9-41st Sts.). Cabeza de Vaca, first European in Texas, shipwrecked about here in 1528; although Mexico established a fleet here in 1816, the pirate Jean Lafitte moved in while the fleet was temporarily away. Lafitte built himself a home (Maison Rouge) and fort (the site is marked at 1417 Water Ave.) and 1817-21 used Galveston as a base for plundering Spanish ships (whose cargo of slaves he sold at $1 a lb). Legend says he buried some of his loot at **Lafitte's Grove** (11 Mile & Stewart Rds.), also site of Battle of Three Trees, ignited by the kidnapping of an Indian woman by one of Lafitte's men—an act the Indians avenged by eating 4 of the pirate crew. The U.S. Navy ended Lafitte's era of gambling, smuggling, slave trading, and pirating, but Lafitte burned the town before fleeing. During the Texas Revolution, the 4-ship Texas Navy was based here, and in 1836 Galveston was briefly the capital of Texas. **Tourist Information Center** (Seawall Blvd at 23rd St.) provides information on self-guided historical tours; air and bus tours; sightseeing cruises; Treasure Isle Tour Train (daily, weather permitting, from Seawall Blvd & 27th St.); Historic Homes Tour (Fri. in July-

Aug.). Along The Strand (20-25th Sts.), once called the Wall Street of the Southwest, 19th-C commercial buildings have been restored to house cafes and boutiques; throughout the old waterfront district (from The Strand to Sealy Ave.) interesting buildings have been marked. Information is available from **Galveston Historical Foundation** (212 22nd St.) in the 1882 Trueheart-Adriance Bldg (restored Victorian law office and other features may be seen Fri. 10-5). The Foundation maintains **Williams House** (3601 Ave. P), built 1837-40, framed in Maine, dismantled and shipped here by schooner, and reassembled; open June-Sept., Tues.-Sun. 1-5; adm.

Bishop's Palace (1402 Broadway), a splendidly ornate 1886 mansion, is outstanding; many rooms were designed around fireplaces purchased from around the globe; mantel and fireplace of the music room are lined with silver; rare woods, marbles, mosaics, crystal chandeliers; tours Memorial Day-Labor Day, Mon., Wed.-Sat. 10-5, Sun. 1-5; rest of yr, Mon., Wed.-Sun. 1-5; closed Good Fri., Thnks, Dec. 24, 25; adm.

Powhatan House (3427 Ave. O at 35th St.), a Greek Revival building erected as a hotel in 1847, has also been a hospital and orphanage; now owned by Galveston Garden Club; open June-Aug., Tues., Sat. 1-5, Fri. 10-5; adm. **Ashton Villa** (2328 Broadway at 24th St.), 1859 Italian-style villa, with cast-iron verandas; period furnishings; carriage house; open Mon., Wed.-Sun. 10-4; closed Easter, Thnks, Dec. 25; adm. Other interesting buildings are: **First Presbyterian Church** (Church St. at 18th St.), splendid Gothic structure, 1840; handsome **St. Mary's Cathedral** (2011 Church St.); ornate **Sacred Heart Church** (918 14th St.); all open daily. **Garten Verein** (in city park at 27th St. & Ave. O) is an 1870s octagonal-shape pavilion.

Rosenberg Library (823 Tremont St.) contains papers of Jean Lafitte, Sam Houston, other Texas notables; open Mon.-Thurs. 9-9, Fri. & Sat. 9-6; free.

American National Insurance Co. (1 Moody Plaza) offers 1-hr guided tours of its fine art exhibits that include scenes of early Galveston, Mon.-Fri. at 2; 20th-floor observation deck open Mon.-Fri. 2-4; closed hols; free.

Texas A & M University—Moody College of Marine Sciences: *Texas Clipper* (moored off Pelican Island), a training vessel, is open Oct.-May, Sat. & Sun. 1-4; free. Marine Science labs and displays (Ft. Crockett campus) is open daily 1-5; free.

GONZALES: Called the "Lexington of Texas" because the first battle of the Texas Revolution was fought here in 1835 when American settlers refused to return a small brass cannon the Mexican government had lent them for defense against Indians; the cannon and the single-star flag are reproduced in mosaic on the municipal building. **Gonzales Memorial**

Museum (E St. Lawrence St.) honors the 32 patriots who answered Travis' call for help at the Alamo even though they knew the cause was lost; Mexican and early Texas relics; information is available here on old homes in the area (including 1848 Eggleston House, a log home with pioneer furnishings); open Wed.-Sun. 1-5; closed hols; donation.

GUADALUPE MOUNTAINS NATIONAL PARK (on US 62, 180 at Pine Springs): **Information office** (open 8-4:40 daily) has schedule of guided walks and horseback trips; ½-m trail leads to Frijoles Historic Site, early Texas ranch buildings being restored; 7-m rough road (four-wheel drive only) leads to Williams Ranch Historic Site (open 8-2); Butterfield Stage Stop Historic Site (1 m W of hq on US 62, 180) has marked ruins of stage station used 1858-9.

HOUSTON: Convention & Visitors Council (suite 1101, 1006 Main St.) provides information. **Market Square** (Congress & Travis) contains the city's oldest building, a trading post, marked with a plaque; the city's early commercial center was here, near the original port on Buffalo Bayou, and was pretty wild when freighters patronized the 50 gambling halls and saloons; now converted to boutiques and nightclubs. **Harris County Heritage Society Tours** (1100 Bagby St. in Sam Houston Historical Park) provides an orientation film and tours to: Long Row, a reconstruction of the city's first shops; Old German Colony Church; 1868 Pillot House, with Victorian laciness; an 1850 Greek Revival home; 1847 brick home; tours Mon.-Fri. 10-4, Sat. 11-3, Sun. 2-5; closed Easter, Thnks, mid-Dec.-Jan. 1; adm. **Alley Theatre** (615 Texas Ave.) is a striking modern structure; tours Mon.-Sat. 12:45; adm. **Rothko Chapel** (1409 Sul Ross St.), an octagonal sanctuary for meditation, houses 14 outstanding panels by Rothko; on grounds is Barnett Newman's memorial to Martin Luther King, Jr.; open daily noon-8; free.

   Museum of Fine Arts (1001 Bissonnet St.), ranging from ancient Egypt to Old Masters and Impressionist to contemporary painting and sculpture; primitive art from Africa and South Pacific; SW Indian and pre-Columbian art; Remington Western art in wing designed by Mies van der Rohe; open Tues.-Sat. 9:30-5, Sun. noon-6; closed hols; free. **Bayou Bend Collection** (1 Westcott St.), a branch of Museum of Fine Arts housed in a Latin Colonial mansion; American decorative arts 1650-1850 arranged in period rooms; open 2nd Sun. of each month 1-5 or by tour reservation for Tues.-Sat. (write Box 13157, zip 77019); closed hols, Aug.; free. **Contemporary Arts Museum** (5216 Montrose Blvd) has contemporary works in all media; films; open Tues.-Sat. 10-5, Sun. noon-6; closed hols; free. **Rice University** (6100 S Main St.), in Mediterranean-style buildings; museum and art gallery with wide-ranging works from

African sculpture to Surrealist painting to modern art; inquire for hrs. **Houston Museum of Natural Science** (5800 Caroline St. in Hermann Park), archaeology, geology, wildlife, space, medical science; Burke Baker Planetarium shows; open Sun. & Mon. noon-5, Tues.-Sat. 9-5; closed Jan. 1, Thnks, Dec. 25; free.

Port of Houston observation deck (Wharf 9 off Clinton Dr.) is open daily 8-5; free boat tours (Tues., Wed.-Fri., Sun.) by reservation (Box 2562, zip 77001); you can drive through the area only on Sun.

San Jacinto Battleground (6 m SE on US 75, I-45, 12 m E on SR 225, 4 m N on SR 134) is site of 18-minute battle in which 910 Texans under Gen. Sam Houston defeated a larger Mexican force under Gen. Santa Anna, ending the Texan struggle for independence. Monument topped with a lone star has elevator (sm adm) to observation deck; historic exhibits on Texas; open Memorial Day-Labor Day, Mon.-Sat. 9:30-5:30, Sun. 10-6; rest of yr, Tues.-Sat. 9:30-5:30, Sun. 10-6; closed Dec. 24, 25; free. Battleground open daily 6 am-9 pm; free. **Battleship Texas** contains exhibits on the Texas Navy, Adm. Nimitz, and a memorial to the USS *Houston,* sunk by the Japanese in 1942; open May-Aug. daily 9-7; Sept.-Apr. daily 11-5; adm.

NASA Lyndon B. Johnson Space Center (21 m SE on I-45, then 5 m E on FM 528, Nasa 1, E of Clear Lake City): Visitor Orientation Center with film and exhibits on space program; booklets for self-guiding tour; open daily 9-4; closed Dec. 25; free. **Northington-Heard Memorial Museum** (42 m SW on US 59, then W on FM 1161 in Egypt), exhibits on regional history 1800-1900; open Mon.-Fri. 8-5; closed hols; free. **Varner-Hogg Plantation State Historic Park** (36 m S on SR 288, 13 m W on SR 35 in W Columbia): pre-Civil War manor of a large sugarcane plantation that was later home of first native governor of Texas; period antiques; Hogg family memorabilia; tours Tues., Thurs.-Sat. 10-noon, 1-5; Sun. 1-5; closed Jan. 1, Thnks, Dec. 25; sm adm. **Brazosport Museum of Natural Science** (42 m S on SR 288 to 101 This Way in Lake Jackson), shells, marine life; fossils and minerals; open Tues.-Sun. 2-5; closed Dec. 25; free. **Shrimp Boat Monument** (head of Brazosport harbor channel on SR 288), former shrimp trawler, *Mystery,* honors the shrimp industry.

Stephen F. Austin State Park (41 m W on I-10, then 2½ m N on FM 1458 at San Felipe), at an old ferry crossing on the Brazos River, was once the town of San Felipe de Austin, first Anglo-American capital of Texas (1823) and site of important conventions. Replica of Stephen Austin's home, restored J. J. Josey Store (built 1847; merchandise of the era; open Sat., Sun., hols; sm adm), hand-dug well, other monuments. Just S is **Our Lady of Frydek Church** (on FM 1458, S of I-10), built by Czech settlers, with a grotto.

HUNTSVILLE: Sam Houston Memorial Park (on Lake Ave. opposite Sam Houston State Univ.) honors the hero of San Jacinto, twice president of the Republic of Texas; here are: **Sam Houston Memorial Museum,** with interesting exhibits on Texas pioneers and the Texas Revolution; relics of Gen. Santa Anna; memorabilia of Houston, including his leopardskin vest. **Houston Residence,** built 1847 with a dog run and occupied until 1858; law office; separate log kitchen. **Steamboat House,** built 1858 to resemble a Mississippi steamboat, where Houston died in 1863. **War & Peace House,** with weapons, pioneer artifacts. Open daily 9-5; closed Thnks, Dec. 25; donation. From here signs lead to **Sam Houston's Grave** (in Oakwood Cemetery), with Andrew Jackson's tribute: "The world will take care of Houston's fame."

JACKSONVILLE: Jacksonville Public Library (310 Bolton St.) has a museum display called Vanishing Texana; open June-Aug., Mon.-Fri. 8-1; Sept.-May, Mon.-Fri. noon-5; closed hols; free. **New Birmingham Trail** (12 m S on US 69 to FM 343 SE of Rusk), 2½-m walking trail, winds partly through ghost town of New Birmingham, hq for early iron industry in the 1880s; the industry died after a furnace explosion and the financial panic of 1893; few remains.

JOHNSON CITY: Lyndon B. Johnson National Historic Site consists of: **Boyhood Home** (1 block off Main St.), a 1901 Victorian frame house where LBJ lived 1913 until he married in 1934; family furnishings. From here a mule-drawn wagon takes you to nearby **Johnson Settlement,** restored ranch of the President's grandfather, who drove cattle up the Chisholm Trail to Abilene, Kansas, 1867-72; stone-and-log buildings are typical of construction used by Anglo and German settlers in this area; demonstrations of ranching and pioneer skills. **LBJ Birthplace** (13 m W on US 290, Park Rd. 49), a typical late-19th-C dogtrot farmhouse where the family lived until LBJ was 5; family cemetery with LBJ's grave. All are open daily 9-5 (longer hrs in summer); closed Dec. 25; free. Also here, but not yet open to the public, is LBJ Ranch, bought by Lyndon and Lady Bird Johnson in 1951.

   Lyndon B. Johnson State Park (14 m W, across the Pedernales River from LBJ Ranch) has a **Visitor Center** (daily 9-6) that interprets the Hill Country and its influence on LBJ; Johnson family and area pioneer memorabilia; dogrun log cabins furnished in frontier style; free buses leave here for tours of LBJ landmarks (daily exc Dec. 25); open June-Aug. daily 8-8; Sept.-May daily 8-5; free.

KINGSVILLE: King Ranch, once the largest in the U.S., was established by riverboat captain Richard King in 1853 on a Spanish land grant called

Santa Gertrudis; Texas Longhorns were the original breed, but the ranch experimented with other breeds and then developed the famous Santa Gertrudis, first strain of cattle originated in the Western Hemisphere; *The King Ranch* by Tom Lea provides background. The ranch is too large to admit visitors, but provides a 12-m loop road (W via Santa Gertrudis Ave. & SR 141) past hq, stables of its prized thoroughbreds and quarter horses, other points of interest; road open daily 6:30-6; free. **John E. Conner Museum** (on campus of Texas A & I Univ., Santa Gertrudis Ave. & Armstrong St.) displays Indian, early Spanish, and Texas pioneer relics; guns and swords; fossils; open Mon.-Fri. 10-5, Sat. 9-noon, Sun. 2:30-5; closed hols; free. **Texas Ranger Museum** (15 m W on SR 141, 22 m S on US 281, adjacent to Chamber of Commerce in Falfurrias) offers pioneer and Texas Ranger displays; open business hrs; free.

LA GRANGE: Monument Hill State Park (2 m S off US 77) marks the tomb of 41 of Capt. Nicholas Dawson's soldiers massacred by Mexicans at Salado Creek in 1842, and 36 men of the Mier Expedition against Mexico, who were captured and forced to draw from a pile of black and white beans—those drawing black beans were executed; open daily 8-5 (8-8 in spring & summer); sm adm. Across the road are 1849 **Kreische Home Museum** (with Indian relics, antique guns and other memorabilia of Bavarian settlers) and ruins of the stone Kreische Brewery; sm adm. **Faison Home** (631 S Jefferson), home of a Dawson Massacre survivor, has mid-19th-C furnishings, relics of Mexican War; open Apr.-Sept., Tues.-Sun. 1-5; Oct.-Mar., Sat. & Sun. 1-5; sm adm.

Winedale Inn Properties (17 m NE on SR 237 to Round Top, then 4 m E via FM 1457, 2714) centers about a restored stagecoach inn of the 1830s, with authentic furnishings and relics, now a center for study of German and other immigrant groups in the area; on grounds are 6 other farm buildings, also furnished; open May-Oct., Thurs.-Sat. 10-6, Sun. noon-6; Nov.-Apr., Thurs.-Sat. 9-5, Sun. noon-5; closed hols; adm.

Koliba Home Museum (26 m SE on SR 71 to 1124 Front St., Columbus), with blacksmith shop and children's house, is open in summer daily 1:30-7; in winter, Sat. & Sun. 1:30-5; sm adm. Information is available here on other Victorian structures, including Seftenberg-Brandon House (usually open summer weekends), Old Water Tower housing local records, Stafford Opera House.

LAREDO: Established 1755 as a ferry crossing on the Rio Grande, Laredo has lived under 7 flags and 1839-41 was capital of an independent "Republic of the Rio Grande." **Capitol** (1000 Zaragoza St.) was built 1755 with 2-ft walls of rock and adobe covered with plaster; displays on the Republic of the Rio Grande, guns, saddles, other frontier relics; open

Wed.-Fri. 9:30-noon; Sat. 9:30-noon, 1:30-4; Sun. 10-1; closed hols; donation. **San Agustin Church** (214 San Agustin Ave.), on the plaza in the heart of the old Spanish section, was rebuilt 1872 on site of 1767 church; open daily 7 am-8 pm; free. Some old buildings of **Fort McIntosh,** established 1848 for border patrol and against Indian attacks, are now on the campus of Laredo Junior College and Texas A & I University (foot of Washington St., on banks of Rio Grande).

LUBBOCK: Museum of Texas Tech University (4th & Indiana Sts.), regional historic displays, art, natural sciences, planetarium; Peter Hurd mural in rotunda. On grounds is **Ranch Headquarters,** a complex of some 20 ranch structures (including dugouts, bunkhouses, barns) illustrating development of ranching in Texas from the 1830s. Open Tues.-Sat. 10-5, Sun. 1-5; closed hols; free.

    Crosby County Pioneer Memorial Museum (38 m E on US 82 in Crosbyton), in replica of rock house built 1876 by a Bavarian-born rancher; Indian, pioneer artifacts; farm equipment; open Tues.-Sat. 9-noon, 2-5, Sun. 2-4; free. **Post Chamber of Commerce** (41 m SE on US 84 to 107 E Main St., Post) provides literature on Post, founded 1907 by C. W. Post, the cereal manufacturer, to demonstrate his economic ideas; he also tried unsuccessful rainmaking experiments here 1910-13. Other local historic relics are in **Borden County Historical Museum** (41 m SE on US 84, 33 m S on SR 669 in Gail), open Thurs.-Sun. 2-5, and in **Dickens County Museum** (61 m E on US 82 in courthouse in Dickens), open Mon.-Fri. 8-5; closed hols; free.

MARSHALL: During the Civil War, while Missouri was in Union hands, Marshall became Confederate capital of Missouri and was an important producer of ammunition and other supplies for the Confederate Army; **Chamber of Commerce** (301 E Austin St.) provides information on historic buildings, including the splendid Victorian Ginocchio Hotel. **Harrison County Historical Museum** (Peter Whetstone Sq), in former courthouse; Caddo Indian artifacts; pioneer and Civil War relics; paintings; musical instruments; clocks; open Sun.-Fri. 1:30-4:30; closed hols & mid-late Dec.; sm adm.

    Caddo Indian Museum (20 m W on US 80 to 701 Hardy St. in Longview), prehistoric and historic Caddo artifacts; 18th-C Spanish trade items; open daily 9-sundown; closed Dec. 24, 25; donation. **Panola County Frontier Jail Museum** 28 m S on US 59 to central square in Carthage), in 1891 jail with old cell block, houses pioneer relics; open in summer, Mon.-Fri. 9-noon, 1-5, Sat. 9-noon; in winter, Mon.-Fri. 3:30-5:30, Sat. 8-noon; free.

Jefferson (12 m N on US 59), on Big Cypress Bayou, established itself as the first river steamboat port in East Texas in the 1830s; just after the Civil War, with as many as 15 sidewheelers lining its docks at one time, and scores of wagon trains passing through on the way West, its population reached 30,000. Jefferson shipped lumber so fast that the area was almost denuded of trees; it had an early brewery, iron foundry, and ice plant. Given such prosperity and confidence in its river traffic, the town rejected Jay Gould's request for a right-of-way for his railroad. The infuriated Gould, who was staying at Excelsior House (211 W Austin St.), wrote in the hotel's register, "This is the end of Jefferson"—and the city did decline as railroads replaced river traffic. **Excelsior House**—which also hosted Presidents Grant and Hayes, Oscar Wilde—is still in use; original furnishings include button and spool beds; lobby is open daily; guided tours daily 9-5 (adm) of the entire building. Opposite is **Atalanta,** Gould's private railroad car, with 4 luxurious staterooms, lounge, dining room, kitchen, butler's pantry, bathroom; open daily 9-5; sm adm. **Jefferson Historical Society Museum** (223 W Austin St.), in a former post office and courthouse, offers 4 floors on early steamboat days, antebellum society; Civil War relics; early painting and sculpture; dolls; memorabilia of famous Texans; open Mon.-Fri. 9:30-noon, 1-5; Sat. & Sun. 9:30-5; closed Dec. 24, 25; adm. Historic buildings include **The Manse** (Delta & Alley Sts.), 1839 Greek Revival structure housing the Jessie Allen Wise Garden Club responsible for much of the city's restoration; **Riverboat Warehouse** (Dallas St.), now a restaurant; **Apothecary Shop & Country Store** (312 E Broadway St.), with 19th-C medicines. During Jefferson Historic Pilgrimage (1st weekend in May), tours of historic houses are conducted and the Diamond Bessie murder trial is reenacted (write Excelsior House for details).

McALLEN: Chamber of Commerce (US 83 & N Broadway) provides information on historic sites. **McAllen International Museum** (2500 Quince in Las Palmas Park) offers local historical, art, natural science displays; open Tues.-Fri. 9-5, Sat. 9-4, Sun. 1-5; closed hols & Aug.; free. **Hidalgo County Historical Museum** (8 m N on US 281 to 121 E McIntyre in Edinburg), in a former jail with hanging tower, depicts the colorful history of this area, once so plagued by bandits that it was known as the Deadline of Sheriffs; pioneer relics; open Wed., Sat., Sun. 2-5; closed hols; sm adm. **Pan American Observatory and Planetarium** (1 m W of Edinburg on SR 107) is open free; shows, sm adm; inquire for schedule. **Old Clock Museum** (929 E Preston St. in Pharr), more than 400 antique clocks dating back to 1690; inquire locally for hrs. Nearby Guadalupe Cemetery is interesting, with Mexican-style graves. **Live Steam Museum** (5½ m E of

McAllen on US 83, then 2 m N on FM 907), also called The Engine Room, displays operating steam engines and pumps; open daily 8-5; closed hols; sm adm. **Donna Hooks Fletcher Historical Museum** (8 m E on US 83 in Chamber of Commerce Bldg., 129 S 8th in Donna), attractive little museum of the city's history; open Mon., Wed., Fri. 2-4; free.

McCAMEY: This town was named for the man whose 1926 wildcat oil well lured 700 people to put up tents and shacks, creating an instant town within 24 hours. **Mendoza Trail Museum** (E on US 67 at entrance to Santa Fe Park) houses relics of the oil boom; ranching; fossils; Indian relics; open Tues.-Sat. 1:30-5; closed hols; free. **Castle Gap Park** (13 m NW of US 385) is barren ground into which are etched the ruts of wagons of pioneers moving West and the trails of ponies following the Comanche War Trail; Emperor Maximilian is said to have buried gold and jewels here as he fled from Mexico.

MIDLAND: Museum of the Southwest (1705 W Missouri) exhibits relics of this area, settled before 1800 at the crossing of Emigrant, Chihuahua, Comanche War Trails; science, art displays; planetarium; open Mon.-Sat. 10-5, Sun. 2-5; closed hols; free. **Permian Basin Petroleum Museum** (1500 I-20W), walk-through representation of an ancient ocean floor; geology and development of oil industry; oil rig; Western historical art; open Tues.-Sat. 10-5, Sun. 2-5; closed hols; adm. **Midland County Library** (301 W Missouri) offers exhibits of ancient Midland Man, Indian and pioneer relics, war memorabilia; open Mon.-Thurs. noon-6, Sat. 9-noon, 1-4; free. **Pliska Museum** (off US 80 at Midland-Odessa Air Terminal) contains plane built 1906 by Johnny Pliska, a local blacksmith; aviation displays; open daily, 24 hrs; free.

NACOGDOCHES: For centuries before whites arrived, this was an Indian center; La Calle del Norte (now North St.) connected a community here with Indian villages to the north; there were Indian mounds, but the only remaining one is on the lawn of a private home (N Mound St. between Park & Hospital Sts.). The Spanish established a mission in 1716, but it was abandoned and the Spanish did not return to settle here until 1779. **Old Stone Fort Museum** (on campus of Stephen F. Austin State Univ., College Ave. & North St.) is a reconstruction of a structure erected about 1779 as a fort and trading post; here 4 unsuccessful attempts were made to establish independent republics, including the 1826 Republic of Fredonia declared by Hayden Edwards; Texas' first 2 newspapers were published here too; historic exhibits, Sam Houston memorabilia, Indian artifacts; open Mon.-Sat. 9-5, Sun. 1-5; closed Thnks, Dec. 25; free. **Hoya Memorial Library & Museum** (211 S Lanana St.), built about

1830 by Adolphus Sterne, a founder of the Republic of Texas, was a pioneer home and store used as a refuge during Indian raids; open Mon.-Sat. 9-noon, 2-5; closed hols; free. **Old Nacogdoches University** (on grounds of Nacogdoches High School, Fredonia & Mound Sts) was founded 1845 by the Republic of Texas; antique furniture, silver, other relics; open June-Aug. daily 10-noon, 2-5, Sun. 2-5; free. **Halfway House** (18 m E on SR 21), an 1840s stagecoach inn, is open daily; inquire for hrs; sm adm. **Mission San Francisco de los Tejas State Historic Park** (38 m SW on SR 21) contains a replica of the first Spanish mission in East Texas, built 1690 as a barrier to French expansion; park open daily; sm adm. **Shelby County Museum** (33 m NE on SR 7 on Shelbyville & Riggs Sts., Center) houses local memorabilia; open Wed.-Sun. 1-5; closed hols; free. **San Augustine** (34 m E on SR 21), founded on El Camino Real (now SR 21), has 36 historic buildings; tours conducted first weekend in June.

ODESSA: Said to have been named by Russian railroad laborers who compared the prairie to the steppes, has a 10-ft Jackrabbit Statue (opposite Chamber of Commerce on 400 block of N Lincoln St.), a re-creation of the Globe Theater (2308 Shakespeare Rd.), relics of the presidents of the Republic of Texas and of the U.S. in Ector County Library (622 N Lee St.; open Mon.-Fri. 10-noon, 1-5; free), and: **Meteorite Museum** (5 m W on US 80, then 2 m S) on site of meteor crater believed formed more than 20,000 years ago; meteorological exhibits with specimens from all over the world; open Thurs.-Mon. 10-6; closed Dec. 25; sm adm. **Monahans Sandhills State Park** (28 m W on US 80, I-20 to Park Rd. 41) contains Sandhills Museum, with historic, geologic, and natural history displays on the sand dune area; open daily 8-5; free.

OZONA: **Crockett County Museum** (404 11th St.), in courthouse annex; frontier and Indian relics, artifacts from Ft. Lancaster; open Mon.-Fri. 11-6; closed Thnks, Dec. 25; sm adm. **Fort Lancaster State Historic Site** (33 m W on US 290), where an army post was established 1855 to guard the San Antonio-El Paso road, is being restored; 25 buildings, wagon ruts; interpretive center; open June-Aug. daily 8-5; Sept.-May, Thurs.-Mon. 8-5; free.

PALESTINE: **Bowers Mansion** (301 S Magnolia St.), an 1878 Steamboat Gothic mansion, has elegant period furnishings; open June-Aug., Mon.-Sat. 10-5; Sept.-May, Sat. 2-5; adm.

PAMPA: **White Deer Land Museum** (116 S Cuyler St.) offers pioneer kitchen, chapel, schoolroom, Victorian parlor; Indian artifacts; model of oil well; pump organ; carriage house with old vehicles; open June-Aug., Fri.-

Sun. 2-5; Sept.-May, Sun. 2-5; closed Dec. 25; free. **Alanreed-McLean Area Museum** (36 m SE on SR 273 at 117 N Main St., McLean) has period rooms in pioneer style, settler mementos; open Mon.-Fri. 9:30-5; closed hols; free. **Wheeler County Museum** (42 m E on SR 152 on Texas St., Wheeler), in 1908 jail; local relics; open Mon., Wed., Fri. 1-5; closed hols; free. **Hemphill County Pioneer Museum** (39 m NE on US 60, 9 m N on US 83 to Main St., Canadian), in Old Moody Hotel; saddles, branding irons, cowboy working gear; guns; pioneer relics; covered wagon; sheriff's office, country store, barbershop; open June-Aug. daily 10-5; Sept.-May, Sat., Sun. & hols 2-5; sm adm.

PARIS: Flying Tigers Air Museum (2 m W on US 82) displays military aircraft; open daily in daylight; free. **Maxey Home** (812 Church St.), built 1867, has original furnishings; open Tues.-Sat. 10-noon, 3-6, Sun. 2-6; closed hols; sm adm. **Museum of Arts & Sciences** (21 m W on US 82 in Honey Grove), paintings; historical relics; manuscripts; open Mon.-Sat. 9-5, Sun. & hols 2-5; free.

PECOS: Until the Pecos River was tamed by impoundment, its treacherous currents were a formidable barrier to stage drivers and wagon trains, and "West of the Pecos" was harsh and hostile country; the town developed as a stop on the Texas & Pacific Railroad, and was known for fast-draw gunmen and rough cowboys. Displays on its colorful history are in **West-of-the-Pecos Museum** (1st St. & US 285), in old Orient Hotel and Saloon, once the finest stopping place in the area; ornate fixtures; site where bartender gunned down 2 outlaws; displays on life in the late 1800s; information on nearby historic sites; open June-Aug., Tues.-Sun. 9-6; Sept.-May, Tues.-Sun. 10-4; closed Jan. 1, Dec. 25; sm adm.

    Comanche Trails Museum & Zoo (17 m NW on US 285, then 26 m E on SR 302) features guns, Indian artifacts, other North Plains relics; open June-Aug. daily 9-8; Sept.-May, daily 9-6; closed some hols; adm.

PORT ARTHUR: Port Arthur Historical Museum (5th & Austin Sts.), displays and relics of the city's history; open Mon.-Fri. 9-4, Sat. 9-noon; closed hols; free. Just NE is **Nederland,** founded by Dutch immigrants, with the **Windmill Museum** (1516 Boston Ave.), built to preserve relics of Dutch heritage; open Tues.-Sun. 1-6; closed hols; free.

SAN ANGELO: Fort Concho Preservation & Museum (along Burges St. & Aves. C & D): fort established 1867 to replace Ft. Chadbourne (see below); troopers protected stagecoaches, wagon trains, and mails, and explored and mapped the region; the fort was hq for the Buffalo Soldiers, the famous black regiment, and for Col. Ranald Mackenzie's campaigns against Indians; buildings, constructed of stone by skilled German artisans from Fredericksburg, are remarkably well preserved; barracks, chapel, powder magazine, other restored buildings; museum features diorama of the post, guns, old vehicles, military and pioneer artifacts; open Mon.-Sat. 9-5, Sun. 1-5; closed hols; sm adm.

Fort McKavett State Historic Site (18 m S on US 277, 28 m SE on FM 2084, 20 m SE off SR 29): extensive ruins, being restored, of fort established 1852; abandoned during the Civil War, the fort was reoccupied in 1868 by Col. Ranald Mackenzie and housed hundreds of men for offensives against Indians; barracks, hospital, magazine, bakery, guardhouse, post office, stables; scale model of fort and other museum displays; open daily.

SAN ANTONIO: Convention & Visitors Bureau (602 HemisFair Plaza Way—or write Box 2277, zip 78298) provides information on this colorful city that grew from a chain of 5 Spanish missions established along the San Antonio River and abandoned about 1793. Unique to the city is **Paseo del Rio**, a walk along the river in the heart of town, landscaped with trees and flowers, lined with shops and cafes, and providing river taxi service.

The Alamo (Alamo Plaza) was established 1718 as Mission San Antonio de Valero, first of the Spanish missions to the Indians, and was later enlarged as a fortress; on Feb. 23, 1836, it was attacked by Mexican Gen. Santa Anna with 2500 soldiers; the 188 defending Texas soldiers (including Jim Bowie, Davy Crockett, and William Travis) refused to surrender and were killed in the 13-day siege; restored mission; museum with Indian, early Texan, and Spanish artifacts; dioramas; library (closed Sun.) with paintings and documents related to Texas history; open Mon.-Sat. 9-5:30, Sun. 10-5:30; closed Dec. 24-25; free. "Remember the Alamo" (across the plaza) is a 30-min multimedia program of the battle; open daily 9-5; adm. Nearby is **Menger Hotel** (on the plaza), where Teddy Roosevelt recruited his Rough Riders and where Robert E. Lee and other notables were guests; still in use.

HemisFair Plaza (200 S Alamo St.), site of '68 HemisFair, contains amusement park, shops, cafes, theater, and: **Institute of Texan Cultures,** maintained by Univ. of Texas; multimedia show on the 26 cultural groups that influenced state history; also 26 exhibits; open Tues.-Fri. 10-4, Sat. & Sun. 1-6; free. **Tower of the Americas,** with 2 observation levels open daily 8 am-midnight; adm. **Convention Center** with exterior mural by Mexico's Juan O'Gorman, symbolizing the union of pre-Columbian, Spanish, and Anglo cultures. **Mexican Cultural Institute,** exhibits of contemporary Latin American artists; open daily 9-5; free. **Lone Star Hall of Texas History,** a historical wax museum, open Apr.-Dec., Mon.-Thurs. 10-7, Fri.-Sun. 10-10; Jan.-Mar., daily 10-6; sm adm. **Witte Confluence**

Museum, with wagons, bicycles, cars, planes, other vehicles tracing the history of transportation; open daily 10-6; closed Jan. 1, Dec. 25; sm adm.

Hertzberg Circus Collection (in Library Annex, 210 W Market St.) has more than 20,000 circus items, including memorabilia of Tom Thumb and Jenny Lind; handbills, paintings, woodcuts; miniature circus; carved ticket wagon; other wagons and equipment; mechanical clown; open Mon.-Sat. 9-5:30; closed hols & Fri. of Fiesta Week; free. **Arneson River Theatre** (on San Antonio River), with the audience on one bank and the stage on the other. **La Villita** (bounded by S. Presa, Alamo, Nueva Sts. & Paseo del Rio), a walled enclosure, was a residential settlement for Spanish soldiers and their Indian wives around Mission San Antonio de Valera; later, aristocrats lived here; authentically restored buildings house craft shops; **Cos House** was where the Mexicans signed the articles of capitulation after Texans had captured San Antonio; **Old San Antonio Museum** (Bolivar Hall) houses life-size dioramas, with authentic relics, of scenes from area history (open Tues.-Sun. 10-4; closed Jan. 1, Dec. 25; free).

Spanish Governor's Palace (105 Military Plaza), a lovely building that housed officials of the Spanish province in Texas; doubleheaded eagle of Hapsburg coat of arms and the date 1749 carved over the entrance; period furnishings; hand-carved doors; patio, chapel; open Mon.-Sat. 9-5, Sun. 10-5; closed Dec. 24-25, Fri. of Fiesta Week; sm adm. **San Fernando Cathedral** (114 Military Plaza) ws completed in 1749 by settlers from the Canary Islands, who organized the first civil government in San Antonio; Santa Anna used the tower as a lookout; some Alamo heros are buried here; open daily. **Jose Antonio Navarro Residence** (228-32 S Laredo St.) was home and office of the Texas patriot; period furnishings; open daily 10-4; closed Jan. 1, July 4, Thnks, Dec. 25; free. **Mexican Quarter** (across San Pedro Creek) has a colorful market. **King William Street Historic District,** settled by wealthy Germans, is named for Wilhelm I of Prussia and is lined with Victorian houses built 1870-1885; one of the fanciest is Steves Homestead (509 King William St.), with ornate period furnishings, natatoriur; carriage house, gardens (open daily 10-noon, 2-4; closed Fri. 10-noon & Dec. 25; sm adm).

Mission Trail (S along the river) is marked: **Mission Concepcion** (807 Mission Rd.), established 1731, features twin towers, intricately carved entrance, rare frescos; still in use; open Apr.-Sept. daily 10-6; Oct.-Mar. daily 9:30-5:30; sm adm. **San Jose Mission National Historic Site** (6539 San Jose Dr.) was one of the most prosperous of the Texas missions and many buildings were added after its 1720 founding; 1768-82 church with fine stone carving and a rose window; 1749 convent with Roman and Gothic arches and cloisters; fortified tower with 3-ft walls and gun ports; granary; stone apartments for Indian families; church still in use; open daily 9-6 (9-8 Apr.-Sept.); sm adm. **Espada Dam** (in Espada Park on Military Dr.

just before bridge over San Antonio River) was built curving the wrong way by the Franciscans about 1731-45 but nevertheless has withstood flood waters. **Mission San Francisco de la Espada** (9800 Espada Rd.), established 1720 and rebuilt 1868; friary and chapel restored; granary and fortified tower in ruins; open daily 10-6; sm adm. **Mission San Juan Capistrano** (off US 181 at Bergs Mill), erected 1731; church still in use; restored missionaries' quarters; open daily 10-6; sm adm.

Temple Beth-El (211 Belknap Pl) was built 1927 with ornate scrollwork on the facade reminiscent of Spanish architecture; marble ark; stained-glass windows; open daily. **National Shrine of the Little Flower** (906 Kentucky Ave.), in Romanesque style, has a replica of the shrine in Lisieux, France; open daily.

Witte Memorial Museum (3801 Broadway in Brackenridge Park) offers displays on archaeology, geology, zoology, other sciences, fine and decorative arts, history; on grounds are 4 restored historic houses dating 1840-60; open Mon.-Fri. 9-5; Sat., Sun. & hols 10-6; sm adm.

Lone Star Brewing Co. (600 Lone Star Blvd) offers guided tours daily in summer, Mon.-Wed. rest of yr; closed hols; free. On grounds are Buckhorn Bar; Buckhorn Hall of Horns; mounted fish, birds; wax museum; weapons; cottage in which O. Henry lived; open daily 9:30-6; closed Jan. 1, Thnks, Dec. 25; free. **Pearl Brewing Co.** (312 Pearl Pkwy) offers tours Mon.-Fri.; replica of Roy Bean's Jersey Lilly saloon, brewery memorabilia, open June-Aug., Mon.-Sat. 10-5; Sept.-May, Mon.-Fri. 10-5; free.

Marion Koogler McNay Art Institute (5 m N on US 81-Bus to 6000 N New Braunfels Ave.), in a Spanish mansion; Post-Impressionist and modern works; Gothic and medieval collection; New Mexico arts and crafts; sculpture pavilion; library; open Tues.-Sat. 9-5, Sun. 2-5; closed Jan. 1, July 4, Thnks, Dec. 25; free.

The following military installations have museums: **Ft. Sam Houston** (3 m NE on Grayson St. & N New Braunfels Ave.), open Mon.-Fri. 9-4, Sat. & Sun. 10-3:30; closed hols. **Brooks AFB** (7 m SE at jct I-37 & Military Dr.), open Mon.-Fri. 8-4; closed hols. **Lackland AFB** (12 m SW on US 90), open Mon.-Fri. 7:30-4:15; Sat., Sun., hols noon-4:15. All free.

New Braunfels (33 m NE on I-35) was founded 1845 by Prince Carl von Solms-Braunfels, who found living conditions too primitive and returned to live in princely style in Germany; as Commissioner-General for the Society for the Protection of German Immigrants in Texas, he encouraged some 5000 Germans to immigrate; these were stranded at their port of entry, Port Lavaca (many tried to walk to New Braunfels), and more than a third died.

Sophienburg Museum (401 W Coll St. at Academy Ave.), on the hilltop where the prince built his home and log fortress; displays on hardships endured by these pioneers; personal effects of the prince; open May-Sept., Mon.-Sat. 3-6, Sun. 2-6; Oct.-Apr., Wed. & Fri. 3-6, Sun. 2-6; closed Dec. 25; sm adm. **Lindheimer Home** (491 Comal Ave.), modest 1852 cottage of fachwerk construction, was home of colorful adventurer and botanist who classified much of Texas' flora; open June-mid-Nov., Tues.-Sun. 2-5; rest of yr, Sat. & Sun. 2-5; closed Jan. 1, Dec. 25; sm adm. **Chamber of Commerce** (Box 180) offers information for walking tours of historic sites, schedule of German festivals.

In **Seguin** (37 m E on I-10), settled by German immigrants in the 1840s and 1870s, Sebastapol (704 Zorn St.) was named for the Crimean War Site; built in early 1850s; V-shape roof stored water and cooled the house; open Sun. 2-5 or through **Chamber of Commerce** (Central Park, W Court St.), which can also arrange for you to see: Los Nogales Museum (E Live Oak & S River Sts.), built of sun-dried brick in 1823 by the Mexican government as a post office (includes historic exhibits and doll house); 1823 Texas Ranger station; 1824 Magnolia Hotel; other historic sites.

Boerne (33 m NW on I-10), settled 1851 by Germans who named it for poet and historian Ludwig Boerne, offers Robert E. Lee Headquarters, a small native-stone building used by Lee during his frontier military service, and the historic Old Kendall Inn, built 1859 as a stagecoach stop (still operating). **Frontier Times Museum** (46 m NW on SR 16 to 506 13th St., Bandera), Old West relics, Western art, Indian artifacts, Chinese temple bells; open Tues.-Sat. 10-noon, 1-4:30, Sun. 1-4:30; closed hols; sm adm. **Castroville Historic District** (20 m W on US 90 in Castroville) preserves quaint buildings with overhanging roofs erected by Alsatian settlers. Landmark Inn (Florence St.), built 1848 as a stagecoach stop, has a separate kitchen and lead-lined bathhouse; small museum of furnishings brought from Europe by settlers; open Mon.-Fri. 9-11:30 am, 1-5:30 pm; Sat. & Sun. 2-6; sm adm. St. Louis Church, erected 1869, has nearby the little stone chapel erected by settlers. **Medina County Museum** (40 m W on US 90 to 18th St. in Hondo), in 1897 railroad depot; local historical artifacts; open Memorial Day-Labor Day, daily 9-5; rest of yr, Sat. & Sun. 9-5; free. **Panna Maria** (50 m S on US 181, then 3½ m E at jct SR 123) has historic markers telling of its founding by Polish Catholics in 1854; a small historical museum is in the former St. Joseph's School building, first Polish school in the U.S. **Helena** (5 m E of Panna Maria), ghost town that once had 3000 people, founded in 1850s near Chihuahua Trail and Ox Cart Road; was famous for its gunfights; in 1884, after a bullet killed the son of a rancher, the rancher vowed to kill the town in revenge; he persuaded the railroad to bypass Helena, which slowly died; courthouse, church, other ruins; historic markers about Helena and Ox Cart Road. **Runge** (SE of Helena on SR 81) also has historic markers telling of its founding by Poles.

STEPHENVILLE: Stephenville Historical House Museum (525 E Washington St.) is an 1869 Victorian home with period furnishings, relics of area history; open June-Aug. daily 2-5; Sept.-May, Sat., Sun., hols 2-5; sm adm. **Thurber Ghost Town** (25 m N on SR 108 off I-20) was founded 1888 by Texas & Pacific Coal Co., which recruited coal miners from 17 countries; most buildings were razed after the mines closed in 1921, but the former company store is now a restaurant with photos of the town. **Hamilton County Museum** (40 m S on US 281 in Hamilton), in county courthouse, has local relics; open daily 8-5; closed hols; free. **Dinosaur Valley State Park** (27 m E on US 67) preserves sauropod, theropod, and duckbilled dinosaur tracks; open daily; sm adm. **Somervell County Historical Museum** (30 m E on US 67 on the square in Glen Rose) offers fossils, regional historic relics; open June-Aug. daily 1-5; rest of yr, Sat. 10-5, Sun. 2-5; free.

SWEETWATER: Nolan County Historical Museum (304 Locust St.), Indian and pioneer artifacts; early regional photos; open Tues.-Sun. 2-5; closed Dec. 25; free. **Colorado City Historical Museum** (26 m SW on I-20 to 3rd & Walnut Sts.), frontier ranch and home items, horse-drawn hearse, early photos; open Tues.-Sun. 2-5; closed hols; free. **Western Heritage Museum** (36 m NW on US 84 on Western Texas College campus, Snyder) has early box-and-strip house, chuck wagon, Indian and ranch relics, regional legend exhibit; open Tues., Thurs., Sun. 2-5; closed hols; free.

TYLER: Goodman Museum (624 N Broadway), in stately 1859 mansion; circular staircase; Empire and Victorian furnishings; pioneer medical equipment; open daily 1-5; closed Dec. 25; free.

Kilgore Chamber of Commerce (26 m E on SR 31 to 107 S Martin St. in Kilgore) offers a map for a 3-hr self-guiding Great East Texas Oil Field Tour through area with 18,000 wells; Howard-Dickinson House (S Main St.), built of brick 1855, with period furnishings, is open Tues.-Sun. 1-5, closed hols, sm adm.

Harmony Hill Ghost Town (33 m SE on SR 64 to Henderson, then 18 m NE on SR 43) was an important trade center known as Nip & Tuck in 1850 that declined when the railroad bypassed it; a 1906 storm destroyed many buildings; a few homes, cemetery survive.

Gov. Hogg Shrine & State Park (26 m N on US 69, then 10 m N on SR 37 to 518 S Main St., Quitman) preserves honeymoon cottage and other buildings connected with the Hogg family; Miss Ima Hogg Museum on the family and history of Northeast Texas; open Tues.-Sun. noon-5; closed Dec. 25; sm adm.

UVALDE: Garner Memorial Museum (333 N Park St.), former home of John "Cactus Jack" Garner, Vice President under FDR; Garner memorabilia, displays on area history; open Mon.-Sat. 9-noon, 1-5, Sun. 2-5; closed Thnks, Dec. 25; free. **City Park** (500 block of N Park St.) has historic markers and graves of settlers killed by Indians; one marker tells of King Fisher, notorious sheriff, rustler, and smuggler, whom local juries refused to convict.

VERNON: R. L. More Bird Egg Collection (2nd floor, 1905 W Wilbarger St.), 10,000 eggs, taxidermy specimens; open Mon.-Fri. 9-5, Sat. 9-noon; closed hols; free. **Red River Valley Museum** (Wilbarger Memorial Auditorium, 2100 Yamparika St.) has archaeological and recent Indian displays; open Mon.-Fri. 7:30-5, Sat. 7:30-noon; closed hols; free. **Foard County Museum** (31 m SW on US 70 to Foard County Courthouse in Crowell) and **Knox County Museum** (31 m SW on US 70, 29 m S on SR 283 in County Courthouse in Benjamin) have regional Indian and pioneer artifacts; open Mon.-Fri. 8:30-5; closed hols; free.

VICTORIA: McNamara-O'Connor Historical & Fine Arts Museum (502 N Liberty St.), in 1869 home; pioneer furniture, art; local historical items; open Wed. 10-noon, 3-5, Sun. 3-5 & by appointment; sm adm. **Memorial Square** (E Commercial & De Leon Sts.), mass burial ground for victims of 1846 yellow fever epidemic; grist mill. **Roadside Park** (10 m W on US 59) has historic marker summarizing county history. At **Fannin Battleground State Park** (16 m W on US 59, then S), 3 weeks after the fall of the Alamo in 1836, Col. James W. Fannin and 342 men surrendered to Mexican troops on the promise they would be treated as prisoners of war; interpretive signs. Fannin and his men were briefly housed at **Presidio La Bahia** (22 m W on US 59 to Goliad, then 2 m S off US 183) and then were massacred on order from Gen. Santa Anna; the fort was established 1749 to protect the nearby mission; chapel (still in use) and other buildings restored; the former Spanish officers' quarters houses a museum of human habitation on this site; the graves of Fannin and his men are nearby; open daily 9-5; closed Good Fri., Dec. 25; sm adm. Also here is a memorial to Gen. Ignacio Zaragoza (1829-62), a liberal leader who was minister of war under Juarez; in 1862 Zaragoza defeated an elite French force that had intended to aid Confederates in Texas. **Mission Espiritu Santo Zuniga** (1 m N of the Presidio on US 183 in Goliad State Park), established 1749, is a replica of the original; museum of mission relics; open daily 8-5. Also at Goliad are: **Goliad County Courthouse** (Court House Sq), an impressive 1894 structure with original carved staircases and wainscoting; on the lawn is a hanging tree used during the 1857 Cart War. **Old Market House** (S Market & Franklin St.), open in summer with historic displays; outside are memorials to Col. Fannin and the Texas Revolution.

Indianola County Historical Park (S of Port Lavaca at end of SR 316) marks the site of Indianola, port of entry for thousands of colonists and goods from around the world; destroyed by an 1886 hurricane; only a few foundations can be seen; historic marker; statue of La Salle, who is believed to have landed here in 1685. **Calhoun County Museum** (in old jail next to courthouse in Port Lavaca) houses exhibits on Indianola; open Mon.-Sat. 10-11:30, 2-5; closed hols; free.

Texana Museum (23 m NE on US 59 in county courthouse in Edna) exhibits regional historic artifacts, art, documents; open Mon.-Fri. 8-5; closed hols; free.

WACO: Baylor University offers: **Texas Collection** (in Carroll Library, 5th & Speight Sts.), relics of Texas pioneers, extensive archives; open June-Aug., Mon.-Fri. 10-4:30, Sat. 8-noon; Sept.-May, Mon.-Thurs. 10-10, Fri. 10-5, Sat. 8-noon; closed school hols; free. **Strecker Museum** (basement, Richardson Science Bldg), Indian displays, minerals, fossils, biology exhibits; open Mon.-Sat. 9-noon, 2-5; closed school hols; free. **Armstrong Browning Library** has one of the world's largest collections on Elizabeth Barrett and Robert Browning; 46 stained-glass windows illustrate Browning themes; paintings, furniture, other Browning relics; open Mon.-Fri. 9-noon, 2-4, Sat. 9-noon, Sun. 2-5; closed school hols; free.

Homer Garrison Memorial Museum (in Ft. Fisher Park, I-35 & University Dr.), in replica of 1837 Texas Ranger fort, houses Ranger memorabilia; open Mon.-Sat. 9-6, Sun. 11-6; closed Dec. 25; sm adm. Also in Fort Fisher Park is **Waco Tourist Information Center,** which provides information on historic homes (open hrs listed below, by appointment, and during Brazos River Festival tours in Apr.): **East Terrace** (100 Mill St.), 1872 home of bricks made from Brazos River sand, Italian villa style, period furnishings; **Earle-Napier-Kinnard House** (814 S 4th St.), 1867 Greek Revival home with period furnishings; **Fort House** (503 S 4th St.), 1868 Greek Revival home with historic exhibits; all open Sat. & Sun. 2-5; closed Easter, Dec. 25; adm. **Earle-Harrison House** (1901 N 5th St.), 1858 Greek Revival home with period furnishings, separate kitchen, gazebo; open 1st & 3rd Sun. of each month 2-5; adm.

Highlands Mansion (25 m SE on SR 6, then 2 m E on FM 147 in Marlin), restored Gay 90s mansion; elegant interior with stained-glass dome, tufted leather paneling; many original furnishings; open Mon.-Sat. 10-4, Sun. 1-4; closed Jan. 1, Thnks, Dec. 25; adm. **Old Fort Parker State Historic Site** (40 m E on SR 164 to Groesbeck, then 4 m N via SR 14, Park Rd. 35) preserves restored log blockhouses and stockade of 1834 fort built to protect settlers; in 1836, Comanches overran the fort, killing 5 and taking captive 9-year-old Cynthia Ann Parker. Cynthia Ann adapted well to

Comanche life, married, and became mother of the last great Comanche chief, Quanah Parker. In 1860 her family recaptured her, along with her 2-year-old daughter Prairie Flower; but Cynthia Ann could not readapt to white life and, after unsuccessful attempts to escape, and an unhappy life as a virtual prisoner, she and her daughter died within 4 years. Historic exhibits in fort; open daily in daylight; sm adm. **Confederate Research Center & Gun Museum** (34 m N on I-35 to Hill Junior College campus, E of Hillsboro), weapons, dioramas, other Civil War displays; library; open Mon.-Fri. 9-5; closed hols; free. Nearby Hill County Courthouse, built 1889, has been called outstanding and a "monstrosity." **Central Texas Area Museum** (53 m S on I-35 to Main & Front Sts., Salado) depicts area history with relics, documents, other exhibits; open daily 10-5 (10-6 in summer); closed Jan. 1, Dec. 24, 25; sm adm. Across the street is the restored Stagecoach Inn where Robert E. Lee, Jesse James, and Shanghai Pierce were early guests; now a restaurant.

Norse Settlement (46 m NW on SR 6 to Clifton, then W on FM 219) was settled by Norwegian immigrants in the 1850s; Norway Mills, Old Norse (Our Savior's) Church, other historic buildings; annual festival (Nov.).

WICHITA FALLS: Wichita Falls Museum & Art Center (2 Eureka Circle) has regional historic exhibits, art, science displays; planetarium; open Mon.-Sat. 9:30-4:30, Sun. 1-5; closed hols; free. **Archer County Historical Museum** (25 m SW on SR 79 in county courthouse, Archer City), frontier relics; open Mon.-Fri. 8-5; closed hols; free. **Fort Belknap** (43 m SW on SR 79, then 12 m S on SR 251), an army post established 1851 to protect settlers, travelers on the Butterfield route, was abandoned 1867; restored buildings include infantry quarters, powder magazine; museum in former commissary displays Indian, military, ranch, and trail artifacts; open daily exc Fri. 9-5; closed hols; sm adm.

WINNSBORO: Caddo Indian Industrial Center (8 m W via FM 852, 269, then unnumbered road S) is on site of prehistoric Indian settlement; tanning yard, corn shellers and mills, area for paint production, other remains; demonstrations; open June-mid-Nov., Sat. & Sun. 10-5; adm.

WOODVILLE: Allan Shivers Library & Museum (302 N Charlton), memorabilia of former governor, historical artifacts; open in summer, Mon.-Fri. 9:30-5:30, Sat. & Sun. 2-4; inquire for shorter winter hrs; sm adm. **Heritage Garden Village** (1 m W on US 190): some 30 homes, shops, other buildings depict Texas life from pioneer days to early 20th-C; buildings are appropriately furnished; old vehicles, other displays; open daily 9-7; closed Jan. 1, Dec. 25; sm adm. **East Texas Indian Reservation**

(16 m W on US 190) offers a museum of Alabama-Coushatta tribes, crafts, village, demonstrations and entertainment; open June-Aug., Mon.-Sat. 9-6, Sun. 12:30-6; Sept.-May, daily 10-4; closed Dec. 25; adm. An outdoor drama based on tribal history is presented in summer. **Polk County Museum** (33 m W on US 190 to 601 W Church St., Livingston), Indian artifacts, early American glass, other historic items; open Tues.-Fri. 1:30-5, Sat. 9:30-12:30; closed hols; free. **Jasper County Museum** (28 m E on US 190 in county courthouse in Jasper), pioneer and Civil War exhibits; open Mon.-Fri. 8:30-5; closed hols; free.

UTAH

BEAVER: Old Cove Fort (22 m N off US 91, I-15) was built by Mormons in 1867 against raids during the Black Hawk War; very well preserved; 12 rooms with period furnishings; museum exhibits include Indian and pioneer artifacts, dolls, guns; open Apr.-Oct. daily 8-7; sm adm. **Old Frisco** (46 m NW on SR 21), a ghost town; boomed after an 1875 silver strike and became known for gambling, prostitution, other vices; shacks, kilns, foundations remain. **Newhouse** (60 m NW on SR 21, then 2 m E) was a more peaceful boom town; the ore gave out in 1910; ruins and mine dumps.

BOULDER: Anasazi Indian Village State Historical Site (NE of town), a large community believed occupied 1075-1275, has been excavated; artifacts in museum; open Apr.-Oct. daily 8 am-7 pm; sm adm.

BRIGHAM CITY: Box Elder Tabernacle (2nd & Main Sts.), on site selected by Brigham Young, was completed 1890; impressive exterior; plasterwork ceilings, 1000-pipe organ; open June-Aug. daily 8-8; free. **Intermountain School** (S edge of town off 7 South St.), secondary boarding school for Navajo children, operated by Bureau of Indian Affairs; tours by appointment Sept.-May, Mon.-Fri. 8:30-3:30; free. Arts & Crafts Shop (on campus) sells Indian-made articles; open Mon.-Fri. 1-5; closed hols; free. **Railroad Museum** (7 m W on SR 83 in Corinne), railroad cars, locomotives, caboose; photos and memorabilia; blacksmith shop; open May-Sept., Tues.-Sat. 9-5, Sun. 2-5; sm adm.

   Golden Spike National Historic Site (30 m W via SR 83 & unnumbered rd to Promontory) commemorates golden spike driven on May 10, 1869 into the last tie joining 1800 m of railway from Omaha, Nebraska, to Sacramento, California; **Visitor Center** with film, exhibits, booklet for self-guiding tour along old railroad bed; ceremony reenacted in summer, daily; open June-Aug. daily 8-6; Sept.-May daily 8-4:30; closed Dec. 25; sm adm. or GEP.

BRYCE CANYON NATIONAL PARK (7 m S of Panguitch on US 89, then 17 m E on SR 12): Famous for vivid, spectacular formations; 17-m drive; **Visitor Center** with orientation programs, geologic displays, is open daily 8-5 (8 am-9 pm in summer); naturalist talks (June-Labor Day); part open all yr; some roads close in winter; sm adm or GEP.

CANYONLANDS NATIONAL PARK, where the rugged canyons of the Green and Colorado Rivers meet, has colorful and fantastically shaped sandstone formations; much of this is wilderness, accessible by four-wheel drive, on foot, or on raft trips; Anasazi ruins, petroglyphs and pictographs; information from Supt. in **Moab** or at ranger offices at **Island in the Sky** (12 m N of Moab on US 163, then 24 m SW on secondary roads), **Needles** (15 m N of Monticello on US 163, then 38 m W). Open all year, free.

CAPITOL REEF NATIONAL PARK (11 m E of Torrey on SR 24): In this colorful sandstone area, pre-Columbian Indians of Fremont Culture lived in open caves reached by handholds and footholds dug into the cliff faces; they also built stone structures in which to store the corn they raised, and left many petroglyphs. In the late 1800s, white settlers established a little community named Fruita. Remains of both peoples are easily accessible. **Visitor Center** offers exhibits and information; open daily 8-5 (8-6 in summer); closed Thnks, Dec. 25; park open all yr.

CEDAR BREAKS NATIONAL MONUMENT (21 m E of Cedar City off SR 14): This gigantic, multicolored natural amphitheater, eroded into fantastic shapes and surrounded by forests of juniper (misnamed cedar by pioneers) and other evergreens, is open (weather permitting) mid-June-mid-Sept.; 5-m rim drive; **Visitor Center** with exhibits on history and natural history of the area (open early June-Labor Day, daily 8-6; free.

CEDAR CITY: Palmer Memorial Museum (75 N 300 West), maintained by Iron County School District; large collection of Piute basketry, beadwork, other artifacts given by Piute to Dr. William Palmer, a Mormon missionary they made a member of the tribe; open Mon.-Fri. 8-5; closed hols, Easter week, July 24; free. **Museum of Southern Utah** (Southern Utah State College Campus, W of Main St. on Center St.) houses Indian and pioneer artifacts; open Mon.-Sat. 9-5; closed hols; free.

Iron Mission State Historical Monument (1 m N on I-15) displays hearse, bullet-scarred stagecoach from Butch Cassidy era, other old vehicles; old spittoons, waffle irons, cheese press, portable bathtub, other frontier relics; open July-Sept. daily 8-7; Oct.-June daily 8-5; closed Jan. 1, Thnks, Dec. 25; free.

Parowan Gap Indian Site (18 m N on I-15 to Parowan, then W on un-numbered road) is a rock art site, probably of Fremont culture; open daily; free.

Ghost towns: **Old Irontown** (17 m W on SR 56, then 3 m S), remains of ill-fated Mormon iron-making venture; ovens, furnaces, house ruins. **Pinto** (2 m S of Irontown) was founded 1867 by Mormon missionaries to the Indians; several houses, cemetery. **Old Fort Harmony** (18 m S on I-15, then 1 m W toward New Harmony), traces of a Mormon fort; by 1862, the disintegration of the fort, Indian raids, and a deluge that washed away homes and land resulted in a move to New Harmony.

DINOSAUR NATIONAL MONUMENT (7 m N of Jensen) is named for fossils of Jurassic dinosaurs found in an ancient river course here; the dinosaurs ranged from the size of chickens to some larger than elephants; crocodile and turtle fossils have also been found. **Dinosaur Quarry Visitor Center** (7 m N of Jensen on SR 149) faces the quarry wall so that you can see fossils in place and watch excavation; exhibits on lives of dinosaurs, scientific methods; open mid-June-Labor Day, daily 8 am-9 pm; Memorial Day-mid-June, daily 8-7; rest of yr, 8-5; free. **Headquarters & Information Center** (on US 40, 2 m E of Dinosaur, Colorado) has exhibits and interpretive programs; open Apr.-Oct. daily 8-5 (longer hrs in summer); Nov.-Mar., Mon.-Fri. 8-5, closed hols; free. Either center can inform you on pictographs and other points of interest in the monument.

FILLMORE: Territorial Statehouse State Historic Monument (50 W Capitol Ave.), a grand red-sandstone building, was left incompleted in 1855 when the government was moved to Salt Lake City; now a museum; period pioneer rooms, Indian artifacts, guns, paintings, documents, other pioneer relics; open June-Aug. daily 8 am-9 pm; Apr.-May & Sept.-Oct. daily 8-5; Nov.-Mar., Mon.-Fri. 8-5; free.

Fort Deseret State Historical Monument (9 m N on I-15, then 18 m NW on SR 26), ruins of an emergency adobe fortification erected in 18 days by 98 men to protect Mormon settlers just before the Black Hawk War; open daily.

Ghost towns: **Hatton** (7 m S on I-15, then SE to road W, just before Kanosh), settled 1854, became a stagecoach stop but was abandoned in 1867 on orders of Brigham Young. **Topaz** (9 m N on I-15, then 27 m NW on SR 26 to Delta, then 15 m NW on county rd) was established 1942 as internment camp for 8778 Japanese and Americans of Japanese descent;

buildings were dismantled and sold at the end of the war; cement foundations and historic marker remain.

HANKSVILLE: Mormon ghost towns are **Giles** (9 m W on SR 24), established in mid-19th-C and abandoned by 1919 due to flooding; **Cainesville** (20 m W on SR 24), once a prosperous agricultural community, still has a few residents; church, old cabins, well-kept pioneer cemetery. **Hog Spring** (36 m SE on SR 95) is a BLM picnic site with a rockshelter containing Indian pictographs; open daily; sm adm.

KANAB: Stunning formations enticed Zane Grey (who wrote *Riders of the Purple Sage* here) and, later, moviemakers to this area; among sites where movie sets were erected are **Coral Pink Sand Dunes** (7 m N on US 89, then 10 m W on gravel rd) and **Johnson Canyon** (9 m E on US 89, then N). **Paria** (30 m E on US 89, then 5 m N) was an 1868 Morman farming community abandoned after Paria River floods; it later had a short gold boom; now a ghost town, it has a cemetery, old log cabins, mining relics.

LOGAN: Mormon Tabernacle (Main & Center Sts.) may be seen on guided tours June-Labor Day, daily 10-9; inquire for hrs other times of yr; free. **Mormon Temple** (175 N 3rd East St.), for which Brigham Young broke ground in 1877, is closed to the public; tours of grounds all yr; free. **Daughters of Utah Pioneers Museum** (in Chamber of Commerce Bldg, Civic Center, 52 W 2nd North St.) offers historical displays on Mormon pioneers; open early June-late Sept., Mon.-Fri. 1-5 or by appointment; closed July 4, 24; free. **Man & His Bread Museum & Historical Farm** (5 m S on US 89, 91) has been designed by Utah State University to illustrate the development of agriculture; demonstrations; open in summer, daily in daylight; free.

MOAB: Moab Museum (118 E Center St.), gems and minerals, fossils; archaeological relics; regional history that includes Butch Cassidy and other outlaws; open daily 3-5, 7-9; closed Jan. 1, Dec. 25; free. **Arches National Park** (5 m NW on US 163) has a **Visitor Center** (open May-Sept. daily 8-6; Oct.-Apr. daily 8-5) explaining the development of natural arches and other stunning red-rock formations here; 21 m of paved road through the formations are open all year; sm adm or GEP. **Dead Horse Point State Park** (12 m N on US 163, then 20 m SW) has a **Visitor Center** with museum of area history and geology; open daily all year; sm adm. **Sego Canyon Petroglyphs** (30 m N on US 163, then 6 m E on I-70 to Thompson, then 4 m N) extend along the red-rock formations called Book Cliffs. Also here is the ghost town of **Sego,** a coal mining town with several ethnic ghettos that suffered from vice and natural disasters; building ruins; primitive homes dug into the canyon walls.

MONTICELLO: Indian Creek State Park (14 m N on US 163, then 10 m W on SR 211) contains **Newspaper Rock**, a large cliff with ancient petroglyphs and pictographs from at least 3 distinct periods. **Edge of the Cedars** State Historical Site (22 m S, just NW of Blanding) and **Westwater Ruins** (just SW of Blanding) are dwellings from the Anasazi period; also rock art. Information on these and other archaeological sites is obtainable from **San Juan County Travel Council** (Box 425, Monticello 84535) or **Chamber of Commerce** in Blanding. For ruins on the Navajo Indian Reservation (22 m S of Blanding on US 163), contact tribal hq in Arizona.

Natural Bridges National Monument (26 m S on US 163 to SR 95, then 45 m W): Brilliant cliffs, pinnacles, and canyons may be seen from Bridge View Drive, an 8-m loop; at least 200 Anasazi sites, accessible only by hiking; displays and information are at the **Visitor Center,** open mid-Mar.-mid-Nov. daily 8-4:30 (also open other times of yr if weather permits); sm adm or GEP.

OGDEN: Daughters of Utah Pioneer Relic Hall (Tabernacle Sq. at 2150 Grant Ave.), pioneer furnishings and relics; cabin of Miles Goodyear, built about 1841 by a trapper who had a trading post here; open June-Sept., Mon.-Fri. 1-4:30; free. **John M. Browning Gun Collection** (4 m S on US 89 at 450 E 5100 South), past and current models of Browning firearms; open Mon.-Sat. 8-5; closed hols & July 24; free.

PRICE: Chamber of Commerce (Municipal Bldg) offers maps for self-guiding tours of this area; crevices and canyons here were used as hideouts by Butch Cassidy and the Sundance Kid, Deaf Charlie Hanks, Kid Curry, other outlaws; **Nine Mile Canyon** (off US 6, 50, S of town) was a center of Fremont Indian culture about 1000 AD, and Indian petroglyphs abound as well as log cabins and other relics from the turn of the century, when it was a coach and freight route; **Cleveland-Lloyd Dinosaur Quarry** (20 m S on SR 10, then 15 m E on SR 155 & unnumbered rd) has interpretive signs; **Buckhorn Draw** (S on SR 10 to Castle Dale, then E) has Indian rock art on canyon walls; other areas of geological and archaeological interest. **Prehistoric Museum** (room 10 of City Hall, Main & 2 East Sts.) has exhibits on regional Indian cultures, dinosaurs, geology; open June-Aug., Mon.-Sat. 8:30 am-9 pm; Sept.-May, Mon.-Fri. 9-5; closed hols; free.

PROVO: Brigham Young University offers campus tours from Herald R. Clark Bldg; on campus are: Grant Bldg botanical collections including western grasses, mounted animals and insects, birds and eggs; Eyring Science Center exhibits of dinosaurs and other prehistoric animals, minerals, planetarium; Maeser Bldg archaeological and ethnological material from South and Central America, the Near East, Iroquois and

SW American tribes; Harris Fine Arts Center with drawings, paintings, and sculpture (regional artists heavily represented), and rare music and instruments collection. Most buildings are open Mon.-Fri. 8-5; closed hols; free.

Pioneer Museum (500 N, 500 West) has superb regional pioneer artifacts; pioneer village with furnished buildings; open June-mid-Sept. daily 9-5 or by appointment; free. **Springville Museum of Art** (just S at 126 E 400 S, Springville) specializes in American painting and sculpture; open Tues.-Fri. 10-5, Sat. & Sun. 2-5; closed hols; free.

Fairview Museum of History & Art (46 m S on US 89 in Fairview), pioneer relics, old vehicles, Indian artifacts; miniature carvings, painting, sculpture by Utah artists; open Apr.-Oct., Tues.-Sat. 10-5, Sun. 2-5; free.

ST. GEORGE: This area is called the "Dixie" of Utah because in 1861 Mormons attempted to start a cotton industry here. **The Temple** (401 S 300 E), first in the state, was begun in the 1860s on a boggy site that required laying tons of rock for a stable foundation and carting building materials from miles around; but because the site had been chosen by Brigham Young, the Saints persevered until the building was completed in 1877; **Visitor Center** (open June-Sept. daily 8 am-10 pm; Oct.-May daily 9-6; closed Thnks, Dec. 25) provides free tours and films, and information on visiting the Tabernacle (Main & Tabernacle Sts.). **Brigham Young Winter Home State Historical Site** (2 N & 1 West), with period furnishings; open daily 9-5; closed Thnks, Dec. 25; free. **Jacob Hamblin Home State Historical Site** (4 m W off I-15 in Santa Clara), fortified home of the Mormon scout and Indian missionary called the Buckskin Apostle; pioneer furnishings; open daily 9-5; closed Thnks, Dec. 25; free. **Daughters of Utah Pioneers Museum** (McQuarrie Memorial Bldg, 145 N 100 E), photos and relics of pioneers who lived in primitive adobe huts or dugouts while attempting to start the cotton industry; open June-Aug., Mon.-Sat. 7-9 pm; rest of yr, by appointment; free.

Ghost towns: **Toquerville** (7 m NE on I-15, 9 m NE on SR 15, 3 m NW) was issued a permit in 1866 by Brigham Young for making wine (for export only); winery still stands. **Grafton** (7 m NE on I-15, then 24 m NE on SR 15), settled 1859 by Mormon farmers, was abandoned because of Indian attacks and alternating floods and drought; site has been used as a movie set; brick schoolhouse can be seen across the Virgin River. **Harrisburg** (15 m NE on I-15) was founded 1861 by Mormon farmers and prospered until water became scarce; cemetery, ruined stone buildings. **Red Cliffs Recreation Site** (20 m NE on I-15 in Dixie National Forest) has 1/8-m trail to Silver Reef, a boom silver town; $8-million in ore was removed in this area 1875-85; Silver Reef had a mile-long boardwalk flanked by saloons, shops, gambling dens, dance halls, public buildings; a Wells Fargo building and remains of Main Street can be seen. **Pine Valley** (23 m N on SR 18, then 7 m E), settled in mid-19th-C, had 7 sawmills, cheese factory, tannery, and grist mill; it died off as the trees gave out; now a resort; 1868 chapel built by Ebenezer Bryce for whom Bryce Canyon is named. **Mountain Meadow** (27 m N on SR 18 in Dixie National Forest) is a valley at the headwaters of the Santa Clara River once used by trappers and explorers en route to California; victims of the 1857 Mountain Meadow Massacre, 120 members of the pioneer Fancher Party killed by whites and Indian allies, are buried in a common grave. **Hebron** (36 m N on SR 18 to Enterprise, then 5 m W to Shoal Creek), an 1862 Mormon settlement, was abandoned for lack of water; foundations and a cemetery remain.

SALT LAKE CITY: Temple Square (Main & Temple Sts.), hq of the Church of Jesus Christ of Latter-day Saints, and center of this well-planned city, is a walled, 10-acre area open summer daily 6 am-11 pm, in winter daily 6 am-10 pm; on the landscaped grounds are: **Visitor Center** (S Temple & Main Sts.), with murals, film, exhibits, and information on the city and on Mormon life; tours leave frequently; open daily in summer 6:30 am-9 pm, in winter 8-6; free. **Tabernacle,** built 1867, is roofed with an oval dome supported by wooden arches; outstanding acoustics; recitals on the 11,000-pipe organ daily; famed Mormon Tabernacle Choir rehearsals (Thurs. 7:30 pm) and broadcasts (Sun. 8-10 am) are open to the public; building open daily. **Temple,** on site selected by Brigham Young 4 days after his arrival, was begun in 1853 but not completed for 40 years; ornate structure, topped with a statue of Angel Moroni, is used for Mormon ceremonies and closed to non-Mormons. **Assembly Hall,** a place of worship is open to public. The 1847 **Old Log House,** built shortly after the arrival of the first settlers, is protected by a pergola. **Seagull Monument** commemorates birds who arrived in 1848 and devoured hordes of crickets that threatened to consume the settlers' grain. **Statues** of Joseph & Hyrum Smith, killed by a mob in Carthage, Illinois in 1844; Joseph was the first prophet and first president of the Mormon Church.

Brigham Young Monument (Main & S Temple Sts.) was erected 1897. **Beehive House** (67 E South Temple & State Sts.) and adjacent Lion House (not open) housed Brigham Young, his 19 wives, and 56 children; Young's office as first governor of the Utah Territory; tours Mon.-Sat. 9:30-4:30; closed Jan. 1, Thnks, Dec. 25; free. **Eagle Gate** (arching across State St. next to Beehive House) marked entrance to Young's estate. **Brigham Young Grave** (1st Ave. between N State & A Sts.) is open to the public; Young died in 1877 at age 76.

State Capitol (Capitol Hill, State St.) is on landscaped grounds overlooking the city; exhibits on state resources; murals, paintings, statues; Gold Room furnishings are decorated with gold leaf from Utah's mines; guided tours daily; open Memorial Day-Labor Day, Mon.-Fri. 8:30-6, Sat. & Sun. 9:30-6; rest of yr, Mon.-Fri. 8:30-5; closed hols; free.

Utah State Historical Society (603 E S Temple St.), in French Renaissance mansion built by a silver king; elaborate mosaic tile floors, hand-carved woodwork; rare tapestries, silver, paintings; open Mon.-Fri. 8-5; also Sept.-May, Sat. 10-2; closed hols & July 24; free. **Pioneer Memorial Museum** (300 N Main St.), relics of early settlers and Mormon leaders; dolls; manuscripts; carriage house with Brigham Young wagon, other vehicles; open Mon.-Sat. 9-5; also Apr.-early Oct., Sun. 1-5; closed hols; free. **Utah Pioneer Village** (2998 Connor St.) is a complex of more than 35 buildings moved here to depict regional pioneer life; museum; wagon rides; open Apr.-Sept., Mon.-Sat. 9-5, Sun. 1-5; adm. **Liberty Park** (5-7th E & 9-13th S Sts.) has an 1852 mill and small museum of pioneer relics.

"This Is The Place" Monument (E on Sunnyside Ave. to Emigrant Canyon) commemorates the words uttered on July 24, 1847 by Brigham Young after the long trek from Illinois; colossal monument to pioneers is on Mormon Pioneer Trail, blazed earlier by other wagon trains including the Donner Party; **Visitor Center** with mural of the Mormon journey; pioneer displays; open daily; closed hols; free.

University of Utah: Museum of Fine Arts (Art & Architecture Center), 19th-C French and American landscape painting; also Egyptian, Far East art objects, French and English decorative arts, tapestries, other exhibits; open Mon.-Fri. 10-5, Sun. 2-5; closed hols; free. **Museum of Natural History,** anthropological material from prehistoric to recent times; regional natural history; reconstructed dinosaur skeletons; geology displays; open daily 9:30-5:30; closed Jan. 1, Thnks, Dec. 25; adm. Marriott library, with large collection of regional Americana; open Mon.-Fri. 7:30 am-8 pm, Sat. 9-8, Sun. noon-10; closed hols & July 24; free.

Hansen Planetarium (15 S State St.) offers exhibits, library, daily shows (adm); open Mon.-Sat. 9-9:30, Sun. 1-5; closed hols; free.

Salt Lake Art Center (54 Finch Lane in Reservoir Park) displays regional art; open mid-Sept.-mid-July, Tues.-Sun. 1-5; closed hols; free.

Council Hall (State St. & 2 North), completed 1866, elegant building once housed city administrative offices; now houses historic displays and Utah Travel Council; open Mon.-Fri. 8:30-5 (to 6 in summer); closed hols; free. **City & County Bldg** (451 Washington Sq.), completed 1894, is in Romanesque style with turrets, balconies, other ornate decoration inside and out; open business hrs. **Trolley Square** (bounded by 5th & 6th S Sts., 6th & 7th E Sts.), a complex of old trolley barns converted into an attractive center for boutiques and cafes. **Cathedral of the Madeleine** (331 E S Temple St.), completed 1909, is in Roman Gothic style; Christ and

Apostles carved over entry; interior murals, paintings, wood carvings; stained-glass windows from Germany; open daily.

Timpanogos Cave National Monument (26 m S on I-15, then 10 m E on SR 80) consists of 3 chambers covered with multicolored crystals; 3-hr guided tours Memorial Day-Labor Day 8-5, spring & fall 8-3; closed Nov.-Apr.; sm adm. **Visitor Center** provides orientation, museum exhibits, audiovisual program; booklets for self-guiding tours of cave and above-ground trails; open June-Aug. daily 8-5; Sept.-May daily 8-4; closed Jan. 1, Dec. 25.

You can combine some of the following on round-trip loops from Salt Lake City or Provo: **Camp Floyd & Stagecoach Inn State Historical Monuments** (30 m S on I-15, then 27 m SW on SR 73 near Fairfield), contains the commissary and cemetery of the camp where the 3000-man Johnsonton's Army spent 3 years (1857-60) trying to put down the Mormon Rebellion, and the restored and furnished inn built 1858 and used as a stop on the Overland Stage and Pony Express; open Apr.-Oct. daily; free. The **Pony Express route,** with stations 8-15 m apart, has been marked W of Fairfield on a dirt road; highlights include Lookout Station, where the operators buried 3 travelers and 4 dogs, naming only the dogs on the tombstones; stone house remains at Simpson Springs Station, one of the many attacked by Indians; ruins of Boyd Station, with gun portals still visible; buildings preserved at Willow Springs Station; part of the circular walls, with gunports, of Round Station, near a favorite Indian ambush site; Deep Creek Station, last in Utah, where several surviving buildings are still in use.

Iosepa, ghost town (49 m W on I-80 to Rowley Junction, then 14 m S), was established in the late 1800s after 50 Hawaiian converts to the Mormon faith decided to make a pilgrimage to Salt Lake City; they were given 960 acres here in arid Skull Valley, but though the Kanakas built homes and a school-church, most returned to Hawaii after the LDS temple was built there in 1916.

Tooele Grist Mill (22 m W on I-80, then 3 m S on SR 36) was built in 1854 by Mormons; original building still stands with much of its equipment. Information on this area is available from the **Chamber of Commerce,** City Hall, Tooele (9 m S of the gristmill on SR 36); ghost towns include **Stockton** (7 m S of Tooele on SR 36), a mining town that flourished about 1865; **Ajax** (15 m S of Stockton on SR 36), which has almost completely disappeared, was famous for a huge general store built entirely underground; **Ophir** (4 m S of Stockton on SR 36, then 4 m E on SR 73, then NE), a well-preserved town that had a silver boom in the 1860s; **Mercur** (4 m SE of Ophir on SR 73), an 1869 silver town that had later booms in gold and other metals, has shells of rock buildings, ore dumps, tailing piles, a few cabins, and remains of the Manning mill (3 m E).

VERNAL: Utah Field House of Natural History (Natural History State Park, 235 E Main St.) is an outstanding museum with life-size models of dinosaurs; displays on Basketmaker and other prehistoric cultures; fossils; minerals; regional wildlife; pioneer artifacts; open daily 9-6 (8 am-9 pm in summer); free. **Thorne's Photo Studio** (18 W Main St.) displays a mummy, tools, other artifacts of prehistoric Utah; open Tues.-Sat. 9-6; closed hols; free.

   Red Canyon Visitor Center (44 m N & W on SR 44), with glass walls overlooking the Red Canyon of the Green River, offers regional natural history exhibits; **Flaming Gorge Visitor Center** (52 m N on SR 44, 260) provides a relief map of the dam and reservoir, information on recreation; open all year; free.

ZION NATIONAL PARK (42 m E of St. George on SR 15): The beautiful, multicolored canyon, where the awesome formations have been given names such as Angels Landing or Mountain of the Sun, can be seen on a 12-m (round-trip) scenic drive with overlooks and trailheads; **Visitor Center** offers exhibits on the park's natural history, relief map, orientation, interpretive programs, guided walks and trips (daily in summer, several times weekly in spring & fall); open daily 8-5 (8-8 in July-Aug.). Park open all year; sm adm or GEP.

VERMONT

BARRE: Center for world's largest granite quarries, Barre was settled by European stonecutters; Robert Burns Monument on school lawn was cut by Samuel Novelli, with relief panels depicting scenes from poems carved by Elia Corti; Barre Cemetery has wonderful seated figure of Elia Corti on the master carver's grave. **Rock of Ages Quarry & Craftsman Center** (1 m S on SR 14, then follow signs 3 m SE to Graniteville) has observation deck overlooking century-old, 20-acre quarries; you can watch artisans at work, take a quarry train ride (June-Sept., Mon.-Fri.), or take guided tour from visitor center (open May-Oct. daily 8:30-4; free). Craftsman Center is open Mon.-Fri. 8:30-3:30, with guided tours in summer. Adm.

BELLOWS FALLS: Steamtown, USA (2 m N on US 5), locomotives, a steamboat, fire engine, steam shovel, and other steam machines from many countries; exhibits on impact of steam machinery on American history; 26-m steam-train ride to Chester Depot daily in summer-early fall, weekends & hols in spring & fall; open late May-Oct. daily 9-6; adm. **Adams Grist Mill** (Mill St.), 1831 mill still operable; museum of early electrical equipment, other antiques; open July-Labor Day, Sat. & Sun. 2-4; donation. **Vermont Country Store** (5 m N on SR 103 in Rockingham), with 1890s country kitchen and soda fountain, 1810 gristmill, 1972 covered bridge, has old-fashioned goods; open July-Nov., Mon.-Sat. 9-6; Dec.-June, Mon.-Sat. 9-5; closed Jan. 1, Thnks, Dec. 25; free. Nearby 1787 **Rockingham Meeting House** has graveyard with interesting epitaphs and carvings on tombstones; open mid-June-Labor Day daily 10-4; sm adm.

BENNINGTON: Tourist Information booth (507 Main St.) is open in summer 8:30-5:30, in winter 8:30-4:30. **Old Bennington** (2 m W), with lovely Colonial homes, is especially worth visiting. **Bennington Battle Monument** (Monument Ave., Old Bennington) commemorates 1777 victory of Ethan Allen's Green Mountain Boys (who headquartered here); observation tower open July-Sept. 9-6; Apr.-June & Oct. 9-5; sm adm. **Old First Church** (Monument Ave., Old Bennington), designed 1805 by Lavius Fillmore, accurately restored (open July-mid-Oct., Mon.-Sat. 10-5, Sun. 1-5; also some spring weekends; donation); graves of American and Hessian soldiers who fell during Battle of Bennington, grave of Robert Frost.

    Bennington Museum (W Main St., Old Bennington), splendid, with emphasis on Battle of Bennington; military equipment from Revolution and Civil War; outstanding Early American glass; Bennington pottery; early furniture, toys; earliest known Stars and Stripes; Rodin, French, Houdon, other sculpture; painting including special collection of Grandma Moses and Moses family memorabilia; open daily in summer 9-6, in spring & fall 9:30-4:30; closed Thnks, Dec.-Feb.; adm.

    Bennington Potters, Inc. (324 County St.) offers tours (Mon.-Fri. 2:15) and showrooms (Mon.-Sat. 8:30-5:30, longer in summer; Sun. noon-5:30); closed Jan. 1, Thnks, Dec. 25; free.

    Gov. McCullough House (on SR 67A in N Bennington), ornate Victorian mansion built 1865 with California Gold Rush money; carved woodwork; Victorian furnishings; clothing display; carriages; special events; open late June-late Oct., Tues.-Sun. 10-4; adm. **Topping Tavern Museum** (10 m N on US 7 to East Rd., Shaftsbury), 1777 stagecoach inn, restored with taproom, ballroom, bedrooms, outbuildings; period furnishings and memorabilia; open May-Oct., Tues.-Sat. 10-5, Sun. 1-5; adm.

BRATTLEBORO: Brattleboro Museum & Art Center (in Old Union Railroad Station), original settlement, 1724, at Fort Dummer, other historic displays; Estey organs, manufactured here in mid-19th-C;

regional art; open May-Dec., Tues.-Sun. 1-4; closed Jan. 1, Dec. 25; free. **Newfane** (13 m NW on SR 30) has splendid 1825 Courthouse, good historical society museum (open May-Oct., Sun.), and covered bridge (4 m NW off SR 30 at Townshend, across West River). **Brigham Young Memorial** (17 m W on SR 9, then S & W on SR 100, between Jacksonville and Whitingham), birthplace of Mormon leader.

BURLINGTON: Robert Hull Fleming Museum (Colchester Ave. on Univ. of Vermont campus), European, American, and Far East art; primitive works from Africa, South Pacific; ancient works from Egypt, South America; open academic yr, Tues.-Fri. 9-5, Sun. 2-5; free. **First Unitarian-Universalist Church** (141 Pearl St.), built 1816 from plans by Peter Banner, supervised by Bulfinch; open Mon.-Fri., Sun. **Shelburne Museum** (7 m S on US 7), impressive Americana; modest to fancy homes, stagecoach inn, jail, railroad station, all appropriately furnished or devoted to special collections; pewter, glass, weathervanes, cigar-store Indians, snuffboxes, other 18-19th-C items; *Ticonderoga,* a Lake Champlain sidewheeler; carriages, sleighs, coaches, locomotive; fine 18-19th-C paintings in Webb Gallery of American Art; Webb Memorial Bldg, with Georgian furnishings, houses European paintings; open May 15-Oct. 15 daily 9-5; adm.

Old Round Church (10 m E on US 2 to Huntington Rd., Richmond), 16-sided building erected 1813 by 5 different denominations; open daily in summer. **Hyde Log Cabin** (11 m N on I-89, then 14 m NW on US 2 in Grand Isle), built 1783; period furnishings and tools; open early July-Labor Day, daily 10:30-5; donation.

MIDDLEBURY: Middlebury College (W end of town on SR 125) has 19th-C Old Stone Row; Emma Willard House (home of pioneer in women's education; now administrative office); Starr Library, collections on regional writers including Robert Frost. College owns Robert Frost Cabin (4 m SE on US 7, 4 m E on SR 125 to Robert Frost Wayside at Ripton); tours occasionally offered.

Sheldon Museum (1 Park St.), in 1829 brick home with furnished nursery, country store, taproom, has period furniture and household items; glass collection; primitive portraits; pewter; clocks; documents; other collections; open June-mid-Oct., Mon.-Sat. 10-5; rest of yr by appointment; closed July 4, Labor Day; adm. **Congregational Church** (The Common), designed by Lavius Fillmore in 1806, is especially attractive; open June-mid-Oct. daily 8:30-4:30; rest of yr, Sun. 8-12:30; free. **Frog Hollow Craft Center,** shows and demonstrations; open Feb.-Dec., Mon.-Sat. 10-5; closed Dec. 25; free.

Prayer Rock (12 m NE via US 7, SR 17 to picnic area E end of Bristol), boulder on which native had Lord's Prayer carved to atone for swearing by travelers on muddy roads. **Bixby Memorial Library & Museum** (13 m NW off US 7 to 258 Main St., Vergennes), in fine 1911 Greek Revival building; Indian artifacts, Sandwich glass, paperweights, historic exhibits; open Mon., Tues., Thurs. 12:30-5, Wed. 10-5, Fri. 12:30-8; closed hols; free.

MONTPELIER: State House (State St.), with elements of Temple of Theseus in Greece, erected of Vermont granite in 1859; dome covered with gold leaf is topped with statue of Ceres; statue of Ethan Allen; chair in the governor's office carved from timber from USS *Constitution*; open daily 9-4; closed hols; free. Adjoining **Vermont Historical Society Museum**, exhibits on state history in reconstructed 1875 Pavilion Hotel; Indian items; railroad memorabilia; first printing press in state; audiovisual programs; open Mon.-Fri. 8-4:30; closed hols; free. **Vermont State Library** (in Supreme Court Bldg, 111 State St.) also has historic exhibits; open Mon.-Fri. 8-4:30; closed hols; free. **Thomas Waterman Wood Art Gallery** (in Kellogg-Hubbard Library, 135 Main St.), paintings by Wood and other 19th-C American artists; open Mon.-Fri. 2-6; closed hols; free.

Kent Tavern Museum (9 m N & E on unnumbered road to Calais), 1837 inn, has country store, Victorian furnishings, historical exhibits; open July-Labor Day, Tues.-Sun. 1-5; adm. **Bundy Art Gallery** (6 m NW on US 2, then 11 m S on SR 100B, 100), good contemporary painting, including Latin American works; sculpture on 80 acres of woods and lawns; open June-Aug., Mon., Wed.-Sat. 10-5, Sun. 1-5; closed July 4; free. **Northfield Falls** (7 m S on SR 12) has 3 covered bridges. **Norwith University** (9 m S on SR 12 at Northfield) has museum of military items in White Memorial Chapel; open academic yr, Mon.-Sat. 8-4; closed hols; free.

MORRISVILLE: Morristown Historical Society Museum (1 Main St.), in 1830 brick mansion; pitchers, glassware, clocks, other early regional items; Civil War relics; open June-Oct., Mon., Wed., Fri.-Sun. 2-5; donation. **Fisher Bridge** (9 m E on SR 15), spanning Lamoille River, is last covered railroad bridge in state; full-length cupola allowed release of smoke.

NEWPORT: Old Stone House (10 m S on US 5 to Orleans, 2 m NE to Brownington), in 1836 school building; 26 rooms of early New England furniture, farm and household items, war relics; open mid-May-mid-Oct., daily 9-5; adm.

RUTLAND: Chaffee Art Center (16 S Main St.), in Victorian mansion; regional arts and crafts; open June-late Oct., Mon.-Sat. 10-5; closed Labor Day; free.

Wilson Castle (2 m W on US 4, then 1 m N on W Proctor Rd., Proctor), with stained-glass windows and carved woodwork; opulent brick-and-marble mansion built 1867; ornate European and Far East furnishings; art gallery; open mid-May-late-Oct. daily 8-6; adm. **Marble Exhibit** (2 m W on US 4, then 4 m N on SR 3 to Proctor), film, exhibits on history, processing, and uses of marble; world-wide specimens; demonstrations; open late May-mid-Oct. daily 9-6; sm adm. Castleton (11 m W on SR 4A), mid-summer tour of homes and churches built in 18th-C by Thomas Royal Drake.

Hubbardton Battlefield & Museum (11 m W on US 4, 7 m N on road to E Hubbardton), site of only Revolutionary War battle on Vermont soil, fought July 7, 1777 by Col. Seth Warner and the Green Mountain Boys; the short battle, halting the British and Hessian pursuit of Americans retreating from Fort Ticonderoga, was the first successful resistance to Burgoyne and had enormous psychological effect; **Visitor Center** with audiovisual program and museum exhibits; open late-May-mid-Oct. daily 9-5; sm adm.

At **East Poultney** (14 m W on US 4, 6 m S on SR 30 to Poultney, 1½ m E), the Baptist Meeting House, a Federal-style church erected 1805, has notable wood carving and weathervane; Eagle Tavern Inn displays Revolutionary War documents and material on Horace Greeley, who was an apprentice printer's devil here. **Stephen A. Douglas Birthplace** (16 m NW on US 7 to 2 Grove St., Brandon), where the Little Giant was born 1813, is open by appointment (phone 247-5535); free.

Green Mountain National Forest, 240,000-acre preserve through center of state; several points of historic interest, Revolutionary and French and Indian War battlegrounds; information from Supt. (Box 519, Rutland 05701).

ST. ALBANS: Franklin County Museum (Church St.), regional historic items; re-created doctor's office; open July-Aug., Tues.-Sat. 2-5; free. **Greenwood Cemetery** (S Main St.), famous for Brainerd Monument, erected on grave of a young soldier who died in Andersonville Prison. **Chester A. Arthur Homestead** (8 m E on SR 36 to Fairfield, then follow signs 5 m NW), birthplace of 21st President; original furnishings, documents; open June-Sept.; inquire locally for hrs.

ST. JOHNSBURY: Fairbanks Museum of Natural Science (Main St.), mounted wildlife, primitive arts, physical science displays, planetarium shows (Sat. 2:30; adm); open Mon.-Sat. 9-4:30, Sun. 1-5; free. **St. Johnsbury Atheneum** (30 Main St.), paintings by Bierstadt, James and William Hart, others; copies of Madonnas; open Mon.-Fri. 10-5; closed hols; free.

SPRINGFIELD: Springfield Art & Historical Society (9 Elm Hill), Richard Lee pewter; primitive portraits; Bennington pottery; dolls; other exhibits; open early May-Dec., Mon.-Fri. noon-4:30; also July-Aug., Sun. 2-4; closed hols; free. **Eureka Schoolhouse** (Charleston Rd.), 1790, oldest school in state; open mid-May-mid-Oct. daily 10-5; donation. Nearby covered bridge.

Congregational Church (7 m SW on SR 11 in Chester), 1828, is especially handsome. **Farrar-Mansur House** (10½ m SW on SR 11, then 7 m W on unnumbered road to The Common in Weston), 1797 home and tavern; restored kitchen, taproom, ballroom; local historic items; open July-Labor Day, Tues.-Sun. 1-5; late-May-June & mid-Sept.-Oct., Sat. & Sun. 1-5; sm adm.

WHITE RIVER JUNCTION: Woodstock (13 m SW on US 4) is one of the most charming towns in New England; restored homes; covered bridge; **Woodstock Historical Society** (26 Elm St.), interesting local relics, library, and art gallery in 1807 home (open Memorial Day-Oct., Mon.-Sat. 10-5, Sun. 2-5:30; adm); Norman Williams Public Library, books and newspapers on the area.

President Coolidge Homestead (20 m W on US 4, 5 m S on SR 100A in Plymouth Notch), unpretentious frame house where Coolidge was sworn in as President by his father in 1923; next door is his mother's birthplace; Vermont Farmer's Museum with pre-1900 farm tools; open late May-mid-Oct. daily 9:30-6; adm.

Justin Smith Morrill Homestead (16 m NW off I-89 in Strafford), gingerbread home in Gothic Revival style with 19th-C furnishings; open mid-May-mid-Oct., Tues.-Sat. 10-5, Sun. 2-5; sm adm. **Joseph Smith Monument** (21 m NW on SR 14) marks place of birth of Mormon leader; Mormon library and museum open May-Nov. daily 8-6; free. **Walker Museum** (22 m N off I-91 in Fairlee), local historical collections; open June-Oct. daily 10-5; sm adm.

WINDSOR: Old Constitution House (16 N Main St.), tavern where constitution of the Republic of Vermont was adopted in 1777; antique clocks, guns, dolls, other displays; open late May-Oct., Tues.-Sun. 9:30-4:30; free. Nearby is **Old South Church** (Main St.), 1798, lovely building believed designed by Asher Benjamin. **American Precision Museum** (196 Main St.), 1846 brick building, formerly firearms and machine tool factory; hand tools and machines; examples of products; library; open late May-mid-Oct. daily 1-5; adm. **Covered Bridge** (across the Connecticut River) is longest in Vermont.

VIRGINIA

ABINGDON: Barter Theatre (Main St.), in 1830 Town Hall, was started during the Depression, when actors performed in exchange for food; today, State Theatre of Virginia, performances Apr.-Oct.

Saltville (12 m E on I-81, 7 m N on SR 91) supplied salt for Confederacy during Civil War; Chamber of Commerce offers brochures for self-guiding tour of Saltville Museum, First Salt Mine, Salt Furnaces, restored log homes, other sites.

ALEXANDRIA: Although settled in the late 1600s, Alexandria was not established until surveyors, including the young George Washington, had laid out streets and lots in 1749. Because Union troops moved in here early in the Civil War, the city escaped destruction and many old buildings remain. Walking tours of Old Town start at **Ramsay House Visitor Center** (221 King St. at Fairfax St.), yellow clapboard cottage, 1721, by Scottish founder of the city; film; maps; brochures for walking, bicycling; guided tours; open daily 10-4:30; closed Jan. 1, Thnks, Dec. 25. Nearby are: **Carlyle House** (121 N Fairfax St.), stately 1752 stone mansion of well-to-do Scottish merchant and shipowner; family furnishings; architectural exhibit; audiovisual program; open daily 10-4:30; closed Jan. 1, Thnks, Dec.25; adm. **Stabler-Leadbeater Apothecary Shop** (107 S Fairfax St.), unusual medical ware and handblown containers, original furnishings, that have never been moved since shop opened in 1792; ledgers show purchases by Washingtons, Lees, Calhouns, Clays; open Mar.-Oct., Mon.-Sat. 10-5; Nov.-Feb., Mon.-Sat. 10-4:30; closed hols; donation.

Atheneum (201 Prince St.), built in Greek Revival style as a bank about 1850; paintings, sculpture, other works; open early-Sept.-mid-June, Tues.-Sat. 10-4, Sun. 1-4; closed Thnks, Dec. 25; free. **Gentry Row** and **Captain's Row** (Prince St. between Fairfax & Union Sts.), typical of row houses in British seaports; not open to public; cobblestones are believed to have been laid by Hessian POWs. **Old Presbyterian Meeting House** (321 S Fairfax St.) was built 1774 by Scottish founders of Alexandria and served as meeting place for patriots; Washington's funeral sermons were preached here; cemetery with Tomb of the Unknown Soldier of the American Revolution; open Mon.-Fri. 9-4, Sat. 9-noon. **Flounder Houses** (321 S Lee; others at 202 Duke, 317 S St. Asaph St.), flat and windowless on one side, may have been designed to avoid English taxes on window glass; not open to public. **Lafayette House** (301 St. Asaph St.), fine Federal building, was lent to Lafayette for use during his last visit to America in 1825.

George Washington Bicentennial Center (201 S Washington St.), exhibits and audiovisual program on Virginia's role in the Revolution; tourist information; open daily 9-5; closed Jan. 1, Dec. 25; free. **Gadsby's Tavern** (128 N Royal St.), handsome Georgian inn; George Washington recruited troops here for his first command and held his last military review here in 1798; authentic furnishings; open daily 9-5; adm. Gen. Henry (Lighthorse Harry) Lee Home (611 Cameron St.) is not open to public. **Christ Church** (118 N Washington St.), whose construction costs were paid in tobacco on its completion in 1773, has marked the Robert E. Lee and Washington pews; open Mon.-Sat. 9-5, Sun. 2-5; closed Jan. 1, Thnks, Dec. 25. **Robert E. Lee Boyhood Home** (607 Oronoco St.), where Lee lived from 1810 (age 3) until he entered West Point in 1825, is a Federal-style house built 1795; period furnishings; open Mar.-Nov., Mon.-Sat. 10-4, Sun. noon-4; sm adm.

Friendship Veterans Fire Engine Co. (107 S Alfred St.) was organized 1774; Washington donated its first fire engine, a $400 hand-pumper; other antique equipment; open Tues.-Sat. 10-4; closed hols; free. **George Washington Masonic National Memorial** (W end of King St. on Shooter's Hill), modeled on an ancient lighthouse in Alexandria, Egypt, has observation platform; Washington was Master here, and relics include clock stopped at the time of his death; murals and stained-glass windows depict events in his life; open daily 9-5; closed Jan. 1, Thnks, Dec. 25; free. **St. Paul's Cemetery** (W end of Wilkes St.) is famous for tomb of "Female Stranger"; many stories have been invented to explain her elaborate monument; also here is Alexandria National Cemetery, including graves of 4 civilians who drowned in the Potomac attempting to chase Lincoln's assassin. **Fort Ward Museum & Park** (4301 W Braddock Rd.) was one of a ring of 68 forts and batteries, connected by miles of trenches, built to protect the capital during the Civil War; restored fort; museum of relics (open Mon.-Sat. 9-5, Sun. noon-5; closed Thnks, Dec. 25); park open daily 9-sunset; free. **Alexandria Gazette** (717 N St. Asaph St.), oldest newspaper in the U.S., is open Mon.-Sat. 9-5; closed Dec. 25.

Gunston Hall (18 m S on US 1, then 4 m E on SR 242 in Lorton) was estate of George Mason, author of Virginia's Declaration of Rights which became model for U.S. Bill of Rights; built 1755 under supervision of William Buckland, whose designs became very influential; restrained exterior; impressive interior with extraordinary carved woodwork; Chippendale Chinese dining room; Hepplewhite, Queen Anne, Chippendale pieces; boxwood gardens; open daily 9:30-5; closed Dec. 25; adm.

Occoquan (20 m S on US 1, then 1 m SW on SR 123), charming village with craft boutiques, 1758 Rockledge (all-stone house), and 1793 Mill House (operated as museum).

AMELIA COURT HOUSE: Sayler's Creek Battlefield State Park (9 m SW on US 360, then 7 m W on SR 307, 2 m N on SR 617) was site of Apr. 6, 1865, battle where 7700 of Gen. Lee's men were killed or captured; Lee surrendered 3 days later at Appomattox; Hillsman House, used as hospital for wounded of both sides, is museum (open June-Labor Day, Tues.-Sun. 10-6; park open all yr; free. **Haw Branch Plantation** (9 m N on SR 681, then 3 m E on SR 667), beautiful Georgian-Federal mansion built by patriots Thomas and John Tabb in 1745; tobacco-leaf carvings; family furnishings; outbuildings; open daily 10-5; closed Thnks, Dec. 25; adm.

APPOMATTOX COURT HOUSE NATIONAL HISTORICAL PARK (3 m NE of Appomattox on SR 24): Here, on Palm Sunday, Apr. 9, 1865, Lee surrendered the Army of Northern Virginia. Trying to unite with Johnston's forces in N Carolina, he was blocked by 80,000 Union men here, just short of reaching supplies at Appomattox Station; when an attempt to break through failed, Lee felt further bloodshed was useless. Grant and Lee met about 1:30 in McLean House—Grant, arriving on his black horse Cincinnati, was mud-spattered and in a common soldier's uniform; Lee was immaculate, with his sword buckled at his side; they spoke of their old army days before Grant offered generous surrender terms. By 4 they were through, and Lee mounted Traveller to tell his men he had surrendered. Three days later, 28,231 Confederate soldiers laid their arms down at the edge of the village. **McLean House** (reconstructed on its original site, with original and period furnishings) and the quiet village (restored to its 1865 appearance, with period shops and other buildings) are movingly evocative. The famous Guillaume painting of the surrender is in the **Visitor Center** in the reconstructed Court House), which offers exhibits, audiovisual program; open June-Labor Day daily 8:30-6; rest of yr, daily 8:30-5; closed Dec. 25; sm adm or GEP.

ARLINGTON: Arlington National Cemetery, established 1864, has graves of many notables, including Presidents Taft and Kennedy; no cars (tram service); **Visitor Center;** open Apr.-Oct. daily 8 am-7 pm; Nov.-Mar. daily 8-5; free. Here are: **Tomb of the Unknowns,** with elaborate precautions taken to assure anonymity; first soldier buried here was chosen from American WW I cemeteries in France, placed on Lincoln catafalque, and buried with honors on Armistice Day 1921; unknown soldiers of WW II and the Korean conflict were later added to the shrine. **Arlington House,** built 1802-17 by George Washington Parke Custis, adopted son of George Washington, as place for perpetuating Washington's memory and traditions of warm hospitality. In 1831, Custis' daughter Mary married Robert E. Lee in the parlor; she raised their 7 children here while Lee was away on military assignments. After Custis died in 1857, leaving the plantation to Mary, Lee returned to manage it; but in 1861, despite his opposition to dissolution of the Union, Lee resigned from the U.S. Army and left to offer his services to Virginia. With Union occupation imminent, Mrs. Lee left after removing many possessions; the rest were looted when Union forces occupied the house. In 1864, when Mrs. Lee was unable to appear in person to pay property taxes, the estate was confiscated by the Federal government (the family later regained the house after appealing to the Supreme Court), which designated a section Arlington National Cemetery. Family heirlooms and other period pieces; wine cellar and slave quarters; open Apr.-Sept. daily 9:30-6; Oct.-Mar. daily 9:30-4:30; closed Dec. 25; free.

   Great Falls Park (12½ m N off SR 193 on Old Dominion Dr.), with overlook for Falls of the Potomac, has **Visitor Center** offering audiovisual programs and exhibits on history and ecology of area; ranger-conducted tours; trails to remnants of canal, ruins of Matildaville, canal town sponsored by Lighthorse Harry Lee. **Falls Church** (3 m W on US 29, 211), crossover point between N and S for Indians, traders, armies, and pioneers, has many homes from late 18th-19th-C and The Falls Church (115 E Fairfax at Washington Sts.), a recruiting station during the Revolution, hospital during the Civil War, and later a stable (open daily 9-5); Memorial Fountain (in National Memorial Park), dedicated to 4 chaplains who gave their lifejackets to soldiers when the USS *Dorchester* was torpedoed off Greenland in 1943. **Fairfax Court House** (12 m W on US 29, 211 at 4000 Chain Bridge Rd., Fairfax) displays wills of George and Martha Washington; open Mon.-Fri. 8-4; closed hols; free. **Sully Plantation** (19 m W on US 50, then N on SR 28, Sully Rd., near Chantilly), 1794, home of Richard Bland Lee, brother of Lighthorse Harry and uncle to Robert E. Lee; many family pieces; outbuildings; craft demonstrations in May; open daily 10-5; closed Dec. 25; sm adm. **Reston** (11 m NW on SR 7, then W on SR 606), a new town, offers maps for walking and driving tours at Information Center (Lake Anne Center, off SR 606); open daily.

   George Washington Memorial Parkway stretches 17 m S along the Potomac to Mount Vernon; picnic areas; overlooks; historic sites with interpretive signs.

BIG STONE GAP: Southwest Virginia Museum (in Historic State Park, W. 1st St. & Wood Ave.), handmade tools, antique firearms, pioneer gadgets, early medical instruments, folk paintings and crafts, illustrating life of the area; open Tues.-Sat. 9:30-5, Sun. 2-5; closed Jan. 1, Dec. 25;

free. **June Tolliver House** (Jerome St. & Clinton Ave.), home of heroine of *Trail of the Lonesome Pine*; period furnishings; regional crafts; 1890 school; open Apr.-Dec. 24, Tues.-Sat. 10-5, Sun. 2-6; free.

BLUE RIDGE PARKWAY runs 451 m S from Waynesboro (at the S end of the Skyline Dr.) to the Great Smoky Mountains. Highlights (miles are from Rockfish Gap at the N end) include: **Humpback Rocks Visitor Center** (5.8 m) with reconstructed mountain cabin, exhibits on mountain life; **Otter Creek Visitor Center** (63.6 m) with self-guiding trail to James River, exhibits, lock of James River & Kanawha Canal; **Rocky Knob Visitor Center** (176.1 m) with self-guiding trail to operating Mabry Mill and blacksmith shop; **Puckett Cabin** (189.8 m), home of midwife from 1865 until her death at 102 in 1939 (she assisted at births of over 1000 mountain infants, but her own 24 children died in infancy). For information, write Supt. (P.O. Box 7606, Ashville, NC 28807). See also N Carolina.

CHARLOTTESVILLE: Chamber of Commerce (100 Citizen Commonwealth Center) offers maps for self-guiding walking and auto tours; many homes (some designed by Jefferson) are open to the public during Historic Garden Week (late Apr.-May). Born here were Jefferson; George Rogers Clark (monument on W Main St.), who opened up the Northwest Territory, and his explorer brother William Clark; Meriwether Lewis (monument to Lewis & Clark in Midway Park, Ridge & Main Sts.). **Albemarle County Court House** (Court Sq.), designed by Jefferson, has a wing used for services of several sects; Jefferson, Monroe, and Madison worshiped here; nearby statue of Stonewall Jackson on Little Sorrel. **University of Virginia** (W end of Main St.), founded and designed by Jefferson, has attractive campus; Edgar Allan Poe room (No. 13, W Range), open to public; tours start at the Rotunda daily at 11, 2, 4; no tours during school hols & exam periods. **Historic Michie Tavern** (2m SE on SR 53), probably built by Patrick Henry's father in 1735; visited by Jefferson, Monroe, Madison, Jackson, Lafayette; ballroom, bar, other rooms have period furnishing; open daily 9-5; closed Jan. 1, Dec. 25; adm.

Monticello (3 m SE on SR 53), Thomas Jefferson's handsome estate, which he designed and built; begun in 1769, but remodeled over next 40 years; he believed the simple lines of classic Roman architecture were appropriate to a new democratic republic; house on mountaintop, with outbuildings hidden on lower terraces; many interesting inventions by Jefferson; original furnishings; Jefferson died here on July 4, 1826; family cemetery; open Mar.-Oct. daily 8-5; Nov.-Feb. daily 9-4:30; closed Dec. 25; free.

Ash Lawn (5 m SE on County rd 795), designed and built by Jefferson in 1798 for his friend James Monroe, is within sight of Monticello; Monroe family furnishings; fine gardens; open daily 7-7; adm. **Castle Hill** (11 m NE on US 250, SR 22, 231 in Cismont), 2 houses built back-to-back—charming 1765 clapboard home of Dr. Thomas Walker, friend of Jefferson, and 1824 neoclassical section; outbuildings; gardens; open Mar.-Nov., Tues.-Sun. 10-5; adm. Grounds open all yr, free. **Montpelier** (22 m NE on SR 20), home of James Madison, is private, but cemetery with graves of James and Dolley Madison is open daily in daylight; free. **Orange County Courthouse** (28 m NE on US 20 to Main St., Orange) contains records on German settlers who arrived 1714-19 under leadership of Alexander Spotswood.

Roaring Twenties Antique Car Museum (16 m N on US 29, then 11 m W on US 33, SR 230 in Hood), antique carriages, engines, cars; 1900-35 household items; other Americana; open Mon.-Fri. 9-5, Sat. & Sun. 9-6; adm. **Scottsville Museum** (17 m S on SR 20), in 1846 Disciples Church; prehistoric Indian relics; pre-Revolutionary-19th-C historic relics; open Apr.-Dec., Sat. & Sun. 2-5; sm adm.

CLARKSVILLE: Prestwould House (2 m N on US 15), Roanoke River Museum; stone mansion built 1795 by Virginia-born baronet Sir Peyton Skipwith, who had extensive holdings along the river; N of here, at **The Forks,** the Christian Social Colony was established in late 1800s, but stored insufficient food for the first winter and quickly disbanded; cultural societies housed here provide area historic information; open weekdays and some weekends; inquire locally for hrs.

CULPEPER: Historic markers designate sites that made this area known for its fighting spirit; Culpeper Minute Men, famous for their flag with a coiled rattlesnake and the motto "Don't tread on me," were organized 1775 and took part in the first battle on Virginia soil at Great Bridge. During the Civil War, many churches and other buildings were turned into hospitals for the 1862 Battle of Cedar Mountain and the 1863 Battle of Brandy Station (with 20,000 horsemen, the largest cavalry battle ever fought in this hemisphere). **Warrenton** (25 m NE on US 15, 29), former center of activity for guerrilla leader John Mosby, the Grey Ghost of the Confederacy, who is buried here.

DANVILLE: Last Capitol of the Confederacy (975 Main St.) was private home where Jefferson Davis met with his cabinet Apr. 3-10, 1865, after fleeing Richmond; historic, arts and craft exhibits; open Mon., Wed., Fri. 9-5, Sun. 2-5; closed some hols; free. **National Tobacco-Textile Museum** (615 Lynn St.), exhibits and library; open Mon.-Fri. 10-noon, 2-4, possibly other hrs; closed hols; adm. Tobacco auctions at warehouses welcome visitors; check for exact dates (usually late-Aug.-mid-Nov.,

Mon.-Thurs 9-2:30; closed hols); free. **Wreck of the Old 97** (W on US 58), 1903 accident that inspired folk song, has marker on site.

FREDERICKSBURG: Although settlers erected a fort here in 1676, and this was an important terminus for Rappahannock River traffic, the town was not officially founded until 1727. Being midway between Washington and Richmond, the city was an armed camp throughout the Civil War, changing hands 7 times, and scene of major battles; despite frightful casualties (in the end the dead were simply buried in the streets), surprisingly many pre-Revolutionary buildings survive. Brochures for self-guiding walking tours, and combination tickets to buildings, are available at **Fredericksburg Information Center** (2800 Princess Anne St. at US 1 N of town).

  Mary Washington House (1200 Charles St.) was bought by Washington for his mother in 1772 so that she would be close to her only daughter, Mary, at Kenmore; Washington stopped on the way to his inauguration in New York, his last visit; his mother died in 1789 here; original woodwork; many original furnishings; open Mar.-Oct. daily 9-5; Nov.-Feb. daily 9-4:30; closed Jan. 1, 2, Dec. 25, 26; adm. **Old Slave Block** (Williams & Charles Sts.), a 3-ft-high stone from which women mounted horses and where slaves stood to be auctioned. **James Monroe Museum & Memorial Library** (908 Charles St.), 1758 building where the 5th President practiced law 1786-89, has French furnishing Monroe used in the White House, desk (with secret compartment) on which Monroe Doctrine was signed; lovely glass, silver, porcelain, portraits, jewelry; library; open daily 9-5; closed Dec. 25; adm. **Presbyterian Church** (George & Princess Anne Sts.) bears cannonballs and other Civil War scars; pews were used as beds for wounded, whom Clara Barton nursed; open daily 9-5:30. **St. George's Episcopal Church** (George & Princess Anne Sts.) has graves of prominent Virginians in cemetery; open daily 7-5.

  Fredericksburg Masonic Lodge No. 4, AF & AM (803 Princess Anne St.), memorabilia of Washington, initiated as a Mason here in 1752; Gilbert Stuart portrait of Washington; open Mon.-Sat. 9-noon, 1-4, Sun. 1-4; closed Jan. 1, Thnks, Dec. 25; sm adm. **Hugh Mercer Apothecary Shop** (1020 Caroline St.) belonged to the Scots immigrant who became a Brigadier General and was mortally wounded at the Battle of Princeton in 1776; room where his friend Washington used to work on visits to Fredericksburg; open daily 9-5; closed Jan. 1, Dec. 25; sm adm. **Rising Sun Tavern** (1306 Caroline St.), built about 1760 by Washington's youngest brother Charles, was stagecoach stop and post office, and center where Jefferson, Patrick Henry, George Mason, Hugh Mercer and others met to discuss the end of British rule; period furnishings, pewter, gaming tables, boot racks; open Mar.-mid-Nov. daily 9-5; mid-Nov.-Feb. daily 9-4:30; closed Jan. 1, 2, Dec. 24, 25; adm. **Stoner's Store Museum** (1202 Prince Edward St.), replica of 19th-C general store; 13,000 items of Americana; open mid-Mar.-Oct. daily 9-5; rest of yr, daily 9-4:30; closed Jan. 1-5, Dec. 25; adm.

Kenmore (1201 Washington Ave.), stately 1752 manor, home of Col. Fielding Lewis and wife Betty Washington Lewis, George's sister; stunning restoration of original woodwork, molded plaster ceilings; lovely furnishings; open Apr.-Oct. daily 9-5; Nov.-Mar., Tues.-Sun. 10-4; closed Jan. 1, 2, Dec. 25, 26; adm. Mary Washington Monument (Washington Ave. & Pitt St.) marks her grave.

Court House (Princess Anne St. near George St.), hand-carved walnut woodwork, historic documents; open Mon.-Fri. 9-5; free. **Historic Fredericksburg Museum** (818 Sophia St.), audiovisual program and exhibits on city history; open Mar.-mid-Nov. daily 9-5; rest of yr, daily 9-4:30; closed Jan. 1, 2, Dec. 25, 26; sm adm. **John Paul Jones Home** (Caroline St. & Lafayette Ave.) is private.

Fredericksburg & Spotsylvania National Military Park, sites of 4 major Civil War battles. Confederates won the first 2—Fredericksburg (where in Dec. 1862 Federals made a pontoon landing but were driven back across the Rappahannock River within a few days, after which Lincoln relieved Gen. Burnside of command) and Chancellorsville (where in Jan. 1863, Gen. Hooker, having reorganized the demoralized Union forces, crossed the Rappahannock to attack Lee; but Lee anticipated Hooker and drove him back across the river). The other 2 battles—the Wilderness and Spotsylvania Court House—produced no decided victories but turned into a relentless war of attrition that culminated in the destruction of the Army of Northern Virginia. The Battle of the Wilderness pitted Grant against Lee for the first time on May 4, 1864. With twice the manpower, Grant began to attack Lee on all fronts at once; here he moved between Lee and Richmond; fighting ended in a stalemate broken by Grant, who again cut between Lee and Richmond, causing both armies to race for the key road junction at Spotsylvania Court House. Confederates arrived first, and the struggle raged bitterly May 8-21; at one point the sides engaged in savage hand-to-hand combat for 24 hours in an area now called Bloody Angle; again Grant moved on, to weaken Lee by applying pressure E and S, destroying Lee's offensive power. **Fredericksburg Visitor Center** (Lafayette Blvd & Sunken Rd.) offers information for self-guiding tours of all battle sites; summer living history program; museum with dioramas and electric map of battlefield; **Frederiksburg National Cemetery,** where 13,000 of the 15,000 Union burials are of unknowns. **Chancellorsville Visitor Center** (9 m W on SR 3) offers a film, dioramas, exhibits. Both open mid-June-Labor Day, daily 9-6; rest of yr, daily 9-5; closed Jan. 1, Dec. 25; free. Sites include: **Angel of Marye's Heights** (near stone wall where battle was fought) honors Richard Kirland, a 20-year-old Confederate from S Carolina who took water to dying Union men during Battle for Fredericksburg despite hundreds of muskets leveled at him; he was killed 9 months later at Chickamauga. **Old Salem Church** (4 m W on SR 3) around which much of Chancellorsville battle took place. **Stonewall Jackson Memorial Shrine** (12 m S on I-95, then 5 m E on SR 606 in Guinea), plantation outbuilding where Jackson died; he had been mortally wounded by his own men at Chancellorsville, while reconnoitering at night, when his party was mistaken for a Union patrol; he died here 8 days later, on May 10, 1863; his last words were, "Let us cross over the river and rest under the shade of the trees." Open Memorial Day-Labor Day, daily 9-5; mid-Apr.-late May & Sept.-Oct., Thurs.-Mon. 9-5; rest of yr, Fri.-Sun. 9-5; free.

George Washington Birthplace National Monument (38 m SE off SR 3): The house in which Washington was born in 1732 burned in 1799 (foundations have been excavated); Memorial House is not a reconstruction but illustrates the environment into which sons of moderately wealthy planters were born in 18th-C Tidewater country; separate kitchen is on site of the original. Surrounding the house is Colonial Living Farm, designed to show the livestock, crops, agricultural methods of Tidewater plantations. Nearby is Family Burial Ground (1 m NW on Bridges Creek), where at least 32 of Washington's ancestors are buried. Open daily 9-5; closed Jan. 1, Dec. 25; adm or GEP in summer, free in winter.

Stratford Hall Plantation (43 m SE on SR 3), birthplace of 4 generations of Lees, including 2 signers of Declaration of Independence, Colonial hero Lighthorse Harry Lee, and Confederate hero Robert E. Lee (born here 1807); built of brick in Flemish bond, the Great House has 4 massive chimneys connected to form tower platforms; kitchen, other outbuildings; original and period furnishings; 1200-acre plantation still in operation; Reception Center with audiovisual program, museum exhibits; open daily 9-4:30; closed Dec. 25; adm. Plantation lunch available Apr.-Oct.

Warsaw (61 m SE on SR 3) has many Colonial mansions, including 1730 Sabine Hall, Mt. Airy (famous for horses since Colonial days); 1737 Farnham Church; tours during Garden Week. **Lancaster** (31 m S of Warsaw on SR 3) was home of Mary Ball Washington, George's mother; she was born in the 1680 Epping Forest (4 m W on SR 3), open Apr.-Nov. daily 9-5, adm; she attended St. Mary's White Chapel (5 m W on SR 622), where many of her family are buried in the churchyard; her portrait is in Lancaster County Courthouse.

FRONT ROYAL: Warren Rifles Confederate Museum (95 Chester St.), Civil War memorabilia; story of beautiful Confederate spy, Belle Boyd;

open Apr.-Oct. daily 9-6 (longer hrs in summer); sm adm. **Elizabeth Furnace** (NW on SR 55 to Water Lick, then S on George Washington National Forest rd) has interpretive trail explaining pig iron manufacture; maps for sites of other furnace ruins may be obtained from forest hq in Harrisonburg (zip 22801).

HAMPTON: Oldest English settlement, 1610, still in existence (Jamestown, settled 1607, was abandoned); Hampton Monument (between Hampton River & Mill Creek on grounds of VA Center) commemorates landing of settlers; open daily 6:30 am-9 pm; free. City was beset by pirates in late 17th-C, attacked by British in 1775 and 1813, and burned by citizens in 1861 to prevent its falling into Union Hands. **Hampton Information Center** (413 W Mercury Blvd), maps for marked, self-guiding auto tour; bus tours; open late May-early Oct., Mon.-Fri. 8-6, Sat. & Sun. 10-6; rest of yr, Mon.-Fri. 8-5; closed Jan. 1, Dec. 25. Adjacent is **Aerospace Park** with aircraft exhibits; open daily 8-5; free. **Hampton Roads Harbor Tours** (Navy dock, Healy Memorial Park, Settler's Landing Rd.), daily in summer, weekends in spring & fall. **Lightship Hampton** (Settlers Landing Rd. & Wine St.), restored Coast Guard vessel may be boarded; open Mon.-Fri. 9-3; Sat., Sun., hols 9-5; free. **Syms-Eaton Museum** (418 W Mercury Blvd.) of first free schools in America; open Mon.-Fri. 8-5, Sat. & Sun. 1-5; closed Dec. 25; free. **Hampton Institute** (E end of Queen St.), 1868, to teach former slaves; Booker T. Washington was alumnus; first buildings made by students; Indians were also educated here 1878-1923; museum (1 Shore Rd.) houses Indian and African artifacts; open Sept.-July, Mon.-Fri. 8-5; closed hols; free. **St. John's Church** (W Queen & Court Sts.) has a memorial window to Pocahontas; open daily 8-4; free.

   Kicotan Indian Village (3 m N on W Mercury Blvd), reproduction of Kecoughtan Indian village the first settlers encountered; artifacts on display; open Mon.-Fri. 8-5, Sat. & Sun. 1-5; closed Jan. 1, Dec. 25; free.

   Fort Monroe (3 m SE on US 258), on site of 2 earlier forts; massive structure designed by aide to Napoleon took 15 years to build (partly under the supervision of Robert E. Lee); the Union held it throughout the Civil War, and Lincoln and McClellan conferred here. Fort Monroe Casement Museum, in a series of casements (chambers in the walls), contains historic exhibits on the fort; Jefferson Davis was confined for several months after the Civil War in one of these casements, on false charges of having plotted Lincoln's assassination; exhibits on the Monitor and Merrimack; open daily 8-5; free.

   NASA Langley Research Center (3 m N on SR 134 on Langley AFB), not open to public, but Visitor Center has exhibits on space exploration; open Tues.-Sat. 9-4, Sun. noon-4; closed Dec. 25; free.

HARRISONBURG: Rockingham County Historical Society (345 S Main St.) has electric map depicting Stonewall Jackson's Valley Campaign of 1862; other regional historic displays; open early June-Labor Day, Tues.-Sat. 10-4; closed hols; sm adm.

Eastern Mennonite College (2 m NW on Mt. Clinton Pike & Parkwood Dr. in Park View), founded by Mennonite farming community; library contains rare volumes on Mennonite history (open Mon.-Sat. 8-5; closed hols; free); gallery, planetarium, natural history museum. **Bridgewater College** (7 m SW on SR 42 in Bridgewater) has museum with history of Church of the Brethren; open Mon.-Fri. 8-5; closed hols; free. **Lincoln Homestead** (9 m N on SR 42), where Abraham Lincoln's father was born; brick house partially built by his grandfather; privately owned.

New Market Battlefield Park (19 m N off I-81), memorial to 247 VMI cadets, sent out in face of heavy Confederate losses, who exhibited courage and discipline the first time under fire; restored Bushong Farm where battle took place has 19th-C furnishings, historic markers; Hall of Valor depicts through films and artifacts the Civil War in the Shenandoah Valley; open daily 9-5; closed Dec. 25; adm.

JAMESTOWN (Colonial National Historical Park), first permanent English settlement in the New World, was established May 13, 1607 by 105 men who, anxious to have their ships within easy reach for escape, laid out their town on a swamp. Few were equipped to survive in wilderness; their intention to make their living from glassmaking, silkworm culture, and gold finds was dashed after the "Starving Time," the winter of 1609-10, when 440 of the then 500 colonists died; they turned to raising food and especially tobacco (planted along the streets, in the marketplace, on every clearing that could be spared). Although Jamestown served as the political, social, and cultural center of the royal colony of Virginia, it was never a big town, and persistent friction eventually led to the Bacon Rebellion of 1676, when much of the town was burned; although colonists rebuilt the city, when the statehouse burned in 1699 they reestablished the capital inland, at Williamsburg, and Jamestown was abandoned. **Visitor Center,** artifacts unearthed in the park, audiovisual programs, excellent conducted tours (almost essential here, as the remains of Jamestown are scanty); open daily 9-5 (8:30-5:30 in summer); closed Dec. 25. In the park are: statue of Pocahontas, daughter of chief Powhatan, whose 1614 marriage to John Rolfe did much to improve Indian-settler relations; statue of John Smith, who held colony together in its first 2 years; shrine to Robert Hunt, minister who also helped hold down strife; ruins of what was probably the church, only surviving structure of 17th-C Jamestown, with a church built 1907 by Colonial Dames of America on part of the foundations; cemetery; foundations of other buildings; Confederate earthworks dating from 1861; other monuments, interpretive signs, recordings. Gate open daily 8-4:30 (8-5 in summer); closed Dec. 25; adm or GEP. Nearby, also run by the NPS, is **Glasshouse,** near the site of a glass works established 1608 by 8 English glassmakers as one of Jamestown's first industries; demonstrations of colonial glassmaking daily; finished products on sale.

Also nearby is **Jamestown Festival Park,** a re-creation of early Jamestown erected by the state to celebrate the 350th anniversary of its founding; full-size replica of the triangular palisade encloses wattle-and-daub structures; **Old World Pavilion** uses wax figures and other exhibits to illustrate English heritage; **New World Pavilion** depicts history and contributions of Indians and settlers to the nation; **Powhatan's Lodge** is a ceremonial building reconstructed from early descriptions; pottery demonstrating colonial methods; full-size replicas of the *Susan Constant, Godspeed,* and *Discovery,* the cramped ships in which settlers arrived, may be boarded; changing-of-the-guard and other events; open daily 9-5 (later in summer); closed Jan. 1, Dec. 25; adm.

LEESBURG: Loudoun County Museum & Visitor Information Center (16 W Loudoun St.), historic exhibits and booklets for walking tours; open Mon.-Sat. 10-5, Sun. 1-5; free. **Morven Park** (N on Old Waterford Rd.), 1200-acre estate with nature trails; fine furnishings in Greek Revival mansion once owned by Gov. Westmoreland Davis; carriage house with horse-drawn vehicles; open Apr.-Oct., Tues.-Sat. 10-5; Sun. 1-5; adm.

Oatlands (6 m S on US 15), property of National Trust for Historic Preservation, was built 1800-3 by George Carter; Greek Revival details added later; superb English and French furnishings; open Apr.-Oct., Mon.-Sat. 10-5, Sun. 1-5; adm.

Waterford Restoration (3 m NW on SR 7, then 3 m on SR 9, 662), quaint mill town settled by Quakers 1773; many structures are pre-Revolutionary War; in early 1800s, Waterford was known for its craft industries; Waterford Foundation sponsors craft shows and demonstrations, plus house tours, annually in Oct.; Waterford Mill offers craft shops and demonstrations June-Sept., Sat. & Sun. 1-5; free.

LEXINGTON: Visitor Information Center (107 E Washington St.) has maps for self-guiding walking and auto tours. **Stonewall Jackson House** (8 E Washington St.), modest brick house built in 1800, was only home Jackson ever owned; he lived here 2½ years while teaching at VMI; Jackson memorabilia; open Mon.-Sat. 9-4:30, Sun. 2-4:30; closed Jan. 1, Dec. 25; free. Jackson is buried in Lexington Presbyterian Cemetery (Main St.), with 400 Confederate soldiers.

Washington & Lee University (W Washington St.) has lovely buildings with white columns and mannered brick; originally Augusta Academy, it changed its name to Washington Academy after Washington gave it stock in his James River Canal Co., and changed its name again after Robert E. Lee had served as president 1865-70. On grounds is Lee Chapel, where Lee is buried in the family crypt; Washington and Lee family art collection; Lee's office; open Apr.-Sept., Mon.-Sat. 9-5, Sun. 2-5; Oct.-Mar., Mon.-Sat. 9-4, Sun. 2-5; closed Jan. 1, Thnks, Dec. 25; free.

Virginia Military Institute (off US 11) museum depicts history of the institute and distinguished graduates (open Mon.-Fri. 9-4:30; Sat. 9-noon, 2-5; Sun. 2-5; closed Jan. 1, Easter, Dec. 25; free); 1850 Gothic-style Cadet Barracks has entrance arches named for Washington, Jackson, George C. Marshall. Facing parade grounds is George C. Marshall Memorial Research Library with exhibits on the life and career of Marshall, WW II, and Marshall Plan; open daily 9-4; free.

Natural Bridge (13 m S on US 11) was long worshiped by Indians; George Washington, sent to survey it in 1750, carved his initials into it; and in 1774 Jefferson bought it and the surrounding 157 acres from King George III for 20 shillings; musical, *Drama of Creation,* is enacted nightly under the 215-ft span (adm); bridge open daily 7 am-dark; adm.

LURAY: Chamber of Commerce will make arrangements for you to see privately owned buildings constructed in frontier times with fortifications in case of Indian attack; the fortified section was usually in the basement, had a fireplace, and was kept stocked with food; some where built over springs, others had an underground tunnel leading to the well; **Fort Song** (S of Stanley on SR 616) was built about 1733; it is separated from the house and reached through a tunnel. Basement forts are in 1735 Egypt House (4 m W on SR 615); 1764 Fort Rhodes (4 m W on SR 615), in which the occupants were killed; 1733 fort in Shirley Home (8 m W on SR 762); 1735 Fort Paul Long (9 m W on SR 615); 1790 Fort Stover (4 m N on SR 660), now a Girl Scout building.

LYNCHBURG: This city grew up around a ferry established by John Lynch, who in 1791 built what was probably the first tobacco warehouse in the nation; courthouse has small museum; 1798 Quaker Meeting House is open to public; in Riverside Park are Miller-Claytor House (open Wed. 10-noon or by appointment), where Jefferson tasted his first tomato (then considered poisonous), and the packet boat *Marshall,* typical of those used on the James River & Kanawha Canal, which carried Stonewall Jackson's body to Lexington (daily 7 am-11 pm); Fort Early (Fort & Vermont Aves.), restored earthwork, was site of Gen. Jubal Early's victory over Union forces that saved Lynchburg, a vital supply center, for the Confederacy.

Patrick Henry Shrine (31 m S on US 501 to Brookneal, then 5 m SE) is in Red Hill, Henry's last home; law office and outbuildings; grave; open Apr.-Oct. daily 9-5; Nov.-Mar. daily 9-4; closed Dec. 25; adm. **Patrick Henry Museum & Library** (in Charlotte Court House) is primarily a research facility.

MANASSAS (BULL RUN) NATIONAL BATTLEFIELD PARK (25 m SW of Washington, D.C. off I-66 at SR 234): Along the pretty stream, Bull Run, 28,000 men were killed or wounded in 2 major battles of the Civil War for control of the vital Manassas railroad junction. **First Manassas**, July 21, 1861, was the first major land battle of the war; on both sides, men were untrained, and only Gen. Jackson stood "like a stone wall," earning his nickname; after considerable confusion, the Union retreated—right into the carriages of Washingtonians who had come out to watch the war; the retreat turned into a panic, but Confederates were too disorganized to follow up. **Second Manassas** (Aug. 28-30, 1862), with seasoned troops, was a bloodier battle, where the brilliant Lee out-maneuvered Gen. Pope. Lee had sent Jackson ahead to destroy Union supplies at Manassas; Jackson entrenched behind the embankment of an unfinished railroad and kept Pope occupied while Lee poured in reinforcements; Pope, concentrating on Jackson's line, allowed the Confederate reinforcements to march in unopposed, and spent the last of the battle simply trying to keep his retreat lines open. **Visitor Center** (N of I-66 off SR 234), on Henry Hill, overlooks the battlefield; museum with audiovisual program, exhibits; open daily 9-6; closed Dec. 25; free. From here a 5-m self-guiding trail of First Manassas and a 9-m trail of Second Manassas lead through battle lines; Stone Bridge, where the first shot was fired and across which Union forces retreated in First Manassas; Stone House, originally a tavern, used as a field hospital in both battles and as Gen. Pope's hq; Jackson's Line, an excellent defensive position; Dogan House, caught in the fire of Second Manassas; Sudley Church and the ruins of Chinn House, both also used as hospitals. Open daily 9-6; closed Dec. 25; free.

MARTINSVILLE: Fairy Stone State Park (21 m NW on US 220, SR 57, 822), named for staurolites, cross-shaped crystals that legend says were shed as tears by fairies on learning of the Crucifixion, found at S end of park; at N end, an interpretive trail leads to a small cemetery and ruins of a forge, all that remains of the iron-mining boomtown of Fayerdale, which supplied cannonballs for the Confederacy and made illegal whiskey.

MOUNT VERNON: Mount Vernon was a modest pre-1735 house when George Washington inherited it from his half-brother Lawrence in 1752;

over the years, he more than doubled its size and added service buildings; 8000 acres he farmed scientifically, keeping copious notes on crop rotation and other experiments. Here he and Martha reared 2 of her children by a previous marriage and adopted 2 of her grandchildren. Although military and political duties kept him away a great deal, Washington remained passionately attached to Mount Vernon and died here 1799; he and Martha are buried on the grounds. More than half the furnishings in the house are original; memorabilia of George, Martha, and of Nelly Custis; sound-and-light program on summer evenings, otherwise open daily, Mar.-Sept. 9-5, Oct.-Feb. 9-4; adm.

Woodlawn Plantation (3 m W on SR 235), George Washington's gift to his foster daughter Nelly Custis; the Georgian-style house, completed 1803, was designed by Dr. William Thornton; fine woodwork; many original furnishings; portraits; open daily 9:30-4:30; closed Dec. 25; adm. On grounds is Pope-Leighey House, designed in 1940 by Frank Lloyd Wright as one of his ideal Usonian houses for working people; open Mar.-Nov., Sat. & Sun. 9:30-4:30; adm. **George Washington Grist Mill Historical Park** (3 m W on SR 235), rebuilt grain mill on site of the original, operated by Washington most of his life; replica of machinery; audiovisual exhibits; open Memorial Day-Labor Day, daily 10-6; sm adm. **Phick Episcopal Church** (on US 1 between SR 617, 242), where Washington was a vestryman, was used as a stable during the Civil War; open daily; donations.

NEWPORT NEWS: Mariners Museum (jct J Clyde Morris Blvd & US 60), established by shipbuilding family, displays items from many eras and regions; figureheads, whaling exhibit, scrimshaw, watercolors and other art works, relics and tales of famous mariners and solo voyages, outstanding ship models; displays on Port of Hampton Roads (comprised of Newport News, Norfolk, Portsmouth); open Mon.-Sat. 9-5, Sun. noon-5; closed Dec. 25; adm.

War Memorial Museum of Virginia (9285 Warwick Blvd. in Huntington Park), weapons, equipment, memorabilia of all U.S. wars since Revolution; open Mon.-Sat. 9-5, Sun. 1-5; closed Jan. 1, Dec. 24, 25; free. **Fort Eustis** (NW of city on Mulberry Island), hq of U.S. Army Transportation Center, offers self-guiding auto tours, daily sunrise-sunset; free. On grounds is **Army Transportation Museum,** with items from all over the world, from dog sleds to flying saucers; open Mon.-Fri. 8-5, Sat. & Sun. 1-5; closed hols; free.

Dept. Commerce & Public Relations (City Hall, zip 23607) or Newport News **Information Center** (2 m N to 524 J Clyde Morris Blvd in Deer Park) provide information. Harbor cruises (from S end of Jefferson Ave. & 12th St.) are offered Memorial Day-mid-Oct. **Deer Park** has Peninsula Nature & Science Center with natural history exhibits, including live fish and animals; planetarium shows; open Mon.-Sat. 10-5, Sun. 1-5; closed hols; sm adm.

NORFOLK: Settled in 1682, on a site bought from a pioneer for 10,000 lbs of tobacco, Norfolk became the largest city in Virginia by the early 18th-C; it was shelled by the British in 1776 and then burned by its citizens to prevent capture by the British; during the Civil War the first battle of ironclads—between the Confederate *Virginia* (formerly the *Merrimack*) and the Union *Monitor*—was fought to a draw in Hampton Roads in March, 1862, but in May the city fell to the Union. **Norfolk Tour Information Center** (475 St. Paul's Blvd) has booklets for self-guiding auto and walking tours, bus tours, and the summer Norfolk-Portsmouth Harbor Tours (leave from foot of W. Main St. at Boush St.; for details write 3008 Acres Circle, Portsmouth 23703). Information is also available at **Gardens-by-the-Sea** (8 m E on Airport Rd., adj to airport), with Information Center (open Mon.-Fri. 8:30-5; Sat., Sun., hols 10-5; closed Jan. 1, Dec. 25); observation tower; film on city and gardens (late May-Labor Day, daily); narrated boat and train tours (Apr.-Oct., weather permitting; adm); park open daily sunrise-sunset; sm adm.

Chrysler Museum at Norfolk (Olney Rd. at Mowbray Arch), Oriental, Egyptian, Greek and Roman, Pre-Columbian American, Old Masters, Impressionists, contemporary; American art from Stuart to Warhol; outstanding Sandwich, Steuben, Galle, Tiffany, and other glass; open Mon.-Sat. 10-5, Sun. 11-5; closed Jan. 1, Dec. 25; free. **Hermitage Foundation Museum** (7637 N Shore Rd.), in elegant Tudor-style mansion on landscaped grounds; Oriental and medieval art; contemporary painting and sculpture; Russian icons and silver; lace; ceramics; open daily 10-5; closed Dec. 25; sm adm.

Old St. Paul's Episcopal Church (201 St. Paul's Blvd at City Hall Ave.), only public building to survive the burning of Norfolk in 1776; cannonball embedded in walls; museum of church history; tours Tues.-Sat. 10-4:30, Sun. 2-4:30; closed some hols; free. The following handsome houses are open Apr.-Nov., Mon.-Sat. 10-5, Sun. 11-5; Dec.-Mar. daily noon-5; closed Jan. 1, Dec. 25; sm adm: **Myers House** (323 E Freemason St.), 1792 Georgian home of wealthy merchant; Adams woodwork; china, crystal, silver; family portraits by Stuart and Sully; early 19th-C music. **Willoughby-Baylor House** (601 E Freemason St.), 1794 townhouse of wealthy merchant; period furnishings, Norfolk historical items. **Adam Thoroughgood House** (8 m NE via SR 166, US 13 to 1636 Parrish Rd., Virginia Beach), one of the oldest brick dwellings in the nation.

Gen. Douglas MacArthur Memorial (City Hall Ave. & Bank St.), in 1850 city hall, contains his tomb, memorabilia of his life and career; film; archives; open Mon.-Sat. 10-5, Sun. 11-5; closed Jan. 1, Dec. 25; free.

Norfolk Naval Station & Naval Air Station (Hampton & Admiral

Taussig Blvds), home port for Atlantic and Mediterranean fleets, aircraft squadrons, offers bus tours from main gate (Apr.-mid-Oct. daily 10:30-2:30; rest of yr, Tues., Thurs., Sat. 1:30; no tours Jan. 1, Dec. 25) and open ship (Sat., Sun. 1-5); adm. **Portsmouth Naval Shipyard Museum** (2 High St., on Elizabeth River in Portsmouth) offers ship models, naval equipment and uniforms; open Tues.-Sat. 10-5, Sun. 2-5; closed Jan. 1, Dec. 25; free. **Lightship & Coast Guard Museum** (London Slip & Water St., Portsmouth), Coast Guard relics housed on a 1916 lightship; open Tues.-Sat. 10-5, Sun. 2-5; closed Jan. 1, Dec. 25; donation.

Portsmouth Chamber of Commerce (600 Court St.), open Mon.-Fri. exc hols 9-5, or **Hill House** (212 North St.), open Sat. 9-5, Sun. 1-5, offer booklets for self-guiding tours of historic buildings in Portsmouth; also here is: Trinity Church (Court & High Sts.), whose bell was rung so long and hard at Cornwallis' surrender that it cracked and had to be recast; cemetery with colonial graves; open Mon.-Fri. 9-4; free.

Princess Anne Court House (16 m SW on SR 615, then W on SR 149 in Princess Anne), attractive building erected 1824.

PETERSBURG: Settled about 1645 around an Indian trading post at the falls of the Appomattox River, Petersburg grew into a cluster of little tobacco towns that merged into a center of water, rail, and road commerce; pillaged by the British during the Revolution, it recovered to become a fashionable social center, but was again battered by the 10-month Union siege of the Civil War. **Historic Petersburg Information Center** (400 E Washington St.) provides information on historic buildings, many restored for private residential or commercial use; homes and gardens are open during Historic Garden Week in Apr.; open daily 9-5; closed Jan. 1, Dec. 25. Among interesting buildings are 1815 **McIlwaine House** (Cockade Alley, with period furnishings; 1817 **Trapezium House** (Market St., N of Brown & Williamson plant), with no square corners inside or out because the Irish owner was said to be afraid of spirits hiding in corners; 1839 **Courthouse** (N Sycamore St. near E. Bank); **St. Paul's** Episcopal Church (110 N Union St.), where Lee worshiped during the siege.

Old Blandford Church (319 S Crater Rd.) has 15 Tiffany windows donated by Southern states in memory of 30,000 Confederate dead in the cemetery; interpretive center has audiovisual program on history of Petersburg and people buried in the cemetery; open Mon.-Sat. 9-5, Sun. 1-5; closed Jan. 1, Dec. 25; free.

Farmers Bank (23 Bollingbrook St.), built about 1812, having invested heavily in the Confederacy, failed at end of Civil War; vault; currency printing equipment, other original features; audiovisual program on 19th-C banking; open Mon.-Sat. 9-5, Sun. 1-5; closed Jan. 1, Dec. 25; free.

Fort Lee Quartermaster Museum (3 m NE on SR 36), insignia uniforms, equipment, weapons; exhibit on women's role in wartime; open Mon.-Fri. 8-5; Sat., Sun., hols 1-5; closed Jan. 1, Thnks, Dec. 25; free. **Centre Hill Museum** (Centre Hill), battlefield relics in home once visited by Lincoln; open Tues.-Sat. 10-1, 2-5, Sun. 2:30-5:30; free. **Siege Museum** (W Bank St. off Market), in 1842 Greek Revival building; city artifacts; open Tues.-Sat. 10-5, Sun. 2-5; closed hols; adm.

Petersburg National Battlefield: Robert E. Lee foresaw that if Grant got to the James River he would lay siege and "it will be a mere question of time"; when an all-out attack failed in June, 1864, Grant did lay siege, for 10 months, engaging in battle after battle. An ingenious plan by Pennsylvania coal miners to dig a tunnel to blast a gap through the Confederate line almost worked, creating a crater 170-ft long, 60-ft wide, and 30-ft deep, but the explosion so confused Union soldiers that they blundered and lost the advantage. The siege enabled Grant to bring in troops and supplies, until he had 110,000 men against Lee's hungry 60,000; on Apr. 2, 1865, Grant ordered an all-out assault, and Lee evacuated Petersburg; the campaign had cost 70,000 American lives; Appomattox was only a week away. **Visitor Center** provides lectures, exhibits, information, living history programs (daily in summer); guided hikes (summer); open daily 8-5 (8-8 in summer); closed Jan. 1, Dec. 25. From here a 4-m auto tour, with interpretive signs and foot trails, leads through the battlefields; you can continue along the entire siege line (3 m S on SR 675) to Poplar Grove National Cemetery.

Merchants Hope Church (9 m NE on SR 36, 6 m E on SR 10, ½ m S on SR 641 in Hopewell), noted for stunning colonial brickwork; key in adj house; donation.

RADFORD: Many massacres occurred in settlements along New River, a favorite Cherokee and Shawnee hunting ground; Mary Draper Ingles, taken captive in 1755 to what is now Chillicothe, Ohio, escaped on foot and, following the river, rejoined her husband; on site of their log home (just W of town), her drama, *"The Long Way Home,"* is staged outdoors in summer. **Claytor Lake State Park** (6 m SW on SR 660) hq is in 1876 Howe House, on land settled 1740-45 by Dunkards, a religious sect that had fled from religious persecution in Germany; but Indians who had a campground nearby resented the intrusion and broke up the colony in 1754.

Blacksburg Chamber of Commerce (11 m E on US 11 to Christiansburg, then 9 m N on US 460 to 202 Central Office Bldg, Blacksburg) offers brochures for touring: Virginia Polytechnic Institute, with mineral and art museums; Draper's Meadow, site of 1755 Indian massacre of settlers. Smithfield Plantation (¼ m W off US 460 Bypass) belonged to one of the great land owners of the region; when the house was built in 1772, this was wilderness, and a stockade protected it from Indians and Tories; period furnishings; museum of regional history; Indian artifacts; open mid-Apr.-mid-Nov., Wed., Sat., Sun. 1-5; adm.

RICHMOND: In 1609, Capt. John Smith bought land from chief Powhatan for a settlement here called None Such, but Indian conflict prevented a permanent settlement until 1737; in 1779, when Richmond was chosen state capital, it had only 700 residents, but grew rapidly; as capital of the Confederacy 1861-65, it was a prime Union target but attempts to take it failed until Petersburg fell; when Richmond was evacuated, Confederate troops burned the government warehouses, and much of the rest of the city also burned. **Greater Richmond Chamber of Commerce** (616 E Franklin St., zip 23219) provides maps for self-guiding tours, tobacco plant tours, and tours of James River plantations. **Visitor Information Center** (420 N 6th St.) provides guided tours. **Historic Garden Week in Virginia** (12 E Franklin St., zip 23219) is a well-organized annual event when private homes and gardens in many areas of the state are opened to the public; in many places, luncheons or special events are also provided; takes place in Apr.; write in advance for information.

　　State Capitol (Capitol Sq.), designed by Jefferson and Charles Louis Clerisseau, is modeled on a 1st-C Roman temple in Nimes, France; in Old Hall of House of Delegates, Aaron Burr was tried for treason, the Articles of Secession were ratified, and Robert E. Lee accepted command of the Army of Northern Virginia; historical paintings, statues include Washington and Lafayette made from life by Houdon; open Mon.-Fri. 8:15-5; Sat. & hols 9-5; Sun. in May-Sept. 9-5, in Oct.-Apr. 1-5; closed Dec. 25; free. Also here are: The 19th-C Gothic Revival former City Hall with arcaded galleries in skylighted court; 1813 Governor's Mansion; 1824 Bell Tower; many monuments.

　　St. Paul's Church (9th & Grace Sts.), where Jefferson Davis received news of Appomattox; Lee also worshiped here; many memorials; open Mon.-Fri. 10-4; closed hols. **Robert E. Lee House** (707 E Franklin St.), leased by Lee for his family during the Civil War; he stayed here for 2 months after his surrender; personal possessions; period furnishings; open June-Aug., Tues.-Sat. 10-4, Sun. 2-5; Sept.-May, Mon.-Fri. 10-4; closed hols & Dec. 24; adm. **Museum of the Confederacy** (1201 E Clay St.), official residence of Pres. Jefferson Davis 1861-65, was White House of the Confederacy; possessions of Davis, Lee, other Confederate leaders; exhibits on the Civil War; open Mon.-Sat. 9-5, Sun. 2-5; closed hols & Dec. 24; adm. **Valentine Museum** (1015 E Clay St.), including 1812 Wickham-Valentine House and 1840 Bransford-Cecil House, plus carriage house remodeled as a studio by sculptor Edward V. Valentine; outstanding exhibits on the history of Richmond from 1607; architecture of the early

Republic (with many Robert Mills designs); history of textiles, including laces, embroidery, costumes 1680-present; research library; Indian artifacts from 10,000 BC-present, from many areas; tobacco displays; china, crystal, toys, paintings, other treasures; open Tues.-Sat. 10-4:45, Sun. 1:30-5; closed Jan. 1, Easter, Thnks, Dec. 24, 25; adm. **John Marshall House** (818 E Marshall St.), only 18th-C brick house surviving in Richmond, was home of the Chief Justice 1790 until his death in 1835; he designed the house himself, and much of the furniture is original; open Mon.-Sat. 10-4:30, Sun. 2-5; closed Jan. 1, Easter, Thnks, Dec. 24, 25; adm.

Edgar Allan Poe Museum (1914 E Main St.), in charming 1686 Old Stone House and 3 other buildings; period furnishings; Poe memorabilia; library; on Tues.-Sat. 10-4:30, Sun. & Mon. 1:30-4:30; closed Dec. 25; adm.

Church Hill, once a fashionable residential section, is being restored by Historic Richmond Foundation, in the house of Poe's childhood friend, Elmira Shelton (2407 E Grace St.); some of these houses are open on special tours; area includes: Carrington Square (2300 block of E Grace St.), with 1810-90 homes, and The Mews, a landscaped, cobblestone alley; Carrington Row (2307-11 E Broad St.), oldest row houses in the city, built 1818; Hardgrove House (2300 E Grace St.), 1849 Greek Revival home of tobacco manufacturer; Carrington and Baker Houses (2302, 2306 E Church), 1814 Federal-style homes with Flemish bond brickwork; Adams Double House (2501-3 E Grace), 1809 home of physician; Greek Revival homes (2600, 2602, 2611, 2617 E Franklin), built 1856-7; 1856 Pulliam House (2701 E Franklin) with cast-iron facade. Also here is **St. John's Episcopal Church** (24th & Broad Sts.), where Patrick Henry gave his "Give me liberty or give me death" speech; George Wythe and the mother of E. A. Poe are buried in the cemetery; open Feb.-Nov., Mon-Fri. 10-4; closed Thnks. **Monument Avenue** (between Lombardy St. & Belmont Ave.) has attractive townhouses and monuments to Confederate heros; Lee, on his famous horse Traveller, faces his beloved South; Stuart and Jackson (on Sorrell), battlefield casualties, face North; Jefferson Davis was carved by Edward Valentine; Maury statue is by Sievers. Monument Avenue forms the N border of the **Fan District**, an area of renovated Tudor and Victorian homes. **Hollywood Cemetery** (412 S Cherry St. at Albermarle St.), graves of Jefferson Davis, James Monroe, J.E.B. Stuart, John Tyler, 18,000 Confederate soldiers; open Mon.-Sat. 7:30-5, Sun. 8-5; free.

Battle Abbey, Virginia Historical Society (428 N Blvd): superb portraits, furniture of early Virginia, Confederate military items (many belonging to Lee, Stuart, other heros); Hoffbauer's dramatic murals of the 4 seasons of the Confederacy; Confederate and other historical papers;

open Mon.-Fri. 9-5, Sat. & Sun. 2-5; closed hols; adm. **Virginia Museum of Fine Arts** (Grove Ave. & Blvd) consists of 14 galleries with works from ancient Egypt to contemporary America; highlights include Faberge and Imperial Russian jewels; arts of India, Nepal, Tibet; Art Nouveau; open Tues.-Sat. 11-5, Sun. 1-5; closed hols; sm adm. **Maymont Park** (Hampton St. & Pennsylvania Ave.) offers Dooley Mansion, lavish Victorian home with art collection (Tues.-Sat. 10-4, Sun. 1-4), Nature Center (Mon.-Fri. 9:30-4:15, Sun. 2-5; free).

Virginia House (4301 Sulgrave Rd. in Windsor Farms) is a Tudor building constructed in 1928 from the remains of England's Warwick Priory, built 1125, rebuilt 1565, and demolished in 1920s; the priory had been visited by Elizabeth I and has her coat of arms; 15th-18th-C furnishings; open Tues.-Fri. 10-4, Sat. & Sun. 2-5; closed hols; adm. **Agecroft Hall** (4305 Sulgrave Rd. in Windsor Farms) is a half-timbered Tudor manor built in England in the 1470s, disassembled and reconstructed here in the 1920s; original oak paneling; audiovisual program on history of the house; open Mon.-Fri. 10-4, Sat. & Sun. 2-5; closed hols; adm.

Richmond National Battlefield Park: Richmond was a target for the North because it was capital of the Confederacy, manufacturing and supply center; of 7 major drives launched against the city, the sites of 2 that almost breached it are preserved here: McClellan's Peninsula Campaign of 1862, which included the Seven Days' Battles (during which Robert E. Lee succeeded to the Confederate command) and the panic spread in the city at the appearance of Union gunboats (led by ironclads) in the James River; this ended with Union withdrawal (McClellan's caution so exasperated Lincoln that he telegraphed, "Either attack Richmond or give up the job."). The second was Grant's savage attack in June 1864, with 7000 Union casualties in one 30-minute period, before his withdrawal for the siege of Petersburg. In Sept., Grant returned for a surprise attack on 2 of Richmond's defenses, capturing one and constructing new fortifications. When Petersburg fell on Apr. 1, 1865, Confederates abandoned Richmond. **Headquarters Visitor Center** (in Chimborazo Park, 3215 E Broad St.) offers information, exhibits, audiovisual program; open Apr.-Nov. daily 9-5; Dec.-Mar., Mon.-Fri. 9-5; closed Jan. 1, Dec. 25; free. From here self-guiding auto tour leads through battleground in 10 sections of the city. Museums and Visitor Centers also at **Cold Harbor** (16 m E on SR 156) and at **Fort Harrison** (10 m SE on SR 5), the latter with living history program in summer; both open June-Labor Day, daily 10-6; rest of yr, dawn-dusk daily; closed Jan. 1, Dec. 25; weekends in Dec.-Mar.; free.

Scotchtown—Patrick Henry Home (16 m N off 1-95 to Ashland, 8 m NW on SR 54, 1 m N on county 685), built about 1719, was Henry's home

1771-77 and later the childhood home of his cousin Dolley Payne Madison; open Apr.-Oct., Mon.-Sat. 10-4:30, Sun. 1:30-4:30; adm. Patrick Henry was born at **Hanover** (6 m E of Ashland on SR 54), where a stone marker is on the site (1 ½ m S on US 301 at Studley) and was married at Rural Plains (3 m SE of Studley), a privately owned residence. **Wilton House Museum** (8 m W off Cary St. on S Wilton Rd.), 1753 Georgian mansion; interior is Queen Anne; fine 18th-C furnishings; was hq for Lafayette in 1781; now hq for National Soc. of Colonial Dames of Va.; open Tues.-Fri. 10-4; Sun. 2:30-4:30 exc July-Aug.; Sat. 10-4 exc Aug.; adm. **Derwent** (38 m W off US 60), where Robert E. Lee and his family retired to escape notoriety after his surrender at Appomattox, is being restored; inquire locally for hrs. **Pocahontas State Park** (10 m S on SR 10, then W on SR 655) has a nature center with the story of Pocahontas and exhibits on beaver life.

Historic James River Plantations (see also Surry, Williamsburg): **Shirley Plantation** (20 m SE on SR 5) has been in the Carter family since it was built about 1723 and is probably Virginia's first plantation; fine paneling, oil paintings, rare antiques, silver; kitchen, laundry, and 2 brick barns form an impressive Queen Anne forecourt; was girlhood home of Anne Hill Carter, mother of Robert E. Lee; open daily 9-5; closed Dec. 25; adm. **Berkeley Plantation** (23 m SE on SR 5) was settled 1619, with the Georgian house built 1726; flanked by kitchen and laundry, and bachelor's quarters; birthplace of 9th President, William Henry Harrison, and home of 23rd President, Benjamin Harrison. During the Revolution the estate was plundered by British troops under Benedict Arnold; during the Civil War it was hq for Gen. McClellan; open daily 8-5; adm. **Westover** (24 m SE on SR 5), a truly elegant Georgian house built about 1730 by William Byrd II, tobacco planter and founder of Richmond, is well worth visiting even though only the grounds are open; daily 9-6; adm. **Brandon Plantation** (20 m SE on SR 5, 3 m S on SR 156, 9 m S on SR 10 to Burrowsville, then toward river) was built by Nathaniel Harrison in the 18th-C; only the grounds are open (daily in daylight; adm); house is open during Historic Garden Week by appointment.

ROANOKE: Roanoke Transportation Museum (in Wasena Park, Wiley Dr. & Winchester St.), indoor and outdoor exhibits on early autos, trucks, dogsled, other vehicles; open Memorial Day-Labor Day, daily 10 am-9 pm; sm adm. **Hollins College** (6 m N off US 11), antique silver in Fishburn Library (open July-Aug. daily 8-4:30; Sept.-June, Mon.-Thurs. 8-midnight, Fr. 8-11, Sat. 8:30-6, Sun. 1-11; closed hols; free.

Booker T. Washington National Monument (18 m S on SR 116 to Burnt Chimney, then 5 m E on SR 122) preserves Burroughs Plantation, a small tobacco farm with a 5-room log home that was more typical of

Southern life than the white-pillared mansions on huge land holdings. Here Booker (he had no surname and chose "Washington" much later) was born Apr. 5, 1856 to the slave-cook and slept on rags on the dirt floor of the small, windowless kitchen cabin; he was valued at $400. When emancipation came, Booker's mother moved her children to Malden, W Virginia, where Booker worked in a salt furnace and as a coal miner. He taught himself the alphabet and in 1872 entered Hampton Institute in Virginia; he was so outstanding that after a short stint as a teacher after graduating, he was chosen to found Tuskegee Institute in Alabama; starting with a shanty, an abandoned church, 30 pupils, and $2000 in 1881, he built an institution of more than 100 buildings, 1500 students, and a $2-million endowment by his death in 1915. **Visitor Center** has exhibits and film on Washington's life; restored farm has demonstrations of farm skills in summer; open June-Labor Day, Mon.-Sat. 8-6, Sun. 9:30-8; rest of yr, daily 8-4:30; closed Dec. 25; free.

Historic Fincastle, Inc. (18 m N on US 220 in Fincastle) offers daily guided walking tours of historic area, Apr.-Dec.; fee.

SHENANDOAH NATIONAL PARK stretches 80 m S from Front Royal to Waynesboro; highlight is magnificent 105-m Skyline Drive along mountain crests. Information, exhibits on mountaineer life and natural history, and schedule of activities at **Dickey Ridge Visitor Center** (4½ m S of Front Royal) or **Byrd Visitor Center** (51 m S of Front Royal); information also at several campgrounds and lodges along the drive; or write to Supt. (Luray, VA 22835).

STAUNTON: Woodrow Wilson Birthplace (24 N Coalter St. on US 11) is a Greek Revival dwelling with family furnishings, Wilson memorabilia; film; open daily 9-5; closed Jan. 1, Thnks, Dec. 25, Sun. in Dec.-Feb.; adm. **Trinity Episcopal Church** (214 W Beverley St.) was built 1855 on site where Virginia Assembly took refuge June 7-23, 1781, after escaping the British.

McCormick Reaper Museum (16 m SW on US 11, then E on SR 606 near Steeles Tavern) displays Cyrus McCormick's first reaper, invented 1831, in blacksmith shop in which it was built; his farmhouse birthplace, Walnut Grove; restored 18th-C gristmill; operating farm and livestock research station; open Apr.-Nov. daily 9-5; free.

SURRY: Chippokes Plantation State Park (6 m E on SR 10, 633), a working plantation since 1621, was named for Indian chief who befriended settlers; antebellum mansion and kitchen; early American furnishings; slave quarters; 18th-C coachhouse; open Memorial Day-Labor Day, Tues.-Sun. 10-6; sm adm. **Smith's Fort Plantation** (2 m N on SR 31) was a gift from

Chief Powhatan to John Rolfe in 1614 as dowry for his daughter Pocahontas; 1652 Rolfe-Warren House in Flemish and English bond brick is furnished with 17th-18th-C pieces; nearby Smith's Fort was built 1609 by Capt. John Smith; open Apr.-Oct. daily 9:30-5; adm. **Bacon's Castle** (7 m SE on SR 10, then NE on SR 617), Jacobean manor built about 1655 with fortress-thick walls; outbuildings; audiovisual program on regional history; open Memorial Day-Oct., Sat. & Sun. 10-5; adm.

WEST POINT: King William County Courthouse (18 m NW on SR 30), built 1725 and still in use, has Flemish bond brickwork; open Mon.-Fri. 9-4:30; closed hols; free.

Gloucester (22 m SE on SR 14, US 17) offers: County Courthouse, with historic displays (including Bacon Rebellion of 1676); early portraits; open Mon.-Fri. 8-4:30; closed hols; free. On Court Green are other 18th-C buildings, including Debtors' Prison. Long Bridge Ordinary, a 1730 stage stop, is a women's club. **Ware Church** (2 m E on SR 14) was built about 1700 with 3-ft-thick walls. **Powhatan's Chimney** (10 m SE on US 17) was site of chief Powhatan's village. **Walter Reed Birthplace** (4 m W at jct SR 614, 616), Belroi, where the physician was born 1851; his discovery that mosquitoes carried yellow fever led to eradication of the disease; hrs vary but usually open mid-Mar.-mid-Apr., Memorial Day-July 4, Sat. & Sun. 2-5, or by request; sm adm. Virginia Institute of Marine Science (Gloucester Point), small marine museum, is open daily 8-4:30; free.

WILLIAMSBURG: On this site in 1633, colonists from Jamestown established Middle Plantation, a stockaded outpost against Indian attack; although the College of William & Mary was erected in 1693, Middle Plantation remained a village of only a few homes and shops until, in 1698, the statehouse at Jamestown burned to the ground; seizing the chance to move from the brackish swamps, Jamestown legislators moved the capital here, renaming it Williamsburg in honor of the reigning king, William III. From 1699-1780, Williamsburg was the political, social, and cultural center of the colony—elegant manners, rich furnishings, fine foods and wine, made it a sophisticated wonder when contrasted to the crude life of the frontier. Intellectual stimulation here did much to form the course of American history as Washington, Jefferson, Patrick Henry, and others debated the overthrow of British rule; in 1774 the dissolved House of Burgess here called the First Continental Congress; but while Williamsburg served briefly as hq for Cornwallis, and later for Washington and Rochambeau, the Revolutionary War ended the city's prominence—in 1780 the capital was moved to Richmond, considered safer from British attack and also more central, and Williamsburg went into abrupt decline. Today it is the grandest restoration in America, with 83 original buildings and many others meticulously reconstructed on their original sites; dozens of these, fully and authentically furnished, are open to the public; research has extended even to the plants on the 100 acres of gardens and greens; horse-drawn carriages and costumed attendants help re-create colonial atmosphere. Private cars are banned 8 am-6 pm, but a special bus service is included in the adm. **Colonial Williamsburg Information Center** (Colonial Pkwy & SR 132) provides full information and literature on what to see and do, accomodations, dining, special events; open daily 8:30 am-10 pm. Tickets at several price levels enable you to choose what you want to see from among films and lectures; some 20 shops where costumed craftsmen demonstrate 18th-C trades (including apothecary, gunsmith, cooper, wigmaker, music teacher, pewter caster— all daily 9-5); and:

The Capitol (E end of Duke of Gloucester St.), an impressive building with Queen Anne's coat of arms on the tower; the General Assembly convened here 1704-80; here Patrick Henry denounced the Stamp Act and Virginia's Declaration of Rights was passed; the square outside was scene of celebrations. **Public Gaol** (across Nicholson St.), where criminals were confined 1704-1910, has housed debtors, runaway slaves, marauding Indians, the mentally ill, and 15 of Blackbeard's crew; cells, shackles. **Raleigh Tavern** and **Wetherburn's Tavern** (Duke of Gloucester St.) were social centers for public receptions and balls, political discussions, auctions, and business meetings. **Peyton Randolph House** (Nicholson St.), with paneled rooms, was home of president of First Continental Congress. **Bush-Everard House** (Palace Green), built 1717 by a gunsmith, later housed a dancing teacher and a mayor; kitchen and smokehouse. **Wythe House** (Palace Green) was home of the influential legislator and teacher, mentor of Jefferson and Marshall; Washington's hq before the siege of Yorktown; Rochambeau's hq after the surrender of Cornwallis. **Bruton Parish Church** (Duke of Gloucester St.), in continuous use since 1715; its pastor conceived the restoration of Williamsburg and interested John D. Rockefeller, Jr. in the project; open in summer daily 9-5; in winter daily 10-4. **James Geddy House** (Gloucester St.), home of prominent silversmith with adjacent shop.

Courthouse of 1770 (Market Sq.) was in use until 1932; here start walking tours of gardens, carriage and "wagon" rides, candlelit tours, and children's Tricorn Hat Tours (all extra fee). **Magazine** (Market Sq.), enclosed by a wall and protected by a guard in adjacent Guardhouse, is a sturdy octagonal building that housed the colony's arms and ammunition; antique arms demonstrations.

College of William & Mary (W end of Duke of Gloucester St.), founded 1693 (only Harvard was earlier), was attended by Jefferson, Monroe, Tyler; oldest academic building in the nation is Wren Bldg., begun 1695, with chapel design by Christopher Wren (open daily 9-5); colonial art in Swem Library (open daily 8 am-10 pm; closed hols).

Within the historic district but requiring an additional fee is **Governor's Palace,** the most elegant building in Williamsburg; residence for royal governors from Alexander Spotwood (1710-22) until the Earl of Dunmore fled in 1775; also residents were Patrick Henry, first elected governor of the new state, and his successor Jefferson. During the Yorktown campaign it became a hospital. Destroyed by fire in 1781, it has been reconstructed with many fragments of the original salvaged from the ruins; elegant furnishings; outbuildings; extensive gardens with Revolutionary graveyard.

Outside the historic district are: **Abby Aldrich Rockefeller Folk Art Collection** (S England St. near Williamsburg Inn) with a fabulous collection of painting, sculpture, and objects of everyday use such as shop signs; open June-Oct. daily 10 am-9 pm; Nov.-May daily noon-8; free. **Craft House** (adjacent) sells reproductions of Williamsburg furnishings, silver, glass; open Mon. 9-5; Tues.-Sat. 9-9; Sun. 1-9.

Carter's Grove Plantation (8 m SE on US 60) is a magnificent Georgian mansion on the James River built by a grandson of King Carter on a 300,000-acre estate that was run by 1000 slaves; it was begun in 1750, and a master woodworker was imported from England to spend 6 years supervising the carving and installation of the extraordinary woodwork; it was a social center for wealthy planters and, according to legend, Washington and Jefferson proposed marriage to early loves and were rejected in the Refusal Room; open Mar.-Nov. daily 9-5; adm.

WINCHESTER: Settled by Pennsylvania Quakers 1732, Winchester played an important role in the French & Indian War. As a 16-year-old, Washington arrived in 1748 as surveyor for Lord Fairfax at **Washington's Office** (Cork & Braddock Sts.); during the French & Indian War, Washington used the building as his hq until Ft. Loudoun was completed; open May-Oct. daily 9-5; sm adm. Lord Fairfax, proprietor of the Northern Neck of Virginia, lived at Greenway Court near here 1739-82, and is buried in the cemetery of **Christ Episcopal Church** (Washington St. near Boscawen Court). During the Civil War, Winchester was strategically located to control Confederate supply lines through the Shenandoah Valley and Union routes to Washington; considered vital to both North and South, the city changed hands 72 times (13 times during one day). **Stonewall Jackson's Headquarters** (415 N Braddock St.) was home to Jackson and his wife during the winter of 1861-62; Jackson memorabilia; open daily 9-5; sm adm. The **Valley Pike** (now US 11) was the "race course" of armies during the Civil War; here Jackson waged his Valley Campaign; in 12 weeks he fought 5 major battles (and innumerable skirmishes) and defeated 3 separate armies on a 630-m march; US 11 and US 340, between Winchester and Lexington, are dotted with turnouts where historic markers commemorate the campaign. **General Sheridan's Headquarters** (Braddock & Piccadilly Sts.) was the starting point for Sheridan's Ride of 1864 to rally his retreating army at Cedar Creek and turn the Confederate victory into a rout; now houses Order of Elks. **Old Stone Presbyterian Church** (306 E Piccadilly St.), built 1788, was used as a stable by Union troops during Civil War; it has also been a school and armory; open daily 7 am-8 pm; free. **Abram's Delight** (1 m E on US 50 at Rouss Spring Rd.), the 1754 Hollingsworth House, has period furnishings; log cabin; open May-Oct., Tues.-Sat. 9-5, Sun. 2-5; sm adm.

Chamber of Commerce (29 S Cameron St.) offers maps on historic sites and the many Revolutionary-era buildings (some are open Historic Garden Week); interesting are: 1783 **Red Lion Tavern**, built by a member of Morgan's Riflemen. **Springdale** (5 m S on US 11), 1753 home of Col. John Hite, son of first settler; privately owned; Hite's Fort (just S) ruins. **Saratoga** (11 m E on SR 7 in Berryville), said to have been built by Hessian prisoners of the Revolution for Gen. Daniel Morgan.

Belle Grove (13 m S on US 11), a National Trust property, is a late Georgian house constructed of hewn limestone in 1794 with the guidance of Thomas Jefferson; hq for Gen. Sheridan; Battle of Cedar Creek raged around it; still a working farm, it is a center for interpretation of rural life and crafts; demonstrations; special events; open Apr.-Oct., Mon.-Sat. 10-4, Sun. 1-5; adm.

Trinity Episcopal Church (22 m SE on US 50 in Upperville), begun in 1951, is modeled on medieval French country churches, erected by local craftsmen who learned medieval methods; wonderful carvings of mythological animals and early Christian symbols; stained-glass windows from Amsterdam; open daily.

WOODSTOCK: Shenandoah County Court House (Main St.), built of native limestone 1792, was designed by Thomas Jefferson; open Mon.-Fri. 8:30-5; closed hols; free. **Hoffman's Military Museum** (768 S Main St.), pistols, rifles, other arms; inquire locally for schedule; donation.

WYTHEVILLE: Scene of many Civil War encounters over its lead and salt mines; local heroine was Molly Tynes, the Paul Revere of the South, who rode 40 miles across the mountains to warn of approaching Union cavalry. **Shot Tower Historical Park** (6 m E on I-81, 7 m S on US 52): built about 1807 on a hilltop on the banks of New River; lead melted in the tower was dropped through the hill into a kettle of water to harden; shot was extracted through a tunnel dug into the hill from the river bank; open mid-June-Labor Day, Tues.-Sun. 10-6; free.

YORKTOWN: In the 7th year of the Revolutionary War, in Aug. 1781, Cornwallis moved his troops into this busy port to establish winter hq for himself and the British fleet. But French and American troops ringed the city, laying siege by land, while a French fleet arrived to block the harbor. The siege began Oct. 9. After failure to break the blockade, and loss of 2 strategic redoubts, Cornwallis realized defeat was inevitable. American, French, and British representatives met on Oct. 18 in Moore House; they argued so long over terms of surrender that the articles were not signed until Oct. 19. One source of argument was the American demand that the defeated army leave the city to the music of a British or German march (in retaliation for British terms at the surrender of Charleston that Americans *not* march to English or German tunes). So at 2 pm on Oct. 19, the British army marched from Yorktown playing the old British tune, "The World Turned Upside Down." **Visitor Center** (end of Colonial Pkwy) has historical exhibits on Yorktown and the siege; audiovisual programs; booklets for self-guiding tour of marked battlefield sites in and around town; open daily 8:30-5 (to 6:30 in summer); closed Dec. 25; free. Highlights of the area are: **Observation deck** for panoramic view of battlefield. **Moore House** (on SR 238 E of town), damaged by shelling, stripped of wood for use as fuel by soldiers, restored to colonial appearance; original and period furnishings; open Apr.-Nov. daily; sm adm. Yorktown National Civil War Cemetery; half the graves are of unknowns.

Monument to Alliance & Victory (E end of Main St.) honors French aid during the Revolution. **York County Courthouse** (Main St. at Ballard), reconstruction of 1792 original; records dating back to 1633; open Mon.-Fri. 9-5; closed hols; free. **Swan Tavern** (Main & Ballard Sts.), reconstruction of tavern, kitchen, smokehouse and stable built before 1722 and blown up in 1863; houses antique shop. **Grace Church** (Church St.), built 1697 of native marl, was used by the British as a magazine; Thomas Nelson, signer of Declaration of Independence, is buried in the cemetery; open daily 9-5; free.

WASHINGTON

ABERDEEN—HOQUIAM: Hoquiam's Castle (515 Chenault Ave., Hoquiam), mansion of lumber czar, built 1897; Victorian woodwork; impressive antique furnishings; open June-Labor Day, daily 11-5; rest of yr, Mon.-Fri. 11-5; closed Jan. 1, Dec. 25; adm.

ANACORTES: Anacortes Museum of History & Art (1305 E 8th St.), photographs, furniture, regional historic relics; old-time doctor's office; open Wed., Sun. 2-4; closed Easter, Dec. 25; free. **La Conner** (10 m E on SR 20, then S), an old fishing village; craft boutiques; Skagit County Historical Society Museum with early fishing and industrial displays (open Wed. 1-4, Sun. 1-5; closed hols; free).

Coupeville (25 m S on SR 20), settled in the 1850s and one of the oldest cities in the state, is center of the Whidbey Island Historic District; **Chamber of Commerce** (Front St.) provides information on many restored homes and the log blockhouses built to protect settlers from Indian attack (Alexander Blockhouse is on the waterfront near Front St.); **Island County Historical Museum** (Alexander St.) displays 19th-C Skagit Indian artifacts and settler relics (open May-Sept., Sat. & Sun. 1-4:30; free). **Fort Casey State Park** (28 m S on SR 20), site of a coastal artillery post established in the 1890s, houses interpretive exhibits at the old lighthouse; open Apr.-Sept. daily 10-6.

BELLINGHAM: Whatcom Museum of History & Art (121 Prospect St.), in 1892 building; exhibits on early settlement; art by Northwest artists; open Tues.-Sun. noon-5; closed Jan. 1, Dec. 25; free. Another Victorian building, **Gamwell House** (1001 16th St.) is not open, but it's worth seeing for its turrets and gingerbread. **International Peace Arch** (24 m NW on I-5 at Canadian border), begun with donations (limited to 10¢) by Canadian and U.S. schoolchildren, is on international territory.

BREMERTON: USS Missouri (Naval Shipyard, Pier G) has a plaque indicating spot on which Japanese signed surrender terms ending WWII; top deck open to public; open in summer daily 10-8; rest of yr. Mon.-Fri. noon-4; Sat., Sun., hols 10-4; free. **Naval Shipyard Museum** (Ferry Terminal Bldg), models and photos of naval vessels, displays of shipyard history; open Wed.-Sun. noon-4; closed hols; free. **Kitsap County Historical Museum** (837 4th St.), local displays and relics; intricately hand-carved furniture made by local resident; open Tues.-Sat. 1-4; closed hols; donation.

In **Suquamish Memorial Cemetery** (12 m N on SR 3, then SE off SR 305 in Suquamish) is grave of Chief Seattle (1786-1866) for whom the city was named in recognition of his friendship; interpretive shelter at Old Man House (½ m SW) marks site of his home. **Port Gamble** (21 m N at jct SR 3, 104), old mill town with many buildings dating back to the 1870s.

CENTRALIA: Borst Blockhouse (W of town in Ft. Borst Park), moved here from original site at the confluence of Skookumchuck and Chehalis Rivers, is a log fortification built 1852 against Indian attack; final refuge was the 2nd floor, with gunports in the floor; other settler exhibits; open daily 7:30-10; free. **Historic Claquato Church** (4 m S on I-5 to Chehalis, 3 m W on SR 6), on its original site on Claquato Hill, is oldest church in state, entirely hand-hewn; open daily on request. **Lewis County Historical Society Museum** (4 m S on I-5 at 1070 Washington St., Chehalis) has lumbering and historic exhibits; open Thurs., Sun. 1-4; closed hols; free.

ELLENSBURG: Olmstead Place State Park (4 m E on I-90, then S on Squaw Creek Trail Rd.) preserves a farm homesteaded in 1875; 1875 log cabin with family furnishings; 1892 barn and granary; outbuildings; 1908 home; being developed to interpret early agriculture in the region; open Apr.-Nov., Tues.-Sun. 9-5; sm adm. **Ginkgo Petrified Forest State Park** (27 m E on I-90 in Vantage), with trees petrified in molten lava; museum interpretive trails; Indian petroglyphs; open in summer daily 8 am-7 pm; rest of yr, daily 9-5; closed Dec.-Jan.; free. **Wanapum Dam Tour Center** (29 m E on I-90, then 3 m S on Sr 243), displays of Columbia River life, Wanapum Indian artifacts, Indian wars, fur trade, mining, steamboating; self-guiding tour of center, fish viewing area (May-Sept.); open in summer daily 8-8:30; spring and fall daily 8-4:30; closed Nov.-mid-Apr.; free. **Cle Elum Historical Museum** (22 m NW on SR 10 to Cle Elum) has displays on early history of the telephone; dolls, other items; open Memorial Day-Oct., Tues.-Sun. 1:30-4:30; closed hols; free.

GOLDENDALE: Klickitat County Historical Society Museum (127 W Broadway), in Victorian home with regional pioneer furnishings; cattle brands, other local items; open May-late-Oct., daily 10-5; sm adm.

Maryhill Museum of Fine Arts (11 m S via US 97 to SR 14, W of Maryhill) was begun 1913 by a local Quaker, Samuel Hill, as a center of a 7000-acre colony for Belgian Quakers; but Quakers who arrived found the soil too poor to farm and left; the castle-like building (named for Hill's wife, Mary, who was rumored to be insane) was dedicated in 1926 by Queen Marie of Rumania, who donated the Gold Throne Room and other royal possessions from her summer palace near Bucharest; other of Hill's royal friends also contributed; outstanding Northwest Indian arts and crafts; chess sets; dolls; guns; boat models; French mannequins; Impressionist paintings; open mid-Mar.-mid-Nov. daily 9-5:30; free. Nearby, Hill constructed a replica of Stonehenge (he sent workmen to England to make casts of the original stones), which he considered a symbol of senseless human sacrifice, as a memorial to the county's war dead.

GRAND COULEE: Coulee Dam National Recreation Area extends from Grand Coulee Dam 151 m along Roosevelt Lake and the Columbia River to the Canadian border. **Grand Coulee Dam Tour Center** provides information for self-guided tours of observation points (especially spectacular is Crown Point on SR 174), powerplant, pump-generator plant; displays, relief map, and tape recorded narration; open daily late-May-Labor Day 7 am-11 pm (dam and spillway illuminated at night); spring and fall, 7 am-8 pm; winter, 8:30-5; closed Dec. 25; free. **Fort Spokane Visitor Center** (19 m SE on SR 174, 30 m E on US 2, 24 m N on SR 25); fort established 1880 to protect settlers from Indians on the Colville Reservation; later the fort was unpopular headquarters of the Colville Indian Agency and hospital; exhibits on colorful frontier history, including 1807-21 fur trading era and fort life; self-guiding tour booklets; open daily 8-5 (8-6 in summer); closed some hols & some winter weekends: free. Information on the N end of the recreation area may be obtained at **Kettle Falls**; artifacts dating back 7000 years have been found on the old Indian trail (now SR 20) along which thousands of Indians came from their winter homes to fish. Also at Kettle Falls is **St. Paul's Mission**, established by Jesuits in 1845; during the fur trade it served as social and religious center; exhibits on fur trade, Indian life, missionaries, settlers, and gold miners; open May-Oct. daily 9-5; free. This area experienced 2 gold rushes (a gold mine still operates at Republic, 44 m W of Kettle Falls), and ghost town remains can be found in the surrounding mountains.

Dry Falls (33 m S on SR 155, 17) interpretive center houses fossils, geologic displays on the area; open Apr.-Sept., Tues.-Sun. 10-5; free. **Lake Lenore Caves** (10 m S of Dry Falls on SR 17) were used by men in prehistoric times; reached via footpath from parking area.

LONG BEACH: Fort Canby (7 m S on SR 103): Here at Cape Disappointment, Lewis and Clark first saw the Pacific in 1805 (their previous campsite, used Nov. 15-25, is marked on US 101, 2 m S of Chinook); defensive works, overlooking the mouth of the Columbia River, were constructed 1862 and used off and on during the Civil War, Spanish-American War, and WW I and II; open all year. **Fort Columbia** (11 m SE on US 101), also built to guard the Columbia; several buildings remain; interpretive center exhibits on the river's exploration and on the Chinook Indians whose homeland this was; open late May-early Sept. daily 10-5; donation.

LONGVIEW: Wahkiakum County Historical Society Museum (29 m W in Cathlamet City Center) has settler, logging, and other exhibits; open June-Aug., Tues.-Sun. 1-4; Sept.-May, Thurs.-Sat. 1-4; closed hols; free. **Cowlitz County Historical Museum** (W to 4th & Church Sts., Kelso), in courthouse annex, reconstructs frontier kitchen, parlor; split-log cabin, barbershop, country store, livery stable; dolls, quilts, guns, Indian artifacts, other items; open Tues.-Sat. 10:30-4:30, Sun. 2-5; closed hols; free. **Vader** (17 m N on SR 411), once a prosperous trading center, is now almost a ghost town; famous at turn of the century for an alcoholic husky dog.

MOSES LAKE: Adam East Museum (401 5th St. at Balsam St.) has fossil animal and marine life, relics of prehistoric man and Indians; open May-Aug., Tues.-Sun. 9-noon, 1-5; Mar.-Apr. & Sept.-Oct., Tues.-Sun. 1-5; closed Easter, Memorial Day, July 4; free. **Adams County Historical Museum** (28 m E on I-90, 11 m S on SR 21 in Lind) has regional pioneer displays; open Mon., Wed., Fri. 1:30-3; closed hols; free. **Grant County Museum** (21 m NW on SR 17, 282 to 742 Basin St. NW in Ephrata) has regional Indian artifacts; displays on settlement; furnished frontier rooms and country store; open late May-mid-Sept., Thurs.-Tues. 1-4:30; sm adm.

MOUNT RAINIER NATIONAL PARK, surrounding glacier-clad Mt. Rainier, offers exhibits, films, information, and ranger-conducted programs at the following **Visitor Centers:** Longmire (61 m E of Tacoma on SR 7, 706), open daily all year, is park hq (write Longmire 98397). Paradise (13 m E of Longmire), open all year. Sunrise (78 m from Tacoma via SR 410) and Ohanapecoch (69 m from Yakima via SR 410, US 12, SR 123), open daily in summer, weekends in fall.

NORTH CASCADES NATIONAL PARK: offers exhibits and naturalist programs; write hq (Sedro Woolley, WA 98284), open weekdays 8-4:30; information also at ranger station in Marblemount, open daily all year 8-4:30 (to 6 in summer).

OLYMPIA: Surrounded by low hills, the state capital is an attractive city with many parks; monument marking end of the Oregon Trail is in Sylvester Park; you may visit the famous oyster beds in Mud, Oyster, and Big and Little Skookum Bays, and watch salmon runs (mid-Aug.-Oct.) at Tumwater Falls Park (S off I-5) or Capitol Lake (formed by a dam where the Deschutes River empties into Budd Inlet); Deschutes Pkwy circles Capitol Lake, providing a good view of the Capitol Group on the E shore: **Legislative Bldg,** with imposing Corinthian columns, has lavish interior; huge Tiffany chandelier in rotunda; open Mon.-Fri. 8-5 (tours daily 9-5 in summer); closed hols; free. **Temple of Justice,** with Doric columns, houses state Supreme Court; open Mon.-Fri. 8-5; closed hols; free. **State Library** has marble mosaic by James Fitzgerald in the lobby; historical murals by Kenneth Callahan in Washington Room; rare books and documents on the Northwest; open Mon.-Fri. 8-5; closed hols; free. On landscaped grounds are memorials and a replica of Tivoli Gardens fountain in Copenhagen.

State Capitol Museum (211 W 21st Ave.), in Spanish-style mansion, traces history of the Northwest; Indian cultural exhibits include Northwest Coast and Plateau tribes, Eskimo; early guns, musical instruments, glass, other exhibits; fossils, shells, other natural history displays; art gallery; open Tues.-Fri. 10-4, Sat. noon-4, Sun. 1-4; closed hols; free. **State Board of Pharmacy** (319 E 7th St.) has a restored 1860s pharmacy; open Mon.-Fri. 8-5; closed hols; free.

OLYMPIC NATIONAL PARK is a 1400-sq-m wilderness with a varied landscape of mountains, rain forests, glaciers, and seacoasts; 3 Indian reservations and several resort complexes; park is open all year, but write ahead for information as many roads close in winter and others are not suitable for trailers even in summer. **Port Angeles Visitor Center** (Park Ave. & Race St., Port Angeles) is park hq; relief model of park; exhibits on history, natural history, and Indian culture; guided walks and other ranger programs; open mid-June-Labor Day, daily 8-7; rest of yr, daily 8-4:30; closed Jan. 1, Thnks, Dec. 25; free. Exhibits and information also at **Hoh Rain Forest Visitor Center** (14 m S of Forks on US 101, then 19 m E), open daily 9-6 (to 7:30 Fri. & Sat. in summer); and at **Storm King Visitor Center** (on US 101, 21 m SW of Port Angeles), open mid-June-Labor Day, Sun.-Thurs. 9-6, Fri. & Sat. 9-7:30.

OMAK: Ruby Ghost Town (NW to Conconully, then S on forest road) is one of many remains from the gold rush in the area. **Fort Okanogan** (27 m S on US 97) was established 1811 as a trading post by John Jacob Astor's Pacific Fur Co., and like his other post (see Spokane House, Spokane) eventually became part of the Hudson's Bay Co.; interpretive center details history of the fur trade and the Okanogan-Caribou trail; open May-Sept. daily 8-6; free.

PASCO—KENNEWICK—RICHLAND: Hanford Science Center (Federal Bldg, 825 Jadwin, Richland): models, animated and graphic displays, depict development of nuclear power; open June-Aug., Mon.-Thurs. 9-noon, 1-5, 6-9, Fri. & Sat. 9-9, Sun. 1-9; Sept.-May, Tues.-Sat. 9-noon, 1-5, Sun.1-5; closed Jan. 1, July 4, Thnks, Dec. 25; free. **Sacajawea State Park** (5 m SE of Pasco off US 12, 395), on site of Lewis and Clark camp, is named for their guide; interpretive center with Indian artifacts; open daily in summer 6:30 am-10 pm; in winter, daily 8-5; closed some hols; free. **Benton County Historical Society Museum** (30 m W on US' 12 to Prosser City Park, Prosser) has Indian artifacts, homestead interior, dollhouse, hand-painted china, other exhibits; open Tues.-Sat. 10-4, Sun. 1-5; closed Thnks, Dec. 25; sm adm.

PORT TOWNSEND: A thriving port in the 1870s-80s; handsome Victorian buildings in the downtown section; **Chamber of Commerce** (2139 Sims Way) provides a map of historic sites and information on house tours. **Jefferson County courthouse** (Jefferson & Cass Sts.), Romanesque building of brick and carved stone, 100-ft clock tower; open Mon.-Fri. 8-4:30; closed hols; free. **Jefferson County Historical Museum** (in City Hall, Water & Madison Sts.), in former 1890s courtroom; displays on town history; library; legend says Jack London was once a prisoner in the basement jail; open mid-Apr.-May, Fri.-Sun. noon-5; June-Sept., Wed.-Sun. 11-5; Oct., Wed.-Sun. noon-5; Nov., Sun. noon-5; closed hols; free. **Rothschild House State Heritage Site** (Franklin & Taylor Sts.), 1868 merchant's home; period furnishings; open mid-May-mid-Sept. daily 10-6; free. **Old Fort Townsend Historical State Park** (3 m S on SR 113), site of 1856 fort built to protect settlers against Indian attack, abandoned in 1893 and burned in 1895; historic marker.

    Fort Flagler Historical State Park (10 m NE of Chimacum on Marrowstone Point), site of 1890s fort established to guard Puget Sound and occupied through WW II; only gun batteries and guns remain; interpretive shelter. **Fort Worden State Park** (1 m N) was also site of Puget Sound harbor defenses; active until WW II; many buildings from 1898-1914 remain and are being restored; gun emplacements.

PULLMAN: **Washington State University** offers tours from Office of Information (448 French Administration Bldg), Mon-Fri, 8-noon, 1-5; inquire here for exact hrs for the following, generally open Mon.-Sat. 8-5 but closed school hols: Library (historical material on territory; papers of Father De Smet); Charles R. Conner Museum (herbarium, mounted birds and mammals, other natural history displays); Museum of Anthropology (prehistory and recent Indians of Northwest; Ashanti and New Guinea artifacts).

SAN JUAN ISLANDS (accessible by Washington State Ferry all year from Anacortes or by plane from Seattle or Bellingham): On Orcas Island, **Orcas Island Historical Society** maintains museum displays in 6 original homestead cabins; open Memorial Day-Labor Day, daily 1-4; donation. On San Juan Island, **University of Washington Marine Laboratories** welcomes visitors (mid-June-late Aug., Wed., Sat. 2-4; free) and **San Juan Island National Historical Park** commemorates struggle for control of the territory; from 1825-46, American pioneers intent on Manifest Destiny battled British fur traders for the region N of the 42nd parallel, giving rise to the slogan "Fifty-four Forty or Fight." An 1846 treaty left unclear ownership of San Juan Island, where Americans were homesteading and Hudson's Bay Co. had a sheep ranch and salmon-curing station, so friction continued; on June 15, 1859, an American found a British-owned pig destroying his little potato patch and shot the animal; the incident exploded into the Pig War, as American infantry and 5 British warships converged on the island. Luckily the British admiral refused to go to war over a pig, and so did the U.S. and British governments when they heard about the incident. Nevertheless, San Juan Island remained under joint military occupation for the next 12 years until Kaiser Wilhelm I of Germany mediated the dispute and ruled in favor of the U.S. in 1872, ending the war in which the pig remained the sole casualty. Park Headquarters (near ferry landing in Friday Harbor) is open all year, Mon.-Fri. 8-4:30; closed Jan. 1, Dec. 25. At **American Camp** (5 m S of Friday Harbor) only earthworks survive, while at **English Camp** (10 m N of Friday Harbor), barracks, commissary, and blockhouse survive; both areas have exhibits, interpretive signs, and information centers open June-Aug., Mon.-Fri. 9:30-6, Sat. & Sun. 8-8. Near American Camp, other marked sites are Old San Juan Town (first settlement in Griffin Bay area, destroyed by 1890 fire) and Bellevue Farm (site of the Hudson's Bay Co. sheep ranch). Park open daily all year, sunrise-sunset; free.

SEATTLE: Information on this historic Pacific Northwest gateway, built on hills and surrounded by mountains, is available from **Seattle & Kings County Convention & Visitors Bureau** (1815 7th Ave., zip 98101), open daily 9-5; closed some hols. (In summer, information centers are also open in Pioneer Square and in Seattle Center, daily 9-5.) They will provide you with maps for marked scenic drives that take you past most attractions, including many water-oriented points of interest—floating bridges, houseboat colonies in Lake Union, the huge Chittenden Locks (only the Panama Canal's are larger), Fishermen's Terminal (winter home of the Alaskan fishing fleet), commercial piers, and private boat docks. The city also has commercial tours, plant tours, a superior park system, special events, and good public transportation; from here a wealth of tour and transportation services will take you to national parks and points of interest in Canada and Alaska. **Washington State Ferries** (Pier 52, Seattle 98104) offer many excursions, including Olympic Peninsula, San Juan Island, and Victoria (B.C.). City avenues run N or S, streets run E to W—and most addresses carry area designations (N, E. etc) to help you find your way. Overviews are available from: **Smith Tower Observatory & Chinese Temple** (506 2nd Ave. at Yesler Way), 35th floor, usually open daily 8:30 am-10:30 pm; sm adm. **Volunteer Park** (15th Ave. E & E Prospect St.) has a 520-ft water tower open daily 9-dusk.

Old Seattle's core is **Pioneer Square** (1st Ave. at James St.), with an iron pergola erected 1909, a fountain, and a horse-watering trough; here

Henry Yesler in 1853 built a steam sawmill, the city's first industry; the term "skid road," later corrupted elswhere to Skid Row, originated here when logs were slid downhill to the waterfront. A fire in 1889 destroyed the mill town. When the city was rebuilt, the new street level was raised 10 ft above the old, leaving many of the old shops intact; an interesting 2-hr guided tour of this 5-block area, above and below ground, is provided at a reasonable price by **Bill Speidel's Underground Tours** (601 1st Ave., zip 98104), daily exc Jan. 1, Easter, Dec. 25; reservations advised. This area, rebuilt with unusual harmony because it was influenced by one architect, became the heart of business and social activity as the Alaskan gold rushes brought new prosperity at the turn of the century; but within a decade the area declined. Today, this Victorian section, with cobblestone streets, gas lamps, surprise arcades, and fine brickwork, is being preserved as the Pioneer Square Historic District (Alaska Way S to 3rd Ave. S, Cherry to S King Sts.), with boutiques, restaurants, and art galleries occupying the old buildings. **King Street Station** (303 S Jackson St. at 3rd Ave. S), the 1906 railroad station, has a wonderful tower copied from the campanile of Venice's Piazza San Marco, with tile roof, 4-faced clock, and cast stone and terra cotta ornamentation. **International Settlement** (5-8th Aves. off E Yesler Way), settled by Chinese, Japanese, and other nationalities, has Oriental shops and restaurants; street festival in Aug.

Gold Rush Strip (mostly between Pier 50 at foot of Yesler Way to Pier 60 near foot of Union St., but extends beyond, as at Pier 70) is the water-front, where in 1897 the steamship *Portland* docked with "a ton of gold" and 68 miners excited about fortunes to be made in the Yukon. Seattle became a boom town, as wharves were built to accommodate the thousands sailing to the Klondike gold rush. Although deep-water docks away from downtown serve today's cargo ships, the gold rush piers have been revitalized with a park (Pier 57), shops, and restaurants. Here are: **Ye Old Curiosity Shop** (Pier 51), established 1899 and still operated by the same family, with Eskimo and Northwest Indian curios; open 7 days a week. Washington State Ferries (Pier 52), offering many excursions. **Seattle Harbor Tours** (Pier 56), operating June-Sept. daily. **Tillicum Village Excursion** (Pier 56) to Blake Island State Park for an Indian baked salmon dinner, Indian dances, craft demonstrations and sales, early June-Labor Day, daily. **Kiana Lodge Excursion** (Pier 56), a similar excursion for dinner, dances, crafts to Sand Hook, early June-Labor Day, daily. **Seattle Marine Aquarium** (Pier 56), open daily 10-dusk; adm. Nearby is **Pike Place Public Market** (between Stewart & Pike Sts., W of 1st Ave.), a historic frontier market for farmers and fishermen; arts and crafts have been added to the traditional flower, vegetable, and fish offerings.

Seattle Center (along 5th Ave N between Mercer St. & Denny Way) was

74-acre site of '62 World's Fair; monorail shuttles between downtown and the center (Mon.-Thurs. 10 am-midnight, Fri. & Sat. 10 am-12:30 am, Sun. & hols 10-10); International Fountain is operated daily 11-11; **Space Needle,** with views from revolving restaurant or observation deck 500-ft high (open daily in summer, 7:30 am-1:30 am; in winter 9 am-midnight; adm); facilities for opera, theater, trade shows, sports events; amusement park; also here are: **Seattle Art Museum Pavilion** (2nd Ave. N & Thomas St.), branch of Seattle Art Museum with contemporary, regional, temporary exhibits; open Tues.-Thurs, Sat., Sun. 10-5, Fri, 10-9; closed Jan. 1, Thnks, Dec. 25; free. **Pacific Science Center** (200 2nd Ave. N), outstanding museum using working models and devices, puzzles, walk-in and other participatory exhibits to explain life sciences, physical sciences, and space; also reconstructed Northwest Indian longhouse made of original totems and house poles, with exhibits on Indian life; open mid-June-Labor Day, daily 11-8; rest of yr, Mon.-Fri. 9-5, Sat. & Sun. 11-8; closed Jan. 1, Thnks, a week at Christmas; adm. **Center House** (305 Harrison St.) has international bazaar and museum; shops with delicacies from around the world; open Sun.-Thurs. 11 am-9 pm, Fri. & Sat. 11-10; free. **Washington State Fire Museum,** with hand-drawn and horse-drawn apparatus, photos, displays on history of firefighting; open in summer daily noon-8; in winter, Sat. & Sun. noon-8; sm adm. **Museum of Flight,**with antique to modern aircraft; open in summer daily noon-8; in winter, Sat. & Sun. noon-8; sm adm. **Northwest Craft Center,** open in summer daily 11-6; rest of yr, Tues.-Sun. 11-6; closed Jan. 1, Thnks, Dec. 25; sm adm.

University of Washington Visitor Center (University Way NE & NE Campus Pkwy) provides information on library collections and other facilities; on campus are: **Henry Art Gallery,** outstanding 19-20th-C American art, including Hassam and Homer; 19th-C European works; Japanese folk pottery; Northwest contemporary prints, ceramics, other crafts; open Tues.-Sat. 10-5, Sun. 1-5; free. **Thomas Burke Memorial** (Washington State Museum) emphasizes human culture and the natural history of the Pacific Rim, with animals, birds, insects, plants; Indian art; open Tues.-Sat. 10-5, Sun. 1-5; free. **Costume and Textile Study Center,** fabrics from all over the world, ancient to modern examples, may be seen on request; free.

Seattle Art Museum (14th Ave. E & E Prospect St.): astounding collection of Far East art from 4000 B.C.—screens, ceramics, painting, sculpture, lacquer, exquisite jade carvings; also European Renaissance and Baroque works; American art includes primitives and works by Mark Tobey and Morris Graves; on grounds are animal figures (tigers, lion-gods, camels) that once lined the paths to tombs of Chinese emperors; open Tues.-Sat. 10-5, Sun. & some hols noon-5; closed Jan. 1, Thnks,

Dec. 25; free. **Charles & Emma Frye Art Museum** (704 Terry Ave. at Cherry St.) houses late-19th-C Munich School paintings; other European works; excellent 19-20th-C American art; open Mon-Sat. 10-5, Sun. & hols noon-6; closed Thnks, Dec. 25; free. **Museum of History & Industry** (2161 E Hamlin St. in McCurdy Park); figureheads, ships' bells, ship models, Indian canoes, Gold Rush artifacts, other relics of Seattle's first 100 years and history of the Pacific Northwest; natural history, transportation, exploration, aerospace sections; open Tues.-Fri. 11-5, Sat. 10-5, Sun. noon-5; closed Jan. 1, Thnks, Dec. 25; free.

Northwest Seaport (Waterway 19, Northlake Way at Lake Union) has steam-driven lightship, 3-masted sailing schooner that transported lumber and cod, and other vessels; exhibits of maritime history, fishing gear, lifesaving; open mid-June-mid-Sept., Tues.-Sun. noon-9; rest of yr, Tues.-Sun. noon-5; closed Jan. 1, Easter, Thnks, Dec. 25; sm adm. **Lake Washington Shipyard** (across Lake Washington in surburban Kirland), an 1889 building, is being restored with examples of early Lake Washington boats and other displays; inquire for hrs.

SPOKANE: Chamber of Commerce (W 1020 Riverside, zip 99210) provides information on industrial tours and special events.

Eastern Washington State Historical Society (W 2316 1st Ave.) preserves 1898 Campbell House, of brick and stucco with half-timber trim, typical of the elegance developed on gold mining fortunes (fine woodwork, a fireplace embellished with gold, period furnishings); art gallery; historical displays include dioramas of 1818 Fort Spokane, 1850s Cataldo Mission; regional archaeological artifacts and Indian arts; pioneer relics; minerals; regional wildlife; open Tues.-Sat. 10-5, Sun. 2-5; closed hols; free. **Pacific Northwest Indian Center** (E 500 Cataldo Ave.), in 5-story circular tower; outstanding collections; furnished longhouse; weapons; clothing; tools; artifacts from Marmes Rock Shelter; petroglyphs set into lobby wall; inquire locally for hrs.

Gonzaga University (E 502 Boone Ave.), with Bing Crosby library and memorabilia; documents on Jesuit missionary work in the Northwest; open daily 8-5 in summer, Mon.-Sat. 8 am-10 pm & Sun. 1-5 during academic year; free. **Cathedral of St. John the Evangelist** (127 E 12th Ave. at Grand Blvd), a 1925 Gothic church; outstanding interior wood carving; English carillon; 5000-pipe organ; lovely baptismal font; stained-glass windows; open daily; guided tours Mon-Fri. 10-4; carillon and organ recitals.

Spokane House (9 m NW on SR 291 in Riverside State Park) is a modern museum on site of first permanent white settlement in Washington, a trading post of the same name built 1810 by the North West Co.; in 1812, John Jacob Astor's Pacific Fur Co. opened a competing fort nearby, and eventually the posts combined under Hudson's Bay Co. aegis; but the site, 60 m from the main artery of transportation, the Columbia River, was inconvenient, and in 1826 the post was moved to Kettle Falls; Spokane House was stripped to provide building materials for the new post; excavated foundations; artifacts; exhibits on the fur trade; open late May-Sept., Tues.-Sun. 10-5; free.

   Steptoe Battlefield (32 m S off US 195) was site of an 1858 defeat of the army, which fled during the night, by area Indians; interpretive signs. **Spokane Plains Battlefield** (10 m W on US 2 at Dover Rd.) was site of 1858 defeat of Coeur d'Alene, Palouse, and Spokane Indians by U.S. troops; interpretive marker. **Spokane Painted Rock** (9 m NW on Little Spokane River near Rutter Pkwy Bridge) are Indian Pictographs; interpretive marker.

TACOMA: Chamber of Commerce (752 Broadway, zip 98401) provides information; **Totem Pole** (9th & A Sts.) carved by Alaskan Indians. **Old Tacoma City Hall** (7th & Pacific), handsome 1893 brick building in ornate Italianate style with bell tower; now houses boutiques and cafes. **Northern Pacific Passenger Station** (1713 Pacific Ave.), built 1911, has terrazzo floors, Italian marble walls, copper-faced ceiling in waiting room.

   State Historical Society Museum (315 N Stadium Way) depicts life in the area from prehistoric to pioneer times; illuminated photomurals; dioramas, models; also exhibits on Alaska; Oriental displays; excellent library contains journal by missionary Narcissa Whitman and other rare works; open Tues.-Sat. 9-4; closed hols; free. **Tacoma Art Museum** (12th St. & Pacific Ave.), 19-20th-C American works, temporary exhibits; children's gallery; open Mon.-Sat. 10-4, Sun. noon-4; closed hols; free. **St. Peter's Chapel-at-Ease** (2909 N Starr St. at N 29th St.), built 1873, organ and bell were shipped around Cape Horn; 9-11th-C manuscripts displayed; open June-Labor Day, daily 11-7; rest of yr, Sat. & Sun. 11-7; free.

   Point Defiance Park (4 m N at end of Pearl St.) contains: **Fort Nisqually,** replica of the Hudson's Bay Co. fur-trading post built 1833, incorporating original Factor's House and Granary; authentically furnished buildings (open Tues.-Sun. 8-dark; closed day after hols); museum with displays on fur trade, early agriculture, Hudson's Bay Co. artifacts (open Tues.-Sun.1-5; closed Dec. 25 & day after hols); free. **Camp Six Logging Museum,** reconstructed logging camp typical of those in Washington from 1880-1940; rare equipment; historic exhibits; logging locomotive; open daily 10-dark; free. **Job Carr House,** first home in Tacoma, built 1865; open daily dawn-dark; free.

   Ezra Meeker Mansion (6 m SE to 321 E Pioneer Ave. in Puyallup), built 1890, was home of the Hop King of the World; Meeker crossed the plains by covered wagon and named the city (Puyallup means "generous people"); in the early 1900s he recrossed the Oregon Trail, marking it and erecting monuments in a campaign to preserve it; at age 76 he crossed the trail by ox-drawn wagon, later by automobile, and, at age 94, by plane; his home has Victorian carved woodwork, ornate fireplaces, stained-glass windows; open in summer, Sat. & Sun. 1-5; rest of yr., Sun. 1-5 closed Dec.-Jan; adm. A statue of Meeker is in Pioneer Park (S Meridian St. & 3rd Ave.). **Frontier Museum** (2301 23rd Ave. SE., Puyallup) houses exhibits on logging; pioneer and Indian artifacts; open Wed.-Sun. 9-5; closed Easter, Thnks, Dec. 25; adm.

VANCOUVER: Clark County Historical Museum (1511 Main St. at 16th St.) offers dioramas of Ft. Vancouver and Hudson's Bay Co. history; 1890 country store; pioneer doctor's office; dolls; early printing press; Indian and pioneer artifacts; railroad exhibit; open Tues.-Sun. 1-5; closed hols; free. **St. James Church** (12th & Washington St.), 1884 Gothic-style structure, has Belgian hand-carved reredos and altar; ornate pulpit; open daily. **Covington House** (4303 Main St.), built 1846, was log home of English family that came to teach the children of Hudson's Bay Co. employees at Ft. Vancouver; open June-Aug., Tues. Thurs. 10-4; free. Several other buildings in town, and Cedar Creek Grist Mill (10 m E on county rd 16) also date from the 19th-C.

Ulysses S. Grant Museum (1106 E Evergreen Blvd), log house erected 1849, was Grant's office while he was quartermaster here 1852-3; officers' mess and offices were downstairs, living quarters upstairs; Grant furniture, petroglyphs and Indian artifacts; pioneer and military relics; open Fri.-Wed. 1-4; closed Thnks, Dec. 25; sm adm.

Fort Vancouver National Historic Site (E Evergreen Blvd); fort was established 1825 by the Hudson's Bay Co. to strengthen British claims to territory N of the Columbia River; it remained the economic, political, and social hub of the Pacific Northwest for 2 decades, and was center of the British commercial empire W of the Rockies, S to California, and N to Alaska. The fort was surrounded by mills, forges, and other early industry; its orchards and cultivated fields stretched for miles along the river. Here were the first school, circulating library, theater, and church of the NW. The fort was stockaded and mounted with cannon (never needed); within its walls were company storehouses, shops, workshops, church, jail, powder magazine, and dwellings for company officers; outside the stockade, in wooden houses, lived tradsmen, artisans, boatmen, and laborers; in 1866 the fort burned; it is being authentically reconstructed through excavation of the original building sites; bakery, blockhouse, and other structures completed; **Visitor Center** has exhibits and audiovisual program; open Mon.-Fri. 8-5; Sat., Sun., hols 9-5; closed Jan. 1, Thnks, Dec. 25; free.

WALLA WALLA: Fort Walla Walla Park (W edge of town off SR 125) occupies site of 1818 trading post erected on old Indian trail that became important pioneer route; a fort was erected during the Indian Wars of 1855-58; **Pioneer Village Museum** consists of original buildings and replicas—log cabins, railroad depot, blacksmith shop, school, doctor's office, blockhouse—with authentic furnishings and historic displays; covered wagon; open early May-late Sept., Sat. & Sun. 1-5; adm.

Whitman Mission National Historic Site (7 m W off US 12): Narcissa Whitman and Eliza Spalding were the first American women to cross the continent overland, arriving with their husbands in the NW in 1836 to establish missions to the Indians. The Spaldings began work at Lapwai (Idaho) among the Nez Perce, while Marcus and Narcissa Whitman worked among the Cayuse here at Waiilatpu. Devising an alphabet, the Whitmans and Spaldings printed, in Nez Perce and Spokan, the first books published in the Pacific Northwest. But the Indians proved indifferent to Christianity; also, they left for long periods on buffalo hunts, and the Whitmans failed to convince them to adopt a sedentary farming life near the mission. Meanwhile, the mission became an important station on the Oregon Trail, and the Whitmans cared for the ill and exhausted. These whites brought measles, to which the Cayuse had no resistance, and half the tribe died. Although Whitman treated whites and Indians alike, the Cayuse, noting that his medicine worked only on whites, concluded he was poisoning them to make way for white settlement; in 1847 they attacked the mission, killing the Whitmans and 11 others, taking 50 captives (later ransomed by the Hudson's Bay Co.), and destroying the mission buildings. The massacre ended Protestant missionary work among the Oregon Indians and led to the settler war against the Cayuse. **Visitor Center** depicts missionary activity in the NW; self-guiding trails to partially restored mission site, common grave of massacre victims, and Whitman memorial; open Memorial Day-Labor Day, daily 8-8; rest of yr, daily 8-4:30; closed Jan. 1, Thnks, Dec. 25; free. (Marcus Whitman's letters and papers are housed in the library of Whitman College, at 345 Boyer Ave., Walla Walla.)

WENATCHEE: North Central Washington Museum (2 S Chelan at Douglas Sts.), with totem pole at door, houses petroglyphs and other prehistoric and recent Indian artifacts; pioneer room and displays; exhibits on local apple industry; minerals; mounted regional fauna; memorabilia of Hugh Herndon and Clyde Pangborn, who made first transpacific flight in 1931; regional art; open Mon.-Fri. 10-5, Sat. 1-5; closed hols; free.

Rocky Reach Dam (7 m N on US 97) offers Information Center with underwater fish viewing gallery; observation deck; history of electricity in powerhouse; archaeological displays, Indian artifacts; geology exhibits; open daily 8-sunset; free.

Willis Carey Historical Museum (12 m NW on US 2 to E end of Cashmere); outstanding Indian artifacts from prehistoric times to present; 19th-C Western buildings moved here to create typical community (log mission, miners' assay office, homesteaders' cabins, other buildings); demonstrations and special events; open Apr.-Oct., Mon.-Sat. 10-5, Sun. 1-5; free.

YAKIMA: Yakima Valley Museum (2105 Tieton Dr. in Franklin Park); artifacts of Yakima Indians; exhibits, including restored post office, blacksmith shop, pioneer kitchen, trace history of white settlement; glassware, minerals, other displays; open Wed.-Fri. 10-4, Sun. 2-5, but check for closings around hols; free. The Naches Pass Wagon Road, used 1853-97 and requiring 68 crossings of the turbulent Naches River, is marked W of town.

Fort Simcoe Historical State Park (15 m S on US 97 to Toppenish, then 28 m W on SR 220): At this ancient Yakima Indian center, know as Mool-Mool (bubbling water), U.S. infantry established a fort 1856-9 as a consequence of Indian hostility toward settlers and gold miners. It took 2 years to bring in building materials by mule train from Ft. Dalles; original fort buildings include the rather grand commandant's house, 3 lesser homes for captains, and a log blockhouse; interpretive center with exhibits and relics; open Apr.-Aug., Tues.-Sun. 10-5; free.

Union Gap Pioneer Cemetery (3 m SE on US 97), site of first trading post in area, has monuments marking battles between Yakima Indians and settlers. **Ahtanum Mission** (9 m SW on local rds), founded 1852, was destroyed in the Yakima Indian Wars and rebuilt in 1867. **Sunnyside Museum** (35 m SE on US 12 to 4th St. & Grand Ave. in Sunnyside) has Indian artifacts; pioneer kitchen and relics; local historic exhibits; open Mar.-Dec., Tues., Thurs., Sun. 1:30-4:30; sm adm. **Yakima Painted Rocks** (5 m NW on US 12) are Indian rock art on the old Yakima trail to the Wenas Mountains; interpretive marker.

WEST VIRGINIA

BECKLEY: Exhibition Coal Mine (in New River Park, N Oakwood Ave.) offers tours of underground tunnels; exhibits; open May-Sept. daily 10-6; adm. *Honey in the Rock,* a Civil War drama, and *Hatfields & McCoys,* a musical about the famous family feud, are presented in summer. At **Talcott** (31 m SE on SR3) is Big Bend Tunnel, where John Henry died trying to beat the steam drill; John Henry Memorial Park is being developed.

BERKELEY SPRINGS: Berkeley Springs Park, with warm springs and state-owned baths, is oldest spa in nation; popular in colonial times, after Washington had surveyed the area for Lord Fairfax in 1748. On hill above the springs is Old Castle, built 1887, a replica of a Norman castle.

BLUEFIELD: Pocahontas Exhibition Mine (9 m NW on SR 102) has tunnels you can walk or drive through; guided tours; open mid-Apr.-Nov. daily 8-6; sm adm. At **Skyland** (2 m S on US 21), Museum of the Hills displays antique loom, guns, other Appalachian relics (June-Labor Day, daily 10-5; sm adm); Mountain Crafts Shop displays and sells merchandise hand-made in the mountains (June-Aug. daily 9-9; Apr.-May & Sept.-Dec. 25, weather permitting, daily 10-5). **Alexander Arts Center** (12 m NE on US 19, 460 on Concord College campus, Princeton), weaving display and art gallery; open daily 8-4:30; closed Jan. 1, Thnks, Dec. 25; free.

CHARLESTON: State Capitol (on E Kanawha Blvd.), on the river, is a fine design by Cass Gilbert; golden dome; guided tours; contains State Museum with historical artifacts, natural history displays; open Mon.-Sat. 9-5, Sun. 1-5; closed Jan. 1, Thnks, Dec. 25; free. **Sunrise** (746 Myrtle Rd.), mansion and other buildings housing art gallery, planetarium, children's museum, library, garden center; open June-Aug., Tues.-Sat. 10-4, Sun. 1-5; Sept.-May, Tues.-Sat. 10-5, Sun. 1-5; closed hols; free exc planetarium. **West Virginia State College** (8 m W on SR 25 in Institute) has Asian art exhibited in library (Mon.-Sat. 9-5, Sun. 1-5) and temporary exhibits in Davis Fine Arts Gallery; free.

CHARLES TOWN: Laid out 1786 by George Washington and named for his brother Charles, with streets named for other family members, this aristocratic old town in best known as site of the John Brown trial and hanging. **Jefferson County Courthouse** (N George & E Washington Sts.), built 1836 on land donated by Charles Washington, was scene of John Brown's 1859 trial for treason after his raid on Harpers Ferry; open Mon.-Fri. 9-5, Sat. 9-noon; closed hols; free. Site of Old Jail (S George & W Washington Sts.) in which John Brown was held awaiting trial is marked with a tablet. **Jefferson County Museum** (E Washington & N Samuel Sts.) displays John Brown memorabilia; open Apr.-Oct., Tues.-Sat. 10-4; free. Gallows (S Samuel & Hunter Sts.) on which John Brown was hanged is marked with a pyramid of stones from his jail cell; 1500 militiamen (including John Wilkes Booth and Stonewall Jackson) surrounded the scaffold during the execution to maintain order.

Zion Episcopal Church (E Congress & S Church Sts.) cemetery has graves of about 75 Washington family members; open daily 7-5. **Claymount Court** (Summit Point Rd.), home of George Washington's grandnephew Bushrod, and **Happy Retreat** (Blakely Pl.), home of Charles Washington 1774 until his death in 1797, are privately owned.

CLARKSBURG: This was Stonewall Jackson's birthplace in 1824 (the site is marked with a tablet at 328 W Main St), and his statue is in front of the courthouse. **Amy Roberts Vance House** (123 W Main St.) houses collections of Harrison County Historical Society; open June-Aug., Mon.-Sat. 2-4; Sept.-May, Sat. 2-4; sm adm.

Watters Smith Memorial State Park (9 m SE off US 19), pioneer farm of late 1700s on Duck Creek; Visitor Center exhibits on early farming. **Salem College** (12 M W in Salem) has restored Fort New Salem with exhibits in 20 log cabins from throughout the state; open daily 10-4; closed school hols; sm adm. **West Virginia Wesleyan College** (7 m E on US 50, 22 m S on I-79, 10 m E on US 33 to College Ave., Buckhannon) is noted for Wesley Chapel with pink marble altar, sculptures of 12 disciples; artifacts of United Methodist Church history; open daily. **Andrews Church** (20 m E on US 50 in Grafton) is known as Mother's Day Church; here Mother's Day was first celebrated in 1908 at the request of Anna Jarvis, still in mourning for her mother who had died 3 years earlier; she spent the rest of her life and all her money promoting Mother's Day, and died penniless in 1948. **Jackson's Mill Museum** (20 m S on US 19 on grounds of Jackson's Mill State 4-H Camp), where Stonewall Jackson spent his boyhood, has exhibits on the area in his day; open June-Sept., Mon.-Sat. 10:30-5, Sun. 1:30-5; free.

HARPERS FERRY: The gap where the Shenandoah and Potomac Rivers meet—a view Thomas Jefferson claimed was worth "a trip across the Atlantic" to see—was chosen by Robert Harper in 1747 as site for his home, flour mill, and ferry; by mid-19th-C it was an important arms-producing center with armory, arsenal, and mills, and an important rail center. On Oct. 16, 1859, abolitionist John Brown—fresh from bloody antislavery campaigns in Kansas—attempted to mount a slave rebellion here. Taking the town by surprise, he and 18 followers seized the arsenal and barricaded themselves in the engine house. On Oct. 19, Col. Robert E. Lee and Lt. J.E.B. Stuart stormed the engine house with 90 Marines, killing 10 of the raiders (including 2 of Brown's sons) and capturing Brown. Tried in Charles Town for murder, treason, and conspiring with slaves to commit treason, Brown was found guilty and hanged on Dec. 2, 1859. The incident sharpened tension in North and South. When Virginia seceded from the Union in Apr. 1861, Confederates planned to take this strategic town and its store of arms, but Federals set fire to the arsenal and armory, destroying weapons and machinery, as they retreated. Throughout the Civil War, Harpers Ferry continued to be occupied intermittently by North and South, and its remaining industrial capacity was destroyed. An attempt to rebuild the town after the war was defeated by devastating floods in 1870 and 1889. **Harpers Ferry National Historical Park** preserves some 1500 acres of the town, with homes, shops, and other buildings restored as they were in John Brown's day. **Visitor Center** (in 1826 Stagecoach Inn, Shenandoah St.) offers exhibits, audiovisual program, brochures for auto and walking tours; living history programs; open daily 8-5 (longer in summer); closed Jan. 1, Dec. 25; free. Among restored buildings are: **Master Armorer's House Museum,** built 1859 as home of chief gunsmith; exhibits on gunmaking; among weapons produced at Harper's Ferry were breech-loading flintlock rifles, with interchangeable parts, an early example of mass production. **Arsenal Square,** with remains of arsenal and muskets burned in the Federal retreat of 1861. **John Brown's Fort** (the fire engine house where Brown and his followers barricaded themselves.) **Gerald B. Wager Bldg.,** built 1836-8, with museum of John Brown's life. **Harper House,** oldest surviving structure in town, built by John Harper 1775-82; period furnishings. **Marmion Row Houses,** 3 buildings erected 1832-50, with pre-Civil War furnishings. **Lockwood House,** built 1848 for the armory paymaster, was one of the best (and best insulated) homes of the period; during the Civil War it was used as hq, barracks and stable by North and South; in 1864-5 it was opened as a school for freed slaves by Julia Mann (niece of educator Horace Mann) and later was a college.

HUNTINGTON: Huntington Galleries (2033 McCoy Rd., Park Hills), with wing designed by Walter Gropius; European painting, many American works; contemporary art; sculpture court; European decorative arts; Georgian silver; arms; prayer rugs; mountain arts and crafts; pre-Columbian works; open Tues.-Sat. 10-4, Sun. 1-5; closed Jan. 1, Dec. 25;

free. **Marshall University** (4th Ave. & 16th St.), named for Chief Justice John Marshall, has geology museum and Shakespeare Room (open Mon.-Sat.; closed hols); free.

MARLINGTON: National Radio Astronomy Observatory (9 m SE on SR 39, then 21 m N on SR 28 in Green Bank) offers film and guided bus tour; mid-June-Labor Day, daily 9-4; after Labor Day-Oct. Sat. & Sun. 9-4; free. **Cranberry Mountain Visitor Center** (8 m S on US 219 to Mill Point, then 7 m NW on SR 39), in Monongahela National Forest, offers exhibits on ecology and forestry; open June-Sept. daily 9:30-5:30; free. **Pearl S. Buck Birthplace Museum** (10 m S on US 219 at Hillsboro), memorabilia of novelist who won Pulitzer and Nobel prizes; open May-Oct., Mon.-Sat. 9-5, Sun. 1-5; adm. **Droop Mountain Battlefield State Park** (13 m S on US 219), site of 1863 victory over Confederate forces that ended resistance to the Union in West Virginia, is marked with monuments, breastworks, graves.

MOOREFIELD: Lost River State Park (33 m SE via SR 55, 259) contains an original log cabin, restored as a museum, of Lee's White Sulphur Springs, a once-famous spa; open Memorial Day-Labor Day, Daily 10-6; free.

MORGANTOWN: West Virginia University offers: Archaeological Museum (White Hall, downtown campus) with artifacts from the Stone Age to the 19th-C; open Mon.-Fri. 8-4:30; closed hols; free. Pharmacy Museum (room 1132 of Basic Sciences Bldg., Medical Center campus) with display of old medications; open Mon.-Fri. 8:15-5; closed hols;

MOOREFIELD: Lost River State Park (33 m SE via SR 55, 259) contains an original log cabin, restored as a museum, of Lee's White Sulphur Springs, a once-famous spa; open Memorial Day-Labor Day, daily 10-6; free.

MORGANTOWN: West Virginia University offers: Archaeological Museum (White Hall, downtown campus) with artifacts from the Stone Age to the 19th-C; open Mon.-Fri. 8-4:30; closed hols; free. Pharmacy Museum (room 1132 of Basic Sciences Bldg., Medical Center campus) with display of old medications; open Mon.-Fri. 8:15-5; closed hols; free.

POINT PLEASANT: Tu-Endie-Wei Park (100 Main St.), Indian name meaning "point between 2 waters," commemorates first battle of the American Revolution, at the point where the Ohio and Kanawha Rivers meet; here on Oct. 10, 1774, the British incited Shawnees, commanded by the great chief Cornstalk, to battle 1100 frontiersmen for the area; the one-day battle was won by the settlers. Mansion House, built as an inn in 1796, is a log building restored as a museum (open Apr.-Nov. daily 9-5; donation). Also in park is the grave of Mad Anne Bailey, a pioneer woman soldier and border scout.

SUMMERSVILLE: Carnifex Ferry Battlefield State Park (6 m S on US 19, then NW off SR 129) was site of 1861 victory by Federals under Gen. Rosecrans over a smaller Confederate force; Patterson House Museum displays relics of the Civil War; open May-early Sept., daily 8 am-10 pm; free.

WHEELING: Fort Henry Site (Main St. near 11th St.) is marked with a plaque; here the last battle of the Revolution was fought at a fort built 1774 by Col. Ebenezer Zane and named for Patrick Henry; in 1782, not having heard that the war was over, British and Indians attacked the fort, which soon ran out of powder. Betty Zane, Ebenezer's younger sister, ran through the fire to the Zane cabin for powder that saved the fort. Her heroism has been recorded in a novel by Zane Grey, a descendant. **Oglebay Park** (5 m NE on SR 88) contains Mansion Museum of early Ohio Valley life; good collection of glass; period rooms; open Mon.-Sat. 9:30-5, Sun. & hols 1:30-5; closed Jan. 1, Thnks, Dec. 24, 25, 31; adm. The park also has art gallery, nature center, zoo, outdoor theater, other facilities; special events. **Campbell Mansion** (12 m NE on SR 88 to Bethany College campus in Bethany) was home of founder of the Disciples of Christ and of the college; antique furnishings; study; schoolhouse; open Apr.-Nov. daily 10-noon, 2-5; donation.

WHITE SULPHUR SPRINGS: Greenbrier Hotel owns the springs popular in colonial days for curative vacations; the former hotel on the site, Old White, hosted many presidents and was honeymoon site for John Tyler. **Coal House** is made of coal; inhabited; privately owned. Nearby **Sweet Springs** (5 m E on I-64, then 14 m S on SR 311) and **Salt Sulphur Springs** (10 m W on I-64, 20 m S on US 219, then 5 m SE), no longer spas, were also popular in colonial times and have buildings surviving from what era. **Lewisburg** (10 m W on I-64, 2 m S on US 219), settled before the revolution by Scots-Irish from Virginia, has restored Colonial buildings and streets with gas lamps; restored pioneer Fort Savannah; Old Stone Church; Lewisburg Museum & Library with pioneer displays; Chamber of Commerce provides brochures for walking tours.

WISCONSIN

APPLETON: Dard Hunter Paper Museum (1043 E South River St.), papermaking from AD 105 to 20th-C; early handmade papers; replica of German mill, model of village mill from India; open Mon.-Fri. 8-noon, 1-5; closed hols; free.

Doty Grand Loggery (6 m S on SR 47 to Doty Park, 5th & Lincoln Sts., Neenah), home of state's second territorial governor; personal belongings, Indian relics, area historic displays; open mid-June-Aug., Tues.-Sun. 1-5; donation. **Bergstrom Art Center & Museum** (165 N Park Ave., Neenah), in Tudor-style former residence on Lake Winnebago; 900 paperweights, many rare examples; antique glass from Austria and Germany; Victorian glass; regional painting; open June-Aug., Tues.-Thurs., Sat., Sun. 1-5; rest of yr, Wed., Thurs., Sat., Sun. 1-5; closed hols; free. **Grignon Home Historical Museum** (8 m E off US 41 on Augustine St. in Kaukauna), 1836 frame home of settler family; family pieces from French period; Indian relics; open Memorial Day-Labor Day, Tues.-Sun. 11-5; sm adm. **New London Public Museum** (18 m NW on SR 76, US 45 to 412 S Pearl St., New London) has Indian and pioneer relics; wildlife display; open June-Aug., Tues.-Fri. 1-5, Sat. 11-4; Sept.-May, Wed.-Fri. 2:30-5, Sat. 11-4; free.

BALSAM LAKE: Polk County Historical Museum (in Polk County Center) has regional historic exhibits (open Mon.-Fri. 8:30-4:30; closed hols; free); a block W is Polk County Rural Life Museum (open Memorial Day-Labor Day, Mon.-Fri. 10-12, 1-3; free).

BARABOO: Circus World Museum (426 Water St.), outstanding collection of circus memorabilia covering 15 acres of what was once Ringling Bros. winter quarters; over 100 gilded and carved wagons; miniature circus; costumes; rigging; tools; photos, posters; materials come from many countries; life-size re-created sideshow includes Tom Thumb; demonstrations of circus skills and crafts, performances, rides, annual parade; extensive library with archives of circus families, companies; open mid-May-mid-Sept. daily 9:30-6; adm. **Sauk County Historical Museum** (531 4th Ave.), minerals, Indian artifacts, Civil War relics, guns, pioneer memorabilia; open mid-May-late Sept., Tues.-Sun. 2-5; sm adm.

Old Indian Agency House (17 m E on SR 33 to Portage, then 1 m E on

Agency House Rd.) was erected in 1832 at portage where Indian had to carry their canoes between the Fox and Wisconsin Rivers; the portage was used by explorers and trappers until a canal was built to connect the rivers; the house was built for John Kinzie, agent to the Winnebago Indians; furnishings include Hitchcock chairs, banjo clock, piano, all made before 1833; Winnebago artifacts; open May-Oct. daily 9-5; rest of yr on request; closed Dec. 25; adm. Nearby **Fort Winnebago Surgeons' Quarters** (on SR 33) is only surviving building from 1828 fort; frontier furnishings, historic exhibits; on grounds in furnished 1850 Garrison School; open May-Oct. daily 9-5; adm.

Devil's Lake State Park (3 m S on SR 123): Ice Age Nature Center with exhibits on regional glaciation, naturalist programs, interpretive trails; several Indian mounds. **Sauk-Prairie Museum** (17 m S on US 12 to 626 Water St., Sauk City) has historic displays on this old river port; open Memorial Day-Labor Day, Sun. & hols 2-5; free. **Mid-Continent Railway Museum** (6 m W off SR 136 near N Freedom): locomotives, coaches, cars, cabooses; steam-train rides; open Memorial Day-Labor Day, daily 10-6; Sun. 10-6 in fall; adm. **Winnebago Public Indian Museum & Settlement** (18 m N off US 12 to jct SR 13, River Rd.) has Winnebago artifacts and historic displays; open June-Aug. 8 am-10 pm; rest of yr, 8-6; free.

BAYFIELD: Apostle Islands National Lakeshore has a Visitor Center (11 m NW at Sand Bay) open Memorial Day-Labor Day daily 8-5; rest of yr, Sat. & Sun. 8-5. **Madeline Island** (frequent ferries Apr.-Dec. from Bayfield) was home of Chippewa Indians and fur trading base for Voyageurs and English traders; Madeline Island Historic Museum consists of 4 hand-hewn-log structures near the old fur company dock, surrounded by a stockade; old jail, pioneer barn, American Fur Co. building, all with memorabilia of logging and fur trade; Old Sailor's Home with period furnishings; open mid-May-mid-Sept. daily 11-4; sm adm. **Red Cliff Indian Reservation** (3 m N on SR 13) has an Arts & Crafts Museum with Chippewa beadwork, painting, crafts. **Cornucopia** (21 m W on SR 13) has one of Wisconsin's few Russian Orthodox churches.

BEAVER DAM: Dodge County Museum (127 S Spring St.), in 1882 railroad depot; early autos; exhibits on railroads; pewter, spinning wheels, dolls, china; open Mon.-Sat. & 2nd Sun. of month, 2-5; closed hols; free.

BELOIT: Beloit College (on US 51) offers: **T. L. Wright Art Center,** with Lucas Cranach painting, German Expressionist and Post-Impressionist graphics; Korean pottery; Oriental art objects; open Mon.-Fri. 10-5, 7-9, Sat. 10-5, Sun. 2-5; free. **Logan Museum of Anthropology:** excellent collection of Stone Age artifacts from Europe and America; full-scale reproduction of Pueblo dwelling; N and S American Indian arts and tools; miscellaneous pieces from Africa and New Guinea; open Mon.-Fri. 9-noon, 1-4, Sat. 9-noon; closed school hols; free. On campus are prehistoric Indian mounds.

Rasey House (517 Prospect Ave.), built of cobblestones by Beloit College in 1850; Early American pressed glass goblets, other exhibits; open on request (phone 362-2419); sm adm. **Bartlett Memorial Historical Museum** (2149 St. Lawrence Ave.), in barn and house built of limestone in 1850, has fine relics of pioneer life and Norwegian settlers; Indian artifacts; farm machinery; early glass; dolls; excellent library; relics from 4 wars; open Wed.-Sun. 1-4; closed hols; sm adm.

DOOR COUNTY: Door County Historical Museum (18 N 4th Ave. at Michigan St., Sturgeon Bay): Indian and pioneer artifacts; farm tools; maritime relics; country store; open mid-May-mid-Oct., Tues.-Sat. 10-noon, 1-5; closed hols; free. **Robert La Salle County Park** (SE of Sturgeon Bay on Lake Michigan) has monument on site where the La Salle party was saved from starvation by Indians. **The Farm** (5 m N of Sturgeon Bay on SR 57), a pioneer homestead with farm animals; open Memorial Day-Labor Day, daily 9-5; adm. **Boynton Chapel** (19 m N on SR 57 in Baileys Harbor) is a replica of a Scandinavian stavkirke.4**Eagle Bluff Lighthouse Museum** (18 m N of Sturgeon Bay off SR 42 in Peninsula State Park), 1868 lighthouse; original furnishings; exhibits on life of lightkeepers; open mid-June-Labor Day, daily 10-6; sm adm. **Ephraim** (28 m N of Sturgeon Bay on SR 42) has furnished Pioneer Schoolhouse (open July-Labor Day, Mon.-Sat. 9-5; free); Anderson Store & Museum, a restored pioneer country store (open July-Labor Day, Mon.-Sat. 10-noon, 2-5; donation); monument commemorating landing of Moravians in 1853. **Washington Island** (reached by ferry from Gills Rock, 42 m N of Sturgeon Bay on SR 42) offers: Washington Island Museum (Little Lake Rd.), with Indian artifacts, fossils and minerals, relics of Icelandic settlers, who arrived here in 1869; open mid-June-mid-Sept. daily 10-4; Memorial Day-mid-June & mid-Sept-mid-Oct., daily 11:30-2; sm adm. Rock Island State Park contains summer home of C. H. Thoradarson in Icelandic style, and 1836 lighthouse.

EAU CLAIRE: Paul Bunyan Logging Camp Museum (Carson Park) is a re-created 1890s logging camp with bunkhouse, cook's shanty, dining hall, blacksmith shop, stables, all authentically furnished; open mid-May-Aug. daily 9:30-5:30; Sept., Thurs.-Mon. 9:30-5:30; free.

Durand Railroad Depot (29 m SW on SR 85 to 407 W Wells St., Durand), in 1882 depot with ticket office; exhibits on early railroads, county history; open early June-Sept., Sat., Sun., hols 2-5;

free. **Independence** (33 m S on SR 93), Polish community on Bugle Lake, has 1895 S.S. Peter & Paul Church with lovely stained-glass windows.

ELKHORN: Webster House (9 E Rockwell St.), an 1830s land office, was later home of J.P. Webster, composer of "In the Sweet By and By"; family mementos; county historical items; open May-Sept., Tues.-Sat. 10-noon, 1-5, Sun. & hols 1-5; Oct., Sat. & Sun. 10-5; sm adm. **Yerkes Astronomical Observatory** (6½ m S on SR 67 to Williams Bay) with 40-in refracting telescope and astronomical exhibits, offers lectures June-Sept., Sat. 1:30-3; rest of yr, Sat. 10-noon; closed hols; free. **East Troy Trolley Museum** (12 m NE on SR 15 to 300 Church St., E Troy): railway exhibits in former depot; trolley rides; open Memorial Day-Labor Day daily noon-5; after Labor Day-Dec. 24, Sat., Sun., hols noon-dusk; adm. Also in E Troy is **Obie's Cobblestone Inn** (town square), built 1843 by a man who gathered stones in nearby river and lake beds and hauled them to town by wagon; Lincoln was a guest here.

FOND DU LAC: Historic Galloway House & Village (336 E Pioneer Rd.): Replica of 1890s village with 30-room Victorian mansion noted for stenciled ceilings, ornate woodwork, square tower, original furnishings; pioneer tools, household items, dolls, other period displays are in log house, country store, workshops, school, gristmill, printshop, other buildings; open Memorial Day-Sept., Tues.-Sun. 1-4; adm. **St. Paul's Cathedral** (51 W Division St.), fine stained-glass windows; life-size wood carvings of Apostles made in Oberammergau, Germany; cloister garden; open daily 7-5:30.

    Old Wade House State Park (17 m E on SR 23, 2 m N on County P, then SW via County P & A in Greenbush) honors pioneers; mid-19th-C Wade House, stagecoach inn, restored with period furnishings; Butternut House, smokehouse, blacksmith shop, sugaring cabin, carriage museum with horse-drawn vehicles; open May-Oct. daily 9-5; adm. **Little White Schoolhouse** (19 m W on SR 23 to Blackburn St. in Ripon): here the Republican Party was first organized; open Memorial Day-Labor Day, Mon.-Sat. 9-4, Sun. noon-4; rest of Sept., Sat. & Sun. 9-4; sm adm. Nearby **Long House** (W edge of town) is a replica of one built by followers of 19th-C French socialist Francois Fourier; the 600-acre settlement soon disbanded.

GREEN BAY: Cotton House (2632 S Webster Ave.), fine example of Greek Revival architecture, built 1840; period furnishings; on grounds is Baird Law Office, erected in the 1830s, first law office in state; open May-Oct., Tues.-Sat. 10-5, Sun. 2-5; closed hols; sm adm. **Hazelwood** (1008 S Monroe Ave.), built 1837; here state constitution was drafted;

modest building, but interior reflects lifestyle of prosperous frontier living; open Apr.-Oct., Tues.-Sat. 10-5, Sun. 2-5; closed hols; sm adm. **Roi-Porlier-Tank Cottage** (860 5th St. at 10th Ave.), oldest house in Wisconsin, built 1776; period furnishings; open May-Oct., Tues.-Sat. 10-noon, 1-4, Sun. 2-4; closed hols; sm adm. **Fort Howard Hospital Museum** (402 N Chestnut St. at Kellog St.): 1816 hospital and ward building (open May-Oct.) and Officers' quarters (open June-Aug.) housing antique silver, cherry furniture, crystal, relics of fort life, displays on Green Bay; open Tues.-Sat. 10-11:30, 1-4:30, Sun. 2-4:30; closed hols; sm adm. **Neville Public Museum** (129 S Jefferson St.), anthropology exhibits including Old Copper Culture and cultures of Mississippi Indians; regional history, natural history, art, geology; open Mon.-Sat. 9-5, Sun. 2-5; free. **National Railroad Museum** (2285 S Broadway on the Fox River) has fine display of locomotives, cars, engines; hundreds of relics in depot; rides; open Memorial Day-Labor Day, daily 9:30-5; also weekends in spring & fall; adm.

Von Stiehl Winery (23 m E on SR 54 to 115 Navarino St., Algoma) offers tours May-Oct. daily 9-5; free. **Kewaunee County Jail Museum** (28 m E on SR 29 to courthouse square in Kewaunee), in 1876 jail, has 9 rooms displaying regional relics; open Memorial Day-Labor Day, Thurs.-Sun. 12:30-4; sm adm.

HAYWARD: Historyland (E on County B) offers tours of Chippewa Village, where Indians demonstrate trapping, leather-tanning, other skills; tours of Wisconsin logging camp with lumbering demonstrations; excursions on paddlewheel steamboat; open late June-Labor Day, Sun.-Fri. 10-8 for tours; area open daily mid-May-mid-Oct.; separate adm for each section.

HUDSON: Octagon House (1004 3rd St.), authentically furnished 1855 home; doll collection; Carriage and Garden House, country store, blacksmith shop, lumbering exhibits, sleighs, farm machinery, other exhibits; open May-Oct., Tues.-Sat. 10-12, 2-5, Sun. 2-5; adm.

JANESVILLE: Tallman Restorations (440 N Jackson St.) is highlighted by Tallman House, an Italian-style villa built 1857 by a land speculator; grandest home in Wisconsin before Civil War, with hidden attic room where escaping slaves stayed; Lincoln stayed a weekend in 1859 when he came to debate the slavery issue in Janesville; many original furnishings. Also here are 1842 Stone House in Greek Revival style and a carriage house converted into museum of local history; open Memorial Day-Labor Day, Tues.-Fri. 1-4, Sat. & Sun. 11-4; May-Memorial Day & after Labor Day-Oct., Sat. & Sun. 11-4; adm.

Milton House Museum (8 m NE to 18 S Janesville St. in Milton), hex-ogonal building constructed of grout in 1844 as an inn; it was a stop on the Underground Railway; country store; open June-Labor Day, daily 11-5; May & after Labor Day-mid-Oct., Sat. & Sun. 11-5; adm. **Hoard Historical Museum** (17 m NE on SR 26 to 407 Merchant Ave., Ft. Atkinson): displays on local history; open Tues.-Sat. 9:30-3:30; closed Jan. 1, Thnks, Dec. 25; free. On grounds are: 1841 **Foster House**, home of city's founder, with period furnishings; open Wed., Sat. 8:30-5; sm adm. Dairy Exhibit Building, tracing development of the dairy industry; open same hrs as museum; free. **Sheepskin School** (13 m N on I-90 in Albion), restored 19th-C rural school with displays on early education; open May-Oct., Sat. & Sun. 1-6; donation. **Jefferson Historical Museum** (23 m N on SR 26 to 333 E Ogden St., Jefferson), displays on local history; open mid-June-late-Oct., daily 1-5; free.

KENOSHA: Kenosha County Historical Society & Museum (6300 3rd Ave.), Chinese snuff bottles among regional historic relics; Indian ar-tifacts; open Tues., Thurs., 1st Sun. each month 2-4:30; closed hols; free. **Kenosha Public Museum** (5608 10th Ave.), interesting dioramas by Lorado Taft of art studios of Praxiteles and other famous artists; Chinese ivory carving; fossils; Indian artifacts; wildlife displays; open Mon.-Fri. 9-noon, 1-5, Sat. 9-noon, Sun. 1-4; closed hols; free. **Civil War Museum** (Lentz Hall on Carthage College campus, on lake at N end of town) is open daily 9-5; closed hols, Aug.; free. **Harmony Hall** (6315 3rd Ave.), hq of Society for Preservation of Barber Shop Quartet Singing, offers exten-sive library; open Mon.-Fri. 8-5; closed hols; free.

LA CROSSE: Hixon House (429 N 7th St.), built 1857 by a successful lumber baron and banker; walls covered with velvet and hand-painted can-vas; Oriental and other original Victorian furnishings; County Historical Museum collections in outbuilding; open June-Labor Day, daily 1-5; adm. **Viterbo College** (815 S 9th St.), changing exhibits on history and natural history; open daily 2-5; closed hols; adm. **St. Joseph the Workman Cathedral** (530 Main St.), fine stained-glass windows; Blessed Sacrament Chapel with black marble walls, ornate altar of mosaic glass; open daily. **St. Rose Convent** (912 Market St.), elaborate Maria Angelorum Chapel with onyx pillars, marble altars, mosaic and gold bronze ornamentation; open daily.

MADISON: State Capitol (Capitol Park), imposing Roman Renaissance building with murals and lavish decoration; observation platform (Memorial Day-Sept.); D.A.R. Memorial Hall (room 419 N) displays relics of Civil War, Spanish-American War (Memorial Day-Labor Day, daily 9-4; rest of yr, Mon.-Fri. 9-4; closed hols; free); open daily 9-4:30;

free. **University of Wisconsin** (W of Capitol along S shore of Lake Mendota) offers campus maps and free tours from information center (Memorial Union, N Park & Langdon Sts.), open Mon.-Sat. 7:30-5, Sun. noon-5; closed Dec. 24-26. Campus includes Library with many rare volumes, former Civil War training center of Camp Randall, carillon, and: **State Historical Society Museum** (816 State St.), archaeological finds; Plains Indian artifacts; exhibits and dioramas on exploration, fur trading, settlement; period rooms and shops; excellent library on the early West; library of United Artists films; open Mon.-Fri. 8 am-10 pm, Sat. 10-5; closed hols; free. **Elvehjem Art Center** (800 University Ave.), 16-17th-C Dutch and Italian works among its European paintings; prints, drawings, sculptures; arts from Greece, Tibet, India; fine library; open Mon.-Sat. 9-4:45, Sun. 1-4:45; closed hols; free.

First Unitarian Church (900 University Bay Dr.), designed by Frank Lloyd Wright; dramatic building set above Lake Mendota; open Tues.-Sun. 9-4; closed hols; free.

Little Norway (18 m W, 1 m N off US 18, 151), 1856 homestead of a Norwegian settler, consists of about 12 log buildings in Norwegian style; replica of 12th-C stave church; Norwegian wooden furnishings, silver, leather-crafts, embroidered wall hangings, other items; open July-Aug. daily 9-7; May-June & Sept.-late-Oct. daily 9-5; adm. **Swiss Historical Village** (23 m SW on SR 69 to 6th Ave. & 7th St., New Glarus): church, cheese factory (37 still operate in the county), store, school, printshop other buildings erected in mid-19th-C by settlers who arrived in 1844 from Swiss canton of Glarus; buildings furnished with settler possessions; open May-Oct. daily 9-5; adm. **Chalet of the Golden Fleece** (618 2nd Ave. & 7th Ave.), replica of Swiss chalet; thousands of Swiss items, including dolls, books, kitchen utensils, glassware; open Apr.-Oct. daily 9:30-4:30; adm. New Glarus also has a floral clock (jct SR 39, 69) and offers a variety of Swiss festivals.

MANITOWOC: Rahr Civic Center & Public Museum (610 N 8th St.) houses Indian and pioneer relics; military artifacts; Chinese ivory carvings; other items; open Tues.-Fri. 9-4:30, Sat. & Sun. 2-5; closed hols; free. **Maritime Museum** (809 S 8th St.) depicts history of Great Lakes shipping with dioramas, ship models, relics; many of the ships described were built at boatyards in Manitowoc; open Memorial Day-Labor Day daily 10-5; rest of yr, daily noon-4; closed Jan. 1, Dec. 25; sm adm. Nearby **Submariners Memorial** (foot of S 9th St. at river), tours of the WW II sub U.S.S. *Cobia*; open Memorial Day-mid-Sept. daily 10-5; rest of yr, Sat. & Sun. 10-5; closed Jan. 1, Dec. 25; adm.

MARINETTE: Marinette County Historical Museum (on Stephenson Is., US 41 at state border) has hand-carved miniature logging camp, other logging displays; Indian relics; open late-May-mid-Oct. daily 10-5; adm. **Peshtigo Fire Museum** (5 m S at 400 Oconto Ave., Peshtigo) describes forest fire of Oct. 8, 1871, that consumed the town and took 800 lives; other historic displays; open late-May-early-Oct. daily 9-5; donation. Nearby Peshtigo Fire Cemetery has a monument to fire victims.

MENOMONIE: Mabel Tainter Memorial Building (205 Main St.) was constructed as civic center in 1889 by a lumber baron in memory of his daughter; ornate Victorian furnishings; baroque theater; collections of Dunn County Historical Society (which also maintains a schoolhouse and child's playhouse); tours June-Aug. 10-5; open Mon.-Fri. 9-5:30, Sat. 9-noon; closed hols; sm adm.

MILWAUKEE: Convention & Visitors Bureau (828 N Broadway) provides information on the many special events, industrial tours, other activities; open Mon.-Fri. 8:30-5, Sat. & Sun. 9:30-5. **Free brewery tours** (Miller at 4000 W State St., Pabst at 901 W Juneau Ave., Schlitz at 235 W Galena St.) are generally offered Mon.-Fri. 9 or 10-3:30 or 4, and sometimes Sat.; closed hols; breweries prefer that you phone first. **Lincoln Memorial Drive,** along the lakefront, offers fine views, including harbor, yacht club, Eero-Saarinen-designed War Memorial. Other interesting buildings: **Annunciation Greek Orthodox Church** (9400 W Congress St.), designed by Frank Lloyd Wright; open daily 10-4; closed Jan. 1, Thnks, Dec. 25; sm adm. **St. John Cathedral** (802 N Jackson St.), elaborate Spanish Renaissance-style church erected 1853; open daily. **St. Joan of Arc Chapel** (601 N 14th St.), 15th-C French church reconstructed on Marquette Univ. campus; tours daily 9:30-4:30; free. The nearby Court of Honor (just E off Wisconsin Ave.), a 3-block area honoring Civil War dead.

  Milwaukee County Historical Center (910 N 3rd St.), in former bank built in French Renaissance-style about 1913; exhibits on early settlers; transportation; city history; 19th-C life of children; military relics; antique fire-fighting equipment; brewer's Victorian home; library; open Mon.-Sat. 9-5, Sun. 1-5; closed hols; free. **Milwaukee Public Museum** (800 W Wells St.), natural history displays; time and space; ocean life; walk-in exhibits, some with recordings, illustrate cultures from around the world, including igloo, Guatemalan market, Melanesian ceremonial house, African cultures; Old Milwaukee street scene with shops; open daily 9-5; closed hols; adm.

  Milwaukee Art Center (750 N Lincoln Memorial Dr.) features Old Masters and contemporary works; American art from Colonial times to the present; open Mon.-Wed., Fri., Sat. 10-5, Thurs. 10-10, Sun. & hols 1-5; closed Jan. 1, Dec. 25; free. **Villa Terrace Decorative Arts Museum**

(2220 N Terrace Ave.), in handsome Mediterranean-style villa; period rooms with wide variety of decorative arts; open Sat., Sun. 1-5; also July-Labor Day, Wed.-Fri. 1-5; also Apr.-Dec., Wed. 1-5; closed Jan. 1, Dec. 25; free. **Marquette University Art Gallery** (in Memorial Library off Wisconsin Ave.), religious arts, with Flemish and Italian Renaissance pieces, tapestries; European ivory carvings; bronzes; crystal, silver, antique furniture; open Mon.-Sat. 9-5, Sun. noon-5; closed hols; free. **University of Wisconsin Art Museum** (3 m NE on lakefront on Downer Ave.) is open Sept.-mid-May, Mon.-Fri. noon-4, Sun. 1-4; free. **Charles Allis Art Library** (1630 E Royall Pl.) offers exhibits from the Allis collection; open Tues.-Sun. 1-5; closed hols; free.

Lowell Damon House (2107 Wauwatosa Ave.), New England-style pioneer home with period furnishings; open Wed. 3-5, Sun. 1-5; closed hols; free. **West Allis Historical Museum** (8405 W National Ave., W Allis), Romanesque-style school built 1887; local relics; open Tues. 7-9 pm, Sun. 2-4; free. **Kilbourntown House** (in Estabrook Park, Shorewood), furnished Greek Revival antebellum home; open in summer Tues., Thurs., Sat. 9-5, Sun. 1-5; free.

EAA Air Museum (SW to 11311 W Forest Home Ave., Franklin), almost 100 aircraft from many countries and from earliest models; also engines, models, photos; open Mon.-Fri. 8:30-5, Sat. 10-5, Sun. 1-5; closed Jan. 1, Easter, Thnks, Dec. 25; adm. **Heg Memorial Park** (16 m SW on SR 36 to Heg Park Rd. & Loomis Rd., Waterford): 1837 hand-hewn cabin, period furnishings; museum on Norwegian heritage; Civil War memorabilia; park is named for commander of Norwegian Regiment of the Civil War; open May-mid-Oct., Sat. 11-4, Sun. & hols 11-5:30; free. **Voree** (24 m SW on SR 36, then 1 m W) is a ghost town, founded as Garden of Peace by Mormons under James Strang; after dissention broke out, the colony moved to Beaver Island, where Strang declared himself king; members of his colony mortally wounded him in 1856, and he asked to be returned to Voree to die.

Old Falls Village (8½ m NW to County Line Rd., Menomonee Falls), 1858 Greek Revival farmhouse with early American furnishings; log cabin, museum exhibits in barn; open May-Oct., Sat. & Sun. 1-4; or by appointment; sm adm. **Brooks Stevens Automotive Museum** (10 m N on US 141 to 10325 N Port Washington Rd., Mequon), antique cars and racing cars; open June-mid-Sept., daily 10-5; rest of yr, Sat. & Sun. 10-5; closed Jan. 1, Dec. 25; adm. **Covered Bridge** (10 m N via SR 57 to SR 143, just beyond jct SR 60 on Covered Bridge Rd.), erected 1876 as a wagon crossing over Cedar Creek, is one of the few remaining in Wisconsin; also in this area are several surviving octagonal barns. **Lizard Mound State Park** (27 m N via US 45 to W Bend, then N on SR 144), Indian mounds in the form of panther, turtle, bird, lizard, other shapes; restored and marked.

Waukesha County Historical Museum (10 m W on SR 59 to 101 W Main St. at N East Ave.), local historical relics; open Mon.-Fri. 9-4:30; closed hols; free. **Delafield** (19½ m W off I-94): **Hawks Inn** (428 Wells St.), 19th-C stagecoach tavern, local historic displays (open late May-early Sept., Sat. & Sun. 1-4; Sept.-Oct., Sun. 1-4; sm adm); **Church of St. John Crysostom** (Genesee & Church Sts.), a solid oak frontier church with stone altar (open daily); other historic buildings.

OCONTO: Copper Culture Indian Cemetery (W of town off Mill St. on the river), with at least 200 burials from 5000 BC, associated with a prehistoric people known for their copper tools and weapons; interpretive sign; open daily. In historic times, this was a Menominee Indian fishing village, first visited by French fur trader Nicholas Perrot (monument to him at Main & Congress Sts.) in 1668; Indians honored his arrival with a festival. In 1669, Father Claude Allouez (monument to him on US 41) founded a mission here, and about 1825 John Jacob Astor founded a trading post. **Oconto County Historical Museum** (917 Park Ave.) offers exhibits on Copper Culture people, the mission, and fur trade and trading post; also lumbering relics; adjacent is Beyer Home, a Civil War mansion with furnishings from local pioneers; open Memorial Day-mid-Sept., Mon.-Sat. 9-5, Sun. noon-6; sm adm.

First Church of Christ, Scientist (Main & Chicago Sts.), first Christian Science church in the world; 1886 Gothic-style building; original Kimball reed organ; reading room has historical displays; open June-Aug., Mon., Wed., Fri. 2-4; Sept.-May, Wed., Fri. 2-4; free.

OSHKOSH: Paine Art Center & Arboretum (1410 Algoma Blvd), in Tudor-style mansion of a lumber baron, has period rooms in Gothic, Tudor, Jacobean, Georgian, and Victorian styles with English decorative arts, antique Persian rugs; Greek and Russian icons; Chinese decorative arts; Barbizon and Hudson River schools of landscapists; sculpture; library; open Memorial Day-Labor Day, Tues.-Sun. 2-5; rest of yr, Tues., Thurs., Sat., Sun. 2-5; closed hols; free. **Oshkosh Public Museum** (1331 Algoma Blvd) has outstanding American pressed glass; early steamboat era and other historic exhibits; archaeological relics; natural history; open Tues.-Sat. 9-5, Sun. 1-5; closed hols; free.

PLATTEVILLE: Ann-Wilson Cunningham Museum (204 Market St.), local history from lead mining days, including establishment of a community by freed slaves in 1848; open mid-May-Oct., Wed., Fri.-Sun. 2-4:30; closed July 4; sm adm. **Mitchell-Roundtree Stone Cottage** (W Madison & Lancaster Sts.), 1837 home with original furnishings; open June-Aug., Tues.-Sun. 2-4; adm. **Mining Museum** (385 E Main St.) traces area's mining history with working models, dioramas, other exhibits; restored 18th-C lead mine under the museum (adm); open June-Aug. daily 9-4; Sept.-May, Mon.-Fri. 8-5, weekends by appointment; free.

Mineral Point (20 m NE on US 151) was settled by lead miners from Cornwall in 1830; town was first called Shake Rag because wives would shake rags from their doorways as a signal to the working men that meals were ready. **Pendarvis-Cornish Restorations** (114 Shake Rag St. off SR 23), complex of Cornish miners' homes built of stone and logs in the 1830s; the miners, experienced in stonework, cut building materials from the limestone cliffs here; period furnishings; open May-Oct. daily 9-5; adm. **Mineral Point Historical Society Museum** (Pine & Davis Sts.), displays on town history, lead and zinc mining; open June-Labor Day, daily 9-5: sm adm. **Chamber of Commerce,** or the summer-only tourist booth in Water Tower Park (on US 151), can provide a map for other historic sites.

Badger Mine & Museum (11 m S on SR 80, 10 m E on SR 11 to Badger Park, Shullsburg), guided tour of pioneer lead mine tunnels; museum; open May-Oct. daily 9-5; adm. The mine is named, like the Badger State, for the many small diggings made by hand that resembled badger holes. **First Capitol State Park** (7 m E on US 151 to Belmont, then 3 m N on County G): wooden buildings that housed legislature and supreme court after capital of Wisconsin Territory established here 1836; museum of frontier life; open May-Sept. daily 9-4:30; free.

PRAIRIE DU CHIEN: Originally site of Hopewell Indian culture, with huge burial mound, this spot was named by French explorers for the local chief, whose name meant "dog." A trading post was established in 1673. During the War of 1812, the U.S. constructed Fort Crawford on the mound (among officers stationed here were Jefferson Davis and Zachary Taylor). When the fort was moved, Hercules Dousman, the state's first millionaire, who made his fortune in the fur trade as John Jacob Astor's agent, bought the mound. On it, in 1843, as a gift for his bride, he built **Villa Louis** (off US 18 at 521 N Villa Louis Rd.), a mansion so lavish that it was the talk of the frontier; hand-carved rosewood chairs, Waterford crystal chandeliers, hand-painted china, paintings, sculpture, 3000-volume library are among the elegant furnishings; carriage house is now museum of the Hopewell mound builders, early fur traders, the fort, and other aspects of city history; open May-Oct. daily 9-5; adm. **Museum of Medical Progress & Stovall Hall of Health** (717 S Beaumont Rd.) is in building that was Fort Crawford's hospital; exhibits on Indian, pioneer, and modern medicine; open May-Oct. 9-5 (longer in summer); sm adm.

Phetteplace Museum (16 m E off SR 60 in Wauzeka) displays gems and fossils; open mid-May-mid-Oct. daily 9-5; adm. **Stonefield Village** (35 m

S via US 18, SR 35, 133 in Nelson Dewey State Park 1 m upriver from Cassville), 19th-C Midwest village entered through a covered bridge; around the green are printshop, school, bank, workshops, cheese factory, other buildings; Dewey Home, restored and furnished home of Wisconsin's first governor; State Farm Crafts Museum tells story of area's agriculture with more than 12,000 early farm tools; open May-Oct. daily 9-5; adm.

RACINE: Racine County Historical Museum (701 S Main St.), displays on Danish settlers, regional history; natural history; early vehicles; open Tues.-Sat. 9-5, Sun. 1-5; closed hols; free. **Wustum Museum of Fine Arts** (2519 Northwestern Ave.), painting, sculpture, crafts; open Sun.-Thurs. 11-9, Fr. & Sat. 11-5; closed Jan. 1, Dec. 25; free.

RHINELANDER: Rhinelander Logging Museum (on US 8 in Pioneer Park), modeled on Wisconsin's late-1800s logging camps; fully equipped cook shack; museum of lumbering (includes the imaginary animal "hodag," created as a hoax and now the city's symbol); 1879 Baldwin locomotive, passenger coach, log cars, stamping hammers, road icer used to prepare roads for log-hauling sleds, other exhibits; open May-Labor Day, Mon.-Sat. 9-4, Sun. & hols 11-4; free. **Laona & Northern Railway** (39 m E on US 8 in Laona) offers a steam train ride to Camp Five Farm, with country store, blacksmith shop, logging museum; mid-June-Aug., Mon.-Sat. 10-2:45; fee. **Nicolet National Forest:** 53-m Oconto, 31-m Peshtigo, and 5-m Alvin auto tours; small logging museum (at Wabeno); old logging town of Padus has been restored; marker at site of McCaselin Mountain gold mine; Indian mounds; information from hq (Rhinelander 54501).

    Henkelmann's Museum (29 m NW on SR 47 to Woodruff, then 3 m NE on SR 70) displays mounted game animals; open late May-mid-Oct., daily 9 am-10 pm; adm. **Vilas County Historical Museum** (21 m NE on SR 17, 11 m W on SR 70, 5 m N on SR 155 at Sayner), exhibits on fur trade, lumbering, pioneers; open Memorial Day-Labor Day, Tues., Wed., Fri.-Sun. 10-5; free.

SHEBOYGAN: Sheboygan County Museum (3110 Erie Ave), in 1848 home; displays on local history; open Apr.-Sept., Tues.-Sat. 10-5, Sun. 1-5; sm adm. **Indian Mound Park** (S 9th St. at Panther Ave.) has 18 burial mounds of Woodland culture; open grave exhibit; open all year; free. **Waelderhaus** (4 m W off SR 28 on W Riverside Dr. in Kohler), reproduction of Austrian alpine chalet; typical furnishings; open daily 2-5; closed hols; free. **Cedar Grove** (13 m S on US 141) has windmill com-

memorating Dutch settlers; annual Holland Festival (in July); nearby
Oostburg (2 m NE) was also settled by Dutch.

SPRING GREEN: **Taliesin Fellowship Buildings** (4 m S on SR 23) is summer hq of Frank Lloyd Wright Foundation; tours by appointment (phone
588-2511), mid-July-Labor Day, Mon.-Sat. 10-4; adm. Wright also
designed Spring Green Restaurant (2 m S on SR 23), overlooking Wisconsin River, and a warehouse in Richland Center (22 m NW on SR
14). **House on the Rock** (6 m SW on SR 23) was designed and built over a
20-year period by sculptor Alex Jordan on a 59-ft rock 450-ft above the
valley; Jordan quarried some 5000 tons of sandstone from nearby bluffs,
and attached these with mortar and cables at various levels on the rock, incorporating some for furniture; trees grow through the building; water-
falls and pools; Oriental art objects, music room; on grounds is Mill
House and re-created 1880s street of shops; open Apr.-Nov. daily 9-5;
adm.

STEVENS POINT: **University of Wisconsin** (2100 Main St.): University
Center with historic exhibits on the state; Library with hand press on
which newspapers were printed before 1848; Fine Arts Bldg with art ex-
hibits; Science Hall with Sun. planetarium shows; Museum of Natural
History with mounted birds and preserved eggs. **North Wood County
Historical Society Museum** (34 m W on US 10 S of Marshfield), in wayside
park, is open June-Aug. daily noon-5; Sept.-May, Tues., Thurs., Sun. 1-5;
free. **Hutchinson House** (28 m SE off US 10 on SR 22 to South Park, S
Main St., Waupaca), 1854 frontier home with period relics; open
Memorial Day-Labor Day, Sat., Sun. & hols 2-5; sm adm. Nearby **Cristy
House** (315 E Lake St.), 1893 mansion with family furnishings; open
June-Aug., Fri.-Sun. 1-5; sm adm.

SUPERIOR: **Douglas County Historical Museum** (4 m SE on US 2 to 906
E 2nd St.): Lake Superior shipping; Indian artifacts; photos of Sioux who
took part in the Custer massacre; Japanese ceramics; pioneer displays;
open Tues.-Fri. 10-noon, 1-5, Sat. 1-5, Sun. 2-5; also June-Aug., Mon.
10-noon, 1-5; closed hols & Dec. 15-25; free. **Finnish Windmill** (E on SR
13) is only one in U.S. **Meteor** (Barker's Island), last whaleback freighter,
built 1896, is a maritime museum; inquire locally for hrs.

TOMAH: **Little Red Schoolhouse Museum** (in Gillette Park, Superior
Ave.), built 1864; many original furnishings; open Memorial Day-Labor
Day, daily 1-5; free. **Yuba** (17 m SE on I-90, 94, then 31 m S on SR 80)
has many homes of distinctive Czech architecture. **Thunderbird Museum**

(32 m NW on I-94, then N via SR 54 and county K to Hatfield), exhibits on regional history; Indian relics; minerals; weapons; open May-Oct., Tues.-Sun. 10-4; sm adm.

WATERTOWN: Settled by New Englanders, Watertown later attracted many Germans—including Carl Schurz (Lincoln's Minister to Spain, Sec. of State under Hayes)—who were called Latin Farmers because they were scholarly and often conversed in Latin. **Octagon House & First Kindergarten** (919 Charles St.): 8-sided house built 1854 by a teacher and lawyer; cantilevered spiral staircase, interesting water reservoir; Victorian furnishings; on grounds is first kindergarten in the U.S., established 1856 by Margarethe Schurz (wife of Carl), with period furnishings; barn with farming tools; open May-Oct. daily 10-5; adm. **Farmers' & Merchants' Union Bank** (24 m NW on US 16 to James St., Columbus), built 1919, was designed by Louis Sullivan; open banking hrs. **Aztalan Historical Society Museum** (11 m SW on county rd to Lake Mills) is open May-Oct., Mon.-Sat. 9-5:30, Sun. 1-5:30; sm adm.

WAUSAU: Marathon County Historical Society Museum (403 McIndoe St.), in lumberman's home; Early American glass; historic relics; Indian artifacts; displays on lumbering; regional arts and crafts; open Mon.-Fri. 9-5, Sun. 2-5; closed hols; free.

WYOMING

BUFFALO: Johnson County-Jim Gatchell Memorial Museum (10 Fort St.), dioramas of Johnson County Cattle War of 1892 between big and small ranchers in which Federal troops had to intervene; archaeological artifacts; pictures; ranch life artifacts; open June-Labor Day daily 9-9; closed July 4; free. **Occidental Hotel** (10 N Main St.) was made famous by the Owen Wister novel, *The Virginian.* **Fort Phil Kearney Site** (13 m N off US 87), 1866 fort erected after Sioux and Cheyenne tried to keep miners headed for Montana's gold fields from trespassing on their property; Indians laid siege to the fort again and again, and the soldiers abandoned it in 1868; Indians then burned it; monument to John "Portugee" Phillips, who made a heroic 236-m winter ride through Indian territory to get relief for the beleaguered fort from Ft. Laramie. Nearby are: **Wagon Box Fight Site** (17 m N off US 87 near Story), involving Chief Red Cloud in

1867. **Fetterman Massacre Monument** (15 m S off I-25), site where Chief Red Cloud and his Ogala Sioux ambushed and killed Capt. Fetterman and his 81 soldiers in 1886.

CASPER: Old Fort Caspar Museum (3 m W on W 13th St. & Ft. Caspar Rd.) was established to escort wagon trains on the Oregon Trail; renamed in 1865 for Lt. Caspar Collins, who sacrificed his life to save a fallen comrade while cavalrymen were protecting a wagon train from Sioux and Cheyenne; 26 others also died; fort also was Pony Express stop and guarded the Pacific Telegraph line (Indians disliked "singing" wires as messages were relayed); fort, destroyed by Indians in 1867, restored with exhibits on pioneer life; open mid-May-mid-Sept. daily 9-9; free. **Natrona County Pioneer Museum** (W on fairgrounds), in first church built by settlers (1887); pistols, musical instruments, other frontier relics; open mid-May-mid-Sept., Mon., Wed.-Sun. 9:30-4:30; free. **Central Wyoming Museum of Art** (104 Rancho Rd.), Tues.-Sun. 1-5; closed hols; free. **Ghost Towns:** Bessemer (17 m SW on SR 220), "Queen City of the Plains," disappeared after Casper was chosen as the railroad terminal. Eadsville (atop Casper Mountain), once a thriving mining community, now a popular picnic site. **Oregon Trail,** stage routes, and other trails went SW from here roughly paralleling SR 220, and many remains can be seen. **Independence Rock** (45 m SW on SR 220) has more than 50,000 names carved into it; just N was the Sweetwater Stage Station; just S is **Devil's Gate,** a gorge cut by the river through the Rattlesnake Mountains, with Tom Sun Ranch, built by a French-Canadian frontiersman, typical of early open-range period in Wyoming. In this area are many graves of pioneers who died on the Oregon Trail.

Goss Rock Museum (25 m SW on SR 220 in Alcova), native fossils and minerals; open May-Sept., Tues.-Sun. 9-7; Oct.-Apr., Tues.-Sun. 9-5; closed Jan. 1, Dec. 25; free. **Teapot Rock** (30 m N off US 87) marks Salt Creek Oil Field that started Casper's oil boom in 1888 and for which the Teapot Dome Scandal was named.

CHEYENNE: State Capitol (Capitol Ave.) has gold-leaf dome; paintings of frontiersmen in rotunda; statue of Esther Hobart Morris, fighter for woman suffrage; open Mon.-Fri. 8:30-5; closed hols; free. **State Museum & Art Gallery** (Central Ave. & 23rd St. in State Office Bldg.) has displays on the area's Indian cultures; exhibits on how Cheyenne became an instant town when Union Pacific reached the site in 1867; life of cowboys, pioneers; open June-Labor Day, Mon.-Fri. 8:30-5, Sat. & Sun. 9-5; rest of yr, Mon.-Sat. 9-5; closed Thnks, Dec. 25; free. **Warren Military Museum** (W on Randall Ave. to Bldg. 211 of Warren AFB), history of fort established 1867 to protect railroad construction crews and early ranchers;

usually open Memorial Day-Labor Day, daily 1-5, and weekends rest of yr, but inquire at Information Office; free. Many of the brick colonial-style buildings built here in the 1880s are still standing and in use.

CODY: Buffalo Bill Historical Center (Sheridan Ave. & 8th St.) consists of Buffalo Bill memorabilia; **Whitney Gallery of Western Art** (painting and sculpture of the W by Remington, Catlin, Bierstadt, Russell, others); **Plains Indian Museum** (artifacts from Mummy Cave; full costumes, tribal medicines, ceremonial objects, scalps, weapons, beaded work); open June-Aug. daily 7 am-10 pm; May & Sept., daily 8-5; adm.

Buffalo Bill Village & Western Exhibits (Sheridan Ave. at 16th St.), re-created Western town with melodrama in theater, exhibits; open June-Aug. daily 7 am-10 pm; additional days if weather permits; buildings free, adm to some exhibits.

DOUGLAS: Wyoming Pioneer Museum (fairgrounds, W end of Center St.) traces history of Western settlement with Indian costumes and artifacts, battlefield relics, maps of immigrant trails, settler relics; open July-Aug., Tues.-Fri. 9-8, Sat. & Sun. 1-5; Apr.-June & Sept.-Oct., Tues.-Fri. 9-5, Sat. & Sun. 1-5; closed Memorial Day, July 4; free.

Fort Fetterman State Museum (10 m NW on SR 93 at Ft. Fetterman State Historic Site); lonely outpost established 1867 as Indians objected to whites advancing along the Union Pacific line; log officers' quarters houses authentic furnishings, other relics; living history demonstrations in summer; open in summer, Mon.-Fri. 8-5, Sat. & Sun. 9-8; in winter, Mon.-Fri. 8-5, Sat. 9-5; closed some hols; free.

Glendo Historical Museum (26 m SE on I-25 in Town Hall, Glendo) has fossils, Indian relics, historical displays; open Mon.-Fri. 9-4, Thurs. & Sat. 2-5; free.

FORT BRIDGER STATE HISTORIC SITE (36 m E of Evanston on I-80) preserves 1858 army post on site of trading post opened 1843 by legendary fur trapper and scout, Jim Bridger; while Bridger was away in 1853, his partner sold the post to Mormons, who used it to outfit Mormons on their way to Salt Lake City; officers' quarters, sutler's store, guardhouse; cemetery. **Fort Bridger Museum** details life at the fort; homesteader's cabin; living history demonstrations; open in summer, Mon.-Fri. 8-5, Sat. & Sun. 9-8; in winter, Mon.-Fri. 8-5, Sat. 9-5; free.

FORT LARAMIE NATIONAL HISTORIC SITE (23 m NW of Torrington on US 26, then W on SR 160): Possibly single most important post in history of the Old Wesι, Fort Laramie offered a haven in the wilderness for thousands of emigrants on the Oregon Trail, was a stop on the Pony

Express and Overland Stage, served as base for marches against the Mormons and conquest of the Plains Indians, and oversaw the settlement that closed the frontier. **Visitor Center** offers excellent exhibits and information; self-guiding tour; trader's store, enlisted men's public saloon and poolroom, officer's club, Old Bedlam (bachelor's quarters), guardhouse, baker, other buildings are either original or reconstructions, with period pieces; insights into family life on the fort and attempts to maintain gentility (white gloves were required), and depiction of life as it evolved to meet changing duties of the fort. Living history demonstrations in summer. Open mid-June-Labor Day, daily 7-7; rest of yr, 8-4:40; closed Jan. 1, Dec. 25; free. The Oregon Trail, along the Platte E of here, has many graves; during one cholera epidemic, graves on the 700 m of trail between Westport Landing and the Laramie averaged 1½ to the mile.

GRAND TETON NATIONAL PARK (6 m S of Yellowstone on US 89, 287), whose peaks were named *tetons* (breasts) by French fur trappers, offers: **Moose Visitor Center,** open daily 8-5 (longer hrs in summer); closed Dec. 25. **Fur Trade Museum** tells story of British, French, and Americans who trapped here 1820-40, until beaver hats went out of fashion; also stories of colorful people for whom geographic features of the park are named. Rustic **Chapel of the Transfiguration** has a window above the altar framing the mountains; open 24 hrs. **Menor-Noble Historic District,** where living history demonstrations are sometimes given; Maude Noble Cabin, erected 1916 by woman who championed creation of national park here; Bell Menor Cabin, built by colorful first settler in 1892 (he ran a ferry across the Snake River, and for years never spoke to his brother, who lived on the opposite shore); furnishings and personal belongings of Jackson Hole settlers on display; self-guiding trail. SE of here are Mormon homesteading cabins (on dirt road 1 m N of Gros Ventre campground), from 1889 settlement; 2 m NE is **Kelly,** which had a population of 80 when Slide Lake (see Jackson) broke its dam; remains of crushed homes can be seen among the boulders. **Cunningham Cabin** (12 m N on US 26, 89, 187) was scene of shootout; 2 cowboys arrived in 1893 to winter a herd of fine horses; when rumor spread that the horses were stolen, a posse formed and, without trial or evidence, killed the cowboys; they are buried nearby; cabin restored; self-guiding trail.

Jenny Lake Visitor Center (8 m N of Moose) has museum of history, ethnology, natural history of Tetons, mountain climbing in Tetons; open early June-mid-Sept. daily 8-7.

Colter Bay Visitor Center (on Jackson Lake), with museum exhibits on regional art, history, natural history, is open mid-May-Sept. daily 8 am-9 pm; may be open at other times. Named for John Colter, member of the

Lewis & Clark Expedition, who later became a trapper, first white man to see Yellowstone and Jackson Hole (hole was the trapper word for valley). Jackson Lake was a favorite Indian hunting ground; Crow, Bannock, Shoshone, and other tribes would gather peacefully in summer; later, trappers followed game and Indian trails to the lake. History is told in **Indian Arts Museum.**

GUERNSEY: This was the first stop out of Ft. Laramie for wagon parties on the Oregon Trail; just E of town is **Emigrant's Wash Tub,** a pool where water stayed warm year round, used for laundering by wagon parties; just S (off SR 26) are **Oregon Trail Ruts,** some of the best preserved in the country, worn as deep as 5 ft into the sandstone; just beyond (on SR 26) is **Register Rock,** where thousands of emigrants carved their names; these are all state historic sites with interpretive signs. **Guernsey State Park** (3 m N on SR 270) has a museum on the Oregon Trail, open mid-Apr.-early Sept. daily 9-7; free. **Hartville** (5 m N on SR 270) has false-front buildings and a Boot Hill; near Sunrise (5½ m N on SR 270) are the remains of **Fairbanks,** a ghost town. **Rock Museum** (17 m W on US 26, 18 m S on I-25 to 806 10th St., Wheatland) has fossils, minerals, archaeologic artifacts; open spring-fall daily 9-5; closed hols; free.

JACKSON: The "Old West" is so overdone here, with antlers decorating the town, melodramas at Opera House, and dude shops galore, that you can't help but be charmed. **Jackson Hole Historical Museum** (101 N Glenwood), early photographs, guns, other relics of trappers and settlers; animal trophies; open May-mid-Sept. daily 9-9; adm. **Gros Ventre Slide Geological Area** (8 m NE on US 89, then 10 m E on Gros Ventre Rd.): Within minutes, on June 23, 1925, an entire mountainside broke loose and, cascading from an altitude of 9000 ft, crossed the valley, damned the Gros Ventre River into what is now called Lower Slide Lake, and pushed 300 ft up the slope of Red Bluffs; in 1927 the dam broke, destroying the town of Kelly; interpretive trail.

KEMMERER: Kemmerer City Museum (Triangle Park on US 30N), local historical artifacts, Old West relics; open June-Aug. daily 9-9; free.

LANDER: Fremont County Pioneer Museum (630 Lincoln St.), local gems and minerals, Indian and pioneer relics; open mid-May-mid-Sept. daily 9-9; rest of yr, Tues.-Sun. 2-5; donation. **Wind River Indian Reservation,** N of town, has grave of Sacajawea (7 m N off US 287), Shoshone guide of Lewis & Clark Expedition; **Arapahoe Cultural Museum** (open June-early Sept. daily 8-8) and log church decorated with Indian motifs at Ethete (10 m N on US 287, then 7 m NE on SR 132).

South Pass City (33 m S on SR 28, then 2 m W) boomed as center of Sweetwater Gold Rush of 1867, with 5 hotels, dozens of saloons and sporting houses, a blacksmith who also practiced dentistry, a furrier, and even a crusader for woman suffrage (Esther Hobart Morris) who caused the Territorial Legislature of Wyoming to become the first government in the world to grant equal rights to women in 1869; by 1870 the gold was gone; restored boom-era buildings; museum; open summer daily 8-8, spring & fall daily 9-5; may be open in winter; closed hols; donation. Nearby are ghost towns of Atlantic City (1 m E), Miner's Delight (2 m E), Lewiston (4 m E) and remains of dozens of gold camps.

LARAMIE: Laramie Plains Museum (603 Ivinson Ave. at 6th St.), in banker's Victorian mansion; relics of town's early days, when it was known as Hell-on-Wheels for the boisterous Union Pacific crews that gathered here; furniture hand-carved in Territorial prison; European china; hand-made toys; art; horsehair shirt made by the last train robber; open June-Aug., Mon.-Fri. 2-4, 7:30-9; rest of yr, Mon.-Fri. 2-4; closed hols; adm. **University of Wyoming** (9-15th, Ivinson-Lewis Sts.): Anthropology Museum (2nd floor, Arts & Sciences Bldg); Geology Museum (Geology Bldg.) with Brontosaurus, mammoth, camel, other fossils; Herbarium (3rd floor, Aven Nelson Bldg); Art Museum (Fine Arts Center), 18-19th-C European and 19-20th-C American works; Western History Research Center (Coe Library); most bldgs open Mon.-Fri. 8-5; closed academic hols; free.

Lincoln Monument (12 m E on I-80), 12-ft high bronze head by Robert Russin. **Ames Monument** (18 m E on I-80, then 2 m SE), designed by Henry Hobson Richardson, with medallions by Saint-Gaudens, is a 60-ft-high granite pyramid erected by Union Pacific Railroad in 1882 to honor Oakes and Oliver Ames, who helped finance the transcontinental line; monument once overlooked town of Sherman, but by 1900 the railroad tracks were relocated and now not a trace remains of the town. **Arlington Stage Station** (30 m NW on I-80), important stop on the Overland Trail; combination blacksmith shop-dance hall-saloon, other buildings; interpretive sign. **Rock River** (36 m NW on US 30-287), successor to earlier settlement of Rock Creek that died when railroad bypassed it; Rock Creek Stage Station, cemetery, historic signs. **Como Bluff Museum** (43 m NW on US 30, 287 at Como Bluff) is a private museum housed in small structure made of fossilized bone (the area has produced dinosaur and other fossils); fossils, minerals; owner (in adj house) will open it on request; donation. **Medicine Bow** (56 m NW on US 30, 287), setting of Owen Wister's novel *The Virginian*; Old Carbon Cemetery (10 m W, follow signs) and caved-in coal mines, remains of race track, are all that are left of the prosperous 1868 town of Carbon.

LUSK: Stagecoach Museum (342 S Main St.), Indian artifacts, relics of pioneer days; Concord stagecoach from Cheyenne-Deadwood run; open June-Aug. daily 9-noon, 1-5, 7-9; late May & Sept.-late Oct., daily 1-5, 7-9; sm adm. **Rawhide Buttes Station** (12 m S on US 85), representative of those on Cheyenne-Deadwood route, was important during the Black Hills Gold Rush of 1870s; **Hat Creek Stage Station** (11 m N on US 18, 85), on a Texas Trail crossing, also remains; on US 18 W of town is a monument to a pioneer stage driver. Ghost town of **Jireh** (W on US 18 between Manville & Keeline) was once a prosperous community founded 1908 by Dayton, Ohio, Christian Church members; foundations of college they built (which had peak enrollment of 65) can still be seen; also cemetery. Nearby are Spanish Diggins, an archaeological site, and the ghost town of Silver Cliff.

RAWLINS: Carbon County Museum (in county courthouse on US 30, between Spruce & Pine Sts.), regional artifacts; open summer, Mon.-Fri. 1-4; rest of yr, Fri. 1-4; free. **Rawlins National Bank** (Buffalo & 5th Sts.) has a room with exhibits on local history; open banking hrs; free. **Fort Fred Steele** (15 m E off I-80), now in ruins, protected work crews on the Union Pacific from Indian and outlaw attack 1868-86.

    Grand Encampment Museum (20 m E on I-80, 28 m S on SR 130, 10 m S off SR 230) is a ghost town; this valley, held sacred by Indians, attracted trappers, tie cutters, cattle barons, and Thomas Edison (who conceived the idea for the incandescent light on a hunting trip to Battle Lake), but permanent residents didn't arrive until the 1870s; an 1897 copper strike set off a boom that created a cluster of 8 camps and ended when the mines closed in 1908; Riverside and Encampment survived as tiny towns, but Elwood, Dillon, Rudefeha, Copperton, Rambler, and Battle (directions available here for these) are ghost towns. Buildings preserved in Encampment (some moved from other sites) include the stage station, ranch house, bakery and ice-cream parlor, transportation barn. **Doc Culleton Museum** exhibits ores, mining stocks (some fraudulent), boom-day household relics, photos, other items; open Memorial Day-mid-Oct. daily 1-5; sm adm.

RIVERTON: Riverton Museum (7th & E Park Sts.), Shoshone and Arapaho relics; blacksmith shop, homesteader's cabin; open June-Aug., Mon.-Sat. 9-5, Sun. 1-5; Sept.-May, Tues.-Sun. 1-5; closed Jan. 1, Thnks, Dec. 25; free.

ROCK SPRINGS: Fine Arts Center (301 Blair Ave.), Grandma Moses, Frederic Taubes, other 20th-C American painting; open daily 10-noon, 2-5; closed hols; free.

Sweetwater County Historical Museum (15 m W on I-80 to courthouse, 50 W Flaming Gorge Way) has Indian, Chinese, pioneer relics of the area; open Mon.-Fri. 10-4:30; closed hols; free.

Pacific Springs Interpretive Site (41 m N on US 187 to Farson, then 30 m NE on SR 28), display shows route of Oregon Trail from South Pass City; was also a Pony Express stop. Point of Rocks Stage Station (25 m E on S side of I-80), in ruins, served emigrants and the Overland Stage 1862-69. Granger Stage Station (39 m W on I-80, then 2½ m N at Granger), important stop on Oregon and Overland trails, stop for Pony Express; one building remains.

Flaming Gorge National Recreation Area extends S from town of Green River into Utah and was named by John Wesley Powell for the brilliant red canyon along Green River; "Drive Through the Ages" interpretive signs explain geologic features; Visitor Centers at the S end, at Red Canyon and Flaming Gorge Dam, provide information.

SHERIDAN: Bradford Brinton Memorial Ranch & Museum (7 m S on US 87, then 5 m SW on SR 334): in 1892 ranchhouse later enlarged; Western art by Russell, Remington, Borein, Audubon, Kleiber, Reiss, De Yong, others; Indian costumes and handcrafts; carriage barn with stagecoach once owned by Buffalo Bill, saddles; open mid-May-Labor Day, daily 9-5; free. Connor Battlefield (15 m N on I-25, just S of Ranchester), site of most important battle of 1865 Powder River Expedition; Gen. Connor surprised an Arapaho village, killing 63 warriors, capturing 1100 horses, and destroying 250 lodges and their contents. Medicine Wheel (on US 14A in Bighorn National Forest), extraordinary construction in stone of almost perfect circle 70 ft in diameter, forming a hub from which 28 spokes (also of stone) radiate like a wheel; on the rim are 6 cairns; around the wheel other stone monuments were built. The meaning is unknown, but Medicine Mountains have been regarded as sacred and as sources of power by Indians into the 20th-C.

SUNDANCE: Crook County Museum (in courthouse), exhibits on gold mining in the Black Hills, for which Sundance was gateway; also on Harry Longabaugh (the Sundance Kid), who earned his nickname as top cowboy working for local ranchers (until, in the 1880s, he killed a deputy sheriff and fled to join the Wild Bunch); inquire here for directions to the ghost gold camps of Welcome and Mineral Hill; open Mon.-Fri.; closed hols; free.

Devils Tower National Monument (22 m W on US 14, 7 m N on SR 24), such a strange formation that even geologists still have questions about it, is a huge molten lava intrusion forced up from within the earth; it rises 1280-ft above the Belle Fourche River, dominating the grasslands;

bands of sedimentary rock and masses of brightly colored lichens growing on the rock change color with the angle of the sun; **Visitor Center** offers scientific explanations, recounts tower's role in the folklore of Indians and early whites; open May-Oct. daily 8-4:45 (to 7:45 in summer); self-guiding trail around the base; park open all year; sm adm or GEP.

THERMOPOLIS: Hot Springs County Pioneer Museum (235 Springview Ave.), exhibits on history of this old spa (which still has state bathhouse and medical facilities), Indian relics, fossils, minerals; open Tues.-Sun. 9-5; closed Jan. 1, Thnks, Dec. 25; free. **Gitlitz Memorial** (5th & Arapahoe Sts.) features Western art by Wyoming artists; open June-mid-Sept., Tues.-Sat. 10-4, Sun. 1-4; free.

WORLAND: Washakie County Museum (110 S 11th St.), Indian and pioneer items; open June-Aug., Mon.-Sat. 2-5; free. **Greybull Museum** (38 m N on US 16, 20 to 325 Greybull Ave., Greybull), fossils, archaeology of area, historic exhibits; open June-mid-Sept. daily 9-9; rest of yr, Mon.-Sat. 1-5; closed Jan. 1, Thnks, Dec. 25; free.

YELLOWSTONE NATIONAL PARK, world's first national park, remains one of the most thrilling; only at 3 other locations in the world—Iceland, New Zealand, Siberia—are there comparable thermal wonders; fur trappers who tried to describe, from 1808-1860s, the fantastic geysers, boiling springs, and bubbling mud pots were not believed. The Montana gold rush of the 1860s brought many prospectors to the area, prompting a scientific expedition in 1869; yet the party was so afraid of ridicule that it made few public statements until their findings were confirmed by an 1870 expedition; Congress then protected the area as a national park (1872). Excellent literature, films, many booklets for fascinating self-guiding trails, ranger-conducted walks, campfire programs, other activities are offered at several visitor centers. **Museums** are at Grant Village (natural history), Old Faithful (history and natural history of park), Fishing Bridge (natural history and geology of area), Norris (natural history), Canyon Village (history, natural history, art of area), Mammoth Hot Springs (history, archaeology, ethnology, natural history of park); dates and hrs vary, but usually these are open mid-June-Labor Day or mid-Sept., daily 8-6 or later. Official park season is May-Oct., when, weather permitting, N, E, S, and W entrances are open (the NE entrance on US 212 is usually open only June-mid-Oct.); however, Visitor Centers and other facilities may not open until mid-May-mid-June and may close by Labor Day or mid-Sept. **Mammoth Hot Springs Visitor Center** (N entrance) is open daily all yr, and in winter can inform you if any other facilities are open.